Lecture Notes in Computer Science 7053

Commenced Publication in 1973
Founding and Former Series Editors:
Gerhard Goos, Juris Hartmanis, and Jan van Leeuwen

Pascal Bouvry
Mieczysław A. Kłopotek
Franck Leprévost
Małgorzata Marciniak
Agnieszka Mykowiecka
Henryk Rybiński (Eds.)

Security and Intelligent Information Systems

International Joint Conference, SIIS 2011
Warsaw, Poland, June 13-14, 2011
Revised Selected Papers

Springer

Volume Editors

Pascal Bouvry
ILIAS, University of Luxembourg
E-mail: pascal.bouvry@uni.lu

Mieczysław A. Kłopotek
Institute of Computer Science, Polish Academy of Sciences, Warsaw, Poland
E-mail: klopotek@ipipan.waw.pl

Franck Leprévost
University of Luxembourg
E-mail: franck.leprevost@uni.lu

Małgorzata Marciniak
Institute of Computer Science, Polish Academy of Sciences, Warsaw, Poland
E-mail: malgorzata.marciniak@ipipan.waw.pl

Agnieszka Mykowiecka
Institute of Computer Science, Polish Academy of Sciences, Warsaw, Poland
E-mail: agnieszka.mykowiecka@ipipan.waw.pl

Henryk Rybiński
Institute of Computer Science, Warsaw University of Technology, Poland
E-mail: h.rybinski@ii.pw.edu.pl

ISSN 0302-9743 e-ISSN 1611-3349
ISBN 978-3-642-25260-0 ISBN 978-3-642-25261-7 (eBook)
DOI 10.1007/978-3-642-25261-7
Springer Heidelberg Dordrecht London New York

Library of Congress Control Number: 2011944280

CR Subject Classification (1998): C.2.4, C.2.5, H.2.8, I.2.9, K.3.1, K.4.4, I.5

LNCS Sublibrary: SL 3 – Information Systems and Application, incl. Internet/Web and HCI

Typesetting: Camera-ready by author, data conversion by Scientific Publishing Services, Chennai, India

Printed on acid-free paper

Springer is part of Springer Science+Business Media (www.springer.com)

Preface

This volume contains papers selected from those accepted for presentation at the International Joint Conference on Security and Intelligent Information Systems (SIIS) which was held in Warsaw, Poland, June 13–14, 2011. The conference was organized by the Institute of Computer Science of the Polish Academy of Sciences, the Institute of Computer Science at the Warsaw University of Technology, and the University of Luxembourg as a joint meeting of the Second Luxembourg-Polish Meeting on Security and Trust and the 19th International Conference on Intelligent Information Systems.

The papers submitted to the conference were organized into three thematic tracks: security and trust, data mining and machine learning, and natural language processing. Based on anonymous peer-review of the 60 submissions, 29 papers were accepted for inclusion in this volume. Moreover, the volume contains two invited papers by Gerhard Frey and Joakim Nivre.

New technologies have emerged in these last few decades. They allow better and easier collaboration and interaction between people, which in turn leads to new threats and dangers. In order to enable any economic or social exchange, trust between the actors is a necessity. A formal definition of trust is needed in this context, and the means to enable and measure trust are required. It is also necessary to fight all potential crimes and attacks. Security and trust are therefore two very key topics in our society. Under these circumstances, it is no wonder that the **Security and Trust** track of the SIIS 2011 joint conference was given a *primus inter pares* status.

The scientific part of the SIIS 2011 conference was opened by an invited plenary talk given by Gerhard Frey entitled "Is Arithmetic Geometry Necessary for Public-Key Cryptography?". The talk presented the challenges of current public-key cryptology based discrete logarithm problems (DLP) in finite cyclic groups. G. Frey and E. Kani's paper entitled "Correspondences on Hyperelliptic Curves and Applications to the Discrete Logarithm Problem" — published in these proceedings — addresses these issues. More precisely, the authors recall that divisor class groups of carefully chosen curves over finite fields provide the main source of groups for DLP. They also recall that curves of genus $g \geq 4$ and non-hyperelliptic curves of genus $g = 3$ have to be avoided for security reasons. Furthermore, Smith showed that 'many' hyperelliptic curves of genus 3 have to be avoided too. The deep reason is due to the existence of isogenies of low degrees between the Jacobians of these hyperelliptic curves to the Jacobians of non-hyperelliptic curves (of the same genus), and hence the DLP is 'easily' transferred from one Jacobian to another. G. Frey and E. Kani take the point of view of correspondences and isogenies: for each g, their paper describes how to find a Hurwitz space parametrizing a subspace of those hyperelliptic curves C of genus g which admit a non-trivial correspondence to a curve D of genus g that can be expected to be non-hyperelliptic. Their approach is purely geometric at the beginning (where they assume the ground field to be algebraically closed) and they focus on rationality issues in a second step. In the frontier case $g = 3$, they give a parametrization of these hyperelliptic curves of genus 3 in terms of a Hurwitz moduli space with monodromy group S_4, the symmetric group on 4 letters. In particular, they recover Smith's results, and announce that a future paper of E. Kani extends these results to the situation where the ground field has the characteristic 2. G. Frey and E. Kani's important paper, together with other results, leads to the conclusion stated at the end of his talk: according to today's knowledge, it is safer to avoid curves of genus ≥ 3 for cryptographic purposes and use only elliptic curves or (simple) Jacobians of genus 2 curves.

The **Security and Trust** Track, opened by G. Frey's talk, also included presentations of the following eight papers. In terms of trust metrics in modern ad-hoc networks, M. Seredyński et al. present in "Solving Soft Security Issues in MANETs Using an Evolutionary Approach" new approaches where decentralized strategies are discussed for trust computation. The paper "Camera Sabotage Detection for Surveillance Systems" by D. Ellwart et al. describes new methods for detecting anomalies in camera surveillance systems. A. Poniszewska-Maranda, in the paper "Implementation of Access Control Model for Distributed Information Systems Using Usage Control," presents an enhanced model for access control based on extensions of role-based access control that enables more dynamic management. Nowadays, cryptography is able to help in authentication, signature, encryption, and non-repudiation. But additional mechanisms are required to help erase all available traces of information exchange between partners. The paper "Beyond TOR: The TrueNyms Protocol" by N. Bernard and F. Leprévost introduces TrueNyms that allows the masking of all information during the exchange on an encoded channel that might remain in the packet headers (e.g., source of the packet, number of packets, etc.). The paper "A Signature Scheme for Distributed Executions Based on Control Flow Analysis" by S. Varrette et al. describes a way to help certify the results on distributed platforms such as desktop-based grids. In the paper "Computational Aspects of Attack-Defense Trees," B. Kordy et al., after introducing the extension of attack-trees called attack-defense trees, demonstrate that the computational complexity of this approach remains equivalent to those of attack trees. D. Priemuth-Schmid presents two attacks on simplifed versions of the stream cipher K2 which was introduced at SECRYPT 2007 by S. Kiyomoto, T. Tanaka, and K. Sakurai.

Data Mining and Machine Learning (DM and ML) was the next conference track. It was opened by an invited plenary talk by Alessio Lomuscio entitled "Verification of Multi-Agent Systems." Serial and parallel algorithms for symbolic model checking for temporal-epistemic logic as well as bounded-model checking procedures were discussed in the talk. Moreover, applications of the methodology to the automatic verification of security protocols, Web services, and fault-tolerance were surveyed. (The paper elaborating on the issues presented in the talk will appear elsewhere and hence it is not included in this volume.)

Regarding DM and ML methods, several new methods of model discovery from data are presented. The paper "Model Selection in Logistic Regression Using p-Values and Greedy Search" by J. Mielniczuk and P. Teisseyre proposes a new method of model selection from a set of candidate models, and demonstrates its effectiveness and applicability in step-wise model construction. The paper "Landau Theory of Meta-Learning" by D. Plewczynski aims at creating and applying machine-learning algorithms in such a way that, for a given problem under scrutiny, a multitude of slightly different decision models can be derived, which can then make final decisions based on a majority vote. The author lists a number of such algorithms, proposes new ones, as well as their combinations, and demonstrates their good properties. In the paper "Multi-Test Decision Trees for Gene Expression Data Analysis," M. Czajkowski at al. argue that the voting should be performed at a single attribute level. It deals with ways to surpass the known problem with proper model construction when a number of different attributes have a similar predictive capability. Under such circumstances decision trees may perform worse than other approaches. The authors claim and demonstrate that one can keep the explanatory power of decision trees while at the same time making more reliable decisions by letting many tests vote at a given branching point of the tree. The paper "Rule-Based Approach to Computational Stylistics" by U. Stańczyk suggests on the other hand that one can start building a model (say, a classifier) filling it with a multitude of constituent rules of varying quality, and then identifying poorly performing features and removing rules which contain these features. Significant increases in decision quality are observed.

Another group of papers, pertaining to DM and ML tools, is devoted to issues in evolutionary optimization. The paper "Differential Evolution for High-Scale Dynamic Optimization" by M. Raciborski at al. proposes and explores a new area of application for differential evolution, showing its reliability in tasks with a dynamically changing environment. The paper "Towards an OpenCL Implementation of Genetic Algorithms on GPUs" by T. Puźniakowski and M. Bednarczyk deals with the technical side of the performance of genetic algorithms, demonstrating that the proper choice of an offspring selection method may provide a significant speed-up of the optimization process due to the technical properties of graphic cards. The paper "Evolutionary Algorithm Parameter Tuning with Sensitivity Analysis" by F. Pinel et al. tackles the delicate issue of tuning the many parameters of a typical evolutionary algorithm. The key idea is that sensitivity analysis allows us to identify the parameters that most strongly influence the performance for a given application, allowing the researcher to concentrate on tuning them properly.

The last group of papers in the DM and ML track is application-oriented. The paper "Image Recognition System for Diagnosis Support of Melanoma Skin Lesion" by W. Paja et al. deals with the application of image understanding in the medical domain, in particular for computer-aided automated classification of melanocytic skin lesions. Instead of a simple classification scheme, a mechanism for chaining diverse image processing methods is developed in order to extract features from images. The paper "Playing in Unison in the Random Forest" by A. Wieczorkowska et al. addresses the issues related to the identification of instruments of an orchestra in the very difficult case of unison play (same tune for each instrument). It turns out that the techniques to be applied and features to be used differ significantly from those used for the recognition of a single instrument. Random forest classifiers are trained and used in the identification process. The paper "Scale Invariant Bipartite Graph Generative Model" by S. Chojnacki and M. Kłopotek is devoted to an important issue of modelling social networks with different modalities, such as user-item, author-paper, or actor-film networks. Traditionally used random graph models failed to represent some important aspects of such networks, such as node degree distributions in conjunction with clustering behavior. The newly introduced mechanisms allow for a much easier fitting of a model to real-world data. The last two papers address text/Web mining problems. The paper "Introducing Diversity to Log-Based Query Suggestions to Deal with Underspecified User Queries" by M. Sydow et al. explores the application of a concept of document set diversification, in order to improve responses to search engine queries. It turns out that to achieve a diversification in the response, there is no need to recall the original documents and one can rely on characteristics of previous queries only, enhanced possibly with some Wikipedia-based statistics. Wikipedia data are also valuable when categorizing documents, as K. Ciesielski et al demonstrate in the paper "Wikipedia-Based Document Categorization." A mapping between the words of a language and hierarchical Wikipedia categories is created on the basis of a Wikipedia category graph and page graph. It constitutes a foundation of mapping the whole document to a set of categories which is then rectified based on common supercategories and *tfidf* (term frequency inverse document frequency) like statistics.

The last track of the SIIS 2011 Joint Conference was devoted to **Natural Language Processing** (NLP). It was opened by an invited plenary talk by Joakim Nivre entitled "Bare-Bones Dependency Parsing." The author presented the general methodological and implementational issues connected with inducing parsers on the basis of annotated examples. In contrast to many other experiments, the presented approach does not utilize intermediate phrase structures.

In the Internet era, when more and more electronic texts in many natural languages become available each day, automatic processing of these texts is one of the most important tasks for computer applications. Among the two main approaches to NLP application building — rule-based and machine learning paradigms — the latter has become more popular. These methods are a common denominator of the first group of papers.

Regarding the problems of dependency parsing techniques, in addition to the invited paper by J. Nivre, A. Wróblewska and M. Woliński present preliminary experiments in the induction of a dependency parser for Polish. Although such experiments were already conducted for many languages, there were no results reported for Polish data yet. The next three papers in the NLP section concern various aspects of dealing with natural language semantics. In the first one

B. Broda et al. describe an evaluation methodology for automated Wordnet expansion algorithms. The next paper by Ł. Kobyliński addresses the problem of word sense disambiguation in a limited domain (in this case economy). The author uses class association rules to create an effective and human-understandable rule-based classifier. The third paper is devoted to semantic relations extraction. In this paper, A. Pohl describes an ontology-based method for selecting testing examples for relation extraction, and a method of their validation.

The subsequent four papers in the NLP section describe problems concerning words and phrases: M. Marcińczuk et al. describe the recognition of proper names in texts, using a very rich set of features for training CRF models. E. Hajnicz describes the creation of a semantic valence dictionary. T. Śniatowski and M. Piasecki present the outcomes of combining the results of three Polish taggers. Finally, the problems of lemmatization of nominal phrases in Polish are presented by Ł. Degórski.

In the final two papers included in the NLP section M. Junczys-Dowmunt and A. Szał present the concept of symmetrical word alignment, which outperforms one-way alignment, and A. Wawer and K. Sakwerda describe an experiment with building an ontology for sentiment analysis in the process of text annotation.

We would like to express our thanks to the invited speakers and the authors of papers for their contributions. We would also like to thank all the Program Committee members and invited reviewers for their excellent job. Last but not least, we gratefully acknowledge the generous support from the Office of Naval Research Global and Fonds National de la Recherche Luxembourg.

Pascal Bouvry
Mieczysław A. Kłopotek
Franck Leprévost
Małgorzata Marciniak
Agnieszka Mykowiecka
Henryk Rybiński

Conference Organization

Steering committee

Pascal Bouvry	University of Luxembourg
Mieczysław A. Kłopotek	Institute of Computer Science PAS, Poland
Jacek Koronacki	Institute of Computer Science PAS, Poland
Franck Leprévost	University of Luxembourg
Józef Lubacz	Warsaw University of Technology, Poland
Małgorzata Marciniak	Institute of Computer Science PAS, Poland
Mieczysław Muraszkiewicz	Warsaw University of Technology, Poland
Agnieszka Mykowiecka	Institute of Computer Science PAS, Poland
Björn Ottersten	University of Luxembourg
Henryk Rybiński	Warsaw University of Technology, Poland
Mirosław Słomiński	Warsaw University of Technology, Poland

Publishing Chair

Leonard Bolc	Polish Japanese Institute of Information Technology, Poland

Programme Committee

Witold Abramowicz	Poznań University of Economics, Poland
Stanisław Ambroszkiewicz	Institute of Computer Science PAS, Poland
Alex Biryukov	University of Luxembourg
António Horta Branco	University of Lisbon, Portugal
Luis Miguel de Campos	University of Granada, Spain
Andrzej Czyżewski	Gdańsk University of Technology, Poland
Jan Daciuk	Gdańsk University of Technology, Poland
Tapio Elomaa	Tampere University of Technology, Finland
Piotr Gawrysiak	Warsaw University of Technology, Poland
Marek Gorgoń	AGH University of Science and Technology, Poland
Jerzy W. Grzymała-Busse	University of Kansas, USA
Wojciech Jamroga	University of Luxembourg
Józef Korbicz	University of Zielona Góra, Poland
Zbigniew Kotulski	Warsaw University of Technology, Poland

Anna Kupść	University of Bordeaux 3, France
Alessio Lomuscio	Imperial College London, UK
Ramón López-Cózar Delgado	University of Granada, Spain
Krzysztof Marasek	Polish Japanese Institute of Information Technology, Poland
Nicola Di Mauro	University of Bari, Italy
Sjouke Mauw	University of Luxembourg
Maciej Michalewicz	IBM Netezza Poland
Zbigniew Michalewicz	University of Adelaide, Australia
Karel Pala	Masaryk University, Czech Republic
Wojciech Penczek	Institute of Computer Science PAS, Poland
Maciej Piasecki	Wrocław University of Technology, Poland
Gábor Prószéky	MorphoLogic, Hungary
Adam Przepiórkowski	Institute of Computer Science PAS, Poland
Zbigniew W. Raś	University of North Carolina at Charlotte, USA
Jan Rauch	University of Economics, Czech Republic
Gilbert Ritschard	University of Geneva, Switzerland
Peter Ryan	University of Luxembourg
Abdel-Badeeh M. Salem	Ain Shams University, Egypt
Franciszek Seredyński	Institute of Computer Science PAS, Poland
Andrzej Skowron	Warsaw University, Poland
Marian Srebrny	Institute of Computer Science PAS, Poland
Marcin Sydow	Polish Japanese Institute of Information Technology, Poland
Stan Szpakowicz	University of Ottawa, Canada
Roman Świniarski	San Diego State University, USA
Ryszard Tadeusiewicz	AGH University of Science and Technology, Poland
Jonathan Timmis	University of York, UK
Krzysztof Trojanowski	Institute of Computer Science PAS, Poland
Angelina Tzacheva	University of South Carolina Upstate, USA
Jerzy Urbanowicz	Institute of Computer Science PAS, Poland
Antti Valmari	Tampere University of Technology, Finland
Zygmunt Vetulani	Adam Mickiewicz University, Poland
Alicja Wakulicz-Deja	University of Silesia, Poland
Sławomir T. Wierzchoń	Institute of Computer Science PAS, Poland
Peter Wittenburg	Max Planck Institute for Psycholinguistics, The Netherlands
Karsten Wolf	University of Rostock, Germany
Bożena Woźna-Szcześniak	Jan Długosz University, Poland

Invited Reviewers

Nicolas Bernard
Elżbieta Hajnicz
Eric Joanis
Andrew V. Jones
Hugo Jonker
Alistair Kennedy
Mirosław Kurkowski
Jacek Małyszko
Marek Ostaszewski
Jakub Piskorski
Peter Ryan
Marcin Seredyński
Jarosław Skaruz
Mirosław Szaban
Piotr Świtalski
Sebastien Varrette
Alina Wróblewska

Organizing Committee

Piotr Borkowski
Michał Ciesiołka
Grzegorz Mańko
Marek Miszewski
Antoni Siennicki

Table of Contents

Invited Papers

Security and Trust

Data Mining and Machine Learning

Natural Language Processing

Correspondences on Hyperelliptic Curves and Applications to the Discrete Logarithm

Gerhard Frey[1] and Ernst Kani[2,⋆]

[1] Institute for Experimental Mathematics, University of Duisburg-Essen, 45219 Essen, Germany
frey@iem.uni-due.de
http:www.esaga.uni-due.de/gerhard.frey

[2] Department of Mathematics and Statistics, Queen's University Kingston, Ontario, K7L 3N6, Canada
Kani@mast.queensu.ca
http:www.mast.queensu.ca/~kani/

Abstract. The discrete logarithm is an important crypto primitive for public key cryptography. The main source for suitable groups are divisor class groups of carefully chosen curves over finite fields. Because of index-calculus algorithms one has to avoid curves of genus ≥ 4 and non-hyperelliptic curves of genus 3. An important observation of Smith [17] is that for "many" hyperelliptic curves of genus 3 there is an explicit isogeny of their Jacobian variety to the Jacobian of a non-hyperelliptic curve. Hence divisor class groups of these hyperelliptic curves are mapped in polynomial time to divisor class groups of non-hyperelliptic curves. Behind his construction are results of Donagi, Recillas and Livné using classical algebraic geometry. In this paper we only use the theory of curves to study Hurwitz spaces with monodromy group S_4 and to get correspondences for hyperelliptic curves. For hyperelliptic curves of genus 3 we find Smith's results now valid for ground fields with odd characteristic, and for fields with characteristic 2 one can apply the methods of this paper to get analogous results at least for curves with ordinary Jacobian.

Keywords: hyperelliptic curves, discrete logarithms, curves of genus 3.

1 Introduction

One fundamental need for many applications of public key cryptography is the construction of groups with hard discrete logarithm. Nowadays, the main source for such groups comes from arithmetic geometry and consists of divisor class groups of curves over finite fields $\mathbb{F}_q$ with q elements.

This development was a great stimulus for computational arithmetic geometry. A bit disappointing is that the same methods used for construction of candidates for cryptographically strong curves can be used for attacks (see Section 2).

⋆ Supported by a Discovery Grant from the Natural Sciences and Engineering Research Council of Canada (NSERC).

P. Bouvry et al. (Eds.): SIIS 2011, LNCS 7053, pp. 1–19, 2012.

The outcome is that curves of genus larger than 3 do not provide strong groups. Even more surprising is Diem's result [3] that for genus 3 there is an index-calculus algorithm which makes the divisor class groups of generic curves weak but does not affect the (more special) hyperelliptic curves.

Assume now that the characteristic of the ground field is different from 2. It was Smith [17] who first realized that explicit isogenies for hyperelliptic curves of genus 3 can be used to transfer divisor classes of $\mathcal{O}(q^5)$ hyperelliptic curves to those of non-hyperelliptic curves of genus 3 and so make the discrete logarithm insecure again. In his work he used results from "classical" algebraic geometry due to Recillas, Donagi and Livné [4].

The purpose of this paper is to give an elementary approach to Smith's results which uses only the theory of curves and elementary algebra and is otherwise self-contained. This is based on the observation that the so-called "trigonal construction" of Recillas, Donagi and Smith is a consequence of the study of certain curve covers of $\mathbb{P}^1$ whose monodromy (or Galois) group is the symmetric group S_4. As a result, we find for every g a Hurwitz space (cf. Section 4) which parameterizes a subspace of those hyperelliptic curves C of genus g which admit a non-trivial correspondence to a curve D of genus g that can be expected to be non-hyperelliptic.

Moreover, if the ground field is $\mathbb{F}_q$, then this correspondence is computable in polynomial time in $\log(q)$.

For $g = 3$ we find the results of Smith again (and are able to extend them to the case of characteristic 3 which he excludes.) To be more precise: By our methods we find a rapidly computable isogeny from the Jacobian variety J_C of C to the Jacobian variety J_D of D of small degree. A more detailed study of the correspondence shows that this isogeny has as kernel an isotropic subspace of the points of order 2 of J_C and is indeed the isogeny studied by Smith. (Details will be given in a forthcoming paper of the second author [9].) But we emphasize that for application to cryptography the results given in this paper are sufficient.

In addition we show that the space of hyperelliptic curves for which the correspondence exists is parameterized by the $(g+1)$-fold product of the generic elliptic curve with a point of order 3 which gives immediately and without any heuristic that $\mathcal{O}(q^{g+2})$ isomorphism classes of hyperelliptic curves over $\mathbb{F}_q$ are affected.

Another advantage of our approach is that it can be applied also in characteristic 2 (but at present only to curves with an ordinary Jacobian variety). In the last section we give a short sketch of this generalization; for details we again refer to [9].

1.1 Discrete Logarithms

Many protocols for public key crypto systems are based on discrete logarithms in groups G of prime order ℓ (see [5]).

Definition 1. The *computational Diffie-Hellman problem* (DHCP) for G is: For randomly given elements $a, b \in G$ compute $k \in \mathbb{Z}/(\mathrm{ord}(b))$ such that $b^k = a$. In this case we write: $k := \log_b(a)$.

There are families of algorithms using only the structure "group" (and called *generic*) that compute discrete logarithms (DL) with complexity $\mathcal{O}(\ell^{1/2})$, e.g. the baby-step-giant step algorithm of Shanks and Pollard's ρ-algorithm ([1]). By work of Maurer and Wolf [14] we know that in *black box groups* we cannot do better. This motivates the search for families of "concrete" groups G for which DHCP cannot be solved with algorithms of complexity smaller than $\sim \sqrt{\ell}$, and we shall say that the discrete logarithm in G is "weak" if we find an algorithm that computes discrete logarithms faster, for instance with complexity $\mathcal{O}(\ell^d)$ with $d < 1/2$, or polynomial in $\log(\ell)$ or subexponential in $\log(\ell)$ ([1]).

1.2 Index-Calculus

All known algorithms that compute the DL in groups G' faster than the generic ones are built in the following way. One finds a transfer of the DL in G' to the DL in a group G that is computed in subexponential or even polynomial time and in G one can apply the pattern of index-calculus, which we want to describe now.

One destroys the "homogeneity" of groups and chooses a "factor base" consisting of relatively few elements. Then one computes G as $\mathbb{Z}$-module given by the free abelian group generated by the base elements modulo relations.

Next one has to prove that with high probability every element of G can be written (fast and explicitly) as a sum of elements in the factor base.

So one has to find a method to create sufficiently many relations in a short time. Usually this is done by a kind of "sieving". Crucial for the method is to balance the number of elements in the factor base to make the linear algebra over $\mathbb{Z}$ manageable and to guarantee "smoothness" of arbitrary elements with respect to this base.

The classical example for index-calculus is applied to the discrete logarithm in the multiplicative group of finite fields. The method was discovered by Kraitchik 1922 [12], re-invented several times and named as index-calculus by Odlyzko 1984 [16]. Theorems about the distribution of numbers with only small prime divisors and sieving (algebraic number field sieve and function field sieve) yield an algorithm of subexponential complexity with $\alpha = 1/3$.

2 Discrete Logarithms in Divisor Class Groups

The success of the classical index-calculus method relies on the fact that points on the group scheme $\mathcal{G}_m$, the multiplicative group, can be easily lifted to points defined over number fields. This picture changes radically if we replace the multiplicative group by abelian varieties of positive dimension, for instance by elliptic curves or more generally by Jacobian varieties of curves of genus ≥ 1 because of structural results like the Mordell-Weil theorem, which prevents the existence of "smooth" points over number fields.

To compute in J_C one presents its points by divisor classes of degree 0.

If not otherwise stated, a curve C defined over a perfect field K (i.e. all algebraic extensions of K are separable) is assumed to be projective, smooth and geometrically connected. Its genus is denoted by $g(C)$.

With K_s we denote the algebraic closure of K, and with C_s the curve obtained from C by constant field extension from K to K_s.

By G_K we denote the Galois group of K_s/K, i.e. the group of automorphisms of K_s that fix K elementwise.

A *divisor* on C_s is a formal sum $D = \sum_{P \in C(K_s)} z_P P$ with $z_P \in \mathbb{Z}$ and almost all $z_P = 0$. The degree of D is $\sum z_P$. Two divisors D_1, D_2 are equivalent iff there is a function f on C_s such that the divisor of zeros and poles of f is equal to $D_1 - D_2$. $\mathrm{Pic}^0(C_s)$ is the group of divisor classes of degree 0 of C_s. There is (after the choice of a "point at infinity" $P_\infty \in C(K_s)$) a canonical isomorphism between $J_C(K_s)$ and $\mathrm{Pic}^0(C_s)$.

We now assume that $P_\infty \in C(K)$. Since G_K acts on points, divisors, functions and hence on the divisor class group of C_s in a canonical way, we get that the divisor class group of degree 0 of C is $\mathrm{Pic}^0(C) = \mathrm{Pic}^0(C_s)^{G_K}$ and that this group is canonically isomorphic to $J_C(K)$.

The whole arithmetic in these divisor class groups is ruled by the theorem of Riemann-Roch. As one consequence we state that with fixed P_∞ we can represent (not necessarily uniquely) elements in $\mathrm{Pic}^0(C)$ by divisors $P_1 + \cdots + P_t - t \cdot P_\infty$ with $t \leq g(C)$ and $P_i \in C(K_s)$ such that the natural action of G_K leaves this sum invariant.

To use these groups for cryptographic purposes one chooses C over a finite field $\mathbb{F}_q$ and one has to solve deep problems in computational arithmetic geometry like point counting and addition formulas in divisor class groups. For the needs of cryptography, this has been solved at least partly in a satisfying way. We state in particular that the results of Heß [7] yield algorithms for group operations in divisor class groups that are of polynomial complexity both in $g(C)$ (with fixed q) and $\log(q)$ (with fixed $g(C)$).

As was said above, one of the main motivation for suggesting divisor class groups for DL-systems (by Miller [15] and Koblitz [10],[11] around 1985) was the difficulty to apply the "classical" index-calculus, and this is true till today. But there are various other ways to find "special" elements in $\mathrm{Pic}^0(C)$ if the genus of C is larger than 1: There are classes which are presented by less than $g(C)$ points, and it may happen that the points representing the given class are rational over K. Hence one can find factor bases, do index-calculus in a very refined way and gets the following result:

Theorem 1 (Diem, Gaudry, Thomé, Thériault[2]). *There exists an algorithm which computes, up to* $\log(q)$*-factors, the DL in the divisor class group of curves of genus* $g(C)$ *in expected time of* $\mathcal{O}(q^{(2-2/g(C))})$.

As one consequence of the Hasse-Weil theorem (which is the analogue of the Riemann hypothesis for curves), we get that for $K = \mathbb{F}_q$ the order of $\mathrm{Pic}^0(C)$ is $\mathcal{O}(q^{g(C)})$. It follows that for genus $g(C) > 3$ the index-calculus algorithm is much faster than the generic algorithms, and hence these curves yield rather weak crypto systems and should be avoided.

But a closer look, done by Diem [3], shows that one can alter the factor base such that the *degree* of a plane model of C becomes the essential measure for the efficiency of the index-calculus algorithm.

Theorem 2 (Diem). *If C is given by a plane curve of degree d (singularities allowed) then the DL in the group of divisor classes of degree 0 is, up to $\log(q)$-factors, of complexity $\mathcal{O}(q^{2-\frac{2}{d-2}})$.*

One sees immediately that curves of genus 1 (elliptic curves) and of genus 2 are not affected by these results since for them the order of $\mathrm{Pic}^0(C)$ over $\mathbb{F}_q$ is $\mathcal{O}(q)$ respectively $\mathcal{O}(q^2)$.

3 Isogenies and Correspondences

Let C be a curve over K of genus $g(C) > 0$ with Jacobian variety J_C.

We exploit the fact that $\mathrm{Pic}^0(C)$ is canonically isomorphic to $J_C(K)$ and use the theory of abelian varieties.

Definition 2. Let A, A' be abelian varieties of dimension g over K and let $\eta : A \to A'$ be a K-rational homomorphism[1] whose kernel is a finite group scheme A_0. Then η is called an *isogeny* and A is *isogenous* to A'. The *degree* of η is the order of A_0. Moreover, an isogeny η is *separable* iff A_0 is an étale group scheme, and then the degree of η is $|A_0(K_s)|$.

Remark 1.
- The homomorphisms of abelian varieties are analogous to those of abelian groups. In particular, for any finite (K-) subgroup scheme A_0 of A there is a (K-rational) isogeny of A with $ker(\eta) = A_0$ and this isogeny is, up to isomorphisms, uniquely determined.
- On the other hand, abelian varieties are kind of rigid: If η is a morphism from A to A' mapping the neutral element 0_A of A to the neutral element $0_{A'}$ of A' then η is a homomorphism.
- As above, assume that A, A' are abelian varieties of the same dimension and that A or A' is simple, i.e. has no proper abelian variety as subvariety. Then a morphism $\eta : A \to A'$ mapping 0_A to $0_{A'}$ is an isogeny iff it is not constant.

Let $f : D \to C$ be a non-constant K-rational morphism from the curve D to the curve C. Then f induces an embedding f^* of the function field $F(C)$ of C into the function field $F(D)$ of D, and the degree $\deg(f) := [F(D) : f^*F(C)]$ of this field extension is called the *degree* of f.

As before, let C_s and D_s be the curves over K_s obtained by constant field extension from K to K_s. Then f induces a morphism $f_s : D_s \to C_s$ (which we usually denote by f again).

The morphism $f : D \to C$ induces two homomorphisms f^* and f_* on the associated divisor groups. To define the first, let $P \in C(K_s)$ be a point. Then

[1] i.e. η is a morphism of varieties compatible with the addition morphisms on A and A'.

$f^*(P)$ is by definition the divisor of D_s which is given by the formal sum of the points (with multiplicity in ramification points) lying in $f^{-1}(P)$. By linear extension f^* defines a homomorphism from the divisor group of C_s to the divisor group of D_s, called the *conorm map* (associated to f).

It is a basic fact of curve theory that divisors of degree n are mapped to divisors of degree $\deg(f) \cdot n$ and that principal divisors are mapped to principal divisors. We thus obtain an induced homomorphism from $\mathrm{Pic}^0(C_s)$ to $\mathrm{Pic}^0(D_s)$ which is again denoted by f^*. This map is Galois invariant, and so it maps $\mathrm{Pic}^0(C)$ to $\mathrm{Pic}^0(D)$.

The map f_* is by definition the linear extension of f to the group of divisors of D_s. Since f_* maps a principal divisor (t) to the principal divisor $(N(t))$ of its norm, we see that f_* induces a homomorphism, again denoted by f_*, from $\mathrm{Pic}^0(D_s)$ to $\mathrm{Pic}^0(C_s)$ that is Galois invariant. It is called the *norm map* (associated to f).

Using the functorial properties of Jacobians, one can show that f^* induces an (algebraic) homomorphism from J_C to J_D and that f_* induces an (algebraic) homomorphism from J_D to J_C.

Now assume that C_1, C_2, D are curves over K. Let $f_i : D \to C_i$ be non-constant K-rational morphisms. It follows that $T_{f_1,f_2} := (f_2)_* \circ f_1^*$ induces a homomorphism from J_{C_1} to J_{C_2} that we call *the correspondence attached to* (f_1, f_2).

We shall describe T_{f_1,f_2} explicitly in the special case that f_1 is fully ramified in a point $P_\infty \in C_1(K_s)$; i.e., that there is a unique point Q_∞ of D_s that is mapped to P_∞ by f_1.

We can represent a divisor class c of degree 0 of C_1 by $\sum_{i \le g_1} P_i - g_1 P_\infty$, where $g_1 = g(C_1)$. Let $(Q_{i,j})_{1 \le i \le g_1, 1 \le j \le \deg(f_1)}$ be the set of points (listed with multiplicities) in $D(K_s)$ which are mapped to $P_1, \ldots, P_{g_1}$ by f_1. Then $T_{f_1,f_2}(c)$ is the divisor class of $\sum_{i,j} f_2(Q_{i,j}) - \deg(f_1) g_1 f_2(Q_\infty)$.

Lemma 1. *In the above situation, assume in addition that J_{C_1} is a simple abelian variety, and that there is no non-constant morphism of degree $\le \deg(f_1)$ from C_2 to the projective line. Then T_{f_1,f_2} has a finite kernel, and if $g(C_1) = g(C_2)$, then T_{f_1,f_2} is an isogeny.*

Proof. Since J_{C_1} is simple, it is enough to show that T_{f_1,f_2} is not the zero map. So take a point $Q_1 \in D(K_s) \setminus f_2^{-1}(f_2(Q_\infty))$ and let c be the class of $P - P_\infty$, where $P = f_1(Q_1)$. Then $T_{f_1,f_2}(c)$ is the class of the divisor $D_P := \sum_{Q \in f_1^{-1}(P)} f_2(Q) - \deg(f_1) \cdot f_2(Q_\infty)$. Note that $D_P \neq 0$ (as a divisor). If the class of D_P is trivial, then we find a non-constant function on C_2 with pole order $\le \deg(f_1)$ and hence a non-constant map of C_2 to the projective line of degree $\le \deg(f_1)$, contradiction.

4 Hurwitz Spaces Attached to Hyperelliptic Curves in Odd Characteristic

4.1 The Case of Algebraically Closed Ground Field

In this subsection we *assume that $K = K_s$ is algebraically closed.*

For the first statements of this section K is allowed to have arbitrary characteristic but for the major part it is necessary to assume that the characteristic of K is odd. This hypothesis will be done in due time.

We first review the following concepts and terminology.

Let $f : D \to C$ be a non-constant separable morphism of curves. We call f (or D, if the context is clear) a *cover* of C. Let $\tilde{F}$ be the splitting field (or Galois closure) of the associated extension $F(D)/f^*F(C)$ of function fields. Since K is algebraically closed, it follows that $\tilde{F} = F(\tilde{D})$ is the function field of a curve $\tilde{D}/K$. Moreover, the inclusion $F(D) \subset \tilde{F}$ induces an (essentially unique) cover $f' : \tilde{D} \to D$. We call the composition $\tilde{f} = f \circ f' : \tilde{D} \to C$ the *Galois closure* of the cover $f : D \to C$.

The *monodromy group* of $f : D \to C$ is the group $G_f := \mathrm{Aut}(\tilde{f}) = \{\alpha \in \mathrm{Aut}(\tilde{D}) : \tilde{f} \circ \alpha = \tilde{f}\}$ of automorphisms of its Galois closure $\tilde{f}$. Thus, G_f is (isomorphic to) the Galois group of the Galois field extension $\tilde{F}/f^*F(C)$, i.e., $G_f \simeq \mathrm{Gal}(\tilde{F}/f^*F(C))$.

If $P \in \tilde{D}(K)$, let $G_P = G_P(\tilde{f}) = \{\alpha \in G_f : \alpha(P) = P\}$ be the ramification group (or decomposition group) at P. Thus $|G_P| = e_P(\tilde{f})$ is the ramification index of P. The set $\mathrm{Ram}(\tilde{f})$ of ramified points Q of $\tilde{f}$ on C is the set of points in $C(K)$ for which one (and hence each) point in $\tilde{f}^{-1}(Q)$ has ramification index > 1.

We recall that a cover $f : D \to C$ is *tamely ramified* if it is separable and if all ramification indices are prime to the characteristic of the ground field. In this case all ramification groups G_P are cyclic, the contribution of the point $P \in D(K)$ to the discriminant divisor of f is $|G_P| - 1$ and the *Riemann–Hurwitz genus formula* (used many times in the following) is very easy to handle. Moreover the compositum of tamely ramified covers is tamely ramified, and the so-called Lemma of Abhyankar holds. For all these facts we refer to [18].

The cover $\tilde{f}$ (respectively f) is *unramified* if $\mathrm{Ram}(\tilde{f}) = \emptyset$.

We observe:

Lemma 2. *If* $C = \mathbb{P}^1$, *then* $G_f = \langle G_P \rangle_{P \in \tilde{D}(K)}$.

For $U := \langle G_P \rangle_{P \in \tilde{D}(K)}$ has as its fixed field the function field of an unramified cover of $\mathbb{P}^1$, so $U = G_f$ because $\mathbb{P}^1$ has no non-trivial unramified covers.

The collection $(\{G_P\}_{P \in \tilde{f}^{-1}(Q)} : Q \in \mathrm{Ram}(\tilde{f}))$ of the conjugacy classes of the ramification subgroups of G_f (indexed by the set $\mathrm{Ram}(\tilde{f})$) is called the *ramification type* $\mathbf{C}$ of the cover $\tilde{f}$ (or of the cover f).

A *Hurwitz space* is a moduli space which parameterizes (isomorphism classes) of covers $h : C \to \mathbb{P}^1$ of the projective line of given degree n and given ramification type. Hence Hurwitz spaces are moduli spaces for covers with given ramification type and monodromy group.

We now turn to the construction of certain covers (and associated Hurwitz spaces) whose monodromy group is S_4, the symmetric group of degree 4. For this, *we shall assume for the rest of this subsection that* $\mathrm{char}(K) \neq 2$.

Lemma 3. *Assume that $f : C \to \mathbb{P}^1$ is a tamely ramified cover of degree n and that for every ramified point $Q \in \mathbb{P}^1(K)$ the number of points in $f^{-1}(Q)$ with even ramification order is even. Then $G_f \subset A_n$, the alternating group of degree n.*

Proof Let $\{P_1, \ldots, P_t\}$ be the ramified points over Q. Let e_i be the ramification index of P_i. Since e_i is prime to the characteristic of K by hypothesis, the multiplicity of the discriminant divisor of f at Q is $\sum_{i=1}^{t}(e_i - 1)$ and hence is even. So the field discriminant $\mathrm{disc}(F(C)/f^*F(\mathbb{P}^1))$ is a square in $f^*F(\mathbb{P}^1) \simeq K(x)$, and hence by field theory, $G_f \leq A_n$.

Theorem 3. *Let $f_2 : C_1 \to \mathbb{P}^1$ be a cover of degree 3 such that every point on $\mathbb{P}^1$ has at least one unramified extension.*

Let $f_1 : C \to C_1$ be a cover of degree 2 with ramification points $P_1, \ldots, P_{2t}$ on C_1 such that exactly one point in ${f_2}^{-1}(f_2(P_j))$ is unramified with respect to f_1 and such that all ramification points of f_2 are unramified under f_1.

Define $f : C \to \mathbb{P}^1$ by $f = f_2 \circ f_1$. Denote by $\tilde{C}_1$ the Galois closure of the cover given by f_2, by $\tilde{C}$ the Galois closure of the cover $f : C \to \mathbb{P}^1$ and by C_Δ the cover over $\mathbb{P}^1$ obtained by adjoining the square root of the discriminant of f_2 to the function field of $\mathbb{P}^1$.

1. *The monodromy group of f_2 is isomorphic to S_3, the symmetric group of degree 3.*
2. *The cover $\tilde{C}_1/C_\Delta$ is unramified and is cyclic of degree 3.*
3. *The monodromy group G_f of f is isomorphic to S_4.*

Proof. 1. The assumption on the ramification behavior of f_2 forces that f_2 cannot be Galois. Since $\deg(f_2) = 3$, it thus follows that its Galois closure has Galois group S_3.
2. From part 1. (or otherwise), we see that that the discriminant divisor $\mathrm{disc}(f_2)$ of f_2 cannot be a square, and hence C_Δ is the unique quadratic cover of $\mathbb{P}^1$ over which $\tilde{f}_2$ factors. By Galois theory, $\tilde{C}_1/C_\Delta$ is a Galois extension with cyclic Galois group of order 3. Since all ramification indices of f_2 (and hence of $\tilde{f}_2$) are ≤ 2, we see that $\tilde{C}_1/C_\Delta$ is unramified.
3. Let $F = F(\mathbb{P}^1)$, $F_1 = F(C_1)$ and $F_2 = F(C)$ be the function fields of the curves $\mathbb{P}^1$, C_1 and C. Then f_1 and f_2 induce inclusions $F \subset F_1 \subset F_2$. Since the assumptions of Lemma 3 are satisfied for f, we see from the proof of the lemma that $\mathrm{disc}(F_2/F)$ is a square in F, and so the hypotheses of the following Proposition 1 are satisfied. It thus follows from that proposition that $G_f \simeq S_4$, as claimed.

Proposition 1. *Let $F \subset F_1 \subset F_2$ be a tower of separable field extensions, and let $\tilde{F}_2/F$ be the Galois closure (or splitting field) of F_2/F. Assume that F_i/F is not normal for $i = 1, 2$ and that $[F_2 : F_1] = 2$ and $[F_1 : F] = 3$. If the discriminant $\mathrm{disc}(F_2/F)$ is a square in F and if $\mathrm{char}(F) \neq 2$, then $\mathrm{Gal}(\tilde{F}_2/F) \simeq S_4$.*

Proof. Let $\tilde{F}_1$ be the Galois closure of F_1/F. Since $[F_2 : F_1] = 2$, we see that $\tilde{F}_2/\tilde{F}_1$ is a compositum of quadratic extensions which are all conjugate to $F_2\tilde{F}_1$, and so $N := \mathrm{Gal}(\tilde{F}_2/\tilde{F}_1)$ is an elementary abelian 2-group.

Since $\mathrm{disc}(F_2/F)$ is a square, we know that $G := \mathrm{Gal}(F_2/F)$ is a subgroup of the alternating group A_6. Thus also $N \leq A_6$. But every non-cyclic elementary abelian 2-group of A_6 is of the form $\{g_i g_j\}$, where $g_1, g_2, g_3 \in S_6$ are 3 disjoint transpositions, and hence $|N| \leq 4$. Now $N \neq 1$ because otherwise $F_2 = \tilde{F}_1$, so F_2/F would be normal, contradiction. Moreover, $|N| \neq 2$ because otherwise $N = \langle g \rangle \trianglelefteq G$, where $g \in A_6$ is a $(2,2)$-cycle. Since $3 = [F_1 : F] \mid |G|$, $\exists \sigma \in G$ of order 3 which therefore centralizes g. But no such pair (g, σ) exists in A_6, contradiction. Thus $|N| = 4$, and hence $|G| = [\tilde{F}_2 : \tilde{F}_1][\tilde{F}_1 : F] = |N| \cdot 6 = 24$.

Let $P_3 = \langle \sigma \rangle$ be a 3-Sylow subgroup of G. If $P_3 \trianglelefteq G$, then the "Normalizator/Centralizator theorem" [8] yields that $G/C_G(P_3)$ with $C_G(P_3)$ the centralizer of P_3 would be a subgroup of $\mathrm{Aut}\ P_3$ and hence $C_G(P_3)$ would have index dividing 2. So it would contain N. This is a contradiction because as was mentioned above, the elements of N do not centralize σ. Thus, by Sylow, G has 4 distinct 3-Sylow subgroups $P_{3,i}$ and so the conjugation action on the set $\{P_{3,i}\}_{i=1}^4$ defines a homomorphism $\varphi : G \to S_4$ whose kernel is $N_1 := \cap_{i=1}^4 N_G(P_{3,i})$. Clearly, $3 \nmid |N_1|$, so $|N_1| \mid 2$ (because $|N_G(P_{3,i})| = 6$). If $|N_1| = 2$, then $N_1 \not\leq N$ because N has no subgroup of order 2 which is normal in G. But then $N_1 N$ is an elementary abelian subgroup of order 8 in A_6, contradiction. Thus $N_1 = 1$, so φ is injective and hence yields an isomorphism $G \simeq S_4$.

Remark 2. In the situation of Theorem 3, assume that s points $Q_1, \ldots, Q_s$ of $\mathbb{P}^1$ ramify in the cover f_2. Then the Riemann-Hurwitz formula [18] shows that $g(C_1) = s/2 - 2$ and $g(C_\Delta) = s/2 - 1$. In particular, $s \geq 4$ because $g(C_1) \geq 0$.

Moreover, if (as in Theorem 3) $2t$ points of C_1 ramify in the cover f_1, then $g(C) = 2g(C_1) - 1 + t = s + t - 5$.

We thus see that $s + t$ points of $\mathbb{P}^1$ ramify in the S_4-cover $\tilde{f} : \tilde{C} \to \mathbb{P}^1$. Since all have ramification index 2, we see by the Riemann-Hurwitz formula that $g(\tilde{C}) = 6(s + t - 4) + 1$.

The ramification structure of $\tilde{f}$ is a follows. If $Q' \in \tilde{C}(K)$ lies above some Q_i, then Q' is unramified over $\tilde{C}_2$ so $G_{Q'}$ is generated by a transposition (because $\mathrm{Gal}(\tilde{C}/\tilde{C}_2) = N$ contains all $(2,2)$-cycles of S_4). On the other hand, if $P' \in \tilde{C}(K)$ lies above some $f_2(P_i)$, then P' is ramified over $\tilde{C}_2$, so $G_{P'}$ is generated by a $(2,2)$-cycle. Thus, the ramification type $\mathbf{C}$ of $\tilde{f}$ consists of s conjugacy classes of transpositions and t conjugacy classes of $(2,2)$-cycles of S_4.

The covers considered in Theorem 3 naturally give rise to Hurwitz spaces $\tilde{\mathcal{H}}_{s,t}$ and $\mathcal{H}_{s,t}$ as follows. For a given $s \geq 4$ and t, let $\tilde{\mathcal{H}}_{s,t}(K)$ denote the set of isomorphism classes of covers $f = f_2 \circ f_1 : C \to \mathbb{P}^1$ of the type defined in Theorem 3. (As usual, two covers $f : C \to \mathbb{P}^1$ and $f' : C' \to \mathbb{P}^1$ are called isomorphic if there is an isomorphism $\alpha : C \to C'$ such that $f' \circ \alpha = f$.) Moreover, since the group $\mathrm{Aut}(\mathbb{P}^1)$ acts on $\tilde{\mathcal{H}}_{s,t}(K)$ (via $(\alpha, f) \mapsto \alpha \circ f$), we can also consider the orbit space $\mathcal{H}_{s,t}(K) := \mathrm{Aut}(\mathbb{P}^1) \backslash \tilde{\mathcal{H}}_{s,t}(K)$. Then we have

Theorem 4. *The moduli problem $\tilde{\mathcal{H}}_{s,t}$ is finely represented by a Hurwitz space $\tilde{\mathbb{H}}_{s,t}/K$ of dimension $s+t$ and the moduli problem $\mathcal{H}_{s,t}$ is coarsely represented by the quotient space $\mathbb{H}_{s,t} = \mathrm{Aut}(\mathbb{P}^1) \backslash \tilde{\mathbb{H}}_{s,t}$ of dimension $s + t - 3$.*

Proof. By Theorem 3 and Remark 2 we see that we can identify $\tilde{\mathcal{H}}_{s,t}(K)$ with the set $\mathcal{H}^{in}(S_4, \mathbf{C})$ of S_4-covers with ramification type $\mathbf{C}$ as in Remark 2. Since this extension is tamely ramified, the assertions follow from the work of Fried/Völklein and Wewers, as was discussed in [6], p. 37.

4.2 Rationality

We now investigate to what extent the constructions of the previous subsection can be done over an arbitrary perfect ground field K (with $\mathrm{char}(K) \neq 2$). Here a basic difficulty is that the technique of Galois closure does not lead in general to curve covers.

To explain this in more detail, let $f : D \to C$ be a K-cover of curves, i.e. f is a separable, non-constant K-morphism of curves over K. As before, f gives rise to a separable extension $F(D)/f^*F(C)$ of the associated function fields, and so we can consider the splitting field (or Galois closure) $\tilde{F}$ of the extension $F(D)/f^*F(C)$.

However, $\tilde{F}$ in general does not need to be the function field of a (geometrically connected) curve $\tilde{D}/K$. For this it is sufficient and necessary that K is algebraically closed in $\tilde{F}$. In this case we say that f *admits a Galois closure*, for we have as before two induced Galois covers $f' : \tilde{D} \to D$ and $\tilde{f} = f \circ f' : \tilde{D} \to C$. It is immediate that if $\tilde{f}$ exists, then this construction commutes with base-change, and so $G_f := \mathrm{Aut}(\tilde{f}) \simeq G_{f_s}$ is the (geometric) monodromy group of the K_s-cover $f_s : D_s \to C_s$

Theorem 5. *Let $f_2 : C_1 \to \mathbb{P}^1_K$ and $f_1 : C \to C_1$ be two K-covers of curves such that their base-changes with K_s satisfy the hypotheses of* Theorem 3.

Then $f = f_2 \circ f_1 : C \to \mathbb{P}^1_K$ admits a Galois closure if and only if the field discriminant $\delta := \mathrm{disc}(F(C)/f^*F(\mathbb{P}^1_K))$ is a square in $f^*F(\mathbb{P}^1_K) \simeq K(x)$. If this is the case, then the Galois closure of f is an S_4-cover $\tilde{f} : \tilde{C} \to \mathbb{P}^1_K$.

Proof. Let $F := f^*F(\mathbb{P}^1_K) \subset F(C) =: F_2$, and let $\tilde{F}$ be the splitting field of the extension F_2/F.

Suppose first that f admits a Galois closure, i.e. that K is algebraically closed in $\tilde{F}$. Then $\tilde{F}$ and K_s are linearly disjoint over K, so $\tilde{F}K_s$ is the splitting field of the extension F_2K_s/FK_s, and $\mathrm{Gal}(\tilde{F}/F) = \mathrm{Gal}(\tilde{F}K_s/FK_s)$. By the proof of Theorem 3 we know that $\mathrm{Gal}(\tilde{F}K_s/FK_s) \leq A_6$, and so also $\mathrm{Gal}(\tilde{F}/F) \leq A_6$. By field theory, this means that $\delta \in (F^\times)^2$.

Conversely, assume that δ is a square in F. Then the tower $F \subset F_1 := f_1^*F(C_1) \subset F_2$ of field extensions satisfies the hypotheses of Proposition 1, and so $\mathrm{Gal}(\tilde{F}/F) \simeq S_4$. Since also $\mathrm{Gal}(\tilde{F}K_s/FK_s) \simeq S_4$ by Theorem 3, it follows that $\tilde{F}$ and K_s are linearly disjoint over K, so K is algebraically closed in $\tilde{F}$ and hence f admits a Galois closure.

Remark 3. In the situation of Theorem 5, suppose that δ is not a square in $F \simeq K(x)$. Since δ is a square in $FK_s = K_s(x)$ (cf. Theorem 3), we see that $F' := F(\sqrt{\delta})$ is a quadratic constant extension of F, i.e., $F' = FK'$, where $K' = K(\sqrt{c})$, for some $c \in K$. Thus, it follows that the cover $f_{K'} : C_{K'} \to \mathbb{P}^1_{K'}$ (which is obtained from f by base-change with K') does admit a Galois closure.

Moreover, by replacing the quadratic cover $f_1 : C \to C_1$ by its quadratic twist $f_1^\chi : C^\chi \to C_1$ (associated to the extension K'/K), we see that the twisted cover $f^\chi = f_2 \circ f_1' : C' \to \mathbb{P}^1_K$ satisfies the hypotheses of Theorem 5 and hence admits a Galois closure $\tilde{f}^\chi : \tilde{C}' \to \mathbb{P}^1_K$ with group S_4.

So we get: Either $f : C \to \mathbb{P}^1$ or its twist $f^\chi : C' \to \mathbb{P}^1$ admits a Galois closure, which is a S_4-cover.

4.3 The Hyperelliptic Case

For the rest of this section and for the whole following section we take $s = 4$. This is equivalent to the hypothesis that $g(C_1) = 0$ or to the hypothesis that C is a hyperelliptic curve of genus $t-1$ with hyperelliptic cover f_1. The curve C_Δ is an elliptic curve E, and we can choose as the origin of E for instance the unique point over Q_1. Then the cover $E/\mathbb{P}^1$ is given by computing modulo $-id_E$, i.e., by mapping a point on E to its $x-$coordinate, if E is given by a Weierstraß equation.

The moduli space of hyperelliptic curves $\mathcal{M}_{H,t-1}$ of genus $t-1$ has dimension $2t-3$.

For $t = 3$ Theorem 4 shows that the dimension of $\mathbb{H}_t := \mathbb{H}_{4,t}$ is 4 and hence larger than the dimension of the moduli space $\mathcal{M}_{H,2}$ of curves of genus 2. (Recall that all curves of genus 2 are hyperelliptic.). We can interpret this by the fact that there are infinitely many covers f_2 which give rise to the same isomorphism class of curves of genus 2. In fact for a given set of 6 points on $\mathbb{P}^1$ there are infinitely many maps of degree 3 such that pairs of these points have the same image.

For $t > 4$ the dimension of $\mathbb{H}_t$ is smaller than the dimension of $\mathcal{M}_{H,t-1}$, and so we will get only very special hyperelliptic curves attached to points on $\mathbb{H}_t$.

But the interesting case is $t = 4$. We get hyperelliptic curves of genus 3, and the moduli space of such curves is irreducible and has dimension 5.

By elementary linear algebra we shall see in Subsection 5.1 that every hyperelliptic curve of genus 3 covers $\mathbb{P}^1$ by a map f such that f corresponds to a point in $\mathbb{H}_t$, and that, generically, to given hyperelliptic curve C there are exactly 2 such covers up to equivalence. Hence we get a 2-fold cover map from $\mathbb{H}_t$ to the moduli space of hyperelliptic curves of genus 3.

Construction of Points on $\mathbb{H}_t$. Take $f = f_2 \circ f_1 : C \to \mathbb{P}^1$ as above. It follows that both C_Δ and $\tilde{C}_1$ are elliptic curves E and E', respectively, which come equipped with an isogeny $\rho : E' \to E$ of degree 3.

We have a bit more: The monodromy group of f_2 is S_3. We embed it into the group of automorphisms $\mathrm{Aut}_K(E')$. Let φ be such an automorphism. Then φ is of the form $\pm id_{E'} + t_V$ where t_V is the translation on E' by a point V.

Let $\sigma \in S_3$ be an element of order 2 and $\tau \in S_3$ be an element of order 3. Since $\langle \sigma, \tau \rangle = S_3$, we have $\sigma = -id_{E'} + t_R$ with $R \in E'(\mathbb{F}_q)$ and $\tau = t_{V_3}$, where V_3 is a point of order 3 of E'. By an appropriate choice of the neutral elements of E and E' (we use that $K = K_s$) we can assume that $V = 0$ and that f_2 is an isogeny.

Let $R_1, R'_1, R_2, R'_2, \ldots, R_{2t}, R'_{2t}$ be the set of points on E' which ramify in $C \times_{C_1} E'/E'$. Then we find $\epsilon_j \in \{-1, 1\}; 1 \leq j \leq t$ such that after a suitable ordering we get $R_k = -R'_k$ for $k = 1, \ldots, 2t$ and $R_j = R_{t+j} + \epsilon_j \cdot V_3$ for $j = 1, \ldots, t$.

Conversely, begin with an elliptic curve E with $Q'_1, \ldots, Q'_4 \in E(K)[2]$, the group of points of order 2 of E. We normalize and assume that Q'_1 is the neutral element of E and denote by π_E the map from E to $E/\langle -id_E \rangle = \mathbb{P}^1$. Define $Q_j := \pi_E(Q'_j)$.

Take E' with point V_3 of order 3 such that $\rho : E' \to E$ is an isogeny of degree 3 with kernel $\langle V_3 \rangle$.

Since $\rho(0_{E'}) = 0_E$, the curve $E'/\langle -id_{E'} \rangle$ is a projective line covering $E/\langle -id_E \rangle$ by a map f_ρ of degree 3 that is ramified exactly in $Q_1, \ldots, Q_4$ in the following way: In the inverse image of Q_i under f_ρ there is one point with ramification index 2 and one unramified point. Hence the discriminant divisor of f_ρ is $Q_1 + \cdots + Q_4$.

Define Γ_ρ as the subset of E'^t consisting of all the t-tuples $(R_1, \ldots, R_t)$ for which $\{\pm R_j, \pm(R_j + \epsilon_j \cdot V_3)); \; 1 \leq j \leq t\}$ (the signs $\pm$ taken independently) has strictly less than $4t$ elements.

Next choose t points $R_1, \ldots, R_t \in E'(K) \setminus \Gamma_\rho$.

Take $P_1, \ldots, P_{2t}$ as the images under $\pi_{E'}$ of $\{R_j, R_j + \epsilon_j \cdot V_3, \; j = 1, \ldots, t\}$. By assumption, these points are distinct and we have $f_\rho(P_j) = f_\rho(P_{j+t})$ for $j = 1, \ldots, t$.

It follows that $f_\rho, P_1, \cdots, P_{2t}$ give rise to a point in $\mathbb{H}_t$.

From the above considerations we know that we get all points of $\mathbb{H}_t$ by this construction.

Before we summarize we make one remark. We have to look at covers f modulo the equivalence relation induced by automorphisms of $\mathbb{P}^1$. But applying such an automorphism does not change the isomorphism class of the elliptic curve E. Moreover elliptic curves with points of order 3 are parameterized by the modular curve $X_1(3)$ (which has genus 0).

Theorem 6. *We get a surjective map from the set of points of* $\{(E', V_3) \in X_1(3)(K), (R_1, \ldots, R_t) \in E'(K)^t \setminus \Gamma_\rho\}$ *to* $\mathbb{H}_t(K)$ *with finite fibres.*

Hence there is a rational dominant morphism from $(\mathcal{E}_3)^t_{X_1(3)}$ *(the t-fold fibre product over* $X_1(3)$ *of the universal elliptic curve* $\mathcal{E}_3$ *over* $X_1(3)$*) to* $\mathbb{H}_t(K)$ *with finite fibres.*

4.4 The Trigonal Construction

The basic task of the classical "trigonal construction" of Recillas, Donagi and Livné (cf. [4]) is the following. Given a curve C/K equipped with cover $f = f_2 \circ f_1 : C \to \mathbb{P}^1$ with degree $f_1 = 2$ and $f_2 = 3$ (for short this is called usually a (2,3)-cover), construct another curve D/K equipped with cover $g : D \to \mathbb{P}^1$ that has degree 4 and a surjective homomorphism $h : J_C \to J_D$ (of a specific type). In the cases studied by these authors, $g(C) = 3$, but this hypothesis is not necessary. Here we shall see that the construction of the S_4-cover via Galois closure (cf. Subsection 4.1) naturally solves this task.

Thus, let $f = f_2 \circ f_1 : C \to \mathbb{P}^1$ be a $(2,3)$-cover as in Theorem 3, and let $\tilde{f} = f \circ f' : \tilde{C} \to \mathbb{P}^1$ be its Galois closure. Thus $G_f = \mathrm{Aut}(\tilde{f}) \simeq S_4$. The Galois group $H := \mathrm{Aut}(f')$ of $\tilde{C}/C$ has order 4 and contains two transpositions; let σ be one of these. Then σ is contained in precisely two of the stabilizers $T_1, \ldots, T_4$ of the elements $\{1,2,3,4\}$ on which S_4 acts. If $T = T_i$ is one of these, then we have $T \cap H = \langle\sigma\rangle$.

Let $\pi_T : \tilde{C} \to D := \tilde{C}/T$ be the quotient map. Then $\tilde{f}$ factors over π_T as $\tilde{f} = g \circ \pi_T$, where $g : D \to \mathbb{P}^1$ has $\deg(g) = 4$. Note that g is primitive (does not factor over a quadratic subcover).

We can use the Hurwitz genus formula to compute the genus of D. (Assume $s = 4$.) Since the Galois closure of $g : D \to \mathbb{P}^1$ is $\tilde{f} : \tilde{C} \to \mathbb{P}^1$, we see that exactly the points on $\mathbb{P}^1$ ramified in $\tilde{C}$ are ramified in D. Since the fixed field of the subgroup A_4 is $C_\Delta = E$, the discriminant divisor of g equals the discriminant divisor of $C_\Delta/\mathbb{P}^1$ plus 2 times another divisor. This is enough to conclude that the points $Q_1, \ldots, Q_4$ have one ramified extension of order 2 and the t points in $\{f_2(P_1), \ldots, f_2(P_{2t})\}$ (recall that the image under f_2 of $\{P_1, \ldots, P_{2t}\}$ consists of exactly t points) have 2 ramified extensions. It follows that the genus of D is equal to $t-1$, and hence is equal to the genus of C.

Finally, we construct a correspondence from J_C to J_D. For this, let $\pi_\sigma : \tilde{C} \to D' := \tilde{C}/\langle\sigma\rangle$ be the quotient map. Then f' factors over π_σ as $f' = \varphi_1 \circ \pi_\sigma$ and similarly π_S factors as $\pi_S = \varphi_2 \circ \pi_\sigma$.

We remark that φ_1 cannot be unramified. For otherwise the compositum of the function fields $F(D')$ and $F(\tilde{C}_1)$ would be unramified over $F(C) \cdot F(\tilde{C}_1)$. But the discussion in the proof of Theorem 3 shows that this is not true. We choose one of these ramification points as P_∞ on C and so the assumptions of Lemma 1 are satisfied for $\varphi_1 : D' \to C$.

Definition 3. The correspondence $T_C(f) := T_{\varphi_1,\varphi_2}$ is the homomorphism from $\mathrm{Pic}^0(C)$ to $\mathrm{Pic}^0(D)$ induced by $\varphi_{2*} \circ \varphi_1^*$.

Using Lemma 1, we obtain:

Theorem 7. *Assume that the Jacobian J_C is a simple abelian variety and that D is not hyperelliptic. Then $T_C(f)$ is an isogeny.*[2]

4.5 Rationality Questions over Finite Fields

Let K be the finite field $\mathbb{F}_q$ with q elements (q odd), and let K_s be its separable closure. Let C be a hyperelliptic curve of genus $g(C) > 1$ defined over $\mathbb{F}_q$ with cover $f : C_s \to \mathbb{P}^1$ defined over K_s as above. We want to give conditions for the rationality of the isogeny of J_{C_s} induced by the correspondence $T_C(f)$.

Given C, there is a uniquely determined $\mathbb{F}_q$-rational 2-cover f_1 of C to the projective line, denoted by C_1, with $2t = 2g(C)+2$ ramification points $P_1, \ldots, P_{2t} \in$

[2] A closer study ([9]) of the situation shows that the theorem is true without the extra assumptions, and that the kernel of T_C is a maximally isotropic subgroup of $J_C[2]$. In addition it is shown that $T_C(f)$ induces the isogeny constructed in [4].

$C_1(K_s)$. The discriminant divisor $\mathrm{disc}(f_1) = P_1 + \cdots + P_{2t}$ is K-rational, so in particular the set $\{P_1, \ldots, P_{2t}\}$ is invariant under G_K.

Conversely, to a given Galois invariant set $\{P_1, \ldots, P_{2t}\}$ of points on $C_1 = \mathbb{P}^1$ we find (in general) two hyperelliptic covers $C/\mathbb{P}^1$ and $C'/\mathbb{P}^1$ whose branch loci are $\{P_1, \ldots, P_{2t}\}$. These two curves are twists of each other and become isomorphic over K_s.

We now assume that the set $\{P_1, \ldots, P_{2t}\}$ is given and that we have a 3-cover $f_2 : \mathbb{P}^1 \to \mathbb{P}^1$ defined over $\mathbb{F}_q$ which maps $\{P_1, \ldots, P_{2t}\}$ pairwise to t points on $\mathbb{P}^1$. Then we know from Remark 3 that there is exactly one $\mathbb{F}_q$-rational quadratic cover f_1 of $\mathbb{P}^1$ such that $f := f_2 \circ f_1$ admits a Galois closure with Galois group S_4 and so there is a uniquely determined hyperelliptic curve cover $C/\mathbb{P}^1$ defined over $\mathbb{F}_q$ with branch points $\{P_1, \ldots, P_{2t}\}$. By the discussion of the "trigonal construction" in Subsection 4.4, it is clear that the constructed curve D and the correspondence $T_C(f)$ from J_C to J_D are both defined over $\mathbb{F}_q$. Hence the question about rationality of curve C with rational $T_C(f)$ boils down to the question of finding f_2.

This motivates the study of covers $h = f_2 : C_1 = \mathbb{P}^1 \to \mathbb{P}^1$ with h of degree 3 defined over $\mathbb{F}_q$ with discriminant divisor $Q_1 + \cdots + Q_4$, $Q_i \neq Q_j \in \mathbb{P}^1(K_s)$ for $i \neq j$. First we see that $\{Q_1, \ldots, Q_4\}$ is Galois invariant. Let $Q'_1, \ldots, Q'_4$ be the *unramified* extensions of $Q_1, \ldots, Q_4$ under h. These 4 points are exactly the ramification points of $\tilde{C}_1/C_1$ where as usual $\tilde{C}_1$ is the Galois closure of $h : C_1 = \mathbb{P}^1 \to \mathbb{P}^1$. Hence $\tilde{C}_1$ is an absolutely irreducible curve over $\mathbb{F}_q$ of genus 1. Moreover, since our ground field is $\mathbb{F}_q$, the curve $\tilde{C}_1$ is an elliptic curve E' defined over $\mathbb{F}_q$. The monodromy group of h is S_3. As was seen in the discussion before Theorem 6, this implies that E' has an $\mathbb{F}_q$-rational point V_3 of order 3.

Lemma 4. *Let $h : \mathbb{P}^1 = C_1 \to \mathbb{P}^1$ be as above. Then $\tilde{C}_1$ is characterized as the elliptic curve E' which is uniquely determined by an affine equation $Y^2 = g'_4(X)$ with zeroes $Q_1, \ldots, Q_4$ and which has an $\mathbb{F}_q$-rational point V_3 of order 3.*

Let $E = E'/\langle V_3 \rangle$. Then h induces an isogeny of degree 3 from E' to E and E has an $\mathbb{F}_q$-rational point of order 3. This determines uniquely the twist class of E.

Conversely: Let E' be an elliptic curve with a K-rational point V_3 of order 3 and let $\rho : E' \to E$ be the isogeny with kernel $\langle V_3 \rangle$. Let $\sigma' = -id_{E'} + t_R$ with some point $R \in E'(\mathbb{F}_q)$ be an automorphism of E' of order 2 and $C_1 := E'/\langle \sigma' \rangle$. Take $\sigma = -id_E + t_{\rho(R)}$ and $\mathbb{P}^1 = E/\langle \sigma \rangle$. Then ρ induces a map $h' : C_1 \to \mathbb{P}^1$ with $\tilde{C}_1 = E'$ and the required properties.

Theorem 8. *Let $\{P_1, \ldots, P_t\}$ be a $G(K_s/\mathbb{F}_q)$-invariant set of t points in $\mathbb{P}^1(K_s)$. Let $g_4(X)$ be a polynomial of degree 4 over $\mathbb{F}_q$ with distinct roots such that the elliptic curve $E' : Y^2 = g_4(X)$ has an $\mathbb{F}_q$-rational point Q of order 3. Let $\tilde{P}_1, \ldots, \tilde{P}_t$ be points on E' with X-coordinates $P_1, \ldots, P_t$. Choose $\epsilon_1, \ldots, \epsilon_t \in \{1, -1\}$ and define P_{t+j} as the X-coordinate of $\tilde{P}_j + \epsilon_j Q$. Assume that the cardinality of $\{P_1, \ldots, P_t, P_{t+1}, \ldots, P_{2t}\}$ is $2t$ (this is generically true).*

Then there is an (up to $\mathbb{F}_q$-isomorphism) unique hyperelliptic curve cover $C/\mathbb{P}^1$ with branch points $\{P_1, \ldots, P_t, P_{t+1}, \ldots, P_{2t}\}$ that has an $\mathbb{F}_q$-rational correspondence of the form $T_C(f)$.

Remark 4. From the point of view of Hurwitz spaces Theorem 8 is a satisfying result. But it does not solve the problem: For given C decide whether E' exists and compute the equation for E'.

We shall see an explicit result for $g(C) = 3$ in the next section.

4.6 Computational Aspects

We continue to take $K = \mathbb{F}_q$ and we assume that the conditions of Theorem 8 are satisfied for the curve C.

Precomputation

1) We know equations for E'/C_1 and we can compute the isogeny ρ.
2) Next compute an equation for $H := C \times_{C_1} E'$ (i.e. compute the compositum $F(C)F(E')$ of the function fields of C and E' over the rational function field $\mathbb{F}_q(T)$ embedded by the cover maps $C \to C_1$ and $E' \to C_1$).
3) Knowing ρ, we can compute an equation for a conjugate H^τ of H with respect to the automorphism τ of order 3 of E' and hence for the Galois closure $\tilde{H} = \tilde{C}$ of f.
4) Determine a subcover $D' = \tilde{C}/\langle\sigma\rangle$ of degree 2 of $\tilde{C}$ which covers C but not E' and compute an equation of the cover $\varphi_1 : D' \to C$.
5) Choose a point $P_\infty \in C(\mathbb{F}_q)$ (this exists in all interesting cases) and compute $\varphi_1^*(P_\infty) = R_\infty^1 + R_\infty^2$.
6) Determine a subcover D of degree 3 over D' and compute an equation for D and for the cover $\varphi_2 : D' \to D$.
7.) Compute $S_\infty^j = \varphi(R_\infty^j)$.

All these computations can be performed (cf.[7]) in time and space polynomial in $\log(q)$.

Transfer of DL: Let c be a divisor class group of C. Present c by

$$\sum_{j=1,\dots,g(C)} P_j - g(C) \cdot P_\infty.$$

Lift the points P_j to points $R_{i,j}$ on D' by using the equation of the curve cover $\varphi_1 : D' \to C$ (or of the extension $F(D')/F(C)$).
Determine the images $S_{i,j}$ of $R_{i,j}$ on the curve to D by using the equation of the curve cover $\varphi_2 : D' \to D$.
Then $T(f)(c)$ is the class of $\sum_{j=1,\dots,g(C),i=1,2} S_{i,j} - g(C)(S_\infty^1 + S_\infty^2)$.
By methods of [7] one finds a representative of $T(f)(c)$ as difference of divisors of degree bounded by $g(D)$ in polynomial time in $\log(q)$.

Result: For a known map $f : C \to \mathbb{P}^1$ one can compute $T_C(f)$ in polynomial time in $\log(q)$.

5 Curves of Genus 3

5.1 The Construction of Trigonal Subcovers

We recall that to every $\mathbb{F}_q$-rational point on $\mathbb{H}_4$ we have an attached hyperelliptic curve C of genus 3 and a map $f : C \to \mathbb{P}^1$ of degree 6 such that $T_C(f)$ is

$\mathbb{F}_q$-rational. C is determined up to $\mathbb{F}_q$-isomorphisms, and $T_C(f)$ is computable in time and space polynomial in $\log(q)$.

Let us look at the situation over K_s. Since the dimension of $\mathbb{H}_4$ is 5 we get a dominant map from $\mathbb{H}_4$ to the moduli space of hyperelliptic curves of genus 3. In other words: For given Weierstraß points $Q_1, \ldots, Q_8$ of a "generic" hyperelliptic curves C we find a cover $f_2 : \mathbb{P}^1 \to \mathbb{P}^1$ *over* K_s that maps these points pairwise to 4 different points. In fact, there will be generically 2 such covers ([4]). We give a proof for this fact by elementary linear algebra.

Theorem 9. *Over K_s there is a rational dominant map of degree 2 from $\mathbb{H}_4$ to $\mathcal{M}_{H,3}$, the moduli space of hyperelliptic curves of genus 3.*

Proof. We fix 8 different points on $\mathbb{P}^1(K_s)$ lying in an affine part with affine coordinates $u_1, \ldots, u_8$.

We look for a rational function $h(U) = \frac{U^3+x_1U^2+x_2U+x_3}{x_4U^3+x_5U^2+x_6U+x_7}$ with $x_i \in K_s$ such that (without loss of generality) $h(u_1) = h(u_2) = 0; h(u_3) = h(u_4) = \infty, h(u_5) = h(u_6) = 1$ and $h(u_7) = h(u_8) = t$ where t is an appropriately chosen element in K_s.

Hence $(x_1, \ldots, x_7)$ has to be a solution of the system of linear equations

$$\begin{pmatrix} u_1^2 & u_1 & 1 & 0 & 0 & 0 & 0 \\ u_2^2 & u_2 & 1 & 0 & 0 & 0 & 0 \\ 0 & 0 & 0 & u_3^3 & u_3^2 & u_3 & 1 \\ 0 & 0 & 0 & u_4^3 & u_4^2 & u_4 & 1 \\ u_5^2 & u_5 & 1 & -u_5^3 & -u_5^2 & -u_5 & -1 \\ u_6^2 & u_6 & 1 & -u_6^3 & -u_6^2 & -u_6 & -1 \\ u_7^2 & u_7 & 1 & -t \cdot u_7^3 & -t \cdot u_7^2 & -t \cdot u_7 & -t \\ u_8^2 & u_8 & 1 & -t \cdot u_8^3 & -t \cdot u_8^2 & -t \cdot u_8 & -t \end{pmatrix} \begin{pmatrix} x_1 \\ x_2 \\ x_3 \\ x_4 \\ x_5 \\ x_6 \\ x_7 \end{pmatrix} = \begin{pmatrix} -u_1^3 \\ -u_2^3 \\ 0 \\ 0 \\ -u_5^3 \\ -u_6^3 \\ -u_7^3 \\ -u_8^3 \end{pmatrix}$$

The parameter t occurs linearly exactly in two rows of the system and hence the determinant of the extended matrix of the system is a polynomial of degree 2 in t over K_s. The condition of solvability of the system, namely that the rank of the extended matrix is ≤ 7, is satisfied if t is a zero of this polynomial, and so generically two values are possible for t.

Now take a hyperelliptic curve C over $\mathbb{F}_q$ given by an equation $Y^2 = f_8(X)$ and let $\{u_1, \ldots, u_8\}$ be the set of roots of f_8. On this set we have an action of the absolute Galois group of $\mathbb{F}_q$. We know that these values come in pairs u_j, u_{4+j} $(j = 1, \ldots, 4)$ with members behaving in the same way under the Galois action, and we look for a $\mathbb{F}_q$-rational map h with $h(u_j) = h(u_{4+j}) = t_j$.

A first condition is that the set $\{t_1, \ldots, t_4\}$ is Galois invariant, too.

In addition, one knows that the absolute Galois group of $\mathbb{F}_q$ is generated by the Frobenius automorphism ϕ_q, and so the cycles induced by this action on $\{t_1, \ldots, t_4\}$ induce cycles of quadratic polynomials defined over $\mathbb{F}_q(t_1, \ldots, t_4)$ with zeros $u_j, \ldots, u_{4+j}$. This is enough to list necessary and sufficient conditions for the rationality of h (over a possibly quadratic extension of $\mathbb{F}_q$) in terms of the decomposition of $f_8(X)$ in irreducible factors over $\mathbb{F}_q$.

For a detailed discussion we refer to [17].

Algorithmic Aspects. For a given $f_1 : C \to \mathbb{P}^1$, we first check whether the Weierstraß points satisfy the Galois condition from above. If so, we solve the linear system found in the proof of Theorem 9 if possible, and hence we obtain the rational map h ($= f_2$ in our notation above). These computations are done in an extension field of $\mathbb{F}_q$ of degree at most 8. Next we compute the discriminant of h and so we find the elliptic curves E and E'. To determine the twist class of C, we compute the class of the discriminant of $h \circ f_1$ modulo squares (alternatively, one can check whether there is a point on $\mathbb{P}^1(\mathbb{F}_q)$ that is completely split under $h \circ f_1$). Now we can proceed as in subsection 4.6.

5.2 Application to Discrete Logarithms

We now apply our results to hyperelliptic curves C of genus 3 with the additional assumption that the Jacobian J_C is a simple abelian variety. (This is the interesting case for cryptography and is true generically.) First assume that $K = K_s$. We shall use two facts about curves of genus 3.

- The moduli space of curves of genus 3 is connected and has dimension 6. Generic curves of genus 3 can be given by plane curves of degree 4 (without singularities).
- The moduli space $\mathcal{M}_{H,3}$ of hyperelliptic curves of genus 3 is connected and has dimension 5 and the generic hyperelliptic curve has no primitive cover to $\mathbb{P}^1$ of degree 4.[3]

Thus, if C is a generic hyperelliptic curve of genus 3, then the curve D constructed by the above trigonal construction cannot be hyperelliptic because D is a primitive cover of $\mathbb{P}^1$ of degree 4.

Consequence
There is a 5-dimensional subvariety U of $\mathcal{M}_{H,3}$ such that for $C \in U$ the curve D is not hyperelliptic.

Now take $K = \mathbb{F}_q$ and q large. Then the number of isomorphism classes of hyperelliptic curves C of genus 3 defined over $\mathbb{F}_q$ and satisfying

1. J_C is a simple abelian variety
2. $C \in U$
3. $T_f(C)$ is rational over $\mathbb{F}_q$

is of order $\mathcal{O}(q^5)$.[4]

By Theorem 7 $T_C(f)$ is an isogeny over K_s and hence over $\mathbb{F}_q$ if $C \in U$. Even a very coarse and elementary estimate of the degree of this isogeny shows that for cryptographically interesting primes ℓ we get a transfer of the DL in $\mathrm{Pic}^0(C)[\ell]$ to the DL in $\mathrm{Pic}^0(D)[\ell]$ in polynomial time and Theorem 2 yields that the complexity of the discrete logarithm in $\mathrm{Pic}^0(C)[\ell]$ is, up to logarithmic factors, $\mathcal{O}(q)$.

---

[3] The authors would like to thank Lange ([13]) for pointing out this result.
[4] For a sharper estimate see [17].

Theorem 10 (Smith). *There are $\mathcal{O}(q^5)$ isomorphism classes of hyperelliptic curves of genus 3 defined over $\mathbb{F}_q$ for which the discrete logarithm in the divisor class group of degree 0 has complexity $\mathcal{O}(q)$, up to log-factors.*

Since $|\mathrm{Pic}^0(C)| = \mathcal{O}(q^3)$, the DL system of these hyperelliptic curves of genus 3 is weak.

6 The Case of Characteristic 2

The above method extends to the case of $\mathrm{char}(K) = 2$ with some minor modifications, provided that C is an *ordinary* hyperelliptic curve of genus 3. Two of the main differences here are that (i) the S_4-extension is now wildly ramified and that (ii) we cannot use the arguments involving the square roots of field discriminants. But both these problems can be circumvented in the ordinary case. We briefly outline the main ideas involved.

Let $K = \mathbb{F}_q$, where $q = 2^n$, and let C/K be a hyperelliptic curve of genus 3 with hyperelliptic cover $f_1 : C \to C_1 = \mathbb{P}^1$. Then C is *ordinary* (i.e. its Hasse-Witt invariant σ_C (or the 2-rank of J_C) equals 3) if and only if the discriminant divisor of f_1 is of the form $\mathrm{disc}(f_1) = 2(P_1 + \cdots + P_4)$, where $P_1, \ldots, P_4 \in C_1(K_s)$ are 4 distinct points.

By the linear algebra method of Subsection 5.1 it is easy to construct (many!) degree 3 subcovers $f_2 : C_1 \to \mathbb{P}^1$ such that $f_{2*}(\mathrm{disc}(f_1)) = 4(\bar{P}_1 + \bar{P}_2)$, with $\bar{P}_1 \neq \bar{P}_2 \in \mathbb{P}^1(K_s)$.

As before, put $f = f_2 \circ f_1 : C \to \mathbb{P}^1_K$, and let $f_s : C_s \to \mathbb{P}^1$ be the cover induced by base-change. Then one can show that the monodromy group of f_s is again S_4. To see this, note that the hypothesis of "ordinary" implies that all non-trivial ramification groups G_P are still cyclic of order 2, and that each is generated by a (2, 2)-cycle in S_6. Thus, by Lemma 2, it follows that $G_{f_s} \leq A_6$, and so the proof of Proposition 1 can be modified to show that $G_{f_s} \simeq S_4$.

By Galois theory (and group theory), the splitting field $\tilde{F}$ of $F(C)/f^*F(\mathbb{P}^1_K)$ is a Galois extension of $F := f^*F(\mathbb{P}^1_K)$ of order dividing 48. Since we know by the above that $\mathrm{Gal}(\tilde{F}K_s/FK_s) \simeq S_4$, we see that either $\mathrm{Gal}(\tilde{F}/F) \simeq S_4$, and that hence f has a Galois closure with group S_4, or that there is a quadratic twist f_1^χ of $f_1 : C \to C_1$ such that $f^\chi := f_2 \circ f_1^\chi$ has a Galois closure $\tilde{f}^\chi$ with group S_4.

Thus, up to a quadratic twist, $f : C \to \mathbb{P}^1_K$ has a Galois closure $\tilde{f} : \tilde{C} \to \mathbb{P}^1_K$ with monodromy group S_4. By the method of the trigonal construction of Subsection 4.4, we thus obtain a K-rational curve D equipped with a primitive cover $g : D \to \mathbb{P}^1_K$ of degree 4 and a correspondence $T_C(f) : J_C \to J_D$ which turns out to be an isogeny. This latter fact requires the arguments mentioned in the footnote to Theorem 7. It is to be hoped that D turns out to be non-hyperelliptic, but at present the authors do not know if the analogue of the second "known" fact of Subsection 5.2 is true in characteristic 2.

Acknowledgment. The authors would like to thank very much the referee for encouragement, careful reading of the manuscript and for very helpful comments.

References

1. Cohen, H., Frey, G. (eds.): Handbook of Elliptic and Hyperelliptic Curve Cryptography. CRC (2005)
2. Diem, C., Gaudry, P., Thomé, E., Thériault, N.: A double large prime variation for small genus hyperelliptic index calculus. Math. Comp. 76, 475–492 (2007)
3. Diem, C.: An Index Calculus Algorithm for Plane Curves of Small Degree. In: Heß, F., Pauli, S., Pohst, M. (eds.) ANTS 2006. LNCS, vol. 4076, pp. 543–557. Springer, Heidelberg (2006)
4. Donagi, R., Livné, R.: The arithmetic-geometric mean and isogenies for curves of higher genus. Ann. Scuola Norm. Sup. Pisa Cl. Sci(4) 28(2), 323–339 (1999)
5. Frey, G.: Relations between Arithmetic Geometry and Public Key Cryptography. Advances in Mathematics of Communications (AMC) 4(2), 281–305 (2010)
6. Frey, G., Kani, E.: Curves of genus 2 with elliptic differentials and associated Hurwitz spaces. Contemp. Math. 487, 33–81 (2009)
7. Hess, F.: Computing Riemann-Roch spaces in algebraic function fields and related topics. J. Symbolic Comp. 33(4), 425–445 (2002)
8. Huppert, B.: Endliche Gruppen I. Springer, Heidelberg (1967)
9. Kani, E.: On the trigonal construction (in preparation)
10. Koblitz, N.: Elliptic curve cryptosystems. Mathematics of Computation 48, 203–209 (1987)
11. Koblitz, N.: Hyperelliptic cryptosystems. Journal of Cryptology 1, 139–150 (1989)
12. Kraitchik, M.: Théorie des nombres, vol. 1. Gauthier-Villars (1922)
13. Lange, H.: e-mail to G. Frey (March 24, 2009)
14. Maurer, U.M., Wolf, S.: Lower bounds on generic algorithms in groups. In: Nyberg, K. (ed.) EUROCRYPT 1998. LNCS, vol. 1403, pp. 72–84. Springer, Heidelberg (1998)
15. Miller, V.: Short programs for functions on curves (1986), `http://crypto.stanford.edu//miller/`
16. Odlyzko, A.M.: Discrete logarithms in finite fields and their cryptographic significance. In: Beth, T., Cot, N., Ingemarsson, I. (eds.) EUROCRYPT 1984. LNCS, vol. 209, pp. 224–314. Springer, Heidelberg (1985)
17. Smith, B.: Isogenies and the Discrete Logarithm Problem in Jacobians of Genus 3 Hyperelliptic Curves. In: Smart, N.P. (ed.) EUROCRYPT 2008. LNCS, vol. 4965, pp. 163–180. Springer, Heidelberg (2008); Revised version in: J. Cryptology 22, 505–529 (2009)
18. Stichtenoth, H.: Algebraic function fields and codes. Springer, Berlin (1993)

Bare-Bones Dependency Parsing

Joakim Nivre

Uppsala University
Department of Linguistics and Philology
Box 635, 75126 Uppsala, Sweden
joakim.nivre@lingfil.uu.se
http://stp.lingfil.uu.se/~nivre/

Abstract. If all we want from a syntactic parser is a dependency tree, what do we gain by first computing a different representation such as a phrase structure tree? The principle of parsimony suggests that a simpler model should be preferred over a more complex model, all other things being equal, and the simplest model is arguably one that maps a sentence directly to a dependency tree – a bare-bones dependency parser. In this paper, I characterize the parsing problem faced by such a system, survey the major parsing techniques currently in use, and begin to examine whether the simpler model can in fact rival the performance of more complex systems. Although the empirical evidence is still limited, I conclude that bare-bones dependency parsers can achieve state-of-the-art parsing accuracy and often excel in terms of efficiency.

Keywords: natural language parsing, dependency parsing.

1 Introduction

The notion of dependency has come to play an increasingly central role in natural language parsing in recent years. On the one hand, lexical dependencies have been incorporated in statistical models for a variety of syntactic representations such as phrase structure trees [10], LFG representations [51], and CCG derivations [9]. On the other hand, dependency relations extracted from such representations have been exploited in many practical applications, for example, information extraction [11], question answering [3], and machine translation [12]. Given these developments, it is not surprising that there has also been a growing interest in parsing models that map sentences directly to dependency trees, an approach that will be referred to as *bare-bones dependency parsing* to distinguish it from parsing methods where dependencies are embedded into or extracted from other types of syntactic representations.

The bare-bones model can be motivated by the principle of parsimony, which says that we should prefer the simplest of two models that explain the same phenomena. If we can show that bare-bones dependency parsers produce dependency trees with at least the same accuracy and efficiency as more complex models, then they would be preferred on grounds of simplicity. In this paper, I will begin by explaining how the parsing problem for bare-bones dependency parsers

P. Bouvry et al. (Eds.): SIIS 2011, LNCS 7053, pp. 20–32, 2012.

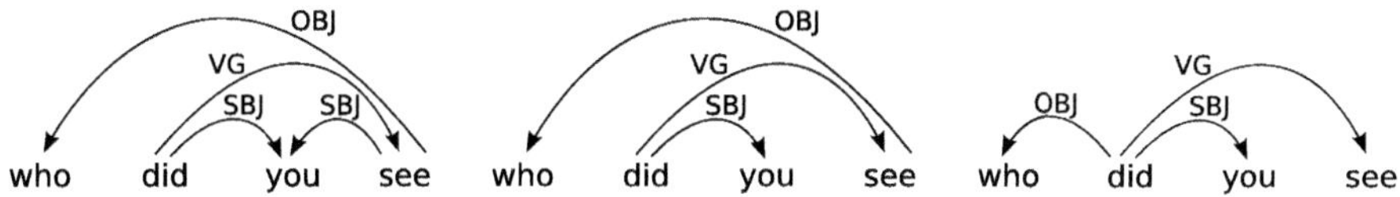

Fig. 1. Dependency graphs: dag (left), tree (middle), projective tree (right)

differs from the more familiar parsing problem for phrase structure parsers. I will go on to survey the main techniques that are currently in use, grouped into four broad categories: chart parsing, constraint-based parsing, transition-based parsing, and hybrid methods. Finally, I will examine a number of recent studies that compare the performance of different types of parsers, demonstrating that bare-bones dependency parsers achieve strongly competitive results.

2 Parsing Problem

In this section, I will define the formal syntactic representations used by bare-bones dependency parsers, discuss the parsing problem they face, and briefly review metrics and data sets used to evaluate them.

2.1 Dependency Graphs

We will take a dependency structure for a sentence $S = w_1, \ldots, w_n$ to be a directed graph $G = (V, A)$, where

1. $V = \{1, \ldots, n\}$ is a set of nodes, with the node i representing the token w_i,
2. $A \subseteq V \times R \times V$ is a set of arcs, with the arc (i, r, j) representing the syntactic relation r from the head w_i to the dependent w_j (given some relation set R).

Sometimes, unlabeled dependency graphs are used, in which case an arc is simply a pair of nodes (i, j). I will use the notation $i \rightarrow j$ to indicate that there is an arc from i to j (with or without a label).

Depending on what additional constraints we want to impose on dependency structures, we get different classes of dependency graphs, with different expressivity and complexity.

- If we only require graphs to be connected and acyclic, then words can have more than one head, which is convenient for representing deep syntactic relations, as exemplified in Figure 1a, where the word *you* is analyzed as the subject not only of the finite auxiliary *did* but also of the main verb *see*.
- If we require the graph to be a tree, then each word can have at most one head, but we can still represent extraction phenomena using non-projective arcs, as shown in Figure 1b, where the word *who* is analyzed as the direct object of the main verb *see*.
- If we require every subtree to have a contiguous yield, finally, we get the class of *projective* trees, where long-distance dependencies cannot always be represented directly, as illustrated in Figure 1c, where the word *who* is analyzed as a dependent of the auxiliary *did* instead of the main verb *see*.

	OBJ	ROOT	SBJ	VG	RELATION $r_i \in R$
OUTPUT	4	0	2	2	HEAD $h_i \in V \cup \{0\}$
INPUT	1	2	3	4	NODE $i \in V$
	who	did	you	see	WORD $w_i \in S$
	WP	VBD	PRP	VB	TAG $t_i \in T$
	...	...	...	...	...

Fig. 2. Dependency parsing as assignment of heads (h_i) and relations (r_i) to nodes (i)

Formally, an arc $i \rightarrow j$ in a dependency tree is projective if there is a path from i to every node k that occurs between i and j in the linear order. A dependency tree is projective if all its arcs are projective. Equivalently, a dependency tree is projective if every subtree has a contiguous yield, that is, if the nodes in every subtree form a contiguous substring of the sentence. Hence, the tree in Figure 1b is non-projective because the arc *see* → *what* spans the words *did* and *you*, which are not reachable from *see*, and the subtree rooted at *see* has the discontiguous yield *who* ... *see*.

2.2 Parsing

Regardless of what restrictions we put on dependency graphs, the basic parsing problem for a bare-bones dependency parser consists in finding the optimal set of arcs, given the nodes as input. This is different from phrase structure parsing, where only the terminal nodes are given as input and where both internal nodes and edges have to be inferred during parsing. Many algorithms for dependency parsing are restricted to projective trees, which reduces the complexity of the parsing problem, but a number of systems are capable of handling non-projective trees, either by using non-standard algorithms or through post-processing. Very few systems can deal with directed acyclic graphs.

If we restrict our attention to trees, then the parsing problem can be simplified further and reduced to finding a head h_i and a dependency relation r_i for every node i (including a dummy head and relation for the root of the tree). Figure 2 gives a schematic representation of the input and output for a parse of the sentence *who did you see* with the non-projective tree in Figure 1b. Note that the input is typically a sequence of words annotated with part-of-speech tags and possibly preprocessed in other ways.

2.3 Evaluation

Dependency parsers are usually evaluated by measuring precision and recall on dependency relations (arcs), with or without labels. When dependency graphs are restricted to trees, precision and recall coincide and are often referred to as the attachment score (AS).

Dependency parsers for English are standardly evaluated on data from the Penn Treebank (PTB) [28], which requires that the original phrase structure annotation is converted to dependency graphs. Two widely used conversions are

Penn2Malt [41], which uses the head-finding rules to produce strictly projective trees with a restricted set of generic dependency labels, and Stanford Typed Dependencies [29], which uses a richer inventory of labels and is not restricted to trees. Another important benchmark corpus is the Prague Dependency Treebank (PDT) [18], which is the largest treebank annotated with dependency trees, 25% of which are non-projective.[1] Finally, the CoNLL shared tasks on multilingual dependency parsing created data sets for 13 languages in 2006 [4] and 10 languages in 2007 [43]. Many of these data sets are converted from other types of annotation, most of them contain non-projective dependencies, and all of them are restricted to dependency trees.

3 Parsing Techniques

In this section, I will review the major approaches that are currently used for bare-bones dependency parsing, grouping them into chart parsing, constraint satisfaction, transition-based parsing, and hybrid methods that combine two or more of the basic techniques.

3.1 Chart Parsing Techniques

A straightforward method for dependency parsing is to view it as a restricted form of context-free parsing and reuse chart parsing algorithms like CKY and Earley, an idea that is implicit already in [21] and [16] and that has been exploited in a number of grammar-based dependency parsers [55,56,22,27,2]. The widely used algorithm of Eisner [13,14] exploits the special constraints on dependency trees to reduce parsing complexity to $O(n^3)$ for lexicalized parsing – as opposed to $O(n^5)$ for the naive application of CKY or Earley – by using a split-head representation where chart items represent a head and its dependents on one side only.

Statistical models for disambiguation are used to score candidate dependency trees for a given sentence, and the parsing problem amounts to finding the highest scoring tree $T^*(S)$ for a given sentence S:

$$T^*(S) = \operatorname*{argmax}_{T \in \mathcal{T}(S)} \mathcal{F}(S, T)$$

where $\mathcal{F}(S, T)$ is the score of the dependency tree T for S and $\mathcal{T}(S)$ is the space of possible dependency trees for S. When combined with chart parsing techniques, the global scoring function needs to factor by subgraphs corresponding to chart items and usually takes the following form:

$$\mathcal{F}(S, T) = \sum_{g \in T} f(S, g)$$

[1] This refers to the analytical (surface syntactic) annotation layer, as opposed to the tectogrammatical (deep syntactic) annotation layer, where all trees are projective.

Table 1. First-, second- and third-order models for chart-based dependency parsing (UAS = unlabeled attachment score on PTB under the Penn2Malt conversion)

Model	Subgraph	Complexity	UAS	Reference
1st-order		$O(n^3)$	90.9	McDonald et al. [32]
2nd-order		$O(n^3)$	91.5	McDonald and Pereira [34]
3rd-order		$O(n^4)$	93.0	Koo and Collins [24]

where $f(S, g)$ is the score of the subgraph g for S.[2] The score $f(g)$ is typically computed as a linear combination of a high-dimensional feature vector $\mathbf{f}$, which captures salient properties of g, and a corresponding weight vector $\mathbf{w}$, which indicates the relative importance of these properties in distinguishing good parse trees from bad. Weights are normally estimated using empirical data in the form of a treebank, and the maximal scope of features is determined by the size of the subgraphs. A first-order model has subgraphs corresponding to single arcs [32]; a second-order model scores pairs of arcs, usually sibling arcs on the same side of the head [34]; and a third-order model scores triples of arcs, for example, sibling arcs plus a grandparent arc [24]. As shown in Table 1, models of higher order tend to give better parsing accuracy but also lead to increased parsing complexity. Third-order grand-sibling models currently constitute the state of the art for this kind of parsing technique.

One drawback of the chart parsing approach, besides the strict limitations on feature scope, is that it does not easily extend to non-projective trees, let alone directed acyclic graphs. Algorithms have been proposed for restricted subsets of non-projective trees, but the best parsing complexity is $O(n^7)$, which is of little practical use [26,17]. However, as shown by McDonald and Pereira [34], it is possible to recover both non-projective arcs and multiple heads through post-processing, a technique that was used in one of the two top-ranked systems in the CoNLL shared task 2006 [33].

3.2 Parsing as Constraint Satisfaction

A different approach is to view dependency parsing as a constraint satisfaction problem, where we start from a compact representation of all dependency graphs compatible with the input and successively eliminate invalid graphs through the propagation of grammatical constraints, as originally proposed by Maruyama [31]. By adding numerical weights to constraints, Menzel and Schröder [37] turned this into an optimization problem:

$$T^*(S) = \underset{T \in \mathcal{T}(S)}{\operatorname{argmax}} \prod_{c:\neg c(S,T)} f(c)$$

Here $c(S, T)$ is true if S and T satisfies the constraint c, $f(c)$ is the weight of c, and $T^*(S)$ is again the optimal dependency tree for S. The main difference

[2] When scores represent probabilities and the natural operation is multiplication, we can use a logarithmic transformation to turn this into an additive model.

with respect to the scoring model considered earlier for chart parsing is that the factorization is over constraints, not subgraphs of the tree. In addition, weights are multiplied instead of added, because constraint weights range from 0 to 1 and weights closer to 0 indicate more severe constraints.

Constraint-based parsing can easily accommodate different classes of dependency graphs and does not have the same inherent limitations on features or constraints and chart parsing, because the constraint model is independent of any particular algorithm for constructing dependency trees. The downside of this, however, is that constraint satisfaction is computationally intractable in general, so exact search methods cannot be used except in special cases. Hence, Foth et al. [15] use transformational search, starting from an arbitrary tree and trying to improve the score through tree transformations. Other techniques that have been explored with promising results are integer linear programming [50,30], Gibbs sampling [39], and loopy belief propagation [57].

An interesting special case of the constraint-based approach is the maximum spanning tree parser of McDonald et al. [35], which can be regarded as a constraint-based model:

$$T^*(S) = \underset{T \in \mathcal{T}(S)}{\operatorname{argmax}} \sum_{c:c(S,T)} f(c)$$

where the constraint $c_{i \to j}(S,T)$ is true just in case the arc $i \to j$ is in the tree T for S. Under this model, finding the optimal dependency tree is equivalent to finding the maximum directed spanning tree in a complete graph containing all possible arcs, a problem that can be solved exactly in $O(n^2)$ time using algorithms from graph theory. A distinct advantage of this approach is that it gives us a very efficient parser for (possibly) non-projective trees, and McDonald et al. [35] showed that this significantly improves unlabeled attachment score for PDT compared to a projective chart parsing model with the same feature scope. Unfortunately, however, the spanning tree technique is restricted to first-order models, as any attempt to extend the scope of constraints beyond single arcs makes the parsing problem NP complete [36].

3.3 Transition-Based Parsing

A third prominent method is to view parsing as deterministic search through a transition system (or state machine), guided by a statistical model for predicting the next transition, an idea first proposed by Yamada and Matsumoto [59]. By way of example, Figure 3 shows the arc-eager transition system for projective dependency trees first described in [40]. In transition-based parsing, dependency graphs are scored indirectly by scoring the sequence of transitions that derive them. If $s(S)$ is the start state for sentence S, then the optimal parse is defined by the transition sequence $t_1, \ldots, t_m$ that maximizes the sum of scores for each transition t_i given the result of applying all the previous transitions:

$$T^*(S) = \underset{T=[t_m \circ \cdots \circ t_1](s(S))}{\operatorname{argmax}} \sum_{i=1}^{m} f(t_i, [t_{i-1} \circ \cdots \circ t_1](s(S)))$$

Start state: $([\,], [1, \ldots, n], \{\,\})$
Final state: $(S, [\,], A)$

Shift:	$(S, i\|B, A)$	$\Rightarrow$	$(S\|i, B, A)$
Reduce:	$(S\|i, B, A)$	$\Rightarrow$	$(S, \mathrm{B}, \mathrm{A})$
Right-Arc:	$(S\|i, j\|B, A)$	$\Rightarrow$	$(S\|i\|j, B, A \cup \{i \rightarrow j\})$
Left-Arc:	$(S\|i, j\|B, A)$	$\Rightarrow$	$(S, j\|B, A \cup \{i \leftarrow j\})$

Fig. 3. Transition system for arc-eager dependency parsing. A parser state consists of a stack S of partially processed nodes, and input buffer B of remaining input nodes, and a set A of dependency arcs defining the (partially built) dependency graph. The parser starts in a state where S and A are empty and applies one of four transitions repeatedly until it reaches a state where B is empty. Whatever arcs have been accumulated in A then defines the output dependency graph. The transitions Shift and Right-Arc both move a node from B to S but the latter first adds an arc connecting the top node of S to the first node in B. The transitions Reduce and Left-Arc both pop the stack but the latter first adds an arc connecting the first node in B to the top node in S.

Finding the optimal transition sequence is often intractable, and transition-based parsers therefore use greedy, often completely deterministic search, just taking the highest-scoring transition out of every parser state. This approach has two distinct advantages. The first is that it avoids the limited feature scope of chart parsing, since parsing decisions can be based on very rich feature representations of the derivation history (including the partially built tree). The second is that it avoids the efficiency problems in constraint-based parsing and chart-parsing with higher-order models or non-projective trees. Transition-based parsers run in $O(n)$ time for projective trees [40] and limited subsets of non-projective trees [1]. For arbitrary non-projective trees, the worst-case complexity is $O(n^2)$, but observed running time can still be linear with an appropriate choice of transition system [42]. Moreover, transition systems can be extended to handle directed acyclic graphs, still in linear time [54].

The main drawback with transition-based parsing is that it may suffer from error propagation due to search errors especially if the scoring model is only trained to maximize the accuracy of local transitions rather than complete transition sequences. Nevertheless, a locally trained, completely deterministic system was one of the two top-ranked systems in the CoNLL shared task 2006 [45]. More recently, Zhang and Clark [61] have shown how these problems can be alleviated by training models to maximize the accuracy of complete transition sequences and by using beam search instead of strictly deterministic parsing. Huang and Sagae [23] report further improvements by using a graph-structured stack for ambiguity packing.

3.4 Hybrid Methods

For parsing as for many other problems, it is often possible to improve accuracy by combining methods with different strengths. Thus, Zeman and Žabokrtský

Table 2. Parsing results for English (PTB, Penn2Malt); unlabeled attachment scores. An asterisk (*) indicates that the evaluation score is not included in the paper cited.

Parser	Type	UAS
Yamada and Matsumoto [59]	Transition-Local	90.3
McDonald et al. [32]	Chart-1st	90.9
Collins [10]*	PCFG	91.5
McDonald and Pereira [34]	Chart-2nd	91.5
Charniak [7]*	PCFG	92.1
Koo et al. [25]	Hybrid-Dual	92.5
Sagae and Lavie [53]	Hybrid-MST	92.7
Petrov et al. [48]*	PCFG-Latent	92.8
Zhang and Nivre [62]	Transition-Global	92.9
Koo and Collins [24]	Chart-3rd	93.0
Charniak and Johnson [8]*	PCFG+Rreranking	93.7

[60] reported substantial improvements in parsing Czech by letting a number of parsers vote for the syntactic head of each word. A drawback of this simple voting scheme is that the output may be a cyclic graph even if all the component parsers output trees. This problem was solved by Sagae and Lavie [53], who showed that we can use the spanning tree method of McDonald et al. [35] for parser combination by letting parsers vote for arc weights in the first-order model, a technique that was used by the top-ranked system in the CoNLL shared task 2007 [19]. Essentially, the same idea was exploited by Koo et al. [25], who used the framework of dual decomposition to combine a first-order spanning tree parser, which ensures the tree constraint, with a third-order approximate chart parser, which has a much richer feature model but may produce ill-formed dependency trees, thereby improving the state of the art for PDT and other data sets containing non-projective dependency trees. A different hybrid technique is parser stacking, where one parser is used to generate input features for another parser, a method that was used by Nivre and McDonald [46] to combine chart parsing and transition-based parsing, with further improvements reported by Torres Martins et al. [58].

4 Comparative Evaluation

When Yamada and Matsumoto [59] presented the first comparative evaluation of dependency parsing for English, using data from PTB with the Penn2Malt conversion, they observed that although their own bare-bones dependency parser had the advantage of simplicity and efficiency, it was not quite as accurate as the parsers of Collins [10] and Charniak [7]. However, as the results reported in Table 2 clearly show, there has been a tremendous development since then, and bare-bones dependency parsers now perform at the same level of accuracy as PCFG-based methods and are usually superior in terms of efficiency. As shown in

Table 3. Parsing results for Czech (PDT); unlabeled attachment scores. An asterisk (*) indicates that the evaluation score is not included in the paper cited.

Parser	Type	UAS
Collins [10]*	PCFG	82.2
McDonald et al. [32]	Chart-1st	83.3
Charniak [7]*	PCFG	84.3
McDonald et al. [35]	MST	84.4
Hall and Novák [20]	PCFG+Post	85.0
McDonald and Pereira [34]	Chart-2nd+Post	85.2
Nivre [42]*	Trans-Local	86.1
Zeman and Žabokrtský [60]	Hybrid-Greedy	86.3
Koo et al. [25]	Hybrid-Dual	87.3

Table 3, a similar development has taken place in the case of Czech dependency parsing but with a greater advantage for bare-bones dependency parsers due to the presence of non-projective dependencies.

Cer et al. [6] evaluated systems for producing Stanford typed dependencies [29] and found that bare-bones dependency parsers like MaltParser [44] and MSTParser [34] had considerably lower accuracy than the best phrase structure parsers like the Berkeley parser [48,49] and the parser of Charniak and Johnson [8]. However, the evaluation was performed after converting the parser output to so-called collapsed dependencies, a conversion process that is less accurate for dependency trees than for phrase structure trees. More importantly, the bare-bones dependency parsers were run without proper optimization, whereas most of the phrase structure parsers have been optimized for a long time not only for English but in particular for the type of Wall Street Journal text that was used in the evaluation. It is therefore likely that the results, although representative for out-of-the-box comparisons on this particular data set, do not generalize to other settings. Evidence for this conclusion comes from a similar study by Candito et al. [5], where parsers were evaluated on data from the French Treebank, and where there was practically no difference in accuracy between the best bare-bones dependency parsers (MaltParser, MSTParser) and the best phrase structure parser (Berkeley), although the transition-based MaltParser was about ten times faster than the other two parsers.

Rimell et al. [52] evaluated a number of statistical parsers specifically on their capacity to recover unbounded dependencies like those involved in different types of relative clauses, interrogative clauses and right node raising. The evaluation was extended to bare-bones dependency parsers in [47], and the overall results show that systems like MaltParser and MSTParser, augmented with simple post-processing for inferring multiple heads, perform at least as well as other types of treebank parsers, although not quite as well as grammar-driven systems like those of Clark and Curran [9] and Miyao and Tsujii [38].

5 Conclusion

Although the available evidence is still scattered and incomplete, the empirical results so far seem to support the hypothesis that bare-bones dependency parsers can achieve the same level of accuracy as more complex systems. Since they have the advantage of simplicity and efficiency, they should therefore be the method of choice in contexts where the main requirement on syntactic analysis is to produce a dependency tree, especially if run-time efficiency is crucial.

References

1. Attardi, G.: Experiments with a multilanguage non-projective dependency parser. In: Proceedings of the 10th Conference on Computational Natural Language Learning (CoNLL), pp. 166–170 (2006)
2. Barbero, C., Lesmo, L., Lombardo, V., Merlo, P.: Integration of syntactic and lexical information in a hierarchical dependency grammar. In: Proceedings of the Workshop on Processing of Dependency-Based Grammars (ACL-COLING), pp. 58–67 (1998)
3. Bouma, G., Mur, J., van Noord, G., van der Plas, L., Tiedemann, J.: Question answering for dutch using dependency relations. In: Peters, C., Gey, F.C., Gonzalo, J., Müller, H., Jones, G.J.F., Kluck, M., Magnini, B., de Rijke, M., Giampiccolo, D. (eds.) CLEF 2005. LNCS, vol. 4022, pp. 370–379. Springer, Heidelberg (2006)
4. Buchholz, S., Marsi, E.: CoNLL-X shared task on multilingual dependency parsing. In: Proceedings of the 10th Conference on Computational Natural Language Learning (CoNLL), pp. 149–164 (2006)
5. Candito, M., Nivre, J., Denis, P., Henestroza Anguiano, E.: Benchmarking of statistical dependency parsers for French. In: Coling 2010: Posters, pp. 108–116 (2010)
6. Cer, D., de Marneffe, M.C., Jurafsky, D., Manning, C.: Parsing to stanford dependencies: Trade-offs between speed and accuracy. In: Proceedings of the Seventh Conference on International Language Resources and Evaluation, LREC 2010 (2010)
7. Charniak, E.: A maximum-entropy-inspired parser. In: Proceedings of the First Meeting of the North American Chapter of the Association for Computational Linguistics (NAACL), pp. 132–139 (2000)
8. Charniak, E., Johnson, M.: Coarse-to-fine n-best parsing and MaxEnt discriminative reranking. In: Proceedings of the 43rd Annual Meeting of the Association for Computational Linguistics (ACL), pp. 173–180 (2005)
9. Clark, S., Curran, J.R.: Parsing the WSJ using CCG and log-linear models. In: Proceedings of the 42nd Annual Meeting of the Association for Computational Linguistics (ACL), pp. 104–111 (2004)
10. Collins, M.: Head-Driven Statistical Models for Natural Language Parsing. Ph.D. thesis, University of Pennsylvania (1999)
11. Culotta, A., Sorensen, J.: Dependency tree kernels for relation extraction. In: Proceedings of the 42nd Annual Meeting of the Association for Computational Linguistics (ACL), pp. 423–429 (2004)
12. Ding, Y., Palmer, M.: Synchronous dependency insertion grammars: A grammar formalism for syntax based statistical MT. In: Proceedings of the Workshop on Recent Advances in Dependency Grammar, pp. 90–97 (2004)

13. Eisner, J.M.: Three new probabilistic models for dependency parsing: An exploration. In: Proceedings of the 16th International Conference on Computational Linguistics (COLING), pp. 340–345 (1996)
14. Eisner, J.M.: Bilexical grammars and their cubic-time parsing algorithms. In: Bunt, H., Nijholt, A. (eds.) Advances in Probabilistic and Other Parsing Technologies, pp. 29–62. Kluwer (2000)
15. Foth, K., Daum, M., Menzel, W.: A broad-coverage parser for German based on defeasible constraints. In: Proceedings of KONVENS 2004, pp. 45–52 (2004)
16. Gaifman, H.: Dependency systems and phrase-structure systems. Information and Control 8, 304–337 (1965)
17. Gómez-Rodríguez, C., Weir, D., Carroll, J.: Parsing mildly non-projective dependency structures. In: Proceedings of the 12th Conference of the European Chapter of the Association for Computational Linguistics (EACL), pp. 291–299 (2009)
18. Hajič, J., Vidova Hladka, B., Panevová, J., Hajičová, E., Sgall, P., Pajas, P.: Prague Dependency Treebank 1.0. LDC, 2001T10 (2001)
19. Hall, J., Nilsson, J., Nivre, J., Eryiğit, G., Megyesi, B., Nilsson, M., Saers, M.: Single malt or blended? A study in multilingual parser optimization. In: Proceedings of the CoNLL Shared Task of EMNLP-CoNLL 2007, pp. 933–939 (2007)
20. Hall, K., Novák, V.: Corrective modeling for non-projective dependency parsing. In: Proceedings of the 9th International Workshop on Parsing Technologies (IWPT), pp. 42–52 (2005)
21. Hays, D.G.: Dependency theory: A formalism and some observations. Language 40, 511–525 (1964)
22. Holan, T., Kuboň, V., Plátek, M.: A prototype of a grammar checker for Czech. In: Proceedings of the 5th Conference on Applied Natural Language Processing (ANLP), pp. 147–154 (1997)
23. Huang, L., Sagae, K.: Dynamic programming for linear-time incremental parsing. In: Proceedings of the 48th Annual Meeting of the Association for Computational Linguistics (ACL), pp. 1077–1086 (2010)
24. Koo, T., Collins, M.: Efficient third-order dependency parsers. In: Proceedings of the 48th Annual Meeting of the Association for Computational Linguistics (ACL), pp. 1–11 (2010)
25. Koo, T., Rush, A.M., Collins, M., Jaakkola, T., Sontag, D.: Dual decomposition for parsing with non-projective head automata. In: Proceedings of the 2010 Conference on Empirical Methods in Natural Language Processing, pp. 1288–1298 (2010)
26. Kuhlmann, M., Satta, G.: Treebank grammar techniques for non-projective dependency parsing. In: Proceedings of the 12th Conference of the European Chapter of the Association for Computational Linguistics (EACL), pp. 478–486 (2009)
27. Lombardo, V., Lesmo, L.: An Earley-type recognizer for dependency grammar. In: Proceedings of the 16th International Conference on Computational Linguistics (COLING), pp. 723–728 (1996)
28. Marcus, M.P., Santorini, B., Marcinkiewicz, M.A.: Building a large annotated corpus of English: The Penn Treebank. Computational Linguistics 19, 313–330 (1993)
29. de Marneffe, M.C., MacCartney, B., Manning, C.D.: Generating typed dependency parses from phrase structure parses. In: Proceedings of the 5th International Conference on Language Resources and Evaluation (LREC) (2006)
30. Martins, A., Smith, N., Xing, E.: Concise integer linear programming formulations for dependency parsing. In: Proceedings of the Joint Conference of the 47th Annual Meeting of the ACL and the 4th International Joint Conference on Natural Language Processing of the AFNLP (ACL-IJCNLP), pp. 342–350 (2009)

31. Maruyama, H.: Structural disambiguation with constraint propagation. In: Proceedings of the 28th Meeting of the Association for Computational Linguistics (ACL), pp. 31–38 (1990)
32. McDonald, R., Crammer, K., Pereira, F.: Online large-margin training of dependency parsers. In: Proceedings of the 43rd Annual Meeting of the Association for Computational Linguistics (ACL), pp. 91–98 (2005)
33. McDonald, R., Lerman, K., Pereira, F.: Multilingual dependency analysis with a two-stage discriminative parser. In: Proceedings of the 10th Conference on Computational Natural Language Learning (CoNLL), pp. 216–220 (2006)
34. McDonald, R., Pereira, F.: Online learning of approximate dependency parsing algorithms. In: Proceedings of the 11th Conference of the European Chapter of the Association for Computational Linguistics (EACL), pp. 81–88 (2006)
35. McDonald, R., Pereira, F., Ribarov, K., Hajič, J.: Non-projective dependency parsing using spanning tree algorithms. In: Proceedings of the Human Language Technology Conference and the Conference on Empirical Methods in Natural Language Processing (HLT/EMNLP), pp. 523–530 (2005)
36. McDonald, R., Satta, G.: On the complexity of non-projective data-driven dependency parsing. In: Proceedings of the 10th International Conference on Parsing Technologies (IWPT), pp. 122–131 (2007)
37. Menzel, W., Schröder, I.: Decision procedures for dependency parsing using graded constraints. In: Proceedings of the Workshop on Processing of Dependency-Based Grammars (ACL-COLING), pp. 78–87 (1998)
38. Miyao, Y., Tsujii, J.: Probabilistic disambiguation models for wide-coverage HPSG parsing. In: Proceedings of the 43rd Annual Meeting of the Association for Computational Linguistics (ACL), pp. 83–90 (2005)
39. Nakagawa, T.: Multilingual dependency parsing using global features. In: Proceedings of the CoNLL Shared Task of EMNLP-CoNLL 2007, pp. 952–956 (2007)
40. Nivre, J.: An efficient algorithm for projective dependency parsing. In: Proceedings of the 8th International Workshop on Parsing Technologies (IWPT), pp. 149–160 (2003)
41. Nivre, J.: Inductive Dependency Parsing. Springer, Heidelberg (2006)
42. Nivre, J.: Non-projective dependency parsing in expected linear time. In: Proceedings of the Joint Conference of the 47th Annual Meeting of the ACL and the 4th International Joint Conference on Natural Language Processing of the AFNLP (ACL-IJCNLP), pp. 351–359 (2009)
43. Nivre, J., Hall, J., Kübler, S., McDonald, R., Nilsson, J., Riedel, S., Yuret, D.: The CoNLL 2007 shared task on dependency parsing. In: Proceedings of the CoNLL Shared Task of EMNLP-CoNLL 2007, pp. 915–932 (2007)
44. Nivre, J., Hall, J., Nilsson, J.: Maltparser: A data-driven parser-generator for dependency parsing. In: Proceedings of the 5th International Conference on Language Resources and Evaluation (LREC), pp. 2216–2219 (2006)
45. Nivre, J., Hall, J., Nilsson, J., Eryiğit, G., Marinov, S.: Labeled pseudo-projective dependency parsing with support vector machines. In: Proceedings of the 10th Conference on Computational Natural Language Learning (CoNLL), pp. 221–225 (2006)
46. Nivre, J., McDonald, R.: Integrating graph-based and transition-based dependency parsers. In: Proceedings of the 46th Annual Meeting of the Association for Computational Linguistics (ACL), pp. 950–958 (2008)
47. Nivre, J., Rimell, L., McDonald, R., Gómez Rodríguez, C.: Evaluation of dependency parsers on unbounded dependencies. In: Proceedings of the 23rd International Conference on Computational Linguistics (Coling 2010), pp. 833–841 (2010)

48. Petrov, S., Barrett, L., Thibaux, R., Klein, D.: Learning accurate, compact, and interpretable tree annotation. In: Proceedings of the 21st International Conference on Computational Linguistics and the 44th Annual Meeting of the Association for Computational Linguistics, pp. 433–440 (2006)
49. Petrov, S., Klein, D.: Improved inference for unlexicalized parsing. In: Proceedings of Human Language Technologies: The Annual Conference of the North American Chapter of the Association for Computational Linguistics (NAACL HLT), pp. 404–411 (2007)
50. Riedel, S., Clarke, J.: Incremental integer linear programming for non-projective dependency parsing. In: Proceedings of the Conference on Empirical Methods in Natural Language Processing (EMNLP), pp. 129–137 (2006)
51. Riezler, S., King, M.H., Kaplan, R.M., Crouch, R., Maxwell III, J.T., Johnson, M.: Parsing the Wall Street Journal using a Lexical-Functional Grammar and discriminative estimation techniques. In: Proceedings of the 40th Annual Meeting of the Association for Computational Linguistics (ACL), pp. 271–278 (2002)
52. Rimell, L., Clark, S., Steedman, M.: Unbounded dependency recovery for parser evaluation. In: Proceedings of the 2009 Conference on Empirical Methods in Natural Language Processing, pp. 813–821 (2009)
53. Sagae, K., Lavie, A.: Parser combination by reparsing. In: Proceedings of the Human Language Technology Conference of the NAACL, Companion Volume: Short Papers, pp. 129–132 (2006)
54. Sagae, K., Tsujii, J.: Shift-reduce dependency DAG parsing. In: Proceedings of the 22nd International Conference on Computational Linguistics (COLING), pp. 753–760 (2008)
55. Sleator, D., Temperley, D.: Parsing English with a link grammar. Tech. Rep. CMU-CS-91-196, Carnegie Mellon University, Computer Science (1991)
56. Sleator, D., Temperley, D.: Parsing English with a link grammar. In: Proceedings of the Third International Workshop on Parsing Technologies (IWPT), pp. 277–292 (1993)
57. Smith, D., Eisner, J.: Dependency parsing by belief propagation. In: Proceedings of the Conference on Empirical Methods in Natural Language Processing (EMNLP), pp. 145–156 (2008)
58. Torres Martins, A.F., Das, D., Smith, N.A., Xing, E.P.: Stacking dependency parsers. In: Proceedings of the Conference on Empirical Methods in Natural Language Processing (EMNLP), pp. 157–166 (2008)
59. Yamada, H., Matsumoto, Y.: Statistical dependency analysis with support vector machines. In: Proceedings of the 8th International Workshop on Parsing Technologies (IWPT), pp. 195–206 (2003)
60. Zeman, D., Žabokrtský, Z.: Improving parsing accuracy by combining diverse dependency parsers. In: Proceedings of the 9th International Workshop on Parsing Technologies (IWPT), pp. 171–178 (2005)
61. Zhang, Y., Clark, S.: A tale of two parsers: Investigating and combining graph-based and transition-based dependency parsing. In: Proceedings of the Conference on Empirical Methods in Natural Language Processing (EMNLP), pp. 562–571 (2008)
62. Zhang, Y., Nivre, J.: Transition-based parsing with rich non-local features. In: Proceedings of the 49th Annual Meeting of the Association for Computational Linguistics (ACL) (2011)

Solving Soft Security Problem in MANETs Using an Evolutionary Approach

Marcin Seredynski[1] and Pascal Bouvry[2]

[1] University of Luxembourg,
Interdisciplinary Centre for Security, Reliability and Trust,
6, rue Coudenhove Kalergi, L-1359, Luxembourg, Luxembourg
marcin.seredynski@uni.lu
[2] University of Luxembourg,
Faculty of Sciences, Technology and Communication,
6, rue Coudenhove Kalergi, L-1359, Luxembourg, Luxembourg
pascal.bouvry@uni.lu

Abstract. Local trust systems are used independently by participants of a mobile ad hoc network in order to build direct and indirect reciprocity-based cooperation in packet forwarding. They enable nodes to distinguish between selfish (untrustworthy) and cooperative (trustworthy) users. The type of information used to evaluate the behaviour of other network participants impacts the performance of such systems. Depending on whether the information considers the status of a node's own packets or the packets of others, it can be partitioned into personal and general classes. In this paper we show that the size of the network should have an influence on a node's decision whether to use personal or general data classes by its trust system. To demonstrate this we use an evolutionary approach based on replicator dynamic. The results obtained using the approach and computer simulation allow us to predict how data classes might be used for trust evaluation by independent network users acting out of self-interest. Our simulation studies demonstrate that, in the presence of a small number of nodes, a node should evaluate the level of cooperation of other network participants using personal and general data. However, if the network size is large, then relying on personal data only is the best choice for the node.

Keywords: MANETs, cooperation, trust management, direct and indirect reciprocity, evolutionary approach, replicator dynamic.

1 Introduction

Mobile ad hoc networks (MANETs) are composed of a set of devices (nodes) wirelessly connected without a support of any fixed infrastructure. Packet delivery is based on a multi-hop routing, therefore nodes act as both terminals and routers. This means that users which are not within the radio range of their communication devices can still exchange information using some intermediate nodes. Therefore, cooperation in packet forwarding is one of the network's silent requirements. Due to the fact that most of the devices in MANETs rely

P. Bouvry et al. (Eds.): SIIS 2011, LNCS 7053, pp. 33–44, 2012.

on batteries, one of their most important characteristics is energy-constrained operation. As a result, the probability that nodes are going to be reluctant to packet forwarding responsibility in order to conserve their energy is very high. In *civilian applications* MANETs nodes belong to different authorities. Therefore, its users act out of self-interest. In consequence, a top down approach, which assumes direct control of the behaviour of each entity in the system, is not possible. In order to avoid free-riding behaviour nodes can collectively create a distributed *cooperation enforcement mechanism.* Such mechanism can be either *pricing* or *trust/reputation-based* [4]. The pricing-based approach can be seen as an economic view of the problem. The general idea is that nodes have to pay for receiving service and are paid for providing it. The work presented in this paper is limited to the second category – trust/reputation-based mechanisms, where the general idea is that intermediate nodes forward packets only on behalf of cooperative (therefore trustworthy) nodes. Several trust-based cooperation enforcement mechanisms have been proposed in the literature (e.g. [1,10,6,11,19]). The key components of such mechanisms are *trust systems.* They enable cooperative nodes to be distinguished from selfish. Trust systems are often extended with reputation systems. The main difference between the two is that, in the former, a node evaluates a subjective view of the entity's level of cooperation, while in the latter the view of the whole community is taken into account [8]. Trust systems can be combined with routing protocols in order to bypass misbehaving nodes (see e.g. [9,7]). Trust/reputation management in the context of cooperation enforcement mechanisms can be seen as a *soft security* approach (similar to the *social control mechanisms* [13] used in Internet commerce). Its goal is to create a network that is resistant to the behaviour of *selfish* (but not malicious) users wanting to exploit it. This differs from the goal of hard security mechanisms, which is to provide protection against malicious nodes [8]. This paper deals only with the problem of selfish nodes.

A node evaluates the trustworthiness of others using *trust data.* Such data refer to the forwarding behaviour of other networking participants and are collected during the executions of a routing protocol. They can be classified into *personal* and *general* [17]. Personal data refer to the status of packets originated by a node itself, while general data refer to the status of packets sent by other nodes. Hence, personal data contribute to a development of cooperation on the basis of direct reciprocity, while general data on the basis of indirect reciprocity. The question that we want to answer in this article is how should nodes use these classes together to evaluate the trustworthiness of other network participants. Four modes of a trust system differing in the use of trust data classes are evaluated. The approach based on replicator dynamic introduced in our previous work [18] is used to discover the best mode for a given size of the network.

The article is structured as follows. The next section provides a survey of the related work. Section 3 introduces the model of the network. Section 4 provides information about the approach used to discover the best mode of a trust system and computer simulation procedure. Section 5 provides a specification of parameters and simulation results. The final section summarises the main conclusion.

2 Related Work

The most closely-related work is concerned with the classification of data classes for the evaluation of the cooperation level of nodes. A distinction is made between *first-* and *second-hand information*. In general, first-hand observations are more reliable than second-hand [8]. The question of whether to use second-hand information or not is basically related to the trade-off between the speed of the evaluation of the level of cooperation and the robustness of such an evaluation [12]. In [10], a cooperation enforcement mechanism called CORE is presented. According to the proposal, the level of cooperation is evaluated using first- and second-hand evaluations (both having the same significance). However, the second-hand ratings include only information about cooperative behaviour. Consequently, the possibility of the malicious broadcast of negative ratings for legitimate nodes is avoided. The reliability of the trust evaluation is also positively correlated with the number of evaluations taken into account and its variance. In [1] the authors propose a protocol called *CONFIDANT*, where negative second-hand rating is allowed. However, a node's own experience is rated higher than second-hand reports. In [2,3] the use of second-hand information is further investigated. A Bayesian approach is introduced: opinions that deviate from the first-hand observations and from the opinion of the majority are excluded. As a result, the reputation system is much more robust against false accusations and benefits from a faster detection of selfish nodes. In [12] the authors apply the mean-field approach to a proposed stochastic process model to demonstrate that liars have no impact unless their number exceeds a certain threshold. In the SORI algorithm of [6], ratings are only exchanged between neighbours. The level of cooperation of the rater is positively correlated with its ratio of packets forwarded to packets discarded on behalf of the evaluator.

The rationale behind a further classification of trust-related information into *personal* and *general* classes in the presence of selfish and colluding nodes is investigated in our previous paper [17]. The work demonstrates that in the presence of a large number of selfish and colluding nodes, prioritising the personal data improves the performance of cooperative nodes and creates a better defence against colluding free-riders.

A direct reciprocity-based cooperation with several forwarding strategies present in the network is analyzed in [21,22,15]. In these works the authors demonstrate that cooperation is very likely to be developed on the basis of defection-tolerant versions of the reciprocal tit-for-tat approach.

In [16] we demonstrate that, if nodes use general trust data for the evaluation of the level of cooperation of network participants, then discarding packets can be seen as an act of altruistic punishment. In such a situation an intermediate node that discards packets from selfish senders pays a cost expressed as a decrease of the level of cooperation among other nodes. If the cost of punishing free-riders is too high, then nobody has an incentive to be the punisher.

3 System Model

We use a simple reciprocity-based model of behaviour of nodes introduced in [16]. It is defined by two elements: a trust data capture mechanism (specifying how nodes collect and classify information about behaviour of other network participants) and a response mechanism (defining whether a packet received for forwarding should be passed-on to the next hop or dropped). The response mechanism includes a trust system. In this paper the following assumptions about the network are made: it is self-organising and the network layer is based on a reactive, source routing protocol. Its topology is unpredictable and changes dynamically. Each device is equipped with an omnidirectional antenna with similar radio range, bi-directional communications and promiscuous mode. Network users pursue their own self-interest.

3.1 Data Collection and Modes of a Trust System

Trust data collection is based on the commonly used *watchdog* (WD) mechanism introduced in [9]. The observable elements used to derive the level of cooperation of the source of the message are two network events: "packet forwarded" and "packet discarded". As a source routing protocol is used, a list of intermediate nodes is included in the header of the packet. Information regarding the packet forwarding behaviour of other nodes (trust data) is gathered only by nodes directly participating in the *communication session*. There is no exchange of ratings between nodes. The communication session involves a source node (sender), several forwarders (nodes that forward packets) and a destination node. Trust data collection is performed in the following way: nodes are equipped with a *watchdog mechanism* that enables them to check whether a packet was delivered to its destination. A node that requests another node to forward a packet verifies by means of a *passive acknowledgement* whether the requested node actually forwarded the packet. As an example, let us assume that node A originates a message to node D via intermediate nodes B and C, and the message is eventually discarded by node C. This event is recorded by the watchdog mechanism of node B, which next informs A about the selfish behaviour of C. As a result, the trust system of node A is updated with two events – "packet forwarded by B" and "packet discarded by C", while the trust system of B is updated with the event "packet discarded by C". However, these events have different meanings to nodes A and B. In the case of node A, they are related to its own packets, therefore, data gathered from these events are referred to as *personal*. The situation of node B is different. In this case it only witnesses the status of packets originated by node A, hence, it collects general data. Thus, senders collect personal, while forwarders collect general trust data. Such a distinction allows to define four basic modes of a trust system [17]. In the first mode, a node evaluates the level of cooperation of others using only general trust data (the mode is denoted by G). In the second one (denoted by P), only personal trust data are taken into account. In the third one (denoted by PG), both data classes are considered (with no distinction between them being made). In the final mode (denoted by PPR), personal data are preferred over general, i.e. general data are used only if personal ones are unavailable.

3.2 Reciprocity-Based Response Mechanism

Each time an intermediate node i receives a packet for forwarding it checks whether its source (node s) is trustworthy or not. The trustworthiness is defined as a ratio of packets forwarded by s to all packets received for forwarding by the node. If the ratio is greater or equal to the value of a parameter called *cooperation threshold* (specified by the trust system of node i), the packet is forwarded. Otherwise, it is discarded. The range of data used by i for the evaluation is defined by the mode of its trust system. For instance, if i uses the system in the P mode, then it only verifies whether s forwarded its packets (that is, the behaviour of s towards packets of other nodes is not taken into account).

There are two special cases concerning messages received for forwarding from unknown nodes. If a node receives a packet in the initial period of the existence of the network (specified by a threshold parameter t_{unkn}), the packet is forwarded with a probability p_1. When the network is established, the packet from an unknown node is forwarded with a probability p_2. The value of p_1 is high so that the network could be easily created. On the other hand, the value of p_2 is low in order to discouraged network participants from whitewashing attack [5]. The attack is defined as a situation, where a selfish node repeatedly rejoins the network under new identities in order to take advantage of cooperative approach towards unknown nodes.

When a nodes wishes to send its own packets it first chooses a route with the best *rating*. The rating is calculated as an arithmetic mean of trustworthiness of all nodes belonging to the route.

3.3 Types of Nodes

Three types of nodes are defined. The nodes of the first type are referred to as R-type. They use the reciprocity-based scheme described above. Depending on the modes of their trust systems, these nodes are denoted by R-P, R-PPR, R-PG or R-G. The remaining two types represent two particular patterns of behaviour that one might expect to be present to some extent in a typical MANET. These are *selfish* and *altruistic* nodes. The former forward packets with a probability equal to 0.2, while the latter unconditionally cooperate (i.e. accept all forwarding requests).

4 Evaluation Model and Computer Simulation Procedure

In order to evaluate the influence of trust data classes on the performance of nodes we use the approach introduced in our previous work [18]. The network is modelled as an evolutionary game, where players correspond to nodes. The strategy set of each player is composed of the modes of his trust system (P, PG, PPR and G). Games are played between a source of a packet and intermediate nodes that can either transmit the packet to the next hop or discard it. Payoffs obtained by players using a particular strategy are translated into fitness. Strategies are passed through nonoverlapping generations. The frequency of a given strategy within the population is positively correlated with the average fitness of individuals using that strategy in the preceding generation. The growth rate of a given strategy is described by replicator dynamic [14].

Two populations of players are defined. Players that belong to the first one are referred to as LEARNERS. They are of R-type, thus they can choose one of the four strategies of their trust systems. The goal of these players is to continuously adapt to the networking conditions by selecting appropriate strategies. The adaptation is modelled by the evolutionary process simulating the survival of the fittest. Therefore, strategies of these players converge to a solution (understood as the best mode of a trust system for given networking conditions according to a fitness function). Players that belong to the second population are referred to as TESTERS. Their goal is to preserve certain properties of the network by employing behaviours (selfishness and altruism) that one could expect to be present in a typical MANET. Hence, TESTERS are composed of selfish and altruistic nodes (see Section 3.3). Their behaviour does not change through generations. Overall conditions of the network are determined by all players, that is, by coevolving population of LEARNERS and fixed (in terms of behaviour) population of TESTERS.

The scheme of the computer simulation is composed of three steps. Its overview is shown in Fig. 1. In the first step, strategies are assigned to LEARNERS. All strategies are represented in equal proportion. In the second step they are evaluated in a MANET. The third step updates the strategies of LEARNERS. Steps 2 and 3 are repeated for a predefined number of times (referred to as *generations*). Detailed procedure description can be found below.

Step 1: Set Values of the Parameters

1. Specify values of the parameters: M as a number of players participating in the network and R as a number of rounds.
2. Setup the population of LEARNERS: specify L as its size and assign the initial strategies to the players.
3. Setup the population of TESTERS: specify T as its size and assign players with types.

Step 2: Evaluate the Strategies

1. Specify r (round number) as $r := 1$.
2. Specify i (source node) as $i := 1$.
3. Randomly select player j (destination of the packet) and intermediate players, forming several possible paths from player i to j.
4. If more than one path is available, calculate the rating of each path and choose the path with the best rating.
5. Let player i initiate a communication session (originate a packet). The packet is next either passed on or dropped by intermediate players according to their forwarding approaches.

6. After the completion of the communication session update trust data.
7. If $i < M$, then choose the next player ($i := i + 1$) and go to point 3. Else go to point 8.
8. If $r < R$, then $r := r + 1$ and go to point 2 (next round). Else, go to point 9.
9. For each strategy calculate the average payoff and stop the evaluation procedure.

Step 3: Update of Strategies of LEARNERS Using Discrete Replicator Dynamic.

1. Let x_s^g denote the proportion of players in the population that use strategy s in generation g.
2. The new proportion of players using strategy s in the subsequent generation (x_s^{g+1}) is given by the following equation:

$$x_s^{g+1} = x_s^g \frac{f_s}{\bar{f}}, \tag{1}$$

where f_s is the average fitness of players that used strategy s and $\bar{f}$ is the average population fitness.

The fitness of a strategy is calculated as an average payoff received by nodes that used the strategy. The payoff of node i is calculated as follows:

$$payoff_i = \frac{nps_i}{npf_i}, \tag{2}$$

where nps_i is a number of packets successfully sent by node i and npf_i is a number of packets forwarded by i.

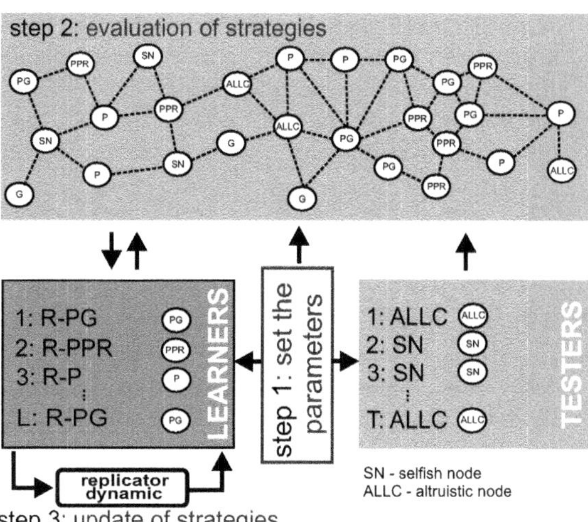

Fig. 1. Overview of the experimental procedure

5 Numerical Results

The computational experiments were carried out to study the influence of personal and general data classes on the performance of players in the function of the size of the network. Strategies corresponding to the four modes of the system were evaluated in different network sizes (ranging from 30 to 600 players). LEARNERS were composed of R-P, R-PPR, R-PG and R-G players, while selfish and altruistic players constituted the population of TESTERS. In the initial generation, all six types of forwarding behaviours were represented in equal proportions. As generations passed, the distribution of strategies used by LEARNERS changed, because these players adapted their behaviour to the networking conditions. Each experiment was repeated 100 times (referred to as runs). The mean value of performance measure of players was calculated over all runs of the experiment. Simulation time was set to 600 rounds. The path length ranged from 1 up to 5 hops with the following probabilities: one hop – 0.1, two hops – 0.3 and three to five hops – 0.2. The number of available paths from a source to a given destination ranged from 1 to 4 (randomly chosen). Forwarding probability of selfish players was set to 0.2. The *cooperation thresholds* ranged from 0.85 to 1 (randomly chosen from the interval). The parameter specifications of the experiments are given in Table 1.

Table 1. Specification of the simulation parameters

Parameter	Value
number of all nodes in the network (M)	60
simulation time (number of rounds (R))	600
strategy set of LEARNERS	P, PG, PPR, G
cooperation threshold	0.85-1 (equiprobable)
forw. prob. of LEARNERS towards unknown (p_1)	1.0
forw. prob. of LEARNERS towards unknown (p_2)	0.3
t_{unkn} of LEARNERS	round # 50
trust of an unknown node in for path rating	0.5
path length/probability of a given # of hops	1/0.1, 2/0.3, 3-5/0.2
number of available paths	1-4 (equiprobable)

Fig. 2 shows the evolutionary outcomes under the continuous replicator dynamics for a small network of 30 players. At first, all defined types of players of LEARNERS and TESTERS were uniformly distributed: 5 players of each type (R-PG, R-P, R-PPR, R-G, selfish and altruistic) were present in the initial generation. As the time passed the distribution of strategies of LEARNERS changed. The first thing that happened was that after 23 generations the G strategy disappeared from the population. On the other hand, the PG strategy grew in popularity, so that after about 100 generations it dominated the population of LEARNERS by being used by 96% of the players. As generations went by, the shares of P and PPR strategies decreased slowly. By the 213th generation the PPR strategy completely disappeared. On the other hand, after about

100 generations the P strategy established its presence (4% share). These outcomes were observed in a small network. The question remains, what happens if network size increases?

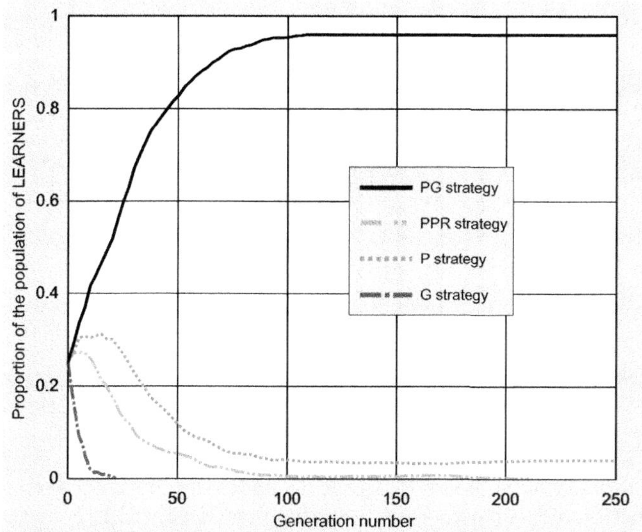

Fig. 2. Evolutionary outcomes of LEARNERS under the continuous replicator dynamics: network is composed of 30 players (5 players of each type). The outcome is the PG strategy.

This issue is addressed in Fig. 3, where the evolutionary outcomes in the function of the network size are shown. Again, all types of players were represented in equal proportions in the initial generation. Four outcomes were observed. In a small network (below 40 players) PG was a dominant strategy. However, some copies of the P strategy managed to survive until the last generation. In the second outcome, when the network's size was between 40 and 65 players, PG was the only strategy that lasted until the end. When the network was composed of 65 up to 100 players, two strategies, PG and P, evenly shared the population. Finally, when the network size was greater than 100 players, P was a dominant strategy. In general, the bigger the network was, the better the P strategy did. For instance, in a network composed of 120 players it took the P strategy around 150 generations to overtake the population. As soon as the size of the network was increased to 600, the same outcome was achieved after only 40 generations.

Additional experiments were carried out to tell whether the outcomes shown in Fig. 3 are evolutionary stable against the other three strategies. A strategy is said to be an evolutionary stable strategy (ESS) if a population of individuals adopting that strategy cannot be invaded by individuals adopting different strategy, i.e. the ESS is the most profitable in a population of players, where almost everyone is using it [20]. The verification procedure was as follows: 95% of

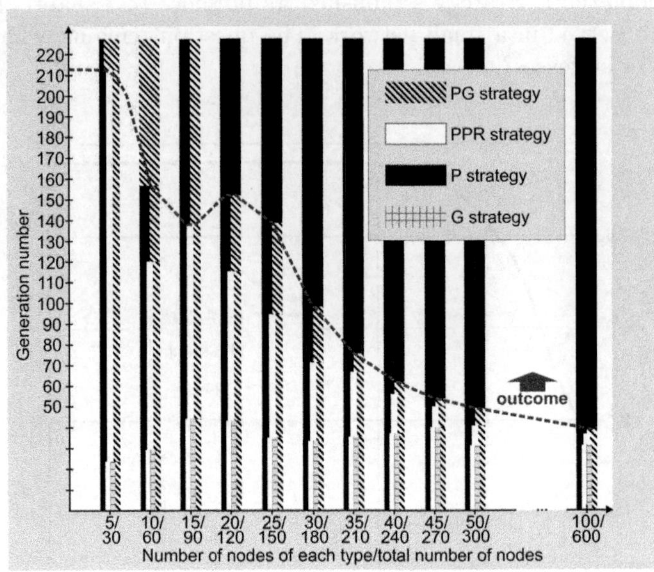

Fig. 3. Evolutionary outcomes of LEARNERS under the continuous replicator dynamics in the function of the network size. In a small network, the PG strategy is the best choice. However, as the network grows in size, the P strategy is the final outcome.

LEARNERS used the strategy discovered for a network of a given size, hereafter referred to as the main strategy. The remaining players belonging to LEARNERS used one of the alternative strategies. Therefore, three independent cases corresponding to each of the three alternative strategies were analysed. Table 2 shows the average payoff of each strategy.

Table 2. Average payoffs of strategies used by the majority (95% of the population of learners) and the alternative strategy (used by 5% of the population of learners)

popularity of main strategy	popularity of alternative strategy	PG	PPR	P	G
19 (PG)	1	**0.537-0.549**	0.502	0.518	0.420
38 (PG)	2	**0.518-0.524**	0.498	0.510	0.432
57 (PG/P)	3	**0.501-0.506**	0.488	**0.501-0.504**	0.429
76 (P)	4	0.497	0.480	**0.503-0.506**	0.434
...					
380 (P)	20	0.497	0.483	**0.603-0.604**	0.418

These results demonstrate that the outcomes shown in Fig. 3 are evolutionary stable. In every case the players that used the alternative strategy obtained worse payoffs than the players that used the main strategy. For instance, in the smallest network, 19 TESTERS used the main strategy (PG) and 1 TESTER used the alternative strategy. In such a case, the PG strategy obtained payoffs ranging from 0.537 to 0.549 (depending on the alternative strategy), while the payoffs of the alternative strategies where equal to 0.502 (PPR), 0.518 (P) and 0.420 (G). For a network size of 90, where PG and P strategies were previously found to perform equally well, the PG strategy obtained slightly higher payoff than P when G was the alternative strategy (0.506 vs. 0.504). Nevertheless, in such a setting both strategies (in any proportion) are evolutionary stable.

6 Conclusion

In order to avoid free-riding behaviour, users of a MANET can collectively create a reciprocity-based cooperation enforcement mechanism. In such a case, each node uses a local trust system that enables cooperative nodes to be distinguished from selfish. The question is what kind of information regarding the behaviour of nodes should be used by the system to evaluate the cooperation level of other network participants. In this paper we have investigated the significance of the partitioning of trust data into personal and general classes in the function of the size of the network. As shown in our simulation studies, in the presence of a small number of nodes, the evaluation of the level of cooperation of network participants should rely on personal and general data. However, if the network size is large, the use of personal data only is the best choice for a node.

References

1. Buchegger, S., Boudec, J.Y.L.: Performance analysis of the CONFIDANT protocol. In: Proc. 3rd International Symposium on Mobile Ad Hoc Networking and Computing (MobiHoc 2002), pp. 226–236 (2002)
2. Buchegger, S., Boudec, J.Y.L.: The effect of rumor spreading in reputation systems for mobile ad-hoc networks. In: Proc. Workshop on Modeling and Optimization in Mobile, Ad Hoc and Wireless Networks (WiOpt 2003), pp. 131–140 (2003)
3. Buchegger, S., Boudec, J.Y.L.: A robust reputation system for p2p and mobile ad-hoc networks. In: Proc. Second Workshop on the Economics of Peer-to-Peer Systems (2004)
4. Carruthers, R., Nikolaidis, I.: Certain limitations of reputation-based schemes in mobile environments. In: Proc. 8th ACM international symposium on Modeling, analysis and simulation of wireless and mobile systems (MSWiM 2005), pp. 2–11 (2005)
5. Feldman, M., Papadimitriou, C., Chuang, J., Stoica, I.: Free-riding and whitewashing in peer-to-peer systems. IEEE Journal on Selected Areas in Communications 24(5), 1010–1019 (2006)
6. He, Q., Dapeng, W., Khosla, P.: SORI: a secure and objective reputation-based incentive scheme for ad-hoc networks. In: Proc. Wireless Communications and Networking Conference (WCNC 2004), vol. 2, pp. 825–830 (2004)
7. Jensen, C.D., Connell, P.O.: Trust-based route selection in dynamic source routing. In: Stølen, K., Winsborough, W.H., Martinelli, F., Massacci, F. (eds.) iTrust 2006. LNCS, vol. 3986, pp. 150–163. Springer, Heidelberg (2006)

8. Jøsang, A., Ismail, R., Boyd, C.: A survey of trust and reputation systems for online service provision. Decision Support Systems 43(2), 618–644 (2007)
9. Marti, S., Giuli, T., Lai, K., Baker, M.: Mitigating routing misbehavior in mobile ad hoc networks. In: Proc. ACM/IEEE 6th International Conference on Mobile Computing and Networking (MobiCom 2000), pp. 255–265 (2000)
10. Michiardi, P., Molva, R.: CORE: A COllaborative REputation mechanism to enforce node cooperation in mobile ad hoc networks. In: Proc. 6th Conference on Security Communications, and Multimedia (CMS 2002), pp. 107–121 (2002)
11. Milan, F., Jaramillo, J., Srikant, R.: Achieving cooperation in multihop wireless networks of selfish nodes. In: Proc. Workshop on Game Theory for Communications and Networks (GameNets 2006). ACM (2006)
12. Mundinger, J., Boudec, J.Y.L.: Analysis of a reputation system for mobile ad-hoc networks with liars. Performance Evaluation 65(3-4), 212–226 (2008)
13. Rasmusson, L., Jansson, S.: Simulated social control for secure internet commerce. In: Proc. 1996 Workshop on New Security Paradigms (NSPW 1996), pp. 18–26. ACM (1996)
14. Samuelson, L.: Evolutionary Games and Equilibrium Selection. MIT Press (1998)
15. Seredynski, M., Bouvry, P.: Evolutionary game theoretical analysis of reputation-based packet forwarding in civilian mobile ad hoc networks. In: Proc. 23th IEEE International Parallel & Distributed Processing Symposium, NIDISC Workshop (2009)
16. Seredynski, M., Bouvry, P.: The cost of altruistic punishment in indirect reciprocity-based cooperation in mobile ad hoc networks. In: Proc. Sixth IEEE/IFIP International Symposium on Trusted Computing and Communications (TrustCom/EUC 2010), pp. 749–755 (2010)
17. Seredynski, M., Bouvry, P.: Trust management for collusion prevention in mobile ad hoc networks. In: Proc. GLOBECOM Workshops, Workshop on Management of Emerging Networks and Services (MENS 2010), pp. 523–528 (2010)
18. Seredynski, M., Bouvry, P.: Nature inspired approach for the evaluation of data types for trust management in MANETs. In: Proc. 25th IEEE International Symposium on Parallel & Distributed Processing, NIDISC Workshop, pp. 361–368 (2011)
19. Seredynski, M., Ignac, T., Bouvry, P.: Probabilistic packet relaying in wireless mobile ad hoc networks. In: Wyrzykowski, R., Dongarra, J., Karczewski, K., Wasniewski, J. (eds.) PPAM 2009. LNCS, vol. 6067, pp. 31–40. Springer, Heidelberg (2010)
20. Smith, J.M.: Evolution and the Theory of Games. Cambridge University Press (1982)
21. Yan, L., Hailes, S.: Cooperative packet relaying model for wireless ad hoc networks. In: Proc. 1st ACM International Workshop on Foundations of Wireless Ad Hoc and Sensor Networking and Computing, pp. 93–100. ACM (2008)
22. Yan, L., Hailes, S.: Designing incentive packet relaying strategies for wireless ad hoc networks with game theory. In: Wireless Sensor and Actor Networks II, pp. 137–148. Springer, Boston (2008)

Camera Sabotage Detection for Surveillance Systems

Damian Ellwart, Piotr Szczuko, and Andrzej Czyżewski

Gdańsk University of Technology, Multimedia Systems Department
Narutowicza 11/12, 80-233 Gdańsk, Poland
{ellwart,szczuko,andcz}@sound.eti.pg.gda.pl

Abstract. Camera dysfunction detection algorithms and their utilization in real-time video surveillance systems are described. The purpose of using the proposed analysis is explained. Regarding image tampering three algorithms for focus loss, scene obstruction and camera displacement detection are implemented and presented. Features of each module are described and certain scenarios for best performance are depicted. Implemented solutions are evaluated as independent events and final results are discussed. A detection efficiency improvement method is proposed.

Keywords: surveillance, tampering, defocus, displacement, obstruction.

1 Introduction

Video surveillance systems are commonly used as a mean of safety. Researchers develop complex methods allowing for so called smart or intelligent systems to be built. The recordings from monitoring systems often serve as an evidence in case of crimes. Therefore vital areas need to be observed continuously and the acquired videos should meet a good quality level requirements. There are many recommendations describing as how the cameras should be located and what additional conditions should be fulfilled to acquire the highest area coverage and yield best system performance. Hence, stationary cameras placed once should not be moved providing reliable image at all times. Most of the currently produced outdoor cameras are equipped with a weather and damage proof enclosure securing the camera itself, and guarantying proper work in various conditions. Despite these precautions the video provided by the camera can be damaged in different ways, for example by painting the camera lens or enclosure. In case of indoor monitoring, the cameras might be accessed quite simply making them an easy target susceptible of being tampered or damaged. To deal with this kind of threats, tamper detection algorithms are developed. There are some hardware implemented solutions already on the market but most of them require additional processing card and a dedicated software. Currently much work is dedicated to video analysis which enables detection of threat related situations. The tampering detection algorithms described in this paper are considered as a part of a larger smart surveillance system. Therefore, besides the algorithm detection accuracy, its low complexity is important making it useful for real-time processing.

P. Bouvry et al. (Eds.): SIIS 2011, LNCS 7053, pp. 45–53, 2012.

2 Camera Dysfunction Detection

The main purpose of detecting camera dysfunctions is to assure that reliable video is being recorded. The problem of camera sabotage detection is mentioned in the literature briefly. Only a few methods for detecting camera tampering were proposed [1][2][3][4]. This task is difficult as the problem itself is hard to define. As it was mentioned in the introduction, this algorithm is to be integrated as a part of a larger smart surveillance system. Typically, the first operations in such systems include background subtraction and object detection. Hence, during tampering detection a background model is being used, utilizing Gaussian Mixture Model based method [5]. Such model becomes the template to compare the analyzed frame to during processing. Detailed description of detecting each tampering event is presented in the following sections. The detection process is performed by three separate modules called in a certain order. In the literature [3] it is shown that the detection of camera occlusion should be performed first, then camera focus loss, and finally the scene shift detection. Our experiments show that the focus analysis of already displaced camera leads to errors, therefore the sequence of these modules is changed. First the camera obstruction is detected, then displacement and finally focus loss.

2.1 Obstruction Detection

To assure that the observed area is visible at all times a module for detecting camera occlusions is used. It utilizes the information from a grey scaled analyzed frame and the corresponding background model. Misting over the camera view causes the entropy of the image to be reduced. This assumption stays true as long as the obstructing object is placed close to the camera or directly on the cameras lens, resulting in lower light exposure (Fig. 1). In such situations entropy of the image (1) reduces dramatically.

Fig. 1. Sample camera view under normal conditions (left) and after camera occlusion (right)

$$E = -\sum_{K} P(I_k) log_2[P(I_k)] \tag{1}$$

where: $P(I_k)$ is the probability of k-level pixel intensity.

The camera occlusion detection occurs by comparing the entropy of currently analyzed frame and the background model, to a defined sensitivity related factor (2):

$$Occlusion = \begin{cases} true, & \dfrac{E_{frame}}{E_{background}} < \propto \\ false, & \dfrac{E_{frame}}{E_{background}} > \propto \end{cases} \quad (2)$$

where: α is the detection sensitivity,
E_{frame} denotes the entropy of current image entropy,
$E_{background}$ is the entropy of background model built and updated according to the literature description [5].

This condition allows detecting only a specified set of situations. To extend the detected cases additional condition based on the comparison of both images histograms is used. If this difference in the meaning of Bhattacharyya distance continues for a set number of frames, camera obstruction alert is triggered despite high frame entropy. This situation can occur if an object is placed in close proximity to the camera.

2.2 Displacement Detection

Moving the camera from its original position can result in a loss of vital information. An example of a shifted camera is shown in the Fig. 2. For the purpose of camera translation detection a popular block matching method is used. Although it was developed for motion estimation in video compression field, it performs well for this application.

Fig. 2. Originally oriented camera view (left) and the view after camera shift (right)

There are several shift detection algorithms beside the block matching method. As it is required to operate in real-time system a compromise between the computational time and acquired accuracy has to be reached [6]. Therefore a slightly simplified Three Step Search (TTS) algorithm is implemented fulfilling this assumption. The procedure describing the algorithm is presented in Fig. 3.

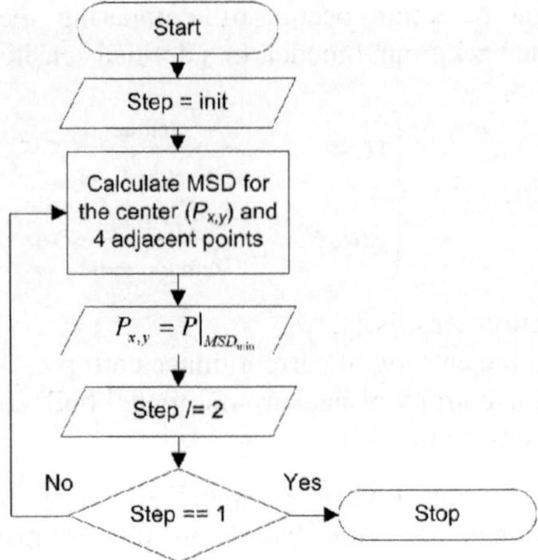

Fig. 3. Three Step Search algorithm calculation procedure. As the result image shift estimation is acquired.

As the minimization criteria the Minimum Squared Difference (MSD) (3) is estimated in each block-matching step.

$$MSD = \frac{1}{XY}\sum_{i}^{X}\sum_{j}^{Y}\left(\mathrm{I}(i,j) - \mathrm{B}(i,j)\right)^2 \tag{3}$$

where: *I(i,j)* is the gray scaled analyzed frame,
B(i,j) depicts the background image.

Using this approach currently processed image is compared with the scene background model. To reduce the image shift calculation time further the analyzed video frame is downscaled. If cameras within the system are not equipped with hardware or software stabilization, a small tolerable transpositions of the observed scene can occur. Therefore, before triggering camera displacement alert, a threshold for minimal detected shift is applied (4):

$$Displacement = \begin{cases} true, & P_{x,y} > th_{min} \\ false, & P_{x,y} < th_{min} \end{cases} \tag{4}$$

where: $P_{x,y}$ denotes the estimated analyzed frame displacement
th_{min} is the minimum shift threshold.

This approach allows detecting camera shifts assuming low and medium object movement in the scene. If the camera observes a small area, the visible objects can cover a greater part of the view resulting in errors. Therefore, as well as for two other modules, time averaging is applied reducing the false positive errors.

2.3 Defocus Detection

In surveillance systems focus loss may occur in various situations. The least possible one is caused by an electro-mechanic failure in the camera itself. More often it may be a result of the system operator error or by atmospheric conditions such as fog. Focused image contains relevant details allowing people and vehicle identification. A camera observing an entrance gate is presented in Fig. 4, where the vehicle license plate becomes unreadable if the camera is out of focus.

Fig. 4. Illustration of the focus loss problem. The defocused image (right) shows the lack of detailed information making it impossible to read the license plate.

The method utilized for focus loss detection in this work is based on a slightly modified solution proposed in the literature [3], as the original version of this algorithm was proven to be quite robust for variously changing light conditions. For the purpose of processing, input RGB image is being reduced to its gray scale representation. Edges present in the image are detected utilizing Sobel operator and the Canny algorithm. The result acquired in this way is accumulated using the weighted sum (5):

$$B_{edges} = \mu \cdot I_{edges} + (1 - \mu) \cdot B_{edges} \tag{5}$$

where: B_{edges} represents the accumulated edges image,
I_{edges} are the edges of the currently processed frame,
μ is the learning rate factor.

The acquired image contains a set of edges, but after thresholding only "strong edges" are present. This process is presented in Fig. 5. As the camera losses focus, gradients in the process image decrease simultaneously, especially for the strong edge parts of the image.

In the literature [3] a measure of focus based on a gradient energy along these edges is proposed. As the activity in the observed scene rises, a large amount of the edges can be covered resulting in a non-reliable energy estimation. It is noticed that even in case of highly defocused images a set of edges can be detected. Therefore, in this work the gradient energy of a common part of frame edges and strong edges is calculated (6):

$$G = \frac{\sum_i^X \sum_j^Y S(i,j) \cdot C(i,j)}{\sum_i^X \sum_j^Y I(i,j) \cdot C(i,j)} \tag{6}$$

where: *I(i,j)* is the input gray scaled image,
S(i,j) is the same image after applying Sobel operators,
C(i,j) denotes the common part of the strong edges and the edges in currently processed frame.

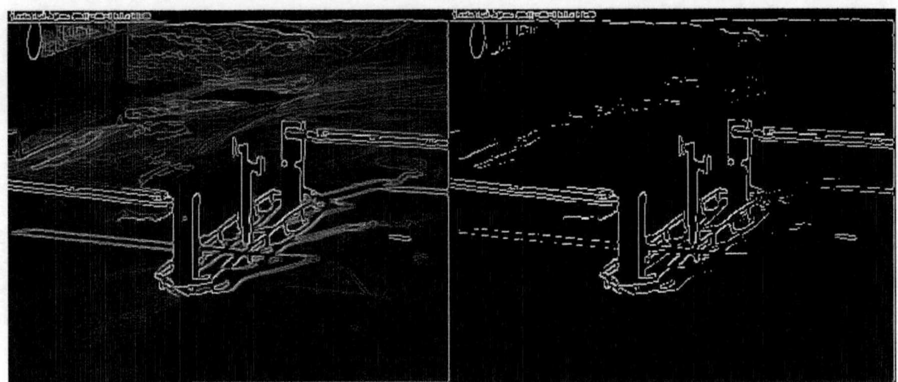

Fig. 5. Examples depicting averaged image edges and the result of applying a threshold

The normalized gradient measure is calculated for the processed frame and the background image. By comparing these values with a set sensitivity, the level of the camera focus loss can be detected (7):

$$Defocus = \begin{cases} true, & \dfrac{G_{frame}}{G_{background}} < \beta \\ false, & \dfrac{G_{frame}}{G_{background}} > \beta \end{cases} \tag{7}$$

where: G_{frame} and $G_{background}$ are the normalized gradient energy for the analyzed frame and the background image,
β denotes the detection sensitivity.

Before any detection occurs, strong edges need to be learnt. Therefore the detection process in this module is started after at least 1/μ frames (μ is the learning rate factor). Similarly to the previous detection algorithms, the results are averaged over a set number of frames before an alert is triggered.

3 Experiments

Two parameters for each tampering event were evaluated during experiments - the algorithm accuracy for a set of prepared recordings and the average calculation time. Algorithms were run using a regular PC with 2GB of RAM memory and 2.4GHz dual core processor. Approximately 6 hours of recordings were processed. The test recordings included scenes at different camera viewpoints shown in Fig. 6. Various weather and variable lightning conditions were considered as well. The original recordings resolution (704x576) was reduced for the purpose of processing to 352x288. During the recordings preparation camera focus as well as the white balance were set manually. It is important to keep these settings at a set value so they do not vary resulting in unwanted image changes.

Fig. 6. Sample frames of the test recordings presenting various camera viewpoints

All three modules were tested using same settings for all the prepared recordings. As to the focus loss and occlusion detection the sensitivity parameter was set to 0.9. Regarding displacement detection, the minimum shift was set to 4 pixels. As it was briefly mentioned in the module description, the detections results are averaged. The time window corresponding to 4 seconds of recording is utilized. Hence, the detection alert is expected to be slightly delayed. The evaluation results are presented in Tab. 1.

Table 1. The results of modules efficiency evaluation

Tampering event	True detections	False alarms	Calc. time [ms]
Occlusion	12/16	2	$0{,}55 \pm 0{,}03$
Displacement	20/26	5	$11{,}20 \pm 0{,}58$
Defocus	20/22	12	$6{,}33 \pm 0{,}25$

The most time-consuming module is the camera displacement detector, although a simplified version of TTS is utilized. Still the overall algorithms calculation time analysis show that the presented approach is possible of being applied along with other complex video processing methods utilized in smart surveillance systems.

As to the detection accuracy, a lot of false alarms are present. Displacement detector as well as the focus loss detector seem to fail often for closed-up views. The shift detection errors manifest especially when a great part of the view is occupied by a moving object. This situation often occurs at the vehicle entrance gate. This problem can be dealt with by extending the average time window length. Moreover, the algorithm can fail if the shifted camera view has no significant common parts with the original scene. In such a case, depending on the view, defocus or occlusion detection may occur. For a precise camera displacement detection in this situation, further research needs to be done to solve the problem. Omitting close-up views in the testing set results in a decrease in false alarms, what makes the result more acceptable. Focus loss detection algorithm proposed in the literature turns out to be more quite dependent to the light changes variations. Hence, a high count of false alarms occurs during the mentioned algorithm testing.

4 Conclusions

A set of methods for camera tampering events detection was presented in the paper. Three processing modules were introduced for camera focus loss, displacement and view occlusion detection. As the conducted experiments show the algorithms are suitable of being used in real time processing with a large margin. Therefore, their application as a part of a complex smart surveillance system is possible. Unfortunately the system accuracy needs to be improved further before being applied in real monitoring systems, especially regarding still too high false positive error rate. Various approaches for close ups and distance views should be introduced in the future for better performance.

Acknowledgements. Research funded within the project No. POIG.02.03.03-00-008/08, entitled “MAYDAY EURO 2012 – The supercomputer platform of context-dependent analysis of multimedia data streams for identifying specified objects or safety threads”. The project is subsidized by the European regional development fund and by the Polish State budget.

References

1. Ribnick, E., Atev, S., Masoud, O., Papanikolopoulos, N., Voyles, R.: Real-Time Detection of Camera Tampering. In: IEEE International Conference on Video and Signal Based Surveillance, Australia (November 2006) ISBN: 0-7695-2688-8
2. Gil-Jiménez, P., López-Sastre, R., Siegmann, P., Acevedo-Rodríguez, J., Maldonado-Bascón, S.: Automatic Control of Video Surveillance Camera Sabotage. In: 2nd International work-conference on Nature Insired Problem-Solving Methods in Knowledge Engineering: Interplay Between Natural and Artificial Computation, Spain (June 2007) ISBN: 978-3-540-73054-5

3. Harasse, S., Bonnaud, L., Caplier, A., Desvignes, M.: Automated camera dysfunctions detection. In: 6th IEEE Southwest Symposium on Image Analysis and Interpretation, USA (March 2004) ISBN: 0-7803-8387-7
4. Sağlam, A., Temizel, A.: Real-time Adaptive Camera Tamper Detection for Video Surveillance. In: 6th IEEE International Conference on Advanced Video and Signal Based Surveillance, Italy (September 2009) ISBN: 978-0-7695-3718-4
5. Czyżewski, A., Dalka, P.: Moving object detection and tracking for the purpose of multimodal surveillance system in urban areas. In: Proc. 1st Int. Symp. on Intell. Interactive Multim. Syst. and Services, Piraeus, Greece (2008)
6. Turage, D., Alkanhal, M.: Search Algorithms for Block-Matching in Motion Estimation, Mid-Term project (1998), http://www.ece.cmu.edu/~ee899/project/deepak_mid.htm

Implementation of Access Control Model for Distributed Information Systems Using Usage Control

Aneta Poniszewska-Maranda

Institute of Information Technology,
Technical University of Lodz, Poland
anetap@ics.p.lodz.pl

Abstract. Currently, the rapid development of information technology requires also the additional features for access control domain. The information is more and more distributed through the networks or federation of numerous information systems located in different places in a country or on the globe. In order to meet the requirements and problems of modern access control, a new implementation of access control model, called implementation of Role-based Usage Control (iRBUC) model is proposed. Proposed iRBUC assures the usage control in accessing data, which is very important especially in distributed information systems, and assures the organization of access control strategies well-described in RBAC (Role-Based Access Control) model or its extensions.

1 Introduction

Currently, the modern information systems evolve very quickly. The information, that is very important and precious resource, is more and more distributed through the networks or federation of numerous information systems located in different places in a country or on the globe. The rapid development of information technology requires also the additional features for access control domain. Not less important is the protection of data against improper disclosure or modification in the information systems. This requirement is always obligatory in development process of information system and its security approach. But nowadays the information technology, as well as other information science domains, changes very quickly and new products appear every day. The access modes to the information have been also changed. New protocols appeared to exchange the information. All these changes cause new security problems against which the existing models or architectures of access control security should make a stand.

On the other side, distributed information systems or federation of information systems provide the access of many different users to huge amount of data, sometimes stored in different localizations and secured by different strategies, security policies and models or inner enterprise rules. These users have different rights to the data according to their business or security profiles that depend

P. Bouvry et al. (Eds.): SIIS 2011, LNCS 7053, pp. 54–67, 2012.

on their organization positions, actual localizations and many others conditions. Also, the system's data is transferred between particular nodes of distributed system. On the other hand, it is also important to protect the information against non-controlled utilization and control the usage and diffusion of this information. It gives the possibility to specify how it can be used and to specify the utilization constraints. All these new problems are connected with traditional access control models and usage control. They necessities new mechanisms to apply in distributed information systems.

The problems with access control in domain of distributed information systems can be caused by many reasons. Each local component of such system can be secured by another security strategy (e.g. centralized vs. decentralized authorization, ownership vs. administration paradigm), by other access control model (e.g. DAC, MAC, RBAC). The security heterogeneities can be caused also by different kinds of access rights (positive, negative or mixed), different authorization units (subjects, users, group, roles) or different access administration concepts (Grant, Revoke, etc.). In order to meet these requirements and problems in modern access control, a new implementation of access control model, called implementation of Role-based Usage Control (iRBUC) model is proposed.

Proposed iRBUC model assures the usage control in accessing data, which is very important especially in distributed information systems, and assures the organization of access control strategies well-described in RBAC (Role-Based Access Control) model or its extensions. We propose the new implementation of access control model for distributed information systems that additionally provides the common coherence of distributed information system's components on the global level of access control strategy.

The paper is structured as follows: first part presents the related works on access control models and deals with existing traditional access control models and usage control model. The second part describes our proposition of new implementation of access control model for information systems that can become the access control approach comprehensible for the components of information system.

2 Access Control to Secure Information Systems

The security policies of a system generally express the basic choices made by an institution for its own data security. They define the principles on which access is granted or denied. The access control imposes the constraints on what a user can do directly, and what the programs executed on behalf of user are allowed to do. A security access system can be defined using two parts that cooperate with each other: strategy of security access that describes all the environments and specifications of entire organization on the security level (i.e. organizational and technical aspects), and access model with:

- set of concepts to describe objects (data access) and subjects (users),
- definition of users' access rights to the data,

– access control policy which describes how users can manipulate data, defines data structure and administers the users' access rights to data.

2.1 Related Work on Access Control Policies

The development of access control models has a long history. There are two main approaches in this field. The first one represents the group of traditional access control models. Discretionary Access Control (DAC) model [1, 11, 12] was the first model in this group. However, DAC model has the inherit weakness that information can be copied from one object to another and it is difficult for DAC to enforce the safety policy and protect the data against some security attacks.

In order to prevent the shortcomings of DAC model, the Mandatory Access Control (MAC) model was created to enforce the lattice-based policies [1, 13]. MAC does not consider the covert channels but they are expensive to eliminate. Next, Sandhu et al. proposed Role-Based Access Control (RBAC) model [2–4] that has been considered as an alternative to DAC and MAC models. The RBAC model was a progress in access control but it is still centered around the access control matrix [11].

The second approach of access control models corresponds to temporal models that introduce the temporal features into traditional access control. The temporal authorization model was proposed by Bertino and al. in [14] and it is based on temporal intervals of validity for authorization and temporal dependencies among authorizations. Next, Temporal-RBAC (TRBAC) model was proposed in [15]. This model introduces the temporal dependencies among roles. Other model - Temporal Data Authorization model (TDAM) was presented in [16] and extends the basic authorization model by temporal attributes associated to data such as transition time or valid time. Recently, the TRBAC model was extended to Generalized Temporal RBAC (GTRBAC) model in [17] to express the wider range of temporal constraints.

However, all these models propose still the static authorization decisions that are based on subject's permissions which can be performed on target objects. If the access to an object is permitted, the subject can access it repeatedly at the valid time intervals, i.e. during the logging session. The Usage Control (UCON) was proposed to solve these problems [18–20]. The UCON model consider the temporal attributes as mutable attributes of subjects or objects. The model permits to evaluate the usage decision also during the access to information to which we want to control the usage. It is realized based on three decision factors: authorizations, obligations and conditions.

2.2 Access Control Policies and Their Models

There are some access control policies and models that can be used for securing the information systems. Sometimes, traditional access control models are not sufficient and adequate for actual distributed information systems, which connect different environments by the network. We can find some disadvantages of these models in security domain of information systems:

- *authorization only* - traditional access control models do not provide the mechanisms for definition of obligations or conditions in access control,
- *access rights can be only pre-defined* by the developers or security administrators and granted to the subjects,
- *no ongoing control* - decision about the access are made before the required access,
- *no consumable rights* - it is not possibly to define the mutable attributes of subjects and objects.

These disadvantages and needs caused the creation of unified model that can encompass the use of traditional access control models, trust management and digital right management (DRM). We have chosen two access control models in our studies to develop the new implementation model for distributed information systems: extended RBAC model and UCON model. The first one allows to represent the whole system organization in complete, precise way while the second one allows to describe the usage control with authorizations, obligations, conditions, continuity (ongoing control) and mutability attributes.

Role-Based Access Control (RBAC) model [2–4] requires the identification of roles in a system. The role is properly viewed as a semantic structure around which the access control policy is formulated. The role can represent the competency to do a specific task and it can embody the authority and responsibility of the system users. The roles are created for various job functions in an organization and the users are assigned to the roles based on their responsibilities and qualifications.

In *extended RBAC (eRBAC)* model [8, 9] each role realizes a specific task in enterprise business process and it contains many functions that the user can take. For each role it is possible to choose the necessary system's functions. Thus, a role can be presented as a set of functions that this role can take and realize. Each function can have one or more permissions, and a function can be defined as a set or a sequence of permissions. If an access to an object is required, then the necessary permissions can be assigned to the function to complete the desired job. Specific access rights are necessary to realize a role or a particular function of this role. Therefore, we extended classical RBAC model by addition of some elements, i.e. function, object, method, class, operation, to express more complex elements of enterprise information system that are secured by this model (Fig. 1).

The *Usage Control (UCON)* model [18, 19, 22] is based on three decision factors: authorizations, obligations and conditions that have to be evaluated for usage decision. It consists of eight main components: subjects, objects, subject attributes, object attributes, rights, authorizations, obligations and conditions (Fig. 2). The traditional access controls use only the authorizations for a decision process. The obligations and conditions are added to the model to resolve certain shortcomings characteristic for traditional access control strategies.

The UCON strategy is characterized by two features: mutability and continuity. Mutability means the mutability of subject and object attributes - with a mutability property the attributes can be either mutable or immutable. The mutable attributes can be modified by subjects' actions and immutable attributes

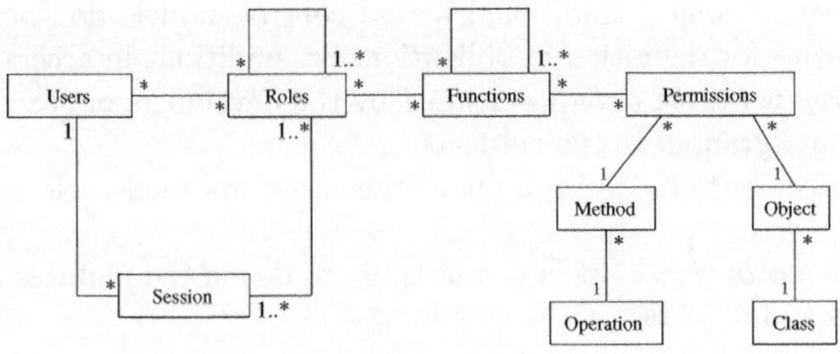

Fig. 1. Extended RBAC model

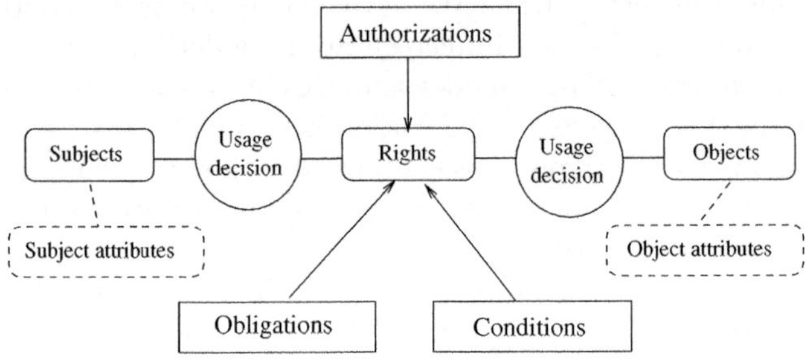

Fig. 2. UCON model

can be modified only by administrative actions. The continuity means that a decision can be made even after an access [18, 22].

3 Access Control Model for Distributed Information Systems

The access control in information systems is responsible for granting direct access to system's objects in accordance with the modes and principles defined by protection policies and security model.

In distributed information systems the stage of checking of access rights and principles should be realized depending on an object(s) to which a user (i.e. subject) wants to access. If the object operates in the same component of information system as the user, then only the local security rights should be examined. If not - if the object and the user are attached to two different components - the security rights for these two components should be checked on local or/and global level.

It is necessary to have more expressive access control model to define better the access control of distributed information systems. Such model should allow to define the complex structure of actual information systems on logical security level and also should provide the concepts for identification of dynamic approach of access control [21, 23].

Therefore, there is the need to create access control model, which will describe the secured organization, their structure in proper and complex way, like extended RBAC model does, and on the other side it will be appropriate and sufficient for dynamic distributed information system, like UCON model.

3.1 Proposition of New Implementation of Access Control Model

The proposed implementation of access control model was based on two models: extended RBAC model and UCON model. It was named *implementation of Role-based Usage Control* (**iRBUC**) model. General structure of proposed iRBUC model is shown in figure 3.

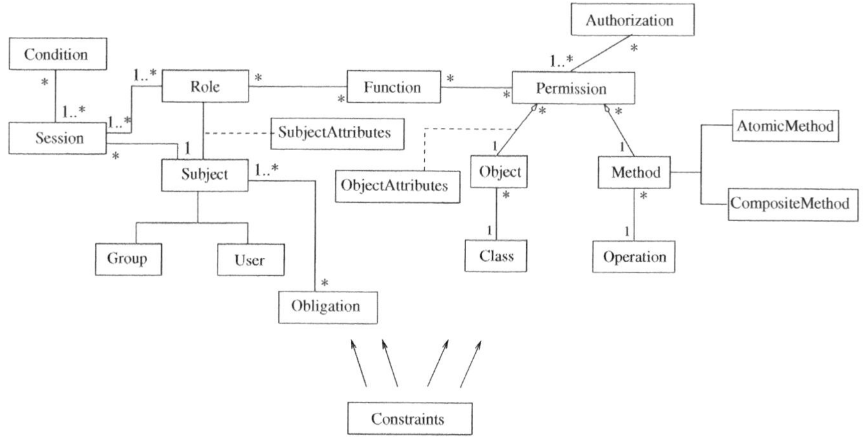

Fig. 3. Implementation of Role-based Usage Control model

The iRBUC model was defined using the elements came from extended RBAC model [8–10] and from UCON model [18, 19]. The core part of the model essentially represents the extended RBAC model. We distinguished two types of users in iRBUC model: single user (*User*) and group of users (*Group*). These two elements are represented by the element **Subject** that is superclass of User and Group. *Subject* permits to formalize the assignment of users and groups to the roles. *Subject* can be viewed as base type of all users and groups in a system. It can be presented as an abstract type, so it can not has direct instances - each subject is either a user or a group. A **User** is a human being, a person or process in a system, so it represents the system's entity, that can obtain some access rights in a system. A **Group** represents a group of users that have the same rights. Subjects can be assigned to the groups by aggregation relation *SubjectGroup* that represents an ordering relation in the set of all system's subjects.

The subject can be associated with the obligations **Obligation** which represent different access control predicates that describe the mandatory requirements performed by a subject. These requirements should be verified before or during a usage realized by a user. They can represent the security constraints that are defined on the subjects (i.e. users or/and groups) and they can be static or dynamic.

The **Session** element represents the period of time during which a user is logged in a system and can execute its own access rights. In our model the *Session* is assigned directly to a *Subject*. On the other hand a session is connected with the *roles* and this association represents the roles that can be activated during one session. Session is also connected with the set of conditions **Condition** that represent the features of a system or application. They can describe current environmental or system status and states during user's session that are used for usage decision.

A **Role** is a job function or a job title within the organization with some associated semantics regarding the authority and responsibility conferred on a member of the role. The role can represent a competency to do a specific task, and it can embody the authority and responsibility. The roles are created for various job functions in an organization. The users are assigned indirectly to the roles, based on their responsibilities and qualifications. The direct relation is established between roles and subjects that represent the users or groups of users. The user can take different roles on different occasions and also several users can play the same role (*Group* element). It is also possible to define the hierarchy of roles, represented by aggregation relation *RoleHierarchy*, which provides the hierarchical order of system roles. Hierarchy of roles represents also the inheritance relations between the roles. The role of the part end of the association inherits all privileges of the aggregate.

The association relation between the roles and subjects is described by association class **SubjectAttributes** that represents additional subject attributes (i.e. subject properties) as in UCON model.

Each role defined in extended RBAC model [8, 9] allows the realization of specific task associated to enterprise process. The same we have in iRBUC model. A role can contain many functions **Function** that a user can apply. Consequently, a role can be viewed as a set of functions that this role can take to realize a specific job. It is also possible to define the hierarchy of functions as the hierarchy of roles has been specified for roles. It is represented by aggregation relation named *FunctionHierarchy*, which provides the hierarchical order of system functions. Hierarchy of functions, just like hierarchy of roles, represents also the inheritance relations between the functions. The function of the part end of the association inherits all privileges of the aggregate.

Because each function can perform one or more operations, a function needs to be associated with a set of related permissions **Permission**. A function can be defined as a set or sequence (depending on the particular situation) of permissions. To perform an operation one has the access to required object, so necessary permissions should be assigned to the corresponding function. Therefore, all the tasks and required permissions are identified and they can be assigned to users to give them the possibility to perform the responsibilities involved when they play a particular role. Due to cardinality constraints, each permission must be assigned to at least one function.

One or more permissions **Permission** can be associated with each function. The permission determines execution right for a particular method on particular object. In order to access the data stored in object a message has to be sent to this object. This message causes the execution of particular method **Method** on this object **Object**. We can say that *permission* is the possibility of method's execution on an object in order to access the data stored in this object. Very often the constraints have to be defined in assignment process of permissions to the object. Such constraints are represented by the authorizations. **Authorization** is a logical predicate attached to permission that determines the permission's validity depending on access rules, object attributes and subject attributes. A constraint determines that some permission is valid only for a part of object's instances. Therefore, the *permission* can be presented as a function $p(o, m, c)$ where o is an object, m is a method that can be executed on this object and c is a set of constraints that determine this permission. According to this, the permission is given to all instances of the object class except the contrary specification.

The relation between objects and their permissions are additionally described by association class **ObjectAttributes** that represents the additional object attributes (i.e. object properties) that can not be specified in the object's class and they can be used for usage decision process. The examples of object attributes are security labels, ownerships or classes. They can be also mutable or immutable as subject attributes do.

Extended RBAC model [8] has also the concept of class and operation. A method is a particular instance of an **Operation**, so each operation can have one or more methods that can differ in number of attributes. The same situation exists for the objects. An object is an instance of particular **Class** and each class can have a few objects.

The *Method* element can be also differentiated between two types of methods: atomic method and composite method. The first one, **AtomicMethod** represents the low-level actions that can be directly mapped to the objects, e.g. *read*, *write* or *execute*. The **CompositeMethod** are high-level actions that represent more complex activities that can be realized on the objects. Moreover, it is also possible to define the aggregation relation between *Method* and *CompositeMethod*, named *MethodHierarchy*. It is used to order the composite methods in groups of methods.

The last element of the model is a set of constraints. The **constraints** can be defined for each element of model presented above, and also for the relationships among these elements. The concepts of *Conditions*, *Obligations* and *Authorizations* represent the idea of constraints related to selected elements of iRBUC model, i.e. *Conditions* are constraints related to *Session*, *Obligations* are related to *Subject* and *Authorizations* are related to *Permissions*. The other elements, such as *Roles*, *Functions* can have the constraints defined for them.

The concept of constraints is described widely in the literature [6, 7]. It is possible to distinguish different types of constraints, static and dynamic that can be attached to different model elements. The most popular type of constraints are *Separation of Duty (SoD)* constraints [6].

The metamodel of iRBUC model with the set of all elements and relationships presented above are shown in figure 4.

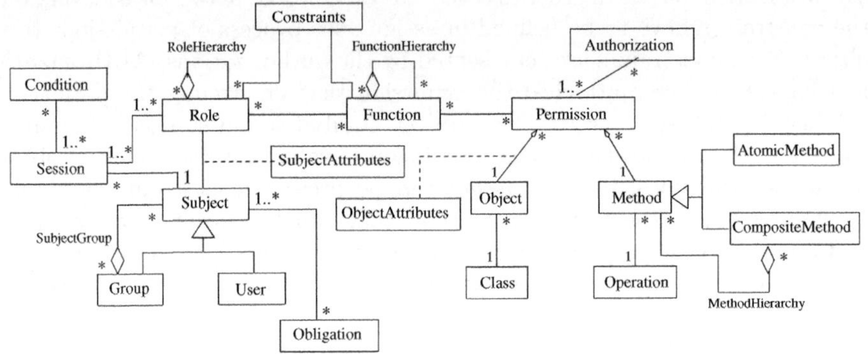

Fig. 4. Metamodel of iRBUC model

3.2 Formal Definition for Implementation of Role-Based Usage Control Model

The formal definition for implementation of Role-based Usage Control model is based on description presented above.

Definition 1. The iRBUC model can be defined with the use of following components:

- main sets of elements: U - users, G - groups, S - subjects, R - roles, F - functions, P - permissions, M - methods, O - objects and Sn - sessions,
- additional sets of elements: Cl - classes, Op - operations, $ATT(S)$ - subject attributes, $ATT(O)$ - object attributes, AM - atomic methods and CM - composite methods,
- functional decision predicates: A - authorizations, B - obligations and C - conditions,
- $UA \subseteq U \times R$ is many-to-many user-to-role assignment relation,
- $GA \subseteq G \times R$ is many-to-many group-to-role assignment relation,
- $RH \subseteq R \times R$ - a partial order on R set, called the role hierarchy or role dominance relation,
- $FA \subseteq F \times R$ - many-to-many function-to-role assignment relation,
- $FH \subseteq F \times F$ - a partial order on F set, called the function hierarchy or function dominance relation,
- $PA \subseteq P \times F$ - many-to-many permission-to-function assignment relation,

- $user : Sn \rightarrow U$ is a function mapping each session sn_i to single user $user(sn_i)$,
- $group : 2^{Sn} \rightarrow G$ is a function mapping set of sessions Sn to the group of users $group(users(sn_i))$,
- $roles : Sn \rightarrow 2^R$ is a function mapping each session sn_i to a set of roles $roles(sn_i) \subseteq \{r|(user(sn_i), r) \subseteq UA\}$ and session sn_i has the functions $\bigcup_{r \in roles(sn_i)} \{f|(f, r') \subseteq FA\}$,
- taking into consideration the hierarchy of roles: $roles : Sn \rightarrow 2^R$ is a function mapping each session sn_i to a set of roles $roles(sn_i) \subseteq \{r|(\exists r' \geq r)[(user(sn_i), r')] \subseteq UA\}$ and session sn_i has the functions $\bigcup_{r \in roles(sn_i)} \{f|(\exists r'' \leq r)[(f, r'') \subseteq FA]\}$,
- $functions : R \rightarrow 2^F$ is a function mapping each role r_i to a set of functions $functions(r_i) \subseteq \{f|(f, r_i) \subseteq FA\}$ and role r_i has the permissions $\bigcup_{f \in functions(r_i)} \{p|(p, f) \subseteq PA]\}$,
- taking into consideration the hierarchy of functions: $functions : R \rightarrow 2^F$ is a function mapping each role r_i to a set of functions $functions(r_i) \subseteq \{f|(\exists f' \geq f)[(f, r_i)] \subseteq FA\}$ and role r_i has the permissions $\bigcup_{f \in functions(r_i)} \{p|(\exists f'' \leq f)[(p, f'') \subseteq PA]\}$,
- $permission : M \times O \rightarrow P$ is a function mapping a pair: method m_i and object o_j to the permission $p(m_i, o_j)$,
- $AUTH \subseteq 2^A \times P$, many-to-many assignment relation of authorizations to a permission,
- $OBLIG \subseteq 2^B \times S$, many-to-many assignment relation of obligations to a subject,
- $COND \subseteq 2^C \times Sn$, many-to-many assignment relation of conditions to a sessions.

3.3 Access Control Elements Using iRBUC Model - Case Study

It is necessary to have more expressive access control model in order to define the access control for distributed information systems. Such model should allow the greatest structure of security policy to make possible the decomposition of this policy and make easy its definition. It should be possible to express more then simple authorizations but also the interdictions or obligations that should be fulfilled in order to obtain an access to data of information system. The model should also allow the expressing of rules assigned to conditions for system state or for access context of a system.

The complexity of actual organizations (i.e. matrix based organizational structure) has guided our proposition to extend the standard RBAC model by role management facilities that allow a finer distribution of responsibilities in an enterprise (Fig. 1) [9].

On the other side, the dynamism of actual information systems, especially distributed information systems or federation of information systems was the reason to use the concepts of Usage Control to develop the new implementation of access control models to support the management of information system security.

Persons employed by a company can have many professional responsibilities. Therefore, a set of roles can be attached to them. Each role defined in iRBUC model allows the realization of specific task associated with an enterprise process. Since every role can contain many functions that a user can apply, it is possible to choose functions of the system that are necessary for it. Consequently, a role can be viewed as a set of functions that this role can take to realize a specific job. Because each function can perform one or more operations, a function needs to be associated with a set of related permissions. To perform an operation one has the access to a required object, so necessary permissions should be assigned to the corresponding function.

This function level allows more flexibility in the security management and partition of responsibilities. For example, the necessity arises to set up a new organization in an enterprise or to integrate a new application in the information system. This situation generally causes the necessity to redistribute the functions to different actors of this enterprise. In this case, the security administrator should only modify the allocations of functions to the roles, with the new reorganization in mind. The users will always have the same roles but with new assigned functions. Likewise, if a function should be changed in the enterprise, it is possible to update the allocations of its permissions without any changes for the roles that use this function.

The example of distribution of roles can be presented by an application found in typical university information system. The user "professor" can have two roles: Teacher and Researcher, to perform his teaching activity and researching activity. The teaching role has a number of functions: prepare lectures, give lectures, prepare exams, record results, modify results, etc. The researching role contains functions like: create a theory, test the theory, document the results, etc. These functions are mapped to sets of permissions that grant the accesses to perform the works required by each function (Fig. 5).

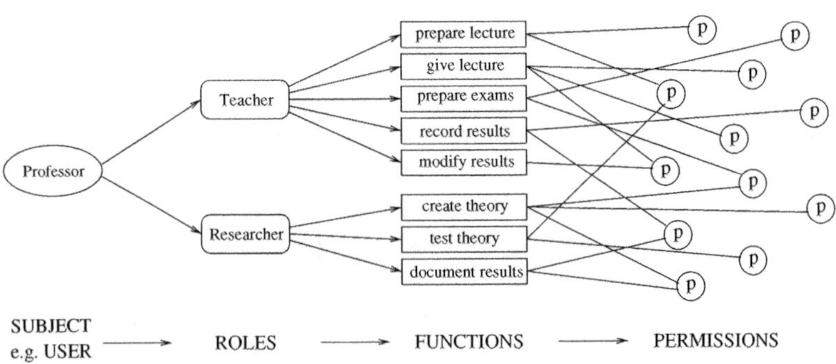

Fig. 5. Example of roles-functions-permissions mapping

This example gives the possibility to identify some elements of iRBUC model, for example:

subject := Professor
listRoles := Teacher, Researcher
listFunctions := prepare lectures, give lectures, prepare exams, record results, modify results, create theory, test the theory, document the results

The examples of other elements of iRBUC model can be proposed basing on elements determined above:

user := Prof. Tomas Smith
group := professors at IT department
SubjectAttribute := position (role) of "Professor" at the department
Condition := role "Dean" can be taken only during one Session at the particular moment of time

Another example, an application "Management of grades" to manage the results of students in university information system is presented in figure 6 using the use case diagram of UML (Unified Modeling Language). This diagram contains the actors (Teacher, Student, etc.) representing the roles and the use cases (visualization, edition, etc.) representing the functions of iRBUC model.

Therefore, it is possible to obtain the list of roles from this diagram:
listRoles := Dean, Teacher, Secretary, Student
and the list of functions:
listFunctions := visualization of grades, edition of grades, presentation of results, configuration, user validation

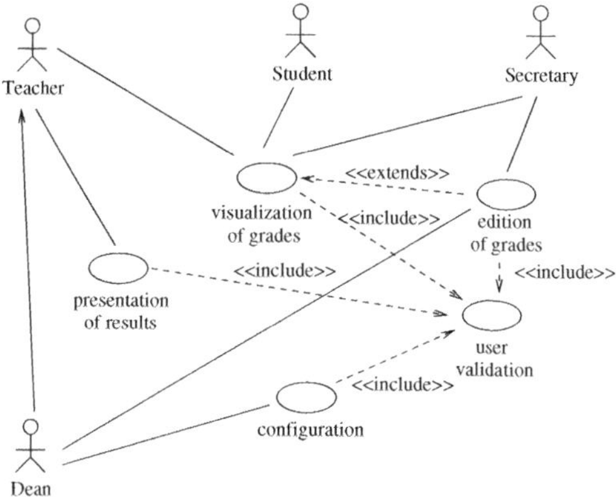

Fig. 6. Example of use case diagram

Next, each function (use case) can be described by means of scenario to find the permissions of iRBUC model associated to the function. For example the scenario of function "Visualization of grades" determines the behavior of following elements: a role (*Student*), some objects (one of class *WShowGradeStudent*, one of class *WShowListStudent*, one of class *listStudent*, one of class *listLectures*, one of class *listExams*, one of class *Exam* and one of class *Grade*) and the messages sent from the actor or objects to another objects. It is possible to obtain from such scenario the set of permissions for the function "Visualization of Grades" and attach them to role "Student":

role := Student
function := visualization of grades
listMethods := active(), content(), chose(), validStudent(), getLecture (Student), getExam(Lecture, Student), getGrade(Student, Lecture, Exam), getValue(), close()
listObjects := :WShowGradeStudent, :WShowListStudent, :listStudent, :listLectures, :listExams, :Exam, :Grade
listPermissions := (active(), :WShowGradeStudent), (active(), :WShowListStudent), (content(), :listStudent), (getLecture(Student), :listLecture), (getExam (Lecture, Student), :listExam), (getGrade(Student, Lecture, Exam), :Exam), ...

The examples of remaining elements of iRBUC model assigned to above elements can be defined as follows:

Authorization := "Student" can visualize only his own Grades
ObjectAttribute := weight (importance) of particular grades for the total grade

4 Conclusions

The presented implementation of Role-based Usage Control model allows defining the access control policy based on access request, as traditional access control models, and access decision can be evaluated during the access to information to which we want to control the usage. The model takes into consideration the provisional aspects in access security.

All the elements of iRBUC model, presented in the previous section form fairly complex model to present the whole organization of each enterprise on access control level. The components of iRBUC model can create the framework for classifying the family of models. Such classification can be based on three criteria: functional decision predicates (i.e. authorizations, obligations and conditions), continuity feature (control decision can be taken before or during the access) and mutability feature (updates of subject or object attributes can be done at different time).

It seems that iRBUC model can also support the security of dynamic information systems, such as distributed information system. It can be done thanks to mutable concept came from Usage Control approach where dynamic change of security policy can be translated to the change of values of subject attributes or object attributes. Moreover, these modifications can be realized before the information access, during information access or at the end of such access.

The future works on iRBUC model will focus on its realization with the use of object-oriented techniques, for example the Unified Modeling Language and next on creation of iRBUC family models.

References

1. Castaro, S., Fugini, M., Martella, G., Samarati, P.: Database Security. Addison-Wesley (1994)
2. Sandhu, R.S., Coyne, E.J., Feinstein, H.L., Youman, C.E.: Role-Based Access Control Models. IEEE Computer 29(2), 38–47 (1996)

3. Sandhu, R.S., Samarati, P.: Access Control: Principles and Practice. IEEE Communication 32(9), 40–48 (1994)
4. Ferraiolo, D., Sandhu, R.S., Gavrila, S., Kuhn, D.R., Chandramouli, R.: Proposed NIST Role-Based Access control. ACM TISSEC (2001)
5. Booch, G., Rumbaugh, J., Jacobson, I.: The Unified Modeling Language User Guide. Addison Wesley (1998)
6. Ahn, G.-J.: The RCL 2000 Language for Specifying Role-Based Authorization Constraints. ACM Transactions on Information and Systems Security (1999)
7. Ahn, G.-J., Sandhu, R.S.: Role-based Authorization Constraints Specification. ACM Transactions on Information and Systems Security (2000)
8. Poniszewska-Maranda, A., Goncalves, G., Hemery, F.: Representation of extended RBAC model using UML language. In: Vojtáš, P., Bieliková, M., Charron-Bost, B., Sýkora, O. (eds.) SOFSEM 2005. LNCS, vol. 3381, pp. 413–417. Springer, Heidelberg (2005)
9. Goncalves, G., Poniszewska-Maranda, A.: Role engineering: from design to evaluation of security schemas. Journal of Systems and Software 81(8), 1306–1326 (2008)
10. Poniszewska-Maranda, A.: Access Control Models in Heterogeneous Information Systems: from Conception to Exploitation. In: Proc. of IEEE International Multiconference on Computer Science and Information Technology, Wisla, Poland (2008)
11. Lampson, B.W.: Protection. ACM Operating Systems Review 8(1), 18–24 (1974)
12. Dows, D., Rub, J., Kung, K., Jordan, C.: Issues in discretionary access control. In: IEEE Symposium on Research in Security and Privacy, pp. 208–218 (1985)
13. Bell, D., Lapadulla, L.: Secure computer systems: Unified exposition and multics interpretation, Mitre Corporation (1975)
14. Bertino, E., Bettini, C., Samarati, P.: A Temporal Access Control Mechanism for Database Systems. IEEE TKDE 8(1) (1996)
15. Bertino, E., Bonatti, P., Ferrari, E.: A Temporal Role-based Access Control Model. ACM TISSEC 4(3), 191–233 (2001)
16. Gal, A., Atluri, V.: An Authorization Model for Temporal Data. ACM Transaction on Information and System Security 5(1) (2002)
17. James, B., Joshi, E., Bertino, U., Latif, A., Ghafoo, A.: A Generalized Temporal Role-Based Access Control Model. IEEE Transitions on Knowledge and Data Engineering 17(1), 4–23 (2005)
18. Park, J., Sandhu, R.: The UCON ABC Usage Control Model. ACM Transactions on Information and System Security 7 (2004)
19. Park, J., Zhang, X., Sandhu, R.: Attribute Mutability in Usage Control. In: 18th IFIP WG 11.3 Working Conference on Data and Applications Security (2004)
20. Lazouski, A., Martinelli, F., Mori, P.: Usage control in computer security: A survey. Computer Science Review 4(2), 81–99 (2010)
21. Pretschner, A., Hilty, M., Basin, D.: Distributed usage control. Communications of the ACM 49(9) (2006)
22. Zhang, X., Parisi-Presicce, F., Sandhu, R., Park, J.: Formal Model and Policy Specification of Usage Control. ACM TISSEC 8(4), 351–387 (2005)
23. Jiang, Z., Hu, S., Gan, S., Shu, Y.: Research on an UCON model supporting distributed management. In: Proc. of ICIA 2008, pp. 1520–1524 (2008)

Beyond TOR: The TrueNyms Protocol

Nicolas Bernard and Franck Leprévost

University of Luxembourg, LACS, 162 A, Avenue de la Faïencerie,
L-1511 Luxembourg
{Nicolas.Bernard,Franck.Leprevost}@uni.lu

Abstract. How to hide who is communicating with whom? How to hide when a person is communicating? How to even hide the existence of ongoing communications? Partial answers to these questions have already been proposed, usually as byproducts of anonymity providing systems. The most advanced one available today is Onion-Routing and is implemented in Tor and I2P. Still, Onion-Routing is exposed to a series of serious attacks. The current paper classifies these series of attacks, and announces the TrueNyms unobservability protocol. We describe here how TrueNyms handles one of the families of attacks applying to the current Onion-Routing system, namely traffic analysis on the "shape", and give some evidence on its performance. Developed since 2003, TrueNyms is not anymore an academic answer to a privacy problem, but is a heavily tested and efficient product providing unobservability and anonymity. Although it cannot be used (for the time-being) for *very low-latency* applications like telephony over IP, TrueNyms can be efficiently used for most *low-latency* applications like Web browsing and HTTP-based protocols (RSS for instance), Instant Messaging, File transfers, audio and video streaming, remote shell, etc. TrueNyms allows parties to communicate without revealing anything about the communication — including its very existence — to any observer, despite how powerful such an observer might be.

1 Introduction

For low-latency communications, protocols like SSL [25] or IPsec [16] allow the encryption of data and authentication of parties. Still, these protocols do not protect all aspects of communication over the Internet. Notably, an observer is still able to learn the identity of the communicating parties, or the nature of the content (Web browsing, file transfer, VoIP, etc.).

The questions we address here are: How to hide who is communicating with whom? How to hide when a person is communicating? How to even hide the existence of ongoing communications?

Partial answers to these questions have already been proposed, usually as byproducts of anonymity providing systems. The most advanced one available today is Onion-Routing [6,12,24] and is implemented in Tor [8] and I2P [15]; enhancements to these systems have been proposed (e.g. [27]). Still, Onion-Routing is not sufficient, and is exposed to a series of serious attacks.

P. Bouvry et al. (Eds.): SIIS 2011, LNCS 7053, pp. 68–84, 2012.

In this paper, we recall in section 2 how Onion-Routing works, raise the performance issues, and classify its security issues into three families of attacks. In section 3 we address one of these security issues, namely preventing traffic analysis on the "shape", and introduce our protocol TrueNyms. Although based on Onion-Routing, TrueNyms bypasses all its security drawbacks [3]. In section 4 we provide the first performance measurements of our protocol after a very intensive testing phase. As a consequence, TrueNyms provides a concrete, practical, and efficient answer to the questions addressed above, which can be resumed as looking for the missing link to privacy. In other words:

- TrueNyms solves all the security issues applying to Onion-Routing;
- In terms of perfomance, although TrueNyms's latency suffers from the security improvements over Onion-Routing, TrueNyms is more efficient than the Onion-Routing implementations (Tor, and I2P), as far as the establishment of communications, and the throughput are concerned ;
- The current version of TrueNyms can be used for most applications like Web browsing and HTTP-based protocols (RSS for instance), Instant Messaging, File transfers, audio and video streaming, remote shell, etc. The applications excluded (for the time-being) are those needing a very low latency (like telephony over the Internet).

Henceforth, with TrueNyms, it is now possible to communicate without revealing anything about the communication — including its very existence — to any observer (passive or active), as powerful as such an observer may be.

A more complete description of our TrueNyms protocol will appear elsewhere [3], where we will further detail the adopted methods not only against traffic analysis but against all three families of attacks applying to Onion-Routing, the in-depth security architecture of the TrueNyms program itself, and further performance data.

2 Description of Onion-Routing and Its Weaknesses

Alice and Bob want to communicate in a very secure way. They want to keep secret not only the content of their communications, but the very fact that they are communicating should be itself a secret too: they want *unobservability*. We suppose nothing about the observers, which may be the computer engineer in the company you are working in, the intelligence service of a very powerful nation-state, or even a combination of such intelligence services like Echelon (see e.g. [9], especially Chapter 2, and [5]). The monitoring of the observers can be targeted on Alice and / or Bob or can be a global and ubiquitous system. Eve is a passive observer; Mallory is an active one.

2.1 From Encryption to Onion-Routing

Let us recall that using some encryption to ensure unobservability is not sufficient. It usually protects only the content of the data packets, and not the headers. As a consequence, an observer sees that the communication takes place between Alice and Bob.

A natural approach to overcome this weakness is to introduce a *relay* R between Alice and Bob. The sender Alice first encrypts her original message M with Bob's key k_B, then encrypts the result $\{M\}_{k_B}$ with the relay's key k_R, and finally sends the newly encrypted message $\{\{M\}_{k_B}\}_{k_R}$ to the relay. Now, when the relay R receives this message, he removes one layer of encryption, recovers hence the message $\{M\}_{k_B}$, which he sends to Bob, who in turn is able to recover the original message M sent by Alice. With this approach, the message sent by Alice to R is distinct from the message resent by R to Bob, and hence an observer cannot *a priori* be able to make the link between the messages sent to R, and the messages sent by R. Moreover, the headers containing the IP addresses of the sender and of the receiver, added at the beginning of each encrypted packet, are *a priori* misleading the observer. Such systems are available on a commercial basis, but with encryption only between Alice and the relay R (see e.g. `anonymizer.com`, `swissvpn.net`, `xerobank.com`).

However, this approach suffers from some serious drawbacks, as R knows the identities of both Alice and Bob, who furthermore must trust R.

2.2 Brief Description of Onion-Routing

One can rely on nested tunnels established through multiple relays R_1, R_2, etc. (in what follows, a *node* denotes either a relay or Alice or Bob). These relays accept to take part in an anonymity system, but are not necessarily trusted. Indeed, some of them can cooperate with Eve or Mallory. Relays see only enciphered traffic and know only the previous and next nodes on the route. They do not know if those nodes are other relays or end-points. This approach, known as Onion-routing (see [12,24]), or as Pipenet [6], and is illustrated in Figure 1.

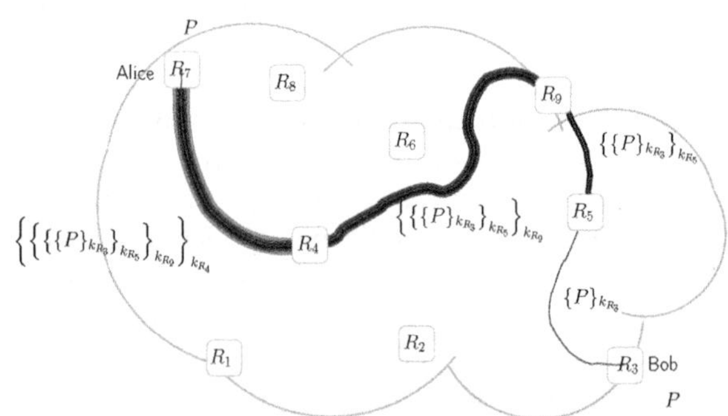

Fig. 1. illustrates how Onion-Routing works, using the notations of 2.1 in an obvious way: to communicate with Bob, Alices creates a set of nested encrypted tunnels. For every packet, each relay removes the outermost encryption layer (hence the name of this scheme).

Throughout this article, an encrypted tunnel between Alice and one of the nodes is called a *connection*. Then, a set of nested connections between Alice and Bob is called a *route*. Despite being created by Alice, those routes are not related to IP source routing or other IP-level routing. Standard IP routing is still used between successive nodes if these nodes are on an IP network as we consider here. A *communication* is a superset of one or more routes between Alice and Bob that are used to transmit data between them. A communication can use multiple routes simultaneously and / or sequentially.

The concept of Onion-Routing goes back to 1996, and is the most advanced system available today. A few implementations of Onion-Routing exist, the better known being probably Tor [8] and I2P [15]. Still, Onion-Routing is not sufficient to achieve unobservability. Onion-routing is subject to a set of serious attacks, and has also performance issues described in the following sections.

2.3 Performance Issues

Establishment time, latency and throughput lead to performance issues for Onion-Routing.

The **establishment time** is the first issue in Onion-Routing. If Alice creates a route with n relays to communicate with Bob, she has to create $n+1$ connections instead of only one as she would do in a classical TCP-connection. Moreover, the time to establish these connections is impacted by key-establishment and partial authentication protocols.

The **latency** considered here is the time for a packet to go from one end of the route to the other end. Latency depends mostly on the path taken by the packets on the network. With a standard communication using standard routing mechanisms, latency between Alice and Bob would probably be low if Alice and Bob are close (in a network sense) to each other. However, with Onion-Routing, the total latency L_{AB} between Alice and Bob is the sum of the latencies between each couple of consecutive nodes on the route (notwithstanding some processing time), and is given by the following formula, assuming there is an average latency $\hat{L}$ between two nodes:

$$L_{AB} = L_{AR_1} + \sum_{i=1}^{n-1} L_{R_iR_{i+1}} + L_{R_nB} \approx (n+1)\hat{L} \,. \qquad (1)$$

Finally, the **throughput** between two nodes measures the amount of data transmitted between these nodes per time unit. Clearly, the throughput T_{AB} between Alice and Bob is limited by the lowest throughput between two successive nodes:

$$T_{AB} \leq \min \left\{ T_{AR_1}, \left\{ T_{R_iR_{i+1}}, 1 \leq i < n \right\}, T_{R_nB} \right\} \,. \qquad (2)$$

These three issues have multiple consequences, ranging from minor annoyances to the user (delays, slower downloads, etc.) to the point where some protocols can hardly be used (e.g. Telephony over IP) with Onion-Routing.

2.4 Classification of Security Issues

The security issues of Onion-Routing may be classified in three categories of attacks:

- Analysis of connection creation;
- Replay attacks;
- Analysis of the shape of the traffic.

None of these attacks is exactly new [1,7,11,22,26,28,29,30,33,34], but no low latency system was solving all of them before TrueNyms.

While it would be easier to perform these attacks by monitoring the whole network, note that it is not needed to make pretty accurate guesses. Even if the observer (passive or active) is not able to observe every node or even every node on a route, correlation on the connections going through the part(s) of the network the observer monitors will give him important information, notably if both Alice and Bob are part of the area the observer looks at [21].

Beginning / End of Connections. Let us assume that Eve can view a part of the network, and let us consider Figure 2, representing this part. When a

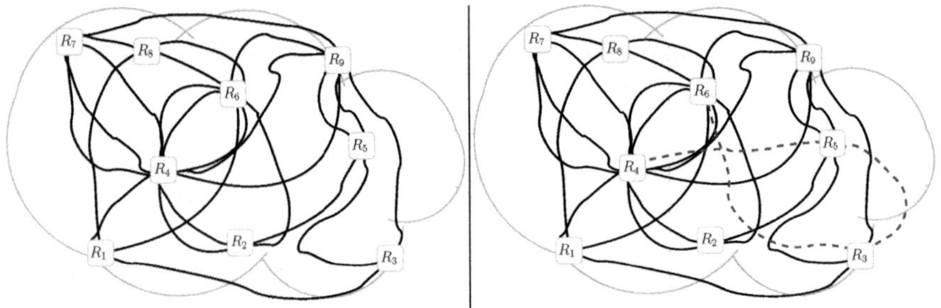

Fig. 2. Background activity at time t (left) and a new route (right)

route is established over the network, even if there are other routes, there will be little change in these while the new route is established if the connections are made without pausing. For instance, let us assume that at some point the network looks like the left part of Figure 2. Then imagine that an activity is ongoing leading to the situation depicted on the right, with the establishment of a connection between the node R_4 and the node R_5, then from R_5 to R_3, then R_3 to R_6, and assume that the background picture of the network stays globally invariant like in the left part of Figure 2. If there is no further activity for some times, Eve will guess that the dashed route has just been established between the nodes R_4, and R_6. The situation is similar when a route is no longer needed and is destroyed.

Replay Attacks. An issue with standard cryptography modes when used in Onion-Routing is that they allow an active replay attack[1]. Let us examine the situation at a relay at a given time: for instance, let us assume that this specific relay is a part of three routes, as depicted in Figure 3.

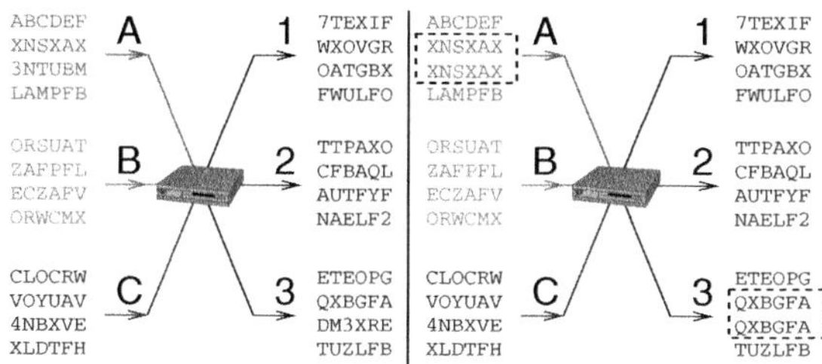

Fig. 3. Cryptography hides connection bindings to a passive observer (left), but not to an active observer able to inject duplicate packets (right)

On the left of Figure 3, Mallory sees three distinct incoming connections (A, B, C). As an encryption layer is removed on each connection, he does not know the corresponding outgoing connections. However, as cryptography is deterministic, a given packet entered twice through the same incoming connection will be output twice — in its form with an encryption layer removed — on the corresponding outgoing connection. So Mallory takes a packet and duplicates it, say on the connection A, which leads to the right side of Figure 3. He then looks for two identical packets on the output, and finds them on the connection 3, so he learns that connection A and connection 3 are part of the same route. Obviously, depending on the interest of Mallory, he can perform a similar attack on the next relay having the connection 3 as an incoming connection, and then see where this leads ultimately. Or he can perform the same attack on the other incoming connections B and C, and figure out exactly which outgoing connection 1 or 2 corresponds to them. Other attacks, depending on the encryption mode, are also considered in [3].

Analysis of the "Shape" of the Traffic. The third class of security issues stems from what could be called "the shape" of the traffic (see e.g. [26]). Indeed, each connection has a very specific signature given by a graph having as x-coordinate the moment when a packet is observed, and its size as y-coordinate. Moreover, this signature shape reveals, despite the encryption, the kind of traffic passing over this connection. For instance, figure 4 illustrates this, where the incoming connection A (resp. connection B, resp. connection C) probably encapsulates Web traffic (resp. VoIP, resp. File transfer).

[1] This is different of the replay attacks well known in cryptography, where an attacker can play part of a protocol back from a recording, and that are usually prevented by the use of nonces or timestamps.

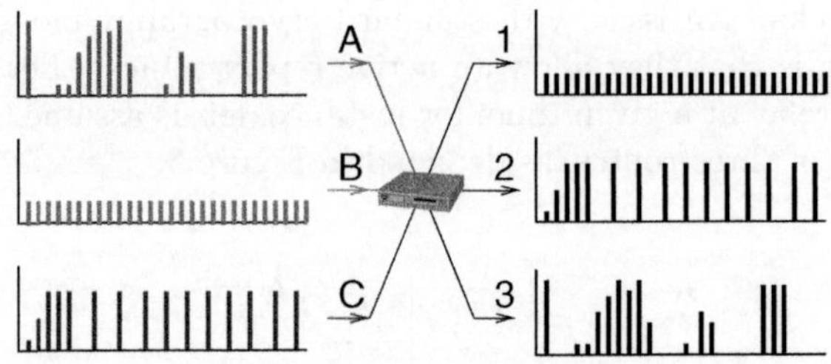

Fig. 4. It is easy to match connections when there is no traffic shaping

Obviously, Eve can easily match the shapes of the incoming connections to the shapes of the outgoing ones to discover that connection A corresponds to connection 3, connection B to connection 1, and connection C to connection 2.

In fact, if an attacker is only able to observe Alice (i.e. far less powerful than what we have assumed so far) and hence is not able to observe any relay, he still can use the shape of the traffic to know what Alice does, for instance by combining attacks like those described in [4,13,14,17,31,32].

3 The TrueNyms Protocol and Its Approach to Traffic Analysis

The previous section described three families of security issues in Onion-Routing that must be solved. This section considers only the last one (a more complete description of the countermeasures against the other families of attacks will appear in [3]), and introduces our TrueNyms protocol.

The shape of the traffic on a connection depends on the specific number of packets this connection sends and receives, the size of each packet, and the time distribution of the packets being related to the ongoing traffic. While it is easy to impose a specific shape of the traffic, this has consequences that have to be addressed, as we see below.

3.1 Traffic Shaping

The problem of the different size for the packets can be solved by imposing the size: each and every packet will be of the same size. Shorter packets will be padded before encryption, bigger packets will be split in two or more. Similarly, it is possible to impose a specific number of packets per second on every connection. Doing these two operations is *traffic shaping*.

However, while it solves the visibility of the shape problem, traffic shaping has its own issues that must, in turn, be solved. The first one is an optimization problem: if both packet size and the number of packets per second are imposed, what are the optimal parameters for these? Although the answer can be tricky (see [3]), let us however assume that we have fixed reasonable parameters. Still, two security issues remain:

- first, while the input-output link is not immediate anymore, the issue of the total number of packets on connections is not solved yet. The way this problem is addressed in TrueNyms is described in [3];
- second, the loss, or even the delay, of a single packet can expose the hidden link. This issue and how TrueNyms solves it is described in 3.2.

3.2 What Happens When a Packet Is Lost?

When a packet is lost (and some will be as experience shows), if nothing is done to prevent it, the situation depicted in Figure 5 arises. The relay has nothing to

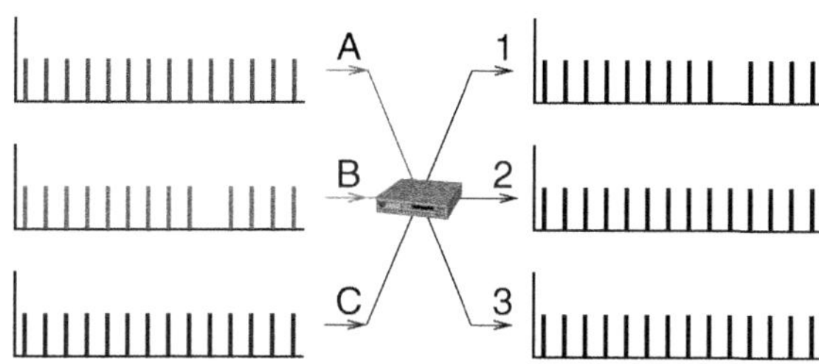

Fig. 5. Lost packets are an issue with traffic shapping

send when it should send the missing packet, and hence sends nothing. Observing this, Eve immediately knows connection B and 1 are parts of the same route. She may even be able to "follow" the missing packet from relay to relay until it "reaches" the end of the route.

A naive approach to solve this issue could be for the relay to drop a packet on each outgoing connection. While it would prevent an observer to see the link, it would amplify the loss of a single packet to all the routes going through this relay, and would lead to obvious problems.

A more suitable approach is for the relay to insert a dummy packet (i.e. consisting of random data) each time a packet is lost. Its content being random, this packet cannot be distinguished from a normal, enciphered packet, by anyone but its destination, either Alice or Bob.

3.3 Issues with Dummy Packets

Assumptions. Let us now clarify the assumptions used, and their first consequences. The idea is to build an *application* allowing unobservable communications. It needs to be an application because the assumptions include:

1. it is not possible to change the core network infrastructure (routers, etc.);
2. users will not change their operating system only to have unobservability.

These assumptions imply the system cannot be at the operating system kernel level (or else it would imply a lot more development work). The system cannot be a mere library either: the need to hide its global use has to be coordinated between applications in the case more than one of them are running, and has also to be ensured in the case no application is running.

Implicit Model. Being an application, the logical choice is to use between relays the default communication mechanism, namely TCP sockets, *i.e.* standard reliable (but insecure) stream oriented connections: this is the implicit model. The reliability of TCP means (apart network failure), all data put at one end of the connection arrive at the other end, the lost packets being retransmitted. If we represent two successive relays on a route, the situation is as depicted in Figure 6.

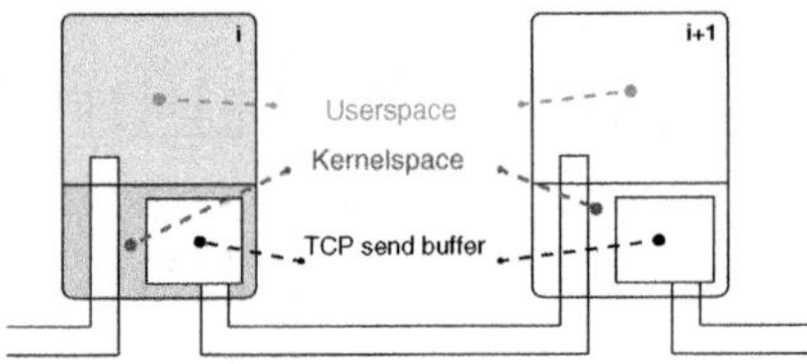

Fig. 6. Implicit model up to now: application level forwarding program linked through TCP connections

TCP is handled at the operating system kernel level ("kernelspace"), while the relaying process is an application (in the "userspace"). The operating system of a relay stores a sent packet in a "send buffer" until the next relay acknowledges its reception (then, it is deleted). While TCP is reliable, the need for reliability on a route from one end to the other end implies that the relaying application must be reliable too, *i.e.* it must not lose or discard packets.

The implicit model will be *discarded* as we need to send dummy packets. Indeed, let us consider what happens with the implicit model if a dummy packet is inserted when a packet is "lost" (or delayed, as reliable underlying TCP connections are used). On each relay, the program alternates between a reading phase, where it receives packets on the network, and a writing phase, where, for each connection, *one and only one* packet is sent. If multiple packets are received on a connection, one only is sent, the other ones are queued. If no packet is received, a dummy one is created and sent.

Let us assume at time t (see Figure 7), that both programs are in their reading phases and receive a packet on each of the two pictured relays (relays i and $i+1$)[2].

[2] Things are presented as synchronized to make the picture clearer. However there is no real synchronization in the actual system, but for a common parameter for the number of packets per second. Clock skew is not an issue, neither at the timescale of a connection (too small) nor between connections (irrelevant).

At time $t+1$, both programs send the previously received packet. Unbeknownst to relay i, the packet it sent is lost. At time $t+2$ (Figure 8, left), both programs

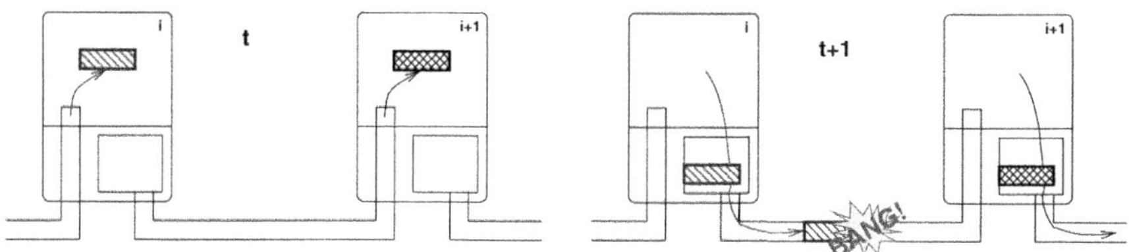

Fig. 7. Packets received (left) are then forwarded (right), but one of them is lost

are, again, in their reading phase. The program on node i gets a packet, but the program on node $i+1$ gets none, as the packet was lost. Meanwhile, the operating system of node $i+1$ receives an "ACK" from node $i+2$, and so it discards the copy of the packet it still had in its send buffer: at time $t+3$ (Figure 8, right),

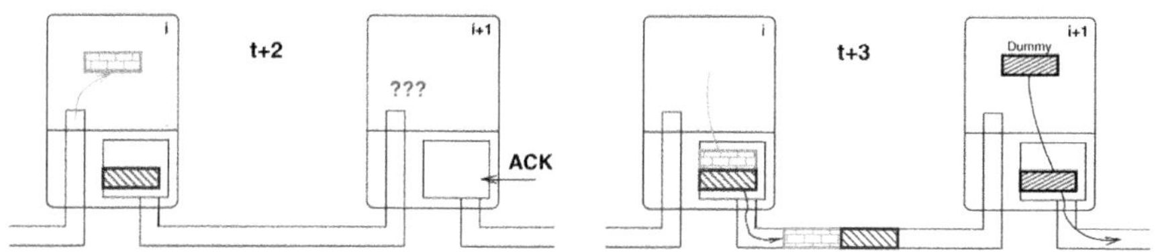

Fig. 8. Due to the lost packet, node $i+1$ does not receive data in time (left). It must then send a dummy packet (right).

both programs are in a new writing phase. Relay program i just sends the packet it got at time $t+2$, which means it gives the packet to the operating system, requesting its delivery to relay $i+1$. The operating system still has the copy of the previous packet in its send buffer. The exact timing can vary, but in essence, the operating system will then send both the new and the old packet on the network. While there are two packets on a connection at the same time, this is not by itself a security issue, as long as there is no correlation with what appeared, appears, or will appear on other connections. Meanwhile, node $i+1$ has to send a packet, but it has received none in the imparted time. Hence, it creates a dummy packet with random data, and sends it. At time $t+4$ (Figure 9, left), both programs are again reading. Relay i receives a new packet, and relay $i+1$ gets at the same time the two packets sent by i. Here is the issue: at time $t+5$ (Figure 9, right), each program, must send one and *only one* packet. This is no issue for relay i, but relay $i+1$ has to send one packet and to queue

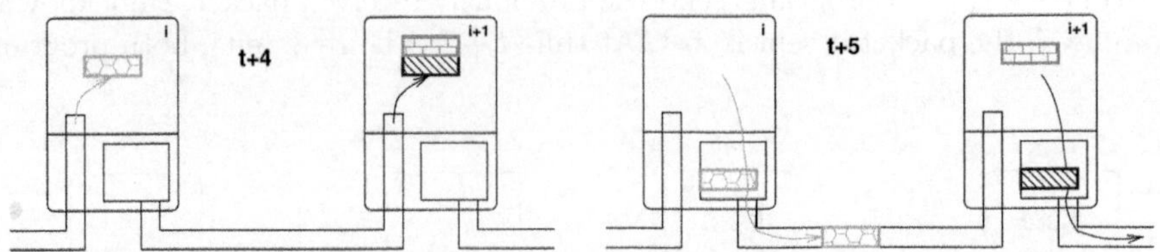

Fig. 9. Relay $i+1$ now receives two packets at the same time (left). But it can send only one (right).

the other one. In the following instants, it will receive the packet sent by relay i. Then it will be able to send the packet in its queue, but then will have to add the new packet, etc. Relay $i+1$ will have to juggle with packets hereafter.

The issue with the implicit model is twofold:

- first, the FIFO queues on the nodes have an impact on the latency: each lost packet, even if it was a dummy packet, increases the latency on the route overtime;
- second, it uses memory; one can imagine a denial of service attack where Mallory ensures some specific packets are lost so that some router is out of memory.

The solution is to abandon the implicit model, and adopt an unreliable model which allows relays to discard packets (while still insuring end-to-end reliability between Alice and Bob).

3.4 Handling Reliability: Our Unreliable Model

The problem caused by sending a dummy packet over a reliable connection as described in 3.3 has no obvious solution. When designing TrueNyms, the choice was made to change the model and to build our system over unreliable channels, leading to our unreliable model. Once relays are able to discard packets and do not have a FIFO queue, the issue caused by dummy packets disappears. It is not even mandatory to change the underlying communication protocol away from TCP. However, except for some cases where it should be used and not another protocol, TCP is now only a second choice. Indeed, the reliability TCP offers between two relays is useless. What counts is the connection of each node of the route with Alice and, except on the first relay, that packets can have been discarded by a previous relay on this connection.

Worse, when a packet is lost between two relays, TCP will retransmit it. However, while the packet is retransmitted, the relay program will not be able to get anything: the packets following the one that was lost are delayed until it is retransmitted. During this waiting time, the relay has to generate dummy packets for traffic shaping. When at last the missing packet is retransmitted, it is given to the program, *at the same time as all the subsequent packets arrived meanwhile.* As the program is anyway unable to forward them all, it will discard most of them. The loss of a packet that may have been a dummy packet is so transformed in the loss of multiple packets, including possibly non-dummy packets. So: *in an unreliable model, TCP must be considered harmful.* In TrueNyms, TCP is only used when another, unreliable, protocol cannot be used.

While either or both the underlying protocol and the relays are able to lose packets, end-to-end reliability is still needed in most cases. To the initial implicit model of host-to-host reliability, TrueNyms substitutes an unreliable model that still provides end-to-end reliability between Alice and Bob. However, even this end-to-end reliability is optional in TrueNyms. This means that when Alice and Bob are communicating through a protocol that does not need end-to-end reliability, it is possible to discard this end-to-end reliability, to the profit of latency for instance. Being able to provide both reliable and unreliable transport to the upper layers, TrueNyms' conceptual position in the TCP/IP network model can be located between IP and the applicative layer. However, to have a better compatibility with existing networks and networking applications (packet filters, etc.), TrueNyms is actually built upon UDP (with TCP as a backup).

This section described how TrueNyms solves the issue of the shape of the traffic. Actually TrueNyms solves the other families of problems as well [3] and is a complete system.

4 Implementing TrueNyms: Addressing Performance Issues

Implementation of TrueNyms started in the last quarter of 2003 as a prototype. TrueNyms is implemented in the C language (ISO C99) and runs on Unix / POSIX systems. TrueNyms consists in a peer-to-peer daemon, to which native clients can connect. A library is provided to write native clients. It is, however, not necessary for most uses: a SOCKSv5 proxy is provided that allows existing software to interface with the daemon.

Regarding the choice of the parameters for our tests, we chose *a priori* sensible values for a generic use of TrueNyms, with 10 packets per seconds and a packet size of 1044 bytes (when over UDP). This packet size gives MTUs of 988 and 996 bytes for respectively reliable and unreliable packets in our unreliable model. Latency could be decreased by sending more packets per second. Unless the size of each packet is decreased, it would also increase the throughput per route, but would increase the burden on the network and disallow the use of the TrueNyms system on slower accesses (like dial-up POTS connections for instance).

During the whole development, the program was constantly tested on a LAN. To gain insights on performance over a real network, we also later deployed (safely) the program on distinct locations linked through the Internet.

4.1 Test Network

Such a test deployment was done by sending small (and secure) computers to miscellaneous universities through Europe (University of Luxembourg, Technische Universität Berlin, University Joseph Fourier in Grenoble, École Normale Supérieure in Lyon, University of Liège, University of Namur). All these universities are connected to the Internet through their national research network, which in turn are themselves connected together through the European research network GÉANT 2. The network links between the relays were both low latency, with an average round-trip time $\hat{t}_{rtt}$ between two relays of about 30 ms, and high throughput. We tested and optimized TrueNyms over this network during more than two years.

4.2 Performance

We measured the performances of the latency and of the time needed to establish a communication.

Latency. With standard Onion-Routing, latency L_{OR} can be approximated by

$$L_{OR} = n \times \hat{t}_{rtt} + 2n \times t_{proc}\,, \tag{3}$$

where n is the number of relays, $\hat{t}_{rtt}$ the average round-trip time between two relays and t_{proc} the average processing time of a packet on a relay. However, when traffic shaping is used, the new important parameter $\hat{t}_{wait}$ must be considered. On average, if the duration between two send phases is called t_{sl}, there is a waiting time of $\hat{t}_{wait} = \frac{t_{sl}}{2}$. As a consequence, TrueNyms' latency L_{TN} becomes

$$L_{TN} = n \times \hat{t}_{rtt} + 2n \times t_{proc} + 2n \times \hat{t}_{wait}\,. \tag{4}$$

Obviously, the dominant term depends on both the chosen parameters, the network and the computers used as relays. On the testbed network, and with a configuration specifying to send 10 packets/sec, the parameters were the following:

$$\hat{t}_{rtt} \approx 30 \text{ ms}, \qquad t_{proc} \approx 5 \text{ ms}, \qquad \hat{t}_{wait} \approx 50 \text{ ms}\,. \tag{5}$$

The graph in Figure 10 shows expected latency as well as latency measured over our tests of TrueNyms. This shows that while this kind of latency will not allow to use some protocols needing a very low latency (e.g.Telephony), TrueNyms is still suitable for most uses with three relays on a route (which provides a more than adequate security).

Time to Establish a Communication. We consider this aspect as important as latency. Indeed, even if both throughput and latency were excellent, if it required to wait a few minutes between the time a request is sent and the time the answer arrives, it would restrict the use of the system to a few aspects (e.g. automated transfers). However, as described in [3], TrueNyms uses a pool of pre-established

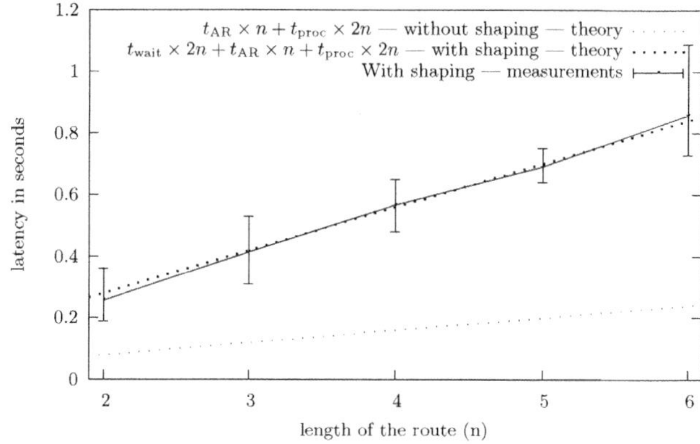

Fig. 10. Theoretical and measured latency for TrueNyms

proto-routes to accelerate the establishment of communications. With six relays, about 90 seconds are needed on average to establish a route. The pool of routes provides a dramatic improvement: it reduces this establishment time to around one second (average 0.75 seconds with three relays, 1.13 with six).

5 Conclusions

The TrueNyms protocol allows Alice and Bob to communicate without any observer knowing it. When parties are using TrueNyms for their communications, an observer, as powerful as he may be, is unable to know who they are communicating with. He is unable to know when a communication occurs. He is even unable to know if a communication occurs at all.

TrueNyms is based on Onion-Routing, to which it adds protection against all forms of traffic analysis. With the current knowledge, it seems out of reach to achieve a formal proof of security of such a system. However, some tried and true principles exist to minimize the risks. These principles and concepts were applied during the design of TrueNyms to make it future-proof, and harden it against yet unknown attacks. To date, this approach was fruitful: since we began our work on TrueNyms, other attacks have been discovered against Onion-Routing or Tor. Some are specific to Tor, due to specific features integrated in it but not related to Onion-Routing [18,19,23]. Others are related to Onion-Routing but, again, specific to Tor. They are due, for instance, to optimizations made to enhance Tor's performance, which in fact lead to the introduction of flaws [2]. At last, some are pretty generic, like [20,10]. While we did not foresee these attacks, none of them worked against TrueNyms, without changing a single line of the code. This is due to the "security over performance" and "security in depth" approaches used when designing TrueNyms. TrueNyms was extensively tested for more than two years on a test network. Its performance is experimentally validated and is appropriate for most uses : Web browsing and HTTP-based protocols (RSS for instance), Instant Messaging, File transfers, audio and video streaming, remote shell, etc.

While focused on *unobservability*, for situations where communicating parties may want to authenticate themselves at a upper layer, TrueNyms provides *anonymity* as a byproduct. This anonymity is at the network level, and is much stronger than what other comparable systems (like e.g. Onion-Routing) provide. The paper [3] completes the present article in providing much more details on TrueNyms, its implementation, its in-depth security, and its performances.

Acknowledgements. The authors thank P. Bouvry, M. Muraszkiewicz, F. Seredynski for their careful reading of [3], and the referees, as well as the Technische Universität Berlin, the University Joseph Fourier of Grenoble, the École Normale Supérieure of Lyon, the University of Liège and the University of Namur for joining the first test campaign. The FNR/04/01/05/TeSeGrAd grant partially supported this research.

References

1. Back, A., Möller, U., Stiglic, A.: Traffic analysis attacks and trade-offs in anonymity providing systems. In: Moskowitz, I.S. (ed.) IH 2001. LNCS, vol. 2137, pp. 245–257. Springer, Heidelberg (2001)
2. Bauer, K., McCoy, D., Grunwald, D., Kohno, T., Sicker, D.: Low-resource routing attacks against Tor. In: Proceedings of the Workshop on Privacy in the Electronic Society (WPES 2007), Washington, DC, USA (October 2007)
3. Bernard, N., Leprévost, F.: Unobservability of low-latency communications: the TrueNyms protocol. Work in Progress (2011)
4. Bissias, G.D., Liberatore, M., Jensen, D., Levine, B.N.: Privacy vulnerabilities in encrypted HTTP streams. In: Danezis, G., Martin, D. (eds.) PET 2005. LNCS, vol. 3856, pp. 1–11. Springer, Heidelberg (2006)
5. Campbell, D.: A new way to do anonymity. STOA European Parliament 168.184/Part.4 (April 04, 1999)
6. Dai, W.: A new way to do anonymity. Post to Cypherpunks Mailing List (February 07, 1995)
7. Danezis, G.: The traffic analysis of continuous-time mixes. In: Martin, D., Serjantov, A. (eds.) PET 2004. LNCS, vol. 3424, pp. 35–50. Springer, Heidelberg (2005)
8. Dingledine, R., Mathewson, N., Syverson, P.: Tor: The second-generation onion router. In: Proceedings of the 13th USENIX Security Symposium (August 2004)
9. Ebrahimi, T., Leprévost, F., Warusfel, B. (eds.): Enjeux de la sécurité multimédia. Informatique et Systèmes d'Information, Hermes-Lavoisier (2006)
10. Evans, N., Dingledine, R., Grothoff, C.: A practical congestion attack on tor using long paths. In: Proceedings of the 18th USENIX Security Symposium (August 2009)
11. Fu, X., Graham, B., Bettati, R., Zhao, W.: Active traffic analysis attacks and countermeasures. In: Proceedings of the 2003 International Conference on Computer Networks and Mobile Computing, pp. 31–39 (2003)

12. Goldschlag, D.M., Reed, M.G., Syverson, P.F.: Hiding Routing Information. In: Anderson, R. (ed.) IH 1996. LNCS, vol. 1174, pp. 137–150. Springer, Heidelberg (1996)
13. Herrmann, D., Wendolsky, R., Federrath, H.: Website fingerprinting: attacking popular privacy enhancing technologies with the multinomial naïve-bayes classifier. In: Proceedings of the 2009 ACM Workshop on Cloud Computing Security (CCSW 2009), pp. 31–42. ACM, New York (2009)
14. Hintz, A.: Fingerprinting websites using traffic analysis. In: Dingledine, R., Syverson, P.F. (eds.) PET 2002. LNCS, vol. 2482, pp. 171–178. Springer, Heidelberg (2003)
15. The Invisible Internet Project: Introducing I2P (200x), http://www.i2p2.de/
16. Kent, S., Atkinson, R.: RFC 2401 Security Architecture for IP. IETF (1998)
17. Liberatore, M., Levine, B.N.: Inferring the Source of Encrypted HTTP Connections. In: Proceedings of the 13th ACM Conference on Computer and Communications Security (CCS 2006), pp. 255–263 (October 2006)
18. McLachlan, J., Hopper, N.: On the risks of serving whenever you surf: Vulnerabilities in Tor's blocking resistance design. In: Proceedings of the Workshop on Privacy in the Electronic Society (WPES 2009). ACM (November 2009)
19. Murdoch, S.J.: Hot or not: Revealing hidden services by their clock skew. In: Proceedings of CCS 2006 (October 2006)
20. Murdoch, S.J., Danezis, G.: Low-cost traffic analysis of Tor. In: Proceedings of the 2005 IEEE Symposium on Security and Privacy. IEEE CS (May 2005)
21. Murdoch, S.J., Zieliński, P.: Sampled traffic analysis by internet-exchange-level adversaries. In: Borisov, N., Golle, P. (eds.) PET 2007. LNCS, vol. 4776, pp. 167–183. Springer, Heidelberg (2007)
22. O'Connor, L.: On blending attacks for mixes with memory. In: Barni, M., Herrera-Joancomartí, J., Katzenbeisser, S., Pérez-González, F. (eds.) IH 2005. LNCS, vol. 3727, pp. 39–52. Springer, Heidelberg (2005)
23. Øverlier, L., Syverson, P.: Locating hidden servers. In: Proceedings of the 2006 IEEE Symposium on Security and Privacy. IEEE CS (May 2006)
24. Reed, M.G., Syverson, P.F., Goldschlag, D.M.: Anonymous connections and onion routing. IEEE Journal on Selected Areas in Communications 16(4), 482–494 (1998)
25. Rescorla, E.: SSL and TLS – Designing and Building Secure Systems. Addison-Wesley (2001)
26. Rybczyńska, M.: Network-level properties of modern anonymity systems. In: Proceedings of the International Multiconference on Computer Science and Information Technology, pp. 837–843 (2008)
27. Rybczyńska, M.: A round-based cover traffic algorithm for anonymity systems. In: 2009 International Conference on Intelligent Networking and Collaborative Systems, pp. 93–99 (2009)
28. Serjantov, A., Sewell, P.: Passive attack analysis for connection-based anonymity systems. In: Snekkenes, E., Gollmann, D. (eds.) ESORICS 2003. LNCS, vol. 2808, pp. 116–131. Springer, Heidelberg (2003)
29. Shmatikov, V., Wang, M.H.: Measuring relationship anonymity in mix networks. In: Proceedings of the Workshop on Privacy in the Electronic Society (WPES 2006) (October 2006)
30. Wang, M.-H.: Timing analysis in low-latency mix networks: Attacks and defenses. In: Gollmann, D., Meier, J., Sabelfeld, A. (eds.) ESORICS 2006. LNCS, vol. 4189, pp. 18–33. Springer, Heidelberg (2006)

31. Sun, Q., Simon, D.R., Wang, Y.M., Russell, W., Padmanabhan, V.N., Qiu, L.: Statistical identification of encrypted web browsing traffic. In: Proceedings of the 2002 IEEE Symposium on Security and Privacy, Berkeley, California (May 2002)
32. Wright, C.V., Monrose, F., Masson, G.M.: On inferring application protocol behaviors in encrypted network traffic. Journal of Machine Learning Research 7, 2745–2769 (2006)
33. Zalewski, M.: Silence on the Wire: a Field Guide to Passive Reconnaissance and Indirect Attacks. No Starch Press (2005)
34. Zhu, Y., Fu, X., Graham, B., Bettati, R., Zhao, W.: On flow correlation attacks and countermeasures in mix networks. In: Martin, D., Serjantov, A. (eds.) PET 2004. LNCS, vol. 3424, pp. 207–225. Springer, Heidelberg (2005)

A Signature Scheme for Distributed Executions Based on Control Flow Analysis

Sébastien Varrette[1], Benoît Bertholon[2], and Pascal Bouvry[1]

[1] Computer Science and Communication (CSC) Research Unit
[2] Interdisciplinary Centre for Security Reliability and Trust,
University of Luxembourg
6, rue Richard Coudenhove-Kalergi
L-1359 Luxembourg, Luxembourg
Firstname.Name@uni.lu

Abstract. This article proposes a dynamic and flexible signature scheme to verify at runtime the execution of a distributed program. Extending [20], the approach relies on the analysis of a trace that represents such an execution using Control Flow Graph (CFG). This mechanism ensures the detection of flow faults that do not correspond to the CFG, *i.e.* that tamper the normal run of the application. Most effects of malicious code injection commonly met on distributed computing platforms such as grids are covered by this approach. The execution engine used in our signature scheme is certified with the TPM-based Certification of a Remote Resource (TCRR) protocol [5].

Our approach has been implemented in KAAPI, a C++ middleware library to execute and schedule fine or medium size grain programs on distributed platforms. The concrete validation on two parallel programs (Fibonacci and NQueens) reveals the scalability of the approach and its relatively low overhead.

Keywords: Distributed Executions, Cloud, Clusters, CFG, DFG, TPM.

1 Introduction

The research presented in this article holds in the context of distributed computing platforms *i.e* clusters, computing grids [7] or Clouds [28]. These infrastructures are subjected to various threats, such as [Distributed] Denial of Services ([D]DoS), malwares, trojan horses or vulnerabilities exploits. These attacks typically lead to crashes, buffer overflows or machine-code injection that, more generally, affect the integrity of the distributed executions carried out over the platform.

Our goal is then to tackle these issues using an abstract representation of a program called Control Flow Graph (CFG). This model is used, for a long time now, to analyze the source code of programs [3]. In complement to this approach, a Data-Flow Graph (DFG) can be used as part of the execution engine on a distributed platform to schedule and execute tasks. Moreover, DFG can be used in a variety of efficient fault-tolerance mechanisms where the objective is to

P. Bouvry et al. (Eds.): SIIS 2011, LNCS 7053, pp. 85–102, 2012.

detect and eventually correct corruptions in order to make the execution resilient against different classes of faults. Historically, the first class of faults addressed by DFG was *crash-faults* that model computing node volatility. Such errors are typically due to hardware or software failures together with nodes disconnections (as a result of a DoS attack for instance). At this level, a general idea relies on checkpoint/rollback mechanisms that store (either periodically or at specific events like communications or task theft) a view of the execution state. DFG precisely provides a consistent global state of the execution and is therefore used in this context to provide efficient checkpoint/rollback algorithms [13,12].

Later on, it was proposed to handle with DFG a more complex kind of faults referred to as *cheating faults*. Generally speaking, the computing resources of the execution platform cannot be fully trusted and such faults represent the consequences of cheaters that alter intermediate or final results of the computation. Whether this is the consequence of malicious code execution or an abnormal yet non-malicious behaviour, they still have been experimented in SETI@Home or BOINC [18], the famous projects that operate on a desktop grid topology. More generally, such a selfish behaviour should not be underestimated on grids, especially when the cloud computing paradigm and its money-oriented incentives raises so much euphoria. In all cases, the detection of cheating faults over a given execution is usually done via result checking techniques. At this level, the only generic approach relies on tasks duplication, either total or partial. By tracking the exact tasks dependencies, DFG analysis permitted to design generic verification algorithms by partial duplication that minimize the number of intermediate result checks *i.e.* the number of tasks duplicated on safe resources. This was proposed for instance in [26,21] with theoretical bounds that proved the efficiency of the approach on Fork-Join or recursive programs but unfortunately a huge overhead in the general case.

To reduce this overhead and noticing that cheating faults commonly lead to the modification of the normal flow of instructions being executed, the purpose of this article is to address *flow-faults* in the context of distributed executions. The motivation behind this work was to evaluate if a weaker model of faults can be handled efficiently over all kind of programs using Control Flow analysis. The answer is positive and this paper describes a concrete signature scheme that checks a distributed execution against flow faults in a distributed environment. As with classical signature schemes for numeric documents, the fingerprint is first elaborated offline by analysing the source code of the program to extract a skeleton that identify the structure of the program to be executed. In practice, we build an automaton derived from the CFG of each task that compose the program. At run-time, the execution of any sub-task of the program (in general on a remote computing node) is accompanied with the evaluation of a specific hash value deduced from the dynamic and distributed execution. This hash is used as a transition value to move between the states of the automaton such that any tampering on the normal flow would result in a move into an invalid state. It follows that abnormal behaviours can be reported in real-time which is of particular importance in a dynamic computing environment. Our signature scheme have been implemented in Kernel for Adaptative, Asynchronous Parallel and Interactive programming (KAAPI), a C++ middleware library that uses a dynamic DFG (unfold at run-time) to execute and schedule fine or medium size grain program on distributed platforms. Being integrated at the middleware level, it makes the approach fully transparent to the user.

This article is organized as follows: §2 recalls the related work. The main contribution of this article *i.e.* a signature scheme for distributed executions is detailed in §3. Implementation aspects in the KAAPI library are described in §4 while §5 expounds the experiments conducted to validate the approach. In particular, we analyse the overhead of the signature process on two parallel applications; firstly a naive Fibonacci to illustrate the impact on a large recursive program; secondly a NQueens solver to evaluate a more realistic application. §6 concludes this article and provides some perspectives.

2 Related Work

This section gives a brief overview of the existing literature in the domain of execution flow checking, more commonly referred as control flow checking. It is important to notice that all the approaches presented here operate on sequential program while the mechanism described in this article deals with parallel or distributed applications. In all cases, two complement approaches can be distinguished: one corresponds to *static* methods applied before or after the execution (see §2.1). The other way relies on *dynamic* techniques that will be detailed in §2.2.

2.1 Static Methods

This approach operates at two levels, firstly on the system reinforcement through various software techniques (sand-boxing, virtualization, quotas, activity scanners etc.) [27]. Secondly, on the detection of malicious codes. In this later context, one idea that dates back to the 90's is to determine a fingerprint that identifies a program or a specific piece of code to detect and/or prevent the execution of malicious code. This approach is typically applied nowadays for malware detections [6]. Signature checkers, for instance, scan the binary file before the run to recognize a known pattern supposed to identify the malware. Integrity checkers complete this process to verify the checksum of the file on pattern recognition to reduce the instances of false positives reported by the scanner.

Instead of detecting a local malware patterns, an alternative approach consists in the construction of a formal proof based on strong mathematical properties able to ensure the integrity of a program prior to its remote execution. In this context, Proof Carrying Code (PCC) [19] is a technique that can be used for safe execution of untrusted code. In a typical instance of PCC, a code receiver establishes a set of safety rules that guarantee safe behavior of programs, and the code producer creates a formal safety proof that proves, for the untrusted code, adherence to the safety rules. Then, the receiver is able to use a simple and fast proof validator to check, with certainty, that the proof is valid and hence the untrusted code is safe to execute.

2.2 Dynamic Methods

Whereas all the previous techniques certify the integrity of the code against flow faults before the run, they do not cover dynamic attacks altering the execution in the run-time. Indeed, the key problem is that although a program at the beginning of its execution can be verified as authentic, while running, its execution flow can be redirected to externally injected malicious code using, for example, a buffer overflow exploit [2]. At this level, one approach consists in modeling the program behavior in order to prevent further malicious computation. For instance, Wagner and Dean [29] provide the first use of statically extracted model of the program behavior (which is control-flow based) to verify security properties at run-time. Yet the generation of the model requires multiple runs of the complete application which is not realistic for distributed executions over large-scale computing platforms. Haldar & al. [10] proposed the remote verification of program behavior using a trusted Virtual Machine (VM). In this sense, the approach is close to oracle-based techniques proposed in the field of result-checking algorithms. It follows that the verification of the full program would require a complete re-execution on the trusted VM such that the computing platform would not be exploited correctly.

In a rather different approach, Kirovski & al. [14] describes a Secure Program Execution Framework that combines architectural and compilation techniques to ensure software integrity at run-time. More precisely, encrypted, processor-specific signatures are embedded into each block of instructions during software installation and then checked at run-time to guarantee the execution of unmodified programs. Yet the validation of this technique demonstrates that the verification of the instructions introduces a very huge overhead. One way to cope with this issue was proposed in [16] by checking only the last signature block. This assumes unfortunately that the memory containing the program instructions is write-protected and that the processor organization is modified to include two hardware resources (a Basic Block Signature Table and a Basic Block Signature Verification Unit). This is currently not realistic for distributed computing environments based on off-the-shelf computers.

In a related perspective, Oh&al. in [20] proposed a scheme to check dynamically that a program is in a valid state. This is done in two steps, firstly by generating the CFG to determine the flow of execution such that in a second phase, a daemon can verify at runtime that each state of the program correspond is valid. Each state is associated with a unique id value and a global register keep track of the current state the program. This verification is done just before or at the same time as the execution of the code. A derived approach (without daemon nor global register) has been used later by Abadi&al [1], this time focusing on context switching via the `jump` commands.

The core of the work presented in this article is to extend the work of Oh&al in [20] in two directions, firstly to operate at the middleware level and secondly over distributed executions (instead of a sequential one) which implies a post-verification instead of a pre-verification as done in [20]. In this context, we present in the next section a flow fault detection mechanism that relies on a signature scheme elaborated though Control Flow analysis.

3 Proposed Framework for a Checkable Signature of Execution Flow

In the sequel, we consider a (parallel) program **P** executed on a computing platform M. Note that M can be a single machine, a cluster or a computing grid.

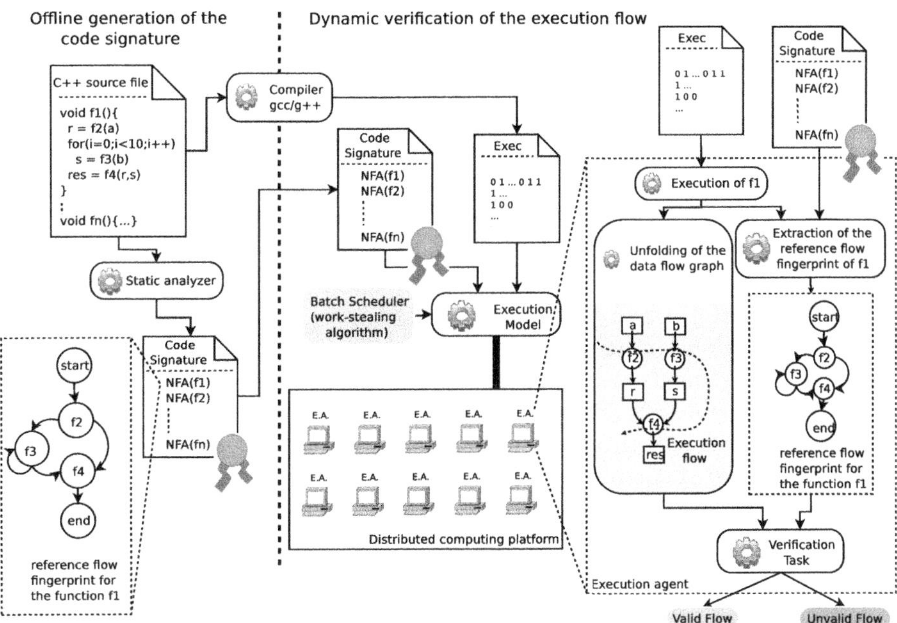

Fig. 1. Overview of the proposed technique for flow-fault detection in distributed executions

3.1 Control Flow Analysis and Fault Model

Our proposal is based on an abstract and portable representation for the distributed execution of **P** for a given granularity which is the trace of the execution.

Definition 1 (Control Flow Graph [3]). *A control flow graph is a directed graph in which the nodes represent basic blocks* i.e. *linear sequence of program instructions and the edges represent control flow paths. The entry point of a given function is associated to the "Start" state in its CFG. The "End" state is further assigned to any legitimate* `return` *step in the function.*

Definition 2 (Flow fault). *Let G denotes the Control Flow Graph of* $\mathbf{P}$ *over* M*. Let T be the trace of an execution of* $\mathbf{P}$ *over* M*. Then T is said faulty or victim of a* flow fault *if T does not end in an end state of the graph G.*

Whereas this definition (and furthermore the signature scheme proposed in this paper) can be applied for any granularity of the graph, we will consider here the smallest program unit of execution *i.e.* a task in G as a middleware function of the source code.

3.2 General Overview

The figure 1 represents an overview of the signature scheme for flow faults detection proposed in this article. As in classical signature schemes, our approach involves two different phases: (1) A static (offline) generation of the reference flow fingerprint for each task that compose the program to be executed (see §3.3 – the set of all fingerprints is referred as the code signature) and (2) a dynamic (online) execution flow verification based on the code signature (see §3.4). This last process is recursive, distributed and handled by execution agents spread on every computing nodes that belongs to the computing platform. The general idea is that when an execution agent is in charge of executing a task t, it will load the control flow graph of each sub-tasks t_i, receive from each t_i a fingerprint and finally use both elements to detect the occurrence of flow faults.

Note that in this signature scheme part, the terms fingerprint and signature **do not** induce classical cryptographic properties. it was decided to use this terminology with regards of their initial meaning (respectively an identifier and a checkable mechanism of validity). Furthermore, this scheme **is not** a result-checking technique. As mentioned in the introduction, we focus here on a weaker model of faults. In particular, an execution with a validated flow could still integrate a data value modification (compared to the execution in a fault-free environment).

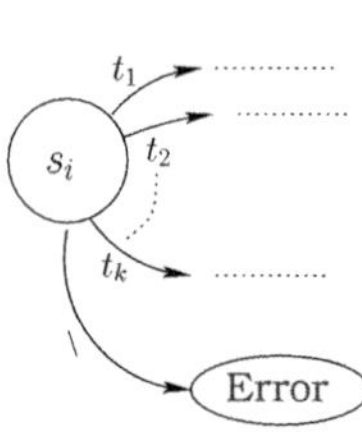

Fig. 2. A state in the automaton signature

Finally, one can immediately argue that this scheme is still vulnerable to mimicry attacks [30] where the attacker compute and return the expected signature to the verification process while executing a completely different task as part of the global program run. But in order to assert the integrity of the Execution Agent we remotely verify the integrity of the node using the TPM-based Certification of a Remote Resource (TCRR) protocol described in [5]. Relying on the Trusted Computing concepts and the Trusted Platform Module (TPM) [25], the TCRR protocol permits to prove that the execution engine running on top of the Operating system (OS) of the remote computing node is reliable *i.e.* that it has not been tampered with. The figure 3 shows how the TCRR protocol's communications ensures that the EA is reliable. This protocol has been verified using two of the reference tools in automatic verifications which are AVISPA and Scyther. Detailing this protocol is clearly outside the scope of this paper. The interested reader can refer to [4] or [5] for its complete analysis.

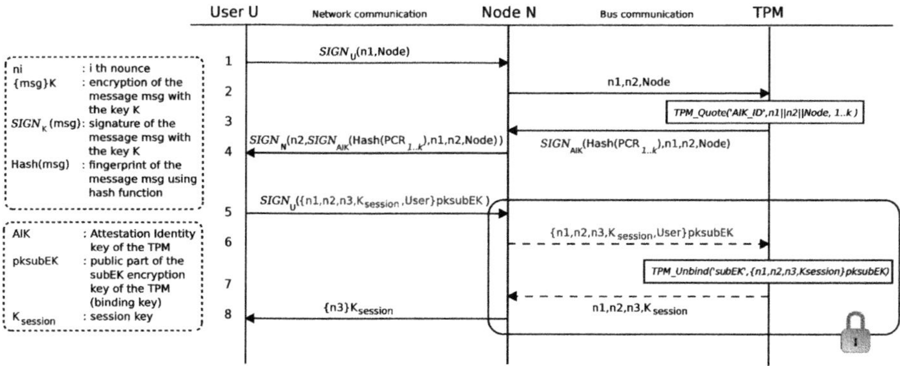

Fig. 3. TPM-based Certification of a Remote Resource (TCRR)

3.3 Offline Execution Fingerprint by Source Code Analysis

In our proposal, the reference fingerprint of **P** also known as its signature, is computed offline by analysing the source code of the program (typically in C or C++ yet with no support for exceptions *i.e.* `throw` clauses and `catch` blocks). More precisely, it consists in a set of non deterministic finite automata (NFA) $\mathcal{A}(t)$ constructed for each task t that compose the program **P**. A path from the initial state `Begin` to the final one `End` corresponds to a path in the execution flow of t to reach a `return` instruction. The states of the automaton are associated to the sub-tasks met in all possible correct execution of t.

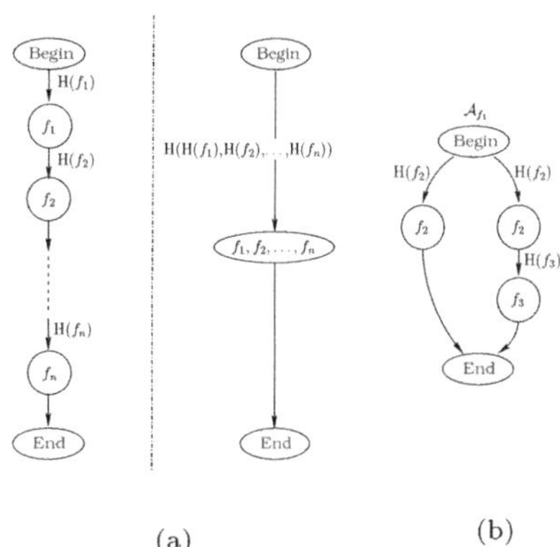

Fig. 4. (a) Optimization phase applied for paths composed by two or more states. (b) Illustration of the non-deterministic aspect of automaton signatures.

Transitions between a state s_i and s_j is authorized for a specific hash values $H(s_j)$ that will be detailed in §3.4. We use a special transition value $H(nil)$ to refer to the `return` instruction. Furthermore, once every legitimate transition from a state s_i are evaluated, an implicit transition to the special state `Error` is added. The special transition value "\" is used for this movement or, more simply, this transition is represented without value but as a dot line.

All those elements are illustrated in figure 2. In particular, in the context of the example given in this figure, the "\" transition value should be understood as "*everything except the values of the set* $\{t_1, \ldots, t_k\}$". Note that in the sequel and unless otherwise specified, the implicit transition to the `Error` state is not represented to improve the readability of the signature automaton.

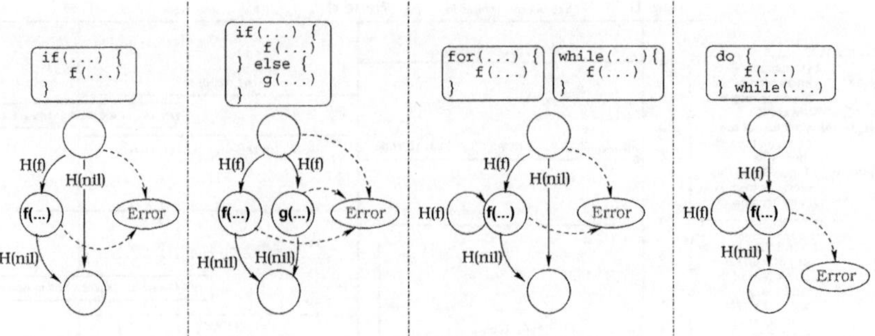

Fig. 5. Structure of control handling for the signature generation

The signature automaton take also into account the control structures and the loops (*i.e.* the sequences `if...else`, `for`, `while` etc.). Those elements affect the construction of the signature as illustrated in figure 5. Once a signature $\mathcal{A}_t$ is built for each task t, we apply an optimization phase for each of them to accelerate the future online verification of paths having more than one state (besides `Begin` and `End`). More precisely, a new branch is added in this case with a single agglomerated state. The transition value to this state derives from those met on the path to synthesize – this process will be detailed in §3.4. In all cases, this optimization phase is shown in the figure 4. Finally, we mentioned that the automaton is non deterministic. This is due to the fact that for some states, a valid transition to distinct states is done with the same hash value as illustrated in the figure 4. Such "conflicts" are solved in the same way Generalized LR parsers handle this kind of issues: at parsing time, we keep in memory all possible paths to drop afterwards those leading to impossible cases [15].

3.4 Online Signature Verification

Hash value construction. The execution of a task t is accompanied with the computation of its hash value defined as follows.

Definition 3 (Flow hash). *Let t represents a task of* $\boldsymbol{P}$ *over* M.
The flow hash *associated to the execution of t is defined by:*

$$H(t) = (\textit{prototype}, \textit{flow\_detail})$$

In this definition, *prototype* details the function prototype *i.e.* the function name together with the typed arguments associated to the function (input, output and return type). At execution time, this information is given by the string `__PRETTY_FUNCTION__` (set at compilation time). *flow_detail* corresponds to information about the executed flow for the task t considered *i.e.* the trace of the execution. In the context of this paper, it consists in the information gathered during the full graph traversal (in the sequential order): the prototype of the sub-tasks executed over this path are collected to form what will be the *flow_detail* part of the hash value. This is illustrated in figure 6.

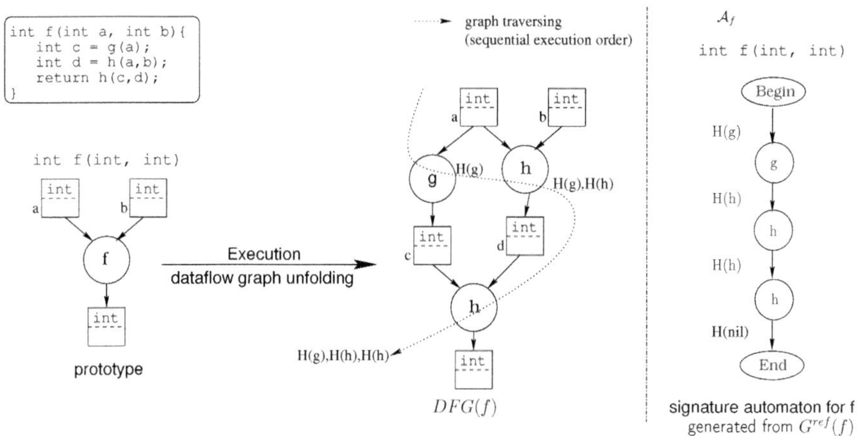

Fig. 6. Elements of the hash value relative to the execution of a task f. For reference, the signature automaton of f is given.

The DFG is used to schedule the tasks to be executed, typically with an online work-stealing algorithm as in KAAPI– see §4. This engine uses agents spread on each computing node. The signature verification is a fully distributed process. Let's suppose the processor p is responsible for running a function f called during the execution of a function F. We describe here the dynamic recursive process that checks the flow of f and returns the hash value $H(f)$ to the agent linked to the execution of F. The execution engine unfolds the graph $DFG(f)$ associated to the execution of f. Let's assume that this graph is composed by the sub-tasks $f_1, \ldots, f_n$ (in the example proposed in figure 6, $n = 3$, $f_1 = g$ and $f_2 = f_3 = h$). Each of them have to be executed, either on p or on another processor. Even if the task may not be executed in the sequential order, as the execution engine uses the DFG to execute tasks, they are called and add in the list of functions to be executed in the sequential order. At the end of the execution of the sub-task f_i on a processor p_i, the hash value $H(f_i)$ is returned from p_i to p, the later being responsible for checking it. This verification is based on f_i's automaton $\mathcal{A}_{f_i}$ and involves two phases: (1) checking that $H(f_i).prototype$ matches the prototype signature of f_i (2) ensuring that the path $H(f_i).flow\_detail$ permits to reach the End state of $\mathcal{A}_{f_i}$.

Whenever one of those conditions does not hold, a flow fault is detected as demonstrated in proposition 2. Otherwise, no flow fault intervened in any of f_i's executions so the hash value $H(f)$ can be computed with the two elements mentioned in the definition 3: (1) the effective prototype of f (for instance using the `__PRETTY_FUNCTION__` string) and (2) the flow summary of f's execution which has been filled during the successive verifications of the sub-tasks $\{f_1, \ldots, f_n\}$ as the sequence: $H(f).flow\_detail = H(f_1).prototype, \ldots, H(f_n).prototype$. Eventually, $H(f).flow\_detail$ does not correspond to this potentially long sequence but to a compressed version.

In all cases, the hash value $H(f)$ is returned to the agent P responsible for the execution of the function F (which again can detect flow faults that may have happened during the execution of f). As it can be seen, the full verification process is fully distributed and permits to reach "leaf" functions for which the hash value is limited to the only prototype. Furthermore, the verification process ends in a finite time as stated in the proposition 1.

Proposition 1. *As soon as the execution of the program **P** ends, the verification process ends in a finite time.*

Proof. If the program **P** ends, then the macro dataflow G representing the execution of **P** is composed by a finite number of tasks. Consequently, a finite number of dataflow graphs have be unfolded and each of them is associated with the verification of a single signature automaton. Furthermore, each automaton owns a finite number of states and checking a signature is linear in the number of states on a critical path. it follows that the verification process of **P** ends in a finite time. The detection of flow faults results from the proposition 2.

Proposition 2. *Let $\{\mathcal{A}_{t_1}, \ldots, \mathcal{A}_{t_n}\}$ denotes the set of automaton signatures elaborated from the analysis of **P**'s source code. Let T be the trace representng of an execution of **P** over M, composed by $t_1, \ldots, t_n$ tasks. $\exists i \in [1, n]$ such that the verification process of T_{t_i} the automaton signature $\mathcal{A}_{t_i}$ ends in the* `Error` *state $\Longrightarrow T$ is faulty.*

Proof. $\Rightarrow \mathcal{A}_{t_i}$ has been constructed to reflect all possible flows in the execution of t_i as a path from `Begin` to `End`. Reaching the `Error` state indicates a abnormal transition value Consequently, $T_{t_i} \notin \mathcal{A}_{t_i}$ and T is faulty. It follows that if any flow fault, which does not correspond to the CFG, that intervenes during the execution of the program **P** is detected by our verification process.

Execution Engine and Signature Verification. In order for this signature scheme to work, the execution agents as to certified, this can be done using the TCRR protocol [4] which verifies that all the code running on the machine correspond to an unmodified code, specially the boot loader, the Operating System and the KAAPI execution engine. We have then a **trustable** execution engine based on dynamic macro dataflow graph construction. In order to gain this property, the machine has to fulfill the hypothesis defined in [4] which is no physical intrusion in the running machine and the correct setup of the machine.

4 Implementation

Our signature scheme have been implemented in KAAPI, a C++ middleware library that uses a dynamic data flow graph (unfold at runtime) to execute and schedule fine or medium size grain program on distributed platforms. We now present the internals of this library relevant for this work, together with the associated programming interface. The elements of the signature scheme implementation are then detailed in §4.

KAAPI stands for Kernel for Adaptive, Asynchronous Parallel and Interactive programming [17]. It is a C++ library for distributed computing that allows to execute multithreaded computation with data flow synchronization between threads. The library is able to schedule fine/medium size grain program on distributed machine. In particular, KAAPI construct dynamically at runtime and with a low overhead the dataflow graph of the tasks to be executed; this description is used to schedule the tasks using a work-stealing algorithm [9]. The KAAPI programming level relies on the Athapascan interface and is based on a global address space called global memory and allows to describe data dependencies between tasks that access objects in the global memory. The language extends C++ with two keywords: the `Shared` keyword which is a type qualifier to declare objects in the global memory and the `Fork` keyword which creates a new task that may be executed in concurrence with other tasks. An example of the use of this programming interface is proposed in the listing 1.1. We will use this program to illustrate the implementation of the signature scheme. The KAAPI low level interface allows to build the macro dataflow graph between tasks during the execution of Athapascan program. This interface defines several objects. A `Closure` object represents a function call (*i.e.* a task t) with a state. An `Access` object represents the binding of an formal parameter in the global memory. All objects are pushed in a stack, called `Frame`, which is associated to each control flow. Finally, `Closure`, `Access` and `Frame` objects are uniquely identified over the network. This will help us to determine the process responsible for the verification of a given task. The execution of a KAAPI program on a distributed platform is done by a dynamic set of processes, one per multi-processor, communicating through a network. These are the execution agents mentioned in §3.4 who will be also responsible for signature checking tasks. Each agent has several threads of control to execute tasks. At deployment step, one of the agent is designed to be the leader which starts the thread that executes the main task. It is therefore the leader that will deliver a potential certification of the correct execution. As precised in the section 3, our approach involves two different phases, one off-line to generate the code fingerprint, the other on-line to check the signature in a fully distributed process.

Listing 1.1. Programming a naive Fibonacci algorithm with the Athapascan interface of KAAPI (simplified view)

```
#include <athapascan-1>
int Fiboseq(int n); // Sequential version
void Sum(Shared_w<int> res,
Shared_r<int> res1, Shared_r<int> res2){
  res = res1+res2;}
void Fibo( Shared_w<int> res, int n,
int threshold int n) {
    if (n < threshold)
        res = Fiboseq(n);
    else {
        Shared<int> res1;
        Shared<int> res2;
/*the Fork keyword => spawn new task */
        Fork<Fibo>(res1, n-1, threshold);
        Fork<Fibo>(res2, n-2, threshold );
        Fork<Sum>(res, res1, res2);
    }
}
```

Off-line fingerprint generation. As mentioned in §3.3, a set of Non-deterministic Finite Automata (NFA) $\mathcal{A}(t)$ are generated off-line for each task t that compose the source code of the KAAPI program. In this context, we developed a dedicated software that parse the preprocessed code of the program (obtained via the GNU Compiler Collection [23] and the command `g++ -E`) with the C++ parser Elsa [22] and the Generalized LR parser Elkhound [15]. From the parse tree it creates the signature automaton for each function (as describe in §3.3). NFAs are stored in encrypted files under the `dot` format [8]. They are read at run time by the KAAPI agents (who hold the key to decrypt them) to operate the signature verification process. The `dot` format The `dot` format simplified the automatic generation of a human-readable view of the signatures. An example of such an output is proposed in Figure 7 by applying this process to the Fibonacci program with the `main` function defined with a for loop calling `Fork<Fibo>(res, n, threshold);`

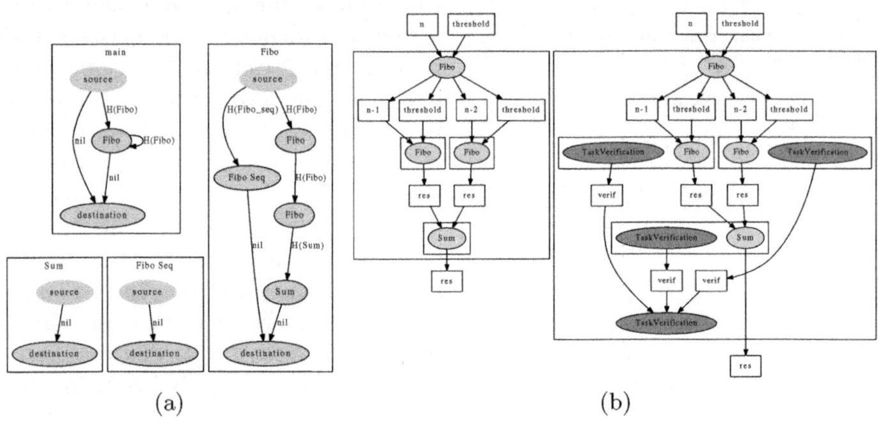

Fig. 7. (a) small Signature automata generated for the Fibonacci program. (b) Dataflow graph without (left) and with (right) the `Taskverification` function responsible for checking the execution flow against the appropriate signature automaton.

On-line signature verification. The flow integrity control is implemented using a dedicated KAAPI `Closure` object called `TaskVerification`. This checking task is added at the end of each frame and is responsible for operating the signature verification of the associated task. Following the mechanism described in §3.4, this task communicates with the `TaskVerification` closures beneath and above it using a KAAPI `Shared` variable `verif` to (1) collect hash values from the agent that executed the sub-tasks *i.e.* the `Closure` objects present in the frame and (2) return the hash value to the frame at the upper level. The effect on the macro dataflow of the program is highlighted in Figure 7. Furthermore, the `Taskverification` closure check the returned hash value of each Closure objects in his frame. As stated in §3.4, this has to be done in the sequential order. This is very simple to operate as KAAPI chains the `Closure` objects in a frame in this precise order. Moreover, and contrary to normal `Closure` in KAAPI, the `TaskVerification` task cannot be stolen by other agents, so as to keep the signature process local to the agent responsible for the execution of the frame checked. Finally, it is important to notice that the approach is fully transparent to the user as the implementation details provided in this paragraph have been applied at the middleware level.

5 Experimental Validation

The proposed signature scheme has been validated on two typical applications (Fibonacci and N-Queens). Version 2.4 of the KAAPI library have been used for those experiments which have been conducted on the clusters of the University of Luxembourg. Each computing node can have one of the following configurations:
C1 Intel Dual Core Pentium D, 3.2 GHz and 4 GBytes of main memory (2 cores)
C2 Two Intel Xeon Quad-Core, 2.0 GHz and 32 GBytes of main memory (8 cores)

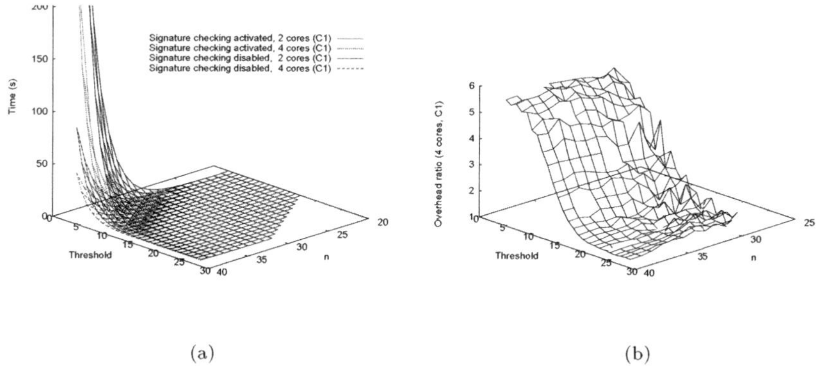

Fig. 8. Overhead of the embedded signature checking process when executing the Fibonacci program (a) absolute (b) relative (for configuration C1 and 4 cores)

Fibonacci computation. A first set of experiments of the folk recursive Fibonacci number computation has been executed based on the code provided in the listing 1.1. This benchmark program demonstrates a configuration with massive task creation, which is the worst configuration for our signature scheme as every new task created is associated with a verification procedure. The granularity of the program is fully controlled by the `threshold` parameter: a small value increases drastically the number of forked tasks, letting the sequential "leaf" functions of the data-flow graph (*i.e.* `Fibosec` tasks) with little work to operate. On the contrary, bigger values for the threshold limits the number of spawned tasks and makes the sequential functions longer, *i.e.* able to cover the task creation process or, in our case, the signature checking operation. This aspect is illustrated in Figure 8 where the Fibonacci program is evaluated for different values of the parameters n and threshold on 1 or 2 computing nodes (each in configuration C1). Figure 8(a) displays the execution time and shows the overhead of activating the signature verification, compared to classical executions where the verification mechanism is also embedded yet disabled. Figure 8(b) derives directly from the previous evaluation and proposes an overview of the relative overhead computed by the formula: $R_{\text{overhead}} = \frac{\texttt{Exec time with sig. checking}}{\texttt{Exec time without sig. checking}}$.

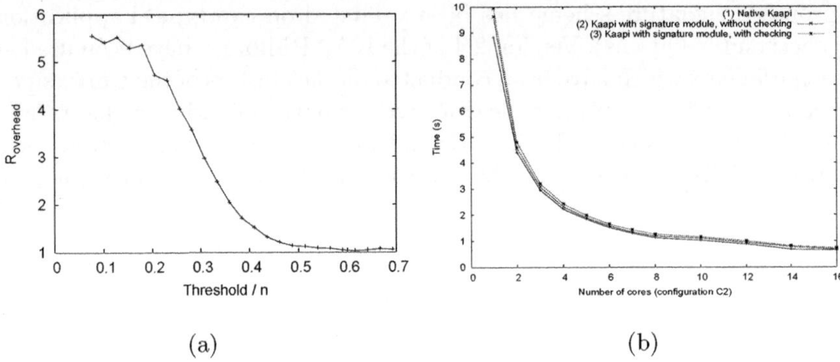

(a) (b)

Fig. 9. (a) Relative overhead vs. relative threshold for a Fibo(39) computation over 2 nodes in configuration C1 with n = 39. (b) Speedup on the computation of Fibo(42) (with threshold=20) in the following configurations: (1) native KAAPI middleware (2) KAAPI middleware with embedded signature module without checking and (3), as (2), but with signature checking.

In particular, we can see that R_{overhead} can go up to a value of 6 which makes the execution accompanied with signature checking 6 times longer than a normal execution. This represents of course a high overhead. Luckily, it is limited to parameters areas unrealistic for an efficient distributed execution, in particular the threshold is very low, leading to a massive task creation where the signature verification applied for each of them is hardly covered by the runtime of the sequential part of the program. This is probably clearer on Figure 9. Anyway, it can be seen that for a relative threshold $r = \frac{\texttt{threshold}}{\texttt{n}}$ greater than 0.5, the overhead of the signature checking is relatively low. Another important aspect illustrated in this experiment is the scalability of the approach in terms of number of tasks handled. Remember that every forked task is associated to a TaskVerification procedure. With a threshold of 1 for the computation of Fibo(39), more than 10^8 tasks have been checked transparently by the system. The speedup of the computation is presented in Figure 9 where we compare the overhead of the signature scheme implementation (with or without checking) against the native KAAPI library. Even if this evaluation was done in a context where we saw a very low overhead for the signature checking (as $r = 0.41$), this experiment still reveals the negligible overhead induced by the signature module implementation inside KAAPI.

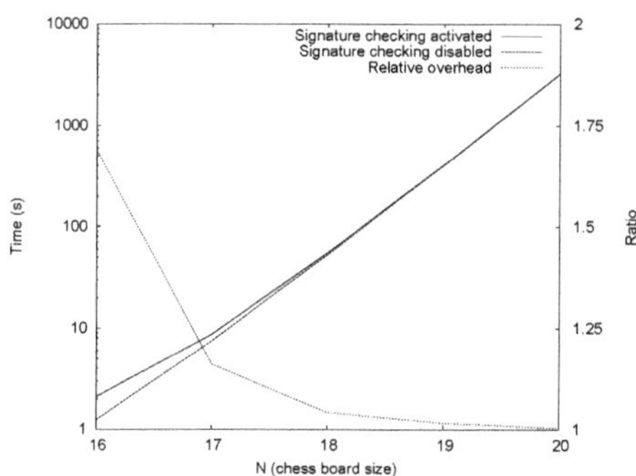

Fig. 10. Overhead of the embedded signature checking process when executing an NQueen parallel solver over 16 cores (configuration C1)

NQueens computation

To illustrate our approach on a more realistic program, we evaluate the signature mechanism on a NQueen solver. The standard NQueen's problem is about how to place N queens on an chess board of N rows and N columns in order to avoid that any of them can hit any other in one move. Note that this is an NP-Complete problem [11]. The parallel NQueens implementation used for this experiment is based on the NQueens sequential code developed by Takaken [24]. This program helped the KAAPI team to be awarded a special prize for the best performances achieved during the Plugtest contest held in 2006 [9].

The results of our experiments are presented in Figure 10. In this problem, the threshold is fixed. We can notice that the relative overhead induced by the signature checking process decrease from a factor 1.68 to 1.004 times. For large instances (*i.e.* for $N > 8$ common in distributed computations), the overhead is negligible. The result for small instances has the same explanation than those corresponding to Fibonacci executions: *i.e.* the computing part is not sufficient to cover the work operated by the signature checking tasks as well as the setting up of the signature scheme which needs to read the NFAs of the different tasks.

```
#include <athapascan-1>
void Fibo( Shared w<int> res,
  int n, int threshold int n);
void main(){
  int n, threshold ;
  Shared<int> res;
  ...
  for(int i = 0 ; i < 10 : i ++)
    Fork<Fibo>(res, n, threshold );
  ...
```

(a)

```
#include <athapascan-1>
void Fibo( Shared w<int> res,
  int n, int threshold int n);
void main(){
  int n, threshold ;
  Shared<int> res;
  ...
  for(int i = 0 ; i < 10 : i ++)
    Fork<Fibo>(res, n, threshold );
  Fork<Fibo>(res, n, threshold );
  ...
```

(b)

Fig. 11. 2 almost similar versions of the main function of the Fibo program

Flow Fault detection

It is hard to get a metric for the detection of fault, without confronting the scheme with the real world. Nonetheless, some Experimentation has been done to verify that a flow fault is detected with this approach. The previous KAAPI version of the naive Fibonacci computation (cf lst. 1.1) has been modified on one of the nodes by add one more "Sum" function in the Fibo function. As expected

This always result in the detection of a flow fault (when this node was used to compute the Fibo function). It also appears to us that all flow fault can't be detected using this scheme because the verification use NFA to check the validity of the signature. For example the two program in listing 11 would result into two different NFA but if we want to execute (a) on a distributed platform and one of the node M execute (b), the scheme won't detect it. Indeed if M execute the main function, the resulted signature $H(f)$ will be valid. This is due to the fact that a `for` statement is represented in an NFA as a loop, it is then impossible to determine that the extra Fibo in (b) is not part of the loop by analyzing flow detail. In all case this last problem, won't trigger any false positive alarm. This scheme is then able to detect most of the flow fault that we can encounter but won't reveal the presence of some of them.

6 Conclusions and Future Work

In this article, a dynamic and flexible signature scheme has been proposed to certify at runtime a distributed execution against flow faults that alter the structure of the graph *i.e.* tamper the normal run of the application. This solution encompasses most of the effects of malicious code execution. Our approach is based on the analysis of the trace that represents the program execution. It involves two phases. The first one is operated offline to generate the fingerprint of the program code. The second phase is operated online in a fully distributed way to assert the execution flow using the program fingerprint. We implement our approach in KAAPI, a C++ middleware library that uses a dynamic data flow graph (unfold at runtime) to execute and schedule a distributed program. The whole scheme is therefore fully transparent to the user. In particular, the source code does not require any modification. The proposed approach has been validated over a Fibonacci computation and a NQueen solver. The experiments confirm the low overhead induced by the signature checking mechanism. In addition, the scalability of the approach has been highlighted for the speedup capabilities on a distributed platform as well as in terms of checked tasks. Our mechanism assumes a trusted execution engine. To ensure this strong property we use the TPM-based Certification of a Remote Resource (TCRR) protocol that rely on the Trusted Computing concepts and TPMs to ensure, using this last tamper-proof cryptographic co-processor, that the execution engine running on top of the system of the remote computing node has not been tampered. As future work, we plan to benchmark the developed signature scheme using other applications, and optimize it to reduce the overhead induced.

Acknowledgments. The authors gratefully acknowledge the KAAPI team and more precisely Thierry Gautier, Xavier Besseron, Serge Guelton and Jean-Noël Quintin for useful discussions and help when implementing the proposed scheme. The present project is supported by the National Research Fund of Luxembourg.

References

1. Abadi, M., Budiu, M., Erlingsson, Ú., Ligatti, J.: Control-flow integrity. In: CCS 2005: Proceedings of the 12th ACM Conference on Computer and Communications Security, pp. 340–353. ACM, New York (2005)
2. Aleph1. Smashing the stack for fun and profit. Phrack (49) (1996), `http://www.phrack.org/phrack/49/P49-14`
3. Allen, F.E.: Control flow analysis, 1–19 (July 1970)
4. Bertholon, B., Varrette, S., Bouvry, P.: The tcrr protocol to certify a remote machine. Technical report, `http://certicloud.gforge.uni.lu/`
5. Bertholon, B., Varrette, S., Bouvry, P.: Certicloud: a novel tpm-based approach to ensure cloud iaas security. In: Proc. of the 4th IEEE Intl. Conf. on Cloud Computing (CLOUD 2011), July 4–9, IEEE Computer Society, Washington DC (2011)
6. Christodorescu, M., Jha, S., Seshia, S.A., Song, D., Bryant, R.E.: Semantics-aware malware detection. In: Proceedings of the 2005 IEEE Symposium on Security and Privacy (Oakland 2005), Oakland, CA, USA, pp. 32–46 (May 2005)
7. Foster, I., Kesselman, C.: The Grid: Blueprint for a new Computing Infrastructure. Morgan Kaufman Publishers (1998)
8. Gansner, E.R., Koutsofios, E., North, S.C., Vo, K.-P.: A technique for drawing directed graphs. IEEE Trans. Software Eng. 19(3), 214–230 (1993)
9. Gautier, T., Besseron, X., Pigeon, L.: KAAPI: a Thread Scheduling Runtime System for Data Flow Computations on Cluster of Multi-Processors.. In: Workshop on Parallel Symbolic Computation 2007 (PASCO 2007). ACM, London (2007)
10. Haldar, V., Chandra, D., Franz, M.: Semantic remote attestation - virtual machine directed approach to trusted computing. In: Virtual Machine Research and Technology Symposium, pp. 29–41. USENIX (2004)
11. Hoos, H.H., Stützle, T.: Stochastic Local Seacrh Funcdations and Applications. Morgan Kaufmann (2005)
12. Jafar, S., Krings, A., Gautier, T.: Flexible rollback recovery in dynamic heterogeneous grid computing. IEEE TDSC 6(1) (January 2009)
13. Jafar, S., Varrette, S., Roch, J.-L.: Using Data-Flow Analysis for Resilence and Result Checking in Peer to Peer Computations. In: Proc. of the 1st Int. Workshop on Grid and Peer-to-Peer Computing Impacts on Large Scale Heterogeneous Distributed Database Systems (GLOBE 2004). IEEE Computer Society (September 2004)
14. Kirovski, D., Drinić, M., Potkonjak, M.: Enabling trusted software integrity. In: ASPLOS-X: Proc. of the 10th Intl. Conf. on Architectural Support for Programming Languages and Operating Systems, pp. 108–120. ACM, New York (2002)
15. McPeak, S., Necula, G.C.: Elkhound: A fast, practical GLR parser generator. In: Duesterwald, E. (ed.) CC 2004. LNCS, vol. 2985, pp. 73–88. Springer, Heidelberg (2004)
16. Milenković, M., Milenković, A., Jovanov, E.: A framework for trusted instruction execution via basic block signature verification. In: ACM-SE 42: Proceedings of the 42nd Annual Southeast Regional Conference. ACM (2004)
17. MOAIS Team. KAAPI (2005), `http://kaapi.gforge.inria.fr/`
18. Molnar, D.: The SETI@Home Problem (November 2000), `http://www.acm.org/crossroads/columns/onpatrol/september2000.html`
19. Necula, G.C., Lee, P.: Proof-Carrying Code. In: Proceedings of the ACM Symposium on Principles of Programming Languages, Paris, France (January 1997)

20. Oh, N., Shirvani, P.P., Mccluskey, E.J.: Control-flow checking by software signatures. IEEE Transactions on Reliability 51, 111–122 (2002)
21. Roch, J.-L., Varrette, S.: Probabilistic Certification of Divide & Conquer Algorithms on Global Computing Platforms. Application to Fault-Tolerant Exact Matrix-Vector Product. In: PPASCO 2007 (2007)
22. Weimer, W., Liblit, B., Foster, J., McPeak, S., Wilkerson, D., Nichols, J.: Elsa: The Elkhound-based C/C++ Parser
23. Stallman, R.M., et al.: Using GCC: The GNU Compiler Collection Ref Man. FSF (2005)
24. Takaken. The NQueens Problem, `http://www.ic-net.or.jp/home/takaken/e/queen/`
25. TCG. TCG Specification Architecture Overview – Rev 1.4. Technical report
26. Varrette, S.: Sécurité des Architectures de Calcul Distribué: Authentification et Certification de Résultats. PhD thesis, INP Grenoble and Universitédu Luxembourg (September 2007) (in French)
27. Varrette, S., Roch, J.-L., Duc, G., Keryell, R.: Building Secure Resources to Ensure Safe Computations in Distributed and Potentially Corrupted Environments. In: César, E., et al. (eds.) Euro-Par 2008. LNCS, vol. 5415, pp. 211–222. Springer, Heidelberg (2008)
28. Viega, J.: Cloud computing and the common man (2009)
29. Wagner, D., Dean, D.: Intrusion detection via static analysis. In: IEEE Symposium on Security and Privacy, pp. 156–168 (2001)
30. Wagner, D., Soto, P.: Mimicry attacks on host-based intrusion detection systems. In: CCS 2002: Proceedings of the 9th ACM Conference on Computer and Communications Security, pp. 255–264. ACM, New York (2002)

Computational Aspects of Attack–Defense Trees

Barbara Kordy*, Marc Pouly, and Patrick Schweitzer**

CSC and SnT, University of Luxembourg,
6, rue Coudenhove–Kalergi, L–1359 Luxembourg
{barbara.kordy,marc.pouly,patrick.schweitzer}@uni.lu

Abstract. Attack–defense trees extend attack trees with defense nodes. This richer formalism allows for a more precise modeling of a system's vulnerabilities, by representing interactions between possible attacks and corresponding defensive measures. In this paper we compare the computational complexity of both formalisms. We identify semantics for which extending attack trees with defense nodes does not increase the computational complexity. This implies that, for these semantics, every query that can be solved efficiently on attack trees can also be solved efficiently on attack–defense trees. Furthermore, every algorithm for attack trees can directly be used to process attack–defense trees.

1 Introduction

Systems become more and more complex as technology is advancing faster and faster. This technological development goes along with more sophisticated attacks on systems. In 1999, Schneier [1] suggested attack trees as a visual method to evaluate the security of complex systems. An attack tree is an AND-OR structure detailing an attack scenario. Schneier advocated attack trees, but he was not the first to suggest such an approach. Weiss [2] and Amoroso [3] were two pioneers in the usage of trees in security analysis. But even as early as the 1960s, tree-like structures were used in risk analysis, see Vesely et al. [4]. In 2005, Mauw and Oostdijk [5] augmented attack trees with semantics, providing a solid, formal and methodological framework for security assessment. Since then, the attack tree methodology has been taken up by numerous researchers, see [6–11].

Attack trees are widely used to evaluate vulnerabilities of systems. However, there are several important aspects of security that they cannot model. Besides the fact that the attack tree formalism only considers an attacker's point of view, it can neither capture the interaction between an attacker and a defender, nor is it well-suited to depict the evolution of attacks and subsequent defenses.

To overcome these limitations, Kordy et al. recently extended the attack tree formalism with defensive measures, by introducing attack–defense trees, see [12]. A main difference between attack trees and attack–defense trees is that the latter allow for a more precise analysis of scenarios by repeatedly changing between

* Supported by grant No. C08/IS/26 from the National Research Fund, Luxembourg.
** Supported by grant No. PHD-09-167 from the National Research Fund, Luxembourg.

P. Bouvry et al. (Eds.): SIIS 2011, LNCS 7053, pp. 103–116, 2012.

an attacker's and a defender's perspective. Thus, the new formalism enlarges the modeling capabilities of attack trees. Moreover, attack–defense trees can be interpreted with several semantics, which allows us to deal with different facets of security. In particular, the choice of an appropriate semantics becomes essential when performing a quantitative analysis of an attack–defense scenario.

An especially important semantics for attack–defense trees is the propositional semantics. It is well-suited to answer feasibility questions, such as whether a system is vulnerable to an attack, whether special equipment is needed to perform an attack, or how many different ways of attacking exist. The propositional semantics has been studied in [13], where it was shown that satisfiability of an attack–defense tree is equivalent to the existence of a winning strategy in a two-player binary zero-sum game.

Our contribution. The main goal of [12] was to enrich the well-established attack tree model, but this work did not consider computational aspects. The following questions therefore remained unanswered:

- How hard is query evaluation on attack–defense trees with respect to query evaluation on attack trees?
- Are there queries that can efficiently be solved on attack trees but not on attack–defense trees?
- Are new algorithms needed to efficiently process attack–defense trees?

In the current paper, we address these problems for a large class of semantics for attack–defense trees. We prove that, when the propositional semantics is used, attack trees and attack–defense trees both represent monotone Boolean functions. Moreover, we show that the same holds if the semantics is induced by arbitrary De Morgan lattices. This lets us conclude that, for every semantics induced by a De Morgan lattice, enriching attack trees with defense nodes has not increased the computational complexity of the model. In particular, we argue that algorithms for attack trees can also be used to process attack–defense trees. Query evaluation on attack–defense trees is thus not harder than the corresponding query evaluation on attack trees. Hence, every query that can efficiently be solved on attack trees, can also efficiently be solved on attack–defense trees.

Structure. In Section 2, we recall basic definitions and introduce necessary notation. Section 3 proves our results for the propositional semantics. In Section 4, we show how to generalize them to semantics induced by De Morgan lattices. We discuss practical consequences and applications of our theoretical results in Section 5. Finally, Section 6 lists possible directions for future research.

2 Preliminaries

We start by recalling necessary facts about attack–defense trees, attack–defense terms and Boolean functions.

2.1 Attack–Defense Trees

Attack trees [1, 5] are a well-known methodology for assessing the security of complex systems. An attack tree is a rooted tree representing an attack scenario.

The root of an attack tree depicts the main goal of an attacker, and the other nodes constitute refinements of this goal into sub-goals. Two kinds of refinements are possible: conjunctive and disjunctive. A conjunctively refined (sub-)goal is satisfied if all its children are fulfilled, and a disjunctively refined (sub-)goal is satisfied when at least one of its children is fulfilled. The leaves of an attack tree represent basic actions which are used to build complex attacks.

Attack–defense trees [12] are attack trees extended with defense nodes. They represent attack–defense scenarios involving actions of an attacker trying to compromise a system and counteractions of a defender trying to protect the system. Consequently, an attack–defense tree can be seen as a game between two players: an attacker and a defender. Each node of an attack–defense tree depicts a (sub-)goal of one of the players, and the root node represents the main goal of an attacker or of a defender, depending on the modeler's perspective. Therefore, instead of talking about attacker and defender, we rather refer to them as *proponent* and *opponent*. By proponent we mean the player related to the root node, and by opponent we mean the other player. As in the case of attack trees, every node of an attack–defense tree can be refined in a conjunctive or a disjunctive way. The refinement is modeled using child nodes of the same type (proponent or opponent) as the type of the parent node. In addition, each node of an attack–defense tree may have one child of the opposite type. Such a child then represents a countermeasure that can be applied to counter or mitigate the (sub-)goal represented by its parent. Finally, every node without any child of the same type represents a basic action. Contrary to attack trees, such a node does not have to be a leaf, because it can still have a child of the opposite type.

2.2 Attack–Defense Terms

Attack–defense trees can formally be represented using so-called attack–defense terms. We briefly recall the construction of these terms and refer to [12], for a more detailed description.

Let $\mathcal{S} = \{\mathrm{p}, \mathrm{o}\}$ be a set of types representing a proponent and an opponent. Given a player $s \in \mathcal{S}$, we write $\overline{s}$ to denote the opposite player. By $\mathbb{B}$ we denote a set of constants called *basic actions*. The set of basic actions $\mathbb{B}$ is partitioned into the set of basic actions of the proponent's type, denoted by $\mathbb{B}^{\mathrm{p}}$, and the set of basic actions of the opponent's type, denoted by $\mathbb{B}^{\mathrm{o}}$. We use the typed operators $\vee^{\mathrm{p}}, \wedge^{\mathrm{p}}$ to model disjunctive and conjunctive refinements for the proponent and the corresponding operators $\vee^{\mathrm{o}}, \wedge^{\mathrm{o}}$ for the opponent. Moreover, to connect actions of one player with counteractions of the other player, we use the counter operators c^{p} and c^{o}.

Definition 1. *Attack–defense terms (ADTerms) are typed ground terms recursively constructed from* $\mathbb{B}$ *using the typed operators* $\vee^{s}, \wedge^{s}, \mathrm{c}^{s}$, *for* $s \in \mathcal{S}$. *The set of all ADTerms is denoted by* $\mathbb{T}$.

Given a player $s \in \mathcal{S}$, we say that an ADTerm t is *of type* s, if its head symbol is $\vee^{s}, \wedge^{s}, \mathrm{c}^{s}$, or if t is a constant from $\mathbb{B}^{s}$. The typed operators $\vee^{s}$ and $\wedge^{s}$ are unranked, i.e., they take an arbitrary number of terms of type s as arguments and return a term of type s. The counter operator c^s is binary. It takes a term of type s as the first argument and a term of type $\bar{s}$ as the second argument, and returns a term of type s. By $\mathbb{T}^p$ we denote the set of ADTerms of the proponent's type and by $\mathbb{T}^o$ the set of ADTerms of the opponent's type. The ADTerms of the proponent's type constitute formal representations of attack–defense trees. Finally, the elements of $\mathbb{T}^p$ which are built by using the operators $\vee^p$ and $\wedge^p$ only represent attack trees and are called *ATerms.*

Example 1. Let $a, b, d \in \mathbb{B}^p$ be basic actions of the proponent's type and let $e, g \in \mathbb{B}^o$ be basic actions of the opponent's type. The ADTerm

$$t = \wedge^p(a, c^p(\vee^p(b, d), \vee^o(e, g)))$$

is of the proponent's type. It expresses a scenario in which, in order to achieve his goal, the proponent has to execute the action a and one of the actions b or d. At the same time, the opponent has the possibility to counter the proponent's actions b and d by executing at least one of the actions e or g. The opponent's ability of countering is indicated by the operator c^p, which takes the term $\vee^p(b, d)$ of the proponent's type as the first argument and the term $\vee^o(e, g)$ of the opponent's type as the second argument.

Different attack–defense trees (and therefore different ADTerms) may represent the same attack–defense scenario. Hence, we consider ADTerms modulo an equivalence relation.

Definition 2. *A semantics for ADTerms is an equivalence relation on* $\mathbb{T}$ *which preserves types.*

Every semantics partitions the set $\mathbb{T}$ into equivalence classes, and ADTerms belonging to the same equivalence class represent the same scenario.

Several distinct semantics for ADTerms have been introduced in [12]. One of them is the propositional semantics discussed in the following section.

2.3 Propositional Semantics for ADTerms

The idea behind the propositional semantics for ADTerms is to first associate a propositional formula with every ADTerm and then deduce an equivalence relation on $\mathbb{T}$ from the canonical equivalence relation of propositional logic.

In this paper, r denotes a countable set of propositional variables. First, with every basic action $b \in \mathbb{B}$, we associate a propositional variable $X_b \in r$. We assume that for $b, b' \in \mathbb{B}$, with $b \neq b'$, we have $X_b \neq X_{b'}$. In particular, since the sets of basic actions of the proponent's and of the opponent's type are disjoint, we have

$$\{X_b \mid b \in \mathbb{B}^p\} \cap \{X_b \mid b \in \mathbb{B}^o\} = \emptyset.$$

Second, a propositional formula $t_{\mathcal{P}}$ is associated with every ADTerm t, as follows

$$t_{\mathcal{P}} = \begin{cases} X_b, & \text{if } t = b \in \mathbb{B}, \\ t^1_{\mathcal{P}} \vee \cdots \vee t^k_{\mathcal{P}}, & \text{if } t = \vee^s_k(t^1, \ldots, t^k), \\ t^1_{\mathcal{P}} \wedge \cdots \wedge t^k_{\mathcal{P}}, & \text{if } t = \wedge^s_k(t^1, \ldots, t^k), \\ t^1_{\mathcal{P}} \wedge \neg t^2_{\mathcal{P}}, & \text{if } t = c^s(t^1, t^2), \end{cases}$$

where $s \in \{p, o\}$ and $k \in \mathbb{N}$. A formula $t_{\mathcal{P}}$ is referred to as *propositional ADTerm*. In case of an ATerm, the corresponding formula is called a *propositional ATerm*.

By $\approx$ we denote the equivalence relation on propositional formulæ. Recall that two propositional formulæ ψ and ψ' are equivalent ($\psi \approx \psi'$) if and only if, for every assignment ν of Boolean values to variables in r, we have $\nu(\psi) = \nu(\psi')$.

Definition 3. *The propositional semantics for ADTerms is the equivalence relation $\equiv_{\mathcal{P}}$ on $\mathbb{T}$ defined, for all $t, t' \in \mathbb{T}$, by $t \equiv_{\mathcal{P}} t'$ if and only if $t_{\mathcal{P}} \approx t'_{\mathcal{P}}$.*

2.4 Boolean Functions

The set of propositional ADTerms can be seen as a representation language for Boolean functions. The analysis of this language, performed in Section 3, allows us to compare the computational complexity of ADTerms and ATerms. The current section gathers necessary definitions and facts about Boolean functions.

A *configuration* with finite domain $d \subseteq r$ is a function $\mathbf{x}\colon d \to \{0, 1\}$ that associates a value $\mathbf{x}(X) \in \{0, 1\}$ with every variable $X \in d$. Thus, a configuration $\mathbf{x} \in \{0, 1\}^d$ represents an assignment of Boolean values to the variables in d.

Definition 4. *A Boolean function f with domain d is a function $f\colon \{0, 1\}^d \to \{0, 1\}$ that assigns a value $f(\mathbf{x}) \in \{0, 1\}$ to each configuration $\mathbf{x} \in \{0, 1\}^d$.*

Given a configuration $\mathbf{x}$ with domain $d \subseteq r$, we denote by $\mathbf{x}^{\downarrow u}$ the projection of $\mathbf{x}$ to a subset $u \subseteq d$. This notation allows us to introduce the following definition.

Definition 5. *Let f and g be two Boolean functions with domains d and u, respectively. The conjunction $(f \wedge g)$ and the disjunction $(f \vee g)$ of f and g are Boolean functions with domain $d \cup u$, defined for every $\mathbf{x} \in \{0, 1\}^{d \cup u}$ by*

$$f \wedge g(\mathbf{x}) = \min\{f(\mathbf{x}^{\downarrow d}), g(\mathbf{x}^{\downarrow u})\}, \qquad f \vee g(\mathbf{x}) = \max\{f(\mathbf{x}^{\downarrow d}), g(\mathbf{x}^{\downarrow u})\}.$$

The negation of f, denoted by $\neg f$, is a Boolean function with domain d, defined for every $\mathbf{x} \in \{0, 1\}^d$ by $(\neg f)(\mathbf{x}) = 1 - f(\mathbf{x})$.

Let $u \subseteq r$ be a finite set of propositional variables. By $e_u\colon \{0, 1\}^u \to \{0, 1\}$ we denote the Boolean unit function, i.e., $e_u(\mathbf{x}) = 1$, for every $\mathbf{x} \in \{0, 1\}^u$. Given a Boolean function f with domain d, we denote by $f^{\uparrow d \cup u}$ the *vacuous extension of f to $d \cup u$*, defined as $f^{\uparrow d \cup u} = f \wedge e_{u \setminus d}$.

Definition 6. *Two Boolean functions f and g, with respective domains d and u, are said to be equivalent (denoted by $f \equiv g$) if and only if, $\forall \mathbf{x} \in \{0, 1\}^{d \cup u}$, we have $f^{\uparrow d \cup u}(\mathbf{x}) = g^{\uparrow d \cup u}(\mathbf{x})$.*

As shown in [14], $f \equiv g$ if and only if $\forall \mathbf{x} \in \{0, 1\}^r$, $f^{\uparrow r}(\mathbf{x}) = g^{\uparrow r}(\mathbf{x})$. The advantage of an equivalence relation using finite sets of variables, as in Definition 6, is that the construction described in this paper is practical and implementable.

Remark 1. Since equivalent propositional formulæ represent equivalent Boolean functions, two ADTerms t and t' are equivalent under the propositional semantics, if they represent equivalent Boolean functions.

Of particular importance for our studies are positive, negative and monotone Boolean functions.

Definition 7. *Let f be a Boolean function with domain $d \subseteq r$, and let $X \in d$ be a propositional variable.*

- *f is positive in X if $f(\mathbf{x}, 0) \leq f(\mathbf{x}, 1)$, for all $\mathbf{x} \in \{0,1\}^{d \setminus \{X\}}$,*
- *f is negative in X if $f(\mathbf{x}, 0) \geq f(\mathbf{x}, 1)$, for all $\mathbf{x} \in \{0,1\}^{d \setminus \{X\}}$,*
- *f is monotone in $X \in d$ if it is either positive or negative in X.*

Note that if $X \in r$ does not occur in the domain of a Boolean function f, then f is insensitive to the values assigned to X. In this case, we may say that f is positive, negative and monotone in X.

Definition 8. *A Boolean function f is positive (resp. negative, monotone) if it is positive (resp. negative, monotone) in every variable $X \in r$.*

The following lemma shows that the classes of positive, as well as negative Boolean functions are closed under conjunction and disjunction.

Lemma 1. *Let f and g be Boolean functions,*

- *if f and g are positive in X, then $f \wedge g$ and $f \vee g$ are positive in X,*
- *if f and g are negative in X, then $f \wedge g$ and $f \vee g$ are negative in X.*

Proof. Both statements follow directly from the monotonicity of minimization and maximization. □

Note however, that the results from Lemma 1 do generally not hold for monotone Boolean functions.

Example 2. The Boolean function $f(X, Y) = X \wedge \neg Y$ is positive in X and negative in Y. Thus, f is monotone. For similar reasons, the Boolean function $g(X, Y) = Y \wedge \neg X$ is monotone. However, it can easily be checked that the function $f \vee g$ is not monotone.

Next we show that monotone Boolean functions are closed under negation.

Lemma 2. *Let f be a Boolean function, and let $X \in r$ be a variable. If f is positive (resp. negative) in X, then $\neg f$ is negative (resp. positive) in X.*

Proof. Let us assume that f is positive in X, and let the domain of f be denoted by d. If $X \notin d$, then, by convention, f is positive in X and $\neg f$ is negative in X. If $X \in d$, then from the positivity of f in X, we have $f(\mathbf{x}^{\downarrow d \setminus \{X\}}, 0) \leq f(\mathbf{x}^{\downarrow d \setminus \{X\}}, 1)$, for all $\mathbf{x} \in \{0,1\}^d$. Therefore,

$$(\neg f)(\mathbf{x}^{\downarrow d \setminus \{X\}}, 0) = 1 - f(\mathbf{x}^{\downarrow d \setminus \{X\}}, 0) \geq 1 - f(\mathbf{x}^{\downarrow d \setminus \{X\}}, 1) = (\neg f)(\mathbf{x}^{\downarrow d \setminus \{X\}}, 1).$$

This shows that $\neg f$ is negative in X. The proof for the other case is similar. □

Note that Lemma 2 holds because negation $\neg$ reverses the order, i.e., for $a, b \in \{0,1\}$, we have $a \leq b$ if and only if $\neg a \geq \neg b$. This is crucial in Section 4, where we generalize this result from the propositional algebra to De Morgan lattices.

From Lemmas 1 and 2, we deduce the following result.

Corollary 1. *If f and g are two Boolean functions, such that f is positive (resp. negative) in a variable X and g is negative (resp. positive) in X, then the Boolean function $f \wedge \neg g$ is positive (resp. negative) in X.*

3 Transformation of ADTerms to ATerms

The objective of this section is to compare the computational complexity of the propositional ADTerms language with the computational complexity of the propositional ATerms language. We achieve this by analyzing the classes of Boolean functions represented by both languages.

3.1 Expressiveness of Propositional ADTerms

We start by analyzing the language of propositional ATerms. ATerms constitute formal representations of attack trees, which are AND-OR trees containing only proponent's nodes. Therefore, every propositional ATerm is a formula generated by the following grammar $\mathcal{AT}$

$$P: \quad X^{\mathrm{p}} \quad | \quad P \vee P \quad | \quad P \wedge P, \qquad (\mathcal{AT})$$

where $X^{\mathrm{p}} \in \{X_b \mid b \in \mathbb{B}^{\mathrm{p}}\}$. Theorem 1 characterizes propositional ATerms using Boolean functions.

Theorem 1. *Boolean functions represented by propositional ATerms are positive.*

Proof. Consider the grammar $\mathcal{AT}$. The Boolean function represented by X^{p} is positive. The positivity of the Boolean functions represented by $P \vee P$ and $P \wedge P$ is a direct consequence of Lemma 1. □

In order to characterize the language of propositional ADTerms, we extend the grammar $\mathcal{AT}$ to the grammar $\mathcal{ADT}$ generating all propositional ADTerms

$$\begin{array}{llllllll} P: & X^{\mathrm{p}} & | & P \vee P & | & P \wedge P & | & P \wedge \neg N \\ N: & X^{\mathrm{o}} & | & N \vee N & | & N \wedge N & | & N \wedge \neg P, \end{array} \qquad (\mathcal{ADT})$$

where $X^{\mathrm{p}} \in \{X_b \mid b \in \mathbb{B}^{\mathrm{p}}\}$ and $X^{\mathrm{o}} \in \{X_b \mid b \in \mathbb{B}^{\mathrm{o}}\}$. The formulæ of the form P (resp. N) are propositional ADTerms for the terms of the proponent's (resp. opponent's) type. Theorem 2 characterizes propositional ADTerms using Boolean functions.

Theorem 2. *Boolean functions represented by propositional ADTerms are monotone.*

In order to prove Theorem 2, we use the following Lemma.

Lemma 3. *Consider the grammar $\mathcal{ADT}$. Every Boolean function represented by a formula of the form P (resp. N) is*

- *positive (resp. negative) in every variable X_b, for $b \in \mathbb{B}^{\mathrm{p}}$,*
- *negative (resp. positive) in every variable X_b, for $b \in \mathbb{B}^{\mathrm{o}}$.*

Proof. We provide a proof in the case of P. A proof for N is analogous. We reason by induction over the structure of P. If $P = X^{\mathrm{p}} \in \mathbb{B}^{\mathrm{p}}$, then the Boolean function represented by P is clearly positive in X^{p}. According to our convention, P is also positive in every $X_b \in \mathbb{B}^{\mathrm{p}} \setminus \{X^{\mathrm{p}}\}$ and negative in every $X_b \in \mathbb{B}^{\mathrm{o}}$.

Now, consider a formula P which is not a single variable, and assume that the lemma holds for all formulæ composing P. If P is of the form $P \vee P$ or $P \wedge P$, the result follows from Lemma 1 and the induction hypothesis. If P is of the form $P \wedge \neg N$, the result follows from Corollary 1 and the induction hypothesis. □

Since the sets $\mathbb{B}^{\mathrm{p}}$ and $\mathbb{B}^{\mathrm{o}}$ are disjoint, we can conclude that every formula generated by $\mathcal{ADT}$ represents a monotone Boolean function. This proves Theorem 2. Note that the assumption that $\mathbb{B}^{\mathrm{p}}$ and $\mathbb{B}^{\mathrm{o}}$ are disjoint is crucial. Without this assumption, Lemma 3 would not hold, see Example 2.

3.2 From Propositional ADTerms to Propositional ATerms

Since every ATerm is also an ADTerm, it is obvious that all Boolean functions represented by propositional ATerms can also be represented by propositional ADTerms. In this section, we show that the converse holds as well.

Theorem 3. *Let f be a Boolean function with domain d and let $X \in d$. We define a Boolean function g with the same domain, as follows*

$$g(\mathbf{x}, 0) = f(\mathbf{x}, 1) \quad \textit{and} \quad g(\mathbf{x}, 1) = f(\mathbf{x}, 0),$$

for all $\mathbf{x} \in \{0,1\}^{d \setminus \{X\}}$. The function g is positive (resp. negative) in X if and only if the function f is negative (resp. positive) in X.

Proof. If f is positive in $X \in d$, then, for all $\mathbf{x} \in \{0,1\}^{d \setminus \{X\}}$, we have $g(\mathbf{x}, 1) = f(\mathbf{x}, 0) \leq f(\mathbf{x}, 1) = g(\mathbf{x}, 0)$, i.e., g is negative in X. The other case is similar. □

Note that the functions f and g in Theorem 3 are not equivalent in the sense of Definition 6, but there is a one-to-one correspondence between their satisfying assignments, i.e., between the elements of the sets of $f^{-1}(\{1\})$ and $g^{-1}(\{1\})$.

It follows from Theorem 3 that every monotone Boolean function, which is not positive, can always be transformed to a positive form. Moreover, Lemma 3 guarantees that such a transformation is linear with respect to the size of the function's domain. Consequently, whenever we want to reason about a propositional ADTerm, we can analyze a positive Boolean function instead of a monotone one. Hence, the following result holds.

Corollary 2. *Propositional ADTerms represent positive Boolean functions.*

This proves that the language of propositional ADTerms and the language of propositional ATerms both represent positive Boolean functions. Practical consequences of this fact are discussed in Section 5.

4 Generalizations

An important feature of ADTerms is that they can be equipped with different semantics. This allows for the analysis of various security aspects. However, the previous sections focus on the propositional semantics, where basic actions are allowed to take propositional values, and ADTerms over the set of variables d represent Boolean functions of the form $\{0,1\}^d \to \{0,1\}$. Hence, the propositional semantics is a semantics induced by the Boolean algebra $\langle\{0,1\},\wedge,\vee,\neg\rangle$. In this section we show that the transformation from ADTerms to ATerms, presented in Section 3 for the propositional semantics, applies to all semantics induced by more general algebraic structures $\langle A,+,\times,\neg\rangle$, such as De Morgan lattices.

Let $\langle A,+,\times,\neg\rangle$ be an algebraic structure defined over a non-empty set A with two binary operations, $+$ and $\times$, and a unary operation $\neg$. Since we still consider propositional variables, ADTerms and ATerms now represent functions of the form $\{0,1\}^d \to A$. From the isomorphism property of Boolean algebras, we directly obtain the following corollary.

Corollary 3. *For every semantics induced by a finite Boolean algebra $\langle A,+,\times,\neg\rangle$, ADTerms can efficiently be transformed to ATerms.*

In the rest of this section, we show that the transformation even works with less algebraic structure. To distinguish between positive, negative and monotone functions of the form $\{0,1\}^d \to A$, over the structure $\langle A,+,\times,\neg\rangle$, the set A must exhibit a partial order that behaves monotonically under the operations $+$ and $\times$. It is well-known that if $\langle A,+,\times\rangle$ is a lattice it can always be equipped with a canonical partial order, defined for all $a,b\in A$, by

$$a \preceq b \text{ if and only if } a+b=b. \qquad (\preceq)$$

This order is monotonic with respect to the operations $+$ and $\times$, see [15]. This allows us to generalize Lemma 1. We then extend $\langle A,+,\times\rangle$ with a negation operation which reverses the order $\preceq$.

Definition 9. *A tuple $\langle A,+,\times,\neg\rangle$ is called a De Morgan lattice if $\langle A,+,\times\rangle$ is a distributive lattice and, for all $a,b\in A$, we have*

$$\neg(a+b)=(\neg a)\times(\neg b), \qquad \neg(a\times b)=(\neg a)+(\neg b), \qquad \neg(\neg a)=a.$$

To validate Lemma 2, we show that in De Morgan lattices the order $\preceq$ is indeed reversed under negation.

Lemma 4. *In a De Morgan lattice we have $a\preceq b$ if and only if $\neg b\preceq\neg a$.*

Proof. Assume that $a\preceq b$, i.e., $a+b=b$. It follows from the definition of a De Morgan lattice that $\neg b=\neg(a+b)=(\neg a)\times(\neg b)$. Moreover, in every lattice we have $b=a\times b$ if and only if $a=a+b$, see [15]. Therefore, we conclude that $\neg b=(\neg a)\times(\neg b)$ if and only if $\neg a=(\neg a)+(\neg b)$. This proves that $a\preceq b$ implies $\neg b\preceq\neg a$. Conversely, assume $\neg b\preceq\neg a$. From the first part of this proof we know that $\neg b\preceq\neg a$ implies $\neg(\neg a)\preceq\neg(\neg b)$, and therefore we have $a\preceq b$. □

Observe that De Morgan lattices are more general than Boolean algebras, because the former do not have to satisfy the law of the excluded middle and the law of non-contradiction.

Example 3. The tuple $\langle[0,1], \max, \min, \neg\rangle$, where $\neg a = 1-a$, for every $a \in [0,1]$, is a De Morgan lattice which is not a Boolean algebra.

Consider a De Morgan lattice $\langle A, +, \times, \neg\rangle$ and a finite set $d \subseteq r$ of variables. A *De Morgan valuation* with domain d is a function of the form $f\colon \{0,1\}^d \to A$. Note that De Morgan valuations satisfy the properties of valuation algebras, see [16]. Similar to Definition 6, equivalence of De Morgan valuations is again defined by point-wise equality of their vacuous extensions. Furthermore, we obtain positive, negative and monotone De Morgan valuations by modifying Definition 7: we replace Boolean functions by De Morgan valuations and the order $\leq$ by $\preceq$.

The above considerations guarantee that the statements of Corollary 1 and Theorem 3 still hold if Boolean functions are replaced by De Morgan valuations. This means that the transformation of ADTerms to ATerms, described in Section 3 for the propositional semantics, actually holds for a larger class of semantics that we define below.

Let $\langle A, +, \times, \neg\rangle$ be a De Morgan lattice. As in the case of the propositional semantics, we consider the set of propositional variables $\{X_b \mid b \in \mathbb{B}\}$. With every ADTerm t we associate a De Morgan valuation f_t, called a *De Morgan ADTerm*, as follows. If $t = b$ and b is a basic action, then f_t is a function of the form $f_b\colon \{0,1\}^{\{X_b\}} \to A$. With the help of f_b, we express how the value assigned to a basic action b changes depending on whether the basic action b is satisfied ($X_b = 1$) or not ($X_b = 0$). De Morgan ADTerms associated with composed ADTerms are then defined recursively, as follows. For $s \in \{\mathrm{p}, \mathrm{o}\}$, $k \in \mathbb{N}$, we set [1]

$$f_{\vee^s(t_1,\dots,t_k)} = \sum_{i=1}^{k} f_{t_i}, \qquad f_{\wedge^s(t_1,\dots,t_k)} = \prod_{i=1}^{k} f_{t_i}, \qquad f_{\mathrm{c}^s(t_1,t_2)} = f_{t_1} \times \neg f_{t_2}.$$

Definition 10. *The semantics for ADTerms induced by the De Morgan lattice* $\langle A, +, \times, \neg\rangle$ *is the equivalence relation* $\equiv_{\mathcal{DM}}$ *on* $\mathbb{T}$ *defined, for all* $t, t' \in \mathbb{T}$, *by* $t \equiv_{\mathcal{DM}} t'$ *if and only if the corresponding De Morgan valuations* f_t *and* $f_{t'}$ *are equivalent.*

Before presenting the main result of this section, we briefly compare the usability of semantics induced by De Morgan lattices with the propositional semantics. Every Boolean algebra is a De Morgan lattice. Thus, the propositional semantics is the semantics induced by $\langle\{0,1\}, \vee, \wedge, \neg\rangle$, where a basic action b is interpreted as the Boolean function $f_b(X_b) = X_b$. Such a propositional interpretation implies that each action which is present is fully feasible, i.e., $f_b(X_b = 1) = 1$. This shows that the use of Boolean functions is not appropriate when one wants to describe the components of an attack–defense tree with more fine grained

[1] $\sum$ and $\prod$ stand for extensions of sum and product of two valuations to any finite number of valuations. They are correctly defined, due to associativity of $+$ and $\times$.

feasibility levels, such as, fully feasible (T), partially feasible (M) and infeasible (F), for instance. In particular, the propositional semantics cannot be applied to determine up to which level a proposed scenario is actually feasible. However, such a more detailed analysis can be performed using the semantics induced by the De Morgan lattice $\langle\{T,M,F\},\max,\min,\neg\rangle$, where $F < M < T$ and $\neg F = T$, $\neg M = M$ and $\neg T = F$, as shown is Example 4.

Example 4. Consider the ADTerm $t = c^p(b, \wedge^o(d,e))$ and the semantics induced by the De Morgan lattice $\langle\{T,M,F\},\max,\min,\neg\rangle$. We assume that when the actions b, d and e are not present, they are infeasible

$$f_b(X_b = 0) = F, \qquad f_d(X_d = 0) = F, \qquad f_e(X_e = 0) = F.$$

Moreover, the presence of the actions b and e ensures their full feasibility, but the presence of the action d guarantees its partial feasibility, only

$$f_b(X_b = 1) = T, \qquad f_d(X_d = 1) = M, \qquad f_e(X_e = 1) = T.$$

Analyzing the De Morgan valuation associated with t, given by $f_t(X_b, X_d, X_e) = \min\{f_b(X_b), \neg(\min\{f_d(X_d), f_e(X_e)\})\}$, allows us to reason about feasibility of the scenario represented by t. We have

$$\begin{array}{llll} f_t(0,0,0) = F & f_t(0,1,0) = F & f_t(1,0,0) = T & f_t(1,1,0) = T \\ f_t(0,0,1) = F & f_t(0,1,1) = F & f_t(1,0,1) = T & f_t(1,1,1) = M. \end{array}$$

From $f_t^{-1}(\{M,T\})$, we deduce that the scenario is at least partially feasible for the proponent if the action b is present, independently of the actions d and e.

The considerations described in this section imply the following theorem.

Theorem 4. *De Morgan ADTerms are positive De Morgan valuations.*

This proves that the results obtained in Section 3 for the propositional semantics, generalize to every semantics induced by a De Morgan lattice.

5 Consequences

As discussed in [12], an obvious limitation of attack trees is that they cannot capture the interaction between attacks on a system and the defenses put in place to mitigate the attacks. To surpass this limitation, attack–defense trees have been developed. By allowing alternation between attack and defense nodes, attack–defense trees take the effects of existing defensive measures into account and allow us to consider the evolution of a system's security. In contrast to this, the results in Sections 3 and 4 compare attack and attack–defense trees on the computational level. We formally proved that, under a semantics induced by a De Morgan lattice, both models represent positive valuations and therefore exhibit the same computational complexity.

Result 1. *Attack–defense trees extend attack trees to a richer model without increasing the computational complexity, provided that their semantics is induced by a De Morgan lattice.*

Result 1 can be applied, for instance, to query evaluation on ADTerms. A *query* on ADTerms is a function $Q\colon \mathbb{T} \to \mathcal{A}$ which assigns to every ADTerm t an element $Q(t) \in \mathcal{A}$ called the *answer* for Q on t.

Example 5. Consider a function $Q_{\mathrm{SAT}}\colon \mathbb{T} \to \{\top, \bot\}$ which assigns $\top$ to an ADTerm t if the corresponding Boolean function f admits at least one satisfying assignment, i.e., if there exists a configuration $\mathbf{x}$, such that $f(\mathbf{x}) = 1$. Otherwise, $\bot$ is assigned to t. The function Q_{SAT} is an example of a query on ADTerms. It models satisfiability check, when the propositional semantics is used.

Result 2 characterizes how hard query evaluation is on ADTerms with respect to query valuation on ATerms.

Result 2. *When a semantics induced by a De Morgan lattice is used, the complexity of query evaluation on ADTerms is the same as the corresponding complexity for ATerms.*

It follows from Result 2 that, when a semantics induced by a De Morgan lattice is used, a query can efficiently be solved on ADTerms if and only if it can efficiently be solved on ATerms. As an example, when the propositional is used, satisfiability check on ADTerms can be performed in constant time, because all positive Boolean functions are satisfiable.

Theorem 3 and subsequent considerations in Section 4 show that, for a large class of semantics, we can effectively transform ADTerms to ATerms. Therefore, we obtain the following result.

Result 3. *When using a semantics induced by a De Morgan lattice, ADTerms can always be processed by algorithms developed for ATerms.*

Moreover, our constructive transformation guarantees that Result 3 holds for all existing and all future algorithms for ATerms.

Finally, knowing that not all Boolean functions are positive and taking into account Corollary 2, we deduce that there exist Boolean functions which cannot be represented by any propositional ADTerm.

Result 4. *The propositional language defined by propositional ADTerms is not complete.*

For instance, there is no ADTerm corresponding to the Boolean function representing the tautology. This example also shows that the set of propositional ADTerms represents a proper subset of the set of positive Boolean functions.

6 Open Problems

One of the particularities of positive Boolean functions is that they admit a unique modulo associativity and commutativity (AC), complete and irredundant

DNF representation, see [17]. This means that no other DNF representation of a positive Boolean function can be as short as its complete DNF, i.e., the disjunction of all its prime implicants. We can therefore conclude that ADTerms under the propositional semantics possess unique modulo AC normal forms. We believe that this provides a sufficient argument to find a finite axiomatization of the propositional semantics for ADTerms. This would be a first step towards an efficient implementation of an attack–defense tree tool that captures all semantics preserving transformations and is able to execute equivalence check between ADTerms. The importance of such transformations has been pointed out by Mauw and Oostdijk in [5].

Furthermore, we would like to know whether it is possible to apply our results to other classes of semantics. Of particular interests would be to replace propositional variables with multi-state variables, as in [18]. The advantage of multi-state variables is that they can express security levels more accurately than propositional variables. Using them we can, for instance, model nominal values or categories, such as *high*, *medium* and *low*.

We also plan to investigate the relation between modeling capabilities and computational complexity of attack–defense trees under the multiset semantics, introduced in [12]. The importance of this semantics arises from its compatibility with a multitude of attributes, such as the cost of the cheapest attack, the maximal damage caused by an attack or the probability of a successful attack.

Finally, we would like to take a look at other languages for representing Boolean functions. The topic has exhaustively been studied by Darwiche and Marquis. In [19], they established a taxonomy of complete propositional languages, based on the succinctness of the representation, the queries that can efficiently be answered on a given representation and the transformations that can be applied to a given language in polynomial time. Their paper considers several queries, including satisfiability and validity checks, model counting, model and counter-model enumeration. In the spirit of this taxonomy, we would like to answer runtime questions for the corresponding queries on our incomplete language of propositional ADTerms.

7 Conclusion

In this paper we perform an exhaustive analysis of a wide class of semantics for ADTerms. First, by employing known results from propositional logics, we prove that propositional ADTerms and propositional ATerms represent the same class of Boolean functions. We then show that this result can be generalized from Boolean functions to De Morgan valuations. We deduce that, for every semantics induced by a De Morgan lattice, the computational complexity of the attack tree model and the attack–defense tree model is the same. This proves that enriching the attack tree formalism with defense nodes was not done at the expense of computational complexity.

We also discuss several important consequences that can be derived for ADTerms interpreted using De Morgan valuations. In particular, we deduce that the complexity of query evaluation on ADTerms is the same as the corresponding complexity on ATerms. Moreover, by showing that ADTerms can efficiently be transformed to ATerms, we conclude that algorithms for ATerms can be used to reason about ADTerms.

References

1. Schneier, B.: Attack Trees. Dr. Dobb's Journal of Software Tools 24(12), 21–29 (1999)
2. Weiss, J.D.: A system security engineering process. In: 14th Nat. Comp. Sec. Conf., pp. 572–581 (1991)
3. Amoroso, E.G.: Fundamentals of Computer Security Technology. Prentice-Hall, Inc., Upper Saddle River (1994)
4. Vesely, W.E., Goldberg, F.F., Roberts, N., Haasl, D.: Fault Tree Handbook. Technical Report NUREG-0492, U.S. Regulatory Commission (1981)
5. Mauw, S., Oostdijk, M.: Foundations of Attack Trees. In: Won, D.H., Kim, S. (eds.) ICISC 2005. LNCS, vol. 3935, pp. 186–198. Springer, Heidelberg (2006)
6. Cervesato, I., Meadows, C.: One Picture Is Worth a Dozen Connectives: A Fault-Tree Representation of NPATRL Security Requirements. IEEE TDSC 4, 216–227 (2007)
7. Edge, K.S., Dalton II, G.C., Raines, R.A., Mills, R.F.: Using Attack and Protection Trees to Analyze Threats and Defenses to Homeland Security. In: MILCOM, IEEE, pp. 1–7 (2006)
8. Morais, A.N.P., Martins, E., Cavalli, A.R., Jimenez, W.: Security Protocol Testing Using Attack Trees. In: CSE (2), pp. 690–697. IEEE Computer Society (2009)
9. Jürgenson, A., Willemson, J.: Serial Model for Attack Tree Computations. In: Lee, D., Hong, S. (eds.) ICISC 2009. LNCS, vol. 5984, pp. 118–128. Springer, Heidelberg (2010)
10. Bistarelli, S., Peretti, P., Trubitsyna, I.: Analyzing Security Scenarios Using Defence Trees and Answer Set Programming. ENTCS 197(2), 121–129 (2008)
11. Yager, R.R.: OWA trees and their role in security modeling using attack trees. Inf. Sci. 176(20), 2933–2959 (2006)
12. Kordy, B., Mauw, S., Radomirović, S., Schweitzer, P.: Foundations of Attack–Defense Trees. In: Degano, P., Etalle, S., Guttman, J. (eds.) FAST 2010. LNCS, vol. 6561, pp. 80–95. Springer, Heidelberg (2011)
13. Kordy, B., Mauw, S., Melissen, M., Schweitzer, P.: Attack–Defense Trees and Two-Player Binary Zero-Sum Extensive Form Games Are Equivalent. In: Alpcan, T., Buttyán, L., Baras, J.S. (eds.) GameSec 2010. LNCS, vol. 6442, pp. 245–256. Springer, Heidelberg (2010)
14. Kohlas, J.: Information Algebras: Generic Structures for Inference. Springer, Heidelberg (2003)
15. Davey, B., Priestley, H.: Introduction to Lattices and Order. Cambridge University Press (1990)
16. Pouly, M., Kohlas, J.: Generic Inference: A Unifying Theory for Automated Reasoning. John Wiley & Sons, Inc. (2011)
17. Crama, Y., Hammer, P.: Boolean Functions: Theory, Algorithms and Applications. Cambridge University Press (2011)
18. Wachter, M., Haenni, R.: Multi-state Directed Acyclic Graphs. In: Kobti, Z., Wu, D. (eds.) Canadian AI 2007. LNCS (LNAI), vol. 4509, pp. 464–475. Springer, Heidelberg (2007)
19. Darwiche, A., Marquis, P.: A Knowledge Compilation Map. J. Artif. Intell. Res. 17, 229–264 (2002)

Attacks on Simplified Versions of K2

Deike Priemuth-Schmid

LACS, University of Luxembourg
deike.priemuth-schmid@uni.lu

Abstract. In 2007, S. Kiyomoto, T. Tanaka and K. Sakurai presented the stream cipher K2 at SECRYPT. In this paper, we present two attacks on simplified versions of K2. We show a differential chosen IV attack with key recovery on a simplified version with 5 initialization clocks with time complexity of $2^{8.1}$ clocks. For a simplified version with 7 initialization clocks, we show a distinguishing attack with time complexity of $2^{34.8}$ clocks.

Keywords: cipher K2, stream ciphers, cryptanalysis.

1 Introduction

The stream cipher K2 was proposed by S. Kiyomoto, T. Tanaka and K. Sakurai at SECRYPT 2007 [4].

A security evaluation is given in [1] with the conclusion that no weaknesses were found. Some side-channel attacks are applied on K2 in [3] showing that K2 offers reasonable resistance to side-channel attacks even without countermeasures.

In this paper, we present two attacks on simplified versions of K2. We show a differential chosen IV attack with key recovery on a simplified version with 5 initialization clocks with time complexity of $2^{8.1}$ clocks and needed keystream of 28 words. For a simplified version with 7 initialization clocks, we show a distinguishing attack with time complexity of $2^{34.8}$ clocks and needed keystream of 2^{32} words. Both attacks have negligible memory requirements.

This paper is organized as follows. We give a description of the cipher K2 and its simplification $K2^{\oplus}$ in Section 2. The differential chosen IV attack with key recovery on $K2^{\oplus}$ with 5 initialization clocks is presented in Section 3. In Section 4, we describe the distinguishing attack on $K2^{\oplus}$ with 7 initialization clocks. Some conclusions are given in Section 5.

2 Description of K2 and $K2^{\oplus}$

S. Kiyomoto, T. Tanaka and K. Sakurai proposed the stream cipher K2 at SECRYPT 2007 [4]. It consists of two FSRs, a dynamic feedback controller and a nonlinear function as shown in Fig. 1.

P. Bouvry et al. (Eds.): SIIS 2011, LNCS 7053, pp. 117–127, 2012.

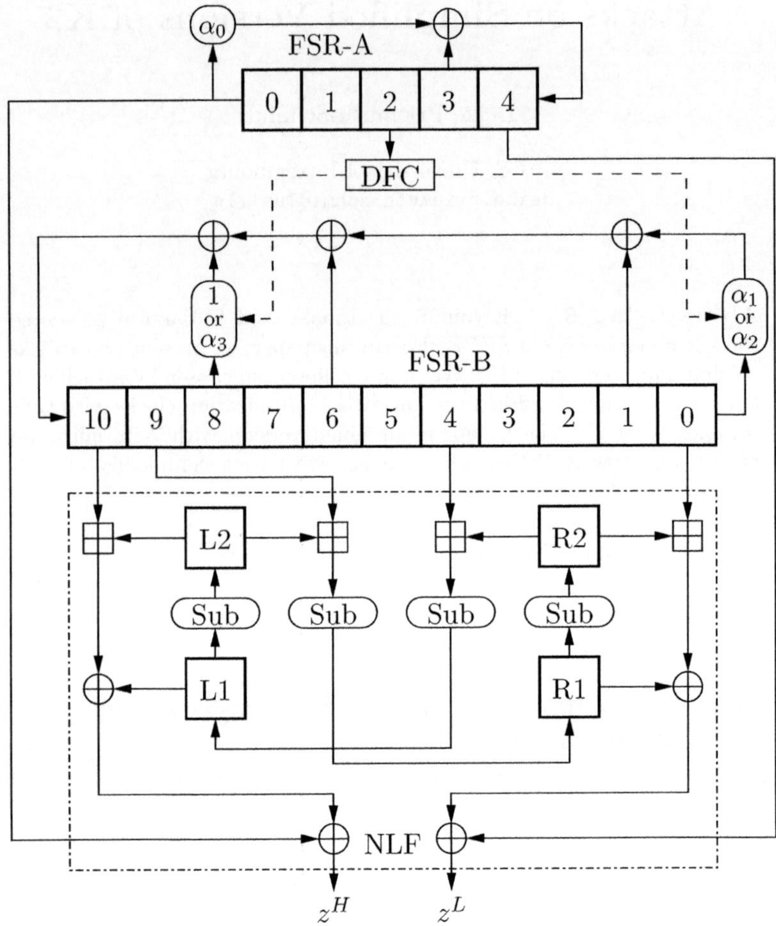

Fig. 1. keystream generation of K2

The first FSR, called FSR-A, has 5 registers $(a_4, \ldots, a_0)$ each of size one word (32 bit). The feedback function is

$$a_4^t = \alpha_0 a_0^{t-1} \oplus a_3^{t-1}$$

where the multiplier α_0 is a constant, chosen as the root of an irreducible polynomial of degree four in $GF(2^8)[x]$. The second FSR, called FSR-B, has 11 registers $(b_{10}, \ldots, b_0)$ each of size one word. The feedback function of FSR-B is selected by the dynamic feedback controller. This controller has two clock control bits $cl1$ and $cl2$ which are described as

$$cl1_t = a_2^t[30] \quad \text{and} \quad cl2_t = a_2^t[31]$$

with $a_2^t[30]$ being the second most significant bit of a_2^t and $a_2^t[31]$ being the most significant bit (abbr. msb) of a_2^t. Then the feedback function of the FSR-B is

$$b_{10}^t = (\alpha_1^{cl1_{t-1}} + \alpha_2^{1-cl1_{t-1}-1})b_0^{t-1} \oplus b_1^{t-1} \oplus b_6^{t-1} \oplus \alpha_3^{cl2_{t-1}} b_8^{t-1}$$

where the multipliers $\alpha_{(1,2,3)}$ are constants, each one chosen as the root of a different irreducible polynomial of degree four in $GF(2^8)[x]$. The nonlinear function (abbr. NLF) has four words memory $(L1, L2, R1, R2)$ and four times a *Sub* function. This *Sub* function operates on a word and uses the 8-bit AES S-box and the AES Mix-Column operation [2]. The exact work flow is: divide the word into four bytes, apply on each byte the 8-bit AES S-box, mix the resulting bytes using the AES Mix-Column operation yielding a word again. To update the memory words of the NLF, compute

$$\begin{aligned} L1^t &= Sub(R2^{t-1} \boxplus b_4^{t-1}) \qquad & L2^t &= Sub(L1^{t-1}) \\ R1^t &= Sub(L2^{t-1} \boxplus b_9^{t-1}) \qquad & R2^t &= Sub(R1^{t-1}) \ . \end{aligned}$$

With each clock, the output of the NLF is the keystream of two words (z_t^H, z_t^L) computed as

$$\begin{aligned} z_t^H &= (b_{10}^t \boxplus L2^t) \oplus L1^t \oplus a_0^t \\ z_t^L &= (b_0^t \boxplus R2^t) \oplus R1^t \oplus a_4^t \ . \end{aligned}$$

The symbol '$\oplus$' denotes the bit-wise xor and the symbol '$\boxplus$' denotes addition modulo 2^{32}.

The K2 cipher uses a four word key $K = [K_0, K_1, K_2, K_3]$ and a four word IV $IV = [IV_0, IV_1, IV_2, IV_3]$. For the loading step, two intermediate results are computed using the *Sub* function

$$\begin{aligned} S1 &= Sub[(K_3 \ll 8) \oplus (K_3 \gg 24)] \oplus 0x01000000 \\ S2 &= Sub[((K_0 \oplus K_1 \oplus K_2 \oplus K_3 \oplus S1) \ll 8) \\ &\quad \oplus((K_0 \oplus K_1 \oplus K_2 \oplus K_3 \oplus S1) \gg 24)] \oplus 0x02000000 \ , \end{aligned}$$

the constants at the end are given in hexadecimal numbers. Then the FSRs are loaded

$$\begin{aligned} a_0 &= K_0 \oplus S1 & b_3 &= IV_1 \\ a_1 &= K_3 & b_4 &= K_0 \oplus S1 \oplus S2 \\ a_2 &= K_2 & b_5 &= K_1 \oplus S2 \\ a_3 &= K_1 & b_6 &= IV_2 \\ a_4 &= K_0 & b_7 &= IV_3 \\ b_0 &= K_0 \oplus K_2 \oplus S1 \oplus S2 & b_8 &= K_0 \oplus K_1 \oplus K_2 \oplus K_3 \oplus S1 \\ b_1 &= K_1 \oplus K_3 \oplus S2 & b_9 &= K_0 \oplus K_1 \oplus S1 \\ b_2 &= IV_0 & b_{10} &= K_0 \oplus K_1 \oplus K_2 \oplus S1 \ . \end{aligned}$$

The four memory words of the NLF are initialized with zero. Then, during the initialization the cipher is clocked 24 times doing

1. get the output from the NLF (z_t^H, z_t^L),
2. update the NLF,
3. update FSR-A with z_t^L is xored to the new word of FSR-A,
4. update FSR-B with z_t^H is xored to the new word of FSR-B.

After this initialization, the K2 cipher produces the keystream and the FSRs are updated without feedback from the NLF.

For the rest of the paper, we consider a simplified version of K2 where all additions modulo 2^{32} are replaced with xor and denote this version with K2$^{\oplus}$.

In our attacks, we only need to compute equations similar to the equations computed for the keystream and the update of the FSRs. In each clock of K2$^{\oplus}$, four such equations are computed (two equations for the keystream and two equations for the FSRs update). We measure the time complexity for our attacks in K2$^{\oplus}$ clocks.

3 Differential Chosen IV Attack with Key Recovery

Considering a differential chosen IV scenario, we choose two different IVs IV_a and IV_b. We know the keystream from both pairs (K, IV_a) and (K, IV_b) with unknown key K. Both IVs only differ in IV word IV_1 which takes the longest until it enters the NLF. The dynamic feedback controller always takes the most and second most significant bit of a_2. Thus, we do not want to have a difference there. Accordingly, we choose the starting difference Δd with most and second most significant bit equal to zero. Our goal is to recover the whole internal state right after the loading step which means we get the unknown key K.

From the differences in the keystream and the partially known differences in the FSRs, we compute the differences in the words of the NLF. We then need to know how the differences in the NLF words propagate through the Sub function. Let v_a^{t-1} and v_b^{t-1} be two arbitrary words at time $t-1$ with the following equations

$$\Delta v^{t-1} = v_a^{t-1} \oplus v_b^{t-1}, \qquad w_a^t = Sub(v_a^{t-1}), \qquad w_b^t = Sub(v_b^{t-1}),$$
$$\Delta w^t = w_a^t \oplus w_b^t = Sub(v_a^{t-1}) \oplus Sub(v_b^{t-1}) \; .$$

We define a new notation

$$\overset{\text{out}}{\Delta} Sub(\Delta v^{t-1}) \overset{\text{def.}}{=} Sub(v_a^{t-1}) \oplus Sub(v_b^{t-1}) \; .$$

During the keystream generation, we have the following equations for the differences at clock t

$$\Delta z_t^H = \Delta b_{10}^t \oplus \Delta L1^t \oplus \Delta L2^t \oplus \Delta a_0^t \qquad \Delta z_t^L = \Delta b_0^t \oplus \Delta R1^t \oplus \Delta R2^t \oplus \Delta a_4^t$$
$$\Delta L1^t = \overset{\text{out}}{\Delta} Sub\left(\Delta R2^{t-1} \oplus \Delta b_4^{t-1}\right) \qquad \Delta R1^t = \overset{\text{out}}{\Delta} Sub\left(\Delta L2^{t-1} \oplus \Delta b_9^{t-1}\right)$$
$$\Delta L2^t = \overset{\text{out}}{\Delta} Sub\left(\Delta L1^{t-1}\right) \qquad \Delta R2^t = \overset{\text{out}}{\Delta} Sub\left(\Delta R1^{t-1}\right) \; .$$

Any fixed input difference $(\Delta R2^{t-1} \oplus \Delta b_4^{t-1}) \neq 0$ results in nearly 2^{28} possible output differences $\Delta L1^t$, because any input difference in the small 8-bit AES S-box results in 127 different output differences. If we know or fix the input-output difference of Sub at clock $t-1$ and t meaning $(\Delta R2^{t-1} \oplus \Delta b_4^{t-1}) \xrightarrow{Sub} \Delta L1^t$, we can recover on average $(2 \cdot \frac{126}{127} + 4 \cdot \frac{1}{127})^4 = 16.51$ sorted pairs of individual values for Sub. This means that we have $\frac{16.51}{2} \approx 8$ possible values for $\Delta L2^{t+1}$. If we know or fix this difference as well, then we have only one sorted pair of individual values left which satisfies the sequence $(\Delta R2^{t-1} \oplus \Delta b_4^{t-1}) \xrightarrow{Sub} \Delta L1^t \xrightarrow{Sub} \Delta L2^{t+1}$.

The same holds for the sequence $(\Delta L2^{t-1} \oplus \Delta b_9^{t-1}) \xrightarrow{Sub} \Delta R1^t \xrightarrow{Sub} \Delta R2^{t+1}$. If we have collected enough individual values for the NLF, we can derive some words for the FSR-B from the update equations $L1^t = Sub(R2^{t-1} \oplus b_4^{t-1})$ and $R1^t = Sub(L2^{t-1} \oplus b_9^{t-1})$ of the NLF. The insertion of the individual values of the NLF together with some words of FSR-B in the keystream equations yields some words for FSR-A. At the end, we know enough words of the NLF, FSR-B and FSR-A to clock backwards and reveal the secrect key.

We reduce the number of initialization clocks of $K2^{\oplus}$ to 5. After these 5 clocks of initialization, the starting difference Δd enters the word $R1$ of the NLF. During the keystream computation, there is no more feedback from the NLF to the FSRs anymore. Therefore, we know all differences of FSR-A as Δd enters it in clock 4 and then propagates linearly. For FSR-B, the computation of the differences only depends on the unknown bits of the dynamic feedback controller which select the multipliers for the FSR-B feedback.

The work flow of K2 has two steps, first displaying the keystream words, then updating the internal state. Thus, the differences of the keystream words for clock 0 are

$$
\begin{aligned}
\Delta z_0^H &= \Delta b_{10}^0 \oplus \Delta L1^0 \oplus \Delta L2^0 \oplus \Delta a_0^0 \\
\Delta z_0^L &= \Delta b_0^0 \oplus \Delta R1^0 \oplus \Delta R2^0 \oplus \Delta a_4^0 \ ,
\end{aligned}
$$

where the differences in $\Delta L1^0, \Delta L2^0, \Delta a_0^0, \Delta b_0^0, \Delta R2^0$ are zero and $\Delta a_4^0 = \Delta d$. Hence, we know Δb_{10}^0 and $\Delta R1^0$. The update equation of FSR-B implies $\Delta b_{10}^0 = \Delta b_{10}^{-1} = \Delta b_9^0$ and $\Delta b_{10}^0 = \Delta b_9^1$. With $\Delta R1^0$, we know the input-output sequence $(\Delta L2^{-1} \oplus \Delta b_9^{-1}) \xrightarrow{Sub} R1^0$ and as explained above on average we can recover 16.51 sorted pairs of individual values for Sub resulting in 8 possible values for $R2^1$.

Clock 1 gives us $\Delta z_1^H = \Delta b_{10}^1 = \Delta b_9^2$ because all other differences are zero. For Δz_1^L, we can rewrite the keystream equation in the following way

$$
\begin{aligned}
& & \Delta z_1^L &= \Delta b_0^1 \oplus \Delta R1^1 \oplus \Delta R2^1 \oplus \Delta a_4^1 \\
\Leftrightarrow & & \Delta R1^1 &= \Delta R2^1 \oplus \Delta b_0^1 \oplus \Delta a_4^1 \oplus \Delta z_1^L \\
\Leftrightarrow & & \overset{\text{out}}{\Delta}\, Sub(\Delta L2^0 \oplus \Delta b_9^0) &= \Delta R2^1 \oplus \Delta b_0^1 \oplus \Delta a_4^1 \oplus \Delta z_1^L \ ,
\end{aligned}
$$

that we know all differences at the right side. Here we can insert all 8 possibilities of $\Delta R2^1$, then undo the Mix Column operation by multiplying with its inverse and check byte by byte whether the computed value on the right side is a valid difference for the left side. The time complexity for this check is 2 clocks and only one pair $(\Delta R1^1, \Delta R2^1)$ will remain due to $\frac{2^{28} \cdot 8}{2^{32}} < 1$. The known difference $\Delta R2^1$ leaves only one sorted pair which fulfills the sequence

$(\Delta L2^{-1} \oplus \Delta b_9^{-1}) \xrightarrow{Sub} \Delta R1^0 \xrightarrow{Sub} \Delta R2^1$. The known difference $\Delta R1^1$ fixes the sequence $(\Delta L2^0 \oplus \Delta b_9^0) \xrightarrow{Sub} \Delta R1^1$ which results in nearly 16.51 sorted pairs of individual values following 8 possible differences for $R2^2$.

In clock 2, Δb_{10}^2 has two possibilities because in its update equation

$$\Delta b_{10}^2 = (\alpha_1^{cl1_1} + \alpha_2^{1-cl1_1-1})\Delta b_0^1 \oplus \Delta b_1^1 \oplus \Delta b_6^1 \oplus \alpha_3^{cl2_1} \Delta b_8^1$$

all differences are equal to zero except for Δb_8^1. Hence, we have $\Delta b_{10}^2 = \Delta b_8^1$ or $\Delta b_{10}^2 = \alpha_3 \Delta b_8^1$ because we have a zero in the msb of $\Delta a_2^1 = \Delta d$. We can rewrite the keystream equation in the following way

$$\begin{aligned} \Delta z_2^H &= \Delta b_{10}^2 \oplus \Delta L1^2 \oplus \Delta L2^2 \oplus \Delta a_0^2 \\ \Leftrightarrow \quad \Delta L1^2 &= \Delta b_{10}^2 \oplus \Delta L2^2 \oplus \Delta a_0^2 \oplus \Delta z_2^H \\ \Leftrightarrow \quad \overset{\text{out}}{\Delta}\, Sub(\Delta R2^1 \oplus \Delta b_4^1) &= \Delta b_{10}^2 \oplus \Delta L2^2 \oplus \Delta a_0^2 \oplus \Delta z_2^H \ , \end{aligned}$$

that we know all differences at the right side. We insert both possibilities for Δb_{10}^2, undo the Mix Column operation and check byte by byte whether the computed value on the right side is a valid difference for the left side. The time complexity for this check is $\frac{1}{2}$ clock and only one pair $(\Delta b_{10}^2, \Delta L1^2)$ will remain. We know $\Delta b_{10}^2 = \Delta b_9^3$ and $\Delta L1^2$ fixes the sequence $(\Delta R2^1 \oplus \Delta b_4^1) \xrightarrow{Sub} \Delta L1^2$ which results in nearly 16.51 sorted pairs of individual values following 8 possibilities for $\Delta L2^3$. For Δz_2^L, we do exactly the same as described for Δz_1^L at clock 1.

For clock 3, we have two possibilities for Δb_{10}^3 and 8 possibilities for $\Delta L2^3$. Thus, we rewrite the equation

$$\begin{aligned} \Delta z_3^H &= \Delta b_{10}^3 \oplus \Delta L1^3 \oplus \Delta L2^3 \oplus \Delta a_0^3 \\ \Leftrightarrow \quad \overset{\text{out}}{\Delta}\, Sub(\Delta R2^2 \oplus \Delta b_4^2) &= \Delta b_{10}^3 \oplus \Delta L2^3 \oplus \Delta a_0^3 \oplus \Delta z_3^H \ , \end{aligned}$$

insert all listed possibilities, undo the Mix Column operation and check byte by byte. The time complexity for this check is 4 clocks and only one triple $(\Delta b_{10}^3, \Delta L1^3, \Delta L2^3)$ will remain due to $\frac{2^{28} \cdot 2 \cdot 8}{2^{32}} = 1$. We know $\Delta b_{10}^3 = \Delta b_9^4$ and $\Delta L1^3$ fixes the sequence $(\Delta R2^2 \oplus \Delta b_4^2) \xrightarrow{Sub} \Delta L1^3$ which results in 8 possibilities for $\Delta L2^4$. The known difference $\Delta L2^3$ fixes the pair of individual values for the sequence $(\Delta R2^1 \oplus \Delta b_4^1) \xrightarrow{Sub} \Delta L1^2 \xrightarrow{Sub} \Delta L2^3$. For Δz_3^L, we do exactly the same as described for Δz_1^L at clock 1.

In clock 4, 5 and 6 we do exactly the same as described for clock 3.

Now we have collected enough individual values for the NLF. So far, the time complexity is $2 + \frac{1}{2} + 2 + 4 \cdot 4 = 20.5$ clocks.

We have to insert these individual values in the keystream and update equations. Since we collected 10 sorted pairs of individual values and two keystreams with the corresponding system of equations, we need to decide for each value to be filled in into which equation system. Wrong allocations will have contradictions somewhere in the equations and are dispelled this way. This would result a time complexity of 2^8 clocks. For the right allocation at clock 6, we can clock backwards and receive the secret key with time complexity of 6 clocks.

The overall time complexity in $K2^{\oplus}$ clocks is

$$20.5 + 2^8 + 6 = 2^{8.1} \ .$$

The needed keystream amounts to 2 words per clock for 7 clocks for each pair (K, IV_a) and (K, IV_b) which yields 28 keystream words. The memory requirements are negligible.

4 Distinguishing Attack

We now consider $K2^{\oplus}$ with the number of initialization clocks reduced to 7. To distinguish the cipher from a random function, we build a multiset over all possible 2^{32} values of one word using 2^{32} different key-IV-pairs and check whether the xored sum over all first keystream words z_0^H is equal to zero. For a random function the probability is 2^{-32} that this sum is zero.

For all 2^{32} key-IV-pairs, we take the same unknown key. The four words of the $IV = [IV_0, IV_1, IV_2, IV_3]$ are loaded in the FSR-B; where the word IV_1 loaded in b_3 takes the longest time until it enters the nonlinear function. For this word IV_1, we make a multiset in a way that all values $[0, 2^{32} - 1]$ occur exactly once. We emphasize that we need the multiset in ascending order starting with zero. Then we know that all IV_1 values in the first half have msb equal to zero whereas all IV_1 values in the second half have msb equal to one. We will use this fact about the msb later. The multiset in IV_1 yields 2^{32} different IVs $IV^i = [IV_0, i, IV_2, IV_3]$, $i = 0, \ldots, 2^{32} - 1$ with arbitrary words $IV_{(0,2,3)}$. For each pair (key, IV^i), we run the $K2^{\oplus}$ cipher with 7 initialization clocks and get the first keystream word ${}^i z_0^H$.

Now we explain why the xored sum over all keystream words is equal to zero. Our goal is to prove the multiset propagation through $K2^{\oplus}$ as shown in Table 1. In this table, we only show the multiset and its behavior. All values which are the same in all 2^{32} key-IV-pairs are omitted (empty in the table). We put the '?' for those sets we do not know anything about. With the symbol 'M^s', we denote the multiset in the starting order. The symbols 'M^1', 'M^2' and 'M^3' denote different multisets. In each of them, each value $[0, 2^{32} - 1]$ occurs exactly once, but we do not know in which order. Thus, also the xored sums over these multisets are zero. The symbol 'S0' denotes a multiset, where the characteristic that each value $[0, 2^{32} - 1]$ occurs exactly once is lost, but the feature that it sums up (xored) to zero still remains. To prove this feature for the 'S0' multisets, it is sufficient to consider the sets in b_{10}^t. We will check them in reverse order. The update equation for the xored sum over all ${}^i b_{10}^t$ is

$$\sum_{i=0}^{2^{32}-1} {}^i b_{10}^t = \sum_{i=0}^{2^{32}-1} \Big({}^i m_{msb}^{t-1}\, {}^i b_8^{t-1} \oplus {}^i b_6^{t-1} \oplus {}^i b_1^{t-1} \oplus {}^i m_{smsb}^{t-1}\, {}^i b_0^{t-1} \oplus {}^i b_{10}^{t-1} \oplus {}^i L2^{t-1} \oplus {}^i L1^{t-1} \oplus {}^i a_0^{t-1} \Big) \ . \qquad (1)$$

Here, the variable ${}^i m_{msb}^{t-1}$ denotes the multiplier depending on the msb of ${}^i a_2^{t-1}$. In particular, ${}^i m_{msb}^{t-1} = \alpha_3$ if the msb of ${}^i a_2^{t-1}$ is equal to one and ${}^i m_{msb}^{t-1} = 1$ if msb=0. Likewise, the variable ${}^{i}m^{t-1}_{smsb}$ denotes the multiplier depending on the second most significant bit of ${}^{i}a^{t-1}_{2}$. In particular, ${}^{i}m^{t-1}_{smsb} = \alpha_1$ if the second most significant bit of ${}^{i}a^{t-1}_{2}$ is equal to one and ${}^{i}m^{t-1}_{smsb} = \alpha_2$ otherwise.

Table 1. Propagation of the multiset through K2$^{\oplus}$ during Initialization

clock	FSR-B											FSR-A					NLF			
ini	10	9	8	7	6	5	4	3	2	1	0	4	3	2	1	0	L1	L2	R1	R2
0								M^s												
1									M^s											
2										M^s										
3	M^s										M^s									
4	S0	M^s										M^s								
5	S0	S0	M^s									M^s	M^s						M^1	
6	S0	S0	S0	M^s								S0	M^s	M^s					?	M^2
7	S0	S0	S0	S0	M^s							?	S0	M^s	M^s		M^3		?	?

From now on, we mean always xored sum when we write sum or the sigma sign. The keystream is produced at clock zero after the initialization. For the internal states, we write the number of the initialization clock as superscript, because we need to go backwards through the initialization clocks to prove the multiset propagation. We know about the sum of all words ${}^{i}z^{H}_{0}$

$$\sum_{i=0}^{2^{32}-1} {}^{i}z^{H}_{0} = \sum_{i=0}^{2^{32}-1} \left({}^{i}b^{7}_{10} \oplus {}^{i}L2^{7} \oplus {}^{i}L1^{7} \oplus {}^{i}a^{7}_{0} \right) .$$

For all 2^{32} key-IV-pairs, the values for $L2^7$ and a^7_0 remain constant for all pairs meaning the sum over them is zero. The values ${}^{i}L1^{7}$ form a multiset in which each value $[0, 2^{32}-1]$ occurs exactly once, but in an unknown order. The *Sub* function preserves this property that each value $[0, 2^{32}-1]$ occurs exactly once, but destroys the known starting order. Thus we have

$$\sum_{i=0}^{2^{32}-1} {}^{i}z^{H}_{0} = \sum_{i=0}^{2^{32}-1} {}^{i}b^{7}_{10} . \tag{2}$$

Now we will prove that the sum over all ${}^{i}b^{7}_{10}$ is zero. We look up the values for (1) at clock 7 in Table 1 and see which values remain constant meaning the sum over them is zero. We omit those zero sums and get (1) for clock 7

$$\sum_{i=0}^{2^{32}-1} {}^{i}b^{7}_{10} = \sum_{i=0}^{2^{32}-1} {}^{i}m^{6}_{msb}\, {}^{i}b^{6}_{8} \oplus \sum_{i=0}^{2^{32}-1} {}^{i}m^{6}_{smsb}\, {}^{i}b^{6}_{0} \oplus \sum_{i=0}^{2^{32}-1} {}^{i}b^{6}_{10} . \tag{3}$$

We take a closer look on the sum over ${}^{i}b^{6}_{10}$. After omitting all zero sums (empty values in Table 1), (1) is

$$\sum_{i=0}^{2^{32}-1} {}^{i}b^{6}_{10} = \sum_{i=0}^{2^{32}-1} {}^{i}m^{5}_{msb}\, {}^{i}b^{5}_{8} \oplus \sum_{i=0}^{2^{32}-1} {}^{i}m^{5}_{smsb}\, {}^{i}b^{5}_{0} \oplus \sum_{i=0}^{2^{32}-1} {}^{i}b^{5}_{10} .$$

The choice for the multipliers depends on the value of a_2^5 which remains constant. Thus, we do not know which multiplier is chosen but we know it is the same for all 2^{32} key-IV-pairs. The values for b_0^5 remain constant meaning the sum is zero. Therefore, our equation reduces to

$$\begin{aligned}\sum_{i=0}^{2^{32}-1} {}^ib_{10}^6 &= m_{msb}^5 \sum_{i=0}^{2^{32}-1} {}^ib_8^5 \oplus \sum_{i=0}^{2^{32}-1} {}^ib_{10}^5 \\ &= m_{msb}^5 \sum_{i=0}^{2^{32}-1} {}^ib_{10}^3 \oplus \sum_{i=0}^{2^{32}-1} {}^ib_{10}^5 \ .\end{aligned} \tag{4}$$

For the sum over all ${}^ib_{10}^5$, (1) reduces to

$$\sum_{i=0}^{2^{32}-1} {}^ib_{10}^5 = \sum_{i=0}^{2^{32}-1} {}^ib_{10}^4 \tag{5}$$

because the choice for the multipliers is constant due to the constant value of a_2^4. For clock 4, the choice for the multipliers in (1) is constant as well yielding

$$\sum_{i=0}^{2^{32}-1} {}^ib_{10}^4 = m_{smsb}^3 \sum_{i=0}^{2^{32}-1} {}^ib_0^3 \oplus \sum_{i=0}^{2^{32}-1} {}^ib_{10}^3 \ . \tag{6}$$

With the constant choice for the multipliers at clock 3, (1) reduces to

$$\sum_{i=0}^{2^{32}-1} {}^ib_{10}^3 = \sum_{i=0}^{2^{32}-1} {}^ib_1^2 \ . \tag{7}$$

Now we take (5), (6) and (7) and include them in (4) which yields

$$\begin{aligned}\sum_{i=0}^{2^{32}-1} {}^ib_{10}^6 &= m_{msb}^5 \sum_{i=0}^{2^{32}-1} {}^ib_1^2 \oplus m_{smsb}^3 \sum_{i=0}^{2^{32}-1} {}^ib_0^3 \oplus \sum_{i=0}^{2^{32}-1} {}^ib_1^2 \\ &= m_{msb}^5 \sum_{i=0}^{2^{32}-1} {}^ib_3^0 \oplus m_{smsb}^3 \sum_{i=0}^{2^{32}-1} {}^ib_3^0 \oplus \sum_{i=0}^{2^{32}-1} {}^ib_3^0 \\ &= m_{msb}^5 \sum_{i=0}^{2^{32}-1} i \oplus m_{smsb}^3 \sum_{i=0}^{2^{32}-1} i \oplus \sum_{i=0}^{2^{32}-1} i \ = \ 0 \ .\end{aligned} \tag{8}$$

Here, we can directly see our multiset and know that the sum is zero.

Equation (3) now has only two summands left both depending on the value of a_2^6. From the update equation for $a_2^6 = a_4^4$, we know

$$\sum_{i=0}^{2^{32}-1} {}^ia_4^4 = \sum_{i=0}^{2^{32}-1} \left({}^ia_3^3 \oplus \alpha_0 {}^ia_0^3 \oplus {}^ib_0^3 \oplus {}^iR2^3 \oplus {}^iR1^3 \oplus {}^ia_4^3 \right) \ .$$

The values for a_3^3, a_0^3, $R2^3$, $R1^3$ and a_4^3 remain constant for all pairs. We denote the sum of them with $C = a_3^3 \oplus \alpha_0 a_0^3 \oplus R2^3 \oplus R1^3 \oplus a_4^3$ which does not depend on i and is unknown to us. With this simplification, we obtain

$$\sum_{i=0}^{2^{32}-1} {}^i a_4^4 = \sum_{i=0}^{2^{32}-1} \left({}^i b_0^3 \oplus C \right) = \sum_{i=0}^{2^{32}-1} \left(i \oplus C \right) . \tag{9}$$

As a result of the multiset, we know that in each bit of i the number of ones and zeros occurring is exactly 2^{31} which is an even number. This means that the second most significant bit of a_4^4 has 2^{31} ones and 2^{31} zeros. Taking this and the fact that the value of b_0^6 remains constant, we obtain for the second summand of (3)

$$\sum_{i=0}^{2^{32}-1} {}^i m_{smsb}^6 \, {}^i b_0^6 = \sum_{i=0}^{2^{31}-1} \alpha_1 b_0^6 \oplus \sum_{i=0}^{2^{31}-1} \alpha_2 b_0^6 = 0 . \tag{10}$$

Altogether (3) simplifies with (8) and (10) to

$$\sum_{i=0}^{2^{32}-1} {}^i b_{10}^7 = \sum_{i=0}^{2^{32}-1} {}^i m_{msb}^6 \, {}^i b_8^6 = \sum_{i=0}^{2^{32}-1} {}^i m_{msb}^6 \, {}^i b_{10}^4 \tag{11}$$

where the choice of the multiplier depends on the msb of the value $a_2^6 = a_4^4$ and the value of b_{10}^4 does not remain constant. We emphasized at the beginning the ascending order of our multiset. This means that the first half of our multiset has msb zero and the second half has msb one. Accordingly, the msb of all ${}^i a_4^4$ with $i = 0, \ldots, 2^{31} - 1$ is the msb of unknown constant C, see (9), whereas the msb of all ${}^i a_4^4$ with $i = 2^{31}, \ldots, 2^{32} - 1$ is the opposite of the msb of unknown constant C. Thus, we divided the sum into a first and a second half. We need to check whether we can also divide the set of ${}^i b_{10}^4$. From (6) with (7) we know

$$\sum_{i=0}^{2^{32}-1} {}^i b_{10}^4 = m_{smsb}^3 \sum_{i=0}^{2^{32}-1} {}^i b_0^3 \oplus \sum_{i=0}^{2^{32}-1} {}^i b_1^2 = m_{smsb}^3 \sum_{i=0}^{2^{32}-1} i \oplus \sum_{i=0}^{2^{32}-1} i .$$

The choice of the multipliers is constant but unknown to us. We can divide both sums into a first and a second half.

Now with the two possibilities of the msb of a_4^4 (first half zero and second half one, or the other way around), for (11) we can compute two values

$$X_1 = \left(m_{smsb}^3 \sum_{i=0}^{2^{31}-1} i \oplus \sum_{i=0}^{2^{31}-1} i \right) \oplus \alpha_3 \left(m_{smsb}^3 \sum_{i=2^{31}}^{2^{32}-1} i \oplus \sum_{i=2^{31}}^{2^{32}-1} i \right)$$

$$X_2 = \alpha_3 \left(m_{smsb}^3 \sum_{i=0}^{2^{31}-1} i \oplus \sum_{i=0}^{2^{31}-1} i \right) \oplus \left(m_{smsb}^3 \sum_{i=2^{31}}^{2^{32}-1} i \oplus \sum_{i=2^{31}}^{2^{32}-1} i \right) .$$

For the sums over exactly one ordered half of the multiset the property of summing up to zero is preserved. Accordingly, the values X_1 and X_2 are both zero.

Thus, we have proven the assumed multiset propagation through $K2^{\oplus}$ which results in

$$\sum_{i=0}^{2^{32}-1} {}^{i}z_0^H = \sum_{i=0}^{2^{32}-1} {}^{i}b_{10}^7 = 0 \ .$$

We have shown that we can distinguish the $K2^{\oplus}$ from a random function with probability $1 - 2^{-32}$. The time complexity is $2^{32} \cdot 7 \approx 2^{34.8}$ clocks of $K2^{\oplus}$. We need the first keystream word for all 2^{32} pairs (key, IV^i) with $(i = 0, \ldots, 2^{32}-1)$. The memory requirements are negligible.

5 Conclusions

We have shown a differential chosen IV attack with key recovery on $K2^{\oplus}$ with 5 initialization clocks. The complexity for this attack is $2^{8.1}$ clocks of $K2^{\oplus}$ with needed keystream of 28 words and negligible memory requirements. The extension of this attack to 6 or 7 initialization clocks is the topic of ongoing research.

A distinguishing attack on $K2^{\oplus}$ with 7 initialization clocks is also presented. With a multiset and its predictable propagation through these 7 clocks, we can distinguish $K2^{\oplus}$ from a random function with probability $1 - 2^{-32}$. The complexity for this attack is $2^{34.8}$ clocks of $K2^{\oplus}$ with needed keystream of 2^{32} words and negligible memory requirements. We can not extend this attack to 8 initialization clocks because in $L1^8$ we will get a set we do not know anything about and therefore resulting in a random sum.

Acknowledgements. I would like to thank Alex Biryukov and Ralf-Philipp Weinmann for helpful comments.

References

1. Bogdanov, A., Preneel, B., Rijmen, V.: Security Evaluation of the K2 Stream Cipher (March 2011), `http://www.cryptrec.go.jp/estimation/techrep_id2010_2.pdf`
2. Daemen, J., Rijmen, V.: The Design of Rijndael: AES - The Advanced Encryption Standard. Springer, Heidelberg (2002)
3. Henricksen, M., Yap, W.S., Yian, C.H., Kiyomoto, S., Tanaka, T.: Side-Channel Analysis of the K2 Stream Cipher. In: Steinfeld, R., Hawkes, P. (eds.) ACISP 2010. LNCS, vol. 6168, pp. 53–73. Springer, Heidelberg (2010)
4. Kiyomoto, S., Tanaka, T., Sakurai, K.: K2: A stream cipher algorithm using dynamic feedback control. In: Hernando, J., Fernández-Medina, E., Malek, M. (eds.) SECRYPT, pp. 204–213. INSTICC Press (2007)

Model Selection in Logistic Regression Using p-Values and Greedy Search

Jan Mielniczuk[1,2] and Paweł Teisseyre[1,*]

[1] Institute of Computer Science, Polish Academy of Sciences,
Ordona 21, 01–237 Warsaw, Poland
{miel,teisseyrep}@ipipan.waw.pl

[2] Warsaw University of Technology, Faculty of Mathematics and Information Science,
Politechniki Sq. 1, 00–601 Warsaw, Poland

Abstract. We study new logistic model selection criteria based on p-values. The rules are proved to be consistent provided suitable assumptions on design matrix and scaling constants are satisfied and the search is performed over the family of all submodels. Moreover, we investigate practical performance of the introduced criteria in conjunction with greedy search methods such as initial ordering, forward and backward search and genetic algorithm which restrict the range of family of models over which an optimal value of the respective criterion is sought. Scaled minimal p-value criterion with initial ordering turns out to be a promising alternative to BIC.

Keywords: logistic regression, model selection, greedy search methods, p-values.

1 Introduction

Model selection and properties of ensuing postmodel selection estimators is one of the central subjects in theoretical statistics and its applications. In particular, variable selection in regression models with dichotomous response e.g. a logistic models is widely used (cf. e.g. [6]). In the paper we focus on the first from the two main related problems of statistical modelling which are explanation (i.e. finding an adequate model) and prediction. The present paper provides some insights into behaviour of logistic model selection criteria based on p-values. In this approach introduced for parametric families of densities by Pokarowski and Mielniczuk ([9]) competing models are viewed as alternative hypotheses with null hypothesis being the minimal model and choosing the model for which appropriately scaled p-value of LRT test statistic is the smallest one. In the paper we investigate basic property of such rules concerning identification of the true model namely their consistency which means that probability of choosing a minimal true model tends to 1. Moreover, we focus on the situation when the number of potential regressors is large and only search of an optimal model over a restricted

* Corresponding author.

P. Bouvry et al. (Eds.): SIIS 2011, LNCS 7053, pp. 128–141, 2012.

family of submodels feasible. That is, we investigate in numerical experiments the performance of the considered criteria coupled with greedy search methods such as initial ordering, forward and backward search and genetic algorithm. We provide some evidence that a scaled minimal p-value criterion introduced in Section 2 in conjunction with forward search compares favourably with Bayesian Information Criterion.

2 Logistic Regression Model and Model Selection Criteria

2.1 Logistic Regression Model

Let $y_1, \ldots, y_n$ be a sequence of independent random variables such that y_i has Bernoulli distribution $P(y_i = 1) = 1 - P(y_i = 0) = \pi_i$. Let $\mathbf{x}_1', \ldots, \mathbf{x}_n'$ be a sequence of associated covariates, $\mathbf{x}_i = (x_{i,1}, \ldots, x_{i,M})'$ with $\mathbf{x}'$ denote a transpose of $\mathbf{x}$. Suppose that the expectations of response variables are related to explanatory variables by the logistic model

$$\pi_i(\boldsymbol{\beta}) = \frac{\exp(\mathbf{x}_i'\boldsymbol{\beta})}{1 + \exp(\mathbf{x}_i'\boldsymbol{\beta})}. \tag{1}$$

Vector $\boldsymbol{\beta} = (\beta_1, \ldots, \beta_M)'$ is an unknown vector of parameters. Denote $\mathbf{Y}_n = (y_1, \ldots, y_n)'$ as the response vector and $\mathbf{X}_n = (\mathbf{x}_1, \ldots, \mathbf{x}_n)'$ as the design matrix. The conditional log-likelihood function for the parameter $\boldsymbol{\beta}$ is

$$l(\boldsymbol{\beta}, \mathbf{Y}_n|\mathbf{X}_n) = \sum_{i=1}^{n} \{y_i \log[\pi_i(\boldsymbol{\beta})] + (1 - y_i) \log[1 - \pi_i(\boldsymbol{\beta})]\}. \tag{2}$$

The maximum likelihood estimator (MLE) is $\hat{\boldsymbol{\beta}} = \arg\max_{\boldsymbol{\beta} \in \mathbf{R}^M} l(\boldsymbol{\beta}, \mathbf{Y}_n|\mathbf{X}_n)$. Let $\Pi(\boldsymbol{\beta}) = \text{diag}\{\pi_1(\boldsymbol{\beta})(1 - \pi_1(\boldsymbol{\beta})), \ldots, \pi_n(\boldsymbol{\beta})(1 - \pi_n(\boldsymbol{\beta}))\}$. A useful quantity is the Fisher information matrix for the parameter $\boldsymbol{\beta}$ which is defined as

$$\mathbf{I}_n(\boldsymbol{\beta}) = -\mathbf{E}\frac{\partial^2 l(\boldsymbol{\beta}, \mathbf{Y}_n|\mathbf{X}_n)}{\partial\boldsymbol{\beta}\partial\boldsymbol{\beta}'} = -\frac{\partial^2 l(\boldsymbol{\beta}, \mathbf{Y}_n|\mathbf{X}_n)}{\partial\boldsymbol{\beta}\partial\boldsymbol{\beta}'} = \mathbf{X}_n'\Pi(\boldsymbol{\beta})\mathbf{X}_n.$$

Define also the score function $s_n(\boldsymbol{\beta}) = \frac{\partial l(\boldsymbol{\beta}, \mathbf{Y}_n|\mathbf{X}_n)}{\partial\boldsymbol{\beta}}$.

Suppose now that some covariates do not contribute to the prediction of expectation of $\mathbf{Y}$ in a sense that the corresponding coefficients are zero. It is assumed that the true model is a submodel of (1). As any submodel of (1) containing p_j variables $(x_{i,j_1}, \ldots, x_{i,j_{p_j}})'$ is described by set of indexes $j = \{j_1, \ldots, j_{p_j}\}$ it will be referred to as model j. The minimal true model will be denoted by t. So p_t is the number of nonzero coefficients in equation (1). The empty model for which $P(y_i = 1) = 1 - P(y_i = 0) = \frac{1}{2}$ will be denoted briefly by 0 and the full model (1) by $f = \{1, \ldots, M\}$. Vector $\boldsymbol{\beta}_j$ of parameters for model j is augmented to $M \times 1$ vector in such a way that $\beta_k = 0$, for $k \notin j$. Let $\hat{\boldsymbol{\beta}}_j$ be a Maximum Likelihood Estimator (MLE) of $\boldsymbol{\beta}$ calculated for the model j also augmented by zeros to $M \times 1$ vector. We denote $\hat{\boldsymbol{\beta}}_f$, MLE in the full model, briefly by $\hat{\boldsymbol{\beta}}$. Let $\mathcal{M}$ be a family of all subsets of a set f.

2.2 Model Selection Criteria

The main objective is to identify the minimal true model t using data $(\mathbf{X}_n, \mathbf{Y}_n)$. Consider two models j and k such that the j model is nested within the model k. Denote by D^n_{jk} likelihood ratio test (LRT) statistic, based on conditional likelihoods given $\mathbf{X}_n$, for testing H_0 : model j is adequate against hypothesis H_1 : model k is adequate whereas j is not, equal to

$$D^n_{jk} = 2[l(\hat{\beta}_k, \mathbf{Y}_n|\mathbf{X}_n) - l(\hat{\beta}_j, \mathbf{Y}_n|\mathbf{X}_n)]. \tag{3}$$

Let F and G be univariate cumulative distribution functions and T be a test statistic which has distribution function G not necessarily equal to F. Let $p(t|F) = 1 - F(t)$. By p-value of a test statistic T given the reference distribution F (which will correspond to the approximate null distribution) we will mean $p(T|F)$. We consider p-values of statistic D^n_{jk} given chi square distribution with $p_k - p_j$ degrees of freedom in view of Fahrmeir (1987) ([4]) who established asymptotic distribution of D^n_{jk} for generalized linear model (cf. Theorem 1 for the logistic regression). In order to make notation simpler, $p(D^n_{jk}|\chi^2_{p_k - p_j})$ will be denoted as $p(D^n_{jk}|p_k - p_j)$. Deviance D^n_{jk} of the model k from the model j will be formally defined by (3) even if j is not nested within k.

We define the model selection criteria based on p-values of D^n_{jk} (cf [9]).

Minimal P-Value Criterion (mPVC)

$$M^n_m = \text{argmin}_{j \in \mathcal{M}} e^{p_j a_n} p(D^n_{0j}|p_j),$$

where $p(D^n_{00}|0) = e^{a_n}/\sqrt{n}$. Observe that when $a_n = 0$ then from among the pairs $\{(H_0, H_j)\}$ we choose a pair for which we are most inclined to reject H_0 and we select the model corresponding to the most convincing alternative hypothesis. If $a_n > 0$ the scaling factor $e^{p_j a_n}$ is interpreted as additional penalization for the complexity of a model. We will assume throughout that $a_n = O(\log(n))$.

Maximal P-Value Criterion (MPVC)

$$M^n_M = \text{argmax}_{j \in \mathcal{M}} e^{-p_j a_n} p(D^n_{jf}|M - p_j),$$

where $p(D^n_{ff}|0) = 1$, $a_n \to \infty$ and $a_n = O(\log(n))$. The motivation is similar as in the case of mPVC, namely we choose a model which we are least inclined to reject when compared to the full model f. We stress that the additional assumption $a_n \to \infty$ needed for consistency of MPVC is not required to prove consistency of mPVC.

Bayesian Information Criterion (BIC) is defined as

Bayesian Information Criterion (BIC)

$$BIC^n = \text{argmin}_{j \in \mathcal{M}}[-2l(\hat{\beta}_j, \mathbf{Y}_n|\mathbf{X}_n) + p_j \log(n)].$$

2.3 Model Selection Criteria Based on a Restricted Search

Selection rules given above require calculations for all members of $\mathcal{M}$ what for large number of possible regressors carries considerable and often enormous computational cost. In order to mend this drawback we consider the following methods whose aim is to restrict the family of models over which the optimal value of the criterion is sought. The restricted search can be applied for any of the criteria considered above. Assume temporarily that the minimum of the criterion is sought.

1. **Initial ordering (IO).** The covariates $\{j_1, j_2, \ldots, j_M\}$ are ordered with respect to the decreasing values of LRT statistics
$$D^n_{(f-\{j_1\})f} \geq D^n_{(f-\{j_2\})f} \geq \cdots \geq D^n_{(f-\{j_M\})f}.$$
Let $\mathcal{M}_{IO} = \{\{0\}, \{j_1\}, \{j_1, j_2\}, \ldots, \{j_1, j_2, \ldots, j_M\}\}$. The selection criteria with initial ordering $M^n_{m,IO}$, $M^n_{M,IO}$, BIC^n_{IO} are defined analogously as M^n_m, M^n_M, BIC^n. The optimization is now performed over set $\mathcal{M}_{IO}$.
2. **Forward selection (FS).**The procedure begins with the null model and at each stage adds the attribute that yields the greatest decrease in the given criterion function. The final model is obtained when none of the remaining variables leads to the decrease of the criterion.
3. **Backward elimination (BE).** A nested sequence of models of decreasing dimensionality beginning with the full model is constructed. At each step a variable is omitted that yields the greatest decrease in the criterion function. FS and BE are widely used techniques for model selection (see e.g. [7])
4. **Genetic algorithm (GA).** We used an algorithm proposed in [12] with the settings considered there. Each model, also called an individual, is described by a binary vector $\mathbf{z} = (z_1, \ldots, z_M)'$, where j^{th} gene $z_j = 1$ indicates that j^{th} variable is included in the model. Each generation consists of 40 individuals (models) . The initial population is randomly generated in such a way that $z_j = 1$ with probability 0.9. Instead of using fitness proportionate selection as in [12] we applied truncation selection (see e.g. in [8]) which performed better. Namely the two individuals with the smallest values of the given criterion function are selected as parents. To create the offspring two integer points are randomly selected from the interval $[0, M-1]$, and ordered so that $v_2 \geq v_1$. The offspring gets the first v_1 genes from the first parent, the next $v_2 - v_1$ genes from the second parent and the last $M - v_2$ genes again from the first parent. This procedure is repeated 40 times to match the size of the previous generation.The individuals of each generation are also mutated before model estimation. Each gene of each individual is flipped, from zero to one or vice versa, with probability 0.01. The procedure outlined above is repeated until convergence is achieved.

3 Consistency Properties of Introduced Criteria

We first state some properties of LRT statistic D^n_{jk}. They are necessary to prove the consistency of selection rules M^n_m and M^n_M introduced in the previous section. We discuss now some technical conditions imposed on the logistic model. We assume throughout that $\mathbf{X}_n'\mathbf{X}_n$ has full rank. This condition will ensure that the information matrix $\mathbf{I}_n(\boldsymbol{\beta})$ is positive definite for all $\boldsymbol{\beta} \in \mathbf{R}^M$ as $\Pi(\boldsymbol{\beta})$ is positive definite. Let $\lambda_{\min}$ ($\lambda_{\max}$) denote the smallest (the largest) eigenvalue of a symmetric matrix. Let $\mathbf{A}^{1/2}$ be a left square root of positive definite matrix $\mathbf{A}$, i.e. $\mathbf{A}^{1/2}(\mathbf{A}^{1/2})' = \mathbf{A}$. The right square root is defined as $\mathbf{A}^{T/2} = (\mathbf{A}^{1/2})'$. As a left square root one can take $\mathbf{Q}\Lambda^{1/2}\mathbf{Q}'$, where $\mathbf{Q}\Lambda\mathbf{Q}'$ is a spectral decomposition of $\mathbf{A}$ or the lower triangular matrix from Cholesky decomposition. $\mathbf{A}^{-1/2}$ will denote the inverse of $\mathbf{A}^{1/2}$. $W_n = O_P(1)$ means that the sequence of random variables is bounded in probability and $\xrightarrow{d}$ ($\xrightarrow{P}$) denotes convergence in distribution (in probability). The following conditions will be needed.

(A1) $\gamma n \leq \lambda_{\min}(\mathbf{I}_n(\boldsymbol{\beta}_t)) \leq \lambda_{\max}(\mathbf{I}_n(\boldsymbol{\beta}_t)) \leq \kappa n$ holds for some positive constants γ and κ.
(A2) $\max_{1\leq i\leq n} ||\mathbf{x}_i||^2 \log(n)/n \to 0$, as $n \to \infty$.

As $\log(n)/n$ is decreasing, condition (A2) is equivalent to $||\mathbf{x}_n||^2 \log(n)/n \to 0$. Define the sequence $N_n(\delta)$, $\delta > 0$, of neighborhoods of $\boldsymbol{\beta}_t$ as

$$N_n(\delta) = \{\boldsymbol{\beta} : ||\mathbf{I}_n(\boldsymbol{\beta}_t)^{T/2}(\boldsymbol{\beta} - \boldsymbol{\beta}_t)|| \leq \delta\}, \quad n = 1, 2, \ldots.$$

The following auxiliary condition is assumed for proving Theorem 1.

(F) For all $\delta > 0$,

$$\max_{\boldsymbol{\beta}\in N_n(\delta)} ||\mathbf{I}_n(\boldsymbol{\beta}_t)^{-1/2}\mathbf{I}_n(\boldsymbol{\beta})\mathbf{I}_n(\boldsymbol{\beta}_t)^{-T/2} - \mathbf{I}|| \to 0,$$

as $n \to \infty$.

The following Theorem (cf [4]) states the asymptotic result of LRT statistic D^n_{jk}.

Theorem 1. *Assume $\lambda_{\min}(\mathbf{I}_n(\boldsymbol{\beta}_t)) \to \infty$ as $n \to \infty$ and (F). Then $D^n_{jk} \xrightarrow{d} \chi^2_{p_k - p_j}$ as $n \to \infty$ provided that model j is true.*

Remark 1. *Assume* $\max_{1\leq i\leq n} ||\mathbf{x}_i||^2/n \to 0$*, as $n \to \infty$ and (A1). Then condition (F) holds. Namely letting $\delta_n^2 = \max_{1\leq i\leq n} \mathbf{x}_i'\mathbf{I}_n^{-1}(\boldsymbol{\beta}_t)\mathbf{x}_i$ and in view of (A1)-(A2)*

$$\delta_n^2 \leq \max_{1\leq i\leq n} ||\mathbf{x}_i||^2 \lambda_{\max}(\mathbf{I}_n^{-1}(\boldsymbol{\beta}_t)) \leq \frac{\max_{1\leq i\leq n} ||\mathbf{x}_i||^2}{n\gamma} \to 0.$$

It follows now from Corollary 2 in [5] that the convergence $\delta_n^2 \to 0$ implies (F).

In particular it follows from the above Remark that conditions (A1) and (A2) imply (F). Recall that $\boldsymbol{\beta}_t = (\beta_{t,1}, \ldots, \beta_{t,p_t})'$ is a vector of parameters for model t. Let $d_n^2 = \min\{[\max_{1\leq i\leq n} ||x_i||^2]^{-1}, [\min_k (1/2)\beta_{t,k}]^2\}$ and observe that $d_n^2 n/\log(n) \to \infty$ as $n \to \infty$. Below we state two propositions. The main idea here is to prove that under mild conditions on the design matrix certain properties of averaged deviance hold, which are weaker than its law of large numbers. However, these properties are sufficient for consistency of BIC and p-valued criteria which we prove in Theorem 2. Consider now two models w and c where the first model is a wrong one (i.e. it does not include at least one explanatory variable with corresponding coefficient not equal zero) and the second model is a correct model (although it is not necessarily the simplest one).

Proposition 1. *Under (A1), (A2)* $P(D^n_{wc} \geq \alpha_1 n d_n^2) \to 1$, *as* $n \to \infty$, *for some* $\alpha_1 > 0$.

Proposition 2. *Assume (F) and that for some* $\varepsilon > 0$ *and for some* $\alpha > 0$ $\max_{1\leq i\leq n} ||\mathbf{x}_i|| n^{-\varepsilon} \leq \alpha$, *as* $n \to \infty$. *Then* $n^{-(1+\varepsilon)} D^n_{0c} = O_P(1)$ *as* $n \to \infty$.

Note that the larger ε results in a weaker conclusion of the Proposition 2. In view of Remark 1, (A1) and (A2) imply assumptions of the 2 for $\varepsilon = 1/2$. Apart from the asymptotic results of LRT statistic the following approximation of $p(x|p_j)$ for $x \to \infty$ will be used. For $x > 0$ and $p \in \mathbf{N}$ define $C(x,p) = e^{-\frac{x}{2}} \left(\frac{x}{2}\right)^{\frac{p}{2}-1} \left[\Gamma\left(\frac{p}{2}\right)\right]^{-1}$ and $B(x,p) = C(x,p)\left[\frac{x}{x-(p-2)}\right]$.

Lemma 1. *If* $Z \sim \chi^2_p$ *then*

(i) for $p = 1$ *and* $x > 0$, $B(x,1) \leq P(Z > x) \leq C(x,1)$;
(ii) for $p > 1$ *and* $x > 0$, $C(x,p) \leq P(Z > x)$, *if* $p > 1$ *and* $x > p-2$, $P(Z > x) \leq B(x,p)$;
(iii) for $x \to \infty$ $P(Z > x) = C(x,p)[1 + O(x^{-1})]$.

The above Lemma is proved in [9].

Now we state consistency property of Bayesian Information Criterion and the introduced selectors M^n_m and M^n_M.

Theorem 2. *Under (A1), (A2) BIC ,* M^n_m *and* M^n_M *are consistent i.e.* $P(\hat{t} = t) \to 1$, *as* $n \to \infty$ *when* $\hat{t}$ *denotes any one of these selectors.*

The strong consistency of Bayesian Information Criterion is proved in [11] where assumption (A1) is also imposed. Condition (C.2) in [11] after taking into account (A1) can be restated as $\max_{1\leq i\leq n} ||\mathbf{x}_i||^2 \log\log(n)/n \to 0$ i.e. it is slightly weaker than our condition (A2). However, we avoid assuming any extra conditions, in particular condition (C.5) in [11], a certain technical condition which seems hard to verify. From the main result there follows consistency of the greedy counterparts of the method.

Corollary 1. *Under (A1), (A2)* BIC^n_{IO}, $M^n_{m,IO}$ *and* $M^n_{M,IO}$ *are consistent.*

In order to explain the main lines of reasoning we prove Theorem 1 in the case of BIC and Corollary 1 here. More technically involved proofs of the remaining part of Theorem 1 as well as proofs of auxiliary results are relegated to the Appendix.

Proof of Theorem 2 (BIC case). Consider the case $j \supset t$ i.e. model t is a proper subset of a model j. We have to show that

$$P[-2l(\hat{\boldsymbol{\beta}}_t, \mathbf{Y}_n|\mathbf{X}_n) + p_t \log(n) < -2l(\hat{\boldsymbol{\beta}}_j, \mathbf{Y}_n|\mathbf{X}_n) + p_j \log(n)] \to 1,$$

as $n \to \infty$ which is equivalent to $P[D^n_{jt} > \log(n)(p_t - p_j)] \to 1$ as $n \to \infty$. The last convergence follows from the fact that $D^n_{jt} = O_P(1)$ which is implied by Theorem 1. The convergence for $j \not\supset t$ follows directly from Proposition 1 and assumption $nd_n^2/\log(n) \to \infty$.

Proof of Corollary 1. Let j_c be an index corresponding to the variable in t and j_w an index corresponding to the variable which is not in t. Note that

$$P[D^n_{(f-\{j_c\})f} \geq D^n_{(f-\{j_w\})f}] \to 1$$

as $n \to \infty$ which follows from the fact that by Proposition 1 $D^n_{(f-\{j_c\})f} \to \infty$ in probability and by Theorem 1 $D^n_{(f-\{j_w\})f} = O_P(1)$. This implies the convergence $P(t \in M_{IO}) \to 1$ which in conjunction with Theorem 2 yields the consistency of a respective two-step rule with an initial ordering.

4 Numerical Experiments

In this section the finite-sample performance of the discussed variable selection procedures is investigated. We considered Bayesian Information Criterion (BIC) and two scaled p-value criteria with scalings which performed well in the simulations, namely minimal p-value criterion with $a_n = \log(n)/2$ (mPVC2)and maximal p-value criterion with the same a_n (MPVC2). Every of the three pertaining criteria was considered in conjunction with any of four search methods resulting in twelve final methods. Our objective is to study the impact of both a criterion function and a search method on the probability of the minimal true model identification in the case when the number of possible variables M is large compared to the number p_t of the true ones. Let $\hat{t}$ be a model selected by the considered rule. As the measures of performance, besides $P(\hat{t} = t)$, we also consider positive selection rate (PSR) defined as $\mathbf{E}(p_{t\cap\hat{t}}/p_t)$ and and the false discovery rate (FDR) $\mathbf{E}(p_{\hat{t}\setminus t}/p_{\hat{t}})$. The last two measures are more appropriate when the probabilities of correct model selection are low (cf. model S3 below). The simulation experiments were carried out for $n = 100$ and repeated $N = 200$ times.

The following logistic regression models have been considered:

(S1) $t = 1$, $\beta_1 = 1$,
(S2) $t = (1, 2)$, $\boldsymbol{\beta} = (1, -1)'$,
(S3) $t = (1, 2, 3, 4)$, $\boldsymbol{\beta} = (0.75, 0.75, 1, 1.25)'$,
(S4) $t = (1, 2, 3)$, $\boldsymbol{\beta} = (1, 1, 1)'$.

The covariates $\mathbf{x}_1, \ldots, \mathbf{x}_n$ were generated independently from the standard normal M-dimensional distribution and the binary outcome is drawn as Bernoulli r.v. with probability defined in (1). Results of our simulation study show that for the given criterion employed search method can affect considerably the probability of the true model selection. Moreover, the analogous results with variable M (cf. Figures 1 and 2 below) indicate that the differences between search methods become larger with increasing M. It is also interesting to note that the search method for which given criterion works the best depends on the criterion used, e.g. for BIC it is usually initial ordering method, whereas for methods based on p-values it is forward search. When for the given criterion and the model the best search method is chosen we see that MPVC2 criterion (with forward search) works better than BIC with any of the considered search methods in the case of model S1 and the same is true for mPVC2 criterion (with forward search) for models S2 and S4. The latter also behaves comparably to MPVC2 in the case of S1. We have shown in Figures 1 and 2 probabilities of correct identification as a function of horizon M for BIC and mPVC2 for models S1 and S4, whereas in Tables 1 and 2 indices for all the methods and $M = 30$ are given for models S2 and S3.

Note that in the case of the model S3, when $P(\hat{t} = t)$ is small overall and for a fixed search method, both FDR and PSR are larger for BIC than for p-based methods indicating that BIC has a tendency for choosing too large subset of variables, whereas p-value based methods choose a proper subset of true variables but rarely include superfluous ones. This is also true for other considered models. The first observation is concordant with [1] and [2]. We also noted (results not shown) that generating dependent predictors with covariance matrix $\Sigma = (\rho_{ij} = \rho^{|i-j|})$ may result in a change of optimal search method for a given criterion. For $\rho = 0.8$ IO is replaced by FS as the the best search method for BIC (actually, BIC with FS became the best method overall). Note also that the genetic algorithm worked uniformly worst for any of the criteria and model considered.

We also investigated in more detail usefulness of initial ordering as the search method. Figure 3 shows probabilities of correct ordering (i.e. true variables preceding superfluous ones) together with $P(t = \hat{t})$ as the function of M in model S1 with $\beta_1 = 1$ and $\beta_1 = 0.5$ for BIC and mPVC2. For mPVC2 they do not differ significantly indicating that the crucial problem is choice of a restricted family of models over which criterion is optimized. Discrepancy between $P(BIC^n = t)$ and probability of correct ordering is mainly due to choice of too large model.

Summarizing, mPVC2 method turns out to be a worthy competitor for BIC when used with an appropriate search method in the case when the number of potential predictors in logistic model is large. Performance of combined selection rule seems worth investigating. This is also confirmed by a real data example we considered. Namely, we investigated performance of BIC and mPVC2 with IO and FS for `urine` data set ([10], $n = 77$) by the means of parametric bootstrap. Two variables (calcium and mmho having the smallest p-values in the full model) were chosen as predictors and logistic regression model was fitted with $\mathbf{Y}$ being occurrence of crystals in urine. The value of $\hat{\boldsymbol{\beta}}$ equals $(0.5725, -0.1186)'$. A parametric bootstrap (see e.g. [3]) was employed to check how the considered selection criteria perform for this data set. The true model was the fitted logistic model with the original two regressors, $\boldsymbol{\beta} = \hat{\boldsymbol{\beta}}$ from which 200 samples and additional superfluous explanatory variables were created in pairs by drawing from the two-dimensional normal distribution with independent components, which mean and variance vector matched that of the original predictors. We considered $k = 3, 7, \ldots, 19$ additional pairs what amounted to horizons $M = 8, 16, \ldots, 40$ when the true variables were accounted for. Figure 4 shows summary of the results. For both search methods mPVC2 performs considerably better, however in the case of IO it behaves much more stably when M increases.

Table 1. Simulation results for model S2 with $M = 30$

(a) Fractions of correct model selection and their SEs

	IO	BE	FS	GA
BIC	0.40	0.30	0.32	0.18
	(0.03)	(0.03)	(0.03)	(0.03)
mPVC2	0.62	0.68	0.70	0.46
	(0.03)	(0.03)	(0.03)	(0.03)
MPVC2	0.42	0.43	0.51	0.28
	(0.04)	(0.04)	(0.04)	(0.03)

(b) Positive selection rates and false discovery rates

		IO	BE	FS	GA
BIC	PSR	0.945	0.965	0.963	0.958
	FDR	0.261	0.332	0.285	0.407
mPVC2	PSR	0.875	0.917	0.905	0.917
	FDR	0.095	0.086	0.061	0.187
MPVC2	PSR	0.657	0.675	0.760	0.695
	FDR	0.164	0.152	0.019	0.271

Table 2. Simulation results for model S3 with $M = 30$

(a) Fractions of correct model selection and their SEs

	IO	BE	FS	GA
BIC	0.12	0.14	0.19	0.12
	(0.02)	(0.02)	(0.03)	(0.02)
mPVC2	0.08	0.12	0.12	0.10
	(0.02)	(0.02)	(0.03)	(0.02)
MPVC2	0.04	0.02	0.07	0.04
	(0.01)	(0.01)	(0.02)	(0.01)

(b) Positive selection rates and false discovery rates

		IO	BE	FS	GA
BIC	PSR	0.814	0.858	0.845	0.843
	FDR	0.272	0.341	0.214	0.319
mPVC2	PSR	0.631	0.714	0.650	0.698
	FDR	0.102	0.199	0.065	0.204
MPVC2	PSR	0.497	0.545	0.540	0.544
	FDR	0.104	0.186	0.034	0.161

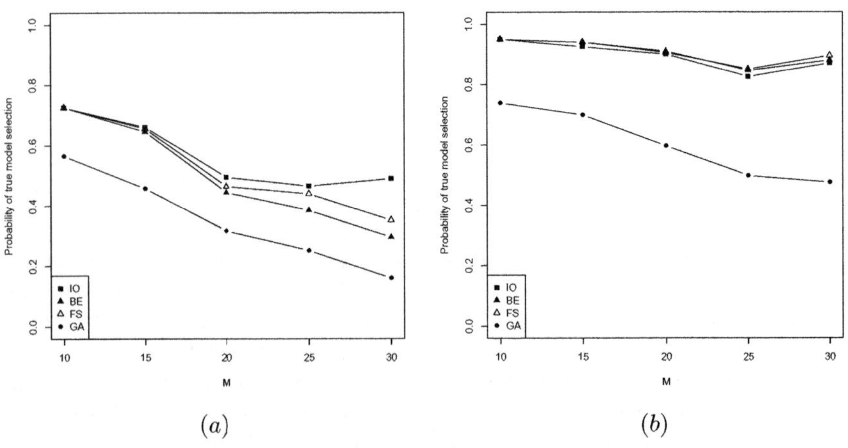

Fig. 1. Estimated probabilities of correct model selection with respect to M for BIC (figure (a)) and mPVC2 (figure (b)) for model S1

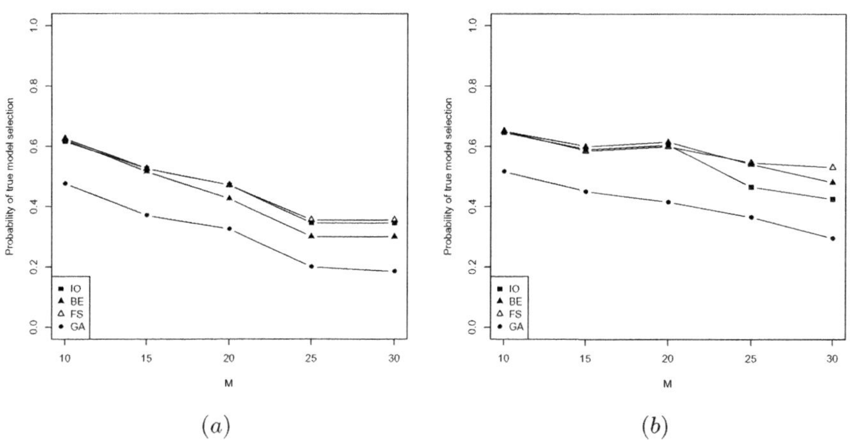

Fig. 2. Estimated probabilities of correct model selection with respect to M for BIC (figure (a)) and mPVC2 (figure (b)) for model S4

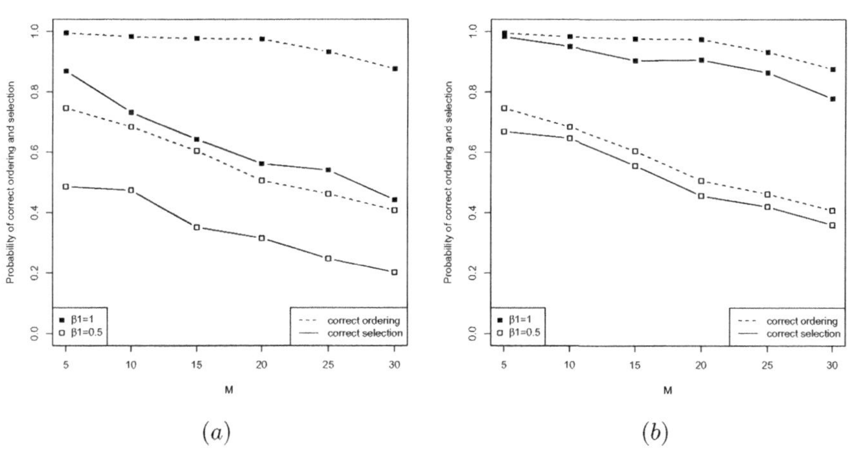

Fig. 3. Estimated probabilities of correct model selection and correct ordering in IO method with respect to M for BIC (figure (a)) and mPVC2 (figure (b)) for model S1 with $\beta_1 = 1$ and $\beta_1 = 0.5$

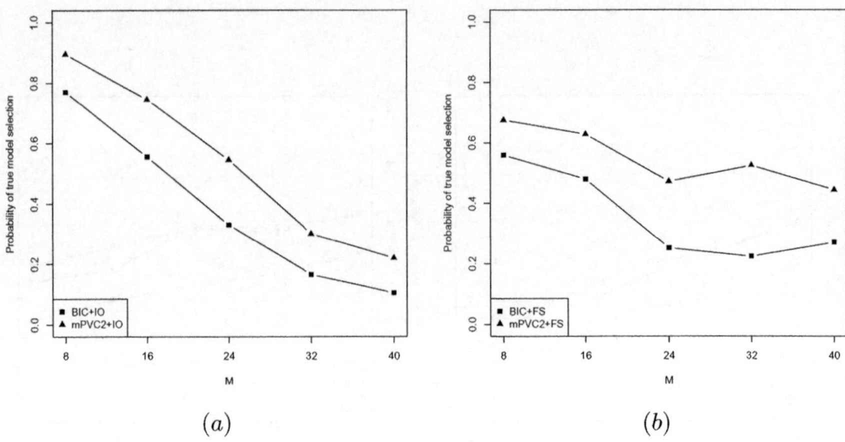

(a) (b)

Fig. 4. Estimated probabilities of correct model selection with respect to M for IO (figure (a)) and FS (figure (b)) for `urine` dataset

Appendix

Proof of Theorem 2. (Consistency of M^n_m). Assume first that $t \neq 0$ and consider the case $j \not\supseteq t$. As the family of logistic models is finite it is sufficient to show that as $n \to \infty$

$$P[e^{p_t a_n} p(D^n_{0t}|p_t) \geq e^{p_j a_n} p(D^n_{0j}|p_j)] \to 0, \tag{4}$$

The probability in (4) does not decrease when D^n_{0j} is replaced by $\max(D^n_{0j}, 2)$ Thus for $p_j > 1$ in view of Lemma 1 (ii) the above probability is bounded from above by

$$P\{e^{p_t a_n} p(D^n_{0t}|p_t) \geq e^{p_j a_n} e^{-\max(D^n_{0j},2)/2} \max(D^n_{0j}/2, 1)^{\frac{p_j}{2}-1} \Gamma^{-1}(\frac{p_j}{2})\}.$$

As $\max(D^n_{0j}/2, 1)^{\frac{p_j}{2}-1} \geq 1$ in view of Lemma 1 (iii) it suffices to show that

$$P\{e^{(D^n_{0t}-\max(D^n_{0j},2))/2} \leq e^{(p_t-p_j)a_n} \Gamma(\frac{p_j}{2})\Gamma^{-1}(\frac{p_t}{2})(D^n_{0t}/2)^{\frac{p_t}{2}-1}[1+O(1/D^n_{0t})]\} \to 0,$$

as $n \to \infty$. The above convergence follows easily form Propositions 1 and 2. For $p_j = 1$ we apply part (i) of Lemma 1 together with

$$e^{-x/2}\left(\frac{x}{2}\right)^{-1/2}\left(\frac{x}{x+1}\right) \geq \frac{2}{3}e^{-x/2-\log(x/2)/2} \geq \frac{2}{3}e^{-x}.$$

for $x = \max(D^n_{0j}, 2) \geq 2$. For $p_j = 0$ the proof is similar. Consider now the case $j \supset t$. We have to show (4). Using Lemma 1 (iii) we obtain for $p_t \geq 1$

$$P\Big[\frac{1}{2}D^n_{jt} \leq \left(\frac{p_t}{2}-1\right)\log\left(\frac{D^n_{0t}}{2}\right) - \left(\frac{p_j}{2}-1\right)\log\left(\frac{D^n_{0j}}{2}\right) + \log\Gamma^{-1}\left(\frac{p_t}{2}\right) -$$

$$\log \Gamma^{-1}\left(\frac{p_j}{2}\right) + \log[1+O(1/D_{0j}^n)] - \log[1+O(1/D_{0t}^n)] + a_n(p_t - p_j)\Big] =$$
$$P\Big[\frac{1}{2}D_{jt}^n \leq \left(\frac{p_t}{2}-1\right)\frac{D_{jt}^n}{2}(D_{jt}^{n*})^{-1} - \left(\frac{p_j}{2}-\frac{p_t}{2}\right)\log\left(\frac{D_{0j}^n}{2}\right) + \log \Gamma^{-1}\left(\frac{p_t}{2}\right) -$$
$$\log \Gamma^{-1}\left(\frac{p_j}{2}\right) + \log[1+O(1/D_{0j}^n)] - \log[1+O(1/D_{0t}^n)] + a_n(p_t - p_j)\Big] \to 0,$$

where D_{jt}^{n*} belongs to the segment joining $D_{0j}^n/2$ and $D_{0t}^n/2$. The above convergence follows from $p_j > p_t$ and Theorem 1 and Proposition 1 which imply that $D_{jt}^n = O_P(1)$ and D_{0t}^n, $D_{0j}^n \to \infty$. For $p_t = 0$ we have to show that $P[e^{a_n}/\sqrt{n} > e^{p_j a_n} p(D_{0j}^n|p_j)] \to 0$, which follows from the fact that $p(D_{0j}^n|p_j) \xrightarrow{d} \mathcal{U}([0,1])$ as $n \to \infty$ and $p_j \geq 1$. □

Consistency of M_M^n. Assume first that $t \neq f$ and consider the case $j \not\supset t$. We have to show that

$$P[e^{-p_t a_n} p(D_{tf}^n|M - p_t) \leq e^{-p_j a_n} p(D_{jf}^n|M - p_j)] \to 0, \tag{5}$$

as $n \to \infty$. It follows from Theorem 1 that $p(D_{tf}^n|M - p_t) \xrightarrow{d} \mathcal{U}([0,1])$ and from Proposition 1 that $D_{jf}^n \to \infty$. Thus using Lemma 1 (iii) it sufficies to show

$$P\Big[\frac{1}{2}D_{jf}^n \leq \left(\frac{M-p_j}{2}-1\right)\log\left(\frac{D_{jf}^n}{2}\right) + \log \Gamma^{-1}\left(\frac{M-p_j}{2}\right)$$
$$+\log[1+O(1/D_{jf}^n)] + a_n(p_t - p_j)\Big] \to 0,$$

as $n \to \infty$. The above convergence follows easily from Proposition 1.
Consider the case $j \supset t$. We have to show (5). For $j \neq f$ the desired convergence follows from Theorem 1 which implies that $p(D_{tf}^n|M - p_t)$, $p(D_{jf}^n|M - p_j) \xrightarrow{d} \mathcal{U}([0,1])$, as $n \to \infty$. For $j = f$ this is implied by $P(e^{-p_f a_n} < (e^{-p_t a_n} p(D_{tf}|M - p_t) \to 1$ which in its turn follows from $p_t < M$ and $a_n \to \infty$. For the case $t = f$ the proof is similar and uses the assumption that $a_n = O(\log n)$. □

Proof of Proposition 1. First we will show that under (A1) and (A2)

$$\mathbf{I}_n(\boldsymbol{\beta}) \geq \tau \mathbf{I}_n(\boldsymbol{\beta}_t) \tag{6}$$

for some positive constant τ and for $\boldsymbol{\beta} \in A_n = \{\boldsymbol{\beta} : ||\boldsymbol{\beta} - \boldsymbol{\beta}_t|| \leq d_n\}$. Recall that $d_n^2 = \min\{[\max_{1\leq i\leq n}||x_i||^2]^{-1}, [\min_k(1/2)\beta_{t,k}]^2\}$. Using Cauchy-Schwarz inequality we have

$$\sup_{\boldsymbol{\beta}\in A_n} |\mathbf{x}_n'(\boldsymbol{\beta} - \boldsymbol{\beta}_t)| \leq \sup_{\boldsymbol{\beta}\in A_n} ||\mathbf{x}_n|| \cdot ||\boldsymbol{\beta} - \boldsymbol{\beta}_t|| \leq 1 \tag{7}$$

In order to prove (6) it suffices to show that there exists a positive constant $\tau > 0$ such that $\pi_i(\boldsymbol{\beta})(1 - \pi_i(\boldsymbol{\beta})) > \tau\pi_i(\boldsymbol{\beta}_t)(1 - \pi_i(\boldsymbol{\beta}_t))$, for all $i = 1, \ldots, n$ and $\boldsymbol{\beta} \in A_n$. This follows easily from (7) as it implies that it is enough to show that

$$\inf_{\boldsymbol{\beta}\in A_n} \frac{1 + e^{\mathbf{x}_i'\boldsymbol{\beta}_t}}{1 + e^{\mathbf{x}_i'\boldsymbol{\beta}}} > \inf_{\boldsymbol{\beta}\in A_n} \max\left(\frac{1}{e^{-\mathbf{x}_i'\boldsymbol{\beta}_t} + e^{\mathbf{x}_i'(\boldsymbol{\beta}-\boldsymbol{\beta}_t)}}, \frac{e^{-\mathbf{x}_i'\boldsymbol{\beta}_t}}{e^{-\mathbf{x}_i'\boldsymbol{\beta}_t} + e^{\mathbf{x}_i'(\boldsymbol{\beta}-\boldsymbol{\beta}_t)}}\right) > 0,$$

for all i which is easy to verify by the second application of (7).

The difference $l(\hat{\boldsymbol{\beta}}_c, \mathbf{Y}_n|\mathbf{X}_n) - l(\hat{\boldsymbol{\beta}}_w, \mathbf{Y}_n|\mathbf{X}_n)$ can be written as

$$[l(\hat{\boldsymbol{\beta}}_c, \mathbf{Y}_n|\mathbf{X}_n) - l(\boldsymbol{\beta}_c, \mathbf{Y}_n|\mathbf{X}_n)] + [l(\boldsymbol{\beta}_t, \mathbf{Y}_n|\mathbf{X}_n) - l(\hat{\boldsymbol{\beta}}_w|\mathbf{X}_n, \mathbf{Y}_n)]. \quad (8)$$

It can be shown using one term Taylor expansion, proof of Theorem 1 in [5] and condition (F) that the first term in (8) is $O_P(1)$. We omit the details. We will show that the probability that the second term is greater or equal $\alpha_1 n d_n^2$, for some $\alpha_1 > 0$ tends to 1. Define $H_n(\boldsymbol{\beta}) = l(\boldsymbol{\beta}_t, \mathbf{Y}_n|\mathbf{X}_n) - l(\boldsymbol{\beta}, \mathbf{Y}_n|\mathbf{X}_n)$. Note that $H(\boldsymbol{\beta})$ is convex and $H(\boldsymbol{\beta}_t) = 0$. For any incorrect model w we have $\hat{\boldsymbol{\beta}}_w \notin A_n$. Thus it suffices to show that $P(\inf_{\boldsymbol{\beta}\in\partial A_n} H_n(\boldsymbol{\beta}) < \alpha_1 n d_n^2) \to 0$, as $n \to \infty$, for some $\alpha_1 > 0$. Consider the following Taylor expansion

$$l(\boldsymbol{\beta}, \mathbf{Y}_n|\mathbf{X}_n) - l(\boldsymbol{\beta}_t, \mathbf{Y}_n|\mathbf{X}_n) = (\boldsymbol{\beta} - \boldsymbol{\beta}_t)' s_n(\boldsymbol{\beta}_t) - (\boldsymbol{\beta} - \boldsymbol{\beta}_t)' \mathbf{I}_n(\tilde{\boldsymbol{\beta}})(\boldsymbol{\beta} - \boldsymbol{\beta}_t)/2,$$

where $\tilde{\boldsymbol{\beta}}$ belongs to the line segment joining $\boldsymbol{\beta}$ and $\boldsymbol{\beta}_t$. Note that $s_n(\boldsymbol{\beta}_t)$ is a random vector with zero mean and the covariance matrix $\mathbf{I}_n(\boldsymbol{\beta}_t)$.

Using the equality above, assumption (A1), (6) and Markov's inequality we have, taking $\alpha_1 < \gamma\tau$

$$P[\inf_{\boldsymbol{\beta}\in\partial A_n} H_n(\boldsymbol{\beta}) < \alpha_1 n d_n^2] \leq P[\sup_{\boldsymbol{\beta}\in\partial A_n} (\boldsymbol{\beta} - \boldsymbol{\beta}_t)' s_n(\boldsymbol{\beta}_t) \geq (\gamma\tau - \alpha_1) n d_n^2) =$$

$$P[||s_n(\boldsymbol{\beta}_t)|| d_n \geq (\gamma\tau - \alpha_1) n d_n^2) \leq \frac{tr(I_n(\boldsymbol{\beta}_t)) d_n^2}{(\gamma\tau n d_n^2 - \alpha_1 n d_n^2)^2} \leq \frac{M\kappa n d_n^2}{n^2 d_n^4 (\gamma\tau - \alpha_1)^2} \to 0,$$

as $n \to \infty$. □

Proof of Proposition 2. Call $\max_{1\leq i\leq n} ||\mathbf{x}_i|| n^{-\varepsilon} \leq \alpha$ assumption (A). We have the following decomposition

$$\begin{aligned} D_{0c}^n &= l(\hat{\boldsymbol{\beta}}_c, \mathbf{Y}_n|\mathbf{X}_n) - l(\boldsymbol{\beta}_c, \mathbf{Y}_n|\mathbf{X}_n) + \\ &l(\boldsymbol{\beta}_c, \mathbf{Y}_n|\mathbf{X}_n) - \mathbf{E}l(\boldsymbol{\beta}_c, \mathbf{Y}_n|\mathbf{X}_n) + \mathbf{E}l(\boldsymbol{\beta}_c, \mathbf{Y}_n|\mathbf{X}_n) - n\log(1/2). \end{aligned} \quad (9)$$

It was proved in the proof of Proposition 1 that under (F) $l(\hat{\boldsymbol{\beta}}_c, \mathbf{Y}_n|\mathbf{X}_n) - l(\boldsymbol{\beta}_c, \mathbf{Y}_n|\mathbf{X}_n) = O_P(1)$ and thus $n^{-(1+\varepsilon)}[l(\hat{\boldsymbol{\beta}}_c, \mathbf{Y}_n|\mathbf{X}_n) - l(\boldsymbol{\beta}_c, \mathbf{Y}_n|\mathbf{X}_n)] \xrightarrow{P} 0$. We will show that

$$n^{-(1+\varepsilon)}[l(\boldsymbol{\beta}_c, \mathbf{Y}_n|\mathbf{X}_n) - \mathbf{E}l(\boldsymbol{\beta}_c, \mathbf{Y}_n|\mathbf{X}_n)] \xrightarrow{P} 0.$$

This follows from the Law of Large Numbers using Schwarz inequality since

$$Var[n^{-(1+\varepsilon)} l(\boldsymbol{\beta}_c, \mathbf{Y}_n|\mathbf{X}_n)] = n^{-2(1+\varepsilon)} Var(\sum_{i=1}^n y_i \mathbf{x}_i' \boldsymbol{\beta}_c) \leq$$

$$||\boldsymbol{\beta}_c||^2 n^{-2(1+\varepsilon)} \sum_{i=1}^n ||\mathbf{x}_i||^2 \to 0$$

as $n \to \infty$ by assumption (A). In view of (9) it suffices to show that $|n^{-(1+\varepsilon)} \mathbf{E}l(\boldsymbol{\beta}_c, \mathbf{Y}_n|\mathbf{X}_n)| \leq \alpha_2$, for $\alpha_2 > 0$. The following inequality holds

$$|n^{-(1+\varepsilon)} \mathbf{E}l(\boldsymbol{\beta}_c, \mathbf{Y}_n|\mathbf{X}_n)| \leq n^{-(1+\varepsilon)} (\sum_{i=1}^n |\mathbf{x}_i' \boldsymbol{\beta}_c| + \sum_{i=1}^n \log(1 + e^{\mathbf{x}_i' \boldsymbol{\beta}_c})). \quad (10)$$

The first term in (10) is bounded in view of the Schwarz inequality and assumption (A). The following inequality holds

$$\log(1+x) \leq 2\log(x)\mathbf{1}\{x>2\} + x\mathbf{1}\{x\leq 2\} \leq 2\log(x)\mathbf{1}\{x>2\} + 2. \quad (11)$$

Using (11) and the Schwarz inequality the second term in (10) is bounded from above by $n^{-(1+\varepsilon)}[2\sum_{i=1}^{n}|\mathbf{x}_i'\boldsymbol{\beta}_c|+2n]$ which is bounded by assumption (A). □

References

1. Broman, K.W., Speed, T.P.: A model selection approach for the identification of quantitative trait loci in experimental crosses (with discussion). J. Roy Stat. Soc. B 64, 641–656, 731–775 (2002)
2. Chen, J., Chen, Z.: Extended Bayesian criteria for model selection with large model spaces. Biometrika 95(3), 759–771 (1995)
3. Davison, A., Hinkley, D.: Bootstrap Methods and Their Applications. Cambridge University Press (1997)
4. Fahrmeir, L.: Asymptotic testing theory for generalized linear models. Statistics 1, 65–76 (1987)
5. Fahrmeir, L., Kaufmann, H.: Consistency and asymptotic normality of the maximum likelihood estimator in generalized linear models. The Annals of Statistics 1(13), 342–368 (1985)
6. Harrell, F.E.: Regression Modelling Strategies: with Applications to Linear Models. Logistic Regression and Survival Analysis. Springer, New York (2001)
7. Hastie, T.J., Pregibon, D.: Generalized Linear Models. Wadsworth and Brooks/Cole (1992)
8. Mühlenbein, H., Schlierkamp-Voosen, D.: Predictive Models for the Breeder Genetic Algorithm, I: Continuous Parameter Optimization. Evolutionary Computation 1(1), 25–49 (1993)
9. Pokarowski, P., Mielniczuk, J.: P-values of likelihood ratio statistic for consistent model selection and testing (2011) (in preparation)
10. SAS datasets, `http://ftp.sas.com/samples/A56902`
11. Qian, G., Field, C.: Law of iterated logarithm and consistent model selection criterion in logistic regression. Statistics and Probability Letters 56, 101–112 (2002)
12. Tolvi, J.: Genetic algorithms for outlier detection and variable selection in linear regression models. Soft Comput. 8(8), 527–533 (2004)

Landau Theory of Meta-learning

Dariusz Plewczynski

Interdisciplinary Centre for Mathematical and Computational Modelling,
University of Warsaw, Pawinskiego 5a Street, 02-106 Warsaw, Poland
darman@icm.edu.pl

Abstract. Computational Intelligence (CI) is a sub-branch of Artificial Intelligence paradigm focusing on the study of adaptive mechanisms to enable or facilitate intelligent behavior in complex and changing environments. Several paradigms of CI [like artificial neural networks, evolutionary computations, swarm intelligence, artificial immune systems, fuzzy systems and many others] are not yet unified in the common theoretical framework. Moreover, most of those paradigms evolved into separate machine learning (ML) techniques, where probabilistic methods are used complementary with CI techniques in order to effectively combine elements of learning, adaptation, evolution and Fuzzy logic to create heuristic algorithms. The current trend is to develop meta-learning techniques, since no single machine learning algorithm is superior to others in all-possible situations. The mean-field theory is reviewed here, as the promising analytical approach that can be used for unifying results of independent ML methods into single prediction, i.e. the meta-learning solution. The Landau approximation moreover describes the adaptive integration of information acquired from semi-infinite ensemble of independent learning agents, where only local interactions are considered. The influence of each individual agent on its neighbors is described within the well-known social impact theory. The final decision outcome for the meta-learning universal CI system is calculated using majority rule in the stationary limit, yet the minority solutions can survive inside the majority population, as the complex intermittent clusters of opposite opinion.

Keywords: Adaptive integration, Artificial Intelligence, Cellular automata, Social strength, Minority survival, Machine Learning, Computational Intelligence, Meta-Learning, Landau theory.

1 Introduction

Several meta-learning approaches were proposed in machine learning (ML) field focusing on the integration of results from different algorithms into single prediction [1-9]. The typical meta-learning procedure is trying to balance the generality of solution and the overall performance of trained model. The main problem with such meta-approaches is that they are static, i.e. adaptivity is not included. The meta-approach is typically optimized for certain combination of single machine learning methods and particular representation of training data. Yet, the actual output of the training should impact the parameters of the method, then allowing for iterative

P. Bouvry et al. (Eds.): SIIS 2011, LNCS 7053, pp. 142–153, 2012.

procedure that is able to adapt to changing environment and further optimization of training model. This dynamical view of machine learning is especially useful for robotic vision applications [10, 11], general robots [10, 12-20], and bioinformatics [6, 21-24]. In those applications, the balance between environment and trained model can be described similarly to ensemble learning theory as the global parameter affecting all learners [25], where each distributed intelligent agent performs training on available input data toward classification pressure described by the set of positive and negative cases. When the query testing data is analyzed each agent predicts the query item classification by “yes”/”no” decision. The answers of all agents are then gathered and fused into the single prediction. The integration scheme allows for adaptive changes when different set of input data is presented to the system by retraining all learners.

The first mathematical approach to the analysis of opinion formation in groups of individuals was made by Abelson [26]. The other class of models that is based on probabilistic cellular automata was later proposed by Nowak et al. [27]. A computer simulation model of the change of attitudes in a population resulting from the interactive, reciprocal, and recursive operation of previously known Latane's theory of social impact [28]. Surprisingly, several emerging macroscopic phenomena were observed, yet resulting from relative simple operation of microscopic rules of opinion change. The mean-field theory, with intermittent behavior, shows a variety of stationary states with a well localized and dynamically stable clusters (domains) of individuals who share minority opinions. The statistical mechanical model of social impact formulated by Lewenstein [29] postulates the impact of a group of N agents on a given learner is proportional to three factors: the *"strength"* of the members of the whole ensemble, their *“social”* distance from the individual, and their number N. The extension of the model was done by Kohring [30, 31], where Latane's theory was extended to include learning. Lewenstein’s class of models of cellular automata with intrinsic disorder was later extended to continuous limit by Plewczynski [32], and proved that even the model of Cartesian social space (therefore not fully connected) and containing no learning rules, one can also observe different phases (small clusters in the sparse phase with large role of strong individuals, and high density phase with almost uniform opinion).

2 Ensemble Learning

We use social impact theory, where individual differences and the *social* influence decaying with distance are assumed [29]. The model of meta-learning is based on several assumptions:

1. Binary Logic

We assume binary logic of individual learners, i.e. we deal with cellular automata consisting of N agents, each holding one of two opposite states (“No” or “YES”). These states are binary $\sigma_i=+/-1$, similarly to Ising model of ferromagnet. In most cases the machine learning algorithms that can model those agents, such as support vector machines, decision trees, trend vectors, artificial neural networks, random forest, predict two classes for incoming data, based on previous experience in the form of trained models. The prediction of an agent address the question: is a query data contained in class A ("YES"), or it is different from items gathered in this class ("NO").

2. *Disorder and random strength parameter*

Each learner is characterized by two random parameters: persuasiveness p_i and supportiveness s_i that describe how individual agent interacts with others. Persuasiveness describes how effectively the individual state of agent is propagated to neighboring agents, whereas supportiveness represents self-supportiveness of single agent. In present work we assume that influential agents has the high self-esteem $p_i = s_i$, what is supported by the fact that highly effective learners should have high impact on others in the meta-learning procedure. In general the individual differences between agents are described as random variables with a probability density $p(p_i,s_i)$.

3. *Learning space and learning metric*

Each agent is characterized by its location in the learning space, therefore one can calculate the learning distance $d(i,j)$ of two learners i and j. The strength of coupling between two agents tends to decrease with increasing learning distance between them. Determination of the learning metric is a separate problem, and the particular form of the metric and the learning distance function should be empirically determined, and in principle can have a very peculiar geometry. In our present manuscript, I will analyze two dimensional Euclidian geometry, with a constant, finite-range metric. In that case, the decay of learning coupling is described by a function $g=1/d(i,j)$, equal to constant value g for $d(i,j)<R$ and ∞ for more distant pairs. In addition we choose $g(0)=1/\beta$, where $\beta=1/kT$, and T represents temperature of the system, that allows for simulating the competition between persuasiveness and supportiveness of each agent.

4. *Learning coupling*

Agents exchange their opinions by biasing others toward their own classification outcome. This influence can be described by the total learning impact I_i that ith agent is experiencing from all other learners. Within the cellular automata approach this impact is the difference between positive coupling of those agents that hold identical classification outcome, relative to negative influence of those who share the opposite state, and can be formalized as

$$I_i = I_p\left(\sum_j \frac{t(p_j)}{g(d(i,j))}(1-\sigma_i\sigma_j)\right) - I_s\left(\sum_j \frac{t(s_j)}{g(d(i,j))}(1+\sigma_i\sigma_j)\right), \tag{1}$$

where $g(d(i,j))$ is a decreasing function of distance $d(i,j)$, and $t(p_i,s_i)$ is the strength scaling function. The strength scaling can be taken to be $t(x)=x$, providing redefinition of the probability density distribution $p(p_i,s_i)$.

The equation of dynamics of the learning model defines the state σ_i of ith individual at the next time step as follows:

$$\sigma_i' = -sign(\sigma_i I_i), \tag{2}$$

with rescaled learning influence:

$$I_i = \sum_j \frac{p_j}{(s+p)g(d(i,j))}(1-\sigma_i\sigma_j) - \sum_j \frac{s_j}{(s+p)g(d(i,j))}(1+\sigma_i\sigma_j) \tag{3}$$

We assume a synchronous dynamics, i.e. states of all agents are updated in parallel. By introducing a weighted majority-minority difference for a system:

$$m_i = \sum_{j \neq i} \frac{(s_j + p_j)\sigma_j}{(s+p)g(d(i,j))},$$

and random parameters to describe effective self-supportiveness of each agent:

$$a_i = \frac{s-p}{s+p} + \frac{\beta}{s+p} s_i,$$

we finally get the dynamical equation in noise absent limit:

$$\sigma_i' = sign(m_i)\theta(|m_i| - |a_i|) + \sigma_i sign(a_i)\theta(|a_i| - |m_i|).$$

5. Presence of *noise*

The randomness of the state change (phenomenological modeling of various random elements in the learning system, and training data) is given by introducing noise into the dynamics:

$$\sigma_i' = -sign(\sigma_i I_i + h_i) \tag{4}$$

where h_i is the site-dependent white noise, or one can select a uniform white noise, where for all agents h_i=h. In the first case, h_i are random variables independent for different agents and time points, whereas in the second case h are independent for different time points. We assume here, that the probability distribution of h_i is both site and time independent, i.e. it has uniform statistical properties. The uniform white noise simulates the global bias affecting all agents (like impurities in training data), whereas site-dependent white noise describes local effects (such as prediction quality of individual learner etc.).

6. The *mean-field approximation*

The mean-field approximation is introduced by replacing the actual value of m_i by its mean value calculated by averaging over disorder values $< m_i >$. This equation is valid for slowly decaying interactions, when the equilibrium solution is not reached rapidly.

The further considerations will be performed using the continuous representation of the above discrete equation in a field-theoretical framework. The sum over agents j translates in this approach into an integral over n-dimensional Euclidean space multiplied by the proper density function. The advantage of mean-field theory is given by the fact that it is able to reduce the full dynamics described by above functional equations with disorder to the averaged functional equation:

$$m'(x) = g(x,[m]) + n_0(x,[|m|]),$$

provided that $m(x)$ does not change its sign, therefore it is for example close to uniform state [29].

The system defined in this way is similar to previously postulated cellular automata models of opinion change in social sciences [29, 32]. The main differences of those approaches from the previously described cellular automata models are given by the short-range interactions. In addition, the random strength parameters are introduced, therefore allowing for more complex behavior of the system. Individual agents are described using probability density $p(p_i,s_i)$, so they differ from each other. Moreover, the n-dimensional learning space geometry presents an interesting real-life case for further analytical analysis. There, the coupling between agents decreases with increasing Euclidean distance between them. The mean-field theory provides very well defined and controlled approximation allowing for solving the dynamical equations of the model. The dynamical "order" parameter has to be defined, to show the decay of minority groups in the form of "staircase" dynamics [29, 32-34].

3 Landau Theory

Now we are ready to introduce continuous limit for the dynamic given by the equation (2). In order to search for analytical solutions in the system we constrain ourselves to the case of Euclidean space with arbitrary dimensionality n, when only nearest-neighbors couplings are taken into account. Our postulates in this simplified case are presented as follows:

1. *Continuous field* of states

A new real value field is introduced $v(x,t)$ that describes the state of the system in the point defined by n-dimensional vector x in the Euclidean space at a given time moment t. The field is an abstract representation of a single agent state, allowing for the search of analytical solutions for the system.

2. Positive *strength function*

The strength of each learning agent is described here using real, positive value, function $f(x)$.

3. *Nonlinearity* in the model

The degree of nonlinearity in the system is governed by the parameter $\beta=1/kT$, which is introduced in order to ensure the stability of two special states $+/-1$ that describe to opposite classification outputs of individual learners. This is crucial for machine learning applications of the model, when the binary classification is selected for predicting class membership for new testing data.

4. *Locality* of interactions

The strength of coupling between neighboring agents is given by the real parameter α, and we assume only the nearest-neighbor interactions. This is strongly supported by the Euclidean metric of the space, where fast decaying coupling function $g(d(i,j))$ ensures that only neighbors are connected. In the case of machine learning ensemble of agents ordered for the purpose of the consensus in the Euclidean space by their training parameters values, this assumption means that algorithms with similar values of parameters tend to have similar results. Such observation can be supported by training similar machine learning algorithms on similar data, or can be modeled as strong coupling between neighbors in the Euclidean space of their parameters values space.

Rewriting the equation (4) similarly as in [32], yet for the more general case of n-dimensional Euclidean space we find:

$$\sigma_i(t+1) - \sigma_i(t) = -\sigma_i(t) +$$

$$sign\left[\begin{array}{l} \dfrac{s_{i+1}+p_{i+1}}{(s+p)g(d(i,i+1))}\sigma_{i+1}(t) + \dfrac{s_{i-1}+p_{i-1}}{(s+p)g(d(i,i1 1))}\sigma_{i-1}(t) + \\ \dfrac{s_{i+1}-p_{i+1}+s_{i-1}-p_{i-1}}{(s+p)g(d(i,i+1))}\sigma_i(t) + 2\beta\dfrac{s_i}{(s+p)}\sigma_i(t) \end{array}\right],$$

with the continuous limit given by the following substitutions:

$$\sigma_i(t+1) - \sigma_i(t) \to v(x,t),$$

$$-\sigma_i(t) \to -v(x,t),$$

$$\frac{s_{i+1}+p_{i+1}}{(s+p)g(d(i,i+1))}\sigma_{i+1}(t) \to f(x+dx)v(x+dx,t),$$

$$\frac{s_{i-1}+p_{i-1}}{(s+p)g(d(i,i-1))}\sigma_{i-1}(t) \to f(x-dx)v(x-dx,t),$$

$$2\beta\frac{s_i}{(s+p)}\sigma_i(t) \to \beta f(x)v(x,t).$$

In addition the third term in the *sign* function argument is approaching zero in the continuous limit.

The continuous form of the dynamical equation for the system is therefore given by the formula:

$$v(x,t) = -v(x,t) + f(x)v(x,t) - \gamma v^3(x,t) + \alpha\frac{\delta^2}{\delta x^2}f(x)v(x,t) \tag{5}$$

This equation governs the dynamics of learning space, i.e. how the state of agent located in space point x and time t is changing during the course of its evolution. The first term describes the process of decaying when there is no coupling to other learners (no self-support). The second one-agent term represents the positive strength function. The third non-linear term weighted by parameter γ introduce the global preference for two stationary solutions uniform for the whole system ("YES" and "NO"). The last two-agent term represents the Euclidean metric using only nearest neighbors scaled by α parameter.

The functional description of the model is given by the equation:

$$w(x,t) = -w(x,t) - \gamma\frac{w^3(x,t)}{f(x)} + \alpha\sqrt{f(x)}\nabla^2\sqrt{f(x)}w(x,t), \tag{6}$$

with

$$w(x,t) = \sqrt{f(x)}v(x,t)$$

as a new field. The dynamics of the system is then governed by the general functional form similar to the Schrödinger equation:

$$\frac{\delta H}{\delta w(x,t)} = \frac{\delta H}{\delta w(x,t)}, \tag{7}$$

where H denotes the Hamiltonian (or Lyapunov function) for the system:

$$H = \int \partial x \left[\frac{w^2(x,t)}{2} + \frac{\gamma w^4(x,t)}{4f(x)} - f(x)\frac{w^2(x,t)}{2} + \frac{\alpha}{2}\nabla(\sqrt{f(x)}w(x,t))^2 \right] \tag{8}$$

Defining the potential energy for the system by

$$V(x,t) = \frac{w^2(x,t)}{2} + \frac{\gamma w^4(x,t)}{4f(x)} - f(x)\frac{w^2(x,t)}{2} + \frac{\alpha}{2}\nabla(\sqrt{f(x)}w(x,t))^2 \tag{9}$$

We get more clear form of the dynamic equation:

$$H = \int \partial t \int \partial x \left[\frac{w^2(x,t)}{2} - V(x,t) \right]. \tag{10}$$

This form of dynamical equation allows for applying the standard mathematical formalisms of statistical physics, the analytical analysis of the system is therefore much easier in comparison to other types of topology.

The stationary solutions for the system can be computed by using the Thomas-Fermi approximation that neglects the kinetic term in the equation (6), i.e. sets α=0. This approximation and further analytical analysis of the system similar to presented in this manuscript is presented elsewhere [32] for the one dimensional case of the nearest neighbors coupling. We will not repeat here the analysis, yet we would like to recapitulate the generic stationary solutions of the system. We will describe here the together with generic phases that can be observed in dynamics governed by the such general equation (6). The presented here results are valid for any dimensionality of the Euclidean learning space and strongly support the existence of stable solutions for the system governed by real Schrödinger equation similarly to one dimensional case. The solutions for the system are given by the minority clusters surrounded by the majority agents, and the dynamic is of the "staircase" character in the presence of small noise [9, 29, 32].

We recapitulate the previous findings by describing three different types of solutions for the equation (6) for different values of parameters γ and α [32]:

1) When $\gamma=\alpha=0$

The equation of dynamic is given by the equation:

$$v(x,t) = -v(x,t) + f(x)v(x,t),$$

with the stationary solution:

$$v(x,t) = e^{f(x)-1}tv(x,t).$$

The subspace of learning space, where $f(x)>1$, are not stable, the learners for which $f(x)=1$ do not change their state, and finally clusters with $f(x)<1$ in the final state agents does not differ in opinion.

2) When $\gamma>0$ $\alpha=0$

The stationary solution for a system is given by the equation:

$$f(x)-1=\gamma v^2(x,t),$$

with two different classes of solutions depending of the sign of $f(x)-1$ term. For larger values of agent strength $f(x)>1$ there are one unstable solution $v(x,t)=0$ and two stable ones:

$$v(x,t)=\pm\sqrt{\frac{f(x)-1}{\gamma}}.$$

Learners with self-strength above average influence from others easily get and maintain their state. For weaker agents we have only one stable, stationary solution $v(x,t)=0$. Such learners rapidly collapses their state into average consensus value, and cannot maintain their own prediction outcome adjusting themselves to average opinion.

3) When $\gamma<0$ $\alpha=0$

The equation of dynamic similarly to one-dimensional case [32] is given by the equation:

$$v(x,t)=-v(x,t)+f(x)v(x,t)-\gamma v^3(x,t),$$

with the two unstable solutions:

$$v(x,t)=\pm\sqrt{\frac{1-f(x)}{-\gamma}},$$

and one stable one given by the $v(x,t)=0$, independent of the actual value of $f(x)$.

Summarizing, three different solutions of the dynamical equation (6) can be observed in the stationary limit. Each agent either support its own prediction outcome, or change its state in accordance with the state of majority of learners. The whole abstract learning space can be divided into subspaces, each with non-zero or zero solution. The clusters with non-zero solution have the mean size proportional to the correlation length in the system.

4 Meta-learning

The meta-learning solution for the system is given by the equilibration of the system, i.e. the solution close to stationary state, can be described by expanding the original equation (5):

$$(f(x)-1)v(x)-\gamma v^3(x)=-\alpha\frac{\delta^2}{\delta x^2}f(x)v(x),$$

around the stationary solution from Thomas-Fermi approximation:

$$v_0(x)=\pm\sqrt{\frac{f(x)-1}{\gamma}},$$

for *f(x)>1* or

$v_0(x) = 0$

otherwise. The dynamical equation is given by the formula:

$$(f(x) - 1 - \gamma v_0^2(x))v(x) = -\alpha \frac{\delta^2}{\delta x^2} f(x)v(x). \tag{11}$$

This equation describes the changes of states on the border of a selected cluster (where *f(x)>1*). Now, we introduce similarly to one-dimensional case [32] the new variable:

$$w(x) = f(x)v(x),$$

namely the state weighted by the strength of the agent, and effective potential:

$$V_{eff}(x) = (f(x) - 1) - \gamma v_0^2(x) = f(x) - 1,$$

for *f(x)>1* or

$V_{eff}(x) = 0,$

otherwise. The linear approximation near the cluster edge is therefore described by equation [32]:

$$\frac{f'(x_0)}{f^2(x_0)}(x - x_0)w(x) - \gamma v^3(x) = \alpha \frac{\delta^2}{\delta x^2} w(x),$$

that has solutions as Airy functions for new variable z

$$z = \frac{1}{h}(x - x_0),$$

where:

$$h^3 = \alpha \frac{f^2(x_0)}{f'(x_0)}.$$

The final stationary solution for the whole cluster given by equation (11) smoothed by the transitory layer with thickness equal to h described by Airy-like function:

$$A_i(z) \sim z^{-1/4} e^{-2/3 z^{3/2}},$$

in the direction perpendicular to the cluster borders in multidimensional space. The thickness h should be much smaller than the average size of the cluster, and the mean distance between clusters.

The statistical description of the whole system can be calculated by averaging a set of variables (such as total area of non-zero clusters, thickness of transitory layer, mean area of one cluster or the number of clusters) over the strength function *f(x)*. For example, the equation for total area of non-zero clusters is given by simple average:

$$P_{tot} = \theta(f(x) - 1),$$

the average thickness of transitory layer is given by the formula:

$$h_{eff} = \langle h \rangle = \left\langle \sqrt[3]{\alpha \frac{f^2(x_0)}{f^{'}(x_0)}} \right\rangle .$$

The order parameter of the system is given by the

$$\eta = S \big/ 2h_{eff} \, ,$$

with S as the mean distance between clusters [32]. Three phases of the system can be therefore observed: a) sparse phase $\eta >> 1$, small minority clusters; b) middle density phase $\eta > 1$, some clusters are close to each other; c) large density phase $0 < \eta < 1$, with clusters close to each other, and uniformity of opinion is almost reached. The time of collapse of the minority cluster (the equilibration of the system) is given by simple, finite value [32]:

$$t_{max} = R_0^2 \big/ 2f\left(R_0\right)$$

The solution for the adaptive integration procedure is given by the minimization of the potential energy for the system (see eq. (9)):

$$\frac{\partial V(x)}{\partial x} = \frac{\partial}{\partial x}[\frac{w^2(x)}{2} + \frac{\gamma w^4(x)}{4f(x)} - f(x)\frac{w^2(x)}{2} + \frac{\alpha}{2}\nabla(\sqrt{f(x)}w(x))^2] = 0$$

i.e. the solution of the stationary state should be given as rewritten equation (6):

$$-w(x,t) - \gamma \frac{w^3(x,t)}{f(x)} + \alpha\sqrt{f(x)}\nabla^2\sqrt{f(x)}w(x,t) = 0 .$$

The minimization of the global solution should be done numerically in respect to the space variables within constrain that both global answers for the system should sum up to one.

5 Concluding Remarks

We showed above that similarly to the original one dimensional case [32], three phases for ensemble learning system emerge: sparse (large isolation of agents), middle density (an interesting transient, meta-stable global configurations), and large density state (large value of learning coupling, near the uniformity edge). In the first case clusters of both types of states exist, and when the weak coupling is present there is no bias toward uniform solution. In this regime the intermittent layer approximation is valid and one can estimate the thickness of transient layer and the approximate size of clusters. In the second case a variety of sophisticated geometries, shapes of clusters are present, some are robust and meta-stable, other disappearing slowly changing their state in agreement with majority rule. Here, no analytical solutions are easy to find, therefore computer simulations have to be applied. The selection of the stationary state, i.e. the adaptive integration procedure, can be described by numerical maximization of the free energy of the system with constrain that the sum of probabilities (the integral over the whole learning space) for both answers should sum up to one.

Acknowledgments. This work is supported by the Polish Ministry of Education and Science (N301 159735) and other financial sources.

References

1. Plewczynski, D.: Brainstorming: Consensus Learning in Practice. Frontiers in Neuroinformatics (2009)
2. Ying, H., et al.: A fuzzy discrete event system approach to determining optimal HIV/AIDS treatment regimens. IEEE Trans. Inf. Technol. Biomed. 10(4), 663–676 (2006)
3. Burton, J., et al.: Virtual screening for cytochromes p450: successes of machine learning filters. Comb. Chem. High Throughput Screen 12(4), 369–382 (2009)
4. Capobianco, E.: Model validation for gene selection and regulation maps. Funct. Integr. Genomics 8(2), 87–99 (2008)
5. Do, C.B., Foo, C.S., Batzoglou, S.: A max-margin model for efficient simultaneous alignment and folding of RNA sequences. Bioinformatics 24(13), i68–i76 (2008)
6. Gesell, T., Washietl, S.: Dinucleotide controlled null models for comparative RNA gene prediction. BMC Bioinformatics 9, 248 (2008)
7. Khandelwal, A., et al.: Computational models to assign biopharmaceutics drug disposition classification from molecular structure. Pharm. Res. 24(12), 2249–2262 (2007)
8. Plewczynski, D., Spieser, S.A., Koch, U.: Assessing different classification methods for virtual screening. J. Chem. Inf. Model. 46(3), 1098–1106 (2006)
9. Plewczynski, D.: Mean-field theory of meta-learning. Journal of Statistical Mechanics: Theory and Experiment 11, P11003 (2009)
10. Joshi, A., Weng, J.: Autonomous mental development in high dimensional context and action spaces. Neural Netw. 16(5-6), 701–710 (2003)
11. Sharma, R., Srinivasa, N.: Efficient Learning of VAM-Based Representation of 3D Targets and its Active Vision Applications. Neural Netw. 11(1), 153–171 (1998)
12. Huang, P., Xu, Y.: SVM-based learning control of space robots in capturing operation. Int. J. Neural Syst. 17(6), 467–477 (2007)
13. Knuth, K.H.: Intelligent machines in the twenty-first century: foundations of inference and inquiry. Philos. Transact. A Math. Phys. Eng. Sci. 361(1813), 2859–2873 (2003)
14. Lau, K.K., et al.: An edge-detection approach to investigating pigeon navigation. J. Theor. Biol. 239(1), 71–78 (2006)
15. Miglino, O., Lund, H.H., Nolfi, S.: Evolving mobile robots in simulated and real environments. Artif. Life 2(4), 417–434 (1995)
16. Peters, J., Schaal, S.: Reinforcement learning of motor skills with policy gradients. Neural Netw. 21(4), 682–697 (2008)
17. Qin, J., Li, Y., Sun, W.: A Semisupervised Support Vector Machines Algorithm for BCI Systems. Comput. Intell. Neurosci., 94397 (2007)
18. Reinkensmeyer, D.J., Emken, J.L., Cramer, S.C.: Robotics, motor learning, and neurologic recovery. Annu. Rev. Biomed. Eng. 6, 497–525 (2004)
19. Roberts, S., et al.: Positional entropy during pigeon homing I: application of Bayesian latent state modelling. J. Theor. Biol. 227(1), 39–50 (2004)

20. Tani, J., et al.: Codevelopmental learning between human and humanoid robot using a dynamic neural-network model. IEEE Trans. Syst. Man Cybern. B Cybern. 38(1), 43–59 (2008)
21. Miller, M.L., Blom, N.: Kinase-specific prediction of protein phosphorylation sites. Methods Mol. Biol. 527, 299–310 (2009)
22. Tang, B.M., et al.: The use of gene-expression profiling to identify candidate genes in human sepsis. Am J. Respir. Crit. Care Med. 176(7), 676–684 (2007)
23. Thomas, G., et al.: IDOCS: intelligent distributed ontology consensus system–the use of machine learning in retinal drusen phenotyping. Invest. Ophthalmol. Vis. Sci. 48(5), 2278–2284 (2007)
24. la Cour, T., et al.: Analysis and prediction of leucine-rich nuclear export signals. Protein Eng. Des. Sel. 17(6), 527–536 (2004)
25. Engelbrecht, A.P.: Computational Intelligence. John Wiley & Sons Ltd. (2007)
26. Abelson, R.P.: In: Frederksen, N., Gulliksen, H. (eds.) Contributions to Mathematical Psychology. Holt, Reinehart & Winston, New York (1964)
27. Nowak, A., Szamrej, J., Latane, B.: From Private Attitude to Public Opinion: A Dynamic Theory of Social Impact. Psychological Review 97(3), 362–376 (1990)
28. Latane, B.: Am. Psychol. (36), 343 (1981)
29. Lewenstein, M., Nowak, A., Latane, B.: Statistical mechanics of social impact. Phys. Rev. A 45(2), 763–776 (1992)
30. Kohring, G.A.: Ising models of social impact: The role of cumulative advantage. Journal De Physique I 6(2), 301–308 (1996)
31. Kohring, G.A.: J. Phys. I France (6), 301–308 (1996)
32. Plewczynski, D.: Landau theory of social clustering. Physica A 261(3-4), 608–617 (1998)
33. Fronczak, A., Fronczak, P., Holyst, J.A.: Mean-field theory for clustering coefficients in Barabasi-Albert networks. Phys. Rev. E Stat. Nonlin. Soft Matter Phys. 68(4 pt 2), 046126 (2003)
34. Lambiotte, R., Ausloos, M., Holyst, J.A.: Majority model on a network with communities. Phys. Rev. E Stat. Nonlin. Soft Matter Phys. 75(3 pt 1), 030101 (2007)

Multi-Test Decision Trees for Gene Expression Data Analysis

Marcin Czajkowski[1], Marek Grześ[2], and Marek Kretowski[1]

[1] Faculty of Computer Science, Bialystok University of Technology, Wiejska 45a, 15-351, Bialystok, Poland
{m.czajkowski,m.kretowski}@pb.edu.pl

[2] School of Computer Science, University of Waterloo, 200 University Avenue West, Waterloo, Ontario, N2L 3G1, Canada
mgrzes@cs.uwaterloo.ca

Abstract. This paper introduces a new type of decision trees which are more suitable for gene expression data. The main motivation for this work was to improve the performance of decision trees under a possibly small increase in their complexity. Our approach is thus based on univariate tests, and the main contribution of this paper is the application of several univariate tests in each non-terminal node of the tree. In this way, obtained trees are still relatively easy to analyze and understand, but they become more powerful in modelling high dimensional microarray data. Experimental validation was performed on publicly available gene expression datasets. The proposed method displayed competitive accuracy compared to the commonly applied decision tree methods.

Keywords: Decision trees, classification, gene expression, univariate tests.

1 Introduction

Decision trees represent one of the most popular classification techniques [19,20]. Their chief advantage is the fact that they are easy to understand by humans which makes them particularly useful when the aim of modelling is to understand the underlying processes of the environment. Decision trees are also applicable when the data does not satisfy rigorous assumptions required by more traditional methods [15,7]. However, existing attempts to apply decision trees to the classification of gene expression data showed that standard decision tree algorithms are not sufficient for inducing competitive classifiers [14].

In this paper, we introduce a new type of decision trees that allow testing more than one feature in a single node of the tree. Every split of such trees is composed of a set of univariate tests and is called a multi-test split. Trees which are based on such tests are called Multi-Test Decision Trees (*MTDT*).

1.1 Background and Motivation

Gene expression data is extremely challenging for computational tools and mathematical modelling [21]. Each observation is described by a high dimensional

P. Bouvry et al. (Eds.): SIIS 2011, LNCS 7053, pp. 154–167, 2012.

feature vector with a number of features reaching even a few dozens of thousands, whereas the number of observations is rarely higher than one hundred. This high ratio of variables/cases requires new era computational tools to extract significant and meaningful rules from this kind of data. Existing decision tree learning algorithms can easily find a split which separates the training data very well at a given level in the tree, but such a split can correspond to noise only. This situation is more probable at intermediate and lower levels of the tree.

A short example will illustrate this problem. Assuming that at a given level of the tree there are 20 observations (10 from class A and 10 from class B) and 2×10^5 features, the number of possible partitions of this training set (the number of combinations of choosing 10 out of 20 instances) is smaller (the exact number is $184,756$) than the number of available features. This makes it very easy to find a split, i.e., an attribute and its corresponding threshold, which can split this data perfectly. When there are only 10 observations in the node, the number of combinations is only 250 whereas the number of attributes is 3 orders of magnitude higher. When there is only one univariate test that splits the data, there is a very high risk of choosing faulty splits which correspond to noise.

In this paper we tackle the problem of improving the performance of decision trees on gene expression data. Our focus is on univariate trees since they are a 'white-box' technique and this fact makes them particularly interesting for scientific modeling. They are much easier to understand than trees with multivariate splits and much easier to learn from data. However traditional algorithms, for example, $C4.5$ [23] or $CART$ [4], fail to produce decision trees with high classification accuracy on gene expression data. Our previous work with various univariate decision tree algorithms showed that these algorithms produce considerably small trees which classify the training data perfectly but fail in classifying unseen instances [14]. Only a small number of attributes is used in such trees and their model complexity is low (high bias) therefore they underfit the training data [20]. Producing bigger trees using standard algorithms such as $C4.5$ does not solve the problem in the case of gene expression data because small trees often classify the training data perfectly [14].

This indicates that the issue of split complexity could be advocated here since not much can be gained from bigger univariate decision trees on this kind of data. Standard techniques of improving the performance of classification algorithms, e.g., ensemble methods when applied to decision trees result in complex classifiers that are almost impossible to understand by humans [8,24]. There are also algorithms which apply multivariate tests [6] based mostly on a linear combination of features. These kinds of decision trees with multivariate splits or bagging/boosting methods often outperform existing univariate algorithms on gene expression data [25,16]. They generate, however, more complex classification rules that from the medical point of view are more difficult to understand and analyze.

Some feature selection should be taken into account especially in the context of microarray data. Providing a group of genes that contributes most to the classification task like in [1,10] may significantly improve the performance of decision trees.

1.2 Related Work

One of the approaches that addresses the issue of the test complexity in decision trees was explored by Berzal et al. [3] who proposed multi-way decision trees using multi-way splits. In [3], a hierarchical clustering of attribute values is combined with the standard greedy decision tree algorithm. The author reduces the tree complexity (in terms of the number of nodes) by using multiple thresholds in each split on a single numerical attribute. This will potentially increase the branching factor of such splits, however such tests will be more expressive and the overall number of nodes in the corresponding decision tree will be smaller. In contrast to our solution, multi-way splits used in [3] are based on a single attribute which is not sufficient to overcome the high ratio of features/observations in the gene expression data.

The specific character of gene expression data and its influence on the process of building decision trees was investigated by Li et al. [18]. This solution was focused on using committees of trees to aggregate the discriminating power of a bigger number of significant rules and make more reliable predictions. Firstly, all features are ranked according to the gain ratio [23]. In the next step, the first tree using the first top-ranked feature in the root node is built. Next, the second tree using the second top-ranked feature in the root node is built and the process continues until the k-th tree using the k-th top-ranked feature is obtained. The classification of the final committee of k decision trees is governed by weighted voting. It was observed that:

- well performing rules often contain features which are globally low-ranked;
- if the construction of a tree is confined to a set of globally top-ranked features, the rules in the resulting tree may be less accurate than rules derived from the entire feature space;
- alternative trees often outperform or compete with the performance of the greedy tree.

This work also supports our approach to use many univariate splits in multi-test decision tree induction algorithm. In particular, our aim is to make use of features which are globally lower-ranked and use them jointly in multi-tests. However, our aim is also to preserve simplicity of final decision trees, which is not the case in [18].

The rest of the paper is organized as follows. In the next section, an algorithm to learn multi-test decision trees is presented. In Section 3, the proposed approach is experimentally evaluated on real gene expression data. The paper is concluded in the last section and future work is also discussed.

2 Multi-Test Decision Trees

Regardless which approach to construct decision trees is used, one of the dimensions by which decision trees can be characterized is the number of features which are tested at each node. Standard algorithms, such as C4.5 [23], use univariate splits, which means that only one feature is checked in each internal node of the tree. In this paper, we introduce a new type of decision trees that allow testing more than one feature in a single internal node of the tree. Every split of our trees is composed of a set of univariate tests and is called a multi-test split. The fact that these elementary splits are univariate and the way they are combined show that our approach is substantially different from multi-variate, e.g. oblique, spits. Trees which are based on our approach are called Multi-Test Decision Trees ($MTDTs$), because several univariate elementary tests can be applied in every internal node of the tree. Every univariate test of the multi-test corresponds basically to one split from classical algorithms such as C4.5, and our extension is about combining such individual tests into more complex multi-test splits. The reminder of this section introduces our algorithm for learning and applying for classification such multi-test splits.

Decision trees can be constructed using different methods among which top-down induction is the most common. In what follows, it is assumed that such top-down induction is used, and the further description focuses on our novel idea of multi-test splits, which could be essentially used with other types of decision tree learning methods as well.

2.1 Learning Multi-Test Splits

Let M be a number of training instances $X = \{x_1, x_2, \ldots, x_M\}$ in a given node. Each instance is described by P attributes denoted as $F = \{f_1, f_2, \ldots, f_P\}$. Let $x_{i,j}$ denote the value of the attribute j of the instance i. Each non-terminal node contains a set of W multi-tests denoted as MT ($MT = \{mt_1, mt_2, \ldots, mt_W\}$) from which only one will be chosen in order to split the training instances into two groups and create a branch for each outcome of the test. Each i-th multi-test is composed of a group of no more than N univariate tests in which one is called a *primary splitter* (PS_i) and the rest $N-1$ *surrogate splitters* ($S_{i,j}$ where $1 \leq j < N$). The parameter denoted as N represents the maximum number of one-dimensional tests that constitute the multi-test.

The $MTDT$ splitting criterion is directed by the majority voting mechanism where the result of each test constitutes a single vote. For this reason, surrogate tests have considerable impact on decisions of multi-tests because they can outvote the primary splitters. It should be noted that this impact can be positive as well as negative and effects the gain ratio for the entire multi-test. Additionally, we create not one but W multi-tests that can compete with each other. Therefore, the best multi-test that will be used as a splitting criterion may not contain the test with highest gain ratio (PS_1). This can happen when a competitive multi-test mt_i ($1 < i \leq W$) has a higher gain ratio than mt_1. The illustration of finding the splitting rule for an internal node of the $MTDT$ is showed in Fig. 1.

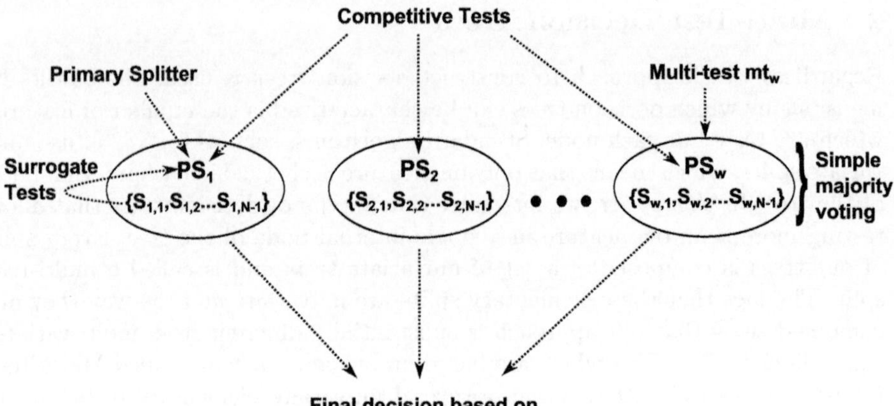

Fig. 1. An example of finding the best multi-test from the set of multi-tests for a non-terminal node in $MTDT$

First, the algorithm searches for the best possible thresholds. This process is similar to the search function in the $C4.5$ algorithm. Next, the W multi-tests are calculated and the one with the highest gain ratio is chosen to split the training instances. The algorithm that finds the splitting rule (the best multi-test) for a given node of the $MTDT$ during top-down induction is presented below.

```
Inputs:
    M - number of training instances X={x1,x2,...,xM} in a node
    P - number of attributes F={f1,f2,...,fP}
    W - number of multi-tests
Initialize:
    V - Vector of pairs: {threshold h, gain ratio gr}
    MT - Empty vector MT={mt1,mt2,...,mtW}
Training:
    FOR i in {1,...,P}
        FOR j in {1,..,M-1}
            h_(i,j) = 0.5*(x_(i,j) + x_(i,j+1))
            IF IsCandidateThreshold(h_(i,j)) is True
                gr = gain ratio of h_(i,j)
            add pair {h_(i,j),gr} to V
        ENDIF
        ENDFOR
    ENDFOR
    Sort V decreasingly according to the highest gain ratio
    MT[1] = BuildMultitest(V[1].h)
    FOR i in {2,...,W}
        h = FindCompetitive(V,MT)
        MT[i] = BuildMultitest(h)
```

```
    ENDFOR
    FOR i in {1,...,W}
        calculate gain ratio for MT[i]
    ENDFOR
RETURN multi-test with the highest gain ratio from MT
```

Specific functions, such as *IsCandidateThreshold*, *BuildMultitest* and *FindCompetitive*, are discussed in detail in subsequent sections.

IsCandidateThreshold. Function *IsCandidateThreshold* guides the search process of the possible thresholds. At the beginning of the algorithm, we search for a vector V that contains pairs of a threshold and a gain ratio that is calculated from the univariate test obtained from that threshold. If the attributes are nominal, the set of possible values an attribute can take is limited and usually small. Finding the potential set of tests for the continuous-valued attributes is somewhat more difficult. In this case, one needs to calculate and rank all tests that involve one feature only. Each single test compares the value of an attribute f_j $(1 \leq j \leq P)$ against a threshold $h_{k,j}$: $f_j \geq h_{k,j}$ where $h_{k,j}$ denotes the value of the k-threshold $(1 \leq k < M - 1)$ on the attribute j. To formulate the test, we sort the training instances based on the values of an attribute f_j in order to obtain a finite set of values $\{x_{1,j}, x_{2,j}, \ldots, x_{M,j}\}$.

Any threshold $h_{k,j}$ between $x_{i,j}$ and $x_{i+1,j}$ $(1 \leq i < M)$ will have the same effect when dividing the training instances, so we need to check only $M - 1$ possible thresholds for each numerical attribute f_j. In Fig. 2, it can be observed that some regular thresholds should not be considered, for example, $h_{1,j}$, $h_{4,j}$ and $h_{M-1,j}$. Tests performed on those thresholds are useless for creating new tests because they split two training instances from the same class. Therefore in order to optimize the performance, we consider only the relevant threshold called candidate threshold [11]. The proposed algorithm performs this optimization using the *IsCandidateThreshold* function. All candidate thresholds are added to the vector V and sorted according to the highest gain ratio. In our work, the gain ratio criterion is used to determine the best possible threshold, and the midpoint, $h_{k,j}$, of the interval $[x_{i,j}, x_{i+1,j}]$ is applied as the value of this threshold: $h_{k,j} = \frac{x_{i,j}+x_{i+1,j}}{2}$. It differs slightly from the implementation in the $C4.5$ algorithm, where the threshold is set to the largest value of f_j in the entire training set that does not exceed the above interval midpoint.

BuildMultitest. Let us consider the first multi-test mt_1. Let PS_1 be a single univariate test performed on a threshold from the input parameter of BuildMultitest function for mt_1. In this particular case, the PS_1 will have the highest gain ratio in the node because it was built on the best possible threshold $(V[1].h)$. However we believe that applying a single test based on one attribute may cause the classifier to underfit the learning data due to low complexity of such a classification rule. For this reason, the multi-test is composed of a group of N univariate tests. The parameter denoted as N represents the maximum number of one-dimensional tests that constitute the multi-test in each non-terminal node.

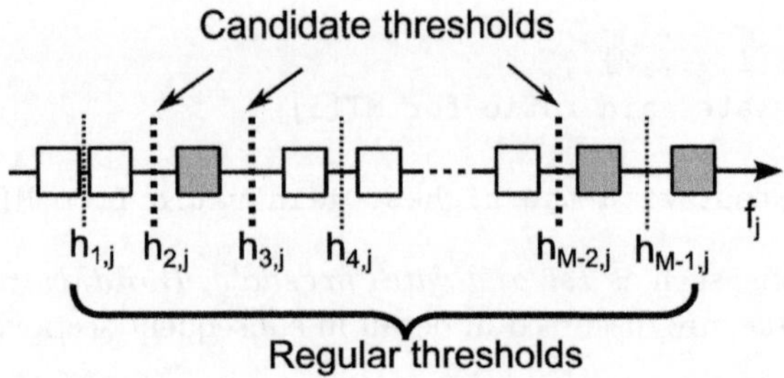

Fig. 2. Candidate thresholds on attribute f_j

Those tests will support the division of the training instances made by the primary splitter PS_1. In other words, the remaining tests of the multi-test should, using the remaining features, branch the tree in similar way to PS_1.

In order to determine surrogate tests, we have adopted a solution proposed in the *CART* system. The use of the surrogate variable at a given split results in a similar node impurity measure. It also mimics the chosen split itself in terms of which and how many observations goes to the corresponding branch. Therefore, the measure of similarity between the primary splitter and remaining tests of the multi-test is the number of observations classified in the same way. In our method, we also consider tests that classify instances in a inverse (opposite) way to PS_1. For such tests, we reverse the relation between attribute and interval midpoint, and recalculate the score. The primary splitter PS_1 and up to $N-1$ surrogate tests $S_{1,l}$ $(1 \leq l < N)$ constitute the single multi-test denoted as mt_1.

FindCompetitive. Function searches for a threshold that will be applied in the *BuildMultitest* function for mt_i where $1 < i \leq W$. This threshold will be used to build an *i primary splitter* (PS) for the i multi-test. The process of obtaining the first multi-test denoted as mt_1, whose primary splitter PS_1 has the highest gain ratio, was shown in previous paragraph. Here we describe alternative multi-tests that are also built in each non-terminal node and which compete with mt_1. The process of building multi-tests, mt_i $(1 < i \leq W)$, requires finding new primary splitters PS_i which together with their surrogate tests may outperform mt_1.

Two factors should be taken into consideration while choosing PS_i. Firstly, the primary splitters PS_i should be competitor splitters to PS_1. Competitor splitters, alike surrogate splitters $S_{1,i}$, yield high gain ratio but are not as good as the primary splitter PS_1. A significant difference between these splits is the way variables are ranked. Surrogate splitters are not evaluated on how much improvement they yield in reducing node impurity but rather on how closely they mimic the split determined by the primary splitter. Competitor splits are runners-up to the primary split and are ranked according to the highest gain ratio. We denote splitters as competitor splitters if their gain ratio is higher than $q\%$ of the best gain PS_1 (the default value equal to 95%). Using more competitor tests in the search process for the primary split (low q value) may lead to the selection of tests with low gain ratio. However, decreasing the number of competitor tests (high q) may cause the PS_i be too similar to PS_1. To sum up: the surrogate splitters are similar to the primary splitter, whereas competitor splitters are those which have highest gain ratio.

The second element that should be taken into consideration is that the same variable is often listed as both a competitor and a surrogate. It may result in obtaining alternative multi-tests, mt_i, that contain similar or identical univariate tests and do not provide any improvement. Therefore competitor splits should be diversified to make the alternative multi-tests also diversified. Function $FindCompetitive$ finds the primary splitter PS_i in a loop for $W-1$ multi-tests. Each PS_i must be a competitor splitter to PS_1 and be the worst average surrogate to all primary splitters PS_j where $j < i$. The next step is to build multi-test mt_i according to PS_i in the same way as in Section 2.1.

2.2 Multi-Test Size and Prediction

The size of the multi-test has a critical impact on its performance and a splitting decision. The parameter denoted as N represents the maximum number of univariate tests in a multi-test and is defined by the user. To classify observations, simple majority voting mechanism is employed in which each test has an equal vote. In the case of a draw, the decision is made in accordance with the primary splitter. In order to determine the final decision, the gain ratio for each of W splits determined by multi-tests, mt_i $(1 \leq i \leq W)$, is calculated and compared. The multi-test with the highest gain ratio is then applied in a given node.

The exact size of the multi-test depends on the difference between the primary splitter and surrogate tests. The main idea of the $MTDT$ is to use a group of similar tests in a single node instead of one test as in the classical approach to univariate decision trees. If there are tests that do not have a right substitute, surrogate tests should not be added in order to avoid discrepancy in the multi-test. An inappropriate set of surrogate tests may dominate the primary splitter and deteriorate the splitting criterion. Therefore, surrogate tests added to the multi-test should not be different from the primary splitter more than b percent. When $b = 0\%$, it means that no surrogates are accepted, which is equivalent to setting $N = 1$. In this case, the decision tree would become similar to the tree generated by the $C4.5$ algorithm as only one attribute will be used in each multi-test. When $b = 100\%$, it means that all $N-1$ surrogates join the multi-test. The threshold, b, can be defined by the user (default value equal 10%).

3 Experimental Results

In this section the proposed solution is experimentally verified using real microarray datasets. The results of the $MTDT$ algorithm were compared with several popular decision tree systems.

3.1 Setup

The performance of the $MTDT$ classifier was investigated using publicly available microarray datasets described in Table 1. These datasets are from the Kent

Table 1. Kent Ridge Bio-medical gene expression datasets

Datasets	Attributes	Training Set	Testing Set
Breast Cancer	24481	34/44	12/7
Central Nervous System	7129	21/39	-
Colon Tumor	6500	40/22	-
DLBCL Standford	4026	24/23	-
DLBCL vs Follicular Lymphoma	6817	58/19	-
DLBCL NIH	7399	88/72	30/50
Leukemia ALL vs AML	7129	27/11	20/14
Leukemia MLL vs ALL vs AML	12583	20/7/20	4/3/8
Prostate Cancer	12600	52/50	27/8

Ridge Bio-medical Dataset Repository [17] and are related to studies of human cancer, including: leukemia, colon tumor, breast and prostate cancer. For datasets that were not pre-divided into the training and testing parts, the 10-fold stratified cross-validation was applied[1]. Leave-one-out cross-validation was also considered however no significant influence on classification accuracy was observed. To ensure stable results, the average score of 10 runs is presented in all experiments.

The classification process for all algorithms was preceded by feature selection using the Relief-F [1] method which is common for microarray data analysis. In the first step, Relief-F draws instances at random and computes their nearest neighbors. Afterwards, Relief-F adjusts a feature weighting vector to give higher weight to those attributes which discriminate the instance from neighbors of different classes. The number of neighbors in Relief-F was equal to 10 and in order to improve the computation time, the number of selected attributes was arbitrary limited to the top 1000. Restriction for the number of attributes has no significant influence on classification accuracy however it speeds the algorithms up.

We have employed two alternative multi-tests mt_2 and mt_3 in addition to the primary test, mt_1, so the number of multi-tests analyzed in each non-terminal node, was equal to 3 ($W = 3$). Performed experiments show that employing a higher number of multi-tests, besides significant increase of the calculation time, did not yield any improvement in classification accuracy. To prevent data over-fitting, $C4.5$-like pessimistic pruning was applied.

3.2 Multi-Test Decision Tree Results

In Table 2, we compare the influence of the multi-test size on the accuracy. Results show that the number of univariate tests N used in a single multi-test has a significant impact on the classifier accuracy. The average score of the

[1] Pre-divided datasets were also tested with cross-validation but since the obtained performance was the same as with the original division into training and testing parts, due to lack of space, we report results with that original division only.

Table 2. A comparison of the *MTDT* accuracy under different numbers of tests in the multi-test

Dataset / Classifier	*MTDT* $N = 1$	*MTDT* $N = 5$	*MTDT* $N = 11$
Breast Cancer	**68.42**	57.89	57.89
Central Nervous System	60.50	72.17	**74.33**
Colon Tumor	80.40	**85.83**	83.92
DLBCL Standford	81.75	85.25	**86.60**
DLBCL vs Follicular Lymphoma	84.82	83.42	**85.42**
DLBCL NIH	51.25	60.00	**62.50**
Leukemia ALL vs AML	**91.17**	**91.17**	88.23
Leukemia MLL vs ALL vs AML	86.67	**100.00**	**100.00**
Prostate Cancer	26.47	**61.76**	44.11
Average score	70.16	77.50	75.89

multi-test with $N > 1$ was higher on most of the datasets. On only one dataset (Breast Cancer), the result of the multi-test algorithm was lower than expected, although the overall improvement is noticeable. We conjecture that the main cause of lower classification accuracy of the *MTDT* approach with $N = 1$ was due to under-fitted decision trees. It is worth emphasizing that the *MTDT* with a single one-attribute test in a node, $N = 1$, behaves similarly to the standard $C4.5$ algorithm. It was also observed that using too many genes in the multi-test may not only induce more complex rules but also over-fit learned trees to the training data.

In order to detect and exclude the possibility of over-fitting in the training phase of our method, we created artificial datasets which were copied from those listed in Table 1 where attributes were left exactly the same but class labels were randomly changed. This is usually referred to as the Y-randomization test [27]. The *MTDT* classification accuracy was significantly lower on randomized data than on original data and therefore this indicates that there is no evidence of over-fitting in our method.

Experiments performed on the Dual-Core CPU 1.66GHz machine with 2GB of RAM showed that the proposed solution is scalable and can manage large datasets. Average computation time on analysed datasets for increasing numbers of tests in the multi-test: $N = 1$, $N = 5$, and $N = 11$ was 2.8, 5.3 and 8.8 seconds correspondingly.

Leukemia MLL vs. ALL vs. AML Dataset. In one of our experiments, the dataset from Armstrong [2] was evaluated. Dataset describes the distinction between Leukemia MLL and other conventional ALL subtypes. There are a total of 57 3-class training samples (20 for ALL, 17 for MLL, and 20 for AML) and 15 test samples (4, 3, and 8 correspondingly). *MTDT* decision trees with $N = 1$ and $N = 5$ when evaluated on the training instances have the classification accuracy equal 100%. The actual trees are illustrated in Fig. 3. Although decision trees compared in this figure have the same performance on the training data, there is a significant difference in results on the testing instances. Table 3 shows the

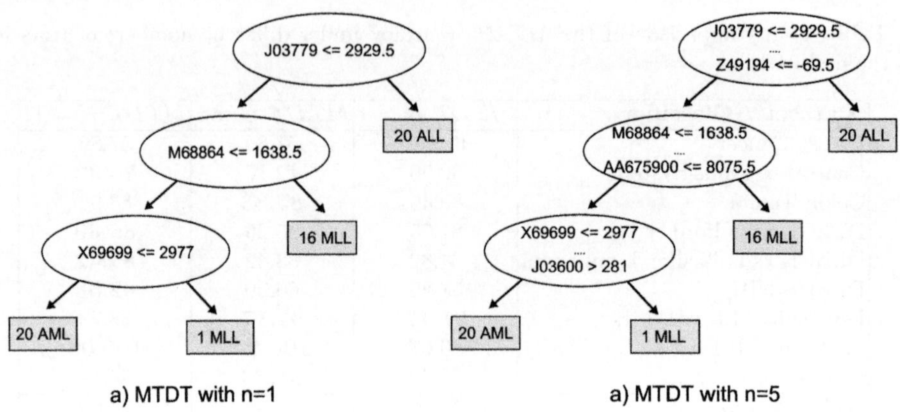

Fig. 3. Multi-Test decision trees with N=1 and N=5 tests in a single node

Table 3. Multi-Test Decision Tree with $N = 1$ and $N = 5$

$MTDT\ N = 1$			$MTDT\ N = 5$			
(a)	(b)	(c)	(a)	(b)	(c)	Classified as:
6	2	0	8	0	0	(a): AML
0	1	2	0	3	0	(b): MLL
0	2	2	0	0	4	(c): ALL
Accuracy 60%			Accuracy 100%			

confusion matrix for decision trees. In this experiment, decision trees with multi-test size $N = 1$ and $N = 5$ have the same structure, number of nodes and the same primary splitters. However, for other values of parameter N or different datasets this may not be the case. Differences in the tree structure may occur when alternative multi-tests outperform the mt_1 test or surrogate splits outvote the primary splitters. In spite of an equal tree size between $MTDT$ with $N = 1$ and $N > 1$, a larger number of univariate tests in a multi-test generates more complex nodes. Hopefully, the multi-tests contain only univariate tests which are easy to understand by human experts. For most datasets shown in Table 1, there is a relevant biological literature which identifies marker genes that are highly correlated with the class distinction. In order to evaluate whether the $MTDT$ results are biologically meaningful, we checked if discovered genes from our model match biological finding in the literature. The comparison showed that most of the genes from our $MTDT$ model were also identified in biological publications. For this particular dataset, 4 out of 5 genes that built $MTDT$ multi-test in the root node were also distinguished in article [2] and patent [13]. Attributes that built multi-tests in the lower parts of the $MTDT$ tree usually do not appear in biological publications as they distinguish only small sets of instances. We believe that $MTDT$ is capable of finding not only the most significant groups of marker genes but also low-ranked genes that when combined may also be meaningful.

Table 4. Comparison of classification accuracy

DT/CL	AD	BF	J48	RF	CT
Breast Cancer	42.10	47.36	52.63	68.42	68.42
Central Nervous System	63.33	71.66	56.66	75.00	73.33
Colon Tumor	74.19	75.80	85.48	75.80	75.80
DLBCL Standford	95.74	80.85	87.23	95.74	82.97
DLBCL vs Follicular Lymphoma	88.31	79.22	79.22	88.31	83.11
DLBCL NIH	50.00	60.00	57.50	52.50	62.50
Leukemia ALL vs AML	91.17	91.17	91.17	82.35	91.17
Leukemia MLL vs ALL vs AML	*	73.33	80.00	86.66	73.33
Prostate Cancer	38.23	44.11	29.41	29.41	44.11
Average score	67.88	69.28	68.81	72.68	72.75

3.3 Comparison of *MTDTs* to Other Classifiers

The comparison of *MTDTs* to other decision trees was also performed. The following classification algorithms were selected for this analysis:

1. *AD Tree* - alternating decision tree [12].
2. *BF Tree* - best-first decision tree classifier [22].
3. *J48 Tree* - pruned *C*4.5 decision tree [23].
4. *Random Forest* - algorithm constructing a forest of random trees [5].
5. *Simple Cart* - *CART* algorithm that implements minimal cost-complexity pruning [4].

The implementation of standard algorithms in the Weka package [26] was used in our evaluation. All classifiers, including the *MTDT* algorithm, were employed with default values of parameters on all datasets. The results are presented in Table 4. AD Tree can be applied only to binary class dataset therefore there are no results for *Leukemia MLL vs ALL vs AML* dataset.

Results in Tables 2 and 4 show that *MTDTs* with $N = 5$ tests in a single node yielded the best average accuracy, 77.50%, over all classification problems. However, the proposed *MTDT* method managed to achieve high accuracy whereas comprehensive decision rules were maintained via univariate tests used in multi-test splits. It is worth emphasizing that the *MTDT* with a single binary test in a node, i.e., $N = 1$, performed similarly to all remaining 'univariate test' methods. It can be compared to the J48 tree algorithm as they both use the gain ratio criterion. Their trees in most cases separated the training data perfectly, but performed considerably worse on testing instances. This may be caused by the under-fitted decision tree model. A slight increase in the number of tests in each split improved classification accuracy which can be observed in Table 2.

4 Conclusion and Future Directions

In this paper, we presented the multi-test decision tree approach to gene expression data classification. A new splitting criterion was introduced with the aim of reducing the under-fit of decision trees on these kind of data and improving classification accuracy. The experimental sections showed that our method led to competitive results as it outperformed the standard decision trees. Additionally, proposed method can be used with incomplete or noisy datasets since it uses internal surrogate tests. The preliminary comparison with the biological literature showed that decision trees learned by the $MTDT$ algorithm have biological interpretation. Therefore, biologists can benefit from using this "white box" approach as it builds accurate and biologically meaningful models for classification. In our future work, we are planning to apply $MTDT$ to solve the problem of missing values.

Even though, our results on the existing version of the algorithm and the current parameter tuning are promising, additional work on the influence of the test size, N, could yield an interesting insight into the behavior of our algorithm. Overall, we observed that the size, N, of the multi-test has significant impact on discovered rules and classification accuracy. We are working at the moment on the algorithm that through internal cross-validation could set this parameter automatically depending on training data. Another improvement concerns the pre-pruning mechanism that will reduce the size of the multi-test in lower parts of the tree. Our observations showed that the split subsets may have an incorrect size which can then increase the tree height and lead to data over-fit. We are planning also to look for adequate values of the percentage threshold b, which measures the similarity between surrogate tests and the primary splitter. We observed that replacing default settings with individually calculated values for each dataset could also improve classification results.

Acknowledgments. We thank Wojciech Kwedlo for reading this paper and providing constructive feedback. This work was supported by the grant S/WI/2/08 from Bialystok University of Technology.

References

1. Aldamassi, M., Chen, Z., Merriman, B., Gussin, D., Nelson, S.: A Practical Guide to Microarray Analysis of Gene Expression. UCLA Microarray Core & Nelson Lab, UCLA Department of Human Genetics (2001)
2. Armstrong, S.A.: MLL Translocations Specify a Distinct Gene Expression Profile that Distinguishes a Unique Leukemia. Nature Genetics 30, 41–47 (2002)
3. Berzal, F., Cubero, J.C., Marín, N., Sánchez, D.: Building multi-way decision trees with numerical attributes. Information Sciences 165, 73–90 (2004)
4. Breiman, L., Friedman, J., Olshen, R., Stone, C.: Classification and Regression Trees. Wadsworth Int. Group (1984)
5. Breiman, L.: Random Forests. Machine Learning 45(1), 5–32 (2001)
6. Brodley, C.E., Utgoff, P.E.: Multivariate Decision Trees. Machine Learning 19, 45–77 (1995)
7. Chen, X., Wang, M., Zhang, H.: The use of classification trees for bioinformatics. Wires Data Mining Knowl. Discov. 1, 55–63 (2011)
8. Dettling, M., Buhlmann, P.: Boosting for tumor classification with gene expression data. Bioinformatics 19(9), 1061–1069 (2003)

9. Demsar, J.: Statistical comparisons of classifiers over multiple data sets. Journal of Machine Learning Research 7, 1–30 (2006)
10. Dramiski, M., Rada-Iglesias, A., Enroth, S., Wadelius, C., Koronacki, J., Komorowski, J.: Monte Carlo feature selection for supervised classification. Bioinformatics 24(1), 110–117 (2008)
11. Fayyad, U.M., Irani, K.B.: On the Handling of Continuous-Valued Attributes in Decision Tree Generation. Machine Learning 8, 87–102 (1992)
12. Freund, Y., Mason, L.: The alternating decision tree learning algorithm. In: Sixteenth International Conference on Machine Learning, Bled, Slovenia, pp. 124–133 (1999)
13. Golub, T.R., Armstrong, S.A., Korsmeyer, S.J.: MLL translocations specify a distinct gene expression profile, distinguishing a unique leukemia, United States patent: 20060024734 (2006)
14. Grześ, M., Kretowski, M.: Decision Tree Approach to Microarray Data Analysis. Biocybernetics and Biomedical Engineering 27(3), 29–42 (2007)
15. Hastie, T., Tibshirani, R., Friedman, J.H.: The Elements of Statistical Learning. In: Data Mining, Inference and Prediction, 2nd edn. Springer, Heidelberg (2009)
16. Hu, H., Li, J., Wang, H., Shi, M.: A Maximally Diversified Multiple Decision Tree Algorithm for Microarray Data Classification. In: I Workshop on Intelligent Systems for Bioinformatics, ACS (2006)
17. Kent Ridge Bio-medical Dataset Repository, `http://datam.i2r.a-star.edu.sg/datasets/index.html`
18. Li, J., Liu, H., Ng, S., Wong, L.: Discovery of significant rules for classifying cancer diagnosis data. Bioinformatics (19 suppl. 2), 93–102 (2003)
19. Murthy, S.: Automatic construction of decision trees from data: A multidisciplinary survey. Data Mining and Knowledge Discovery 2, 345–389 (1998)
20. Rokach, L., Maimon, O.Z.: Data mining with decision trees: theory and application. Machine Perception Arfitical Intelligence 69 (2008)
21. Sebastiani, P., Gussoni, E., Kohane, I.S., Ramoni, M.F.: Statistical challenges in functional genomics. Statistical Science 18(1), 33–70 (2003)
22. Shi, H.: Best-first decision tree learning, MSc dissertation, University of Waikato (2007)
23. Quinlan, R.: C4.5: Programs for Machine Learning. Morgan Kaufmann Publishers, San Mateo (1993)
24. Tan, A.C., Gilbert, D.: Ensemble machine learning on gene expression data for cancer classification. Applied Bioinformatics 2(3), 75–83 (2003)
25. Tan, P.J., Dowe, D.L., Dix, T.I.: Building classification models from microarray data with tree-based classification algorithms. In: Orgun, M.A., Thornton, J. (eds.) AI 2007. LNCS (LNAI), vol. 4830, pp. 589–598. Springer, Heidelberg (2007)
26. Witten, I.H., Frank, E.: Data Mining: Practical machine learning tools and techniques, 2nd edn. Morgan Kaufmann, San Francisco (2005)
27. Wold, S., Eriksson, L.: Statistical Validation of QSAR Results. In: van de Waterbeemd, H. (ed.) Chemometrics Methods in Molecular Design, VCH, pp. 309–318 (1995)
28. Yeoh, E.J., Ross, M.E.: Classification, subtype discovery, and prediction of outcome in pediatric acute lymphoblastic leukemia by gene expression profiling. Cancer Cell 1(2), 133–143 (2002)

Rule-Based Approach to Computational Stylistics

Urszula Stańczyk

Institute of Informatics, Silesian University of Technology,
Akademicka 16, 44-100 Gliwice, Poland

Abstract. Decision algorithms correspond to the rule-based approach to classification and pattern recognition problems. While to shorten the processing time we need as few constituent decision rules as possible, when their number is too low it may lead to a poor performance of the classifier. The decision rules can be found by providing the minimal cover of the training samples, by calculating rules with some genetic algorithms, by the exhaustive search for all rules. This last option offers the widest choice of rules, which enables tailoring the final algorithm to the task at hand, yet this is achieved by the additional cost of rule selection process. Usually there are assumed some measures indicating the quality of individual decision rules. The paper presents a different procedure, which is closer to feature reduction. In the first step there are selected condition attributes that are discarded, then the rules that contain conditions on these attributes are removed from the algorithm. The classifier performance is observed in the domain of computational stylistics, which is a study on characteristics of writing styles.

Keywords: Decision Algorithm, Computational Stylistics, Rough Sets, DRSA, Condition Attribute, Rule Support.

1 Introduction

When invented by Zdzislaw Pawlak in the early 1980s, rough set approach dealt only with abstract or discrete data, which enables only nominal classification [9]. When the input data sets contain continuous values, discretisation becomes problematic and it can be difficult to ensure high coverage of the input space, which in turn can result in the low classification accuracy. What is more, in multicriteria decision making it often happens that the value sets are ordered. To take an advantage of this observation and allow for ordinal classification, Dominance-based Rough Set Approach (DRSA) has been proposed, replacing the indiscernibility relation with dominance [5,4].

Basing on the knowledge contained in a decision table, theory of rough sets offers tools for calculation of decision rules. Their premise parts list conditions on the attributes that describe objects of the Universe, while the conclusion parts state the decisions when the conditions are met. The rules are found by applying the variety of algorithms. Sometimes the minimal cover of the learning samples gives satisfactory results, but far more often some wider selection, even the

P. Bouvry et al. (Eds.): SIIS 2011, LNCS 7053, pp. 168–179, 2012.

exhaustive search, is needed to ensure a high classification accuracy. A selection of rules forms a decision algorithm, which can be applied in a classification task.

To arrive at the smallest set of the most important decision rules typically the research path goes in two ways. In the first the most important attributes are determined, by referring to the concept of reducts and core. A reduct is a subset of condition attributes which keeps intact the quality of approximation of the decision table. The core is found by intersecting all reducts and the attributes included in it are considered to be more important than others [8,6]. However, when the core is empty, the importance of attributes is not necessarily so straightforward and to establish it some domain knowledge can be required.

In the second approach some measures of rule quality are defined and calculated for all individual decision rules, for example based on their parameters such as support, length, conditions specified, or even more elaborated [7].

A rule support indicates for how many learning samples a rule returns the correct decision. As the rule describes some detected pattern, a high support means that this pattern is present in many training samples. Thus it is reasonable to expect that it will also be present in the samples from the testing set. Long rules mean the risk of overfitting the data: decision rules so closely describe the learning samples that they may fail when generalisation for the testing samples is required. Thus shorter rules can be considered as more adaptable.

The paper presents a methodology for construction of a custom decision algorithm by merging these two ways, focusing both on condition attributes and generated decision rules, with selection of rules for the tailored algorithm by assuming indirect rule importance indicators, referring to attributes involved, using them as rule selectors.

Within the methodology firstly the decision rules are found by applying some algorithm, possibly exhaustive search. The condition attributes are used in construction of rules with varying degrees. Some attributes are exploited more often than others, some appear frequently in the rules with a higher support and some with lower. This line of reasoning puts condition attributes in a new perspective. The distribution of rule support for attributes is analysed and it gives base to their ordering that reflects their importance.

Next the established orderings are exploited for attribute reduction, yet with actual target being reduction of rules. When a condition attribute is discarded, all rules referring to it are discarded as well, regardless on their conclusions and other conditions. The methodology results in building tailored decision algorithms, which preserve the classification accuracy. The performance of the modified classifier is compared against the decision algorithm corresponding to the previously found set of rules, with constraints on rule support to maximise the classification accuracy which is typically employed.

The performance of the rule-based classifier is studied in the area of computational stylistics, which belongs with information retrieval, text mining, data mining. Within the textual analysis there are found numerical characteristics that in the quantitative terms express individual writing styles, allowing for author characterisation, comparison and attribution [10].

2 DRSA Methodology

DRSA offers a modification of Classical Rough Set Approach (CRSA) defined by Z. Pawlak [9], by replacing the indiscernibility relation with dominance. The former enables observation of only presence or absence of features (the objects either are or are not indiscernible with respect to their features) thus leading to nominal classification. Dominance allows for ordinal properties in attribute value sets and it has been proposed to deal with multi-criteria decision making problems [11,5].

With $\succeq_q$ standing for a weak preference relation on the set of objects with respect to some criterion q, if for all $q \in P$, $x \succeq_q y$, then x dominates y with respect to $P \subseteq C$ (denoted as xD_Py). A set of objects dominating x is denoted as $D_P^+(x)$, and a set of objects dominated by x is indicated by $D_P^-(x)$.

If the set of decision attributes contains just one attribute $D = \{d\}$, it partitions the Universe into some finite number of classes $\boldsymbol{Cl} = \{Cl_t\}$, for $t = 1, \ldots, n$, which are preference ordered. The increasing preference is indicated with the increasing indices of classes. The sets of objects to be approximated are upward or downward unions of classes, or dominance cones:

$$Cl_t^{\geq} = \bigcup_{s \geq t} Cl_s \qquad (1)$$
$$Cl_t^{\leq} = \bigcup_{s \leq t} Cl_s$$

For $P \subseteq C$, and $t = 1, \ldots, n$, P-lower approximation of $Cl_t^{\geq}$, $\underline{P}(Cl_t^{\geq})$, is the set of objects belonging to $Cl_t^{\geq}$, while P-upper approximation of $Cl_t^{\geq}$, $\overline{P}(Cl_t^{\geq})$, is the set of objects that could belong to $Cl_t^{\geq}$:

$$\underline{P}(Cl_t^{\geq}) = \{x \in U : D_P^+ \subseteq Cl_t^{\geq}\} \qquad (2)$$
$$\overline{P}(Cl_t^{\geq}) = \{x \in U : D_P^- \cap Cl_t^{\geq} \neq \emptyset\}$$

The differences between upper and lower approximations define the boundary regions of $Cl_t^{\geq}$ and $Cl_t^{\leq}$ with respect to P:

$$Bn_P(Cl_t^{\geq}) = \overline{P}(Cl_t^{\geq}) - \underline{P}(Cl_t^{\geq}) \qquad (3)$$
$$Bn_P(Cl_t^{\leq}) = \overline{P}(Cl_t^{\leq}) - \underline{P}(Cl_t^{\leq})$$

Quality of approximation of $\boldsymbol{Cl}$ by the criteria $P \subseteq C$ can be defined as

$$\gamma_P(\boldsymbol{Cl}) = \frac{\left| \left(U - \left(\bigcup_{t \in \{2,\ldots,n\}} Bn_P(Cl_t^{\geq}) \right) \right) \right|}{|U|} \qquad (4)$$

Each irreducible subset $P \subseteq C$ for which the quality of approximation with the selected criteria is preserved ($\gamma_P(\boldsymbol{Cl}) = \gamma_C(\boldsymbol{Cl})$) is called a reduct. The intersection of all reducts is called the core.

Approximations of the dominance cones is the starting point for the process of induction of decision rules. The rules can be certain, possible, or approximate. A set of decision rules is complete when no object of the table remains unclassified. It is minimal when it is complete and irredundant.

Unfortunately, the minimal set of rules does not guarantee the highest classification accuracy. It assumes to include only the rules that are necessary to cover the training samples and they hardly can cover all points of the multidimensional input space. Therefore, instead of always using minimal cover algorithms, there are also tried approaches generating all rules and then by some selection procedure an optimised classifier is built. It contains only some of rules, basing on their length, support, some assumed weights, or measures of importance [8,1].

3 Aims of Computational Stylistics

Authorship attribution is usually regarded as the most important task within computational stylistics or stylometry. Typical applications, both historic and contemporary, comprise proving or disproving the authenticity of documents, establishing authorship for unattributed or disputed texts, detecting plagiarism. Other tasks of stylometric analysis include author characterisation and author comparison [2].

Computational stylistics relies on the fundamental notion that any writing style can be uniquely described by not only qualitative but also some quantitative measures. These measures have to be defined in such a way that, on one hand, enables recognition of an individual writing style, but, on the other hand, makes imitating it if not exactly impossible, then next to impossible. That is why stylometry uses in its processing such features of texts that are employed in rather subconscious way. Instead of observing some striking language patterns that are easily spotted by anyone who reads the text, usually there are exploited more subtle textual markers of lexical or syntactic type [3].

Lexical descriptors give frequencies of usage for single letters, words, or groups of words, while syntactic markers reflect the structure and patterns of sentences by referring to punctuation marks. Past research shows that both these types of textual descriptors perform well as characteristic features of a classifier needed for authorship attribution studies [12].

Wide corpus of texts processed ensures that characteristics found are more reliable. Construction of samples ends the initial pre-processing phase within the stylometric analysis. The next step requires application of some data mining methodology to go through available data, to find some patterns and trends in it, and return a classifier capable of authorship attribution with satisfactory accuracy. Techniques employed come from either statistic-oriented computations or artificial intelligence domain, such as rough set methodology.

When term frequencies are used as characteristic features for the constructed classifier, there is no doubt that the observed values are ordered, yet their preference cannot be established within stylometric domain, as some universal, a priori knowledge about these frequencies with reference to particular authors does not exist. However, as basing on them we definitely can determine authorship, it is reasonable to expect that such preference does exist. That is why the preference order as required by DRSA is either assumed arbitrarily or found in some experimental way.

4 Experimental Setup

In the experiments described in the paper a set of 25 markers was used, with frequencies of usage for the selected function words (17) and punctuation marks (8): but, and, not, in, with, on, at, of, this, as, that, what, from, by, for, to, if, a fullstop, a comma, a question mark, an exclamation mark, a semicolon, a colon, a bracket, a hyphen. The frequencies were calculated for the samples included in the training (180 samples) and two testing sets (60 and 48 samples, respectively named Test60 and Test48). The samples were constructed basing on chapters from the selected novels of two writers, Thomas Hardy and Henry James.

The granules of knowledge considered in DRSA are the dominance cones, hence no discretisation of real-valued input values is required, and in the first step the decision table is constructed from the set of the training samples. Basing on these samples all relative reducts were calculated (6664) and their core turned out to be empty. Next there were built decision rules specifying conditions on attributes involved to arrive at a decision, finding only enough rules to provide a minimal cover of the learning samples, and calculating all rules on examples.

The minimal cover algorithm (found with DOMLEM algorithm implemented in 4eMka software employed in the research) contained only 61 rules, while all rules on examples (exhaustive search) decision algorithm had 46,191 constituent rules. When both were tested without any additional constraints upon them, the first gave only 40% correct decisions while the latter 0%. These results from the fact that all cases with ambiguous decisions corresponding to no rules matching or verdicts with several contradicting decisions were treated as incorrect, and for the full algorithm with its high number of rules it was unavoidable that there were ambiguous decisions.

To reduce at least some rules from the full algorithm, DRSA suggests imposing some threshold value for the minimal support the rules must have to be included in the final algorithm. This threshold value of support was tested in the whole range, giving the performance of the classifier as depicted in Fig. 1a. With increasing values of minimal support required the classification accuracy increases gradually from 0 to the level of 76%, for support equal at least 40 or 41. Then the accuracy starts to decrease as there are not enough rules left in the algorithm to ensure good results.

Limiting support values means obtaining a reduced decision algorithm with fewer rules, so the classifier performance can be observed in relation to the number of rules included in it, as shown in Fig. 1b. Two algorithms with the highest classification accuracy of 76% contain 90 rules (for support at least 40) and 80 rules (for support at least 41) respectively, which is more than in the minimal cover algorithm. Yet, as clearly can be seen in the full algorithm, high

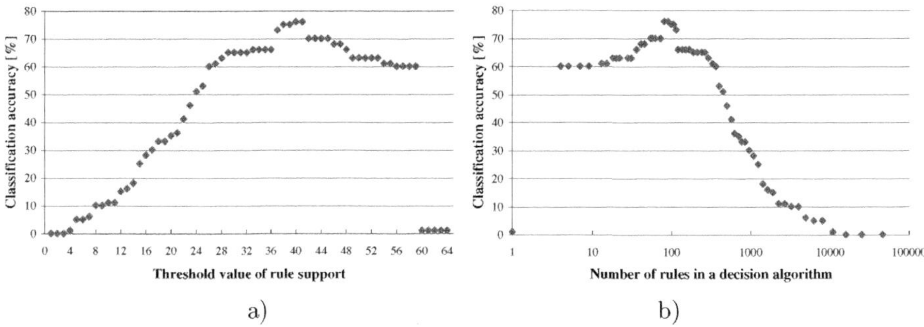

Fig. 1. Classification accuracy in relation to: a) threshold values of support imposed on the rules to be included in a decision algorithm, b) numbers of rules (displayed in logarithmic scale) included in decision algorithms with limited support. All results for the testing set Test60.

number of rules is not necessarily an advantage in itself but only through the much wider choice of rules it subsequently offers.

The selection of decision rules for a reduced algorithm can result from reduction of some of condition attributes by analysing how many times they are used in construction of relative reducts and decision rules, which was described in the past research [13]. Furthermore, both reducts and rules can be studied through their parameters: for reducts it is important to observe their cardinalities, and for rules their length, support, condition attributes or detailed conditions included.

When there are found all rules on examples within the exhaustive search, many of them typically have relatively low support when compared to the maximum obtained. Quite noticeable portion of rules are true for single training samples. Out of the total 46191 decision rules generated within the performed research as many as 20976 have support equal 1, which means 45% of rules supported by single samples.

In order to treat the values of support as indicators of the decision rule significance in the process of classification and recognition, and to establish how this significance in turn reflects on condition attributes the rules refer to, more detailed analysis of support distribution for attributes is needed, as presented in Table 1. Since supports of rules range from 1 to 64, their values were grouped into 7 subranges. In the table for each attribute there is given the total number of rules this attribute is included in, with specifying how many rules have supports belonging to each range. The attributes are ordered according to the increasing number of rules they were included in.

From Table 1 it is clear that the majority of rules have support falling into the lowest range between 1 and 10. In general the higher the range the fewer rules with such supports. Only two attributes are present in rules with support in the range with the highest values. With such overall variety of supports it is necessary to consider which ranges of values should be consulted to provide some base for ordering of attributes. It is possible to treat all ranges independently and

Table 1. Distribution of rule supports for condition attributes

Number of rules	Support in range 1-10	11-20	21-30	31-40	41-50	51-60	61-64	Attribute
3928	3872	42	12	2	0	0	0	but
4173	3256	530	214	95	56	21	1	and
6167	6117	39	6	3	1	1	0	that
6173	6069	91	10	3	0	0	0	what
7450	7370	74	5	1	0	0	0	for
7469	7355	95	12	4	3	0	0	?
7615	6651	669	216	51	25	3	0	from
7692	7545	111	30	3	3	0	0	if
7951	7589	270	54	18	14	6	0	(
7997	7845	127	20	5	0	0	0	-
8451	7575	639	163	48	15	11	0	by
8472	8279	164	26	2	1	0	0	as
8647	8570	55	16	2	2	2	0	with
9083	8953	109	16	5	0	0	0	at
9798	9683	93	17	5	0	0	0	;
10241	9720	376	105	28	10	2	0	in
10306	9736	444	92	24	4	5	1	not
10327	9928	325	59	12	3	0	0	:
10640	10307	260	52	18	3	0	0	!
11005	10795	176	29	5	0	0	0	.
11177	10913	232	26	5	1	0	0	,
11427	11177	188	42	11	8	1	0	this
11839	11579	206	40	8	3	3	0	to
12922	12523	324	57	17	1	0	0	on
13311	12921	303	66	15	6	0	0	of

test within each, or group them together according to some arbitrary fashion, which makes for many possible combinations.

The three orderings used in the performed tests are given in Table 2. In general it was assumed that higher support values are preferred. Firstly there were studied numbers of rules with supports in the median and higher than median range of values, that is equal at least 31 (Table 2a). Secondly, there was observed only the median range of support values for rules (Table 2b), from 31 to 40. And thirdly the focus was on these rules with the highest support and these maximal supports were ordered (Table 2c).

It should be noted that for all three orders given, from the side considered as less significant, as the first one on the list there is always the same feature ("for"), which results in the same version of the decision algorithm. From the more significant side there can also be observed some similarities.

Three orderings of condition attributes, obtained through the analysis of rule support, resulted in three groups of tests performed. Each of these groups could be further divided into two parts, one corresponding to reduction of rules with attributes considered as more important in the current context while keeping

Table 2. Ordering of attributes: a) based on the number of rules with support in median and higher ranges (Order 1) that is at least 31, b) based on the number of rules only with support in median range (Order 2) from 31 to 40, c) based on the maximal support (Order 3).

a)

Attribute	Order 1
for	
.	L1
what	
but	
;	
at	
-	L2 M11
on	L3
,	
as	M10
!	L4
:	M9
if	L5
?	
of	M8
this	L6 M7
that	L7 M6
in	L8
with	
to	M5
from	M4
(	M3
by	M2
not	M1
and	

b)

Attribute	Order 2
for	
with	L1
as	
if	L2
,	L3
.	
what	
that	
but	
;	
?	
at	M7
-	L4
to	M6
this	L5 M5
of	L6
:	M4
on	L7
!	M3
(	L8
not	
in	M2
by	
from	M1
and	

c)

Attribute	Order 3
for	
at	L1
but	L2
.	L3
-	
;	L4
what	L5
as	L6 M11
on	L7 M10
,	L8
!	M9
?	L9 M8
of	L10
:	M7
if	L11 M6
this	L12 M5
in	L13 M4
to	L14 M3
that	M2
with	
from	
by	
(	M1
and	
not	

these less important, another with removing rules with less important features and leaving the ones with more important attributes. The former of the series is denoted by letters *M*, the latter with letters *L*. Increasing numbers indicate more removed attributes and rules and gradual shortening of the decision algorithm. In some cases only single attributes with their rules were discarded, while in other several attributes at the same time. When some condition attribute was disregarded, from the set of rules there were removed all decision rules referring to this attribute in their premise parts, regardless of the particular local conditions, all other attributes (if there were any), and conclusions.

5 Results and Discussion

Tests from M-labelled series were characterised by very fast decrease in the number of decision rules left. As the still remaining rules were these with lower supports, the performance of the resulting classifier was getting steadily worse and worse, quickly becoming unacceptable, not only lower than for the full algorithm, but lower than 50%. For Order 1 only 4 attributes could be reduced, for Order 2 only one (the same as the first in this series for Order 1), and for Order 3 only two (the same as the second in this series for Order 1). This poor performance could not be repaired with restrictions as to the minimal support required for the decision rules, because incorrect decisions were mainly due to no rules matching rather than to ambiguous decisions.

On the other hand, in the initial phase of the reduction process these M series gave base to the algorithms with the highest classification accuracy of all, as listed in Table 3. It should be noted that in M4 decision algorithm just 4 condition attributes were discarded along with their rules, and it resulted in reducing the set of rules by more than half.

Table 3. Best decision algorithms for the first ordering of attributes with reduction of features from more significant side (classification for Test60 set)

Decision algorithms	M1	M2		M3	M4		
Number of attributes	24	23		22	21		
Number of rules left	42018	32175		25388	20173		
Support	33	28	30	20	10	11	14
Number of rules in the shortened algorithm	19	43	31	75	301	244	134
Classification [%]	83	78	76	76	80	78	76

L-labelled series for all three orderings of characteristic features allowed for much more significant reduction of attributes and their rules than M-labelled ones, while at least preserving the original power of the classifier. As stated before, for the full algorithm the highest classification accuracy was 76% and the highest minimal support requested for rules to achieve that was 41 which limited the number of rules to be included to 80. In relation to that threshold support value of 41 there are given parameters of decision algorithms in Fig. 2, the number of condition attributes being reduced and resulting from that reduction the number of remaining decision rules with support equal to or higher than the required threshold.

From these three series plotted in the graph the best performance is for the second ordering, which reflected the number of decision rules with supports in median range for all condition attributes. Within this series the number of rules with support at least 41 is cut by half, from the initial 80 for the full algorithm to 40 rules when there are only 6 condition attributes left, which means keeping only 25% of more important characteristic features and even some increase in the classification accuracy.

Within all three orderings of condition attributes for various values of threshold support required, there were several versions of decision algorithms with higher classification accuracy than for the complete set of attributes. The shortest of these with the highest classification accuracy is obtained when a single

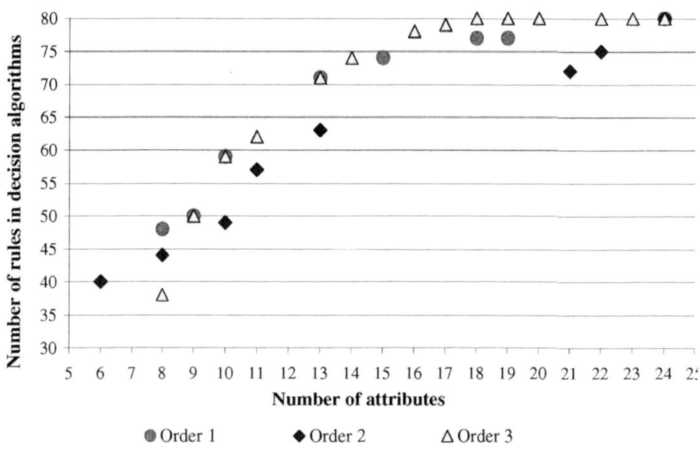

Fig. 2. Number of decision rules in relation to the number of condition attributes for decision algorithms with support limited to at least 41. For Test60 set, for *Order 1* classification accuracy is 76%, only for 9 and 8 attributes it falls to 75%. For *Order 2* classification equals 76% for 24, 22, 21, and 8 attributes, while for 13 and 11 attributes it increases to 78%, and for 6 attributes it is 81%. For *Order 3* classification is 76% till there are 9 or 8 attributes left, when it falls to 75 and 70% respectively.

attribute, corresponding to the frequency of usage of "and", is removed, along with all rules referring to it in their premise parts, and requiring decision rules to have the support equal at least 33. It consists of five rules with the conclusion "hardy", and fourteen for "james". It is as follows.

Decision Algorithm Rus12M1 (24 attributes and 42018 rules, for support≥33 limited to 19 rules containing 12 attributes, for Test60 set classification 83%)

```
Rule 4073 (not >= 0,0061) & (from >= 0,0035) & (!>= 0,0022)
          => hardy
Rule 4190 (of >= 0,0206) & (from >= 0,0035) & (by >= 0,0041)
        & (, >= 0,0629) => hardy
Rule 6015 (by >= 0,0055) & (, >= 0,058) => hardy
Rule 9076 (not >= 0,0059) & (at >= 0,0055) & (from >= 0,0033)
        & (? >= 0,0029) => hardy
Rule 11259 (from >= 0,0038) & (by >= 0,0048) => hardy
Rule 17108 (from <= 0,0025) & (by <= 0,0035) & (! <= 0,0076)
           => james
Rule 18227 (in <= 0,0159) & (on <= 0,007) & (from <= 0,003)
           => james
Rule 18229 (in <= 0,0159) & (from <= 0,003) & (by <= 0,0065)
           => james
Rule 18454 (in <= 0,0155) & (on <= 0,0069) & (from <= 0,0032)
           => james
Rule 19601 (in <= 0,015) & (from <= 0,0034) & (by <= 0,0053)
```

```
        &  ( ( <= 0) => james
Rule 24945 (of <= 0,0271) & (this <= 0,0064) & (from <= 0,0029)
        &  ( ( <= 0) => james
Rule 31626 (not <= 0,0058) & (in <= 0,0162) & (from <= 0,0035)
           => james
Rule 31793 (not <= 0,0058) & (of <= 0,0289) & (from <= 0,0035)
        &  (by <= 0,0045) => james
Rule 39780 (on <= 0,0079) & (from <= 0,0035) & (by <= 0,0032)
        &  (! <= 0,0071) => james
Rule 42141 (on <= 0,0074) & (of <= 0,0289) & (from <= 0,0028)
           => james
Rule 43633 (not <= 0,006) & (in <= 0,0166) & (from <= 0,0029)
           => james
Rule 43635 (not <= 0,006) & (from <= 0,0029) & (by <= 0,0044)
           => james
Rule 43641 (in <= 0,0166) & (from <= 0,0029) & (by <= 0,0044)
           => james
Rule 44499 (on <= 0,0067) & (from <= 0,0032) & (by <= 0,0034)
           => james
```

Since the testing set Test60 was used to find maximal threshold support values, which by limiting the rules of decision algorithms resulted in the highest classification accuracy, for additional verification of conclusions there was performed the second round of tests, for the testing set Test48. The tests confirmed that in all three orderings of condition attributes in L-labelled series when the features were reduced and previously established support threshold values imposed, the classification accuracy was kept at the same (72%) or higher level (75%). In M-labelled series the acceptable results are for the same decision algorithms as for Test60, but for the decision algorithm *Rus12M1* the supports at least 29 are needed to get 75% correct decisions for 54 decision rules remaining. For support of 33 the classification decreases to 66%. On the other hand, for support at least 29 the classification accuracy for Test60 is 83%.

6 Conclusions

The paper presents results of authorship attribution studies for the literary works. The methodology employed bases on rough set theory with dominance relation substituting the original indiscernibility relation, which allows for not only nominal but also ordinal classification. Decision algorithms constructed within DRSA methodology are tailored by exploiting observations on supports for generated rules and how they reflect upon the significance of individual condition attributes. Such analysis of characteristic features does not require any additional domain knowledge or computationally complex calculations and results in noticeable reduction of the decision algorithms while the classification accuracy is either kept at the same level or even increased. Thus considering the attributes from the perspective of rule supports brings more insight as to their role in the classification task and could be treated as an additional feature to the methodology of constructing decision algorithms by limiting rule supports and their lengths.

Acknowledgments. In search for decision rules there was used 4eMka System - a rule system for multicriteria decision support integrating dominance relation with rough approximation, developed in the Laboratory of Intelligent Decision Support Systems, Institute of Computing Science, Poznan University of Technology, (`http://www-idss.cs.put.poznan.pl/`).

References

1. Baszczynski, J., Sowinski, R., Szelaga, M.: Sequential covering rule induction algorithm for variable consistency rough set approaches. Information Sciences 181(5), 987–1002 (2011)
2. Burrows, J.: Textual analysis. In: Schreibman, S., Siemens, R., Unsworth, J. (eds.) A Companion to Digital Humanities. Blackwell, Oxford (2004)
3. Craig, H.: Stylistic analysis and authorship studies. In: Schreibman, S., Siemens, R., Unsworth, J. (eds.) A Companion to Digital Humanities. Blackwell, Oxford (2004)
4. Greco, S., Matarazzo, B., Słowiński, R.: Handling missing values in rough set analysis of multi-attribute and multi-criteria decision problems. In: Zhong, N., Skowron, A., Ohsuga, S. (eds.) RSFDGrC 1999. LNCS (LNAI), vol. 1711, pp. 146–157. Springer, Heidelberg (1999)
5. Greco, S., Matarazzo, B., Slowinski, R.: The use of rough sets and fuzzy sets in Multi Criteria Decision Making. In: Gal, T., Hanne, T., Stewart, T. (eds.) Advances in Multiple Criteria Decision Making, pp. 14.1–14.59. Kluwer Academic Publishers, Dordrecht Boston (1999)
6. Hu, X., Han, J., Lin, T.Y.: A new rough sets model based on database systems. Fundamenta Informaticae 20, 1–18 (2004)
7. Li, J., Cercone, N.: Introducing a rule importance measure. Transactions on Rough Sets 5, 167–189 (2006)
8. Moshkov, M., Piliszczuk, M., Zielosko, B.: On partial covers, reducts and decision rules with weights. Transactions on Rough Sets 6, 211–246 (2006)
9. Pawlak, Z.: Rough sets and intelligent data analysis. Information Sciences 147, 1–12 (2002)
10. Peng, R., Hengartner, H.: Quantitative analysis of literary styles. The American Statistician 56(3), 15–38 (2002)
11. Słowiński, R., Greco, S., Matarazzo, B.: Dominance-based rough set approach to reasoning about ordinal data. In: Kryszkiewicz, M., Peters, J.F., Rybiński, H., Skowron, A. (eds.) RSEISP 2007. LNCS (LNAI), vol. 4585, pp. 5–11. Springer, Heidelberg (2007)
12. Stańczyk, U.: Dominance-based rough set approach employed in search of authorial invariants. In: Kurzyński, M., Woźniak, M. (eds.) Computer Recognition Systems 3. AISC, vol. 57, pp. 315–323. Springer, Berlin (2009)
13. Stańczyk, U.: DRSA decision algorithm analysis in stylometric processing of literary texts. In: Szczuka, M., Kryszkiewicz, M., Ramanna, S., Jensen, R., Hu, Q. (eds.) RSCTC 2010. LNCS (LNAI), vol. 6086, pp. 600–609. Springer, Heidelberg (2010)

Differential Evolution for High Scale Dynamic Optimization

Mikołaj Raciborski[1], Krzysztof Trojanowski[2], and Piotr Kaczyński[1]

[1] Cardinal Stefan Wyszyński University
Faculty of Mathematics and Natural Sciences
Wóycickiego 1/3, 01-938 Warsaw, Poland
[2] Institute of Computer Science, Polish Academy of Sciences
Ordona 21, 01-237 Warsaw, Poland

Abstract. This paper studies properties of a differential evolution approach (DE) for dynamic optimization problems. An adaptive version of DE, namely the jDE algorithm has been applied to two well known benchmarks: Generalized Dynamic Benchmark Generator (GDBG) and Moving Peaks Benchmark (MPB). The experiments have been performed for different numbers of the search space dimensions starting from five until 30. The results show the influence of the problem complexity on the quality of the returned results both in case of varying and constant number of fitness function calls between subsequent changes.

1 Introduction

In [8] uncertainty is divided into four main types. In the first type, a noise is present in the optimized function. Uncertainty of the second type is present when for some reason (for example, high computational costs), instead of using a function, we use approximation evaluation of function values. The third type of uncertainty occurs when the main aim is to find a solution not only of the highest quality, but — more importantly — one whose neighbors are equally good, that is, when the most important issue is the robustness of the returned solution. The last of the four types of uncertainty is observed when the function dynamically changes during the search process. In this case, the main task is an immediate adaptation to the changes. Problems with this type of uncertainty are often referred to as dynamic problems. This last type of uncertainty concerning the search space defined in $\mathbf{R}^n$ is the subject of interest in the presented research.

The number of already published dynamic benchmarks is quite impressive. Benchmarks given in [1,12,17] consisted of a number of moving peaks, cones or hills of varying height and width. Later on, in [6,21] authors used a set of n-dimensional gaussian functions. In [9] authors proposed a dynamic landscape consisting of a number of static component functions which rise up and fall down during the process of search. In [15] authors proposed Continuous Dynamic Optimization Problem Generator (CDOPG) which is a real-valued version of a XOR DOP benchmark [18]. A new type of changes, that is, rotation of fitness

P. Bouvry et al. (Eds.): SIIS 2011, LNCS 7053, pp. 180–189, 2012.

landscape components appeared in Dynamic Rotation Peak Benchmark Generator [10], however, the largest number of deformation types applied to the fitness landscape components can be found in Generalized Dynamic Benchmark Generator (GDBG) mentioned first in [11] and then also in [10].

There were also proposed many heuristic approaches to dynamic optimization problems (DOPs). A review of them can be found, for example, in [19,20]. In spite of significant number of research and published results dynamic optimization is still a subject of interest and new methods devoted to this area are developed. Recently, a number of approaches were presented at the special session *Competition on Dynamic Optimization* accompanying the Congress CEC'09 where the competitors compared their approaches using GDBG mentioned above. The winner was a self-adaptive differential evolution algorithm [4] (called jDE). We decided to study jDE and especially check its performance in high dimensional dynamic optimization benchmarks. The results of our research are presented in this paper.

Differential evolution approach which originated with the Genetic Annealing algorithm [13] has been heavily studied from many points of view (for detailed discussion see, for example, monographs [5,14]). The presented version of the DE algorithm [3] differs form the basic approach in that a self-adaptive control mechanism is used to change the control parameters F and CR during the run. This approach has been studied for static optimization tasks and proved its efficiency and effectiveness [2].

The paper is organized as follows. In Section 2 a brief description of the optimization algorithm is presented. Section 3 includes some details of the selected testing environment and the applied measure. Section 4 shows the results of experiments. Section 5 concludes the presented research.

2 The Algorithm

The differential evolution algorithm is an evolutionary method with a very specific mutation operator controlled by the scale factor F. Three different, randomly chosen solutions are needed to mutate a target solution $\mathbf{x}^i$: a base solution $\mathbf{x}^0$ and two difference solutions $\mathbf{x}^1$ and $\mathbf{x}^2$. Then, a mutant undergoes discrete recombination with the target solution which is controlled by the crossover probability factor $CR \in [0, 1]$. Finally, in the selection stage trial solutions compete with their target solutions for the place in the population. This strategy of population management is called *DE/**rand**/**1**/**bin*** which means that the base solution is **rand**omly chosen, **1** difference vector is added to it and the crossover is based on a set of independent decisions for each of coordinates, that is, a number of parameters donated by the mutant closely follows a **bin**omial distribution.

The jDE algorithm (depicted in Figure 1) extends functionality of the basic approach in many ways. First, each object representing a solution in the population is extended by a couple of its personal parameters CR and F. They are adaptively modified every generation [3]. The next modifications have been introduced just for better coping in the dynamic optimization environment. The

Algorithm 1. jDE algorithm

```
Create and initialize the reference set of (k · m) solutions
repeat
    for l = 1 to k do {for each subpopulation}
        for i = 1 to m do {for each solution in a subpopulation}
            Select randomly three solutions: x^{l,0}, x^{l,1}, and x^{l,2}
                        such that: x^{l,i} ≠ x^{l,0} and x^{l,1} ≠ x^{l,2}
            for j = 1 to n do {for each dimension in a solution}
                if (rand(0,1) > CR^{l,i}) then
                    u_j^{l,i} = x_j^{l,0} + F^{l,i} · (x_j^{l,1} − x_j^{l,2})
                else
                    u_j^{l,i} = x_j^{l,i}
                end if
            end for
        end for
    end for
    for i = 1 to (k · m) do {for each solution}
        if (f(u^i) < f(x^i) then {Let's assume this is a minimization problem}
            x^i = u^i
        end if
        Recalculate F^i and CR^i
        Apply aging procedure for x^i
    end for
    Do overlapping search
until the stop condition is satisfied
```

population of solutions has been divided into five subpopulations of size ten. Each of them has to perform its own search process, that is, no information is shared between subpopulations. Every solution is a subject to the aging procedure protecting against stagnation in local minima and just the global-best solution is excluded form this. To avoid overlapping between subpopulations a distance between subpopulation leaders is calculated and in the case of too close localization one of subpopulations is reinitialized. However, as in previous case the subpopulation with the global-best is never the one to reinitialize. The last extension is a memory structure called archive. The archive is increased after each change in the fitness landscape by the current global-best solution. Recalling from the archive can be executed every reinitialization of a subpopulation, however, decision about the execution depends on a few conditions. For details of the above-mentioned extension procedures the reader is referred to [4].

3 Plan of Experiments

3.1 Benchmarks

Among the existing dynamic benchmarks, we have selected two: Generalized Dynamic Benchmark Generator (GDBG) [10] and the Moving Peaks Benchmark

(MPB) generator [1]. In both cases optimization is carried out in a real-valued multidimensional search space, and the fitness landscape is built of multiple component functions individually controlled by their parameters.

GDBG consists of two generators of benchmarks: Dynamic Rotation Peak Benchmark Generator (DRPBG) and Dynamic Composition Benchmark Generator (DCBG). There are five types of component functions: peak (F_1), sphere (F_2), Rastrigin (F_3), Griewank (F_4), and Ackley (F_5). F_1 is applied for DRPBG whereas all the remaining types are applied for DCBG.

There were also defined six change types of the GDBG control parameters which represent different characteristics of variability. Among them we did our experiments with just three of them: small step change ($\mathbf{T}_1$ — eq. (1)), large step change ($\mathbf{T}_2$ — eq. (2)), and random change ($\mathbf{T}_3$ — eq. (3)). The change Δ of a parameter value is calculated as follows:

$$\Delta = \alpha \cdot r \cdot (\max - \min), \text{where } \alpha = 0.04,\ r = U(0,1), \tag{1}$$

$$\Delta = (\alpha \cdot sign(r_1) + (\alpha_{\max} - \alpha) \cdot r_2) \cdot (\max - \min), \quad \text{where } \alpha = 0.04,\ r_{1,2} = U(0,1),\ \alpha_{\max} = 0.1 \tag{2}$$

$$\Delta = N(0,1) \tag{3}$$

In the above-mentioned equations max and min represent upper and lower boundary of the search space, $N(0,1)$ is a random value obtained with gaussian distribution where $\mu = 0$ and $\sigma = 1$, and $U(0,1)$ is a random value obtained with uniform distribution form the range $[0,1]$.

In the case of MPB, three scenarios of the benchmark parameters control are defined [1]. We did experiments for two versions of the second scenario. In this scenario the fitness landscape has been defined for the five-dimensional search space with the same boundaries for each dimension, namely $[-50;50]$. The fitness landscape consists of a set of moving cones which randomly vary their heights within the interval $[30;70]$, their widths within $[1;12]$ and their positions by the distance of one. In the first version of the scenario 2 there are ten moving cones whereas in the second version 50 moving cones is in use. We extended this definition and did our tests also for ten, 20 and 30 dimensions of the search space for both versions of the selected benchmark instance.

For the experimental purpose we reimplemented the selected benchmarks. A new version is based on the Eigen C++ library [7] which makes execution of the computer program fast. The structure of the C++ code is based on a fitness landscape model where the landscape consists of a number of simple components. The components are individually controlled by a number of unified parameters. This allows to create multiple classes of dynamic landscapes and particularly to simulate easily a number of existing benchmarks like MPB, DRPBG and DCBG.

Our algorithm has no embedded strategy for detecting changes in the fitness landscapes. Simply, the last step in the main loop of the algorithm executes the reevaluation of the entire current solution set. Therefore, our optimization system is informed of the change as soon as it occurs, and no additional computational effort for its detection is needed.

3.2 The Measures

We used measures of the obtained results proposed for both of the benchmarks by their authors. This gave opportunity for fair comparison of the algorithm efficiency. For GDBG there were defined four measures:

$$Avg^{\text{best}} = \sum_{i=1}^{N_{\text{exp}}} \min_{j=1,\ldots,N_{\text{changes}}} E_{\text{last}}^{i,j} / N_{\text{exp}}, \tag{4}$$

$$Avg^{\text{mean}} = \sum_{i=1}^{N_{\text{exp}}} \sum_{j=1}^{N_{\text{changes}}} E_{\text{last}}^{i,j} / (N_{\text{exp}} \cdot N_{\text{changes}}), \tag{5}$$

$$Avg^{\text{worst}} = \sum_{i=1}^{N_{\text{exp}}} \max_{j=1,\ldots,N_{\text{changes}}} E_{\text{last}}^{i,j} / N_{\text{exp}}, \tag{6}$$

$$STD = \sqrt{\frac{1}{N_{\text{exp}} \cdot N_{\text{changes}} - 1} \sum_{i=1}^{N_{\text{exp}}} \sum_{j=1}^{N_{\text{changes}}} (E_{\text{last}}^{i,j} - Avg^{\text{mean}})^2}, \tag{7}$$

where N_{exp} is a number of repeated experiments for the same control parameter settings of the algorithm, N_{changes} is a number of changes in the fitness landscape appearing during a single experiment run, and E_{last}^{j} is an absolute function error value:

$$E_{\text{last}}^{j} = |f(\mathbf{x}_{\text{best}}^{j}) - f(\mathbf{x}^{*j})|, \tag{8}$$

where $\mathbf{x}_{\text{best}}^{j}$ — current best solution which has been found since the last j-th change in the fitness landscape, $\mathbf{x}^{*j}$ — real optimum solution for the fitness landscape after the j-th change.

In the case of MPB most of the publications contain the values of offline error measure obtained for performed experimental research. The offline error represents the average deviation from the optimum of the best solution value since the last change in the fitness landscape. Formally:

$$oe = \frac{1}{N_{\text{changes}}} \sum_{j=1}^{N_{\text{changes}}} \left(\frac{1}{N_{\text{e}}(j)} \sum_{i=1}^{N_{\text{e}}(j)} (f(\mathbf{x}^{*j}) - f(\mathbf{x}_{\text{best}}^{ji})) \right), \tag{9}$$

where $N_{\text{e}}(j)$ is a total number of solution evaluations performed for the j-th static state of the landscape. It should be clear that the measure oe should be minimized, that is, the better result the smaller the value of oe.

3.3 The Tests

We performed experiments with a subset of GDBG benchmark functions as well as with two versions of MPB scenario 2 and for different numbers of dimensions of the search space. The group of tests in the MPB testing environment was repeated twice for two different calculation rules of the number of fitness function calls between subsequent changes. The first group was performed according to the rules as in the CEC'09 competition, that is, for $10^4 \cdot n$ fitness function calls between subsequent changes where n is a number of search space dimensions. The second group — for 5000 calls as it is recommended for experiments with MPB. The group of tests in the GDBG testing environment was performed once just for $10^4 \cdot n$ fitness function calls between subsequent changes.

For each of the environment configurations the experiments were repeated 20 times and each of them consisted of 60 changes in the fitness landscape.

4 The Results

The results can be divided according to the applied measures. Tables 1, 2, 3, and 5 contain values of measures specific for GDBG (Avg^{best}, Avg^{worst}, Avg^{mean}, and STD), whereas, Tables 4, and 6 — offline error (oe) values specific rather for MPB. It must be stressed, however, that both measures were calculated for every experiment. This way we can compare our results with other already published results obtained both for MPB and GDBG.

Table 1. Error values achieved for DRPBG problems F_1 for three change types: $\mathbf{T}_1$, $\mathbf{T}_2$, $\mathbf{T}_3$ and the number of fitness function calls equal $10^4 \cdot n$, where: n — number of dimensions of the search space

Errors	n	10 moving peaks			50 moving peaks		
		$\mathbf{T}_1$	$\mathbf{T}_2$	$\mathbf{T}_3$	$\mathbf{T}_1$	$\mathbf{T}_2$	$\mathbf{T}_3$
Avg^{best}	5	0.0	0.0	0.0	0.0	0.0	0.0
	10	0.0	0.0	0.0	0.0	0.0	0.0
	20	$3.8 \cdot 10^{-7}$	$3.8 \cdot 10^{-7}$	0.0	$7.6 \cdot 10^{-7}$	$1.5 \cdot 10^{-6}$	$7.6 \cdot 10^{-7}$
	30	$7.2 \cdot 10^{-6}$	$8.0 \cdot 10^{-6}$	$8.4 \cdot 10^{-6}$	$8.7 \cdot 10^{-6}$	$1.0 \cdot 10^{-5}$	$8.0 \cdot 10^{-6}$
Avg^{worst}	5	0.294	0.206	0.578	5.864	5.698	6.431
	10	0.101	0.0315	0.143	4.759	5.255	3.906
	20	0.611	1.132	0.159	3.542	4.437	3.631
	30	0.0083	0.586	1.385	3.853	5.598	3.556
Avg^{mean}	5	0.005	0.004	0.016	0.389	0.471	0.930
	10	0.0016	0.0005	0.009	0.272	0.289	0.502
	20	0.014	0.046	0.005	0.235	0.347	0.386
	30	0.0001	0.015	0.093	0.277	0.496	0.374
STD	5	0.165	0.076	0.263	1.229	1.274	2.035
	10	0.0584	0.0176	0.146	1.083	1.081	1.591
	20	0.262	0.396	0.073	0.854	0.984	1.245
	30	0.0047	0.183	0.728	0.993	1.430	1.169

Table 2. Error values achieved for DCBG problems F_2 and F_3 for three change types: $\mathbf{T}_1$, $\mathbf{T}_2$, $\mathbf{T}_3$ and the number of fitness function calls equal $10^4 \cdot n$, where: n — number of dimensions of the search space

Errors	n	F_2: sphere			F_3: Rastrigin		
		$\mathbf{T}_1$	$\mathbf{T}_2$	$\mathbf{T}_3$	$\mathbf{T}_1$	$\mathbf{T}_2$	$\mathbf{T}_3$
Avg^{best}	5	0.0	0.0	0.0	8.41	5.20	4.97
	10	0.0	0.0	0.0	14.97	14.92	14.92
	20	0.0	0.0	$1.9 \cdot 10^{-7}$	51.08	78.11	64.97
	30	$1.6 \cdot 10^{-6}$	$1.3 \cdot 10^{-6}$	$3.7 \cdot 10^{-6}$	166.42	138.13	154.82
Avg^{worst}	5	3.869	4.421	5.758	829.7	861.1	763.5
	10	2.759	7.381	5.864	3687.4	3732.4	3675.1
	20	5.026	6.182	5.274	10312	10567	10264
	30	8.051	15.403	6.806	18237	18521	18101
Avg^{mean}	5	0.138	0.130	0.353	405.5	421.9	389.4
	10	0.085	0.251	0.402	1910.7	1986.1	1941.2
	20	0.257	0.246	0.338	5508.4	5647.3	5585.2
	30	0.472	1.196	0.910	9958	10045	9729
STD	5	0.923	0.882	1.355	184.3	189.3	178.4
	10	0.681	1.398	1.582	850.0	861.6	850.3
	20	1.437	1.457	1.269	2509.3	2546.1	2471.8
	30	2.110	3.834	2.795	4546.7	4563.1	4579.6

Table 3. Error values achieved for DCBG problems F_4 and F_5 for three change types: $\mathbf{T}_1$, $\mathbf{T}_2$, $\mathbf{T}_3$ and the number of fitness function calls equal $10^4 \cdot n$, where: n — number of dimensions of the search space

Errors	n	F_4: Grievank			F_5: Ackley		
		$\mathbf{T}_1$	$\mathbf{T}_2$	$\mathbf{T}_3$	$\mathbf{T}_1$	$\mathbf{T}_2$	$\mathbf{T}_3$
Avg^{best}	5	0.0	0.018	0.0	0.0	0.0	0.0
	10	0.0	0.0	0.0	0.00038	0.00034	0.00038
	20	0.0	0.0	0.0	0.0015	0.0018	0.0017
	30	0.0	0.0	0.0	0.0035	0.0043	0.0042
Avg^{worst}	5	4.785	4.835	5.657	7.84	14.69	6.86
	10	6.378	5.554	9.245	11.58	14.86	6.004
	20	0.104	0.129	0.331	25.03	41.06	40.74
	30	0.244	0.262	0.348	189.2	199.9	189.9
Avg^{mean}	5	1.368	1.371	1.889	0.69	1.05	0.97
	10	0.984	0.602	2.213	0.902	1.491	0.697
	20	0.002	0.003	0.011	3.957	7.159	6.738
	30	0.005	0.004	0.008	93.92	94.239	86.85
STD	5	1.111	1.046	1.284	2.16	3.45	2.05
	10	1.461	1.1001	1.976	2.85	3.83	1.77
	20	0.030	0.0423	0.075	6.52	10.67	9.32
	30	0.055	0.052	0.069	63.11	64.11	63.87

Table 4. Mean values of *oe* achieved for DCBG problems $F_1, \ldots F_5$ for three change types: $\mathbf{T}_1$, $\mathbf{T}_2$, $\mathbf{T}_3$ and the number of fitness function calls equal $10^4 \cdot n$, where: n — number of dimensions of the search space; values in the brackets represent std. error for the series of repeated experiments

P	n	$\mathbf{T}_1$	$\mathbf{T}_2$	$\mathbf{T}_3$
F_1	5	2.500 (0.598)	2.590 (0.616)	3.934 (0.884)
10	10	3.583 (0.395)	4.032 (0.654)	5.121 (0.734)
moving	20	6.008 (0.632)	7.099 (0.665)	6.453 (0.861)
peaks	30	7.411 (1.003)	9.001 (0.635)	8.556 (1.671)
F_1	5	3.473 (0.654)	3.898 (0.509)	5.951 (1.643)
50	10	4.756 (0.584)	5.288 (0.462)	6.481 (1.331)
moving	20	6.843 (0.625)	7.824 (0.376)	7.817 (1.154)
peaks	30	8.835 (0.749)	9.978 (0.831)	9.651 (0.943)
F_2	5	1.730 (0.432)	3.298 (0.974)	8.157 (1.585)
	10	8.414 (2.196)	18.218 (3.159)	41.792 (4.723)
	20	62.17 (9.945)	104.65 (19.509)	168.01 (20.98)
	30	160.47 (22.089)	241.01 (28.88)	348.95 (25.82)
F_3	5	613.58 (43.5)	599.10 (51.6)	389.43 (54.7)
	10	2869 (94.25)	2973.3 (105.0)	3050.4 (100.9)
	20	8137 (242.2)	8534.9 (179.75)	8574.4 (169.3)
	30	14706 (411.6)	14921 (402.16)	14853 (553.9)
F_4	5	0.164 (0.026)	0.140 (0.021)	0.388 (0.050)
	10	0.952 (0.245)	0.631 (0.136)	2.617 (0.511)
	20	1.037 (0.251)	1.181 (0.216)	2.781 (0.222)
	30	1.942 (0.368)	1.593 (0.396)	2.819 (0.234)
F_5	5	9.87 (1.979)	11.41 (1.631)	15.70 (1.137)
	10	18.90 (2.970)	21.078 (3.403)	23.57 (2.202)
	20	57.10 (3.516)	54.88 (3.957)	52.16 (3.783)
	30	142.31 (9.243)	129.91 (7.681)	153.2 (8.189)

Table 5. Error values achieved for two versions of MPB sc. 2: with ten and 50 moving component functions in the landscape and for two max. numbers of fitness function calls between subsequent changes: 5000, and $10^4 \cdot n$, where: n — number of dimensions of the search space

Dim. number:		$n = 5$		$n = 10$		$n = 20$		$n = 30$	
fitness fun. calls:		5000	$10^4 \cdot n$	5000	$10^4 \cdot n$	5000	$10^4 \cdot n$	5000	$10^4 \cdot n$
10	Avg^{best}	0.042	0.0	0.81	$5.15 \cdot 10^{-6}$	1.007	0.618	4.546	2.09
mov.	Avg^{worst}	23.674	12.489	31.172	18.919	62.95	31.937	68.687	32.517
cones	Avg^{mean}	7.869	1.87	14.165	4.889	11.162	13.357	15.091	15.762
	STD	7.673	3.401	10.84	6.365	10.178	10.881	12.107	11.075
50	Avg^{best}	0.006	$3.82 \cdot 10^{-7}$	1.231	$1.106 \cdot 10^{-5}$	2.179	0.801	4.254	0.112
mov.	Avg^{worst}	16.641	10.371	27.38	14.742	64.53	31.778	56.211	26.079
cones	Avg^{mean}	5.39	2.556	13.462	4.491	11.82	12.143	18.586	9.847
	STD	4.909	2.933	10.224	4.231	9.215	9.897	12.233	8.389

Table 6. Mean values of *oe* achieved for two versions of MPB sc. 2: with ten and 50 moving components in the landscape and for two max. numbers of fitness function calls between subsequent changes: 5000, and $10^4 \cdot n$, where: n — number of dimensions of the search space; values in brackets represent std. error

Dim. number n:	$n = 5$		$n = 10$	
fitness fun. calls:	5000	$10^4 \cdot n$	5000	$10^4 \cdot n$
10 moving cones	11.111 (4.119)	2.489 (1.192)	17.022 (6.318)	5.81 (3.6)
50 moving cones	7.112 (1.909)	3.307 (0.893)	15.709 (6.438)	5.183 (1.401)
Dim. number n:	$n = 20$		$n = 30$	
fitness fun. calls:	5000	$10^4 \cdot n$	5000	$10^4 \cdot n$
10 moving cones	21.371 (7.552)	13.994 (6.353)	20.799 (8.115)	16.16 (7.223)
50 moving cones	17.390 (4.0)	12.455 (6.379)	20.297 (7.104)	10.202 (4.497)

5 Conclusions

In the presented research an experimental comparison of the optimization algorithm efficiency has been performed. We observed changes of the algorithm efficiency for higher numbers of the search space dimensions. One of the interesting conclusions is that the formula for the number of fitness evaluations "$10^4 \cdot n$" should be carefully applied. For some test-cases linear dependency of the evaluation number on n did not compensate growth of the errors (see, e.g., values of Avg^{mean} obtained for F_2, F_3 and F_5 — Tables 2 and 3) whereas in others the errors even decreased (F_1 and F_4 — Tables 1 and 3). In the case of *oe*, however, increase was observed for every case which means that the two measures, *oe* and Avg^{mean}, evaluate different features of the search process.

Comparing with the results presented in [4] the values of Avg^{best}, Avg^{worst}, Avg^{mean}, and STD obtained by our version of jDE for DCBG for ten-dimensional search space are smaller for all the test-cases except from F_5 (composition of Ackley functions) and two selected cases: the first one defined as F_1 with 50 moving peaks and dynamics $\mathbf{T}_1$ and the second one — F_3 with dynamics $\mathbf{T}_1$. On the other side, the results for the second benchmark, that is, offline error obtained for both versions of MPB and 5-dimensional search space are worse than those published for example in [16]. This shows, that the features of the two benchmarks represent different demands for the optimized algorithm.

Acknowledgments. This research has been partially supported by the European Regional Development Fund with the grant no. POIG.01.01.02-14-013/09: *Adaptive system supporting problem solution based on analysis of textual contents of available electronic resources.*

References

1. Branke, J.: Memory enhanced evolutionary algorithm for changing optimization problems. In: Proc. of the Congr. on Evolutionary Computation, vol. 3, pp. 1875–1882. IEEE Press, Piscataway (1999)
2. Brest, J., Boskovic, B., Greiner, S., Zumer, V., Maucec, M.S.: Performance comparison of self-adaptive and adaptive differential evolution algorithms. Soft Comput. 11(7), 617–629 (2007)

3. Brest, J., Greiner, S., Boskovic, B., Mernik, M., Zumer, V.: Self-adapting control parameters in differential evolution: A comparative study on numerical benchmark problems. IEEE Trans. Evol. Comput. 10(6), 646–657 (2006)
4. Brest, J., Zamuda, A., Boskovic, B., Maucec, M.S., Zumer, V.: Dynamic optimization using self-adaptive differential evolution. In: IEEE Congr. on Evolutionary Computation, pp. 415–422. IEEE (2009)
5. Feokistov, V.: Differential Evolution. In: Search of Solutions, Optimization and Its Applications, vol. 5. Springer, Heidelberg (2006)
6. Gallagher, M., Yuan, B.: A general-purpose tunable landscape generator. IEEE Trans. Evol. Comput. 10(5), 590–603 (2006)
7. Guennebaud, G., Jacob, B., et al.: Eigen v2.0.15 (2010), `http://eigen.tuxfamily.org`
8. Jin, Y., Branke, J.: Evolutionary algorithms in uncertain environments – a survey. IEEE Trans. Evol. Comput. 9(3), 303–317 (2005)
9. Jin, Y., Sendhoff, B.: Constructing dynamic optimization test problems using the multi-objective optimization concept. In: Raidl, G.R., Cagnoni, S., Branke, J., Corne, D.W., Drechsler, R., Jin, Y., Johnson, C.G., Machado, P., Marchiori, E., Rothlauf, F., Smith, G.D., Squillero, G. (eds.) EvoWorkshops 2004. LNCS, vol. 3005, pp. 525–536. Springer, Heidelberg (2004)
10. Li, C., Yang, S.: A generalized approach to construct benchmark problems for dynamic optimization. In: Li, X., Kirley, M., Zhang, M., Green, D., Ciesielski, V., Abbass, H.A., Michalewicz, Z., Hendtlass, T., Deb, K., Tan, K.C., Branke, J., Shi, Y. (eds.) SEAL 2008. LNCS, vol. 5361, pp. 391–400. Springer, Heidelberg (2008)
11. Liang, J.J., Suganthan, P.N., Deb, K.: Novel composition test functions for numerical global optimization. In: IEEE Swarm Intelligence Symposium, Pasadena, CA, USA, pp. 68–75 (2005)
12. Morrison, R.W., De Jong, K.A.: A test problem generator for non-stationary environments. In: Proc. Congr. on Evolutionary Computation, vol. 3, pp. 1859–1866. IEEE Press, Piscataway (1999)
13. Price, K.V.: Genetic annealing. Dr. Dobb's Journal, 127–132 (October 1994)
14. Price, K.V., Storn, R.M., Lampinen, J.A.: Differential Evolution, A Practical Approach to Global Optimization. Natural Computing Series. Springer, Heidelberg (2005)
15. Tinós, R., Yang, S.: Continuous dynamic problem generators for evolutionary algorithms. In: IEEE Congr. on Evolutionary Computation, pp. 236–243. IEEE (2007)
16. Trojanowski, K.: Properties of quantum particles in multi-swarms for dynamic optimization. Fundamenta Informaticae 95(2-3), 349–380 (2009)
17. Trojanowski, K., Michalewicz, Z.: Searching for optima in non-stationary environments. In: Proc. of the Congr. on Evolutionary Computation, vol. 3, pp. 1843–1850. IEEE Press, Piscataway (1999)
18. Yang, S.: Non-stationary problem optimization using the primal-dual genetic algorithm. In: Proc. of the 2003 IEEE Congr. on Evolutionary Computation CEC 2003, pp. 2246–2253. IEEE Press (2003)
19. Yang, S., Ong, Y.-S., Jin, Y. (eds.): Evolutionary Computation in Dynamic and Uncertain Environments. SCS. Springer, Heidelberg (2007)
20. Yang, S., Yao, X.: Population-based incremental learning with associative memory for dynamic environments. IEEE Trans. Evol. Comput. 12(5), 542–561 (2008)
21. Yuan, B., Gallagher, M.: On building a principled framework for evaluating and testing evolutionary algorithms: a continuous landscape generator. In: IEEE Congr. on Evolutionary Computation, pp. 451–458. IEEE (2003)

Towards an OpenCL Implementation of Genetic Algorithms on GPUs*

Tadeusz Puźniakowski[1] and Marek A. Bednarczyk[2,3]

[1] Institute of Informatics, University of Gdańsk, Gdańsk, Poland
[2] Faculty of Informatics, Polish-Japanese Institute of Information Technology, Gdańsk Campus, Poland
[3] Institute of Computer Science, Polish Academy of Sciences, Gdańsk, Poland

Abstract. The paper compares usual sequential implementations in C of a Genetic Algorithm with parallel implementations in OpenCL. It turns out that the speedup obtained by turning parallel depends on the choice of the selection methods used in GA. In particular the simple tournament selection method yields better results than the selection based on the roulette rule. In case of the latter which requires a synchronization of threads which manipulate individual chromosomes. This is done to compute the joint fitness of a population and find the best specimen. With the help of `scan` method this can be achieved with $O(\log n)$ complexity.

1 About the OpenCL Standard

The OpenCL is a new standard for heterogeneous systems. It appeared in response to the need for a unified framework for conducting computations on graphic cards and specialized computing accelerators. Previously there were many solutions which were not compatible with each other. Each one was created by different company, i.e., AMD had its CTM technology, while NVidia developed CUDA. In 2008 the OpenCL working group has been created and it finished working on the standard in a year time. Current version of the standard is 1.1.

OpenCL allows for computing on any kind of computing device, at least in theory. In practice, it is possible to execute code either on standard CPU, or on GPU, or on a dedicated accelerator (like Tesla cards). In theory it could even be implemented on, for example, audio processors or on processors running on smartphones.

This flexibility is achieved mostly by using embedded programming language – OpenCL C – which is based on C99 and extension schema similar to the one used in OpenGL. The OpenCL applications does not need to be compiled using special compiler like in CUDA. The OpenCL application is compiled using the compiler of choice and linked to library called OpenCL, so compilation on Linux can look like:

Every OpenCL application consists of code that is executed on host (CPU) and the code executed on computing device (usually GPU). The host code is

* Work supported by a Polish MoSaHE project funded in years 2010-2012.

P. Bouvry et al. (Eds.): SIIS 2011, LNCS 7053, pp. 190–203, 2012.

```
gcc -lOpenCL mandelbrot.c -o mandelbrot
```

Listing 1.1. Compilation of OpenCL application in Linux

called host program, the code executed on device is called OpenCL program or program and the whole application is called OpenCL application or application.

2 The Classical Genetic Algorithm

Genetic Algorithms (abbr.: *GA*) are widely used to cope with many optimization problems. Over the years the GA approach proved to give good suboptimal solutions to many practical problems in engineering and science.

The pseudocode of typical sequential implementation of GA is shown in listing 1.2. It consists of a loop in which a *population* of *specimen* or *chromosomes* is forced to evolve. This evolution is performed by `newGeneration` function which implements *selection*, *crossover* and *mutation* methods.

```
oldpop = initializePopulation()
countFitness(oldpop)
countStatistics(max,min,sumfitness,oldpop)
generation = 0
for generation in 1 to maxgen do
begin
    newpop = newGeneration(oldpop)
    countFitness(newpop)
    countStatistics(max,min,sumfitness,newpop)
    oldpop := newpop
end
```

Listing 1.2. Sequential Genetic Algorithm

The implementation of GA in our experiment is almost straight forward translation of the idea presented by Goldberg in its classical book, see [3].

Classical implementation of genetic algorithms described above uses selection based on roulette rule. This selection method requires that the sum of fitness value is computed over all specimens in a polulation.

For the need of the experiment, the tournament selection has also been used instead of the roulette selection. Tournament selection does not need any information about the global statistics of the population. Using this kind of selection allows to skip the countStatistics phase in the loop.

3 An OpenCL Implementation of GA for OneMax

The experiment has been performed on function OneMax, which counts the number of 1's in an array of bits. This function is one of the most common examples in prototyping genetic algorithms.

Formally, given a bit array a of length n OneMax function is defined as follows.

$$OneMax(a, n) = \sum_{i=0}^{n} a_i \tag{1}$$

The fitness function f of a specimen a of length n is defined as follows.

$$fa = \left(\frac{OneMax(a, n)}{n}\right)^5 \tag{2}$$

In the application, the chromosomes were constructed as shown in listing 1.3. The bits were implemented as array of chars containing values 1 or 0.

```
typedef struct specimen {
        char c[specimenbits];
        float fitness;
} specimen;
```

Listing 1.3. OneMax chromosome definition

The OpenCL does not provide any random number generator which can be called from kernels. Common approaches involve sharing one global variable which stores random seed and whenever the random number generator is invoked, the variable is updated to a new seed. In heavily parallel environment such a synchronisation would be a bottleneck. Moreover, in extreme cases change parallel algorithm into sequential algorithm. This problem has been solved here by using a copy of random number generator form GNU libc and temporary global seed which is passed on kernel invocation and updated afterwards. The kernel adds own rank to the global seed (in private memory) and then uses it as usual random function.

3.1 OpenCL Solution

The algorithm implementation consists of multiple kernels. Most kernels are as similar as possible to functions presented in [3].

The problem implementation is in separate files, so the application can be easily set to solve problems other than OneMax.

The host code works as a supervisor for functions executed on OpenCL device and it does not perform any computations. This code is also independent of problem implementation. Even gathering results is done in generic way, so the host code does not need to be compiled in compliance with chromosome representation.

3.2 Initialization of Population

The first step is to create initial population of chromosomes. This is done using kernel shown in listing 1.4

```
__kernel void initPopulation (__global specimen* newpop,
            __global environment * data,
            const int size,
            long random_seed)
{
    const int i = get_global_id(0);
    if (i >= size) return;
    int seed = random_seed + i;
    generateSpecimen(&newpop[i], data, &seed);
}
```

Listing 1.4. Kernel creating initial population

This kernel calls function **generateSpecimen** from problem implementation to generate specimens.

3.3 Counting Fitness

The fitness function is parallelized in the same fashion as initialization of population. This kernel is invoked in as many instances as the size of population, so every thread counts its own specimen fitness. The source code of this kernel is shown in listing 1.5.

```
__kernel void countFitness (__global specimen* pop,
            __global environment * data,
            const int size,
            long random_seed)
{
    const int i = get_global_id(0);
    if (i >= size) return;
    int seed = random_seed + i;
    specimen sp = pop[i]; // Here is copying into provate
        memory
    pop[i].fitness = fitness(&sp, data, &seed);
}
```

Listing 1.5. Kernel counting fitness for each specimen in population

Note the way random seed is used. It is obtained from the host program, copied with addition of kernel instance rank into private variable called *seed*. Then the *seed* is used in usual way passing it to function **fitness** as a parameter.

Note that kernel **countFitness** uses private memory in variable *sp* for storing specimen. According to OpenCL standard this should be the fastest memory available [4].The function **fitness** is provided in problem implementation. In the experiment it was the function in listing 1.6.

```
float fitness(specimen *sp, __global environment * data, int *
    random_seed) {
```

```
        int s = 0;
        int i = 0;
        for (i = 0; i < specimenbits; i++) {
                s += (int)(sp->c[i]);
        }
        float r = ((float)s)/ specimenbits;
        return pow(r,5);
}
```

Listing 1.6. Fitness function utilised in experiment

3.4 Counting Fitness of the Entire Population and the Best Specimen

Our implementation uses massive parallelism for solving the problem, so counting the sum of fitness values of all specimen in a population has also been done in parallel. Note that this can be accomplish only when all fitness values have been computed. This has a negative impact on the speed of computation.

Our first approach to compute the sum was to use so called OpenCL tasks. Unfortunately,this turned out to be a sequential solution. The approach finally adopted involves parallelization which works just like **MPI_Allreduce** in MPI. The source code of kernel performing distributed summation and finding best specimen is in listing 1.7. The sequential implementation iterates through all the specimens and is too simple to be presented here.

```
__kernel void countSummaryFitnessP (__global specimen* pop,
    __global environment * data, __global specimen* best,
    __global float *sumfitness, __global float *tmpfitness,
    const int size, __local float *sumfitnessLocal, __local
    int *bestLocal)
{
    const int wgsize = get_local_size(0);
    const int rank = get_global_id(0);
    int j;
    int bestIndex = 0;
    float bestFitness;
    float sumFitnessPrv = 0;

    // Gathering data into one work item (1)
    if (rank < wgsize) {
        j = rank % wgsize;
        if (j < size) {
            sumFitnessPrv = pop[j].fitness;
            bestIndex = j;
            bestFitness = sumFitnessPrv;
            for (j = j+wgsize; j < size; j+=wgsize) {
                float f = pop[j].fitness;
                sumFitnessPrv += f;
                if (bestFitness < f) {
```

```
                    bestIndex = j;
                    bestFitness = f;
                }
            }
        }
        bestLocal[rank] = bestIndex;
        sumfitnessLocal[rank] = sumFitnessPrv;
    }
    barrier(CLK_LOCAL_MEM_FENCE);

    // scan algorithm (2)
    int currStep = 1;
    for (;currStep < wgsize;) {
        // gathering results in parallel
        if ((rank % (currStep<<1) == 0) && (rank < wgsize))  {
            if ((rank + currStep) < wgsize) {
                sumfitnessLocal[rank] += sumfitnessLocal[rank+
                    currStep];
                if (pop[bestLocal[rank]].fitness < pop[
                    bestLocal[rank+currStep]].fitness) {
                    bestLocal[rank] = bestLocal[rank+currStep
                        ];
                }
            }
        }
        barrier(CLK_LOCAL_MEM_FENCE);
        currStep *= 2;
    }

    if (rank == 0) {
        sumfitness[0] = sumfitnessLocal[0];
        best[0] = pop[bestLocal[0]];
    }
}
```

Listing 1.7. Counting the sum of all specimen fitnesses and finding best specimen

3.5 Selection Algorithms

There are two selection algorithms available – the roulette rule shown in listing 1.9 and the tournament selection shown in listing 1.8. Note that tournament selection does not use *sumfitness* parameter, so this is not computed if this selection algorithm is in use. In both algorithms the random seed is passed as a parameter.

```
int selectSpecimen(float sumfitness, __global specimen *pop,
    int size, int *random_seed, int rank) {
    int i, j;
        i = rand_int(random_seed) % size;
```

```
        j = (rand_int(random_seed) % (size - 1)+i+1)%size;
        if (pop[i].fitness > pop[j].fitness) return i;
    return j;
}
```

Listing 1.8. Tournament selection function

The roulette rule selection is dependent on sum fitness of all specimens. This is the selection method used in first GA implementations. Even though it is more sophisticated method, it does not perform as well as tournament selection in simple function optimizations like OneMax.

```
int selectSpecimen(float sumfitness, __global specimen *pop,
    int size, int *random_seed, int rank) {
    float partsum, rnd;
    int j;
    partsum = 0;
    rnd = sumfitness * rand_float(random_seed);
    for (j = 0; j < size; j++) {
        partsum += pop[j].fitness;
        if (partsum > rnd) {
            return j;
        }
    }
    return 0;
}
```

Listing 1.9. Roulette rule selection function

3.6 New Generation

The algorithm for computing new generation is also heavily inspired by Goldberg's approach. This function can be easily parallelized i a way that every kernel instance calculates two specimens. The selection is done using roulette rule without elite. The source code for new generation is in listing 1.10. The same code is also used in version that uses tournament selection.

```
__kernel void newGeneration (__global specimen* pop, __global
    environment * data, __global specimen* newpop, __global
    float * sumfitness, const int size, long random_seed) {
    const int i = get_global_id(0)<<1;
    if (i >= size) return;
    int seed = random_seed + i;
    specimen parent[2];
    specimen offspring[2];
```

```
    parent[0] = pop[selectSpecimen( sumfitness[0], pop, size,
        &seed, i )];
    parent[1] = pop[selectSpecimen( sumfitness[0], pop, size,
        &seed, i )];
    if (rand_float(&seed) < pcross) {
        crossover(parent, offspring, &seed);
    } else {
        offspring[0] = parent[0];
        offspring[1] = parent[1];
    }
    mutate(&offspring[0], &seed);
    newpop[i] = offspring[0];
    if(i+1 < size) {
        mutate(&offspring[1], &seed);
        newpop[i+1] = offspring[1];
    }
}
```

Listing 1.10. Kernel performing new generation

3.7 Sequential Solution

The sequential solution consists of the same set of functions as in OpenCL version. The implementation of problem is included using C preprocessor directive #include, so the problem is solved in the same way as in OpenCL version. Kernel functions are called in a way simulating the real kernel calls. The fragments showing this approach is shown in listing 1.11. Note that in order to correctly compile the application it is needed to define OpenCL keywords like ***__kernel***. The OpenCL C functions like **get_global_id** are simulated by just declaring appropriate C functions. The fake kernel execution is performed by calling "kernel" function in loop. This allows for OpenCL application and standard C application to share as much code as possible, thus allowing for a better performance comparison.

```
#define __global
#define __constant const
#define __kernel inline
#define __local

int global_id[1] = {0};
void reset_global_id() {
    global_id[0] = 0;
}
int get_global_id(int n) {
    return global_id[n];
}

int get_local_size(int n) {
```

```
    return 1;
}
...
reset_global_id();
for (i = 0; i < pop_size; i++) {
    initPopulation (population_dev, environment_dev, pop_size,
        *random_seed);
    global_id[0]++;
}
```

Listing 1.11. Calling kernel functions from sequential application

4 Results

The experiments aimed to compare two implementations:

- Standard sequential implementation in C compiled with optimizations enabled and kernels compiled in as inline.
- The OpenCL version run on CPU and on GPU.

Each of the implementations had two variants depending on the selection method used, i.e., one for the roulette rule, another for the tournament method.

The sources used in experiment have been compiled with **-O2** optimization enabled and **-mtune=generic**. The hardware configuration details are in appendix. The algorithm has been configured in the following way.

- Crossover probability: 0.8
- Mutation probability (of each gene): 0.000033
- Chromosome length: 63bit
- Selection method: roulette or tournament

Let us start the analysis of the experiments with diagrams presented on Figure 1. Both represent the total execution time of the implementations as a function of the population size. The iteration count is constant and equal to 60. The fitness was 1 (best solution found) for the population size of at least 110 and 220 for tournament and roulette respectively. Diagram on the left describes the results for GA with selection based on the roulette, while on the right GA used selection with tournaments of size 2. On both diagrams we consider the same algorithm run either on CPU or on GPU with and without the cost of pre-compilation taken into account.

One immediate observation is that the initialization phase of the CPU implementation is neglegible — the two curves are almost indistinguishable on both diagrams. In case of OpenCL implementations the overhead related to the pre-compilation of the kernels is substantial. However, in practice the cost would be paid only once. Hence, if one is interested in repeated computation of GA's it does not really matter. Consequently, the cost the initialization phase is omitted from discussion in the sequel.

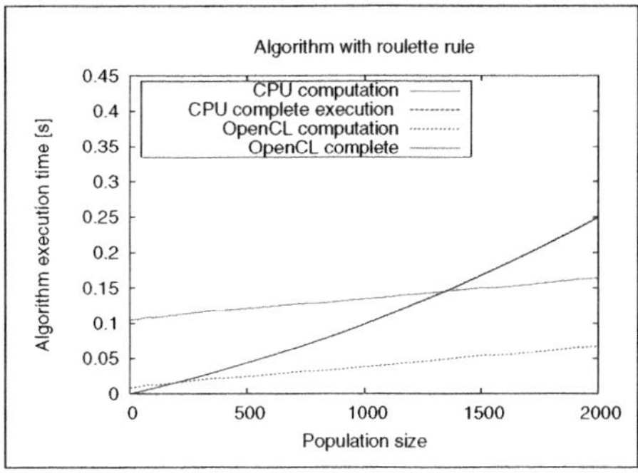

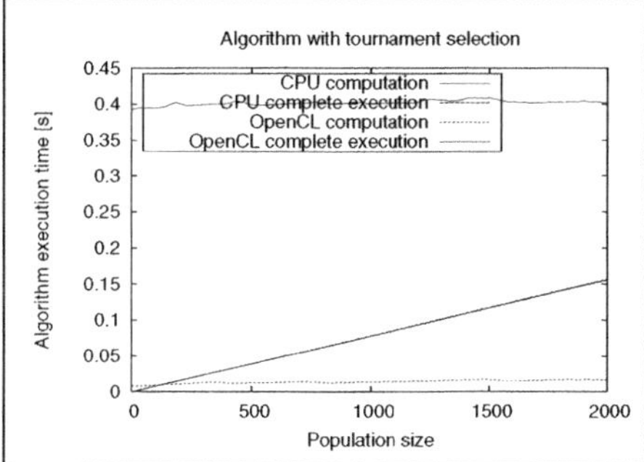

Fig. 1. Comparison of total execution time – sequential code compared to OpenCL code on Nvidia GeForce GTS 250. The iteration count is 60 for both cases.

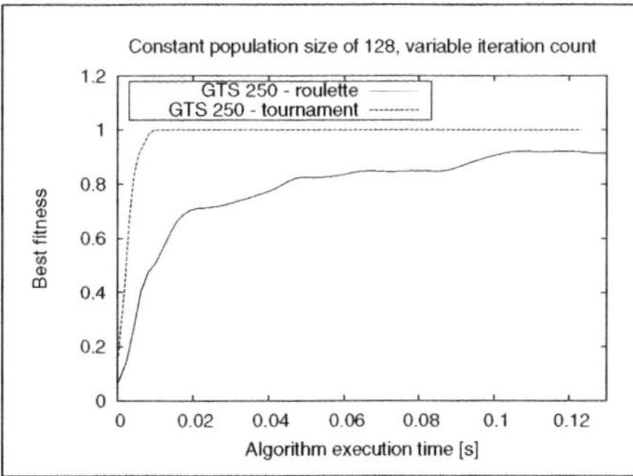

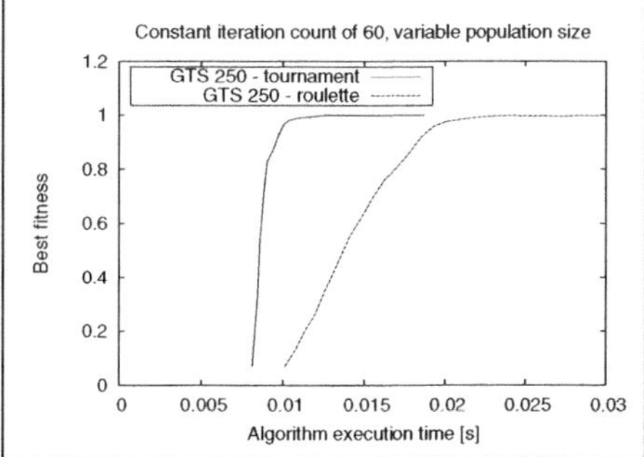

Fig. 2. Comparison of fitness and execution time on two different implementations run on Nvidia GeForce GTS 250

Another observation that can be drawn from Figure 1 is that in case of the GA with roulette the cost of computation grows linearly with OpenCL implementation, and seems worse than linear in case of CPU implementation. In case of the tournament selection the execution on CPU grows linearly with respect to the population size, and seems almost constant in case of OpenCL.

4.1 Roulette Rule versus Tournament Selection on GPU

Let us compare the efficiency of the two OpenCL implementation from the poin of view of the selection method each of them uses, see Figure 2. The diagram on the left demonstrates that in case of tournament selection for a fixed size of population the parallel implementation converges towards solution in, rougly, linear time. In case of the roulette selection the convergence is much slower. This is similar to the sequential case — a comparison of these two selection methods gave similar results, see [5].

4.2 CPU Versus GPU

From the above it follows that GA with tournament selection performs better than the same GA but with selection based on roulette rule. This difference in convergence can be better understood when one looks more closely at the way the two selection methods are implemented on parallel hardware. Our basic idea to distribute chromosomes among threads is at odds with the need to compute the sum of fitness values of each of them. Simply, such sum can only be computed when all these values are known. This introduces a synchronisation point among the threads of the parallel implementation. In case of tournament selection there is no need for such synchronisation.

Nevertheless, even in case of GA with roulette selection the implementation on parallel hardware gives better results than the same implementation run on CPU, see Figure 3. The experiment has been performed on population sizes ranging from 2 to 2000.

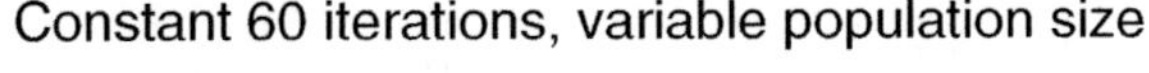

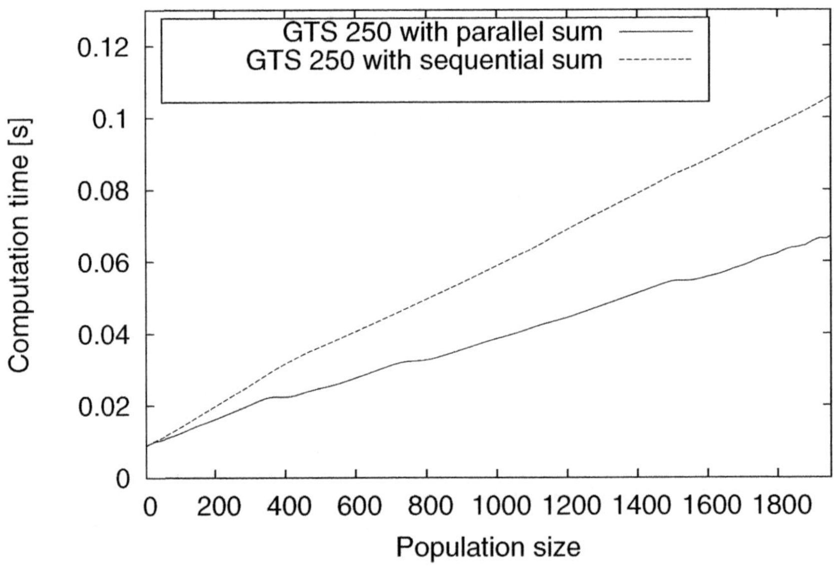

Fig. 3. OpenCL computation time

4.3 Different OpenCL Implementations on the Same Hardware

We have created one experiment in order to compare:

1. NVIDIA OpenCL on GTS 250 in Linux (as reference) (PC 1)
2. AMD OpenCL on Radeon HD5850 (Cypress) in Windows XP (PC 2)
3. AMD OpenCL on Radeon HD5850 (Cypress) in Linux (PC 2)
4. AMD OpenCL on Phenom II x2 3.1GHz in Linux (PC 2)

The results are in figure 4. The tournament selection was used. The population size varied from 32 to 8192 with constant iterations count of 128. Of course it was only performance comparison, because the best fitness was achieved by population of 128. The genetic algorithm implementation was exactly the same on every setup, except for the compilation, which was done on Linux by GCC and on Windows by MinGW. The optimization switches (-mtune=generic -O2 -mpc32) were always used for compilation. The (PC 1) was the computer used in the primary experiment. The (PC 2) was used only for this experiment.

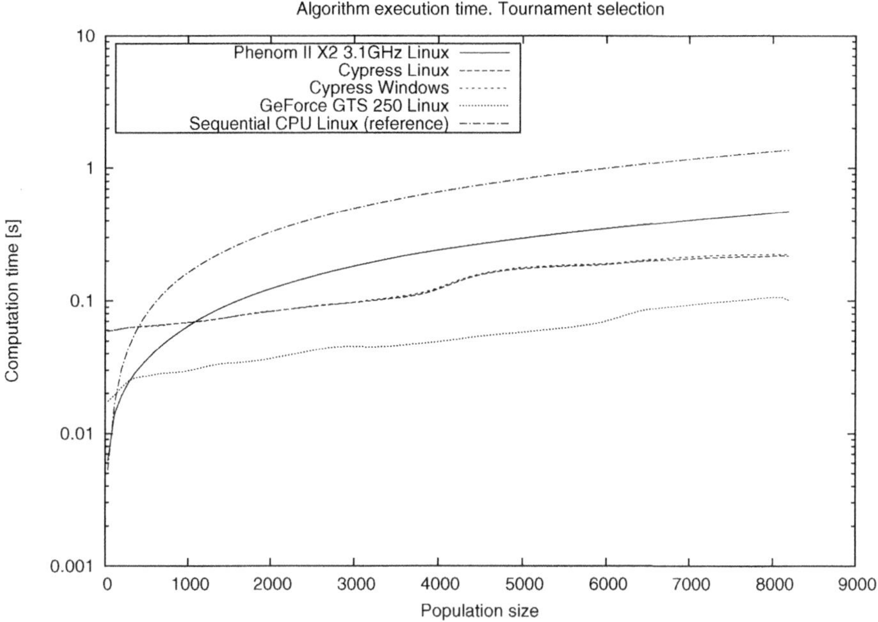

Fig. 4. Different OpenCL implementations

There is slight difference between Cypress on Linux and Windows.

The conclusion is that in order to achieve the best performance, one have to check its program on multiple hardware+software configurations and choose the best one for its problem.

5 Conclusions

The paper shows that OpenCL performs quite well in computing genetic algorithms on parallel hardware offered by today's GPUs.

One has to consider, however, that not all population manipulation mechanisms equally well undergo parallelization. In particular, the roulette wheel selection proved to be very inefficient compared to the much simpler tournament selection.

However, the computation time of OpenCL version GA was faster than the sequential code for large enough computational problems. For example, intensive computations involving GAs have recently been performed in the studies of search paths in SAR operations, see [1]. In order to tune the GA we have created a framework in which many instances of a GA problem can be distributed among many computers, see [2]. In the sequel we plan to investigate a mixture of distribution of of tasks with their efficient computation on parallel hardware provided by GPUs.

When implementing many GA computations in parallel one often has to implement some methods that are needed as well. For instance, we have to provide local instances for computing pseudorandom numbers for each parallel thread.

References

1. Bednarczyk, M.A., Kitowski, Z., Piotrowski, M., Przybyszewska, A., Puźniakowski, T., Pyrchla, J., Siekielski, A., Sławiński, J., Wierzchoń, S.T.: GASPS — genetic algorithm search path simulator. In: Recent Advences in Intelligent Information Systems. Academic Publishing House EXIT, Warsaw (2009)
2. Bednarczyk, M.A., Neumann, J., Pawłowski, W., Siekielski, A., Sławiński, J.: Towards an object-oriented framework for higher order genetic algorithms. In: International Conference on Artificial Inteligence. Publishing House of University of Podlasie (2009)
3. Goldberg, D.E.: Genetic Algorithms in Search, Optimization, and Machine Learning. Addison-Wesley Publishing Company (1989)
4. Group, K.O.W.: The OpenCL Specification. Khronos Group (2010)
5. Zhong, J., Hu, X., Zhang, J., Gu, M.: Comparison of performance between different selection strategies on simple genetic algorithms. In: International Conference on Computational Intelligence for Modelling, Control and Automation, vol. 2, pp. 1115–1121 (2005)

Appendix

A Experiment Configuration

The main experiment (PC 1) has been performed on the following hardware:

- Processor: Dual AMD Phenom(tm) II X2 550 Processor. Cores parameters:
  - Frequency: 3100MHz
  - Cache size: 512Kb
  - bogomips: 6227.80
- Memory: 4096MB
  - Frequency: 1600 MHz
  - Dual Channel
- OpenCL device (video card): nVidia Corporation G92 [GeForce GTS 250]:
  - Driver version: 270.26 Linux-x86
  - Frequency: Graphics 740MHz, Processor 1836MHz, Memory 1100MHz

  - Memory: 512MB
  - Memory interface: 256bit
  - CUDA Cores: 128
  - BIOS Version: 62.92.7d.00.11
  - bus type: PCI Express x16 Gen2

The software configuration:

- Linux distribution: Linux Mint with all updates from 2011-03-14
- Linux x86 kernel 2.6.35-25-generic-pae
- NVIDIA drivers 270.26 Linux-x86
- XOrg 1.9.0

The additional experiment comparing different OpenCL implementations was performed on:

- Processor: Intel(R) Core(TM) i5 CPU 760 @2.80GHz. Cores parameters:
  - Frequency: 2794MHz
  - Cache size: 8192Kb
  - bogomips: 6227.80
- Memory: 4096MB
- OpenCL device (video card): AMD Radeon HD5850 (Cypress):
  - Driver version: 270.26 Linux-x86
  - Frequency: GPU 725Mhz
  - Memory: 512MB
  - OpenCL Driver Version: CAL 1.4.1353
  - OpenCL Version: OpenCL 1.1 AMD-APP-SDK-v2.4 (Windows & Linux)

For both - Windows and Linux there was the current stable driver version as of day 2011-05-12.

Software configuration (Linux):

- Linux distribution: Linux Mint with all updates from 2011-03-14
- Linux x86 kernel 2.6.35-25-generic-pae
- NVIDIA drivers 270.26 Linux-x86
- XOrg 1.9.0

Software configuration (Windows):

- Windows Microsoft Windows XP, Multiprocessor Free, Professional + SP3
- Windows product version 5.1, kernel build 2600

Evolutionary Algorithm Parameter Tuning with Sensitivity Analysis

Frédéric Pinel, Grégoire Danoy, and Pascal Bouvry

FSTC/CSC/ILIAS, University of Luxembourg
6 Rue R. Coudenhove Kalergi, L-1359 Luxembourg
{frederic.pinel,gregoire.danoy,pascal.bouvry}@uni.lu

Abstract. This article introduces a generic sensitivity analysis method to measure the influence and interdependencies of Evolutionary Algorithms parameters. The proposed work focuses on its application to a Parallel Asynchronous Cellular Genetic Algorithm (PA-CGA). Experimental results on two different instances of a scheduling problem have demonstrated that some metaheuristic parameters values have little influence on the solution quality. On the opposite, some local search parameter values have a strong impact on the obtained results for both instances. This study highlights the benefits of the method, which significantly reduces the parameter search space.

Keywords: Evolutionary Algorithm, Parameter Tuning, Sensitivity Analysis.

1 Introduction

Evolutionary Algorithms (EAs) have been used since many years to optimize combinatorial and continuous hard problems. These nature-inspired algorithms function by iteratively applying specific operators in order to modify potential solutions to a problem and converge to an optimal or near-optimal solution. Despite their application success, EAs remain highly dependent on their parameterization but also on the optimization problem class. Moreover, the complexity of recent EAs, such as cellular genetic algorithms (CGAs), implies an increase in the number of parameters to be set. As mentioned by De Jong in [8], the No Free Lunch (NFL) theorem state that no single algorithm will outperform all other algorithms on all classes of problems. This induces several key questions, including: "which parameters are useful to improve the EA performance?". Although a lot of works have been conducted in the field of parameter setting for EAs, most of these focused on independently searching for the best parameter values without considering if these parameters have a direct influence on the EA performance.

The contribution of this paper is the proposal of a generic of sensitivity analysis method to quantitatively study the influence and interdependencies of the parameters of an EA when applied on a specific optimization problem. The objective is to help the algorithm designer in parameter setting by narrowing the

P. Bouvry et al. (Eds.): SIIS 2011, LNCS 7053, pp. 204–216, 2012.

parameter search space prior to optimizing their values. We here focused on a Parallel Asynshronous Cellular Genetic Algorithm (PA-CGA) [22] and analyzed its parameters influence on two different instances of a scheduling problem of independent tasks in a grid.

The paper structure is detailed next. The next section contains a brief survey on parameter setting techniques. Then section 3 presents the sensitivity analysis method. In section 4 a detailed description of the scheduling problem and of the PA-CGA is given. Section 5 and 6 respectively present the experimental setup used and discusses the obtained results. Finally in section 7 the conclusion and perspectives of the work are presented.

2 Related Work

Parameter setting can greatly influence the performance of Evolutionary Algorithms and therefore focused the interest of many researchers. Comprehensive surveys have been introduced by De Jong in [8], Eiben [10] and more recently by Kramer in [17].

As mentioned by Maturana et al. in [19], one of the main problems is to assess which parameters can lead to the algorithm transformation, i.e. improvement. Yet, they proposed a classification of parameters, distinguishing *behavioral parameters* (operators probabilities, population size) and *structural parameters* (encoding, choice of operators). A similar classification was proposed by Smit and Eiben in [27] distinguishing between *numerical* and *symbolic* parameters. In this work we focused on behavioral, respectively numerical parameters setting.

The EA parameter space can be explored in offline (before the search) or online (during the search) setting. Eiben in [9] classified these parameter techniques as parameter *tuning*, and *parameter control*. In this work we are interested in parameter setting before the run (i.e. tuning), for which a taxonomy extension has been proposed by Kramer in [17] (see Fig. 1).

Tuning by hand induces user experience for setting the EA parameters beforehand. This solution is largely predominant in the literature in which parameters are usually set based on empirical evaluations as mentioned in [19].

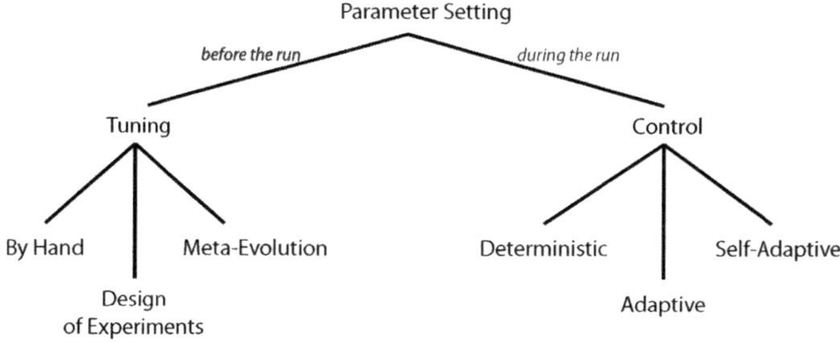

Fig. 1. Parameter setting in EA's taxonomy [17]

The second tuning class, design of experiments (DoE), refers to Bartz-Beielstein work on Sequential Parameter Optimization (SPO) [3] which is a heuristic combining classical and modern statistical techniques (e.g. latin hypercube sampling - LHS). The objective is to design the experimental plan prior to doing the experiments. Some works have focused on analyzing the sensitivity of parameter, but limited to the study of the independent influence of parameters values on the fitness. De Castro et al. in [7] studied the sensitivity of 3 parameters (number of antibodies, number of generated clones and amount antibodies to be replaced) of their Clonal Selection Algorithm (CLONEALG). Similarly, Ho et al. in [13] have analyzed the sensitivity of parameters of their Intelligent Genetic Algorithm (IGA), including mutation and crossover probabilities. In [20] Min et al. analyze the sensitivity of the population size and the termination condition (maximum number of generations) of a standard GA on a reverse logistics network problem. Finally, most lately Geem et al. in [11] analyzed the sensitivity of Harmony Search (HS) parameters (harmony size, memory considering rate and pitch adjustment).

The last parameter tuning class, meta-evolution, is also referred to as nested evolution. This is a two-level evolutionary process in which one algorithm optimizes the parameters of the second one. A recent approach has been proposed by Nannen and Eiben in [21], Relevance Estimation and Value Calibration of EA parameters (REVAC). It estimates the expected performance of the EA when parameter values are chosen from a probability density function (PDF) and includes a measure of the parameter relevance (normalized Shannon entropy).

The contribution of this work lies in the DoE class, in which existing approaches provide information on the best parameter values for the specific problem tackled. However these do not answer to two important questions:

1. Do all EAs parameters influence the algorithm performance on a specific problem instance?
2. What are the interdependencies between the parameters? Since, as Eiben already mentioned in [10] parameters are not independent.

The following section describes how sensitivity analysis can answer the drawbacks of the aforementioned approaches.

3 Sensitivity Analysis

Sensitivity analysis aims to identify how uncertainty in each of the parameters influence the uncertainty in the output [25] of a model. This technique can answer the following question: which factors cause the most and the least uncertainty in the output (also known as screening). This measures the importance of factors in the model analyzed. It is useful when designing experiments (DoE activity) and setting parameter, because it allows to focus on the most influential factors, possibly setting arbitrary values to the least influential ones. Moreover, this knowledge is also useful at design-time. The designer of a model intuitively develops an idea of its behavior. Sensitivity analysis allows the designer to verify his hypothesis, and modify the model accordingly. This work therefore proposes to use sensitivity analysis to study the influential parameters of an EA on a specific problem class, i.e. scheduling problem of independent tasks in a grid. The objective is to reduce the EA parameter search space.

3.1 Desirable Sensitivity Analysis Properties

There are several ways to conduct a sensitivity analysis. Section 2 listed a few. Before presenting the suggested method, the desired characteristics of a method for sensitivity analysis are presented below. The method should:

- be model independent (it does not place requirements on the type of model to work),
- evaluate the effect of a parameter while varying other parameters (most manual analysis vary one parameter at a time, which hides interactions between parameters),
- cope with the influence of scale and shape in the model (the probability density function and its parameters),
- describe the influence of uncertainty in the parameters in a quantitative mode (the relative importance of each parameter should be quantified),
- capture the interaction between parameters.

3.2 Selected Method

These desired properties restrict the possible methods (such as using entropy as a measure of output uncertainty [21]). The chosen method is based on decomposing the variance of the output, as introduced by Saltelli et al. in [25]. The exact implementation used is an extension to the Fourier Amplitude Sensitivity Test proposed by Saltelli et al., called Fast99 [26]. This method allows the computation of first order effects and interactions for each parameter. Parameters interaction occurs when the effect of the parameters on the output is not a sum of their single (first order) effects.

3.3 Application of Sensitivity Analysis

The chosen method benefits from the properties presented in Section 3.1, therefore there are no model specific restrictions.

First, the goal of the analysis must be stated and the output of the model defined accordingly. For an evolutionary algorithm, this can be the quality of the solutions, the number of evaluations, the runtime of the implementation, etc. For each parameter of the model analyzed, the range of possible of values is required, along with their distribution in the range. These values come from experts in the application domain, or from the literature. Unless there are many parameters (greater than 30) or if the evaluation takes too much time (due to the number of parameters combinations), the Fast99 method mentioned in Section 3.2 is suitable. Otherwise, the qualitative method of Morris is better suited (it is a One-At-a-Time method, or OAT). The method then produces a list of parameter combinations, for which the model is evaluated. In the case of an algorithm, the implementation of the algorithm is run with the prepared parameter combinations. The number of combinations is $N_{samples} \times N_{parameters}$ (1000 samples are typical). The method for the sensitivity analysis then collects the evaluation results and presents the linear and non-linear influence of each parameter. The next sections present a worked application.

4 Example Application

The presented sensibility analysis is performed on a parallel asynchronous cellular genetic algorithm [22] for scheduling of independent tasks in a grid. The following section provides a description of the problem and its representation, and section 4.2 presents the algorithm and the parameters used.

4.1 Problem Description

The problem the EA attempts to solve arises quite frequently in parameter sweep applications, such as Monte-Carlo simulations [6]. In these applications, many tasks with almost no interdependencies are generated and submitted to the grid system. Efficiency means to allocate tasks as fast as possible and to optimize some criterion, such as makespan or flowtime. Makespan is among the most important optimization criteria of a grid system. Indeed, it is a measure of its productivity (throughput). Task scheduling is treated as a single objective optimization problem, in which the makespan is minimized. *Makespan*, the finishing time of latest task, is defined as

$$\min_{S} \max\{F_t : t \in Tasks\} \ , \tag{1}$$

where F_t is the finishing time of task t in schedule S.

More precisely, assuming that the computing time needed to perform a task is known (assumption that is usually made in the literature [5,12,16]), the problem is represented with the Expected Time to Compute (ETC) model by Braun et al. [5]. The instance definition of the problem is as follows:

- *nb_tasks*: the *number* of independent (user/application) *tasks* to be scheduled.
- *nb_machines*: the *number* of heterogeneous *machine* candidates to participate in the planning.
- The *workload* of each task (in millions of instructions).
- The *computing capacity* of each machine (in *mips*).
- $ready_m$: ready time indicating when machine m will have finished the previously assigned tasks.
- The Expected Time to Compute (ETC) matrix ($nb\_tasks \times nb\_machines$) in which $ETC[t][m]$ is the expected execution time of task t on machine m.

The two benchmark instances used for this study consist of 512 tasks and 16 machines. Both instances represent different classes of ETC matrices. The classification is based on three parameters: task heterogeneity, machine heterogeneity, and consistency [2]. Instances are labelled as *u_x_yyzz* where:

u stands for uniform distribution (used in generating the matrix).
x stands for the type of consistency (*c* for consistent, *i* for inconsistent, and *s* for semi-consistent). An ETC matrix is considered consistent when the following is true: if a machine m_i executes a task t faster than machine m_j, then m_i executes all tasks faster than m_j. Inconsistency means that a machine is faster for some tasks and slower for some others. An ETC matrix is considered semi-consistent if it contains a consistent sub-matrix.
yy indicates the heterogeneity of the tasks (*hi* means high, and *lo* means low).
zz indicates the heterogeneity of the resources (*hi* means high, and *lo* means low).

4.2 Parallel Asynchronous Cellular GA

The chosen EA is a parallel asynchronous CGA (PA-CGA) [22], based on [23]. Cellular genetic algorithms (cGAs) [1] are a kind of GA with a structured population in which individuals are spread in a two dimensional toroidal mesh and are only allowed to interact with their neighbors. The algorithm iteratively considers as current each individual in the grid, and individuals may only interact with individuals belonging to their neighborhood, so parents are chosen among the neighbors with a given criterion. Crossover and mutation operators are applied to the individuals, with probabilities p_c and p_m respectively. Afterwards, the algorithm computes the fitness value of the new offspring individual (or individuals), and inserts it (or one of them) instead of the current individual in the population following a given replacement policy. This loop is repeated until a termination condition is met.

In the PA-CGA, the population is partitioned into a number of contiguous blocks with a similar number of individuals (Figure 2). Each block contains *pop_size*/*#threads* individuals, where *#threads* represents the number of concurrent threads executed. In order to preserve the exploration characteristics of the CGA, communication between individuals of different blocks is made possible. This neighborhood may include individuals from other population blocks. This allows an individual's genetic information to cross block boundaries.

The different threads evolve their population block independently and do not wait on the other threads to complete their generation (the evolution of all the individuals in their block) before pursuing their evolution. Hence, if a breeding loop takes longer for an individual of a given thread, the individuals evolved by the other threads may go through more generations.

The combination of a concurrent execution model with the neighborhoods crossing block boundaries leads to concurrent access to shared memory. To enable safe concurrent memory access, we synchronize access to individuals with a POSIX [15] read-write lock. This high-level mechanism allows concurrent reads

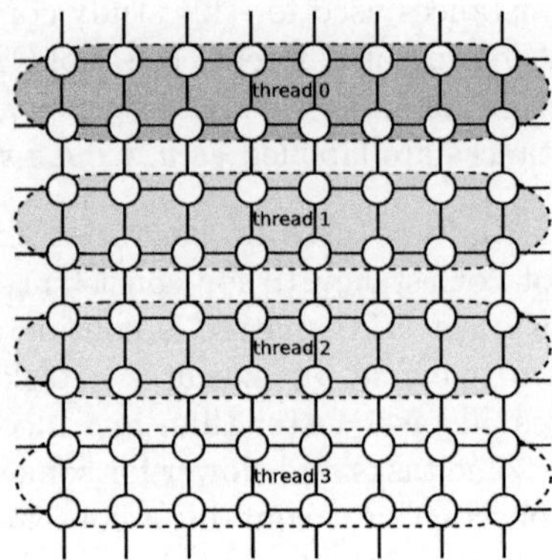

Fig. 2. Partition of an 8x8 population over 4 threads

from different threads, but not concurrent reads with writes, nor concurrent writes. In the two latter cases, the operations are serialized.

The algorithm employs a local search operator, specific to the scheduling problem considered. This operator moves a randomly chosen task from the most loaded machine (a machine's load is the total of the tasks completion times) to a selected candidate machine among the N least loaded (N is a parameter). A candidate machine is selected if its new completion time, with the addition of the task moved, is the smallest of all the candidates. This new completion time must also remain inferior to the makespan. This operation is performed several times (a parameter of the local search).

The following parameters have been used for the PA-CGA. The population is initialized randomly, except for one individual obtained with the *Min-min* heuristic [14]. The selection operator used is binary tournament. The recombination operator used is the one-point (*opx*) crossover and the mutation operator moves one randomly chosen task to a randomly chosen machine. The neighborhood shape used is linear 5 (L5), also called Von Neumann neighborhood, composed of the 4 nearest individuals (measured in Manhattan distance), plus the individual evolved. The replacement strategy is "replace if better", i.e. the newly generated offspring replaces the current individual if it improves the parent fitness value.

5 Experimental Setup

The studied parameters of the PA-CGA, called factors in the context of sensitivity analysis, are summarized in Table 1.

For each factor considered in this study, a uniform distribution of the values is considered since we have no a priori indication of the correct values. Population size represents the dimension of the square shaped grid of the cellular GA, which can range between 8X8 to 32X32 individuals. Crossover rate is defined in a range between 0.1 to 1.0. Mutation is defined by its rate, ranging between 0.1

Table 1. Uncertainty in the model parameters

Factor	Distribution	Range of values
Population size	uniform	8x8 – 32x32
Crossover rate (P_crossover)	uniform	0.1 – 1.0
Mutation rate (P_mutation)	uniform	0.1 – 1.0
Mutation iterations (Iter_mutation)	uniform	1 – 5
Local search rate (P_search)	uniform	0.1 – 1.0
Local search iterations (Iter_search)	uniform	1 – 10
Load for local search (Load_search)	uniform	0.1 – 0.9
Threads	uniform	1 – 4

and 1.0, and the maximum number of mutations, ranging from 1 to 5. Local search is defined by the same properties (rate between 0.1 and 1.0 and maximum number of iterations between 1 and 10). The value range for the number of least loaded machines to consider 4.2 is 0.1 to 0.9. Finally, as the algorithm can be parallelized, the number of threads also varires between 1 and 4.

The stop condition for each run of the EA is 100 generations. Each set of factors generated for the analysis is used for 4 runs. The result is the average of the makespan over those 4 runs. The sensitivity analysis therefore considers a total of 6400 parameters combinations.

Sensitivity analysis is performed on the algorithm for two different instance files for which we provide their Blazewicz [4] notation:

- *u_c_512x16_hihi*: $Q16|26.48 \leq p_j \leq 2892648.25|C_{max}$;
- *u_c_512x16_lolo*: $Q16|1.44 \leq p_j \leq 975.30|C_{max}$.

The intention is to discover if different problem instances modify the factor prioritization results. The Fast99 implementation of the sensitivity analysis is provided by the R Sensitivity Analysis package [24].

6 Results

Figure 3 presents for each factor, their linear and non-linear (or interaction) effects on the output for the problem instance with high tasks and resources heterogeneity: the quality of the solution (the average makespan over 4 independent runs).

The benefits of the sensitivity analyzis are immediately visible. Indeed, the local search parameters and notably the maximum number of iterations, influence the most the output. It is indeed twice more important than the second

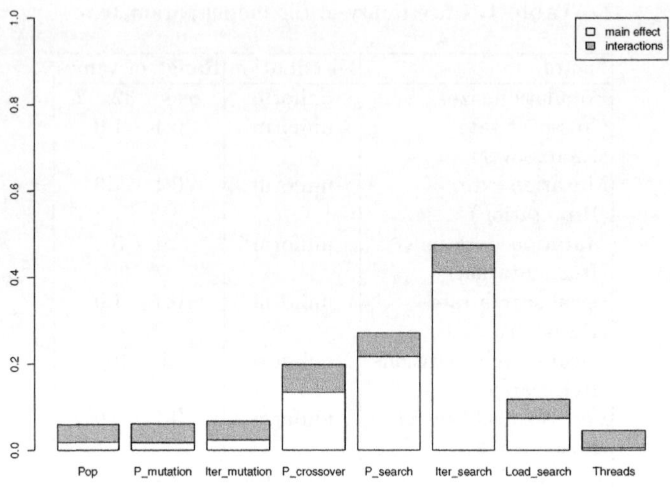

Fig. 3. Sensitivity analysis, hihi instance

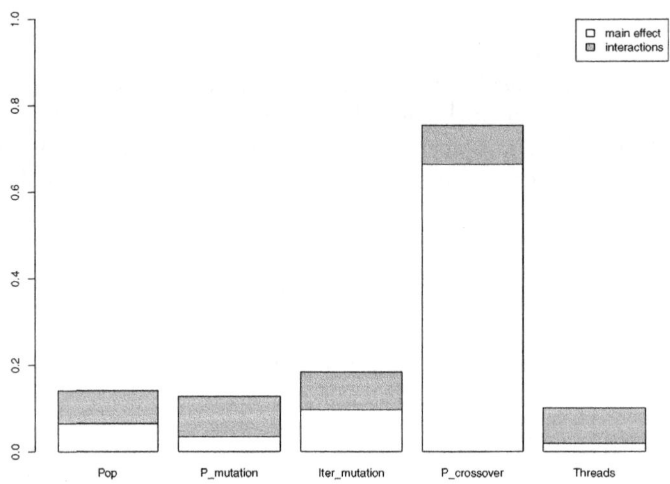

Fig. 4. Sensitivity analysis, hihi instance with fixed local search parameters

most influential parameter, the local search rate. This result is consistent with related works in the scheduling literature which enlightened the importance of the local search when dealing with hybrid metaheuristics. This also justifies the hand tuning of the parameters performed for [22]. The third most important parameter the crossover rate. This is highlighted in Figure 4 which analyzes the effects on the output of the GA parameters, thus using fixed values for the local search. It appears that the crossover rate is at least six times more important than all the other GA parameters.

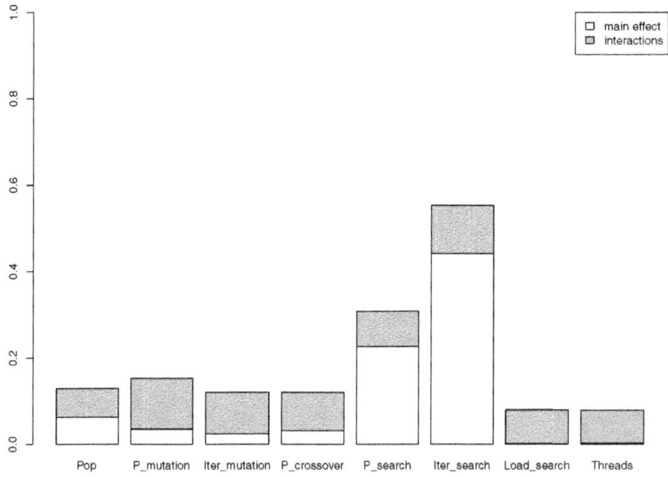

Fig. 5. Sensitivity analysis, lolo instance

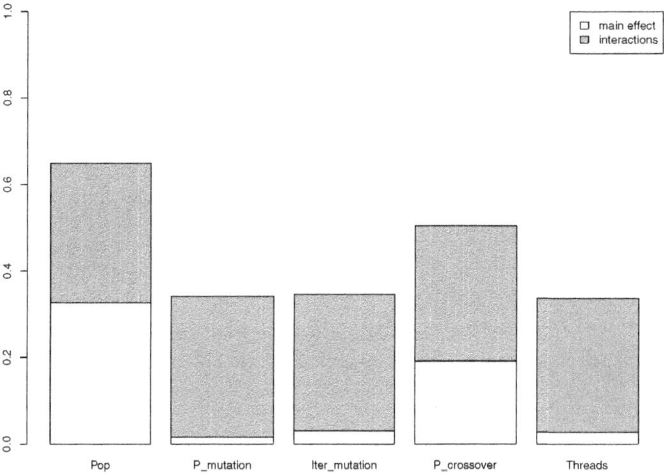

Fig. 6. Sensitivity analysis, lolo instance with fixed local search parameters

These results also highlights that some parameters play a limited role, i.e. population size, mutation rate and iterations as well as the number of threads. This is also beneficial because values which have a positive impact on other aspects of the algorithm, such as runtime, can be selected without impacting the quality of the solutions. Indeed, this algorithm was designed to be run for a limited period of time (wall clock), therefore choosing a smaller population size and a higher number of threads will allow the computation of more generations.

Figure 5 shows the same analysis for the instance with low tasks and resources heterogeneity. The two most influential parameters are similar to the hihi instance, local search iterations followed by the of local search rate. One difference can be noticed at the level of the third parameter in terms of importance. This parameter now consists in the "GA population size" while the "crossover rate" was used for the hihi instance. As can be seen in Figure 6, crossover has indeed 40% less influence than population size. Finally the load for local search has almost no influence on the output in the hihi case. Figure 6 shows that there are significant interaction effects, which mean that the remaining parameters combined, influence the output more than individually. The interaction part shows the total interactions (between two, three, etc parameters).

To conclude, these first results are promising because they brought a first exploration of the relationship between the algorithm's influential parameters and the classes of problem instances.

7 Conclusion

In this paper, a variance based sensitivity analysis has been proposed to study the influence and interdependencies of the parameters of a Parallel Asynchronous Cellular Genetic Algorithm (PA-CGA). Experimental results on two different instances of a scheduling problem of independent tasks on a grid have shown that, for both problem instances, the two most impacting parameters are the local search ones. As expected, the GA parameters have a limited influence on the solution quality, except the crossover rate and the population size, respectively for the hihi and lolo instance. Current implementations are available [24] to make this analysis a systematic step in any EA experiment.

Future works will include studying the cost of the proposed approach and extending the sensitivity analysis of the PA-CGA parameters on a larger set of scheduling problem instances with different properties. Another targeted objective is to study the parameters sensitivity of the scheduling problem model itself.

References

1. Alba, E., Dorronsoro, B.: Cellular Genetic Algorithms. Operations Research/Compuer Science Interfaces. Springer, Heidelberg (2008)
2. Ali, S., Siegel, H.J., Maheswaran, M., Hensgen, D., Ali, S.: Representing task and machine heterogeneities for heterogeneous. Journal of Science and Engineering, Special 50 th Anniversary Issue (3), 195–207 (2000)
3. Bartz-Beielstein, T., Lasarczyk, C.W.G., Preuss, M.: Sequential Parameter Optimization. In: IEEE Congress on Evolutionary Computation, vol. 1, pp. 773–780. IEEE (2005)
4. Blazewicz, J., Lenstra, J.K., Rinnooy Kan, A.H.G.: Scheduling subject to resource constraints: classification and complexity. Discrete Applied Mathematics 5, 11–24 (1983)

5. Braun, T.D., Siegel, H.J., Beck, N., Bölöni, L.L., Maheswaran, M., Reuther, A.I., Robertson, J.P., Theys, M.D., Yao, B., Hengsen, D., Freund, R.F.: A comparison of eleven static heuristics for mapping a class of independent tasks onto heterogeneous distributed computing systems. Journal of Parallel and Distributed Computing 61(6), 810–837 (2001)
6. Casanova, H., Legrand, A., Zagorodnov, D., Berman, F.: Heuristics for scheduling parameter sweep applications in grid environments. In: Heterogeneous Computing Workshop, pp. 349–363 (2000)
7. de Castro, L., Von Zuben, F.: Learning and optimization using the clonal selection principle. IEEE Transactions on Evolutionary Computation 6(3), 239–251 (2002)
8. DeJong, K.: Parameter setting in eas: a 30 year perspective. In: Lobo, F.G., et al. (eds.) [18], pp. 1–18
9. Eiben, A.E., Hinterding, R., Michalewicz, Z.: Parameter control in evolutionary algorithms. IEEE Trans. Evolutionary Computation 3(2), 124–141 (1999)
10. Eiben, A.E., Michalewicz, Z., Schoenauer, M., Smith, J.E.: Parameter control in evolutionary algorithms. In: Lobo, F.G., et al. (eds.) [18], pp. 19–46
11. Geem, Z.: Harmony search algorithm for solving sudoku. In: Apolloni, B., Howlett, R.J., Jain, L. (eds.) KES 2007, Part I. LNCS (LNAI), vol. 4692, pp. 371–378. Springer, Heidelberg (2007)
12. Ghafoor, A., Yang, J.: Distributed heterogeneous supercomputing management system. IEEE Comput. 26(6), 78–86 (1993)
13. Ho, S.Y., Chen, H.M., Ho, S.J., Chen, T.K.: Design of accurate classifiers with a compact fuzzy-rule base using an evolutionary scatter partition of feature space. IEEE Transactions on Systems, Man, and Cybernetics, Part B: Cybernetics 34(2), 1031–1044 (2004)
14. Ibarra, O.H., Kim, C.E.: Heuristic algorithms for scheduling independent tasks on nonidentical processors. Journal of the ACM 24(2), 280–289 (1977)
15. IEEE and The Open Group: Posix (ieee std 1003.1-2008, open group base specifications issue 7) (2008), http://www.unix.org
16. Kafil, M., Ahmad, I.: Optimal task assignment in heterogeneous distributed computing systems. IEEE Concurrency 6(3), 42–51 (1998)
17. Kramer, O.: Evolutionary self-adaptation: a survey of operators and strategy parameters. Evolutionary Intelligence 3, 51–65 (2010)
18. Lobo, F.G., Lima, C.F., Michalewicz, Z. (eds.): Parameter Setting in Evolutionary Algorithms. SCS, vol. 54. Springer, Heidelberg (2007)
19. Maturana, J., Lardeux, F., Saubion, F.: Autonomous operator management for evolutionary algorithms. Journal of Heuristics 16, 881–909 (2010)
20. Min, H., Ko, H.J., Ko, C.S.: A genetic algorithm approach to developing the multi-echelon reverse logistics network for product returns. Omega 34(1), 56–69 (2006)
21. Nannen, V., Eiben, A.E.: Relevance estimation and value calibration of evolutionary algorithm parameters. In: Proceedings of the 20th International Joint Conference on Artifical Intelligence, pp. 975–980. Morgan Kaufmann Publishers Inc., San Francisco (2007)
22. Pinel, F., Dorronsoro, B., Bouvry, P.: A new parallel asynchronous cellular genetic algorithm for scheduling in grids. In: Proceedings of the 2010 IEEE International Symposium on Parallel and Distributed Processing, Workshops and Phd. Forum, IPDPSW 2010 (2010)
23. Pinel, F., Dorronsoro, B., Bouvry, P.: A new parallel asynchronous cellular genetic algorithm for de novo genomic sequencing. In: Proceedings of the IEEE International Conference on Soft Computing and Pattern Recognition (SOCPAR 2009), pp. 178–183 (2009)

24. Pujol, G.: sensitivity: Sensitivity Analysis (2008), r package version 1.4-0
25. Saltelli, A., Tarantola, S., Campolongo, F., Ratto, M.: Sensitivity Analysis in Practice: A Guide to Assessing Scientific Models. Wiley (2004)
26. Saltelli, A., Tarantola, S., Chan, K.: A quantitative, model independent method for global sensitivity analysis of model output. Technometrics 41, 39–56 (1999)
27. Smit, S.K., Eiben, A.E.: Comparing parameter tuning methods for evolutionary algorithms. In: Proceedings of the Eleventh Conference on Congress on Evolutionary Computation, CEC 2009, pp. 399–406. IEEE Press, Piscataway (2009)

Image Recognition System for Diagnosis Support of Melanoma Skin Lesion

Paweł Cudek, Wiesław Paja, and Mariusz Wrzesień

University of Information Technology and Management,
Institute of Bimedical Informatics,
Sucharskiego 2, 35- 225 Rzeszow, Poland
{pcudek,wpaja,mwrzesien}@wsiz.rzeszow.pl

Abstract. In this paper, computer-aided automatic system for classification of melanocytic skin lesions is described. The main goal of our research was to elaborate and to present new approach to classification of melanocytic lesions based on medical images recognition. Here, functionality, structure and operation of this approach is presented. Our approach is based on well known ABCD formula, a very popular medical method to prepare non-invasive diagnosis. Now, we present progress in development of our system and also explanation of applied approach.

Keywords: diagnosis support system, image recognition, teledermatology, Total Dermatoscopy Score, ABCD formula.

1 Introduction

Melanoma is the most deadly form of skin cancer. The World Health Organization estimates that more than 65000 people a year worldwide die from too much sun, mostly from malignant skin cancer [6]. It is the cutaneous tumour with the worst prognosis and its incidence is growing, because most melanomas arise on areas of skin that can be easily examined. Early detection and successful treatment often is possible. Most dermatologists can accurately diagnose melanoma in about 80% of cases according to ABCD process [10]. Meanwhile the incorporation of dermatoscopic techniques, reflectance confocal microscopy and multiespectral digital dermatoscopy have greatly enhanced the diagnosis of this cutaneous melanoma. While these devices and techniques could give dermatologists a closer look at suspicious skin lesions. This, in turn, can help dermatologists find suspicious lesions earlier than before and better determine whether a biopsy is needed. None of these devices can confirm that a suspicious lesion is melanoma. It is, however, not yet possible to tell if a patient has melanoma or any type of skin cancer without a biopsy. It is important to combine the classically ABCDs and biopsy to prevention and diagnosis of melanoma. In recent years there are a lot of available articles about investigation in the domain of non-invasive diagnosis support systems for melanoma classification [3,8,9,1].

In the domain of automatic skin lesion recognition there are some information system available to use for dermatologists. The *MoleExpert* software [5] is

P. Bouvry et al. (Eds.): SIIS 2011, LNCS 7053, pp. 217–225, 2012.

an example of such a system. This system was developed for the support of the diagnostic identification. The system does not give a diagnosis, but instead provides measurement results on expansion, color, net structure, globules and the border which can be evaluated in comparison with many hundred lesions at any time. Another system *SkinSeg* [12] is simple tool used for skin lesion segmentation. First, image is converted to intensity image and then the lesion edges are detected.

Our approach is a part of complementary system for supporting of diagnosis of melanocytic lesions. This main system provides user interface in form of a website to get the access to its three working modules (see Figure 1). The first one is dedicated to medical doctors without specialized medical knowledge, and serves diagnosing using simple dermatoscope. This module allows to determine all symptoms required for correct classification of a given skin lesion.

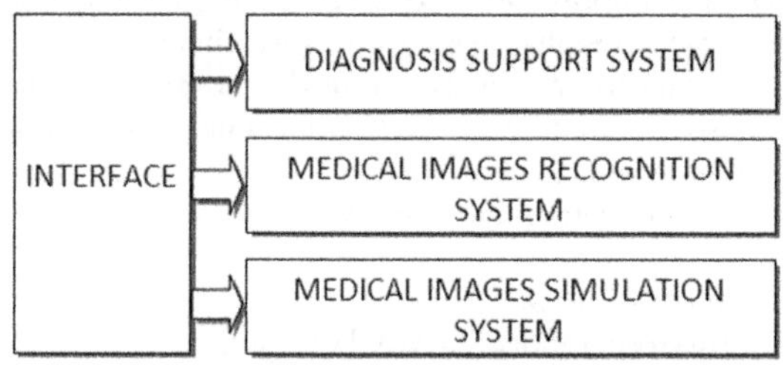

Fig. 1. Structure of the complementary diagnosing support web centered system

The second module, called medical images recognition system, is based on automatic analysis and recognition of medical images. This module is the main subject of our paper. This approach consists of a system solution designed to analyze images of the patient's injury using image processing techniques where the dermatologists will capture the image of a melanoma using a digital dermatoscope. Next, a set of algorithms will process the image and provide an output diagnosis automatically. Detailed information is given in the next sections.

In turn, the third module enables to generate the exhaustive number of simulated images, which considerably broaden the informational source database, and can be used in the process of training less experienced medical doctors. It contains algorithms of semantic conversion of textual description of melanocytic lesion into respective image of the lesion.

2 Melanocytic Skin Lesion Image Classification

According to the previous section one of the main task of our research was to extend the general system with diagnostic module based on automatic analysis of real digital images of melanocytic lesions on the skin. Created tool could be treated as a supplement of diagnosing process and may facilitate suitable medical procedures, giving an indication for the necessity of the lesion's surgical removal. After analysis of methods described in literature [11,2,7], that are used by dermatologists in recognition process of skin lesions we decided to focus on **Stolz** algorithm. It is formally based on the primary version of **ABCD rule**. In this method, four parameters are estimated: **A** (***A****symmetry*) concerns the result of evaluation of lesion's asymmetry, **B** (***B****order*) estimates the character of lesion's border, **C** (***C****olor*) identifies the number of colors (one or more, from 6 allowed) present in the investigated lesion, and **D** (***D****iversity of structures*) identifies the number of structures (one or more, from 5 allowed). Values of ABCD elements are used to calculate **TDS** parameter (***T****otal* ***D****ermatoscopy* ***S****core*) [4] as follow (equation 1):

$$\mathbf{TDS} = (1.3 * \mathbf{A}symmetry) + (0.1 * \mathbf{B}order) + (0.5 * \sum \mathbf{C}olors) + \\ + (0.5 * \sum \mathbf{D}iversity) \tag{1}$$

Depending on the TDS value, investigated lesion could be assigned to one of four accepted categories: *Begin nevus*, *Blue nevus*, *Suspicious nevus* or *Malignant melanoma* (see Table 1).

Table 1. Values of TDS parameter and corresponding lesion's category

TDS value	***Category of lesion***
TDS <4.76 and lack of color blue	Begin nevus
TDS <4.76 and color blue is present	Blue nevus
$4.76 \leq$ TDS <5.45	Suspicious nevus
TDS ≥ 5.45	Malignant melanoma

In this part of article we focus on automatic acquisition of ABCD parameters which is not difficult from the standpoint of a medical specialist but automation of this process is a great challenge.

3 Structure and Operation of the System

Our automated system for lesions classification provides the ability to analyze medical images in different graphic formats like JPG, BMP, PNG, and TIF . After loading of an investigated image (see Figure 2) the preprocessing operation is performed. Next, system locates the lesion's area. If the area of lesion is determined, system tries to estimate the values specified in the ABCD formula. Finally, TDS parameter is calculated and lesion is classified according to rules presented in Table 1. The main structure of our automatic image recognition system is shown on Figure 2. Additionally its graphical interface is presented on figure 3. Details about each operations are presented in next subsections.

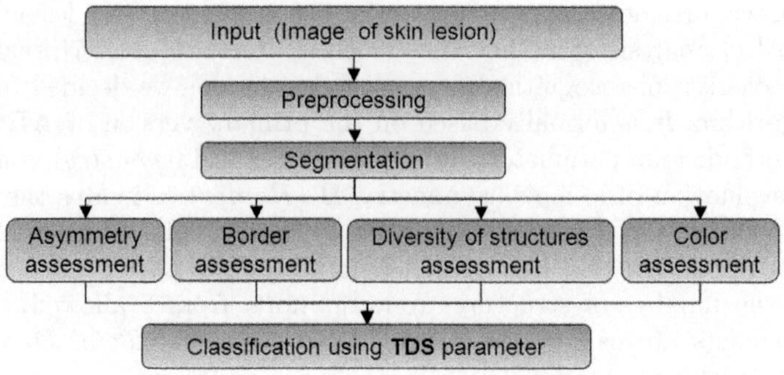

Fig. 2. The main structure of image recognition system

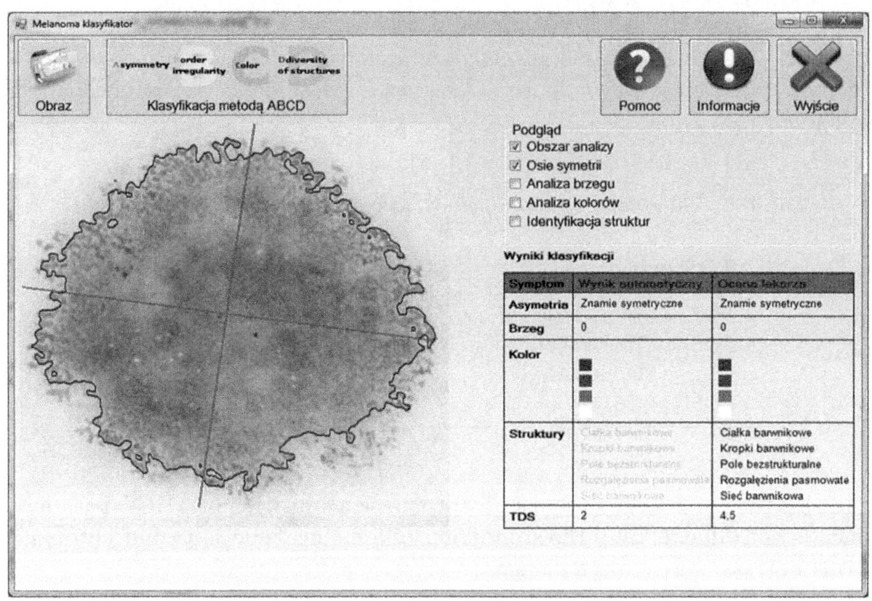

Fig. 3. Graphical interface of image recognition system

3.1 Preprocessing Module

Preprocessing module is responsible for improving the quality of picture and creating the next version of the image used in subsequent stages. First of all algorithm converts color image into grayscale according to equation 2.

$$\mathbf{Y} = 0.299 * \mathbf{R} + 0.587 * \mathbf{G} + 0.114 * \mathbf{B} \tag{2}$$

where: Y - pixel value in grayscale, R, G, B - components of RGB color value

Next step of preprocessing is adaptive histogram equalization used to improve the local contrast in the image. To achieve this, the *Contrast Limited Adaptive*

Histogram Equalization (**CLAHE**) [13] method were applied. This method computes several histograms, each corresponding to a distinct section of the image, and uses them to redistribute the lightness values of the image. At this stage a blurred version of image is also created. This version is used to apply segmentation process.

3.2 Evaluation of Asymmetry Feature

Asymmetry evaluation in **ABCD** formula devotes to information about number of symmetry axes located in lesion's area. There is a three logical values of **Asymmetry** attribute: **symmetric spot** (there are two perpendicular axes of symmetry), **1-axial asymmetry** (there is only one axis of symmetry) and **2-axial asymmetry** (there is no axis of symmetry). The numerical values used in the calculation of **TDS** parameter for the above logical values are 0, 1 and 2 respectively.

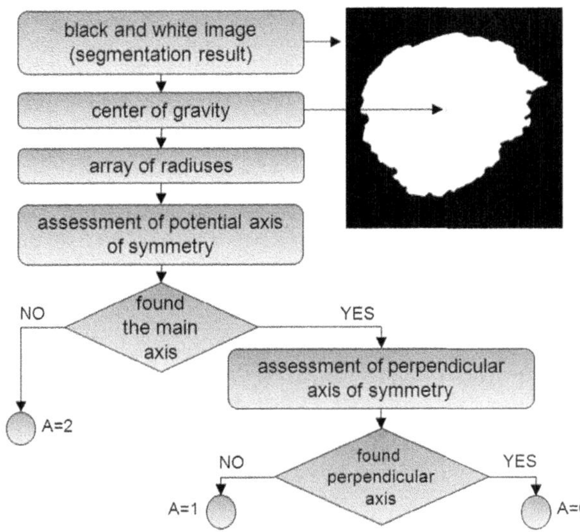

Fig. 4. Diagram of algorithm for the evaluation of lesion's asymmetry

The developed algorithm for evaluation of asymmetry (see Figure 4) is based on the analysis of the black and white image created as a result of segmentation. In this image white dots belongs to lesion area and black dots represents an area of healthy skin. In the first step a center of gravity (**GC**) is determined. Next, algorithm creates an array containing the length of straights (radiuses) outgoing from the GC point with angle in range between 0 and 359 degrees. Next task is to find straights, which can be symmetry axis of lesion. For this purpose, for each of the 180 potential axis of symmetry SFA_α is calculated as a sum of similar radiuses inclined to the tested axis at angles β and -β (see Figure 5). The main axis of symmetry of the lesion is that for which the **SFA** is the largest and exceeds the threshold value agreed in researches (indicating axis as a symmetry axis).

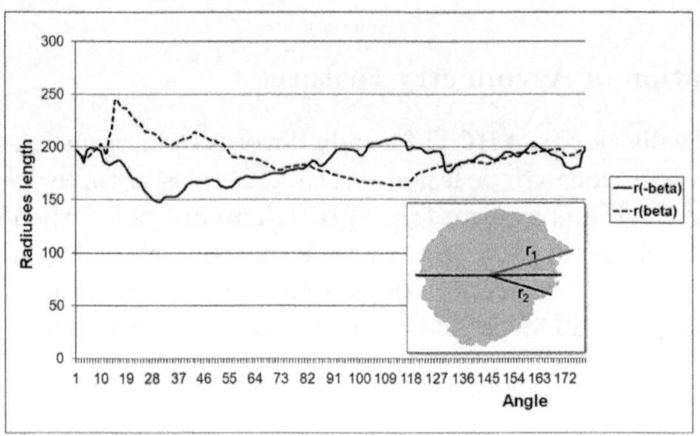

Fig. 5. Comparison of radiuses for the potential axis of symmetry with an angle $\alpha = 0$

3.3 Evaluation of Border Feature

To estimate the character of a border of lesion, the image is divided into eight equal parts by using four lines crossing in the center of gravity (see Figure 6).

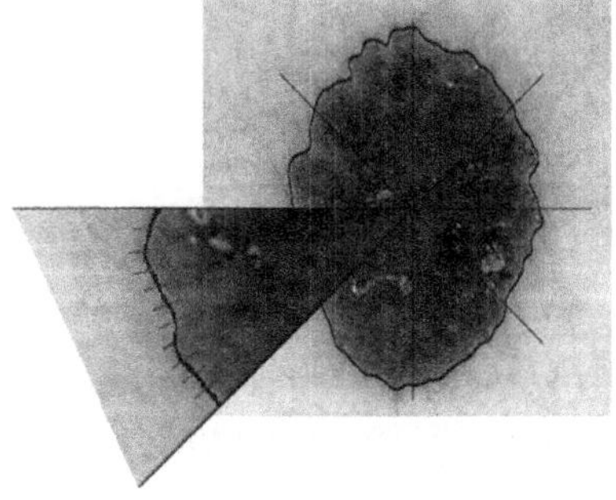

Fig. 6. Lesion divided into eight parts

Next, in each created part of lesion the sharpness of transition between lesion and health skin is evaluated. For this purpose, set of samples containing the pixel values in grayscale are collected within the area of crossing lesion to healthy skin. In our initial research it was about 20 samples in each octal part. Analysis of a single sample acquired from an octal part of lesion apply the least squares method to determine the slope factor **a** (see Equation 3) of the linear function passing through the collected values.

$$a = \frac{n \sum x_i y_i - \sum x_i \sum y_i}{n \sum x_i^2 - (\sum x_i)^2} \tag{3}$$

where: x_i - number of sample, y_i - sample value in grayscale, n - number of all samples

If the slope factor exceeds determined threshold the transition between the lesion and the skin in a given sample then it is considered to be sharp border (see Figure 7). If most of samples in investigated octal part was classified as a sharp transition then this part has value 1 and Border value in ABCD rule increase by one.

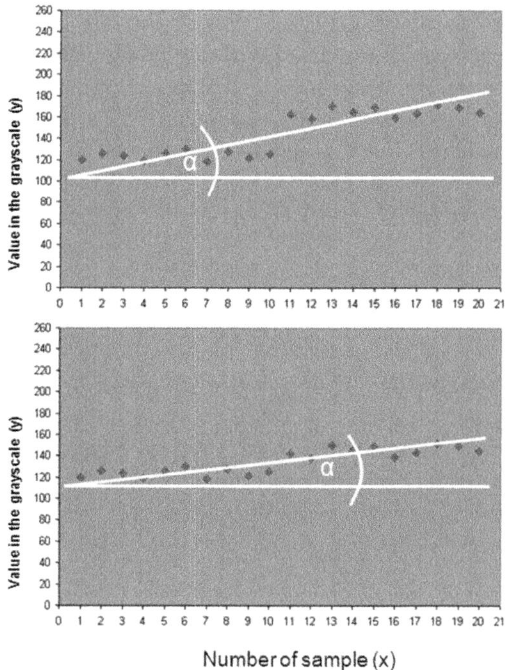

Fig. 7. The slope factor determined for sharp and unsharp border

3.4 Evaluation of Color Feature

In this research, all collected images are saved in the **RGB** color system. Thus, the precise determination of the similarity between colors is not possible. Analysis of literature has shown that the most appropriate and recommended color space for colorimetric purpose is **Lab** system. Direct conversion of colors from RGB to Lab is not possible and requires the transformation through the **XYZ** color space.

In the **Lab** space, the color value is defined by the brightness (**L**) with values from 0 to 100, in turn component **a** specifies position on the green-red axis, and component **b** specifies position on the blue-yellow axis. This color space is based on the perception of color by the human eye and allows calculate the difference between colors as the difference of points in three dimensional space. It is also independent of the hardware device.

After performing transformation to Lab color space the identification of colors is applied using k-means algorithm. In this algorithm difference between colors is measured using city block distance. In the research central values of allowed colors expressed in Lab value which are start points in k-means algorithm were determined. Result of clustering allows to specify the number of colors presented in the area of lesion and use it as a C parameter in ABCD formula.

3.5 Evaluation of Diversity of Structure

This part of the system is in the process of implementation and will be described in future publications. The main goal of this approach is to build classifier, which for selected area of lesion will be able to decide: if in the investigated area are known type of structures. For this purpose, we intend to determine the vector of features of the study area and build a neural network, which makes classification based on the input vector.

4 Initial Results and Conclusions

Initial results of our experiments were gathered using developed information system for image recognition. These results are presented in Table 2. During experiment 53 images of melanocytic lesions were investigated. Accuracy of recognition is presented in second column of Table 2. Most of cases are recognized correctly. Thus, it could be said that applied methods are effective and should be developed by using numerous of testing images.

Table 2. Error rate for classified images

Investigated feature	*Classification error rate*
Asymmetry:	
symmetric spot	6%
1-axial asymmetry	8%
2-axial asymmetry	9%
Border	21%
Color	28%

According to medical doctors [10] correct classification of pigment skin lesions is possible using histopatological research of lesion. The newest trend of diagnosing devoted to using non-invasive methods, has become cause of disseminating of information technology tools supporting this process.

During our research, practical development of a new approach to diagnosis support was applied. This approach is based on automatic recognition of medical images acquired during early examination by dermatologists. This automatic examination is possible only by using images with proper quality and dimension acquired using dermatoscopic devices. In this research, application of ABCD formula were discussed, but in the future research it could be extended to new algorithms or methods of recognition. Additionally, better results of error rate are expected during extensive research and also mobile version of our system could be presented.

References

1. Amalian, B., Fatichah, C., Widyanto, M.R.: Abcd feature extraction for melanoma skin cancer diagnosis. In: Proceedings of the 9th International Conference on Advanced Computer Science and Information System, ICACSIS 2009, pp. 224–228 (2007)
2. Argenziano, G., Fabbrocini, G., Carli, P., De Giorgi, V., Sammarco, E., Delfino, M.: Epiluminescence microscopy for the diagnosis of doubtful melanocytic skin lesions. com-parison of the abcd rule of dermatoscopy and a new 7-point checklist based on pattern analysis. Archives of Dermatology 134, 1563–1570 (1998)
3. Bajcar, S., Grzymaa-Busse, J., Grzymaa-Busse, W., Hippe, Z.: Diagnosis of melanoma based on data mining and abcd formulas. In: Abraham, A., Köppen, M., Franke, K. (eds.) Design and Application of Hybrid Intelligent Systems, pp. 614–622. IOS Press, Amsterdam (2003)
4. Braun-Falco, O., Stolz, W., Bilek, P., Merkle, T., Landthaler, M.: Das dermatoskop. eine vereinfachung der auflichtmikroskopie von pigmentierten hautveranderungen. Hautarzt 40 (1990)
5. Datinf gmbh tubingen: Introduction (12/02/2011), `http://moleexpert.com/micro/intro.shtml`
6. Lucas, R., McMichael, T., Smith, W., Armstrong, B.: Solar ultraviolet radiation. global burden of disease from solar ultraviolet radiation. Environmental Burden of Disease Series 13, 1–17 (2006)
7. Menzies, S.: Surface microscopy of pigmented skin tumors. Australas J. Dermatol. 38, 40–43 (1997)
8. Oka, H., Hashimoto, M., Argenziano, G., Iyatomi, H., Tanaka, M., Soyer, H.: Internet-based program for automatic discrimination of dermoscopic images between melanoma and clark nevi. British Journal of Dermatology 150, 1041 (2004)
9. Papastergiou, A., Hatzigaidas, A., Zaharis, Z., Tryfon, G., Moustakas, K., Ioannidis, D.: Introducing automated melanoma detection in a topic map based image retrieval system. In: Proceedings of the 6th WSEAS International Conference on Applied Computer Science, pp. 452–457 (2007)
10. Rigel, D., Russak, J., Friedman, R.: The evolution of melanoma diagnosis: 25 years beyond the abcds. A Cancer Journal for Clinicians 60, 301–316 (2010)
11. Stolz, W., Braun-Falco, O., Bilek, P., Landthaler, M., Burgdorf, W., Cognetta, A.: Atlas of Dermatoscopy. Czelej Edit. Office (2006)
12. Xu, L., Jackowski, M., Goshtasby, A., Yu, C., Roseman, D., Bines, S., Dhawan, A., Huntley, A.: Segmentation of skin cancer images. Image and Vision Computing 17, 65–74 (1999)
13. Zuiderveld, K.: Contrast limited adaptive histogram equalization, pp. 474–485. Academic Press Professional, Inc., San Diego (1994)

Playing in Unison in the Random Forest

Alicja A. Wieczorkowska[1], Miron B. Kursa[2], Elżbieta Kubera[3], Radosław Rudnicki[4], and Witold R. Rudnicki[2]

[1] Polish-Japanese Institute of Information Technology, Koszykowa 86, 02-008 Warsaw, Poland
alicja@poljap.edu.pl

[2] Interdisciplinary Centre for Mathematical and Computational Modelling, University of Warsaw, Pawińskiego 5A, 02-106 Warsaw, Poland
{M.Kursa,W.Rudnicki}@icm.edu.pl

[3] University of Life Sciences in Lublin, Akademicka 13, 20-950 Lublin, Poland
elzbieta.kubera@up.lublin.pl

[4] The University of York, Department of Music, Heslington, York, YO10 5DD, UK
radek.rudnicki@york.ac.uk

Abstract. In this paper, we deal with the difficult problem of automatic identification of multiple instruments playing sounds of the same pitch, i.e. in unison. Random forests have been selected to be used as a classifier. Training data represent isolated sounds of selected instruments which originate from three commonly used repositories, namely McGill University Master Samples, The University of IOWA Musical Instrument Samples, and RWC. Testing data represent audio records especially prepared by one of the authors for research purposes, and next carefully labeled. The experiments on identification of instruments in a frame-by-frame manner and the obtained results are presented and discussed.

Keywords: Music information retrieval, Random forests, Sound recognition.

1 Introduction

Identification of a musical instrument playing in a polyphonic recording is a challenging task, especially when instruments play in unison, i.e. play sounds of the same pitch. This task is an example of research within the area of interest in the domain of Music Information Retrieval (MIR). MIR research focusses on such tasks as pitch-tracking of a melody sung or whistled by the user (often with errors), in order to find the tune in the database, or identification of a piece of music on the basis of a short excerpt (often noisy), when user wants to know the title and the performer. Such systems already exist, see for example [18] or [22], to facilitate searching through constantly growing audio data sets available in both private collections and in the Internet. The users of such repositories may also want to find tunes/excerpts played by a specified instrument, for example the first flute solo in "Boléro" by M. Ravel. This requires identification of timbre (of musical instrument) in polyphonic and polytimbral environment. The

P. Bouvry et al. (Eds.): SIIS 2011, LNCS 7053, pp. 226–239, 2012.

research on identification of instrument has already been performed, and in the case of recognition of a single instrument playing a single isolated sound it can even reach 100% (if just several instruments are considered), although results vary depending on the number of instruments and sounds investigated (down to 40% for about 30 instruments), as well as the sound parameterization method, the classifier, and the validation method used. However, when instruments play in unison, then the correct identification is much more difficult, because instrument identification is based to a large degree on features describing the sound spectrum, but harmonic partials in the spectrum overlap in the case of unison, see Figure 1. Such sounds can be difficult to discern even for human listeners.

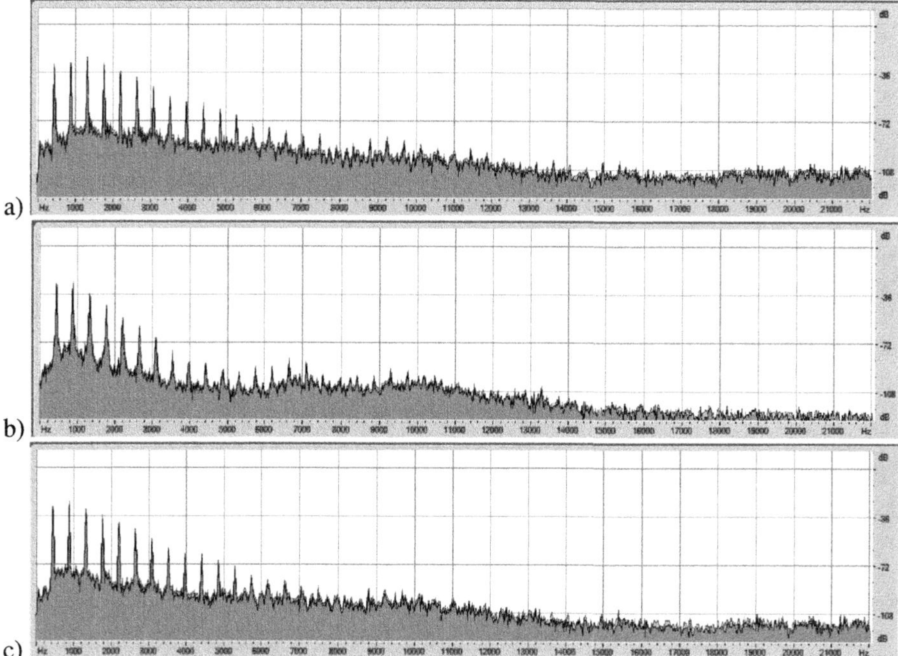

Fig. 1. Spectra of sounds of the same pitch, 440 Hz, and similar timbre: (a) trumpet sound, (b) trombone sound, (c) trumpet and trombone sound. Harmonic peaks represent the fundamental frequency (the first peak, corresponding to the pitch) and its multiples. Since all these sounds are of the same pitch, harmonic partials coincide and the spectra overlap to a large extent.

The starting point of any training of a classifier is sound parameterization, because digitally recorded sound is represented as a sequence of amplitude values interpolating time-domain graph of the sound wave, i.e. amplitude vs. time, in discrete form. In the case of CD recordings, amplitude values are quantized using 16 bits, i.e. 2^{16} amplitude levels, and 44,100 samples per second per channel. Such data are inconvenient to deal with, not only because of long sequences of values, but also because these values may vary significantly even for similar sounds. Therefore, audio data are parameterized. The created feature set can be based on the time-domain representation, or, more often, on the spectrum of the sound, describing frequency content, and changes of the spectrum in time (time-frequency representation, i.e. spectrogram). The spectrum and the spectrogram can be obtained using the Fourier or wavelet transform, or other methods.

Various researchers conducting experiments aiming at identification of musical instrument sounds use various feature sets. Many of these features were included in the MPEG-7 standard as low-level audio descriptors [8]; also, Mel-Frequency Cepstral Coefficients (MFCC), originating from speech recognition, are applied in MIR [5], including the recognition of musical instruments [3]. An overview of parameterization techniques applied in musical instrument sound identification tasks is presented in [7].

The quality of identification of the instrument depends both on the parameterization used, as well as the classifier used. In the case of recognition of single sounds of instruments, many classification methods have already been applied: k-nearest neighbors (k-NN), artificial neural networks (ANN), rough-set based classifiers, support vector machines (SVM), decision trees and random forests, see [7], [9]. However, methods that work well for isolated single sounds (even such simple algorithms as k-NN) may not work as well for polyphonic sounds, and they are prone to errors when tried on duets [17]. In polyphonic and polytimbral (i.e. representing plural instruments) recordings, with more than one sound present at the same time, the recognition of instruments is much more challenging, so more sophisticated algorithms might be needed.

When identification of instruments in polyphonic recordings is performed, sounds of the same pitch pose substantial difficulties. This is because harmonic components of their spectra coincide, as their represent multiples of the same fundamental frequency. When polyphonic music is investigated, harmonic peaks representing interfering tones are unreliable and they can be even excluded from the classification process [4] thus improving the identification of sounds of different pitches. In a different approach [1], prestored independent instrument spectra are used to correct collided harmonics; prior knowledge of instrument spectra is applied. The uncollided harmonics are matched to the ones contained in a pre-stored spectrum library, and then each harmonic series is assigned to the appropriate instrument, so the corrupted harmonics can be restored using data taken from the library. Similar approach is applied in [25], where instruments in polyphonic recordings are identified one by one, starting with the one with most prominent harmonic peaks in the spectrum of the polyphonic recording, on frame-by-frame basis. After identifying the most similar frame in the database, whose set of harmonics is the closest to the set of harmonics corresponding to the most prominent pitch, the found spectrum is subtracted from the investigated one. This procedure is repeated until no useful peaks are left in the spectrum.

So far, we have already performed the research on identification of instruments in mixes and polyphonic recordings, including mixes of musical instrument sounds of the same pitch [11], [13], [24]. The previous research proved that random forests perform very well, better than other classification methods, outperforming such a highly valued methods as SVM by an order of magnitude. Therefore, we decided to continue experiments using random forests as classifiers. In order to make our research independent of the initial audio segmentation into sound events (notes) which is prone to errors, and time consuming when preparing ground-truth data, the investigations described in this paper are performed in a frame-by-frame manner, and no prior information on the borders of notes is required. The data were especially prepared for the purpose of this research, including the recording and the ground-truth labeling of the audio data.

2 Feature Set

In our previous research, we have already performed experiments on identification of musical instruments, including polyphonic sounds, and also unisons [24]. Therefore, we decided to base our work on the parameters we used before, yet adjusting the feature set to capture more details of the investigated sounds.

The feature set we applied in this research is designed to parameterize sounds of definite pitch, containing harmonic partials in their spectra. The feature vector was calculated on frame-by-frame basis, with 30-ms offset (hop size). Fourier transform with Hamming window was applied to obtain the spectrum for each subsequent audio frame. Our features can be grouped into 2 sets: static features, describing properties of 40-ms frame of audio data, and dynamic features, describing changes of sound properties, as they can improve the accuracy of instrument identification [10]. Dynamic features show differences between values of each static feature for a given 40-ms frame and for the 40-ms frame at the position shifted by 20 ms. For consistency, 60-ms frames are taken to calculate both static and dynamic features. Calculations of static features are performed for the first 40 ms of the 60-ms frame, and the remaining 20 ms are ignored.

The features we use represent MPEG-7 low-level audio descriptors [8], and other descriptors used in research on automatic recognition of instruments. Two features from MPEG-7 were also added to the set of dynamic features, namely, $HarmonicSpectralVariation$ and $Flux$. Altogether, the following features constitute our feature vector:

- static features:
  - *AudioSpectrumCentroid* - power weighted average of the frequency bins in the power spectrum; coefficients are scaled to an octave scale anchored at 1 kHz [8];
  - *AudioSpectrumSpread* - RMS (root mean square) value of the deviation of the Log frequency power spectrum wrt. *AudioSpectrumCentroid* for the frame [8];
  - $NonMPEG7 - AudioSpectrumCentroid$ - a differently calculated version - in linear scale;
  - $NonMPEG7 - AudioSpectrumSpread$ - a different version; the deviation is calculated in linear scale, with respect to $NonMPEG7 - AudioSpectrumCentroid$;

- *RollOff* - the frequency below which an experimentally chosen percentage equal to 85% of the accumulated magnitudes of the spectrum is concentrated. It is a measure of spectral shape, used in speech recognition to distinguish between voiced and unvoiced speech;
- *AudioSpectrumFlatness*, $flat_1, \ldots, flat_{25}$ - multidimensional parameter describing the flatness property of the power spectrum (obtained through the Fourier transform) within a frequency bin for selected bins; 25 out of 32 frequency bands were used for a given frame;
- *ZeroCrossingRate* - time-domain descriptor; zero-crossing is a point where the sign of time-domain representation of sound wave changes;
- *Energy* - energy (in logarithmic scale) of the spectrum of the parameterized sound;
- *MFCC* - vector of 13 Mel frequency cepstral coefficients. The cepstrum was calculated as logarithm of the magnitude of the spectral coefficients, and then transformed to the mel scale, used instead the Hz scale, to better reflect properties of the human perception of frequency. Twenty-four mel filters were applied, and the obtained results were transformed to twelve coefficients. The thirteenth coefficient is the 0-order coefficient of MFCC, corresponding to the logarithm of the energy [10], [19];
- *HarmonicSpectralCentroid* - the mean of the harmonic peaks of the spectrum, weighted by the amplitude in linear scale [8];
- *HarmonicSpectralSpread* - represents the standard deviation of the harmonic peaks of the spectrum with respect to *HarmonicSpectralCentroid*, weighted by the amplitude [8];
- *HarmonicSpectralDeviation* - represents the spectral deviation of the log amplitude components from a global spectral envelope, where the global spectral envelope of nth harmonic partial is calculated as the average value of the neighboring harmonic partials: no. $n-1$, n, and $n+1$;
- *FundamentalFrequency*; maximum likelihood algorithm was applied for pitch estimation [26];
- r_1: ratio of the energy of the fundamental to the total energy of all harmonic partials;
- r_2: amplitude difference [dB] between 1st partial (i.e., the fundamental) and 2nd partial;
- r_3: ratio of the sum of energy of 3rd and 4th partial to the total energy of harmonic partials;
- r_4: ratio of the sum of partials no. 5-7 to all harmonic partials;
- r_5: ratio of the sum of partials no. 8-10 to all harmonic partials;
- r_6: ratio of the remaining partials to all harmonic partials;
- r_7: brightness - gravity center of spectrum;
- r_8: contents of even partials in spectrum,

$$r_8 = \frac{\sqrt{\sum_{k=1}^{M} A_{2k}^2}}{\sqrt{\sum_{n=1}^{N} A_n^2}}$$

where A_n - amplitude of nth harmonic partial,
N - number of harmonic partials in the spectrum,
M - number of even harmonic partials in the spectrum;

- r_9: contents of odd partials (without fundamental) in spectrum,

$$r_9 = \frac{\sqrt{\sum_{k=2}^{L} A_{2k-1}^2}}{\sqrt{\sum_{n=1}^{N} A_n^2}}$$

where L – number of odd harmonic partials in the spectrum;

- r_{10}: mean frequency deviation for partials 1-5 (when they exist),

$$r_{10} = \frac{\sum_{k=1}^{N} A_k \cdot |f_k - kf_1| / (kf_1)}{N}$$

where $N = 5$, or equals to the number of the last available harmonic partial in the spectrum, if it is less than 5;

- r_{11}: partial (i=1,...,5) of the highest frequency deviation;

– dynamic features:
  - changes (measured as differences) of the static features for two 40-ms subframes within the 60 ms frame: the starting 40 ms and the last 40 ms (i.e. with 20-ms offset);
  - *Flux* - the sum of squared differences between the magnitudes of the DFT points calculated for the starting 40 ms sub-frame of the given 60 ms frame, and the ending 40 ms sub-frame (starting with 20 ms offset); this feature by definition describes changes of magnitude spectrum, thus it cannot be calculated in a static version;
  - *HarmonicSpectralVariation* (HSV) - the normalized correlation between amplitudes of harmonic peaks of the two 40 ms sub-frames of the 60 ms frame (see *Flux*), calculated in the following way:

$$HSV = 1 - \frac{\sum_{n=1}^{N} A_n(1) \cdot A_n(2)}{\sqrt{\sum_{n=1}^{N} A_n^2(1)} \cdot \sqrt{\sum_{n=1}^{N} A_n^2(2)}}$$

where $A_n(i)$ - amplitude of nth harmonic partial in i^{th} 40-ms subframe, $i = 1, 2$ [8].

We decided to perform identification of instruments on frame-by-frame basis, to stay independent of detection of the beginning and the end of each sound. This is why we did not include features pertaining to whole sounds, for instance *LogAttackTime*, *TemporalCentroid*, even though these features were used in our previous research [14], [13], and they were significant in the instrument recognition process, as shown using the *Boruta* feature selection algorithm [15], [16]. Still, our research on polyphonic multi-pitch identification of musical instruments shows that such a frame-by-frame instrument recognition is possible [12].

3 Audio Data

The purpose of our experiments was to identify musical instruments playing in unison, which is the most difficult situation in case of simultaneously sounding sounds. In order to train classifiers to identify particular instruments, we used recordings of representing single, isolated sounds of these instruments. Three repositories of musical instrument sound were used for this purpose, namely McGill University Master Samples (MUMS) [20], The University of IOWA Musical Instrument Samples (IOWA) [23], and RWC Musical Instrument Sound Database (RWC) [6]. Marimba, vibraphone, piano, trumpet, and trombone sounds were taken from these repositories.

In order to obtain testing data, several recording sessions were performed at the University of York, recorded and mixed by one of the authors (R. Rudnicki) as a mixing project manager. The obtained audio data represent simultaneously played sounds of the same pitch. The recordings include [21]:

1. vibraphone (Enrico Bertelli) and piano (Cheong Li) playing scales in unison, legato and staccato;
2. trumpet (Matthew Postle) and marimba (Enrico Bertelli) playing scales in unison, legato and staccato, recorded in Sir Jack Lyons Concert Hall, The University of York;
3. trumpet (Matthew Postle), trombone (Noah Noutch), and piano (Dave Smyth), playing scales.

Firstly, the scales were recorded 16bit/44.1kHz in the case of recordings no. 1 and no. 2, and 32bit/44.1kHz in the case of the recording no. 3. Piano, vibraphone, and marimba were recorded stereo (with 2 microphones), whereas trumpet and trombone were recorded mono (with 1 microphone). Secondly, after panning and different volume setting applied, each track was rendered to stereo 16bit/44.1kHz (with cross-talks from neighboring instruments). Final mixes containing all the contributing tracks were rendered in .wav format, 16bit/44.1kHz. All these tracks were used as a basis for segmentation, i.e. creation of ground-truth data, with starting and ending points marked for each sound.

The instruments recorded in duos and in trio represent three families of instruments, namely idiophones (marimba and vibraphone), strings/chordophones (piano), and aerophones (trumpet and trombone - brass). Instruments representing the same family sound similar, so we can expect confusing marimba and vibraphone, and also confusing trumpet and trombone. Playing in unison makes discernment yet more difficult and challenging for classifiers.

4 Random Forests

Random Forest (RF) is a classifier consisting of a set of decision trees; weak, weakly correlated and non-biased classifiers. It has been shown that RF are quite good classifiers and they often outperform other methods for various classification problems [2]. RF is constructed using the following procedure, that minimizes bias and correlations between individual trees. Every tree is built using different N-element bootstrap sample of the training N-element set. Since the elements of the bootstrap sample are drawn with replacement from the original set, roughly one-third (called OOB, out-of-bag) of the training data are not used in the bootstrap sample for any given tree.

For a P-element feature vector, p attributes (features) are randomly selected at each stage of tree building, i.e. for each node of any tree in RF ($p \ll P$, often $p = \sqrt{P}$). The best split on these p attributes is used to split the data in the node. The best split is determined as minimizing the Gini impurity criterion, which is a measure how often an element would be incorrectly labeled if randomly labeled according to the distribution of labels in the subset. Each tree is grown to the largest extent possible, i.e. without pruning. After repeating this randomized procedure M times, a collection of M trees is obtained, constituting a random forest. Classification of an object is done by simple voting of all trees in the RF.

4.1 Training of RF in Our Experiments

Each audio file used in training represents a single isolated sound of an instrument; the sound is first normalized to RMS=1. Next, the preceding and the following silence is removed as follows. A smoothed version of amplitude is calculated starting from the beginning of the audio file, as moving average of 5 subsequent amplitude values. When this value increases by more than a threshold, experimentally set to 0.0001, this point is considered to be the end of the initial silence. The ending silence is removed analogously. After removing the starting and ending silence, we perform parameterization, and train RF to identify each instrument – even when accompanied by other sound of the same pitch. Next, we perform training on 60 ms frames of instrument sounds, mixing from 1 to 4 randomly chosen instruments with random weights and then normalized again to RMS=1. The battery of one-instrument sensitive RF binary classifiers is then trained. 3,000 mixes containing any sound of a given instrument are fed as positive examples, and 3,000 mixes containing no sound of this instrument are fed as negative examples. Since we want to obtain random forests which can be applied in a general task of instrument recognition, mixing is done irrespective of the pitch. Therefore, training data include both unisons and mixes of sounds of different pitch. The random forests trained this way yielded good results (precision exceeding 80%, over 93% in most cases) in the task of the recognition of instruments in real polyphonic recordings of 4 instruments [12], when the forests were trained for 8 instruments. Now we decided to check whether random forests trained using this methodology can be successfully applied to a particular case of recordings, i.e. for instruments playing in unison.

When identification of N instruments in recordings is aimed at, we need a battery of N random forests ($N = 5$ in the case of this research), each one trained to identify one instrument. Quality test of the battery is performed on 100,000 mixes, prepared the same way as the training data. The battery trained this way is then ready to be applied in experiments on frame-by-frame recognition of instruments in recordings mentioned in Section 3.

5 Experiments and Results

After preparing audio data (recordings and labeling), the training of the RF classifier was performed, using sounds taken from MUMS, IOWA and RWC repositories. The results of the training for OOB objects are shown in Table 1, and the results of the quality test of this training are shown in Table 2. As we can see, the battery of RF can recognize OOB objects with about 69–95% accuracy, and the quality test yields about 69–87% accuracy at the end of the training.

Table 1. The results of the RF training for OOB objects, for mixes created with weights w exceeding the indicated levels for the target instrument

	$w = 0.5$	$w = 0.3$	$w = 0.1$	$w = 0.0$	Average
Instrument	Accuracy [%]				
marimba	87.1	78.7	71.5	69.3	76.6
piano	85.0	78.9	74.7	71.7	77.6
trombone	92.3	87.3	82.1	78.4	85.0
trumpet	95.1	92.8	88.4	84.9	90.3
vibraphone	88.0	77.9	72.3	70.1	77.1
Average	89.5	83.1	77.8	74.9	

Table 2. The results of the quality test of the RF training, for mixes created with weights w exceeding the indicated levels for the target instrument

	$w = 0.5$	$w = 0.3$	$w = 0.1$	$w = 0.0$	Average
Instrument	Accuracy [%]				
marimba	76.9	73.0	71.2	69.2	72.6
piano	73.5	71.8	73.9	71.4	72.7
trombone	76.9	78.4	81.0	77.9	78.6
trumpet	77.1	82.6	87.3	83.6	82.6
vibraphone	75.6	73.4	71.3	68.7	72.3
Average	76.0	75.8	76.9	74.2	

When the training phase was completed, we performed experiments with identification of instruments in the recordings mentioned in Section 3. General results of these experiments are shown in Table 3. The results were weighted by RMS measured for each instrument track. Therefore, precision was calculated as the sum of the RMS values of the sound frames marked as correct in our ground-truth labeling and found by the RF, divided by the sum of the RMS values of all sound frames found by the RFs, for a given target instrument. Similarly, recall was calculated as the sum of the RMS values of the sound frames marked as correct in our ground-truth labeling and found by the RF, divided by the sum of the RMS values for all frames labeled with this instrument in ground-truth data.

As we can see, instruments of similar timbre are often confused. Vibraphone is mistaken with marimba (recordings no. 1 and no. 2), and trumpet is mistaken with trombone (recording no. 2). On the other hand, the obtained precision is very high, at the cost of quite low recall. However, recall increases and the number of false positives decreases when confusing instruments play together, or if a pair of confusing instruments is not present in the recording: see improved recall when both trombone and trumpet are playing together, and improved false positives when neither marimba nor vibraphone are playing (recording no. 3).

Table 3. Classification results for the recordings of instrument sounds played in unison, weighted by RMS measured for each instrument track

1. Piano and vibraphone					
	marimba	piano	trombone	trumpet	vibraphone
precision [%]	-	99.49	-	-	99.97
recall [%]	-	46.65	-	-	71.72
false positives [%]	85.71	-	03.21	21.87	-
2. Marimba and trumpet					
	marimba	piano	trombone	trumpet	vibraphone
precision [%]	99.38	-	-	100	-
recall [%]	57.00	-	-	13.90	-
false positives [%]	-	08.10	51.61	-	65.68
3. Piano, trombone, and trumpet					
	marimba	piano	trombone	trumpet	vibraphone
precision [%]	-	99.82	97.21	93.96	-
recall [%]	-	28.83	49.83	55.78	-
false positives [%]	24.94	-	-	-	10.94

Since we deal with simultaneously played sounds, no confusion matrix can be produced, because multiple input sounds produce multiple output predictions. Instead, we present the results as graphs (Figures 2 and 3), indicating annotated areas (*Ann*), i.e. ground-truth, and RF-predictions (*RF*), all RMS-weighted. Presence of an instrument is encoded in shades of gray; darker colors represent higher intensities, and white represents absence of this instrument. As we can see, errors mainly happen when the sound intensity is high, i.e. during the attack, which is a transient state, always prone to errors because of non-stationarity of the audio signal. Transients lead to erroneous results even in the case of monophonic sounds (for example, in pitch-tracking), so errors in a difficult task of identification of multiple instruments in unison recordings were actually expected.

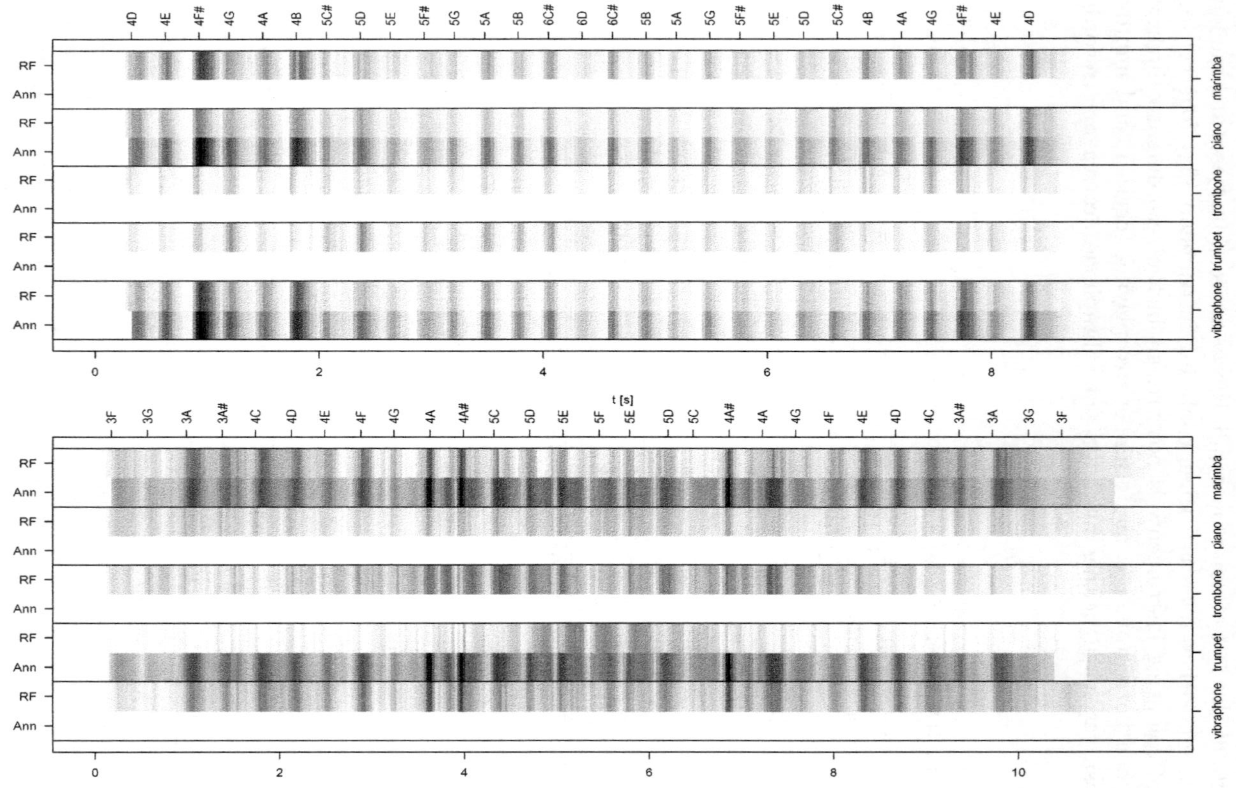

Fig. 2. Results of the recognition of instruments playing in unison, for the battery of RF trained for 5 instruments (marimba, piano, trombone, trumpet, and vibraphone). *Top:* vibraphone and piano; *Bottom:* marimba and trumpet

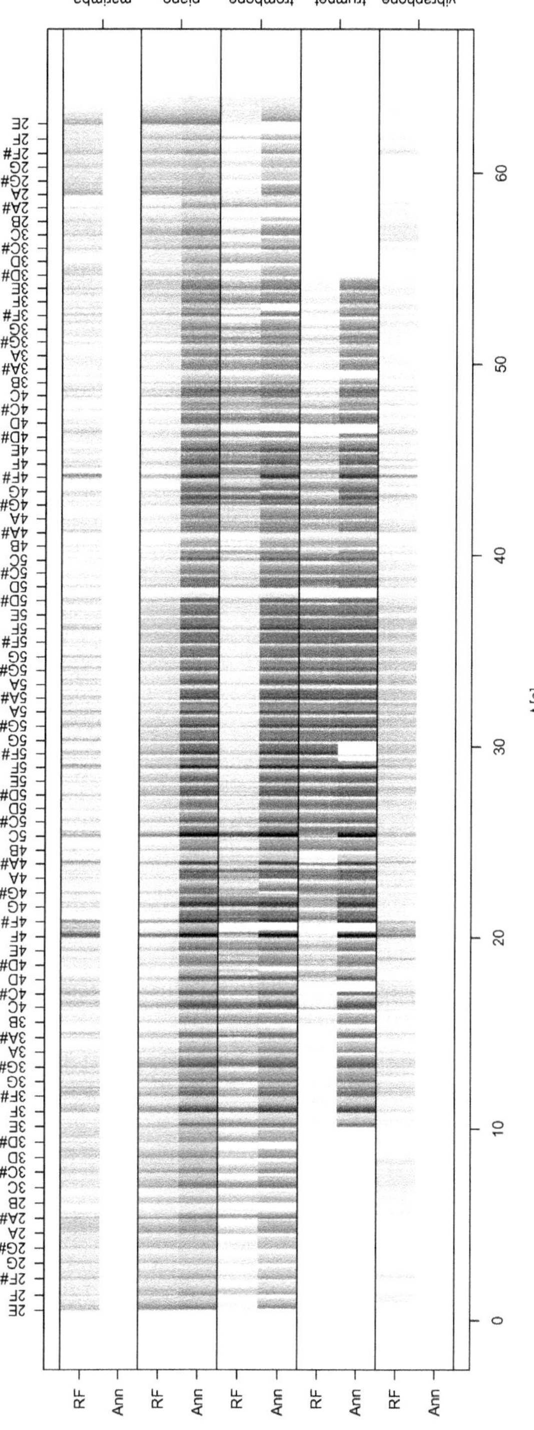

Fig. 3. Recognition of trumpet, trombone, and piano, playing in unison, for the RF battery trained for 5 instruments (marimba, piano, trombone, trumpet, and vibraphone)

6 Summary and Conclusions

In the research reported in this paper, we wanted to check whether a battery of random forests, trained to identify instruments in sound mixes, can be applied to identify instruments playing in unison. This is an extremely difficult case, since partials in spectra of such sounds overlap to a great extent. Moreover, when instruments play together, they can imitate another instrument and be recognized as this another instrument by humans. Therefore, we expected low results, and the obtained high precision is rather surprising, whereas low recall was actually expected. If an instrument is recognized by our battery of random forests, the precision of this recognition is high. False positives stem from similarity of sound timbre to other instruments. Low recall and relatively high false positives rate indicate that probably more advanced methodology is necessary to identify instruments playing in unison.

We are planning to continue our research. This includes expanding the training set, in order to include more unison samples. Also, since the quality of classification depends on parameterization, we consider adding more sophisticated features to describe audio data. If this succeeds, we would also like to add more instruments to the set.

Acknowledgments. The authors would like to express thanks to the musicians who recorded our test audio data: Matthew Postle (trumpet), Enrico Bertelli (marimba, vibraphone), Noah Noutch (trombone), Cheong Li (piano), and Dave Smyth (piano).

This project was partially supported by the Research Center of PJIIT, supported by the Polish National Committee for Scientific Research (KBN). Computations were performed at ICM, grant G34-5.

References

1. Bay, M., Beauchamp, J.W.: Harmonic Source Separation Using Prestored Spectra. In: Rosca, J.P., Erdogmus, D., Príncipe, J.C., Haykin, S. (eds.) ICA 2006. LNCS, vol. 3889, pp. 561–568. Springer, Heidelberg (2006)
2. Breiman, L.: Random Forests. Machine Learning 45, 5–32 (2001), `http://www.stat.berkeley.edu/~breiman/RandomForests/cc_papers.htm`
3. Brown, J.C.: Computer identification of musical instruments using pattern recognition with cepstral coefficients as features. J. Acoust. Soc. Am. 105, 1933–1941 (1999)
4. Eggink, J., Brown, G.J.: Application of missing feature theory to the recognition of musical instruments in polyphonic audio. In: ISMIR (2003)
5. Foote, J.: An Overview of Audio Information Retrieval. Multimedia Systems 7(1), 2–11 (1999)
6. Goto, M., Hashiguchi, H., Nishimura, T., Oka, R.: RWC Music Database: Music Genre Database and Musical Instrument Sound Database. In: Proceedings of ISMIR, pp. 229–230 (2003)

7. Herrera, P., Amatriain, X., Batlle, E., Serra, X.: Towards instrument segmentation for music content description: a critical review of instrument classification techniques. In: International Symposium on Music Information Retrieval, ISMIR (2000)
8. ISO: MPEG-7 Overview, `http://www.chiariglione.org/mpeg/`
9. Klapuri, A., Davy, M. (eds.): Signal Processing Methods for Music Transcription. Springer, New York (2006)
10. Kubera, E.: The role of temporal attributes in identifying instruments in polytimbral music recordings (in polish). Ph.D. dissertation, Polish-Japanese Institute of Information Technology (2010)
11. Kubera, E., Wieczorkowska, A., Raś, Z., Skrzypiec, M.: Recognition of Instrument Timbres in Real Polytimbral Audio Recordings. In: Balcázar, J.L., Bonchi, F., Gionis, A., Sebag, M. (eds.) ECML PKDD 2010. LNCS (LNAI), vol. 6322, pp. 97–110. Springer, Heidelberg (2010)
12. Kubera, E., Kursa, M.B., Rudnicki, W.R., Rudnicki, R., Wieczorkowska, A.A.: All That Jazz in the Random Forest. In: Kryszkiewicz, M., Rybinski, H., Skowron, A., Raś, Z.W. (eds.) ISMIS 2011. LNCS, vol. 6804, pp. 543–553. Springer, Heidelberg (to appear, 2011)
13. Kursa, M.B., Kubera, E., Rudnicki, W.R., Wieczorkowska, A.A.: Random Musical Bands Playing in Random Forests. In: Szczuka, M., Kryszkiewicz, M., Ramanna, S., Jensen, R., Hu, Q. (eds.) RSCTC 2010. LNCS (LNAI), vol. 6086, pp. 580–589. Springer, Heidelberg (2010)
14. Kursa, M., Rudnicki, W., Wieczorkowska, A., Kubera, E., Kubik-Komar, A.: Musical Instruments in Random Forest. In: Rauch, J., Raś, Z.W., Berka, P., Elomaa, T. (eds.) ISMIS 2009. LNCS (LNAI), vol. 5722, pp. 281–290. Springer, Heidelberg (2009)
15. Kursa, M.B., Jankowski, A., Rudnicki, W.R.: Boruta: A System for Feature Selection. Fundamenta Informaticae 101, 271–285 (2010)
16. Kursa, M.B., Rudnicki, W.R.: Feature Selecion with the Boruta Package. J. Stat. Soft. 36, 1–13 (2010)
17. Livshin, A.A., Rodet, X.: Musical Instrument Identification in Continuous Recordings. In: Proc. of the 7th Int. Conference on Digital Audio Effects (DAFX 2004), Naples, Italy, October 5–8 (2004)
18. MIDOMI, `http://www.midomi.com/`
19. Niewiadomy, D., Pelikant, A.: Implementation of MFCC vector generation in classification context. J. Applied Computer Science 16(2), 55–65 (2008)
20. Opolko, F., Wapnick, J.: MUMS – McGill University Master Samples. CD's (1987)
21. Rudnicki, R.: Instrumental duos and trios. Recording and mixing. Trumpet - M. Postle, trombone - N. Noutch, marimba, vibraphone - E. Bertelli, piano - C. Li, D. Smyth (2010)
22. Sony Ericsson: TrackID, `http://www.sonyericsson.com/trackid/`
23. The University of IOWA Electronic Music Studios: Musical Instrument Samples, `http://theremin.music.uiowa.edu/MIS.html`
24. Wieczorkowska, A.A., Kubera, E.: Identification of a dominating instrument in polytimbral same-pitch mixes using SVM classifiers with non-linear kernel. J. Intell. Inf. Syst. 34(3), 275–303 (2010)
25. Zhang, X.: Cooperative Music Retrieval Based on Automatic Indexing of Music by Instruments and Their Types. Ph.D thesis, Univ. North Carolina, Charlotte (2007)
26. Zhang, X., Marasek, K., Raś, Z.W.: Maximum Likelihood Study for Sound Pattern Separation and Recognition. In: 2007 International Conference on Multimedia and Ubiquitous Engineering MUE 2007, IEEE, pp. 807–812 (2007)

Scale Invariant Bipartite Graph Generative Model

Szymon Chojnacki and Mieczysław A. Kłopotek

Institute of Computer Science PAS,
J.K. Ordona 21, 01-237 Warsaw, Poland
{sch,klopotek}@ipipan.waw.pl

Abstract. The purpose of this article is to present new undirected bigraph generator. Bigraphs (or bipartite graphs) contain nodes of two types and there exist edges only between nodes of different types. This data structure can be observed in various real-life scenarios. Random generator can be used to describe and better understand the scenarios. Moreover, the generator can output a wide range of synthetic datasets. We believe that the datasets can be utilized to evaluate performance of various algorithms that are deployed in such settings. The generative procedure is based on the preferential attachment principle. The principle is combined with the iterative growth mechanism and results in the power-law node degree distribution. Our algorithm extends the classic Barabási - Albert model. We obtain the same scaling exponent as in the classic model, when we set equal parameters for both modalities. However, when we abandon the symmetry we are able to build graphs with wider spectrum of scaling exponents.

1 Introduction

Bipartite or affiliation networks describe a situation in which we have two types of nodes and direct links only between nodes of different kinds. The first modality can be users (or actors). The second modality can be interpreted as items (or events). Bipartite graphs are an efficient data structure used to represent sparse matrices. Such matrices are characteristic e.g. for the settings in which recommender systems are deployed. For example, the customers of an internet bookstore are the first modality of the nodes. Books are perceived as the second modality. An edge is drawn between a user and an item if the user bought the item.

More formally, a graph is an ordered pair $G = (V, E)$ comprising a set of vertices (or nodes) V and a set of edges (or links) E. A bipartite network is a graph, whose vertices can be labeled with two types of tags. The set of vertices V can be split into two disjoint sets $V = \{V_A \cup V_B : V_A \cap V_B = \emptyset\}$. An edge can be drawn only between nodes of different types $E \subseteq V_A \times V_B$. The number of direct neighbors of node v is called the *degree of* v. The degree distribution of all nodes in a graph is an important structural measure. It is correlated with such topological properties as the diameter, the size of the largest connected component or the pace of the spread of innovations.

P. Bouvry et al. (Eds.): SIIS 2011, LNCS 7053, pp. 240–250, 2012.

In this article we study node degree distributions in bipartite graphs. We show that the long-tail relation is observed in various real-life datasets. This relation can be quantified by the probability density function of the power-law distribution

$$f(x; a, \varphi) = a \cdot x^{-\varphi}. \tag{1}$$

The parameter φ is called the scaling exponent. The tail of the power-law distribution vanishes slower than the tail of an exponential distribution with the same mean value. The shape of the density function is scale invariant $f(cx) \propto f(x)$. One can verify that $f(cx) = a \cdot (cx)^{-\varphi} = c^{-\varphi} f(x) \propto f(x)$. The node degree distribution of real-life datasets is often drawn in a log-log scale. We can show that $\log f(x) = -\varphi \log(x) + \log a$. Because of this equation the power-law distribution becomes a straight line when drawn in a log-log scale scatter plot.

It is not an easy task to build a random graph with the above distribution. A straightforward approach proposed by Erdös results in the binomial node degree distribution [1]. The first model that was able to output the power-law relation for classic unipartite graphs was described in [2]. We modified this model and placed the algorithm in the bipartite setting.

The rest of the paper is organized as follows: Section 2 surveys the related work. Section 3 contains the analysis of real-life bipartite datasets. In Section 4 we describe in detail the proposed random bipartite graph generator. We verify the properties of the generator with both formal and experimental tools. We conclude and discuss the implications of our findings in the last fifth section.

2 Related Work

In the classic Barabási - Albert model, a graph is initialized with a set of m_0 vertices. The generator runs t epochs. A new node is added to the graph during each iteration. The node comes with p new edges. The edges get connected to the nodes that are already present in the graph. The probability that an existing node is selected by the new node is proportional to the degree of an existing node [2]. This process reflects the rich gets richer phenomenon. It generates the power-law node degree distribution with the scaling exponent equal to 3.

Various extensions of the base model have been introduced. The extended models enable us to build networks with the exponent ranging from 2 to infinity. In the winners don't take all model, the probability that a node is selected is modified and controlled by an additional threshold parameter. If a random number is greater than the threshold, the probability that an existing node is selected becomes uniform [3]. It has been shown that a similar outcome can be obtained by means of the stochastic urn transfer model [4]. The generalization described in [5] allows us to add edges between existing nodes. The most complex extension was described in [6]. The following three actions may happen in one step: adding a node, adding an edge or rewiring an edge. The copying model is an example of a graph generator that gives the power-law distribution, but does not utilize the preferential attachment mechanism [7, 8].

The heavy-tailed node degree distribution is an important property of various networks. In this paragraph we review other properties that have been observed in real-life datasets and are not visible in the graphs analyzed by Erdös. It has been shown by Milgram that an average graph distance between two random people is close to six [9]. The phenomenon of the smallworld is explained by the models that allow local structures to be connected to random distant nodes [10, 11]. Another interesting feature was reported for dynamic networks. It has been shown that the proportion of the number of edges to the number of nodes increases over time. This densification feature was explained by a generic Community Guided Attachment model. This observation was attributed to the hierarchical structure of connections among the nodes [12]. It has also been shown that an effective diameter of a network decreases over time [13]. A very powerful model to simulate this pattern, based on an adjacency matrix multiplication, was proposed [12]. In [8] the users of a social network were divided into three groups: linkers, inviters and passive. This enabled to create a model that simulates the structure of the largest connected component and the middle region in a real network.

Most of the described research was focused on the analysis of classic unipartite graphs. An early analysis of affiliation networks was limited by the size of available data. In [14] a network of only twenty-six CEOs and their club memberships was analyzed. It is a common practice to induce a classic unipartite graph from the data that are bipartite. It is performed by projecting a bigraph onto one of the modalities. This operation preserves some properties (e.g. the relative size of the largest connected component). However, other important measures may differ (e.g. node degree distribution) [15]. Therefore, it is important to distinguish the two situations and build a generator dedicated only for bigraphs. There are not many bigraph generators described in the literature. Two examples can be found in [15] and [16]. In the former, the number of all nodes is fixed. A degree of each node is drawn from a predefined distribution. The edges are created by matching the nodes of opposite modalities. An iterative model for bipartite graph generation was proposed in [16]. Firstly, a node of a preselected modality is added to a bigraph. Secondly, the degree of the new node is drawn from a predefined distribution. Thirdly, the new node is connected to an existing node or to a new node. The drawback of the two models is the fact that one has to preselect the degree distribution of each analyzed node. In the model that we describe the node degree distribution results from an atomic process and does not need to be chosen in advance.

3 Observations

In this section, we analyze eight real-life bipartite graphs. The datasets are defined in the first three subsections. In the last subsection we describe the results.

3.1 BibSonomy Dataset

The BibSonomy dataset was used during ECML/PKDD 2009 Discovery Challenge [17]. It contains a full snapshot of the actions taken by the users of the BibSonomy bookmarking portal until the end of 2008. We processed a tas table, which contains 401 104 tag assignments made by 3 617 users to 235 328 websites using 93 756 distinct tags. This dataset enabled us to build three bipartite graphs: user-resource, user-tag and resource-tag.

3.2 CiteULike Dataset

The structure of the main table in the CiteULike dataset is similar to the BibSonomy dataset. The two datasets differ in the magnitude. Moreover, the users of CiteULike bookmarked publications instead of websites. We also obtained additional table with assignments of CiteULike users to thematic groups. The table contains 2 657 227 tag assignments made by 18 467 users to 557 101 articles by means of 166 504 tags. The second file linking groups with users contains only 2 336 groups and 5 208 users. We created three bipartite graphs from the first table and one from the second table.

3.3 Movies Database

The table contains information about links between actors and films. It was downloaded from Notre Dame Center for Complex Network Research website. The bipartite graph contains information about 383 640 actors and 127 823 films retrieved from The Internet Movie Database.

3.4 Degree Distributions

The node degree distributions of the eight bipartite graphs are presented in Figure 1. In most cases, the points are shaped in a straight line on a log-log scale. It is a necessary condition for the power-law distribution. The levels of the scaling exponents were assessed by means of the least squares regression after removing overly influential observations. This step was done with DFFITS statistic [18]. In most cases, there are outliers at the beginning and at the end of the domain. The values of estimated exponents are between 1 and 4. A good example of how outliers affect the shape of the regression is visible in the last graph. The value of the cleaned exponent calculated for the actors modality equals to 1.84. The value of the exponent obtained without cleaning is 2.41.

4 Proposed Model

In the following subsections we describe the details of the generative procedure. We present formal proof that the node degree distribution is power-law. Finally, we compare the asymptotic scaling exponents to the exponents obtained from generated bigraphs.

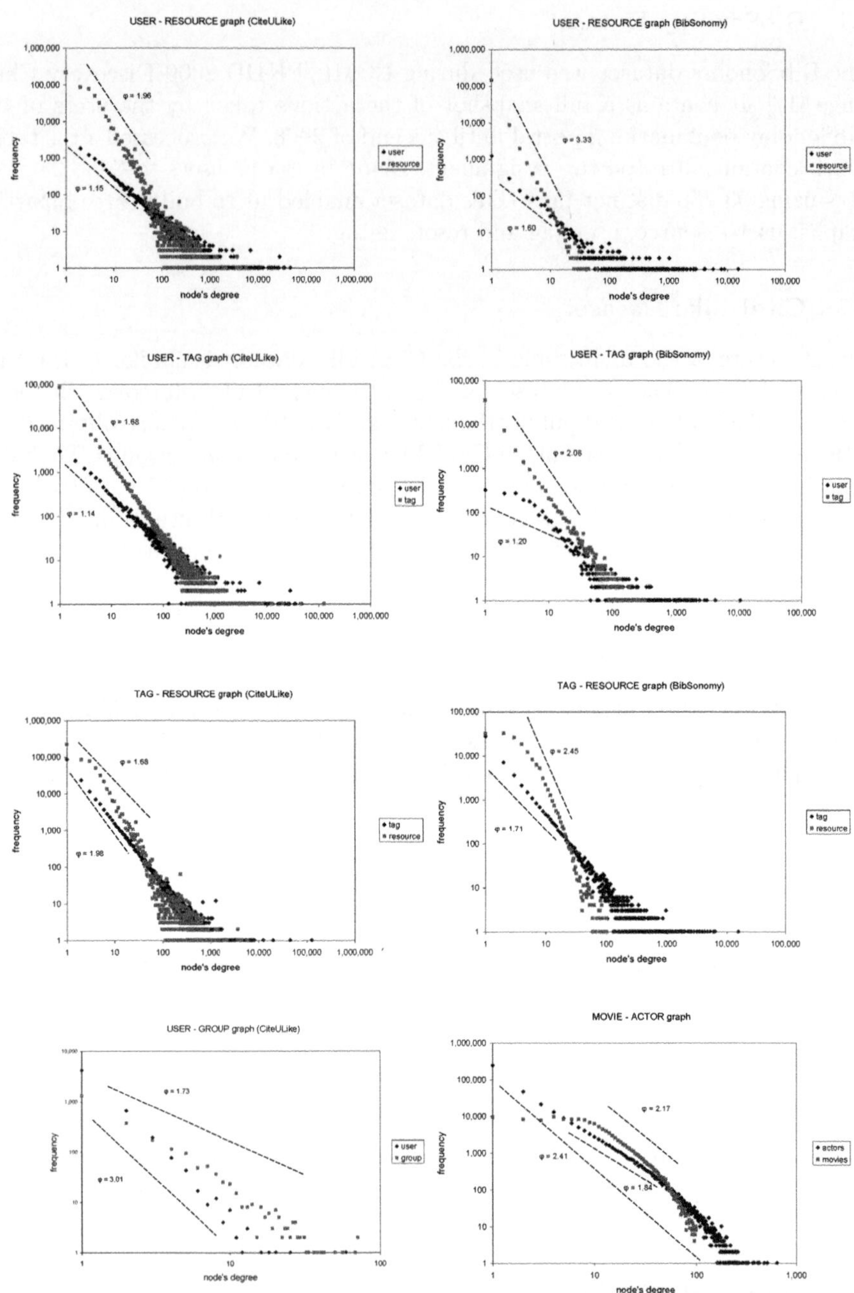

Fig. 1. The node degree distributions calculated for real-world bigraphs. A straight line of points on a log-log scale is characteristic for the power law distributions. The dotted line is a linear regression obtained with the least squares method. The values of the scaling coefficients are given next to the dotted lines.

4.1 Generative Procedure

The graph is initialized with m_0 edges linking vertices of type A with vertices of type B. During each iteration we add a node v of type A and a node w of type B to the graph. We connect v with p existing nodes of type B and w with q existing nodes of type A (Fig. 2).

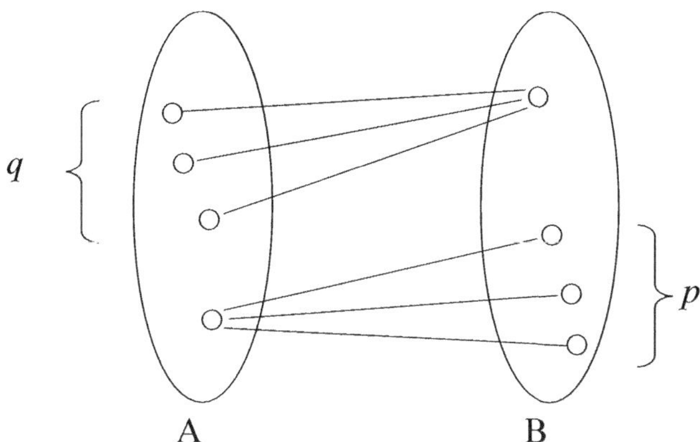

Fig. 2. During each iteration, one node of type A and one node of type B are added to the graph. A node of type A is connected to p existing nodes of type B and a node of type B is connected to q existing nodes of type A. The selection of existing nodes is based on the preferential attachment principle.

After t iterations the number of vertices is equal to $|V(t)| = 2 \cdot (t + m_0)$. The number of edges at epoch t is $|E(t)| = t \cdot (p + q) + m_0$. After relatively many iterations ($t \gg m_0$) we can neglect m_0 and write $|E(t)| \approx t \cdot (p + q)$. Let us denote with k_i the degree of node i. The probability that node $j \in V_B$ is drawn equals to

$$\pi_j = \frac{k_j}{\sum_{x \in V_B} k_x}. \tag{2}$$

The probability that node $i \in V_A$ is drawn equals to

$$\pi_i = \frac{k_i}{\sum_{x \in V_A} k_x}. \tag{3}$$

The number of edges in a bipartite graph can be calculated in two ways

$$\sum_{i \in V_A} k_i = \sum_{j \in V_B} k_j = |E|. \tag{4}$$

Hence, both Eq. 2 and Eq. 3 can be simplified. In the following, we limit our deduction to measuring only the degree distribution of nodes of type B. The degree distribution of the nodes of type A can be obtained in an analogous way. The probability that a node $j \in V_B$ is selected at step t by one of the edges created by new node v is $\pi_j = \frac{k_j}{|E(t)|}$. The node j has p chances to become selected. As a result, the expected growth of the degree of j between t and $t+1$ is

$$p\frac{k_j}{|E(t)|} \tag{5}$$

If we assume that all nodes with degree k evolve with the same pace, we can write down the global evolution rule as

$$\frac{\partial k}{\partial t} = \frac{k \cdot p}{(p+q) \cdot t}. \tag{6}$$

The assumption is referred to as the mean field approach. The differential equation enables us to derive the asymptotic degree distribution of nodes $j \in V_B$. In order to derive the degree distribution of $i \in V_A$, we could use the following equation

$$\frac{\partial k}{\partial t} = \frac{k \cdot q}{(p+q) \cdot t}. \tag{7}$$

In the section 4.2 we will use Eq. 6 and describe the details of the mathematical reasoning.

4.2 Asymptotic Properties

The mathematical technique that we apply in this section is called the *continuum approach* in the field of statistical physics [2].

Theorem 1. *The degree distribution obtained for the nodes of* V_B *is power-law with the scaling exponent equal to* $\varphi = q/p + 2$.

Proof. Let's reorganize Eq.6 and calculate corresponding integrals:

$$\int \frac{1}{k}\mathrm{d}k = \int \frac{p}{(p+q) \cdot t}\mathrm{d}t. \tag{8}$$

The initial degree of node j equals to q. The node was added to the graph at time t_0. Hence, the solution is

$$\log k - \log q = \frac{p}{p+q}[\log t - \log t_0], \tag{9}$$

by using both sides of the above equation as powers of e we get

$$k(t) = q \cdot (t/t_0)^s, \text{ where } s = \frac{p}{p+q}. \tag{10}$$

By means of mean field assumption, the above solution applies to each $j \in V_B$. Let's put this result into a cumulative distribution function of k.

$$P(k_j(t) < k) = P(t_0 > t \cdot (k/q)^{-1/s}) \tag{11}$$
$$= 1 - P(t_0 \leq t \cdot (k/q)^{-1/s}) \tag{12}$$
$$= 1 - t \cdot (k/q)^{-1/s}/2(t + m_0). \tag{13}$$

We can move from step (12) to step (13) as one can assume that new nodes are added to the graph at equal time intervals. We can also assume that $t \gg m_0$ and substitute $t/2(t+m_0)$ with $1/2$. In order to obtain $P(k)$ we make one more step

$$P(k) = \frac{\partial P(k_j(t) < k}{\partial k} = c \cdot k^{-1/s} - 1, \tag{14}$$

and finally

$$P(k) = c \cdot k^{-(2+q/p)}, \tag{15}$$

where c is a positive expression independent on k, hence $\varphi = q/p + 2$.

In particular when $p = q$ we get $\varphi = 3$, which is consistent with the preferential attachment model studied by Barabási.

5 Experiments

In this subsection we verify the impact of initial number of edges on the stability of the scaling exponents in graphs obtained after finite number of iterations. The results let us suspect that the power law distribution is obtained early. However, the value of the scaling exponent differs significantly from the theoretical result, when we use all the observations. Because of this reason, we also evaluate the impact of the overly influential nodes on the exponent estimation and verify that the empirical exponent is close to the theoretical after the removal of the outlying points. We simulated the above described procedure with initial number of edges m_0 varying from 1 to 30. We run 20 000 iterations for each graph. We set $p = 2$ and $q = 3$. The results are given in Fig. 3.

We can see a slightly increasing trend of the values of the exponents for both modalities. The higher the number of initial edges the steeper the distribution is observed. It is a consequence of the fact that some of the m_0 nodes were not selected by the preferential attachment rule even once during 20 000 iterations.

We present in Figure 4 the node degree distribution obtained for a graph with $m_0 = 5$. The points are shaped in a straight line, which indicates the power-law relation. We have observed the straight line in all 30 graphs. However, the value of the estimated scaling exponent in Figure 3 differs significantly from the asymptotic theoretical result. The slope estimated for nodes of type A is around 1.5 and for nodes of type B only around 2.5. According to the Theorem 1. the values should converge to $(2.66 = 2 + 2/3)$ and $(3.5 = 2 + 3/2)$ respectively. It turns out that the level of 2.66 and 3.5 can be obtained when we remove the overly influential observations. The detailed analysis of this phenomenon

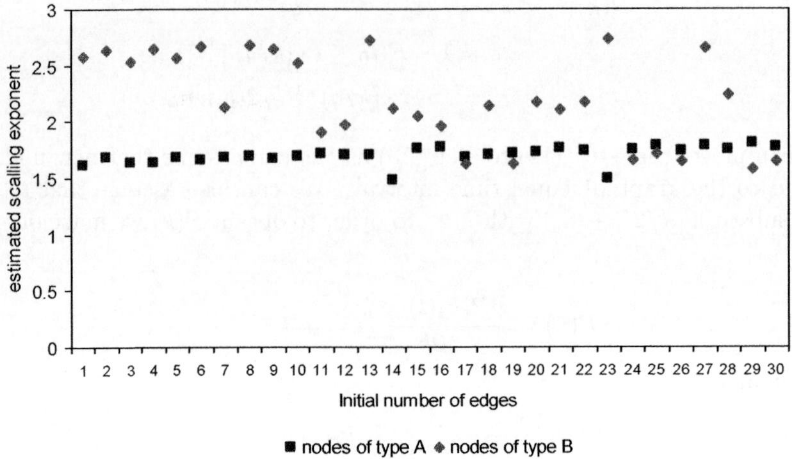

Fig. 3. The values of estimated scaling exponents differentiated by the number of edges. All points of corresponding empirical node degree distributions were used to calculate the slope of the regression.

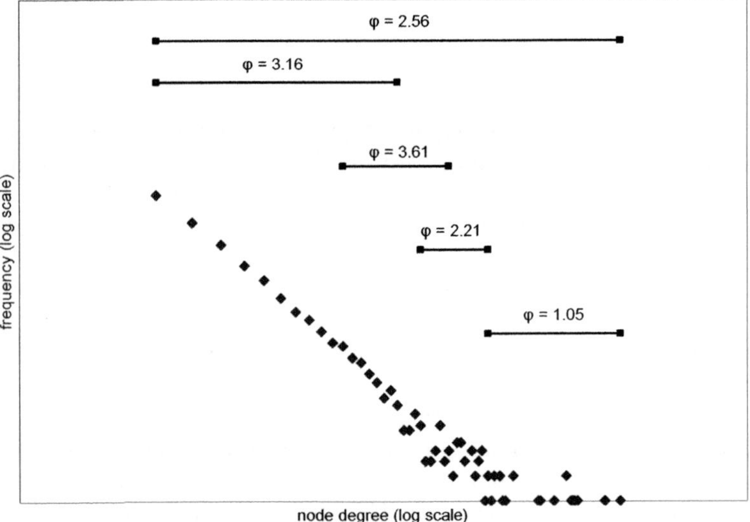

Fig. 4. The degree distribution of node of type B. The graph was generated after 20 000 iterations ($m_0 = 5$, $p = 2$ and $q = 3$). The scaling exponent estimated for all points is 2.56. The scaling exponents estimated for intervals containing twenty subsequent points differ from 1.05 to 3.61

is presented in Figure 4. Let us remark that a point is considered an outlier, when the value of the estimated regression function calculated for the point differs more than three standard errors from the value of the regression function estimated without this point.

6 Conclusion

In this article we have shown that the power-law node degree distribution can be observed in various real-life datasets. We have described a random graph generator, which can output bipartite graphs resembling the properties of real-life datasets. Similarly to the unipartite setting, the power-law property can be attributed to the preferential attachment principle. Formal mathematical reasoning enables us to proof that the node degree distribution of both modalities converge to the power-law relation. The model can build graphs with the exponents between 2 and infinity. There exists a relation between the exponents of both modalities. If an exponent of one modality is $2 + p/q$ than the exponent of the second modality is $2 + q/p$. The results of the simulations suggest that the number of initial edges in random graphs influences the stability of the estimated exponents even after several thousand of iterations. Moreover, we found it very difficult to decide how to estimate the slope of the regression. The results most similar to the theoretical were obtained after the removal of overly influential points at the beginning and at the end of the domain.

Acknowledgments. This work was partially supported by Polish state budget funds for scientific research within research project *Analysis and visualization of structure and dynamics of social networks using nature inspired methods*, grant No. N516 443038.

References

[1] Erdös, P., Renyi, A.: On the evolution of random graphs. Publication of the Mathematical Institute of the Hungarian Academy of Sciences (1960)

[2] Barabási, A., Albert, R.: Emergence of scaling in random networks. Science 286(5439), 509–512 (1999)

[3] Pennock, D.M., Flake, G.W., Lawrence, S., Glover, E.J., Giles, C.L.: Winners don't take all: Characterizing the competition for links on the web. Proc. Natl. Acad. Sci. USA 99(8), 5207–5211 (2002)

[4] Levene, M., Fenner, T.I., Loizou, G., Wheeldon, R.: A stochastic model for the evolution of the web. Computer Networks 39(3), 277–287 (2002)

[5] Dorogovtsev, S., Mendes, J., Samulkin, A.: Structure of growing networks: Exact solution of the barabasi-albert model. Physical Review Letters 85, 4633–4636 (2000)

[6] Albert, R., Barabási, A.: Topology of evolving networks: Local events and universality. Physical Review Letters 85(24), 5234–5237 (2000)

[7] Kleinberg, J.M., Kumar, R., Raghavan, P., Rajagopalan, S., Tomkins, A.S.: The web as a graph: Measurements, models, and methods. In: Asano, T., Imai, H., Lee, D.T., Nakano, S.-i., Tokuyama, T. (eds.) COCOON 1999. LNCS, vol. 1627, pp. 1–17. Springer, Heidelberg (1999)

[8] Kumar, R., Raghavan, P., Rajagopalan, S., Sivakumar, D., Tomkins, A., Upfal, E.: Stochastic models for the web graph. In: Proceedings of the 41st Annual Symposium on Foundations of Computer Science (FOCS), Redondo Beach, CA, USA, pp. 57–65. IEEE CS Press (2000)

[9] Milgram, S.: The small-world problem. Psychology Today 2, 60–67 (1967)
[10] Watts, D.J., Strogatz, S.H.: Collective dynamics of small-world networks. Nature 393, 440–442 (1998)
[11] Waxman, B.: Routing of mulitpoint connections. IEEE Journal of Selected Areas in Communications 6, 1617–1622 (1988)
[12] Leskovec, J., Chakrabarti, D., Kleinberg, J.M., Faloutsos, C.: Realistic, mathematically tractable graph generation and evolution, using kronecker multiplication. In: Jorge, A.M., Torgo, L., Brazdil, P.B., Camacho, R., Gama, J. (eds.) PKDD 2005. LNCS (LNAI), vol. 3721, pp. 133–145. Springer, Heidelberg (2005)
[13] Leskovec, J., Kleinberg, J., Faloutsos, C.: Graphs over time: densification laws, shrinking diameters and possible explanations. In: KDD 2005: Proceeding of the Eleventh ACM SIGKDD International Conference on Knowledge Discovery in Data Mining, pp. 177–187. ACM Press, New York (2005)
[14] Galaskiewicz, J., Wasserman, S., Rauschenbach, B., Bielefeld, W., Mullaney, P.: The influence of class, status, and market position on corporate interlocks in a regional network. Social Forces (1985)
[15] Newman, M., Watts, D., Strogatz, S.: Random graph models of social networks. P. Natl. Acad. Sci. USA 99, 2566–2572 (2002)
[16] Guillaume, J.-L., Latapy, M.: Bipartite structure of all complex networks. Inf. Process. Lett. 90(5), 215–221 (2004)
[17] Eisterlehner, F., Hotho, A., Jaschke, R. (eds.): ECML PKDD Discovery Challenge 2009 (DC 2009). CEUR-WS.org, vol. 497 (September 2009)
[18] Harrell, F.E.: Regression Modeling Strategies, with Applications to Linear Models, Survival Analysis and Logistic Regression. Springer, Heidelberg (2001) ISBN 0-387-95232-2

Introducing Diversity to Log-Based Query Suggestions to Deal with Underspecified User Queries

Marcin Sydow[1,2], Krzysztof Ciesielski[1], and Jakub Wajda[1]

[1] Institute of Computer Science, Polish Academy of Sciences, Warsaw, Poland
[2] Polish-Japanese Institute of Information Technology, Warsaw, Poland
{msyd,k.ciesielski,jakub.wajda}@ipipan.waw.pl

Abstract. This paper presents novel approaches to deal with ambiguous or under-specified user queries in search engines. We propose two algorithms for automatic query suggestion that are based on query logs. Furthermore, we propose a novel approach of diversifying the suggestions in order to improve user experience and present a novel adaptation of the MMR diversification algorithm to this problem. We propose two novel query-similarity measures that are utilised by the algorithm. We also present promising preliminary experimental results that are conducted on real data.

1 Introduction

One of the main problems in information retrieval systems such as web search engines is *underspecification* of the user's information need that is imperfectly represented by a query, which is usually very short. The problem is especially important in case of *ambiguous* or *broad* queries i.e. queries that can be *interpreted* in many different ways or that have many different *aspects*, respectively. The examples of these two cases are: "jaguar" (a car, an animal, etc.) and "toshiba" (a will to purchase a notebook, information about company, etc.), respectively.

One of the approaches to deal with this problem is *personalisation* i.e. utilising some available information concerning the user behind the query in order to clarify their implicit information need. For example, the information that the user is very interested in nature may be utilised to boost the "animal" interpretation of the "jaguar" query when returning the search results (at the expense of the "car" interpretation).

Typically, to implement personalisation the search system records and analyses some additional information concerning the users collected during serving the user operations prior to submitting the query. This information can have many forms such as: user profiles, search history or click history of users. The following issues arise:

- it may be difficult or impossible to collect information or data from the user to successfully build their profile
- collecting such data usually violates *user privacy*

Independently, another (complementary) approach to deal with underspecification of user information need is *query suggestion* i.e. the system automatically suggests a set of queries, based on the original query, such that each proposed suggestion represents

P. Bouvry et al. (Eds.): SIIS 2011, LNCS 7053, pp. 251–264, 2012.

different possible interpretation or aspect of the implicit information need. For example, given the ambiguous query "linux" the system can suggest, for example "linux debian" or "linux installation" to clarify the user's intent.

The subsequent selection of particular suggestion done by the user helps the system to present results that are better suited to particular aspect or interpretation.

Leaving aside (for the moment) the technical problem of how to automatically generate good query suggestions, there is another problem. Usually the limited space available in the interface of the search engine and limited user capacity usually makes the number of query suggestions possible to display significantly smaller than the number of possible interpretations or aspects of the query.

This problem is partially alleviated if personalisation is available, as explained before, by providing the means of narrowing the range of possible aspects/interpretations potentially interesting to the user in order to efficiently reduce the number of query suggestions that are likely to be relevant to the particular user. However, if personalisation is not available or desired (due to one of the problems mentioned earlier) the system has to maximise the likelihood of meeting the needs of particular unknown user in the absence of any knowledge about their profile.

This idea is close to the approach of *search results diversification* that is recently gaining increasing interest in the information retrieval community, e.g.: [3,4,1].

In this approach, the search results are *diversified* so that the system maximises the number of covered aspects or interpretations of the query in the context of unknown actual user information need and the lack of user profile. In this way the average relevance of returned results is sacrificed in order to avoid *query abandonment* i.e. the situation when user finds *no* relevant result among the top ones.

In this paper we propose a novel approach of diversifying *query suggestions* instead of search results (or, perhaps, independently of, as these techniques can be used together). To this end, we propose in this paper to adapt one of the techniques previously used for result diversification to the problem of diversifying query suggestions.

To all the problems discussed above, we propose to use historical search engine query-logs as the basis of automatic computation of query suggestions. Such a solution has numerous advantages. First, it is knowledge-poor, i.e. not much knowledge of natural language, grammar or domain knowledge is necessary prior to operation. In particular, the approach is completely language-independent, provided the logs in appropriate language are available. Second, it is leveraging the "wisdom of the crowds", i.e. the results are guaranteed to be previously used by statistically significant population of human users. Thus it is robust and adaptive to specifics of particular language or even some temporal trends (e.g. some topics might be more important due to recent events). Such adaptivity is very difficult to be automatically obtained.

By definition, the query suggestions provided by such a method will be most likely well formed and represent real trends in information needs of users.

Finally, the approach does not break user privacy since it ignores the information concerning particular users (such as cookie or IP) and uses global statistics instead.

A disadvantage of the method is its limited availability of the real query-log datasets as it is extremely sensitive data that is usually owned only by specific companies like search engines or alike and difficult to be accessed by academic research community.

Related Work. There exists a body of literature devoted to the concept of personalisation in the context of the web, some examples are [2] or [8] in the particular context of web search. The need for diversification in search was identified very early in information retrieval research [6] however the first practical algorithm to diversify search results was presented much more recently [3]. Afterwards, many more diversity-aware measures e.g. [4] or algorithms e.g. [1] were proposed. The connection between web search personalisation and result diversification is discussed in [13]. Utilising query logs to automatically measure the ambiguity of queries is studied in [5]. The idea of applying the analysis of query logs to diversify search results is studied in [14].

Contributions of this paper are as follows:

- novel approach of diversified query suggestions as the substitute of personalisation in the context of missing user profiles
- two novel algorithms for automatic query suggestion based on historical query logs: time-succession-based and suffix-based
- demonstration of the results of a prototype implementation of the algorithms
- adaptation of the MMR diversification technique to diversified query suggestion
- two novel measures of query similarity: edit-distance-based and semantic-based
- preliminary experimental demonstration of the diversified query suggestion approach on unique real dataset

Despite the fact, that the topics of diversification, query suggestion or personalisation are well represented in the research literature, this paper seems to be the first one to discuss the idea of diversification of query suggestions, up to the authors' knowledge.

2 Log-Based Query-Suggestion Algorithms

In this section we propose two algorithms for automatic query suggestion based on appropriately preprocessed dataset that consists of historical query logs of a search engine. Both algorithms work on a directed graph $G(V, E)$ that is automatically built from the dataset in the pre-processing phase. Every query in the logs is represented by some vertex $v \in V$ of the graph and every directed weighted arc $e \in E$ represents some relation between queries that is extracted from the logs. The algorithms differ in the way the relation is defined and in the way of computation of the weights on arcs. The details will be explained in subsections 2.2 and 2.3.

Once the query graph G is built, our query suggestion algorithm works as follows. Given a user query q and the number $k \in \mathcal{N}$, the node $v_q \in V$ representing the query is identified and the set $R(v_q)$ of nodes, that represent suggestions to q is returned. $R(v_q)$ consists of the set of vertices $v \in V$ such that $(v_q, v) \in E$ and that are the top-k such vertices with regard to the value of the weights $w((v_q, v))$ (if $outDeg(v_q) < k$ then respectively smaller number of suggestions is returned).

2.1 Dataset

The data used in the experiments presented in this paper was made available to the authors by two Polish search-engine-related IT companies[1]. The data concerns Polish

[1] Thanks are due to Gemius S.A. and NetSprint S.A., for providing the data.

queries that limits the examples presented in this paper, however by its definition, the method is language-independent and, as we believe, can be successfully applied to other natural languages if appropriate data is available.

The data used to conduct our experiments has been extracted from integrated query logs comprising approximately 1 million records from early 2010. Each line of the query log contained the following fields: `timestamp query hashedUserId`[2]

Since the raw data originated from heterogeneous sources it was subsequently pre-processed and cleaned, including: removing empty queries, re-coding all the queries to common encoding (UTF-8), unification of word separators, removing unreadable queries (due to, for example, uncorrect encoding, etc.), capitalisation, normalisation. The logs were then sorted by timestamp and (hashed) user ID.

2.2 Algorithm Based on Time Succession

The first presented approach is based on *time succession* of the queries in the logs. A graph $G(V, E)$ is build so that each vertex $v \in V$ represents some unique query found in the logs and there is an arc $(v, w) \in E$ iff the following conditions are satisfied:

- the query w occurs at least once *directly after* (in terms of time) the query v in the logs and was submitted by *the same user* (represented by the hashed user ID)
- the difference in time between submitting the queries is not higher than some threshold T, that is one of the parameters

The arc weight is the occurrence frequency of the pair of queries as recorded in the logs.

Provided that there is sufficiently much data available, the following approach is quite powerful since the suggestions are based on real query reformulations done by real users observed sufficiently frequently. The approach has also some negative properties:

- suggestions can be generated only for queries that are found in the historical logs
- since the hashed user ID does not truthfully represent one-to-one mapping between the user IDs and real users (e.g. multiple users can be represented by the same IP, etc.) the "reformulation" relation is contaminated with casual successions, etc.

The approach was implemented and experiments showed that the most important problem with this approach is the sparsity of data. I.e. it turned out that the size of input data that was at our disposal (i.e. approximately 1 million of original logs) is definitely too low to produce results of satisfactory quality except some small fraction of cases.

Selected promising examples results produced by this approach are presented on figure 1. As can be seen from the presented examples, a very strong point of this approach is the ability of the algorithm to suggest queries that are completely dissimilar in terms of "surface" string appearance (e.g. "tyres" -> "rims") or even semantically not very related (such as "Cracow" -> "guest rooms") but that are actually very reasonable as they reflect real mental steps that humans do (e.g.: planning a trip to Cracow and then looking for accommodation, etc.).

On the other hand, we observed that not all the suggestions seemed to be of high quality in this approach, due to data sparsity. We believe that the results would by much

[2] userId was encoded on the company's side due to the sensitivity of the data.

query	total	1st suggestion	2nd suggestion	3rd suggestion
opony	67	felgi (28)	opony samochodowe (5)	opony ciężarowe (3)
Kraków	190	pokoje gościnne (28)	zabytki Kraków (28)	forum Kraków (16)
komputery	70	monitory (10)	notebooki (7)	komputery Warszawa (4)

query	total	1st suggestion	2nd suggestion	3rd suggestion
tyres	67	rims (28)	car tyres (5)	lorry tyres (3)
Cracow	190	guest rooms (28)	Cracow monuments (28)	Cracow forum (16)
computers	70	monitors (10)	notebooks (7)	computers Warsaw (4)

Fig. 1. Time-succession-based query suggestions, examples. Upper part: original queries and corresponding suggestions in Polish; lower part: the same translated to English

more satisfactory, provided that much larger dataset is available. Due to the unavailabilty of larger data, we designed, implemented and tested another approach that is adapted to limited size of query-log dataset and is described in the next subsection.

2.3 Suffix-Based Algorithm

As explained in section 2.2, our preliminary experimental results with the approach to query suggestion based on direct time succession failed seems to have great potential but suffers from sparsity of data if it is not large enough.

Due to the above, another log-based method, that is suffix-based, was designed, that "forgets" time and user dimensions and thus makes the data more dense that can work better for smaller datasets (such as the one available to the authors)

The method uses a large set P of query phrases extracted from query logs, together with some other statistics (e.g. query or word frequencies, etc.). The phrases from P serve as candidates for query suggestions. The phrases can be extracted also from other large text corpora, e.g. by keyword-identification techniques, but using query logs guarantees (to some extent) that suggested queries will be well-formed user queries.

The idea is very simple. Elements of P are sequences of words $c = w_1, w_2, ..., w_l$, where l is the length of phrase (the number of words). The helper graph $G = (V, E)$ is built so that each $v \in V$ represents exactly one phrase $p \in P$ and there is arc (q, c) between two vertices (phrases) $q = v_1, ..., v_m$ and $c = w_1, w_2, ..., w_l$ iff $l > m$ and $\forall_{i=1,...,m} v_i = w_i$ i.e. c constitutes p extended by some suffix (on the word level). For example, if q corresponds to phrase "linux debian" and c corresponds to "linux debian download", then (q, c) is a valid arc of E in $G = (V, E)$. To extend the applicability of the method, we decided also to add to the set of vertices V in the helper graph, all words w that start any phrase in P even if w does not constitute a complete query found in query logs. Each arc (q, c) has associated a weight w_1 that is the frequency of c in P (as derived from the query logs, in our case). Thus, given a user query q such as "linux debian", all phrases found in the logs, that start with words "linux debian" are considered as candidates c for suggestion.

The algorithm returns top-k (where $k \in \mathcal{N}$ is given in input, usually $k = 3, 5, 10$) suggestions sorted non-increasingly by weights (frequency).

In our implementation we also use a helper weight w in order to obtain finer distinction between the suggestions (if the values of v are tied, what happens frequently, the suggestions are secondarily sorted by w). In current implementation, for a candidate suggestion c, its secondary weight w is the number of times c occurs as a prefix in any query in the logs. We also experiment with other, e.g. word-frequency-based definitions of w. We observed that the introduction of the helper weight w seems to improve the quality of the results.

The method has been implemented and our preliminary experimental results demonstrate that it seems to perform satisfactorily (i.e. it produces reasonable and useful suggestions) on all tested cases, even on limited-size dataset that was at our disposal. See selected examples on figure 2.

query→			opony			opony zimowe			zamek
no	v	w	suggestions:	v	w	suggestions:	v	w	suggestions:
1st	9	25	opony zimowe	4	4	opony zimowe ceny	2	4	zamek Czocha
2nd	8	36	opony letnie	1	1	opony zimowe ranking	2	3	zamek Drakuli
3rd	4	15	opony rolnicze	1	1	opony zimowe Warszawa	2	2	zamek noclegi
4th	4	12	opony używane	1	1	opony zimowe Mokotów	2	2	Zamek Królewski na Wawelu
5th	4	4	opony zimowe ceny	1	1	opony zimowe R13	1	1	zamek nie zapina się
6th	4	4	opony letnie wyprzedaż	0	0	-	1	1	zamek w Sorkwitach zdjęcia
query →			tyres			winter tyres			castle
no	v	w	suggestions:	v	w	suggestions:	v	w	suggestions:
1st	9	25	winter tyres	4	4	winter tyres prices	2	4	czocha castle
2nd	8	36	summer tyres	1	1	winter tyres ranking	2	3	dracula's castle
3rd	4	15	agricultural tyres	1	1	winter tyres warsaw	2	2	castle accommodation
4th	4	12	used tyres	1	1	winter tyres mokotow	2	2	king's castle wawel
5th	4	4	winter tyres prices	1	1	winter tyres R13	1	1	**zip does not fasten**
6th	4	4	summer tyres sale	0	0	-	1	1	sorkwity castle photos

Fig. 2. Examples of suffix-based query suggestions in Polish (upper part) and their translations to English (bottom part). The query "zamek" is ambiguous in Polish – the suggestion concerning the meaning other than "castle" is in bold. Notice that the word order can be changed due to translation. "Mokotów" is the district of Warsaw. "Czocha" is the name of a famous castle in southern Poland. "Wawel" is the name of the historical king's castle in Cracow - the former capital of Poland.

Importantly, the method can produce reasonable suggestions in significantly more cases than the time-succession method. The obvious restriction is that the method can produce suggestions only for queries that constitute (word-level) prefixes of any query found in the logs. One possible idea for relaxing this restriction is to use other text corpora (than query logs) to extract candidate phrases from (e.g. Wikipedia).

Motivation for Diversification. As our preliminary experimentation demonstrated, the suffix-based method produces high-quality suggestions and seems to have quite high coverage. However, the "zamek" example shown on figure 2 illustrates another important problem. The word "zamek" in Polish has many very different interpretations concerning: the context of historical architecture ("castle" in English); cars, doors, windows, anything that can be locked, etc. ("lock" in English); garments ("zip" in English); a part of firearms, guns, etc. ("gunlock" in English).

As seen on the figure, the top-6 suggestions are dominated by one interpretation only ("castle") while the other are completely missing (only the 5-th suggestion concerns another interpretation: "zip"). Thus, *a user that is interested in other meanings of the word will not find any relevant query suggestions*. In the remaining part of the paper we propose a solution to this problem by the means of *diversification* of query suggestions in order to improve user experience.

3 Diversification of Suggestions

To improve the coverage of different interpretations or aspects of an underspecified query in the set of query suggestions, we propose to adapt one of the diversification methods proposed in document retrieval.

In this paper we describe novel adaptation of the MMR ("Maximal Marginal Relevance") algorithm [3], usually used to diversify recommendations or search results to the novel application of query suggestion.

The original formulation of MMR can be viewed as finding a balance between the relevance of returned documents D_i to the user query q and pairwise dissimilarity of the results. More precisely, given the user query q and precomputed set R of the relevant "candidates" to the query, the items of the target "diversified" set S are chosen greedily in iterations so that an appropriate objective function is maximised in each iteration (until k "diversified" items are collected).

$$MMR = argmax_{D_i \in R \setminus S}[\lambda sim_1(D_i, q) - (1 - \lambda) max_{D_j \in S} sim_2(D_i, D_j)]$$

where $\lambda \in (0, 1]$ is a parameter; the lower the value of λ the higher emphasis is put on the diversification of the results (at the expense of the relevance). In the extreme case $\lambda = 1$ (no diversification), the results are sorted only by relevance. Experiments reported in [3] show that good practical results were obtained for a small initial value of $\lambda = 0.3$ that was subsequently increased in next iterations.

The key ingredients in the formula are the functions sim_1 and sim_2 that measure similarity between the query and the items and pairwise similarity between the selected items, respectively. There are many possible text-based similarity measures in this context, for example tf-idf vector similarity, etc. We propose to adapt this method to our problem of diversified query suggestions. Thus, the adapted formula is as follows:

$$qSuggMMR = argmax_{q_i \in R \setminus S}[\lambda sim_1(q_i, q) - (1 - \lambda) max_{q_j \in S} sim_2(q_i, q_j)]$$

where q is the original (underspecified) user query and R is the set of candidate query suggestions and q_i represent candidates to be selected to the final set of query suggestions S. We propose to use one of the methods for (undiversified) query suggestion described in sections 2.2 and 2.3 to compute the initial set of candidates R.

Concerning the similarity measures sim_1 and sim_2 between the queries one can first consider some standard text-based similarity measures used in the original result diversification problem. However, as practical experiments shown, such choice does not work well in practice because the queries constitute too short texts to make the standard text-based methods (such as tf-idf) work well, unlike in the case of longer textual documents.

Thus, we propose two query similarity measures adapted to our problem: a fast and "shallow" similarity measure based on comparing strings and "deep" but more computation-demanding "semantic" similarity measure.

3.1 Query Similarity Measure Based on Edit-Distance

The first query similarity measure that we propose is based on string-distance between two queries. After studying the results of extensive experimentation with various string-distance metrics [12,11,10] and their performance on various information-retrieval or extraction tasks on real data, we decided to design and implement a special adaptation of the Levenshtein string-edit distance [7] to our task.

We modified and extended the classic Levenshtein algorithm to better adapt it to query similarity measurement problem and to the specific properties of the Polish language. One of the modifications is to reverse the order of computation (from the end of strings, backwards) in order to allow for arbitrary costs of suffix append operation that is particularly important in Polish. Other features include Polish-diacritic awareness, encoding some typical orthographic errors and treating word separation symbols in a special way so that the cost of splitting or merging two words is significantly higher than other operations. We compute the similarity value as the inverse of the edit-distance.

3.2 Semantic-Based Query-Similarity Measure

An alternative approach to the string-distance-based similarity metrics is taxonomy-based approach. One of the widely used taxonomies is the Wordnet dictionary[3]. Main drawback of Wordnet and alike dictionaries is that they focus on general language, contrary to search engine users' queries, which frequently contain named entities.

Moreover, Wordnet is relatively slowly extended with new entities (i.e. *iPad*). Instead, Wikipedia can be used as an up-to-date source of semantic information.

Wikipedia is less formal than Wordnet, but more intensively updated. In Polish version from January 2011, it contains almost 800K pages, categorised in 75K categories. Categories themselves are organised into a hierarchy[4]. Additional advantage is that Wikipedia contains special disambiguation pages and redirect pages, which can be used to identify semantic similarity between synonymous forms of search queries.

We have adapted semantic similarity measures used to assess similarity between synsets in Wordnet [9] to obtain similarity measures between categories. All of those measures are based on two concepts: *Information Content* (*IC*) and *Most Specific Common Abstraction* (*MSCA*).

In Wordnet, for a given synset s, $IC(s)$ was equal to the number of its hyponyms, i.e. more detailed synsets in the Wordnet taxonomy. In Wikipedia, in place of synsets we used categories and instead of computing just the number of subcategories, we have taken the total number of pages assigned to a given category subgraph. Finally, we have normalised IC to $[0, 1]$ interval. More precisely, for a given Wikipedia category k:

$$IC(k) = 1 - \frac{log(1 + |S(k)|)}{log(1 + WP)}$$

[3] http://wordnet.princeton.edu

[4] http://en.wikipedia.org/wiki/Special:Categories

where WP is the total number of pages in Wikipedia, and $S(k)$ is the set of all pages assigned to a given category or one of its subcategories (direct or indirect). It should be noted that very specific categories have highest IC, while main (root) category has $IC = 1 - log(1 + WP)/log(1 + WP) = 0$.

For the two categories, k_1 and k_2, we can find their generalisation, called a *Most Specific Common Abstraction* (*MSCA*). *MSCA* is the most specific supercategory of both k_1 and k_2. For instance, in case of $Unix$ and $Windows$ categories, *MSCA* is their direct common supercategory: *"operating systems"*. Then value $MSCA$ is calculated as IC for such a common supercategory, i.e. $MSCA(k_1, k_2) = \max\{IC(k) : k \in CA(k_1, k_2)\}$, where $CA(k_1, k_2)$ is the set of all categories subsuming both k_1, k_2.

There exist a number of similarity measures exploiting $MSCA$ and IC concepts in context of Wordnet, e.g. Resnik, Jiang or Lin measures [9]. We have translated all of them to Wikipedia. In our experiments, the most precise appeared to be Pirro-Seco measure, proposed in [9]. Pirro-Seco measure promotes similarity between very specific categories (which carry most of the semantic information):

$$sim_{\text{PirroSeco}}(k_1, k_2) = (1/3) * (2 + (3 * MSCA(k_1, k_2)) - IC(k_1) - IC(k_2))$$

Having defined similarity measure between categories, we have derived another similarity measure, between Wikipedia pages. Every page in Wikipedia is assigned to one or more categories (some pages are not categorised - in this case we have used simple algorithm to assign categories on the basis of categories assigned to the set of pages which are linking to a given page). Similarity measure between Wikipedia pages is then simply defined as the maximal similarity between any pair of the categories of these pages: $sim_{\text{PAGE}}(page_i, page_j) = max\{sim_{\text{PirroSeco}}(k_i, k_j) : page_i \in k_i \wedge page_j \in k_j\}$

Finally, having defined Wikipedia pages similarity, we can define semantic-based similarity between queries. First, we try to map all the terms (i.e. words and phrases) in a given query to a set of Wikipedia pages, which contain given term. For instance, in the query *"robert altman film"*, our algorithm will identify the phrase *"robert altman"* and it will map it to the appropriate Wikipedia page. Then a single word *"film"* will be maped to a set of Wikpedia pages which has this word in their title. Order of words is ignored as long as they are adjacent (i.e. *"altman robert"* will be treated exactly the same way as the *"robert altman"* phrase, while *"altman film robert"* will not be identifed as a phrase).

Obviously, such a mapping of query terms to Wikipedia pages will often be ambiguous. I.e. some terms are mapped to an empty set of pages, some are mapped to exactly one page (unambiguous mapping), and other terms are mapped to multiple pages. The latter case is disambiguated. From a set of mapped Wikipedia pages, we choose exactly one page – the one which maximises similarity with all other mappings. After disambiguation step, each term identified in the query is mapped to exactly one Wikipedia page. For example, in case of *"altman film"* query, the ambiguous word *"altman"* will be disambiguated to Wikipedia page *"Robert Altman"*, and the word *"film"* will be disambiguated to the page *"MASH" (film)*.

At this stage, the query is assigned with a small set of Wikipedia pages, one for each term. Each of the pages is assigned to a set of categories. We aggregate these mappings to obtain query categorisation. Each query term (a word or a phrase) has weight equal to its *idf* (inverse document frequency) in all Wikipedia pages: $idf(t) = log(WP/df(t))$, where WP is the total number of Wikipedia pages and $df(t)$ is the number of pages which contain term t. This weight is divided among categories of the Wikipedia page assigned to this term and is treated as a "weighted vote" for this category. Finally, votes from all terms in the query are summed up and we obtain weighted ranking of categories for a given query. For instance, in case of *"altman film"* query, most voted category would be *"M*A*S*H"*, followed by numerous cinematography-related categories.

Given two queries, q_i and q_j, each query is categorised with the above-described algorithm, which produces two rankings. Semantic similarity between the two queries is calculated as weighted aggregation of those rankings. We decided not to use correlation or cosine measure here, since categories in this ranking are tightly interrelated, i.e. in that case we would disregard information that *"Adaptations"* and *"Adaptations by authors"* are semantically very similar, however they are not exactly the same categories. Precisely speaking, our semantic similarity measure is defined as:

$$sim_{\text{QUERY}}(q_i, q_j) = avg\{w_i \cdot w_j \cdot sim_{\text{PirroSeco}}(k_i, k_j) : q_i \in k_i \wedge q_j \in k_j\}$$

where avg is the weighted average, k_i and k_j and categories in rankings related to queries q_i and q_j, respectively, and w_i and w_j are weights (sums of votes) assigned to the categories k_i and k_j.

3.3 Experimental Results

We have implemented and integrated the algorithms for query suggestion and diversification presented in this paper. This section demonstrates some selected results obtained by this prototype implementation on the real dataset described in section 2.1.

In all experiments the base set R of candidate suggestions was obtained by the suffix-based algorithm described in section 2.3. We considered maximum of 100 candidate suggestions. Next, the suggestions were diversified with the MMR-based diversification algorithm presented in section 3. We experimented with various settings of the diversification parameter λ: $1, 0.875, 0.65, 0.5, 0.375, 0.25, 0.125$ and various combinations of similarity functions sim_1 and sim_2 used by the algorithm. More precisely, we considered the following similarity functions: (L): Levenshtein edit-distance-based similarity function adapted for Polish queries, as described in section 3.1 , (S): semantic-based similarity function described in section 3.2 and additionally (O): occurrence-frequency-based relevance function (only used as sim_1 in some settings of the MMR diversification algorithm) as $1 - 1/v$ (where v is described in section 2.3). We tested the following combinations of similarity function pairs (sim_1,sim_2): (O,L), (O,S), (L,L), (L,S), (S,S), (S,L).

Figure 3 demonstrates the performance of our system for the query "windows" for the (O,L) and (O,S) settings (only suffixes of the suggestions are shown to save space, i.e. "7 download" on the figure corresponds to "windows 7 download", for example). In general, while the platform can be still considered as a prototype and our experimental work is ongoing, the preliminary results are interesting and seem to have significant potential of improving user experience since the novel aspects of queries are brought

Suggested suffixes for query "windows"						
(O,L) (sim_1 =occurrence (log-based frequency), sim_2 = **Levenshtein**-based similarity):						
	lambda: 1.0		lambda: 0.5		lambda: 0.125	
nr	query suggestion:	MMR	query suggestion:	MMR	query suggestion:	MMR
1	**7** download	0.8824	**7** download	0.4412	**7** download	0.1103
2	7	0.833	7	0.4103	7	0.0933
3	7 opinie	0.8	**media player**	0.3901	**media player**	0.0889
4	**media player**	0.7917	7 opinie	0.3898	7 opinie	0.0821
5	**xp** download	0.75	7 aktywator	0.3679	7 aktywator	0.0813
6	7 aktywator	0.75	**xp** download	0.35	**vista** zmiana języka	0.0561
7	media player 10	0.6667	media player 10	0.3095	**movie maker** download	0.0545
8	7 pl	0.6	7 pl	0.2762	**live** messenger	0.0538
9	7 dla studentów	0.5	**vista** zmiana języka	0.2463	**xp** zmiana klucza	0.0538
10	xp zmiana klucza	0.5	**movie maker** download	0.2455	7 dla studentów	0.0533
(O,S) (sim_1 = occurrence (log-based frequency), sim_2 = **semantic**-based similarity):						
	lambda: 1.0		lambda: 0.5		lambda: 0.125	
nr	query suggestion:	MMR	query suggestion:	MMR	query suggestion:	MMR
1	**7** download	0.8824	**7** download	0.4412	**7** download	0.1103
2	7	0.833	7	0.4165	7	0.1041
3	7 opinie	0.8	7 opinie	0.4	7 opinie	0.1
4	**media player**	0.7917	**media player**	0.3958	**media player**	0.099
5	**xp** download	0.75	**xp** download	0.375	**xp** download	0.0938
6	7 aktywator	0.75	xp zmiana klucza	0.25	xp zmiana klucza	0.0625
7	media player 10	0.6667	**vista** zmiana języka	0.25	**vista** zmiana języka	0.0625
8	7 pl	0.6	7 porównanie	0.1667	7 porównanie	0.0417
9	7 dla studentów	0.5	7 starter	0.1667	7 starter	0.0417
10	xp zmiana klucza	0.5	7 aktywator	0.0547	**download** peb.pl	0.0
11	media connect	0.5	**98** pobierz	0.015	**jar 128x160 chomikuj**	0.0

Fig. 3. Suggestions for the query "windows". The left-most column shows non-diversified results ($\lambda = 1.0$) returned by the suffix-based algorithm. Next columns demonstrate increasing levels of diversification with the MMR-based algorithm. The query "windows" has multiple aspects, for example: "windows 7", "windows media player", "windows xp", etc. Each highest occurrence of a new aspect on the list is in bold. One can observe increasing number of new aspects brought to the top results as the value of lambda decreases (i.e. the diversification level increases).

into the top suggestions as the level of diversification increases (i.e. the value of the λ parameter decreases). The results obtained for the (O,L) similarity pair seem to be especially promising, see figure 3, upper part, for an example.

Concerning the semantic-based similarity measure, we believe that it has even more potential than the simple Levensthein-based one. However, at the current stage of the development our implementation cannot compute semantic similarity for some pairs of queries (we temporarily fill these missing values with 0) that significantly deteriorates the performance (figure 3, bottom part). Part of our ongoing work focuses on improving this. Besides this, the semantic-based function produces quite good results too.

Suggested suffixes for query "zamek"						
sim_1 and sim_2: **string-distance**-based similarity measure:						
	lambda: 1.0		lambda: 0.5		lambda: 0.125	
1	**czocha**	0.02	**czocha**	0.01	**czocha**	0.0025
2	drakuli	0.0175	drakuli	0.0013	**ryglowy podwójny**	-0.0038
3	w kręgu	0.0175	w kręgu	0.0013	królewski **wynajęcie sali**	-0.004
4	**noclegi**	0.0175	**ze szkła**	0.0007	królów pruskich wrocław	-0.0041
5	**ze szkła**	0.0156	długa 24	0.0003	w dąbrówce starzeńskiej	-0.0041
6	długa 24	0.0156	książąt legnickich	0.0003	siedlisko wizualizacje	-0.0043
7	w tucznie	0.0141	**patentowy do szafki**	0.0001	obronny zdjęcia malbork	-0.0043
8	w meissen	0.0141	**ryglowy podwójny**	0.0001	kamieniec ząbkowicki	-0.0047
9	**hakowy mcm**	0.0128	obronny zdjęcia malbork	0.0001	w malborku prezentacje	-0.0048
10	w będzinie	0.0128	skibo zdjecia	0.0001	trzy ośmiokątne wieże	-0.0049
11	w krokowej	0.0128	**film** kafka chomikuj	0	**patentowy do szafki**	-0.0049
12	w ujeździe	0.0128	**hakowy mcm**	0	w sorkwitach zdjęcia	-0.005

Fig. 4. Diversified query suggestions for ambiguous Polish query "zamek". English translations of its interpretations include: "castle" (most of the suggestions in the table concern particular historical castles in Poland), "lock" ("patentowy", "ryglowy" in the table). "zamek ze szkła" is the title of a song, "noclegi" means "accommodation" and "wynajęcie" means "hiring".

Figure 4 presents results for the ambiguous query "zamek" with the modified Levenshtein string similarity function applied both as sim_1 and sim_2 ((L,L) setting). Surprisingly, the simple edit-distance performs quite well in this example (and a few other examples that we studied).

Finally, we did a preliminary mini-evaluation experiment of our system as follows. First, by manually inspecting the query logs, we have selected 6 queries that have multiple interpretations ("zamek", "komórka","program") or multiple aspects ("windows", "radio", "money".) in Polish. Next, for any combination of three different similarity function settings ((O,L),(L,L) and (O,S)) and query we generated two lists of suffix-based suggestions: undiversified (equivalently: $\lambda = 1$) and diversified (with very low value of $\lambda = 0.125$). Subsequently, we manually inspected how many new aspects or interpretations of the query were brought into the top-k suggestions (for four different levels of $k = 3, 5, 10, 15$) by the diversifier compared with the undiversified list. The results of this experiment are presented on figure 5.

This preliminary evaluation on a controlled small set of queries clearly shows that there is a potential in all the studied settings as in most cases novel aspects or interpretations are introduced into the top suggestions. On the other hand, one can see that there is still much room for improvement (many non-positive numbers in the table) by tuning the parameters and modifying the suggestion or diversification algorithms.

Due to limitations of this paper, we postpone fuller demonstration of the results and extensive experimental evaluation for future work.

(sim_1,sim_2)=(O,L)					(sim_1,sim_2)=(L,L)					(sim_1,sim_2)=(O,S)				
	new aspects in top k					new aspects in top k					new aspects in top k			
query↓	k=3	k=5	k=10	k=15	query↓	k=3	k=5	k=10	k=15	query↓	k=3	k=5	k=10	k=15
komórka	-1	-1	0	0	komórka	0	0	0	0	komórka	0	0	0	
money	-1	0	3	4	money	1	2	3	2	money	0	0	0	0
program	1	-1	2	1	program	1	2	3	4	program	1	1	1	1
radio	0	0	1	0	radio	0	0	-2	-2	radio	0	0	0	-2
windows	1	-1	3	2	windows	2	2	3	5	windows	0	0	2	3
zamek	0	1	0	-2	zamek	0	0	-1	1	zamek	0	0	1	0
total:	0	-2	9	5		4	6	6	10		1	1	4	2

Fig. 5. Counts of novel aspects or interpretations of queries brought by the diversifier into the top-k suggestions for a selected set of evaluated queries. Negative number means that the number of different aspects/interpretations actually dropped compared to the undiversified list.

4 Conclusions and Further Work

We have presented novel approaches to improve user experience in search engines by means of automatic, log-based query suggestion, in particular, *diversified* query suggestion that can be used as a substitute for search personalisation in the absence of user personal profile data. The demonstrated preliminary experimental results of a prototype implementation of our system that are based on real query logs are quite promising.

One of the most important next steps is to design and conduct systematic experimental evaluation, including user evaluation experiments in order to objectively assess the proposed approaches. Another thing would be to design some performance comparison experiments with some existing query-suggestion systems, although the authors are not aware of publicly available competitors for Polish. To some extent, the results can be compared with those observable on user interfaces of commercial search engines.

If larger datasets are available, it would be interesting to repeat experiments with the time-succession method. The same concerns the datasets in other languages than Polish. There exist some publicly available query logs in English (e.g. KDDCup2005), but they usually lack time, user or even the frequency counts that is crucial to our approach.

Since the time-succession query suggestion algorithm (section 2.2) is generally capable of automatically detecting time search patterns that are very hard to detect by other techniques (such as string or semantic similarity), provided that dataset contains an appropriate case, it may be desired to experiment with a hybrid approach, so that only if time-succession algorithm has no sufficient evidence in the data, another, less data-demanding algorithm (such as the suffix-based one) is applied. This, cascade-style approach can be used with more than two algorithms, of course, or another way of aggregation of suggestions from various algorithms can be used.

A natural extension of the approach described in section 3.2 is the categorisation of the query search results, not the queries themselves. Documents (or snippets) retrieved as a search result bring much more textual content than queries, thus their categorisation (as well as the disambiguation of ambiguous terms) is more precise. Obviously, better categorisation should lead to high-quality semantic similarity identification. We plan to tackle this issue in our further research.

Acknowledgements. The research is supported by POIG.01.01.02-14-013/09 grant at the Institute of Computer Sciences, Polish Academy of Sciences, aiming at building NEKST, an experimental, semantically enhanced web search engine particularly adapted for Polish language.The first author is also supported by the N N516 481940 grant of Polish Ministry of Science and Higher Education. The third author is supported by IEFRR and EU in the MPD programme.

References

1. Agrawal, R., Gollapudi, S., Halverson, A., Ieong, S.: Diversifying search results. In: WSDM, pp. 5–14 (2009)
2. Anand, S.S., Mobasher, B.: Intelligent Techniques for Web Personalization. In: Mobasher, B., Anand, S.S. (eds.) ITWP 2003. LNCS (LNAI), vol. 3169, pp. 1–36. Springer, Heidelberg (2005)
3. Carbonell, J., Goldstein, J.: The use of mmr, diversity-based reranking for reordering documents and producing summaries. In: SIGIR 1998: Proceedings of the 21st Annual International ACM SIGIR Conference on Research and Development in Information Retrieval, pp. 335–336. ACM, New York (1998)
4. Clarke, C.L.A., Kolla, M., Cormack, G.V., Vechtomova, O., Ashkan, A., Büttcher, S., MacKinnon, I.: Novelty and diversity in information retrieval evaluation. In: SIGIR, pp. 659–666 (2008)
5. Paul, C., et al.: Multiple approaches to analysing query diversity. In: Proceedings of the 32nd Annual International ACM SIGIR Conference on Research and Development in Information Retrieval, pp. 734–735. ACM (2009)
6. Goffman, W.: A searching procedure for information retrieval. Information Storage and Retrieval 2(2), 73–78 (1964)
7. Levenshtein, V.: Binary Codes for Correcting Deletions, Insertions, and Reversals. Doklady Akademii Nauk SSSR 163(4), 845–848 (1965)
8. Liu, F., Yu, C., Meng, W.: Personalized web search for improving retrieval effectiveness. IEEE Transactions on Knowledge and Data Engineering 16, 28–40 (2004)
9. Pirrò, G., Seco, N.: Design, implementation and evaluation of a new semantic similarity metric combining features and intrinsic information content. In: Chung, S. (ed.) OTM 2008, Part II. LNCS, vol. 5332, pp. 1271–1288. Springer, Heidelberg (2008)
10. Piskorski, J., Sydow, M.: String Distance Metrics for Reference Matching and Search Query Correction. In: Abramowicz, W. (ed.) BIS 2007. LNCS, vol. 4439, pp. 353–365. Springer, Heidelberg (2007), doi:10.1007/978-3-540-72035-5-27
11. Piskorski, J., Sydow, M., Wieloch, K.: Comparison of string distance metrics for lemmatisation of named entities in polish. pp. 413–427 (2009)
12. Piskorski, J., Wieloch, K., Sydow, M.: On knowledge-poor methods for person name matching and lemmatization for highly inflectional languages. Information Retrieval 12(3), 275–299 (2009)
13. Radlinski, F., Dumais, S.: Improving personalized web search using result diversification. In: Proc. of the 29th Annual International ACM SIGIR Conf. on Research and Development in Information Retrieval, pp. 691–692. ACM, NY (2006)
14. Santos, R.L.T., Macdonald, C., Ounis, I.: Exploiting query reformulations for web search result diversification. In: Proceedings of the 19th International Conference on World Wide Web, WWW 2010, pp. 881–890. ACM, New York (2010)

Wikipedia-Based Document Categorization

Krzysztof Ciesielski, Piotr Borkowski,
Mieczysław A. Kłopotek, Krzysztof Trojanowski, and Kamil Wysocki

Institute of Computer Science, Polish Academy of Sciences,
ul. Ordona 21, 01-237 Warszawa, Poland
{kciesiel,piotrb,klopotek,trojanow}@ipipan.waw.pl

Abstract. A novel method of text categorization for Polish language documents, based on Polish Wikipedia resources is presented. The distinctive feature of the approach is that document labelling can be performed with no additional categorized corpora. Experiments with two different types of document semantic disambiguation have been performed, and evaluated according to the several quality metrics.

1 Introduction

Nowadays growing interest in an automated text document categorization can be observed. There appear multiple practical applications, primarily for assisting in text retrieval tasks, e.g. via expanding queries with new terms (from hierarchical categories), expanding and/or improving ontologies, but also applications of query reformulation, query answering, e-mail and memo organization as well as web page classification and many others. The text document categorization should be understood as an assignment of one or more labels (categories) to a single document, possibly in the context of other documents. The task of the text document categorization may be approached either as a special case of a text classification or as a clustering task. However, the text document categorization requires methodologies on its own because the vocabulary of labels to be used is quite large in most cases.

Typical text categorization methods require an extensive well-structured taxonomy along with a large corpus of categorized texts. Wikipedia ($\mathfrak{W}$) appears to be one such candidate and, what is more, it has already been used in this role successfully for the English language documents. To our best knowledge, Polish version of $\mathfrak{W}$ has not been used for the extensive text categorization yet. There is a couple of good reasons for it: Polish language is characterized with strong flexion, hence for, e.g., the text matching or the phrase identification almost all the words and phrases have to be reformulated. In our method, the categorization is performed just on the graph structure of $\mathfrak{W}$, and beside the titles of $\mathfrak{W}$ pages, no other text content is used, therefore, we can avoid most of the text-related quality problems.

In Section 2 we review previous work. Then we explain our approach to measure $\mathfrak{W}$ page similarity (Section 3), to the document content mapping on $\mathfrak{W}$ structure (Section 4) and to the mapping disambiguation (Section 5). The proposed method of text document categorization is presented in Section 6. In

P. Bouvry et al. (Eds.): SIIS 2011, LNCS 7053, pp. 265–278, 2012.

Section 7 we demonstrate the experimental results of the proposed categorization methods. Section 8 concludes and points at some future research issues.

2 Related Work

In the past, a number of approaches to the document categorization have been proposed. Many of them were based on some kind of clustering mainly. Let us just mention "nonnegative matrix factorization (NMF)", latent semantic analysis (LSA), probabilistic LSA (PLSA), finite mixture of multidimensional Bernoulli distributions and similar, described in an overview [7].

Another branch of the research concentrates around mapping of document contents to some semantic resources, in particular the English language $\mathfrak{W}$. This was used, for example, in *WikipediaMiner Project*[1], developed at the University of Waikato in Hamilton, New Zealand [2,4,5]. Authors of the project proposed a method of keyphrase indexing, which maps document phrases onto related terms of a controlled vocabulary, that is, $\mathfrak{W}$. The method consists of two stages. The former selects a set of possible indexing terms whereas the latter evaluates candidate terms and selects most appropriate ones.

For any term or phrase selected as a keyword candidate (that is, a term or phrase which appears in the anchor test in any $\mathfrak{W}$ entry) the so-called keyphraseness [3] is assigned. Keyphraseness estimates the probability of the term being a link, that is, this is a fraction of the number of $\mathfrak{W}$ articles in which this term appears as a link to the total number of documents in $\mathfrak{W}$ containing it. In case of an ambiguous term (that is, being assigned to multiple $\mathfrak{W}$ pages), the $\mathfrak{W}$ page which is the most similar to the document context represents the term sense.

In the second stage potential "outliers" are selected and eliminated. First, for each of the terms semantic and statistic features are calculated. Then classification algorithm is applied to evaluate final ranking of the terms – see [2] and [5]. The outlier selection is performed based on the results of this ranking. Another approach can be found in [1] where a local random walk PageRank computation is used to point the terms related to the document with the highest probability.

Our work differs from the WikipediaMiner approach in that (1) we use Polish Wikipedia, (2) we do not train any classifiers which means that no additional manually classified texts are needed, and (3) for calculations of the similarity we do not use the structure of links between $\mathfrak{W}$ pages, but instead we apply taxonomic measures fashioned after Wordnet [6], that makes the method more robust and immune to overfluous links.

3 Taxonomy-Based $\mathfrak{W}$ Pages Similarity Measures

3.1 Preparing and Cleansing $\mathfrak{W}$ Graphs

$\mathfrak{W}$ graph consists of two subgraphs: the page graph and the category graph. In this study, we use the Polish $\mathfrak{W}$ graph of January 2011. It consists of 730,180

[1] `http://wikipedia-miner.sourceforge.net/`

pages interconnected with over 30,000,000 hyperlinks. The number of hyperlinks (ca.40 per page on average) is quite high in comparison with many other graphs (e.g. Web graph or social network graphs). It is characteristic for 𝔚 that some links are inserted between semantically weakly related pages.

The frequency information is used to differentiate significance of words and phrases via computation of *inverse document frequency* for the measure *tfidf* (*term frequency inverse document frequency*). As Polish is featured by strong inflection, page content and titles are lemmatized using a Polish lemmatiser Morfologik[2].

In 𝔚 categories also form a connected, (nearly) acyclic graph which consists of 76,154 nodes and 133,774 edges, with a single root, the category *Kategoria*. Categories are linked by relations more general/more specific (in analogy to hyperonymy/hyponymy relations encountered e.g. in Wordnet). The category graph is not a tree; hence a category can have multiple direct hyper-categories and there exist multiple paths from a given category to the graph root. We had to restore graph acyclicity by removing several cycles of length over 1 and nearly 1000 cycles of length one.

𝔚 pages are assigned with categories, what provides the connection between the graph of pages and the graph of categories (taxonomy). One page can be assigned to one or more categories. The total number of page-to-category links is 1,813,498 (on average 2.48 category per page). Regrettably some pages are not assigned to any category.

In our experiments we use the XML-formatted 𝔚 *dumps*[3] as our data source (texts and graphs). The data are loaded to a database and cleaned, that is, the acyclicity of the graph is carefully analyzed and restored where necessary (for example, contradictory links are removed manually).

Cleaning the page graph means also the page title lemmatization and adding 42,356 disambiguation pages as separate graph nodes as well as adding their titles as additional titles of disambiguated pages (after removing disambiguation word from the title). The disambiguated pages are supplemented with a word or phrase expressing the context of a given meaning. Such context phrases represent additional titles, e.g., for a page with the title "Fedora (kapelusz)", we add titles: "Fedora", "Fedora kapelusz" and "kapelusz Fedora", but not just "kapelusz" alone ("hat" in English). Every such a phrase is stored in a dictionary of phrases and used later on during indexing of document content.

Regrettably, disambiguation pages contain also links to pages that do not help in the disambiguation of the main meaning. For example, the page "Olimpiada (ujednoznacznienie)" (Olympiad disambiguation) contains the diverse meanings of the word "olimpiada", but also there is a link to the page "Kalendarz grecki" ("Greek calendar"). Currently we use a simple rule to reject such links: target pages sharing no word with the disambiguation page title are omitted.

In the last phase we process (and lemmatize) the 𝔚 text, and calculate frequencies of words and phrases in such a textual corpus. Anchor texts are extracted and added as additional titles to graph nodes.

[2] `http://sourceforge.net/projects/morfologik`

[3] `http://download.wikimedia.org/plwiki`

We remove superfluous link via a heuristic method which finds nodes in the page graph with the number of ingoing links exceeding a threshold (currently 1,000). For each neighbor of such a page we compute a *categorical similarity* (see Section 3.2) of both of them. If the similarity is less than a threshold (0.5), we remove this link. Using this method we selected over 7,000,000 links to remove (that is almost 20% of all links).

The categorical similarity threshold of 0.5 was chosen based on the analysis of similarity of linked and unlinked pages, depicted in Fig. 1. In this figure the horizontal axis presents the categorical similarity value (more precisely, PIRRO-SECO measure, see Eq. (2) in Section 3.2), and the vertical axis is the frequency of occurring of such a similarity. We can clearly see that links carry some semantic information: in the category graph, linked pages lie more closely to one another than unlinked pages.

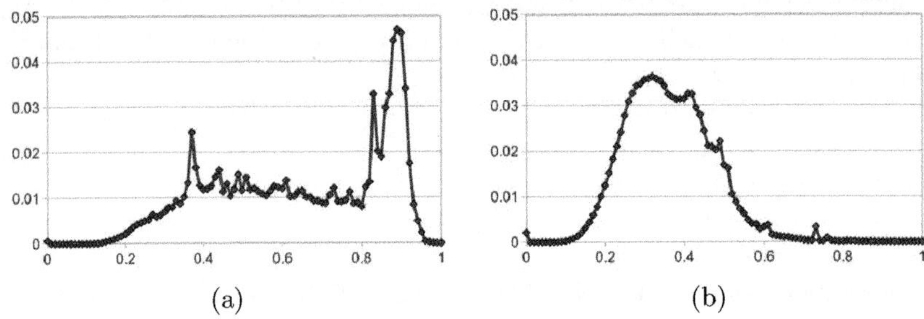

Fig. 1. Semantic link locality in 𝔚𝔚. Category-based similarity of pages (a) connected by a link (b) not connected by a link.

3.2 Similarity Measures of 𝔚𝔚 Categories and Pages

While elaborating a categorical similarity measure for Polish 𝔚𝔚, we followed the experience of authors dealing with Wordnet, described in [6]. These measures exploit two basic concepts: *IC* (*Information Content*) and *MSCA* (*Most Specific Common Abstraction*).

To accommodate these measures to the particular form of 𝔚𝔚, a slight modification, taking into account the number of pages belonging to a category, is proposed here. We define *IC* as follows[4]: $IC(k) = 1 - log\,(1 + s_k)\,/log\,(1 + N)$, where s_k is the number of 𝔚𝔚 pages in the category k and all its subcategories, and the N is the total number of pages in 𝔚𝔚. So the highest values of *IC* are assigned to the categories without any subcategory and with only few pages belonging to. The main category has the value of $IC = 1 - log(1 + N)/log(1 + N) = 0$.

For the given two categories, k_1 and k_2, the $MSCA(k_1, k_2)$ value is equal to $\max\{IC(k) : k \in CA\}$, where CA is the set of super-categories for both

[4] Pirro and Seco proposed formally identical formula, but they considered s_k as the number of hyponyms of a given synset in Wordnet, and N as the total number of synsets.

categories k_1, and k_2. The properties of $IC(k)$ measure ensure that the category chosen is most specific amongst the common super-categories.

In the literature dealing with Wordnet, a number of interesting measures, based on IC and $MSCA$ have been elaborated [6]. Let just mention:

$$sim_{\text{CATEG}_{\text{Lin}}}(k_1, k_2) = \frac{2 \cdot MSCA(k_1, k_2)}{IC(k_1) + IC(k_2)} \tag{1}$$

$$sim_{\text{CATEG}_{\text{PirroSeco}}}(k_1, k_2) = (2 + 3 \cdot MSCA(k_1, k_2) - IC(k_1) - IC(k_2)) \,/\, 3 \tag{2}$$

Characteristic feature of the PIRRO-SECO measure (Eq. (2)) is that its maximum value is not always equal 1 (i.e., $sim_{\text{PirroSeco}}(k, k) = (2 + IC(k)) \,/\, 3)$. The main advantage of $sim_{\text{PirroSeco}}$ lies in its sensitivity to IC, so that similarity between more specific categories is promoted.

To measure similarity between two $\mathfrak{W}$ pages p_i and p_j the similarities between their categories are aggregated using MAX aggregation method (we have also experimented with other types of aggregation, which – contrary to our expectations – led to worse results than simple MAX aggregation):

$$sim_{\text{PAGE}}(p_i, p_j) = max\{sim_{\text{CATEGORY}}(k_i, k_j) : p_i \in k_i \wedge p_j \in k_j\} \tag{3}$$

4 Document Mapping to Semantically Related $\mathfrak{W}$ Pages

The next component of our document categorization algorithm is the method of mapping document content terms (words and phrases) to vertices of $\mathfrak{W}$ graph (i.e. $\mathfrak{W}$ pages). The basic outline of the algorithm, mapping a text T of a query or a document into a list of $\mathfrak{W}$ pages is as follows:

1. The text T is split into a set of words W,
2. $\mathcal{P}(W)$ (see below) is applied to get the set S of $\mathfrak{W}$ pages p containing in the title at least one of the words from W,
3. to each page $p \in S$, the largest set $W_p \subset W$ is assigned, such that all the words from this set are contained in the title of p and, for a document, occur within a window of n words (in this way we approximately identify phrases in the original text T, up to various variants).

The above mentioned algorithm makes use of a function $\mathcal{P}$ which relates words to their sets of $\mathfrak{W}$ pages. The domain of $\mathcal{P}$ is a set of words occurring in a title, redirection or disambiguating page or in any anchor text of any $\mathfrak{W}$ page. To each of the words from the domain the function $\mathcal{P}$ assigns the set of $\mathfrak{W}$ pages containing this word in its title.

Words and phrases (terms) t from $\{W_p; p \in S\} \subset W$ are assigned with weights. Those t for which no corresponding $\mathfrak{W}$ page was found have the weight of 0. For the remaining ones weights are combinations of the following factors:

- tf (term frequency) within the text T,
- $idf = log(N/df(t))$, where N is the number of $\mathfrak{W}$ pages, $df(t)$ is the number of occurrences of the term t in the content of the whole $\mathfrak{W}$,

– the total number of links pointing to pages from the set $\mathcal{P}(t)$ within $\mathfrak{W}$ (an approximation of popularity of the term in page titles),
– indicator of term *keyphraseness*, proposed in the WikipediaMiner project [3].

5 $\mathfrak{W}$-Based Disambiguation

To reduce the number of pages assigned to a single term (word or phrase) by the algorithm described in the previous section, a document/query mapping disambiguation algorithm has been designed.

Two separate cases are distinguished:

1. one or more terms in the document (or search query) have been mapped to exactly one $\mathfrak{W}$ page (unambiguous assignment),
2. all terms suffer from ambiguous mappings.

The second case is beyond the scope of this paper because it very rarely occurs for full-text documents. But it is quite frequent for too general (or ambiguous) user queries.

5.1 Case with Some Unambiguous Terms

This case means that a document or query contains terms that have a unique interpretation (one $\mathfrak{W}$ page). As this is more probable for words than for phrases, unique phrases are rewarded at the expense of single words.

The algorithm proceeds as follows:

1. we divide the terms into unambiguous (with one-element lists of $\mathfrak{W}$ pages) and ambiguous ones. For each ambiguous term we try to select the page best reflecting its meaning.
2. for each $\mathfrak{W}$ page and for each category of this page we assign the fraction of IC of that category (see Section 3.2) to the sum of ICs of all categories of the page. This shall prevent advantage of pages with multiple categories.
3. for each query/document term its weight is computed ($tfidf$, where tf part results from the document, and *idf* refers to the whole Polish $\mathfrak{W}$.)
4. weights are normalized separately for words and multi-word phrases by the highest ranking word/phrase (so both a word and a phrase with highest $tfidf$ has weight 1).
5. For each term from the set of ambiguous terms we proceed as follows:
   - for each of the pages assigned to this term, we calculate the categorical similarity of the page to all the pages assigned unambiguously to some other term in the text.
   - an average of similarities – weighted by term weights – (see Section 3.2) is calculated, and – among the pages assigned to the ambiguous term – the page which maximizes weighted average similarity is selected as the disambiguated mapping for the given term.

6 𝔚-Based Document Categorization

The document categorization algorithm starts with mapping words and phrases found in the text of the document onto lists of 𝔚 pages (see Section 4). Thereafter *tfidf* weights of all found terms (words and phrases) are computed, with *idf* factor being computed in the corps of whole Polish 𝔚. Too rare terms (occurring on less than 5 pages) or too frequent (occurring on more than 50000 𝔚 pages) are dismissed in subsequent steps of the algorithm. The remaining weights are normalized as described in Section 5, separately for words and for phrases, to increase the impact of latter ones, as they carry more precise semantic information than single words.

The second step of the algorithm consists in disambiguation of the lists of pages obtained in the above-described step (see Section 5), in order to obtain unambiguous mapping: one 𝔚 page per term.

At this stage each term is assigned with a vector of categories. The vectors differ in length as the pages may be assigned to the different number of categories. To avoid unnecessary impact of the vector length, the vector of categories is normalized for each term, so that the sum of weights assigned to the categories is equal to *tfidf* value for the associated term (cf. Section 5).

Thus, the impact of each term is proportional to its normalized *tfidf* weight. We compute the category vector for the document by summing up the vectors for the individual terms, weighting the summands by the respective weight (i.e., we do weighted category voting).

We did tests with *two variants of category label assignment* to documents.

1. **Highest Weights:** we take the K categories with the highest weights; we ignore the similarity between the categories occurring on the ranked list which is the main drawback of this method;
2. **SPA approach:** we apply one-step of the **Spreading Activation (SPA)** algorithm on 𝔚 category graph[5] to cluster similar categories; this solution tends to provide with more general labels at the expense of the more detailed ones.

Note that through the application of the SPA algorithm a kind of diversification of the results can be achieved (that is, the results are presented to the user with differing semantic categories to choose from). We will discuss the impact of this diversification on the resulting categorization in the next section.

7 Experimental Results

7.1 Benchmark Dataset

Our test-bed based on the DMOZ[6] taxonomy consists of 2805 text files. Each of them includes complete text from a single Polish language web page containing

[5] For the details, cf. `http://en.wikipedia.org/wiki/Spreading_activation`

[6] Open Directory Project `http://www.dmoz.org`

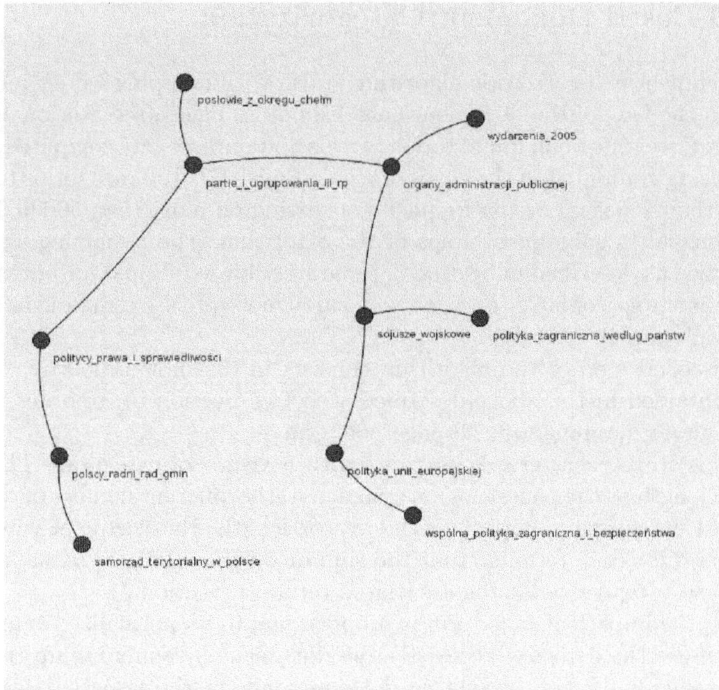

Fig. 2. Political essay: an example of the spanning tree on the similarity graph of predicted categories

at least 1000 characters just with html tags removed but without any additional text preprocessing. The files are divided into 34 categories having their representation in $\mathfrak{W}$ (and in the DMOZ taxonomy as well, cf. Table 3 below). For the detailed description and the benchmark documents saved in CSV format the Reader is referred to the benchmark web page[7].

7.2 Categorization Efficiency Measures

Because of the taxonomical properties of the category graph, neither classical ("flat") classification efficiency measures, nor hierarchy-based classification measures are not directly applicable to the document categorization evaluation. Therefore two new measures have been proposed, generalizing the concepts of *precision* and *recall*. We consider the set of categories predicted by our algorithm and the real ones (that is, categories assigned by a human editor).

For each real category k_i we compute $sim'(k_i) = \max\{sim(k_i, k_{pred}) : k_{pred}\}$, (similarity to the most similar predicted category). Then we average over all real categories to obtain a *generalized precision* saying how close on average a real category matches its best predicted counterpart.

[7] `http://www.ipipan.waw.pl/~kciesiel/iis/DMOZ_PL_dataset.html`

The *generalized recall measure* is obtained by inverting the roles of real and predicted categories. Note that both measures are parameterized with a chosen *similarity measure*. We will discuss some choices in the next section.

Let us show an example. Weights indicate the relative importance of a category, the LIN measure is taken as the similarity measure in precision-recall calculations. The real categories of the 𝔚 page *Organizacja Ukraińskich Nacjonalistów na Ukrainie (Organization of Ukrainian Nationalists in Ukraine)* are: ukraińskie partie polityczne (political parties in Ukraine), nacjonalizm ukraiński po 1991 (ukrainian nationalism after 1991), partie nacjonalistyczne (nationalist parties). Predicted categories are: ukraińscy działacze społeczni (Ukrainian activists; weight: 2), ludzie związani ze Lwowem (people from Lviv; weight: 2), pochowani na Cmentarzu Łyczakowskim we Lwowie (buried in Lychakiv Cemetery; weight: 2), ukraińscy politycy (Ukrainian politicians; weight: 2). Generalized precision in this case is 0.56 and recall – 0.61.

7.3 Methods, Results and Discussion

In our experiments, we compared two term disambiguation methods (cf. Section 5): the first one based on the LIN (eq. (1)) similarity measure and the second one based on the PIRRO-SECO (denoted further as *P-S*) (eq. (2)) similarity measure, both described in Section 3. We have investigated two methods of the final category selection, based on Highest Weights (denoted *No SPA* below) and SPA, both described in Section 6. We have also varied the number of predicted categories, what is denoted with #1 (we predict just a single category) and #3 (3 categories are predicted).

Below we present results of the DMOZ dataset categorization. Tables 1, 2 show generalized precision and recall values averaged respectively over 34 DMOZ categories, listed as shown in Table 3. Pages within each category have been split according to their length, i.e., the number of characters in textual content. *Short* pages have less than 2000 characters, *medium* length pages have at least 2000 characters but less than 10000 characters, and *long* pages have at least 10000 characters. The columns are labeled with type of similarity measure used in the generalized precision/recall calculations (cf. Section 7.2) and with the appropriate page length group.

Generalized precision and recall have been computed in three variants, with the following similarity measures (cf. definitions in Section 7.2):

- the **SHORTEST-PATH** measure, equal to $1/2^{SP}$, where SP is the length of the shortest path in the 𝔚 category graph between DMOZ/𝔚 category node and the node of the category predicted by the proposed algorithm;
- the **SUBCATEGORY** measure, similar to the previous one, but equal to 1 if predicted category is a subcategory of a real DMOZ category, and 0 otherwise. Motivation for this measure is given below;
- the **LIN** similarity measure, from Eq. (1) see Section 3.

The rows are labeled with the type of categorization algorithm used: the final categorization algorithm, the similarity measure used in the disambiguation and the number of predicted categories. Thus, e.g., a row with *P-S NoSPA*

#3 means that PIRRO-SECO measure was used for disambiguation, Highest Weights method for final category selection and three categories have been predicted. *P-S SPA #3* on the other hand means that one-step Spreading Activation has been applied to the results from the previous (that is, NoSPA) experiment.

Table 1. Average values of generalized Precision measure

		LIN			SHORTESTPATH			SUBCATEGORY		
Experiment type	Disambig. measure	short	medium	long	short	medium	long	short	medium	long
SPA#3	*LIN*	0.367	0.437	0.459	0.392	0.435	0.461	0.448	0.723	0.623
	$P-S$	0.388	0.456	0.487	0.416	0.443	0.489	0.441	0.723	0.646
NoSPA#3	*LIN*	0.254	0.359	0.34	0.299	0.359	0.375	0.538	0.716	0.723
	$P-S$	0.271	0.36	0.344	0.33	0.371	0.387	0.572	0.723	0.723
NoSPA#1	*LIN*	0.163	0.202	0.245	0.213	0.225	0.283	0.379	0.458	0.523
	$P-S$	0.168	0.229	0.236	0.225	0.256	0.272	0.386	0.471	0.515

Table 2. Average values of generalized Recall measure (note that the SUBCATEGORY measure makes no sense in this context, thus it has been omitted)

		LIN			SHORTESTPATH		
Experiment type	Disambig. measure	short	medium	long	short	medium	long
SPA#3	*LIN*	0.196	0.231	0.281	0.243	0.272	0.317
	$P-S$	0.21	0.224	0.291	0.258	0.276	0.327
NoSPA#3	*LIN*	0.154	0.199	0.225	0.192	0.227	0.26
	$P-S$	0.16	0.204	0.23	0.209	0.236	0.268
NoSPA#1	*LIN*	0.163	0.202	0.245	0.213	0.225	0.283
	$P-S$	0.168	0.229	0.236	0.225	0.256	0.272

It should be stressed that values coming from the three generalizations of precision and recall measures (i.e. LIN, SHORTESTPATH, SUBCATEGORY) reflect different aspects of categorization output. In case of the LIN measure, presented values are proportional to the generality of the category subsuming both real and predicted categories. In particular, such a measure does not take into account that predicted category can be a very specific subcategory of a real DMOZ category (i.e., the *Black holes* in case of the *Physics* DMOZ category). The more specific is the predicted subcategory, in comparison with generality of the DMOZ category, the lower is the value of the LIN measure. This is obviously undesirable feature, thus we decided to provide two more variants of evaluation based on different category similarity measures.

The SHORTESTPATH evaluation is based on the lengths of the shortest paths between real (DMOZ) and predicted categories, but without taking category specificity into account (i.e., Information Content in our case). Still it has drawback of the LIN measure, since it does not award correct but specific predictions placed within a general DMOZ concept.

The last measure, SUBCATEGORY, captures vertical relations between real (DMOZ) and predicted categories within $\mathfrak{W}$ taxonomy. The SUBCATEGORY measure simply gives 1 if predicted category is a subcategory of a given DMOZ category, and 0 otherwise. Then 1's are summed up and averaged. Such solution is still far from being perfect, however, together with LIN and SHORTESTPATH generalizations gives some insights on the categorization process quality.

In most cases, the PIRRO-SECO based disambiguation of words and phrases gives slightly better results than the LIN-based disambiguation – both in terms of precision and recall. It is mainly due to promotion of specific categories in case of PIRRO-SECO in comparison with the LIN measure. Narrow categories describe a concept space of a given document more precisely, and they allow for better disambiguation of a meaning of ambiguous terms appearing in the text.

Not surprisingly, prediction of more categories (3 instead of 1) results in better precision, and slightly lower recall. Also a quite expected result – especially in the case of the DMOZ high-level categorization – is that application of SPA algorithm increases precision. Since the DMOZ categorization we used is rather general, and using one-step Spreading Activation algorithm replaces more specific predictions with more general ones, i.e. with categories being higher in taxonomy graph, the LIN measure value is increased, and shortest paths lengths are decreased. It has almost no effect on the SUBCATEGORY measure, beside cases when SPA generalization goes above the real DMOZ category in the taxonomy graph (replacing 1 with 0).

Generally speaking, results in Tables 1 and 2 show a very good performance of our categorization methods, to the extent where it can be measured with DMOZ general categories. One can see the high percentage of cases where the predicted category is a subcategory of the real DMOZ category, especially in case of medium-length and long documents. Also the SHORTESTPATH measure shows, that in most cases taxonomy paths between the real category and the predicted one are short. For instance, precision value 0.489, in case of long documents, PIRRO-SECO based disambiguation and *SPA #3* experiment shows, that on average the shortest path has length near 1 ($0.489 = 1/2^{SP}$, i.e., $SP = 1.03$).

Category quality evaluation is strongly related to the quality of the document content and to the quality of the DMOZ categorization itself. Various DMOZ categories we have taken into consideration bring themselves various levels of precision. In Table 3 detailed results are presented, where generalized precision is computed within each DMOZ category. One can notice that some categories (such as science-related categories: "fizyka" (physics),"informatyka" (informatics)) are characterized with much higher precision, while other categories (such as travel-related categories: "azja" (asia), "turystyka" (tourism)) are more frequently missed with our categorization approach. Documents in the latter group more frequently discuss many vague or just unrelated topics, which are captured with our algorithm and are not related by the DMOZ taxonomy. It is another dimension, which should be taken into account during construction of an ideal evaluation measure (as well as benchmark datasets): that is, the fact that in the real world documents are often related to more than one concept simultaneously.

Table 3. Precision within each DMOZ category for the experiment *SPA#3*, i.e., PIRRO-SECO with Spreading Activation and 3 predicted categories (s – short, m – medium, l – long)

	LIN			SHORTESTPATH			SUBCATEG.		
DMOZ category	s	m	l	s	m	l	s	m	l
afryka (africa)	0.326	0.551	0.784	0.191	0.308	0.412	0.4	0.6	1
ameryka północna (n. america)	0.061	0.427	0.6	0.081	0.239	0.36	0	0.6	0.8
ameryka południowa (s. america)	0.323	0.592	0.724	0.25	0.389	0.421	0	0.6	0.8
archeologia (archeology)	0.623	0.618	0.536	0.66	0.7	0.708	0.6	0.6	0.5
astronomia (astronomy)	0.606	0.296	0.636	0.459	0.494	0.721	1	1	0.8
australia i oceania (oceania)	0.037	0.244	0.997	0.037	0.227	0.707	0	0.2	1
azja (asia)	0.103	0.391	0.652	0.069	0.268	0.454	0.2	0.6	1
biologia (biology)	0.23	0.197	0.51	0.331	0.138	0.447	0.2	0.4	0.6
ekologia (ecology)	0.254	0.085	0.174	0.324	0.216	0.234	0.2	0	0
ekonomia (economy)	0.104	0.295	0.234	0.385	0.547	0.624	0.4	0.8	0.8
filantropia (philanthropy)	0.449	0.559	0.103	0.382	0.417	0.108	0.2	0	0
filozofia (philosophy)	0.616	0.409	0.408	0.571	0.441	0.566	0.8	0.6	0.6
fizyka (physics)	0.628	0.321	1	0.766	0.5	1	0.8	0.4	1
geografia (geography)	0.315	0.158	0.099	0.463	0.271	0.427	0.75	0.6	1
geologia (geology)	0.631	0.646	0.089	0.812	0.7	0.375	1	0.8	1
grafika (graphics)	0.015	0.568	0.028	0.053	0.5	0.063	0	0	0
grupy etniczne (ethnic gr.)	0.134	0.259	0.257	0.216	0.327	0.256	0	0.2	0.2
historia (history)	0.425	0.114	0.15	0.46	0.371	0.389	1	1	1
hydrologia (hydrology)	0.086	0.66	––	0.402	0.628	––	0	0.66	––
informatyka (informatics)	0.508	0.521	0.403	0.447	0.55	0.435	0.6	0.6	0.4
internet	0.969	0.74	0.938	0.766	0.433	0.624	0.8	0.8	1
językoznawstwo (linguistics)	0.396	0.552	0.363	0.41	0.199	0.397	0.4	0.6	0.2
matematyka (mathematics)	0.412	0.568	0.998	0.553	0.606	0.927	0.4	0.6	0.75
pedagogika (pedagogy)	0.504	0.701	0.346	0.46	0.655	0.541	0	0.25	0.5
politologia (political science)	0.15	0.647	––	0.5	0.594	––	0	0.75	––
polityka (politics)	0.255	0.424	0.12	0.346	0.512	0.297	0.8	1	1
polonia (polish diaspora)	0.185	––	0.348	0.075	––	0.25	0	––	0
prawo (law)	0.49	0.759	0.819	0.442	0.666	0.654	0.5	1	1
psychologia (psychology)	0.661	0.713	0.552	0.525	0.512	0.543	0.8	0.8	0.6
religioznawstwo (relig. studies)	0.934	0.812	1	0.625	0.625	1	1	1	1
rolnictwo (agriculture)	0.334	0.605	0.012	0.374	0.589	0.088	0	0.2	0
socjologia (sociology)	0.437	0.435	0.237	0.544	0.585	0.36	0.5	0.4	0.2
technika (technology)	0.307	0.433	0.787	0.583	0.512	0.654	0.6	1	1
turystyka (tourism)	0.065	0.307	0.186	0.184	0.25	0.275	0	0	0.2

One can notice that in most cases longer documents are categorized with higher precision (especially within well-defined DMOZ categories).

We have manually inspected some of the categorization results. Some examples of proper and flawed categorizations are presented below. These categorizations were carried out with PIRRO-SECO as a disambiguation measure, with one-step Spreading Activation (SPA) applied to highest-weight categories, and with three predicted categories (i.e., *SPA#3* experiment from the table 1).

The first example of a poor categorization is the page `http://ptaki.ovh.org`, which has the DMOZ category *biologia*. However, it just discusses the fact, that the new bird-related portal has been started, and almost no biology-related terminology is used. The generalized LIN precision equals 0.01 and the recall – 0.01. Three highest-ranked predicted categories are:

- aplikacje internetowe (web applications), weight: 0.243
- strony internetowe (websites), weight: 0.243
- oprogramowanie według producenta (software by company) , weight: 0.181

The next example is the page `http://www.galeriajk.to.pl` with the DMOZ category *turystyka*. The page contains almost no content, just links to author's photos (mainly from Croatia, thus our predicted categories). The generalized LIN precision equals 0.04, the recall – 0.03, and predicted categories are:

- wyspy chorwacji (list of islands of croatia), weight: 0.113
- miesiące (months), weight: 0.108
- podział administracyjny chorwacji (counties of croatia), weight: 0.106

Yet another example is the page of math-related newspaper `http://www.mmm.uni.wroc.pl` with the DMOZ category *matematyka*. The page content is very short and related more to subscriptions and archived volumes of the newspaper, than to math itself. The generalized LIN precision equals 0.02, the recall – 0.02, and predicted categories are:

- wydarzenia (events), weight: 0.179
- biblioteki cyfrowe (digital library), weight: 0.114
- polskie biblioteki (polish library), weight: 0.081

The last example of a poorly evaluated categorization, which as a matter of fact is more precise than the DMOZ categorization is the page `http://www.technologiagps.org.pl`. The page is assigned with the DMOZ category *geografia*, but is focused on GPS issues. However, both the generalized LIN precision and the recall values are low (0.08 and 0.06 respectively), predicted categories are precisely showing GPS topic:

- satelitarne systemy nawigacyjne (satellite navigation systems), weight: 0.630
- przyrządy pomiarowe (measuring instrument), weight: 0.055
- geodezja (geodesy), weight: 0.054

We conclude this section with two examples of categorizations which are coherent with the DMOZ taxonomy. The first one is the page `http://www.adamklimowski.pl/matematyka-wedyjska.html`, which has the DMOZ category *matematyka*. Our predicted categories (the precision equals 1, the recall – 0.83) are:

- matematyka (mathematics), weight: 0.217
- działania (operations), weight: 0.121
- arytmetyka (arithmetic), weight: 0.071

The page `http://psychologia-procesu.org.pl` has the DMOZ category *psychologia*. Our predicted categories (the precision equals 1, the recall – 0.65) are:

- psychologia (psychology), weight: 0.279
- terapie (therapy), weight: 0.142
- psychologia kliniczna (clinical psychology), weight: 0.124

8 Conclusions

In the future we plan to deal with the following issues: (1) minimization of the input data quality (that is, the merit of the content present in the input documents) on the algorithm performance, (2) exploiting other features of $\mathfrak{W}$, like *infoboxes*, being frames for systematic presentation of information on objects of some specific types (e.g., country infobox etc.), (3) improvement of methods used for appropriate mapping terms on the ontology concepts, that is, application of new measures taking into account context of the term appearance, (4) creation of more sophisticated methods of categorization clustering including also diversification of the results in case of multi-topic documents. We also plan to extend $\mathfrak{W}$ taxonomy with other semantic knowledge sources, such as Wiktionary (Wikisłownik), DBPedia, YAGO or Freebase.

Acknowledgement. this research has been partly supported by the European Regional Development Fund with the grant no. POIG.01.01.02-14-013/09: *Adaptive system supporting problem solution based on analysis of textual contents of available electronic resources.*

References

1. Coursey, K., Mihalcea, R.: Topic identification using Wikipedia graph centrality. In: NAACL 2009: Proceedings of Human Language Technologies: The 2009 Annual Conference of the North American Chapter of the Association for Computational Linguistics, Companion Volume: Short Papers, pp. 117–120. Association for Computational Linguistics, Morristown (2009), `http://portal.acm.org/citation.cfm?id=1620887`
2. Medelyan, O., Witten, I.H., Milne, D.: Topic indexing with wikipedia. In: Proceedings of the First AAAI Workshop on Wikipedia and Artificial Intelligence, WIKIAI 2008 (2008)
3. Mihalcea, R., Csomai, A.: Wikify!: linking documents to encyclopedic knowledge. In: Proceedings of the Sixteenth ACM Conference on Information and Knowledge Management, CIKM 2007, Lisbon, Portugal, November 6-10, pp. 233–242. ACM (2007)
4. Milne, D., Witten, I.H.: An effective, low-cost measure of semantic relatedness obtained from wikipedia links. In: Proceedings of the First AAAI Workshop on Wikipedia and Artificial Intelligence, WIKIAI 2008 (2008)
5. Milne, D.N., Witten, I.H.: Learning to link with wikipedia. In: Proceedings of the 17th ACM Conference on Information and Knowledge Management, CIKM 2008, Napa Valley, CA, USA, October 26-30, pp. 509–518. ACM (2008)
6. Pirrò, G., Seco, N.: Design, implementation and evaluation of a new semantic similarity metric combining features and intrinsic information content. In: Chung, S. (ed.) OTM 2008, Part II. LNCS, vol. 5332, pp. 1271–1288. Springer, Heidelberg (2008)
7. Seppänen, J.K., Bingham, E., Mannila, H.: A simple algorithm for topic identification in 0–1 data. In: Lavrač, N., Gamberger, D., Todorovski, L., Blockeel, H. (eds.) PKDD 2003. LNCS (LNAI), vol. 2838, pp. 423–434. Springer, Heidelberg (2003)

Preliminary Experiments in Polish Dependency Parsing*

Alina Wróblewska and Marcin Woliński

Institute of Computer Science, Polish Academy of Sciences, Warsaw, Poland
{alina.wroblewska,wolinski}@ipipan.waw.pl

Abstract. Preliminary experiments presented in this paper consist in the induction and evaluation of a dependency parser for Polish. We train data-driven dependency models with publicly available parser-generation systems (MaltParser and MSTParser) given a converted dependency structure bank for Polish. Induced Polish dependency parsers are evaluated against a set of gold standard dependency structures using labelled and unlabelled accuracy metrics.

Keywords: dependency parsing, Polish parsing, MaltParser, MSTParser.

1 Introduction

In recent years two shared tasks on multilingual dependency parsing have been organised at the Conference on Computational Natural Language Learning (CoNLL 2006 [3] and CoNLL 2007 [13]). Different languages were represented in these tasks, among other some Slavic languages such as Slovene, Bulgarian and Czech. Polish has not been represented in any of these tasks. What is more, dependency parsing is hardly represented by the Polish NLP community[1] and we are not aware of any experiments with data-driven Polish dependency parsing. According to our knowledge, no publicly available Polish dependency parser exists, even if it would be an useful tool in different language processing domains. The predicate-argument structure transparently encoded in dependency-based syntactic representations may be useful in machine translation, question answering or information extraction. As mentioned NLP applications are in the early development stage in Polish, a well performing dependency parser may contribute to improve their quality.

The main goal of our preliminary experiments presented in this paper is the induction and evaluation of a dependency parser for Polish. In order to induce a Polish dependency parser we will proceed according to the following procedure.

* This research is supported by the POIG.01.01.02-14-013/09 project which is co-financed by the European Union under the European Regional Development Fund.

[1] The only dependency parser we are aware of was developed by Obrębski [16,17]. However, this rule-based parser was only tested against a small artificial test set and no wide-coverage grammar seems to accompany the work. An interesting element of Obrębski's thesis is a proposition of a set of relation labels for Polish.

P. Bouvry et al. (Eds.): SIIS 2011, LNCS 7053, pp. 279–292, 2012.

First, we start with the conversion of an existing Polish constituency treebank [21] into dependency-based representations that constitute our training corpus. Second, labelled dependency graphs serve for training and optimising a parsing model which our dependency parser will be based on. The data-driven dependency model training is performed with two freely available parser-generation systems: MaltParser [14] and MSTParser [9]. Finally, we evaluate trained Polish dependency parsers and compare them in terms of parsing accuracy.

Our paper is structured as follows. Section 2 introduces the constituency treebank of Polish and describes its conversion into a Polish dependency bank. In Section 3 we present parsing systems used in our experiments. Section 4 describes the experimental methodology. Section 5 reports achieved results and compares induced dependency parsers. Section 6 concludes with some ideas for future research.

2 Training Data for Our Experiments

2.1 A Constituency Treebank of Polish

A bank of constituency trees for Polish is under preparation at the Institute of Computer Science PAS [21]. The planned size of the bank is 20,000 sentences taken from the balanced hand-annotated subcorpus of the National Corpus of Polish (NKJP, [18]). However, as the project is still ongoing, we have only available trees for about 5000 sentences.

The treebank is being developed in a semi-automatic manner. Candidate parse trees are generated by the parser Świgra [22] and one tree is selected and validated by human annotators. The project uses a new version of Świdziński's formal definition of Polish [20]. The treebank and the grammar are developed in parallel: the feedback given by annotators is used to improve the grammar, which leads to regenerating some trees in the treebank.

The project constructs constituency trees, however, their structure is designed with convertibility in mind. In particular each constituent has its syntactic centre marked, which enables us to convert the trees into dependency structures.

Due to the method of construction the current treebank is biased by the incomplete grammar. It consists only of the sentences accepted by the current version of the grammar. As the grammar is being enriched the bias will be reduced. In consequence it currently makes no sense to test our trained parsers on general text, and so we only use cross validation for evaluation. However, we think it is a good idea to start experiments early, so that any deficiencies leading to problems with conversion to dependency structures can still be cured in the source treebank.

2.2 Conversion of Constituency Trees into Dependency Trees

The process aims at converting the source treebank to a bank of labelled dependency structures. The dependency structure of a sentence is a graph with arcs representing directed binary relations between lexical nodes (tokens). One of related tokens is regarded as a *head* of the dependency relation, while the other one is its *dependent*. Arcs linking lexical nodes are named with dependency labels. We have predefined 29 fine-grained dependency labels in the Polish language. The most important dependency types are represented by subject (*subj*), different objects[2], object in dative (*obj_th*), different obliques[3], sentence predicate (*pred*), adjunct (*adj*), relative clause (*crel*). We also distinguish some incidental dependencies: apposition (*app*), predicative argument (*pd*) and pseudo-dependencies representing agglutinative affixes (*aglt*), auxiliaries (*aux*), complementizer of a finite clausal object (*cobj_fin_form*), conjuncts of a coordination (*conjunct*), conjunction (*coord_form*), punctation mark conjunction (*coord_punct*), negation particles (*neg*), interrogative pronoun (*pron_int*), punctuation marks (*punct*), reflexive markers (*refl*). An example of the Polish dependency structure is given in Figure 1.

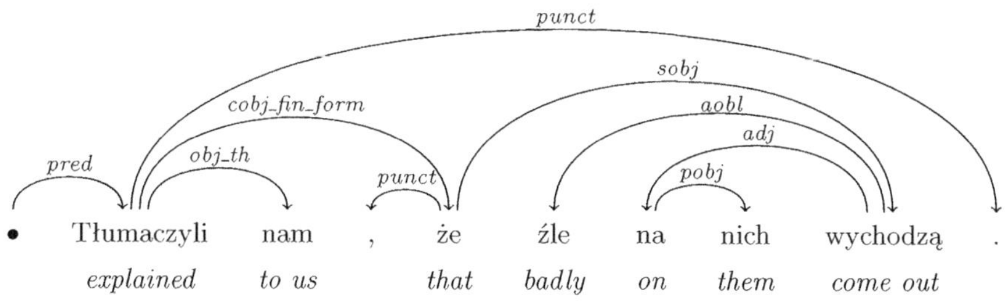

Fig. 1. Dependency structure of the sentence *Tłumaczyli nam, że źle na nich wychodzą.* eng. 'They explained to us that they come out badly on them (photographs).'

Converted dependency structures are stored in the column-based data format of CoNLL shared task [3]. Ten columns contain following data: `ID` (integer token identifier), `FORM` (word form or punctuation symbol), `LEMMA` (lemma of a word form), `CPOSTAG` (coarse-grained part-of-speech tag), `POSTAG` (fine-grained part-of-speech tag), `FEATS` (set of syntactic and/or morphological features separated by a vertical bar), `HEAD` (head `ID` of the current token), `DEPREL` (dependency relation label to the `HEAD`), `PHEAD` (projective head `ID` of the current token) and `PDEPREL` (dependency relation label to the `PHEAD`). All mentioned token attributes except for `PHEAD` and `PDEPREL` are represented in converted dependency structures. If a value is not available from the constituency treebank, an underscore is used as a default value. Since the underlying tagset makes no distinction between `CPOSTAG` and `POSTAG`, we currently use `CPOSTAG` values identical to `POSTAG`.

[2] Object arguments: indirect question object (*cobj_fin*), infinitival clausal object (*cobj_inf*), object of a numeral (*nobj*), (direct) object (*obj*), adjectival/adverbial argument of a preposition (*paobj*), nominal argument of a preposition (*pobj*), argument of a subordinatig conjunction (*sobj*), verbal object (*vobj*).

[3] Oblique arguments: adverbial oblique argument (*aobl*), prepositional oblique argument of an adjective/adverb (*apobl*), nominal oblique argument(*obl*), prepositional oblique argument (*pobl*).

Converted dependency structures stored in the CoNLL data format are basis of our further experiments.

3 Dependency Parsers

Shared tasks on multilingual dependency parsing at CoNLL 2006 [3] and CoNLL 2007 [13] arouse interest in data-driven dependency parsing. The interest has turned into development of different methods for data-driven dependency parsing. Two of them have dominated other methods: *transition-based* dependency parsing and *graph-based* dependency parsing. A transition-based dependency parser uses a deterministic parsing algorithm that builds a dependency structure of an input sentence based on transitions (shift-reduce actions) predicted by a classifier. The classifier learns to predict the next transition given training data and the parse history. A graph-based dependency parser, in turn, induces parameters of a parsing model over substructures of a dependency graph. The parser learns to score correct trees higher than incorrect ones given an annotated input. The parser finds the highest scored dependency tree. Transition-based and graph-based dependency parsing methods have been implemented as *MaltParser* [14] and *MSTParser* [7], [9], respectively. Even if the considered parsers use different parsing methods, they have achieved similar results for a wide range of languages as described in [8]. We are going to compare both methods in the realistic scenario of dependency parsing of Polish, which is a language not included in any CoNLL shared task on dependency parsing.

3.1 MaltParser – Transition-Based Dependency Parser

The data-driven parser-generator MaltParser[4] [14] trains a transition-based dependency parser for a language given a portion of annotated data in this language. The architecture of an induced deterministic parser consists of three main components: a **parsing algorithm** deriving a labelled dependency structure from an input sentence, a **feature model** helping in prediction of the next parser action, and a treebank-induced **classifier** deterministically predicting the optimal next action given a feature representation of a parser configuration in the current state.

Parsing algorithm. A deterministic parsing algorithm provides a basis both for learning and parsing in the MaltParser system. While learning, an *oracle* module maps every tree in the dependency structure bank to a transition sequence that derives this tree, i.e., valid transition sequences are reconstructed from annotated dependency trees. A training oracle is required to train a classifier. While parsing, a transition system builds labelled dependency graphs according to predicted transitions. Transition sequences are predicted by a trained

[4] We use MaltParser 1.4.1 downloaded from `http://maltparser.org`.

classifier that makes use of a history-based feature model. The *MaltParser* system provides some built-in implementations of parsing algorithms for projective[5] (`nivreeager`, `nivrestandard` and `covproj` [10] or `stackproj` [11]), for non-projective[6] (`covnonproj` [10], `stacklazy` [15], and `stackeager` [11]), and for planar[7] (`planar` [6]) dependency structures.

Feature model. The history-based feature model is used by MaltParser classifier to predict next actions at non-deterministic choice points given a feature vector. Features are defined in terms of token attributes, i.e., word form (FORM), part of speech (POS), morphological features (FEATS), and lemma (LEMMA) available in input data or dependency types (DEPREL) extracted from partially built dependency graphs and updated during parsing.

Learning algorithm. The MaltParser system enables switching between two implementations of machine learning algorithms used to induce a classifier given training data: the LIBSVM library [4] being the implementation of *support vector machines* and the LIBLINEAR package [5] with various *linear classifiers* implemented in it.

3.2 MSTParser – Graph-Based Dependency Parser

A data-driven dependency parser may be trained with the graph-based MSTParser system[8] [7] given a sufficient amount of annotated data. The MST parsing consists in searching for the maximum spanning tree (MST) in a directed graph. MSTParser selects the highest scored dependency tree y as the correct analysis of an input sentence x. The score of the dependency tree is the sum of scores of

5 Projective dependency structure – the dependency analysis of a sentence is constrained on the linear word order, i.e., dependency edges are non-crossing with respect to the word order. For example:

w_1 w_2 w_3 w_4

6 Non-projective dependency structure models non-local syntactic constructions such as topicalization, WH-movement, discontinuos NPs, or other resulting in crossing edges, e.g.:

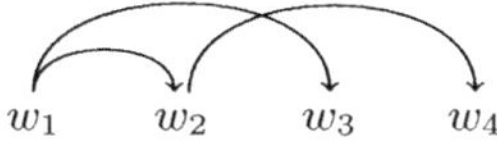

7 The concept of planarity [19] is similar to the projectivity idea regarding the requirement that dependency links drawn above words in a sentence do not cross. The following structure is planar but not projective because of the root node:

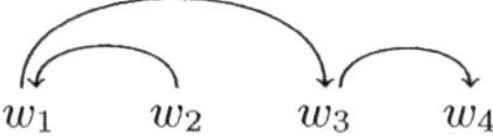

8 We use MSTParser 0.4.3b downloaded from `http://mstparser.sourceforge.net`.

all edges in this tree. The score of an edge $s(i, j)$ is defined by [9] as the dot product between a high dimensional feature representation of this edge $f(i, j)$ and a weight vector w learnt during training. The score of a complete dependency tree y for a sentence x is defined as:

$$s(x, y) = \sum_{(i,j)\in y} s(i, j) = \sum_{(i,j)\in y} w \cdot f(i, j)$$

The parser endeavours to find the highest scored dependency tree using one of two parsing algorithms that are available in the MSTParser system: the algorithm of Eisner [7] which deals with the projective structures and the Chu-Liu-Edmonds algorithm [9] which manages non-projective structures. The Eisner parsing algorithm is a bottom-up dynamic programming algorithm with a runtime $O(n^3)$ and the Chu-Liu-Edmonds maximum spanning tree algorithm is a greedy recursive one with the $O(n^2)$ complexity.

Both presented systems are applied to train Polish dependency parsers as described in following sections.

4 Experiments

In this section we present some experiments carried out with MaltParser [14] and MSTParser [9]. Polish is a highly inflected language with flexible word order, what may cause some difficulties for syntactic parser developing. However, both mentioned parsing systems provide an opportunity for adapting parser to characteristic phenomena of a language. We are going to take this opportunity and tune parser parameters, in order to train optimal parsing models.

4.1 MaltParser

Baseline MaltParser. The baseline parsing model for Polish is induced using default settings of the MaltParser system. At first, we compare outputs by two baseline parsing models with default settings and different machine learning algorithms which a classifier is trained with. Cross-validation shows that a parser with the LIBLINEAR-classifier performs slightly better (79.5% LAS[9] and 85.8% UAS[10]) than the other one with the LIBSVM-classifier (79.1% LAS and 85.6% UAS). The difference between accuracy of baseline parsing models is not considerable. Neverthless, we have decided to use LIBLINEAR library in our further experiments, as it is faster than the other one. The baseline MaltParser for Polish (default settings and LIBLINEAR classifier) with the labelled attachement score of 79.5% constitutes a point of reference to compare optimized parsing models.

[9] Labelled attachment score (LAS) – the percentage of tokens that are assigned a correct head and a correct dependency type.

[10] Unlabelled attachment score (UAS) – the percentage of tokens that are assigned a correct head.

Experiment 1: Transition System Selection. Taking into account that our dependency bank is converted from constituent trees, we only have projective dependency structures. Even if we deal with projective dependency structures, we test out all built-in transition systems, in order to find out the best one applying to the Polish parsing scenario. According to our results (see Table 2 in Section 5), the best performing projection system is `nivrestandard`[11] and the best non-projective system is `stacklazy`. These two transition systems achieve almost the same results with 82.4% LAS and 88.9/89% UAS. Since our data is projective, we have decided to choose the `nivrestandard` projective system for our further experiments.

Experiment 2: Feature Model Estimation. The history-based feature model is a combination of static (FORM, POS, LEMMA, FEATS) and dynamic (DEPREL) features. In this experiment we are going to find out the feature combination that improves the parsing performance. We consider the built-in *NivreStandard* as the baseline feature model. It is based on FORM, POS and DEPREL features. We expand this baseline model by addition of LEMMA and/or FEATS features. The default and additional features used in the experiment are presented in Table 1.

Table 1. Repertoire of history-based features. Rows correspond to tokens in a parser configuration: `TOP` (the token on the top of a stack), `NEXT` (the next token in the remaining input), `HEAD(TOP)` (the head of `TOP` in a partially built tree), `LDEP(TOP/NEXT)` (the leftmost dependent of `TOP` or `NEXT`), `RDEP(TOP/NEXT)` (the rightmost dependent of `TOP` or `NEXT`). Columns correspond to feature types: FORM (word form), POS (part of speech), DEPREL (dependency relation), LEMMA, FEATS (set of morphological features). ⊕ (default features for the NivreStandard model); + (additional features in the optimised model).

		FORM	POS	DEPREL	LEMMA	FEATS
Stack:	`TOP`	⊕	⊕		+	+
Stack:	`TOP-1`		⊕			
Input:	`NEXT`	⊕	⊕		+	+
Input:	`NEXT+1`	⊕	⊕		+	+
Input:	`NEXT+2`		⊕			
Input:	`NEXT+3`		⊕			
Tree:	`HEAD(TOP)`	⊕			+	
Tree:	`LDEP(TOP)`			⊕		
Tree:	`RDEP(TOP)`			⊕		
Tree:	`LDEP(NEXT)`			⊕		
Tree:	`RDEP(NEXT)`			⊕		

4.2 MSTParser

Baseline MSTParser. We induce a baseline parsing model for Polish using default settings of the MSTParser system. The Eisner projective parsing algorithm

[11] The `stackproj` projective transition system scores just as good as `nivrestandard`. We have decided to use `nivrestandard` in further experiments.

is running 10 times during training a parsing model. The baseline MSTParser specifies 1-best parses to create constraints and uses first order features.

MSTParser Optimisation. As we previously mentioned (see Section 3.2), MSTParser enables switching between two built-in parsing algorithms: the Eisner algorithm and the Chu-Liu-Edmonds algorithm. Our baseline model applies the Eisner parsing algorithm designed for projective dependency structures. Although our training data is projective, we test out the Chu-Liu-Edmonds algorithm designed for non-projective structures as well. As expected, MSTParser with the Chu-Liu-Edmonds algorithm performs slightly worse than the baseline MSTParser (see Table 4).

Hereinafter, we concentrate on the *order-of-features* factor used to score dependency trees. We may choose between *first-order* and *second-order* dependency parsing. In case of the first-order factorization, the score for a dependency graph factors only over single adjacent edges, while in the second-order scoring, the tree score is the sum of adjacent edge pair scores (see Figure 2). The second-order function $s(i, j, k)$ scores a pair of adjacent edges on the same side of the parent node. If the middle argument is ignored, the first-order scoring substitutes the second-order scoring. All adjacent edge pair scores are added up to score the dependency tree.

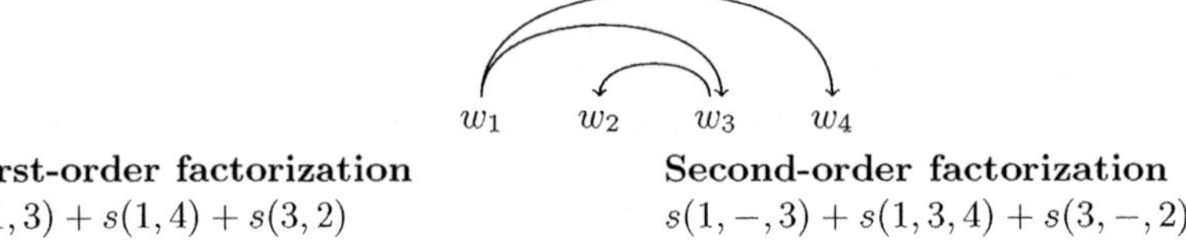

Fig. 2. First-order and second-order factorization

The baseline model applies first-order dependency parsing, as it is a default setting in MSTParser. We are going to test out if the change of the order-of-feature factor influences the Polish MSTParser performance.

The next section reports results of described experiments.

5 Data, Evaluation and Results

The performance of Polish dependency parsers is evaluated with the following metrics: *labelled attachment score* (LAS) and *unlabelled attachment score* (UAS). We evaluate trained parsers in two ways. In the optimisation phase we apply ten-fold cross-validation using the same split of training data for both induced parsers. The final evaluation is performed against the unseen validation data set. We start this section with the presentation of our data and continue with results gained by the Polish MaltParser and the Polish MSTParser.

5.1 Data

The conversion of constituent trees results in 4,601 dependency structures (44,883 tokens). We split the entire dependency bank into a training set with 4,141 sentences (40,346 tokens) and a validation set with 460 sentences (4,537 tokens). As our training data is relatively sparse, we have decided to apply ten-fold cross-validation in the optimisation phase. The validation set is used for the final parser evaluation. It is worth mentioning that sentences in our data set are not long and contain 9.75 tokens on average. Therefore, we suppose to deal with relatively simple syntactic structures in most cases.

5.2 Evaluation of the Polish MaltParser

Experiment 1. Transition System Selection. In section 4.1 we gave an account of our first experiment that consists in verification of the built-in transition systems. Results presented in Table 2 show that two parsing models with default parameters and either `nivrestandard` projective system or `stacklazy` non-projective system perform the best (the highest scores are marked in bold). Both parsers perform better than the baseline (`nivreeager`) and their evaluation scores are about 3 percentage points higher. It is also worth noting that we

Table 2. Evaluation of transition systems built in MaltParser. Evaluation metrics: labelled attachment score (LAS) and unlabelled attachment score (UAS).

Parsing Algorithm	Structures	Cross-Validation	
		LAS	UAS
`nivreeager` (baseline)	Projective	79.5	85.8
`nivrestandard`	Projective	**82.4**	**88.9**
`covproj`	Projective	80.3	87.0
`covnonproj`	Non-Projective	80.2	86.8
`stackproj`	Projective	82.3	88.9
`stackeager`	Non-Projective	82.3	88.9
`stacklazy`	Non-Projective	**82.4**	**89.0**
`planar`	Planar	78.6	84.9

get an improvement of parsing performance compared to the baseline parser in case of all built-in transition systems except for `planar` system.

Comparing labelled and unlabelled attachment scores of considered parsing models, we notice that UAS is about 6.5 percentage points higher than LAS. The difference between LAS and UAS may be influenced by relatively small amount of training data.

Experiment 2. Feature Model Estimation. The second experiment aims at identification of the optimal feature model. The default feature model consists of word form (FORM), part-of-speech (POS) and dependency relation (DEPREL) features as presented in Table 1. A parser with the default feature model, the `nivrestandard` transition system and the LIBLINEAR classifier achieves 82.4% LAS and 88.9% UAS. Addition of the LEMMA feature to the considered default feature model slightly improves the parser performance, but the difference is below 1 percentage point. Much better improvement is achieved, if the FEATS values are taken into account while predicting the next parser action (4 percentage points above accuracy of the parser with the default feature model). According to results presented in Table 3, the optimal feature model consists of all examined attributes. The parser making use of the optimal feature model achieves 86.9% LAS and 90.2% UAS.

Table 3. Feature model estimation. Evaluation metrics: labelled attachment score (LAS) and unlabelled attachment score (UAS).

Feature Model	Cross-Validation		Final Test	
	LAS	UAS	LAS	UAS
nivrestandard (FORM, POS, DEPREL)	82.4	88.9	84.2	90.5
nivrestandard + LEMMA	83.1	89.1	84.4	90.6
nivrestandard + FEATS	86.4	90.1	88.0	91.7
nivrestandard + LEMMA + FEATS	**86.9**	**90.2**	**88.8**	**92.2**

We evaluate the best scoring parser with the `nivrestandard` transition system, the LIBLINEAR classifier and the feature model with all attributes against a final validation set (460 dependency structures) and achieve even better results then in cross-validation. The final Polish MaltParser may achieve 88.8% LAS and 92.2% UAS.

5.3 Evaluation of the Polish MSTParser

In the experiment, we try to optimise the induced MSTParser changing two parameters: the parsing algorithm and the order-of-features factor. According to our conjectures, the non-projective Chu-Liu-Edmonds algorithm should not be used to train a dependency parser given projective data. However, the difference between the baseline model and the Chu-Liu-Edmonds parsing model is not significant (about 1 percentage point). Polish admits non-projective structures and they are quite frequent. We suppose that the Chu-Liu-Edmonds parsing algorithm could be a good starting point while training a dependency parser on Polish non-projective data. What is more, results presented in Table 4 show that the order-of-features factor may slightly improve the parsing quality. However, it is true only in cross-validation of MSTParser and not in the final evaluation performed with the unseen test set of 460 sentences. The final Polish MSTParser achieves the 85% LAS and 92% UAS.

Table 4. Evaluation of MSTParser for Polish. Evaluation metrics: labelled attachment score (LAS) and unlabelled attachment score (UAS). Explanation: the Eisner algorithm (Eisner), the Chu-Liu-Edmonds algorithm (Chu-Liu-Edmonds), first-order dependency parsing (1-order), second-order dependency parsing (2-order).

Parameter Settings	Cross-Validation		Final Test	
	LAS	**UAS**	**LAS**	**UAS**
Eisner + 1-order (baseline)	83.9	90.6	**85.2**	**91.9**
Chu-Liu-Edmonds + 1-order	83.0	89.5	83.8	90.5
Eisner + 2-order	**84.3**	**91.0**	84.4	91.5

5.4 Comparative Error Analysis

The final Polish MaltParser achieves the labelled accuracy score of 88.8% and the unlabelled accuracy score of 92.2%. The best performing Polish MSTParser is our baseline parser at the same time, with 85.2% LAS and 91.9% UAS. It follows that MaltParser has the advantage over MSTParser with regard to the labelled accuracy score (3.6 percentage points). In terms of the unlabelled accuracy score the Polish MaltParser slightly outperforms MSTParser.

We predefined 29 fine-grained dependency labels, which the Polish parsed sentences are annotated with. We evaluate individual labels in terms of *precision*, *recall* and *f-measure*. Automatically labelled dependencies in the final test set are evaluated against the gold standard set. Furthermore, we count the frequency of individual labels in the final set of gold annotated sentences. According to our results, some labels annotated both by MaltParser and by MSTParser have f-score over 90% (*aglt, paobj, cobj_fin_form, cobj_inf, coord_form, neg, pobj, pred, punct, refl, sobj, vobj*). Other labels with the label attachement below 90% (f-score) are listed in Table 5. F-score of about 80% is achieved for following labels: *adj, conjunct* and *nobj*. *pobl* reports f-score above 60% and *cobj_fin* over 40%. Both parsers perform equaly poorly while annotating oblique arguments, especially *aobl* and *apobl*. In case of *aobl*, it is mostly mixed with *adj*, as both of them may be represented by the same part-of-speech tag and morphological features. *apobl*, in turn, is mixed either with *adj* or *pobl* represented by a prepositional phrase. As both *aobl* and *apobl* are sparsely represented in the validation set, they may appear rarely also in the training corpus. The conclusion is that we need more training data to solve this data sparseness problem. The Polish MaltParser considerably outperforms MSTParser in labelling *app, crel, obj_th, obl, pd* and especially in case of *obj* and *subj*, when it achieves over 90% f-score. The Polish MSTParser labels two pseudo-dependency relations more exactly than MaltParser: *coord_punct* and *pron_int*. It is worth noting that we obtain balanced precision and recall values in most cases. If precision and recall values are unequal, than precision value more frequently enhances recall. It follows that if a parser finds a dependency relation between two tokens it is a great chance to label it correctly. The problem is to find all relevant relations what may cause degrade in recall.

Table 5. Labelled accuracy for fine-grained Polish dependency types. Evaluation metrics: precision (Prec), recall (Rec) and f-measure (F).

Dependency	Frequency	MaltParser			MSTParser		
		Prec	Rec	F	Prec	Rec	F
adj	1304	83.9	82.6	83.2	82.0	82.9	82.4
aobl	17	50.0	17.6	26.1	0.0	0.0	0.0
apobl	9	50.0	11.1	18.2	40.0	22.2	28.6
app	26	65.6	80.8	72.4	75.0	23.1	35.3
cobj_fin	9	44.4	44.4	44.4	75.0	33.3	46.1
conjunct	250	77.5	81.2	79.3	76.0	81.2	78.5
coord_punct	23	62.5	65.2	63.8	67.8	82.6	74.5
crel	18	84.2	88.9	86.5	61.1	61.1	61.1
nobj	31	82.9	93.5	87.9	79.5	100.0	88.6
obj	217	89.5	94.0	91.7	71.9	75.6	73.7
obj_th	41	86.0	90.2	88.1	79.3	56.1	65.7
obl	50	66.7	68.0	67.3	46.1	24.0	31.6
pd	54	89.1	75.9	82.0	71.7	61.1	66.0
pobl	168	67.4	72.6	69.9	68.6	63.7	66.0
pron_int	7	62.5	71.4	66.7	75.0	85.7	80.0
subj	354	93.8	93.8	93.8	75.5	81.1	78.2

6 Conclusions and Future Work

In experiments presented in this paper, dependency parsing models for Polish have been trained using two parser-generators: MaltParser and MSTParser. Both the transition-based MaltParser and the graph-based MSTParser are data-driven systems designed for induction of a dependency parser for a language for which an annotated dependency bank exists. As Polish lacks any dependency bank, we automatically converted trees from the existing constituency treebank into dependency structures.

According to final evaluation results, the Polish MaltParser (89% LAS and 92% UAS) slightly outperformed the Polish MSTParser (85% LAS and 92% UAS) taking their labelled accuracy scores into account. Achieved results are quite good, but we may not forget that our dependency bank contains short sentences (9.7 tokens per sentence on average) which do not have to represent complex syntactic structures.

As no Polish dependency parser is publicly available, the accuracy of dependency parsers for Czech and Russian constitutes our point of reference while evaluating Polish dependency parsers. Czech is one of languages that has participated in CoNLL 2006 and CoNLL 2007. Dependency parsers for Czech were trained on *Prague Dependency Treebank* [2] with 72,700 sentences (1,249,000 tokens and 17.2 tokens per sentence on average) in CoNLL 2006 and with 25,400 sentences (450,000 tokens and 17 tokens per sentence on average) in CoNLL 2007. According to results, the Czech MaltParser achieved 78.4% LAS and 84.8% UAS in the first task and 77.2% LAS and 82.3% UAS in the second CoNLL task. MaltParser was outperformed by the Czech MSTParser with 80.2% LAS and 87.3% UAS.

The Russian MaltParser [12] have been trained on the large dependency treebank SynTagRus [1] containing over 32,000 sentences (460,000 tokens) taken from different genres. The best Russian MaltParser achieved 82.2% LAS and 89.1% UAS. Polish parsers seem to perform better than dependency parsers for Russian and Czech. However, we should take into account simplicity of Polish training data. Even if Polish dependency parsers trained on preselected training data perform well, they may not be appropriate for parsing general text.

We need more training data to cover the bulk of syntactic phenomena of the Polish language. As the Polish constituency treebank is going to be completed in a few months, we will gain four times more training data. The full treebank will be comparable in size to treebanks used for training Czech and Russian dependency parsers. So we expect to be able to achieve a reasonable corpus coverage with parsers trained on the entire corpus. It is an interesting question, however, what accuracy scores can we achieve for that future parser.

In case we need still more training data we plan to explore an alternative solution: an automatic annotation using the projection method. As some well-performing dependency parsers for English exist, they may be applied to analyse the English part of a parallel Polish-English corpus. Using automatic generated word alignment links, English dependencies will be projected onto corresponding Polish tokens. As result, a large Polish dependency bank may be induced. Future studies will show, if a well-performing dependency parser may be trained on a great amount of presumably noisy data.

References

1. Boguslavsky, I., Chardin, I., Grigorieva, S., Grigoriev, N., Iomdin, L., Kreidlin, L., Frid, N.: Development of a Dependency Treebank for Russian and its possible Applications in NLP. In: Proceedings of the 3rd International Conference on Language Resources and Evaluation, Las Palmas, Gran Canaria, pp. 852–856 (2002)
2. Böhmová, A., Hajič, J., Hajičová, E., Hladká, B.: The PDT: a 3-level annotation scenario. In: Abeillé, A. (ed.) Treebanks: Building and Using Parsed Corpora, Text, Speech and Language Technology, ch. 7, vol. 20. Kluwer Academic Publishers, Dordrecht (2003)
3. Buchholz, S., Marsi, E.: CoNLL-X shared task on multilingual dependency parsing. In: Proceedings of the Tenth Conference on Computational Natural Language Learning, CoNLL-X 2006, pp. 149–164. Association for Computational Linguistics (2006)
4. Chang, C.C., Lin, C.J.: LIBSVM: a library for support vector machines (2001), `http://www.csie.ntu.edu.tw/~cjlin/libsvm`
5. Fan, R.E., Chang, K.W., Hsieh, C.J., Wang, X.R., Lin, C.J.: LIBLINEAR: A library for large linear classification. Journal of Machine Learning Research 9, 1871–1874 (2008)
6. Gómez-Rodríguez, C., Nivre, J.: A transition-based parser for 2-planar dependency structures. In: Proceedings of the 48th Annual Meeting of the Association for Computational Linguistics, ACL 2010, pp. 1492–1501. Association for Computational Linguistics (2010)

7. McDonald, R., Crammer, K., Pereira, F.: Online large-margin training of dependency parsers. In: Proceedings of the 43rd Annual Meeting on Association for Computational Linguistics, ACL 2005, pp. 91–98 (2005)
8. McDonald, R., Nivre, J.: Characterizing the errors of Data-Driven dependency parsing models. In: Proceedings of the 2007 Joint Conference on Empirical Methods in Natural Language Processing and Computational Natural Language Learning (EMNLP-CoNLL), pp. 122–131 (2007)
9. McDonald, R., Pereira, F., Ribarov, K., Hajič, J.: Non-projective dependency parsing using spanning tree algorithms. In: Proceedings of the Conference on Human Language Technology and Empirical Methods in Natural Language Processing, HLT 2005, pp. 523–530 (2005)
10. Nivre, J.: Algorithms for deterministic incremental dependency parsing. Computational Linguistics 34, 513–553 (2008)
11. Nivre, J.: Non-projective dependency parsing in expected linear time. In: Proceedings of the Joint Conference of the 47th Annual Meeting of the ACL and the 4th International Joint Conference on Natural Language Processing of the AFNLP, ACL 2009, vol. 1, pp. 351–359. Association for Computational Linguistics (2009)
12. Nivre, J., Boguslavsky, I.M., Iomdin, L.L.: Parsing the SynTagRus treebank of Russian. In: Proceedings of the 22nd International Conference on Computational Linguistics, COLING 2008, vol. 1, pp. 641–648 (2008)
13. Nivre, J., Hall, J., Kübler, S., McDonald, R., Nilsson, J., Riedel, S., Yuret, D.: The CoNLL 2007 shared task on dependency parsing. In: Proceedings of the CoNLL Shared Task Session of EMNLP-CoNLL 2007, pp. 915–932. Association for Computational Linguistics, Prague (2007)
14. Nivre, J., Hall, J., Nilsson, J.: Maltparser: a data-driven parser-generator for dependency parsing. In: Proceedings of LREC 2006, pp. 2216–2219 (2006)
15. Nivre, J., Kuhlmann, M., Hall, J.: An improved oracle for dependency parsing with online reordering. In: Proceedings of the 11th International Conference on Parsing Technologies, IWPT 2009, pp. 73–76. Association for Computational Linguistics (2009)
16. Obrębski, T.: Automatyczna analiza składniowa języka polskiego z wykorzystaniem gramatyki zależnościowej. Phd thesis, Institute of Computer Science. Polish Academy of Sciences, Warsaw (2002)
17. Obrębski, T.: Mtt-compatible computationally effective surface-syntactic parser. In: Proceedings of First International Conference on Meaning-Text Theory, Paris, pp. 259–268 (2003)
18. Przepiórkowski, A., Górski, R.L., Łaziński, M., Pęzik, P.: Recent developments in the National Corpus of Polish. In: Proceedings of the Sixth International Conference on Language Resources and Evaluation, LREC 2010, ELRA, Valetta, Malta (2010)
19. Sleator, D.D., Temperley, D.: Parsing English with a link grammar. In: Third International Workshop on Parsing Technologies, pp. 277–291 (1993)
20. Świdziński, M.: Gramatyka formalna języka polskiego. Rozprawy Uniwersytetu Warszawskiego, Wydawnictwa Uniwersytetu Warszawskiego, Warszawa (1992)
21. Świdziński, M., Woliński, M.: Towards a bank of constituent parse trees for polish. In: Sojka, P., Horák, A., Kopeček, I., Pala, K. (eds.) TSD 2010. LNCS (LNAI), vol. 6231, pp. 197–204. Springer, Heidelberg (2010)
22. Świgra – an implementation of the formal grammar of Marek Świdziński (2005), `http://nlp.ipipan.waw.pl/~wolinski/swigra/`

Evaluation Method for Automated Wordnet Expansion*

Bartosz Broda, Roman Kurc, Maciej Piasecki, and Radosław Ramocki

Institute of Informatics
Wrocław University of Technology
Wybrzeże Wyspiańskiego 27,
Wrocław, Poland
{bartosz.broda,roman.kurc,maciej.piasecki}@pwr.wroc.pl

Abstract. Laborious construction of large wordnets (lexico-semantic networks) can be supported by automatic wordnet expansion methods. Several methods were proposed but mostly were not thoroughly evaluated and compared. In the paper an evaluation methodology for automated wordnet expansion algorithms is proposed. Basic requirements for it are formulated in relation to the linguistic process. The general scheme based on the idea of automated wordnet reconstruction is presented. The methodology is illustrated by applying it to the comparison of the two top level wordnet expansion algorithms: Algorithm of Activation-area Attachment and the algorithm of Snow *et al.*. The latter was reimplemented and adopted to the Polish language tools.

1 Introduction

Wordnets[1] became important language resources, even fundamental ones, at least for those languages for which they have been built. Unfortunately, construction of a large wordnet is a laborious process, which requires a lot of efforts of trained linguists. However, huge amounts of available electronic texts and the development of methods of automatic extraction of linguistic knowledge from corpora have created a possibility of supporting manual work with automatic tools suggesting attachment places for new words in the wordnet.

There are two main paradigms of automated extraction of lexico-semantic relations: pattern-based and clustering based, cf [12]. However, methods of both types express some intrinsic limitations, e.g., pattern-based methods offer mostly good precision but low recall while measures of semantic relatedness (clustering paradigm) assign some value to any pair of words but can hardly distinguish between different relations[2]. Clustering based methods are often referred to as

* Work financed by Innovative Economy Programme project POIG.01.01.02-14-013/09.

1 Wordnet is an electronic thesaurus following the structure of Princeton WordNet [5].

2 Measures of semantic relatedness produce high values not only for word pairs expressing synonymy or hypernymy but also for more fuzzy associations.

P. Bouvry et al. (Eds.): SIIS 2011, LNCS 7053, pp. 293–306, 2012.

Distributional Semantics. The core task of automated wordnet expansion is to identify for a word all its senses and all instances of the lexico-semantic relations in which it participates, i.e., respectively, *synsets*[3] (word sets) and word pairs in which the given word should be included. Both tasks require extraction of the significantly precise semantic information. Moreover the large scale of the wordnet requires extensive coverage. Contemporary approaches to the automated wordnet expansion are mostly based on a combination of two or more extraction methods.

Caraballo [4] combined agglomerative hierarchical clustering of words together with the manually constructed patterns. The basic structure was obtained by clustering and the patterns were applied to identify hypernyms for word clusters and refine the structure. The overall accuracy of Caraballo's approach was not high, according to limited manual evaluation.

Several projects have explored building an extended wordnet over an existing one. The advantage is the possibility of using the wordnet structure already in place, especially the hypernymy structure, as a knowledge source.

In [1] Distributional Semantics methods were applied first to assign a meaning representation to synsets. Next, instead of using patterns, the existing hypernymy structure was used as a kind of decision tree. A place for a new word was found by traversing the tree and comparing the word's description with the vectors assigned to synsets. A similar, but more radical approach was presented in [19], in which wordnet is converted into a decision-tree-like structure by upward propagation of meaning descriptions to the root. The descriptions are based on Distributional Semantics. In evaluation on two subtrees from GermaNet, the best accuracy of exact classification was 14% and 11%, comparable to that in [1]. In a similar way, in [18] attach points for a word are suggested in those synsets of the hypernymy hierarchy in which semantic neighbours of the new word are concentrated. The neighbours are identified on the basis of the similarity of the co-occurrence, in a 15-word window, with 1000 most frequent words. Evaluation was on the British National Corpus [2] and randomly selected common nouns of varied frequency. Synsets identified by the algorithm were compared with their exact hypernyms. The best accuracy of finding the direct hypernym, with no intervening nodes, producing exact reproduction of the wordnet (among 4 highest ranked labels) was 15% for $k = 3$ neighbours taken into account, but the overall classification (considering hypernyms located up to 10 links away from the suggested site in the wordnet structure) gave only 42.63%.

In [16] the expansion of wordnet hypernymy structure is described in terms of a probabilistic model. Attachment of new elements transforms the former structure **T** into a new structure **T**'. The most appropriate **T**' maximises the probability of the change in relation to the evidence at hand. This algorithm will be described in details in Sec. 3.1, and, for the needs of this paper, it will be called Probabilistic Wordnet Expansion (PWE). PWE precision equal to 84% was manually assessed on random sample of the 100 words from 10000 added. The evaluation method applied in [16] will be discussed in Sec. 2.1.

[3] Simplifying, a synset is a set of near synonyms.

For the needs of the WordnetWeaver system a wordnet expansion algorithm was proposed and called the Algorithm of Activation-area Attachment (AAA) [10,12]. AAA is capable of utilising heterogeneous knowledge sources characterising word lexico-semantic relations. AAA was applied to a combination of results generated by different pattern-based methods and Distributional Semantics. WordnetWeaver has been supporting large scale wordnet expansion for several years [12]. WordnetWeaver and AAA will be discussed in Sec. 3.2. According to an evaluation method based on automatic wordnet reconstruction, AAA achieved precision of 67.99% in the partial reconstruction of plWordNet[4] version 1.0 in relation to the highest-scoring attachment suggestions.

A taxonomy iterative construction or expansion method called the Metric-based Framework (MF) was proposed [20]. In a similar way to AAA, the method allows for the utilization of many knowledge sources in making decisions concerning subsequent words. Each decision is made on the basis of fifteen features. The features represent results obtained with different extraction methods ("contextual, co-concurrence, patterns, syntactic dependency, word length difference and definition"). Contrary to the unsupervised work of PWE and AAA, MF is based on supervised learning approach according to which parameters of the ontology metric – defining transformation of the feature values into ontological distance – are tuned on the basis of the word pairs acquired from an existing taxonomy. MF is limited to the construction of a taxonomy and hypernymy as the primary relation (however it was also applied to the meronymy). It was tested on taxonomies extracted from, e.g., WordNet. MF precision was calculated on the basis of the number of relation instances (word pairs) correctly rediscovered. The algorithm was compared with some re-implementation of PWE. MF performed slightly better, however the description of the applied PWE version is too general to analyse possible changes introduced. There is also no analysis of the statistical significance of the differences. It is worth to be emphasised that the goal of MF – taxonomy reconstruction, not the whole wordnet – is much more limited in comparison to AAA and PWE.

Several wordnet expansion algorithms (or lexically grounded semantic networks in general) have been proposed. However, the proposed algorithms are mostly evaluated on the basis of different methods and not all of them have been compared with respect to their performance. The goal of the work presented here it to develop a methodology for evaluating wordnet expansion algorithms, and, next, apply it to the selected, best performing algorithms. Moreover, as the comparison can be interesting for wordnet developers by itself, we want to perform it in in an objective and uniform way analysing performance of the algorithms on the identical, large scale data and in a similar setting.

2 Evaluation Methods for Automated Wordnet Expansion

Automated wordnet expansion (or construction) produces complicated relation graphs. Precision calculated in terms of words placed on the 'appropriate'

[4] A large wordnet for Polish, see `www.plwordnet.pwr.wroc.pl`

positions is the first natural candidate for a basic evaluation measure, however several problems appears. Are any 'appropriate' positions defined in a wordnet? A wordnet is a result of a linguistic process and hardly one can get two identical wordnets with two groups of equally trained linguists. How to penalise small differences in the produced wordnets? Should we calculate precision on the level of relation instances, as e.g., [20], or on the level of relation subgraphs? Which relation should be taken into consideration? Before we will present our own approach to evaluating wordnet expansion methods, first, we will make a brief overview of the approaches to this problems as presented in literature.

2.1 Approaches

There are four possible ways of evaluating a language tool: analytical method, manual assessment, comparison with a golden standard and evaluation by application. Analytical examination is hardly conceivable, as the wordnet structure is related to the human language system and hardly any wordnet properties can be formalized except such trivial ones like the lack of cycles in the hypernymy relation. The second option – manual assessment – seems to be the most natural one, and was used in many approaches, e.g. [4,16]. For instances, in [16], evaluators assessed manually 100 samples selected randomly from the first n up to 20000 automatically added hypernymic links. They were asked: "is X a Y?", where $\langle X, Y \rangle$ was an added link. It is not clear in [16] whether only direct hyponym/hypernyms counted as positive. Moreover only the best hit for a word, according to the algorithm, was evaluated. Human judgement is the obvious primary source of knowledge to compare with, however, the manual method can pose several problems: a wordnet is mostly large – only a sample can be assessed; a sample must be drawn from a structure – how to cut off; to distinguish between close (direct) and distant (indirect) relation links (e.g. hypernymic) is very difficult for the evaluator; mostly word pairs are evaluated – guidelines for the evaluation of substructures are much more difficult to be formulated.

The third type – comparison with a golden standard is the most often used one due to the availability of large wordnets, e.g. [18,10,12,20]. For instance, precision measured on the level of extracted relation instances (word pairs) in comparison to the instances encoded in the wordnet was measured in [20]. However, the shape of the extracted structure was only indirectly evaluated in this approach. Distribution of the distances of the suggested attachment sites in relation to the original ones was reported in [18]. In [10,12] several types of measures were used, depending on the distance and type of the relation links. Also, some measures took into account all suggestions generated not only the best ones.

The last possibility – evaluation by application, which is often used, e.g., for assessing measures of semantic relatedness, is very rarely applied to wordnet expansion methods. In [10,12] automated wordnet expansion was used as a supporting tool in wordnet construction by linguists. Linguist decisions were recorded and later compared with the automatic suggestion. The indirect application was the change in the efficiency of the wordnet building process. Thus it was a little step beyond the comparison-based approach, but into the direction of the evaluation of the practical value of the proposed methods.

2.2 Requirements

The main objective of the evaluation of semi-automatic wordnet expansion method is to answer the question: "How useful this algorithm is in practice?". *Wordnet reconstruction* seems to be close to this task. The basic idea is straightforward: first some word w is removed from the wordnet; next the expansion algorithm is expected to re-attach the word w. The closer the proposed attachment to its original position is the better. However, several constraints must be fulfilled in order to make the method useful in practice:

- *Distance weighting* — suggested attachments should be useful for a linguist working on extension of a wordnet, so, first, it should be related by one of the wordnet relations, but also attachments closer to the most appropriate point are trivially better then distant ones. For example, when for *Walker hound* algorithm proposes a *mammal* then it is not very useful in semi-automatic wordnet expansion as the hypernymic path between both synsets is long.[5] A hypernymic path is not the only option for measuring the linguist perceived distance in the wordnet. Distance perception measured along paths including links of different relations should be further investigated.
- An algorithm that identifies multiple word senses is better then an algorithm that finds only one sense of a given word.
- The evaluation methodology should be independent from any single wordnet expansion algorithm.
- The evaluation should focus on the lower parts of the hypernymy hierarchy of a wordnet. For evaluation focused on wordnet expansion, not construction from scratch, this approach seems appropriate. It provides similar settings for the use of the expansion algorithms during evaluation as in future use, i.e., some network structure is present. Moreover, it is hardly possible to create automatically the entire wordnet structure from scratch, cf [12]. On the other hand, automated wordnet construction seems to be a different problem that requires different evaluation setting. This requirement has a side effect of making the evaluation harder for wordnet expansion algorithms as lower parts of hypernymy hierarchy tends to have more specialized words, which are usually less frequent in corpora.
- Evaluation results should be interpreted easily and intuitively. Thus, we favour measures like precision and recall known from the information retrieval. Specifically, we want to avoid the need of setting of thresholds in evaluation phase. This is contrast to approach used in, e.g., [9], where setting of a wrong threshold could result in accepting very broad attachment areas, see [3].

[5] In WordNet 3.0 the path is as follows: Walker hound → fox hound → hound → hunting dog → dog → canine → carnivore → placental → mammal. This assignment would be correct according to methodology used by Snow et al [16] as they ask evaluators a following question "is X a Y ?".

- The evaluation should be performed for words of different frequency in the corpus. Construction of an algorithm that would cope with infrequent words in a robust manner is very hard. Alas, this is the necessity as our experience with wordnet construction shows. The Zipfian nature of words distribution is very evident in this problem, i.e., there is relatively small amount of frequent words which are included in a wordnet during the initial phase. The remaining words are infrequent in general language, but nevertheless, important from the linguistic point of view.
- Even if evaluation focuses on lower parts of the hypernymy hierarchy it should also refer to other relations. For example, *paw* is a part[6] of *canine* in WordNet 3.0, but the path in hypernymy/hyponymy graph is 19 edges long. However, traversal through different relations should be carefully restricted as it could lead to traveling to semantically unrelated synsets in just a few steps — and that kind of attachment proposals are not very useful for linguist working on semi-automatic extension of a wordnet.

2.3 Methodology

It is hard to find works in literature treating the evaluation of wordnet expansion algorithm as a problem independent from any particular method. Mostly, evaluation methods are proposed for a specific expansion algorithm and specific experimental setting.

Our main assumption is that every evaluation is performed on the same lexico-semantic network. All other data may be adjusted accordingly to the expansion method being tested and the data available at the time of the testing. The evaluation method proposed by us consists of the following steps:

1. Draw a sample of the words from the lexico-semantic network.
2. Split words into two disjoint sets. Namely, a set of frequent and a set of infrequent words. Frequencies of words can be collected from any corpus at hand. However they can be strongly biased by the size of the corpus and its content. Comparison between different algorithms should be performed on corpora from the same domain. In this work we focus on the general language because the primary role of a wordnet is to describe general language.
3. For each word set:
   (a) Take a subset S of the sample set. The best option would be if $card(S)$ was 1 but due to the possible limitations on computation time larger values may be used in practice.
   (b) Remove words in S from the lexico-semantic network, but not network nodes. Lacking nodes (e.g., synsets in a wordnet) can significantly alter the structure of a network. Note, that via tuning of depth parameter P (Sec. 4.1) one can evaluate only leaves of the semantic network.
   (c) Run the tested algorithm.
   (d) Evaluate suggestions.

[6] Part holonymy relation.

Point 3d should be described in more details. The tested algorithm returns attachment suggestions for words in S. One word can be associated with zero or more suggestions (*attachment points*). The suggestions are next compared with the original structure of the lexico-semantic network. One should measure the distance from the suggested attachment points to the original positions of the tested words in the network. We set maximal distance $max\_d = 6$ at which suggestion is considered to be informative for linguists. To be precise the path can include up to $max\_d - 1$ hyper/hyponymy links and one additional link of the other type.

The suggested max_d value has been derived from the analysis of the linguist work and was confirmed in discussions with lexicographers. It represents the number of transitions between the suggested attachment and an appropriate place for the word. It was observed that longer distance gives the linguist no real clue and the suggestion at such distance is usually ignored. Aggregated results for all words should be considered in the perspective of the distance histograms. We propose three evaluation strategies:

1. For a given word, only *the attachment of the closest path* to one of the word's original positions in the network is taken into account.
2. Only the position of *the highest scored attachment* (with the *strongest* support from the algorithm) for a given word is considered.
3. All suggestions generated by the algorithm word are counted in relation to their distance.

Concerning strategy 1, the closest path gives insight into usefulness of a given expansion algorithm for a linguist. The question answered here is whether the algorithm presents *any* informative suggestion for a linguist. Attachments located to far deliver too little information and requires too much manual work to be corrected. We call it *Closest* in further experiments. Strategy 2 shows how correlated are the best propositions with human decisions. We call it *Strongest* in further experiments.

The algorithm is not only useful when it returns one or few good propositions for a given word, but also the ability to abstain from making wrong suggestions has very important practical meaning. A naive algorithm can return every node as an attachment suggestion. Strategy 3, probably the most natural one, henceforth called *All*, gives us insight into this aspect.

In addition to *All* and a standard *Recall* defined as the ratio of words with at least one suggestion to the testing sample size, the second type of recall, called *Sense Recall* has been introduced. Sense Recall is defined as a ratio of the different attachment suggestions for one word to all known senses of that word. It measures how good a given algorithm is at finding different senses of a word.

3 Semi-automatic Wordnet Expansion

Among different approaches to automated wordnet expansion those that allow for combining several knowledge sources seem to create the most interesting perspectives. As Metric-based Framework [20] is limited to the taxonomy extraction, we will pay more attention to WordnetWeaver system and its AAA [10,12], as well, as Probabilistic Wordnet Expansion (PWE) of [16]. However, as the implementation of the latter is not available, its thorough re-implementation will be discussed in the next section.

3.1 Snow's Algorithm Revisited

Snow *et al.* proposed an algorithm, called here Probabilistic Wordnet Expansion (PWE) for taxonomy induction based on a formal probabilistic model [16].

PWE is based on the probabilistic model of the taxonomy structure. This probability is expressed in terms of taxonomic relations, i.e., pairs of objects (lemmas or word senses in the case of a wordnet) present in the taxonomy. The probability of a relation instance is based on heterogeneous sources of evidence. For WordNet expansion Snow *et al.* consider two types of relations: (transitive) hypernymy and (m,n)-cousinhood. The second one is a generalization of the co-hyponymy relation. Namely, (m,n)-cousinhood occurs between two word senses i and j if their *least common subsumer*[7] is exactly m links from i and n links from j in the WordNet graph.

The presence of one hypernymy or (m,n)-cousinhood relations imply set of other relations. For example, a direct hypernym of one word sense implies all other indirect hypernyms, because the hypernymy is transitive. Thus, in order to add a new word to the taxonomy, the whole taxonomy must be (locally) searched for an attachment place that maximises probabilities of all the implied relations.

Snow *et al.* use two sources of evidences based on logistic regression to determine probability of a relation (hypernymy or (m,n)-cousinhood) linking two words. The hypernymy classifier was build on the basis of patterns extracted from corpora with the help of generalized syntactic dependency paths from MiniPar parser [8]. The (m,n)-cousinhood classifier is build in a two-step process on the basis of Harris' distributional hypothesis [6]. First, the clusters are formed using a measure of semantic relatedness between words. Second, the classifier is trained with only one feature — a cosine similarity between a word and a cluster centroid. For both classifiers the training data is derived from WordNet [5].

For the need of evaluation we have reimplemented PWE for Polish. Alas, there are a few differences between our implementation and the original PWE implementation [16,15]. They arise either from the lack of certain NLP tools for Polish or unclear description of the original algorithm. More specifically, a parser which is comparable to MiniPar is not available for Polish, so instead of implementing a hypernymy classifier based on MiniPar we followed the approach for classification of lexico-semantic relation proposed in [11], which expresses good results for Polish. The difference between work presented in [11] and here is in the use of logistic regression in a similar way to [16] for classification.

---

[7] Snow *et al.* define the least common subsumer as "a synset that is an ancestor in the hypernym hierarchy of both i and j which has no child that is also an ancestor of both i and j.", cf [16].

Another significant difference was introduced in the implementation of the (m,n)-cousinhood classifier. Snow *et al.* cite the work of Ravichandran *et al.* [14] in the context of clustering. Ravichandran *et al.* are primarily concerned with speeding up computations of the cosine between feature vectors. The evaluation in [14] is done for computing similarity lists, not for clustering[8]. There are a few possible ways in which the step of the (m,n)-cousinhood classification could be performed:

1. Clustering by Committee (CBC) algorithm was used, which was cited in [14],
2. other clustering algorithm was used,
3. the output of the similarity function was used directly.

The use of cluster centroids, explicitly referred to in [16,15], is a strong evidence that one of the first two variants was applied in the original PWE implementation. For similarity lists the centroid is not typically defined.[9] On the other hand, in [15] only similarity function is used for an experiment with coordinate-term classification. We experimented with all the approaches, i.e., we tested improved CBC algorithm [3], several classical clustering algorithms (hierarchical, flat and graph-based) and the usage of a measure of semantic relatedness without referring to "cluster centroid" notion. The preliminary experiments showed that the best results are achieved with the last possibility, i.e., the direct use of the measure of semantic relatedness. Thus, in the further experiments we will use only this variant.

3.2 Algorithm of Activation-Area Attachment

AAA introduces a notion of a *semantic fit* between two lemmas[10]. The semantic fit is calculated on the basis of several knowledge sources and the linear combination of their support. The sources are represented as sets of lemma pairs and are extracted by several methods of different types: a measure of semantic relatedness (only pairs of the highest values of the relatedness are included in the set), hand-written lexico-syntactic patterns, automatically extracted patterns and a classifier recognising pairs representing instances of one of the wordnet lexico-semantic relations, cf [12]. We assume that a weight is assigned to each knowledge source. Weight values can be defined in any way, however in the case of the experiments presented here the weight values equal to the precision of the sets evaluated manually by linguists on the basis of representative samples drawn from the sets.

AAA works in two phases. During the first phase semantic fit between an input lemma x and each synset Y is computed. The semantic fit between a lemma and a synset is calculated on the basis of:

[8] For examples: "We randomly choose 100 nouns and calculate the top N elements closest to each noun in the similarity" [14].

[9] One can calculate a centroid for a similarity list, but this seems to be incorrect and very *ad hoc* approach.

[10] A lemma is a pre-selected basic morphological form representing the whole set of words or multi-word expressions that differ only with respect to values of grammatical categories (like case or gender) but express the same lexical meaning.

- the lemma-to-lemma fit between a given lemma and all lemmas included in the synset,
- as well as, the fit calculated for the synsets in the neighbourhood.

The neighbourhood is defined as encompassing synsets located up to a maximal distance where the distance is calculated as the length of the path consisting of the relation links. The following relations were taken into account during the experiments: hypernymy, hyponymy, part, portion, place, collection's element, material, taxonomic element, type, antonymy, conversion, feminine counterpart, diminutive, young of, expressiveness, conversion, relatedness, troponymy, fuzzynymy, synonymy, aspectuality and causation.

Lemma-to-synset fit values are transformed into *strong fit* according to the weighted voting scheme (higher sum of accumulated 'votes' is required for larger, lower for smaller synsets) and *weak fit* following non-linear filtering with parameters set experimentally. In the later phase synsets that fit the input lemma are grouped into *activation areas* describing the input lemma senses.

During the second phase, on the basis of the strong and weak fit between x and synsets, connected subgraphs of the hypernymic wordnet structure, called *activation areas*, are identified. Each activation area includes only synsets for which semantic fit to x is above some threshold and is assigned its semantic fit value to x which is defined as the maximum of the semantic fit values between x and synsets of the area. The weak fit helps to avoid too fragmented and small activation areas, but it depends on the predefined threshold.

4 Methodology Applied

In this section the proposed methodology is applied to compare two state-of-the-art wordnet expansion algorithms, i.e., AAA [10] and PWE [16].

4.1 Input Data

When evaluating an implementation of a single algorithm one has to prepare both input data for an evaluation framework and for the implementation. This separation comes out of the fact that the evaluation framework is independent from the implementation. Only basic data, i.e., a wordnet and lists of words to be added, are shared between the two.

Input data for the evaluation framework consists of:

- a lexico-semantic network (e.g., a wordnet),
- a test set of words selected from the network.
- corpus frequency of the selected words.

The frequency of words is required for dividing words in two groups, i.e., low and high frequency words. This data can be derived from some available corpus. The words for testing are selected in a straightforward procedure. Let W denotes a list of words that are at least P links away from the root of the lexico-semantic network. The W should be split into two disjoint sets according to the frequency of word occurrences. Namely, words with frequencies higher then some threshold L form the set of high frequency words (W_m) and words with frequencies lower then the threshold form the set of low frequency words (W_l). Usually, $card(W_m)$ and $card(W_n)$ are large, thus we need to select a representative sample of the words from those sets in order to speed up computation, cf. [7]. We will denote those samples for W_l and W_m as $W_{l_{sampled}}$ and $W_{m_{sampled}}$ respectively.

Parameter P represents level of abstraction. We assume that the majority of new lemmas are added at the bottom or in the middle of the network, because top or root senses are rare in the language use. The top-level hierarchy of a lexico-semantic network is usually far too abstract to be properly added in an automatic way. Value of L is usually set heuristically, as it is strongly dependent on the algorithm used and resources available.

Input data for the implementation of an algorithm must be synchronized with the data for the evaluation framework. It must be gathered from the same corpus and if a lexico-semantic network is used by the algorithm, it has to be the same as the network provided for the evaluation framework.

4.2 Evaluation Framework's Data

The methodology is language independent assuming that a corpus and a lexico-semantic network is available for that language. We decided to test our evaluation methodology for Polish as this presents unique opportunity for experiments. A large Polish wordnet – plWordNet [12] – is not yet finished and is being actively built with the support of automatic methods. For the evaluation we used plWordnet in the version 1.2 which consists of 47 402 lexical units (senses) and 34 919 synsets. A frequency list was extracted from the following corpora: the IPI PAN Corpus (254 million tokens) [13], the corpus of the electronic edition of *Rzeczpospolita* (a Polish daily, 113 million) [17], the corpus of documents from Polish Wikipedia (171 million), and a corpus of large electronic text documents in Polish collected from the Internet (500 million). We use words that appear at least 50 times in a corpus, because we noticed that PWE fails for less frequent words. L was set to 200 and P equaled 4. In table 1 we can see size of W_l, W_m, $W_{l_{sampled}}$ and $W_{m_{sampled}}$. The first row represents all words from the wordnet when P threshold is applied. Our experiments were conducted only for nouns. Synonymy, hypernymy and meronymy were considered during the evaluation.

4.3 Results and Their Comparison

The experiments provided us better insights into the performance of both tested algorithms. First, both were compared with respect to the number of word senses (attachments) discovered for lemmas being added. AAA has better Sense Recall than PWE (see Tab. 2 and 3). Second, we can see how the frequency of test lemmas influences the algorithm performance. Comparison between Tab. 2 and Tab. 3 clearly indicates that both algorithms suffer when faced with rare lemmas. The only exception is for PWE when all propositions are considered. In this case

Table 1. Sizes of selected words

frequency	all	sample
	19172	—
> 50	12842	1034
> 200	9473	1000
< 200 ∩ > 50	3369	870

PWE performs a little better for infrequent then for frequent lemmas, but the difference is not significant. This might be related to the fact that recall for PWE is much lower for infrequent then for frequent lemmas (82% vs 94%). Still, the precision for both $W_{l_{sampled}}$ and $W_{m_{sampled}}$ is better for AAA then for PWE.

For both algorithms most correct suggestions are no further away than 3 from the original synset. However, in the case of AAA perfect hits (distance 0) and near perfect hits (distance 1) occurred almost twice as often as for PWE.

Table 2. Results for infrequent lemmas ($W_{l_{sampled}}$ set). AAA recall for all propositions is 99%, the algorithm found on average 72% of all known senses for attached lemmas and returned 4299 propositions for all lemmas. PWE recall for all propositions is 82%, the algorithm found on average 58% of all known senses for attached lemmas and returned 3555 propositions for all lemmas.

	AAA			PWE		
Dist.	**Closest [%]**	**Strongest [%]**	**All [%]**	**Closest [%]**	**Strongest [%]**	**All [%]**
0	9.0	2.4	1.9	2.8	1.0	0.6
1	35.9	20.5	10.1	28.3	16.2	7.1
2	17.6	20.3	23.8	18.0	11.8	10.2
3	6.9	12.0	12.7	12.7	11.4	11.0
4	4.9	5.1	8.0	9.1	11.3	11.6
5	6.0	6.0	6.1	6.5	9.0	9.7
6	0.8	0.6	0.6	2.1	1.5	1.2
Total	81.0	66.8	63.2	79.5	62.2	51.3

Splitting all the lemmas into two sets was meant to simulate two common situations. More frequent words (W_m) are usually attached at the early stage of wordnet construction. In that case, both algorithms worked rather well, even though only AAA achieved overall precision higher than 70% and precision of the closest path over 90%. However, infrequent words (W_l) are added to the wordnet when it reaches certain level of maturity. At such time the majority of new lemmas are infrequent in any corpora. Thus, it is important to gracefully handle rare occurring lemmas. In such an environment AAA were able to produce higher number of correct suggestions. Interestingly, almost half of the correct suggestions where very close to the appropriate attachment points for AAA.

Table 3. Results for frequent lemmas ($W_{m_{sampled}}$). AAA recall for all the propositions is 99%, the algorithm found on average 66% of all known senses for attached lemmas and returned 4949 propositions for all lemmas. PWE recall for all propositions is 94%, the algorithm found on average 52% of all known senses for attached lemmas and returned 4695 propositions for all lemmas.

	AAA			PWE		
Dist.	**Closest [%]**	**Strongest [%]**	**All [%]**	**Closest [%]**	**Strongest [%]**	**All [%]**
0	15.6	4.3	3.4	3.6	1.0	0.7
1	49.2	29.9	15.2	27.7	16.3	7.0
2	12.7	22.3	29.2	14.0	11.3	9.9
3	5.0	9.6	13.6	12.6	10.6	10.5
4	4.2	6.4	8.0	10.5	10.2	10.9
5	4.0	5.4	5.8	10.2	9.6	10.9
6	0.4	0.9	0.5	1.2	1.0	1.2
Total	91.1	78.8	75.7	79.8	60.0	51.1

5 Conclusions

We proposed a new evaluation method that can be applied to a class of algorithms that expand wordnets in an automatic way. The method can be applied to any lexico-semantic network which has a similar structure to Princeton WordNet [5]. The proposed methodology is based on experience collected during several years of plWordNet expansion performed by a team of lexicographers supported by the application of WordnetWeaver – a semi-automatic wordnet expansion system. Source code for the evaluation framework is available at `http://nlp.pwr.wroc.pl/expeval`.

Application of the proposed methodology in testing algorithms enables a straightforward comparison of the approaches without the need of their reimplementation (if the systems are available). Only a few assumptions must be met, i.e., the genre of text used for training the expansion algorithm should be similar and the sample of words should be drawn in a proper way.

The methodology was applied to two state-of-the-art algorithms called Algorithm of Activation-area Attachment (AAA) implemented within Wordnet-Weaver system [10,12], and Probabilistic WordNet Expansion (PWE) [16,15]. Within the evaluation framework AAA performs better then PWE for both frequent and infrequent lemmas using all quality assessment indices. Namely, precision of AAA is higher, AAA returns more propositions for test lemmas and the number of senses found is larger for AAA then for PWE.

This paper focus on Polish language, but the evaluation methodology can be applied to any language. In future work we plan to perform similar study also for other languages. Preliminary results for English are encouraging and support conclusions drawn in this paper.

References

1. Alfonseca, E., Manandhar, S.: Extending a lexical ontology by a combination of distributional semantics signatures. In: Gómez-Pérez, A., Benjamins, V.R. (eds.) EKAW 2002. LNCS (LNAI), vol. 2473, pp. 1–7. Springer, Heidelberg (2002)
2. BNC: The British National Corpus, version 2 (BNC World), distributed by Oxford University Computing Services on behalf of the BNC Consortium (2001)
3. Broda, B., Piasecki, M., Szpakowicz, S.: Extraction of polish noun senses from large corpora by means of clustering. Control and Cybernetics 31(2), 401–420 (2010)
4. Caraballo, S.A.: Automatic construction of a hypernym-labeled noun hierarchy from text. In: Proceedings of ACL 1999, Baltimore, MD, pp. 120–126 (1999)
5. Fellbaum, C. (ed.): WordNet — An Electronic Lexical Database. The MIT Press (1998)
6. Harris, Z.S.: Mathematical Structures of Language. Interscience Publishers, New York (1968)
7. Israel, G.: Determining sample size. Tech. rep., University of Florida (1992)
8. Lin, D.: Principle-based parsing without overgeneration. In: Proc. ACL 1993, Columbus, Ohio (1993)
9. Pantel, P.: Clustering by committee. Ph.D. thesis, Edmonton, Alta., Canada (2003), adviser-Dekang Lin
10. Piasecki, M., Broda, B., Głąbska, M., Marcińczuk, M., Szpakowicz, S.: Semi-automatic expansion of polish wordnet based on activation-area attachment. In: Recent Advances in Intelligent Information Systems, pp. 247–260. EXIT (2009)
11. Piasecki, M., Szpakowicz, S., Marcińczuk, M., Broda, B.: Classification-based filtering of semantic relatedness in hypernymy extraction. In: Nordström, B., Ranta, A. (eds.) GoTAL 2008. LNCS (LNAI), vol. 5221, pp. 393–404. Springer, Heidelberg (2008)
12. Piasecki, M., Szpakowicz, S., Broda, B.: A Wordnet from the Ground Up. Oficyna Wydawnicza Politechniki Wrocławskiej, Wrocław (2009)
13. Przepiórkowski, A.: The IPI PAN Corpus: Preliminary version. Institute of Computer Science PAS (2004)
14. Ravichandran, D., Pantel, P., Hovy, E.: Randomized algorithms and nlp: using locality sensitive hash function for high speed noun clustering. In: Proc. of the 43rd Annual Meeting on ACL, pp. 622–629 (2005)
15. Snow, R.: Semantic Taxonomy Induction. Ph.D. thesis (2009)
16. Snow, R., Jurafsky, D., Ng, A.Y.: Semantic taxonomy induction from heterogenous evidence. In: COLING 2006 (2006)
17. Weiss, D.: Korpus Rzeczpospolitej, corpus from the online edtion of Rzeczypospolita (2008), `http://www.cs.put.poznan.pl/dweiss/rzeczpospolita`
18. Widdows, D.: Unsupervised methods for developing taxonomies by combining syntactic and statistical information. In: Proc. HLT of North American Chapter of the ACL (2003)
19. Witschel, H.F.: Using decision trees and text mining techniques for extending taxonomies. In: Proc. of Learning and Extending Lexical Ontologies by Using Machine Learning Methods, Workshop at ICML 2005 (2005)
20. Yang, H., Callan, J.: A metric-based framework for automatic taxonomy induction. In: Proceedings of the 47th Annual Meeting of the ACL and the 4th IJCNLP of the AFNLP, pp. 271–279. ACL (2009)

Mining Class Association Rules for Word Sense Disambiguation

Łukasz Kobyliński

Institute of Computer Science, Polish Academy of Sciences,
ul. Ordona 21, 01-237 Warszawa, Poland
lkobylinski@ipipan.waw.pl

Abstract. In this paper we propose an approach to the task of Word Sense Disambiguation problem that uses Class Association Rules to create an effective and human-understandable rule-based classifier. We present the accuracy of classification of selected polysemous words on an evaluation corpus using the proposed method and compare it to other known approaches. We discuss the advantages and weaknesses of a classifier based on association rules and present ideas for future work on the idea.

1 Introduction

The task of Word Sense Disambiguation (WSD) consists of correlating a given instance of a polysemous word, used in a particular context (sentence, paragraph, etc.), with one of known senses of this word. It is a problem we face every day communicating, as every natural language seems to contain some lexical ambiguity as its characteristic feature. Typical examples of English language words that may convey multiple senses are "bank" (having a meaning related to geographical feature or a financial institution) and "pen" (a place or an instrument for writing). It is thus necessary to resolve such ambiguities each time they appear in spoken or written text to be able to comprehend the text as a whole.

Automatic WSD is an important problem, for which an accurate solution would greatly simplify implementations of other tasks related to computational linguistics, such as machine translation. Whether it can be solved completely is an open question, having in mind that even humans vary in their decisions about the sense of a particular word in context. From a computational point of view this problem translates to the problem of classification: assigning one of known senses (classes) to each of the polysemous words appearing in a text fragment (instances).

The aim of our contribution is twofold: to present the results of a supervised learning approach to the task of WSD, evaluated on a Polish language corpus constrained to one specific domain and to propose a novel method of word sense classification, based on mining Class Association Rules (CARs). The motivation for the latter approach is creating a classifier that may be understood and modified by a human, which is not possible using the classical best-performing machine learning methods (neural networks, Bayes approaches, SVM, etc.).

P. Bouvry et al. (Eds.): SIIS 2011, LNCS 7053, pp. 307–317, 2012.

In the following chapters we first briefly describe work done previously in the field of Word Sense Disambiguation (Chapter 2). Next, we discuss the corpus used to assess the accuracy of the proposed method, which was created by manually annotating Polish language texts (Chapter 3). In Chapter 4 we describe the approach used to represent the context of disambiguated words in the form of a feature vector. In Chapter 5 we present the idea of using Class Association Rules in the task of WSD for classifying word senses. Finally, we show the results of experiments conducted using the proposed method and compared with other, known approaches (Chapter 6) and conclude with a summary of the contribution and ideas for future work (Chapter 7).

2 Word Sense Disambiguation

The idea of performing WSD automatically seems to have emerged in the late 1940s, when also the work on machine translation began. Many approaches have been proposed since then, including AI-based methods (as a part of larger systems intended for full language understanding), knowledge-based methods (using such language resources as thesauri and machine-readable dictionaries to compare the context of a particular word with definitions of each of the senses) and corpus-based methods (learning on the samples provided by an annotated text corpus) [8]. The Lesk's algorithm [10] is a particularly notable approach to WSD, which prompted evolution of knowledge-based methods and to which corpus-based methods are compared still today. In this algorithm, a list of words from each sense definition from the dictionary is created. Disambiguation is accomplished by selecting the sense, for which the overlap between the word list and the words in disambiguated context is the largest.

Recently, machine learning methods have been used extensively for the task of WSD and these may be further divided into supervised, semi-supervised and unsupervised approaches. Supervised learning methods require a text corpus, annotated with information about the correct sense of each or some of the appearing words. Sense annotation consists of associating a sense label (taken from a sense dictionary) with each instance of a polysemous word in the running text. Methods of this type are first trained on a learning corpus, manually annotated by linguists and then evaluated on another corpus, by automatically assigning annotations for ambiguous words. As reported by [18] these methods usually achieve the best results, compared with semi- and unsupervised approaches. Examples of algorithms used include Naive Bayes, kNN and SVM.

Semi-supervised methods usually require only a small "bootstrap sample" of annotations and large corpus of unannotated data. For example in [12] an approach is presented, where co-training and self-training paradigms are used for WSD, attempting to increase the small amount of available training data and tag new, previously unlabeled samples from a dataset.

Finally, unsupervised methods, which use external knowledge sources, such as WordNet or Wikipedia and unsupervised learning approaches, can be used in situations where very little or no training data in the form of annotated corpus is available. In [2] the authors present a graph-based approach, where WordNet is used as a lexical knowledge base containing hierarchical information about relationships between ambiguous words and other elements of the language.

In the context of Polish language there is very little work done in the field of automatic WSD. One of the first results of WSD for Polish language texts has been presented in [6], where supervised learning methods have been trained and evaluated on a small corpus of 1500 annotated examples, taken from a dictionary of 13 polysemous words. Some experimental results have also been presented in [13], where the classifier comparison environment used also in this contribution has been introduced.

Rule based approaches have been already used in the task of WSD and promising results of experiments have been reported. For example, the performance of several rule-based classifiers (J48, PART, decision table) has been compared in [15]. The authors show that rule-based methods may achieve better results than purely statistical approaches, such as Naive Bayes. The idea of mining association rules in a corpus annotated with word senses has been presented in [16], but for finding correlations between annotations done by different linguists and not for sense classification itself.

3 Evaluation Corpus

We have created a sense-annotated corpus of Polish language texts from the domain of economy. The evaluation corpus has been composed of resources coming from: 1 million subcorpus of the National Corpus of Polish [19], with morphosyntactic annotation and a collection of stock market reports in Polish, collected from the Internet. Details of the corpus may be found in Table 1.

Table 1. Statistics of the evaluation corpus

Corpus	Number of segments	Number of annotated segments
Subcorpus of NCP	87 816	3 821
Stock market reports	282 366	18 719
Overall	370 182	22 540

We have automatically selected a subcorpus from the National Corpus of Polish by choosing the fragments, which had the greatest number of occurrences of words related to the domain of economy. The words have been collected by hand-picking 5100 multi-word economy-related dictionary entries, names of institutions and agencies, as well as stock names from the Warsaw Stock Exchange. While the resources from NCP subcorpus have already been human-annotated morphosyntactically, the market reports have been not. Therefore, we have used the TaKIPI tagger [17] to add the annotation automatically.

To enable the task of annotating the corpus with sense tags, we have created a dictionary of polysemous lexemes. We have gathered 52 polysemous words from the domain of economy (in Polish) and associated them with a list of possible senses. For each word the senses have been grouped into a few broader senses, to lower the granularity of the dictionary. The experience with word sense disambiguation seems to tell us [1] that most automated methods fail with high granularity of senses and it is not needed in real applications. For example, for the word "rynek" the dictionaries offer no less than 14 different definitions. We have combined these 14 senses into 5 broader senses, which are more intuitive, easier to grasp by human annotators and should result in better classification accuracy using automated methods. The dictionary has been created by a linguist and edited using a simple web-based application, to enable easy synchronization of the definitions between the linguists during the annotation phase. Table 2 presents the words included in the resulting dictionary and Figure 1 shows the histogram of the number of senses per each lexeme. There is an average of 3.62 senses per lexeme in the dictionary.

Table 2. Lexemes in the sense dictionary

idx	lexeme	idx	lexeme	idx	lexeme	idx	lexeme
1	agent[n]	14	koszt[n]	27	punkt[n]	40	ubezpieczenie[n]
2	akcja[n]	15	linia[n]	28	rachunek[n]	41	udział[n]
3	baza[n]	16	ochrona[n]	29	rynek[n]	42	umowa[n]
4	cena[n]	17	opcja[n]	30	rząd[n]	43	unia[n]
5	dochód[n]	18	pieniądz[n]	31	sąd[n]	44	wartość[n]
6	efekt[n]	19	podatek[n]	32	siła[n]	45	warunek[n]
7	firma[n]	20	podstawa[n]	33	spółka[n]	46	zasada[n]
8	fundusz[n]	21	polityka[n]	34	stan[n]	47	zmiana[n]
9	gospodarka[n]	22	pomoc[n]	35	stopa[n]	48	zysk[n]
10	granica[n]	23	postępowanie[n]	36	stopień[n]	49	czarny[a]
11	inwestycja[n]	24	praca[n]	37	system[n]	50	specjalny[a]
12	jednostka[n]	25	prawo[n]	38	środek[n]	51	wolny[a]
13	kontrola[n]	26	projekt[n]	39	świadczenie[n]	52	złoty[a]

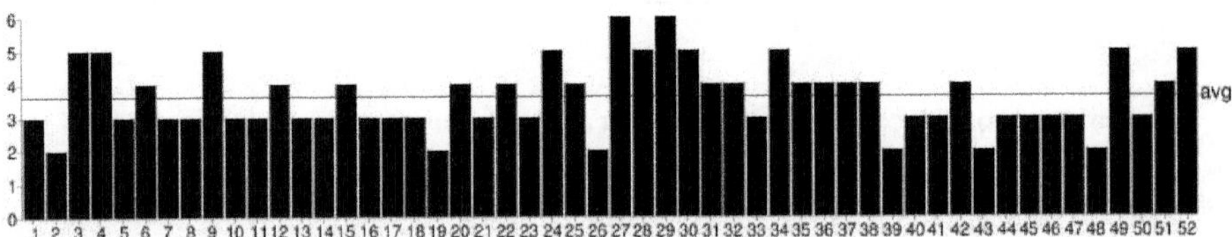

Fig. 1. Histogram of the number of senses per each lexeme in the dictionary. Numbers on the horizontal axis reflect the index of a lexeme from Table 2.

Semantic annotation of the final corpus has been performed by an average number of four linguists. Fragments of the texts (usually paragraphs) have been selected at random from the corpus and assigned to the annotators. Each fragment has been assigned to any of two annotators at the same time. One of the linguists had been assigned the role of a "super-annotator", who has the final decision about a particular annotation in case of a disagreement of two annotators working on a fragment. He or she also had a general overview of the work already done and may have reviewed the statistics of individual annotators' work. The annotation has been performed using a multi-user, web-based application developed for that purpose. The resulting distribution of instances of each of the senses in the annotated corpus is presented on Figure 2.

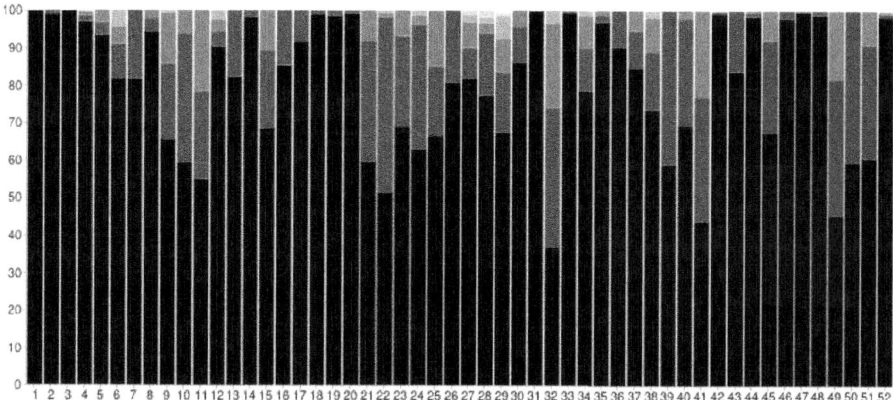

Fig. 2. Percentage of occurrences of each of the senses (per lexeme from the dictionary) in the evaluation corpus. Sense occurrences are sorted in descending order and shades of gray indicate particular senses of the lexemes (e.g. bottom bar – black – most frequent sense of a particular lexeme, dark gray – second most frequent, and so on).

It may be noted that some words from the dictionary were not found in the corpus at all (and have been ignored in the evaluation), while the distribution of senses of other words turned out to be highly skewed towards one or two most frequent meanings. This type of distribution is an example of Zipf's Law, which states that frequency of an object is inversely proportional to its rank in the frequency table.

4 Feature Representation

As we are treating the WSD task as a classification problem, we have to be able to represent the textual data (disambiguated words in context) in the form of a fixed-length feature vector. We have chosen to modify for our needs and use the feature generators implemented in the WSD Development Environment [13].

Thematic Feature Generator (TFG) Existence of a word in a window around the disambiguated lexeme with window size: 5–25 and lemmatization: on/off.

Structural Feature Generator 1 (SFG1) Existence of a word on a particular position in a small window relative to the disambiguated lexeme with window size: 1–5 and lemmatization: on/off.

Structural Feature Generator 2 (SFG2) Existence of part-of-speech on a particular position in a small window relative to the disambiguated lexeme with window size: 1–5 and tagset: full or simplified.

Keyword Feature Generator (KFG) Grammatical form of the disambiguated lexeme with tagset: full or simplified.

Examples of feature vectors created by the generators described above are presented on Figure 3.

TFG

płacić	cena	złotówka	moralność	kilogram	przetwarzać
1	0	1	0	1	1

SFG1

obniżyć-2	obniżyć-1	siebie-1	surowiec+1	praca+1
1	0	1	1	0

SFG2

praet-2	subst-1	adj-1	subst+1
1	0	0	1

KFG

subst	sg	pl	dat	acc
1	0	1	0	1

Fig. 3. Examples of feature vectors

5 Class Association Rules

Association rule mining has been proposed in [3], originally as a method for market basket analysis. This knowledge representation method focuses on showing frequent co-occurrences of attribute values in data. During the last two decades the work on association rules has bloomed, as the technique proved to efficiently provide interesting insights into very large collections of data. Some interesting applications of association rules to real-world problems include: mining medical data to predict heart diseases ([14]), text document categorization ([5]) and image classification ([9]).

Definition. Let's assume the database $\mathcal{D}$ contains data described by binary attributes $I = \{I_1, I_2, \ldots, I_m\}$. We call the set I the itemspace. Database $\mathcal{D}$ is a set of transactions, $\mathcal{D} = \{T_1, T_2, \ldots, T_n\}$ and each transaction T is a set of items (an *itemset*) from the itemspace, $T \subseteq I$. Association rules have the form of an implication over two itemsets, X and Y, where $X, Y \in I$ and $X \cap Y = \emptyset$:

$$R : X \rightarrow Y \tag{1}$$

Itemset X is called the rule's *body*, while itemset Y is called the rule's *head*. A rule of the form shown above indicates, that the occurrence of items in the set X often implicates the occurrence of items in the set Y. The strength of this implication may be measured by two basic parameters: support and confidence. The support of a set of items A is determined by the number of transactions in D, which contain A:

$$\text{supp}(A) = |\mathcal{D}_A| \tag{2}$$

A relative support value, calculated in relation to the size of the database, may also be used:

$$\text{supp}_r(A) = \frac{|\mathcal{D}_A|}{|\mathcal{D}|} \tag{3}$$

The relative support of a rule is defined as the support of its body and head, which is the union of itemsets X and Y, divided by the size of the database:

$$\text{supp}_r(X \to Y) = \frac{\text{supp}(X \cup Y)}{|\mathcal{D}|} = \frac{|\mathcal{D}_{X \cup Y}|}{|\mathcal{D}|} \tag{4}$$

The confidence of a rule is a conditional probability that a transaction containing the rule's body also contains its head.

$$\text{conf}(X \to Y) = \frac{\text{supp}(X \cup Y)}{\text{supp}X} = \frac{|\mathcal{D}_{X \cup Y}|}{|\mathcal{D}_X|} \tag{5}$$

We say that an itemset A is *frequent* in database $\mathcal{D}$, when its support in $\mathcal{D}$ is greater than a certain threshold, called *minimum support*, $\text{supp}(A) > minSup$. Similarly, we say that a rule R is *strong* in database $\mathcal{D}$ if its support and confidence are greater than minimum rule support and confidence, $\text{supp}(X \to Y) > minSup$ and $\text{conf}(X \to Y) > minConf$.

Use in classification. Association rules used for classification, frequently referred to as Class Association Rules (CARs), are rules constrained to have a class label in its head. Having $I = \{I_1, I_2, \ldots, I_m\}$ (the set of items) and $C = \{c_1, c_2, \ldots, c_k\}$ (the set of class labels), $X \subset I$, $c \in C$, CAR is rule of the following form:

$$CAR : X \to c \tag{6}$$

The first method of building a classifier based on a set of mined association rules, named CBA, has been introduced in [11]. The process is divided into two parts: rule generation (CBA-RG) and building the classifier (CBA-CB). During the rule generation step frequent itemsets (having support greater than a specified *minsup* value) are being found in the data, using the Apriori algorithm [4] to avoid searching the entire feature space. Apriori principle tells us that no superset of an infrequent itemset can be frequent. The difference in the approach to finding general frequent itemsets for building association rules and the CBA-RG algorithm consists in considering also the category label as an item in the formed itemsets. Next, rules are created from the itemsets, which have a confidence higher than a set minimum value *minconf*.

In the second step of the process the generated rules are sorted according to a precedence relation. This relation is defined as follows:

$$\begin{aligned} r_i \prec r_j \Leftrightarrow & [\mathrm{conf}(r_i) > \mathrm{conf}(r_j)] \vee \\ & [\mathrm{conf}(r_i) = \mathrm{conf}(r_j) \wedge \sup(r_i) > \sup(r_j)] \vee \\ & [\mathrm{conf}(r_i) = \mathrm{conf}(r_j) \wedge \sup(r_i) = \sup(r_j) \wedge \\ & r_i \text{ generated earlier than } r_j] \end{aligned} \tag{7}$$

Next, for each of the rules in the sorted order all matching examples from the training set are found and number of correct classifications is noted. Rules, which classify at least one example correctly are added to the final classifier and the matching examples are removed from memory. This step is iterated until no data is available in the current memory.

6 Experimental Results

We have adapted the framework described in [13] to carry out a series of classification experiments using a selection of supervised learning methods and text feature representation approaches. Specifically, we have added the ability to use a CARs-based classifier to be able to compare its effectiveness against other well-known methods.

Each experiment has been conducted using the ten-fold cross-validation methodology to be able to use the evaluation corpus as a source for both training and testing data. At first, we have calculated the Most Frequent Sense (MFS) minimum classification accuracy baseline to be able to relate the achieved results to the characteristics of the available corpus. We have also noted the Inter-Annotator Agreement (ITA) value, which reflects the percentage of annotations, for which two annotators provided the same sense labels and no conflict resolution was necessary. This value is frequently described as a good candidate for an upper bound of classification accuracy, as we cannot expect that the system trained on annotated data will perform better than human linguists, who provided the annotation. Abovementioned statistics are presented in Table 3 and for each of the lexemes from the dictionary on Figure 4.

We have performed experiments of classification of the entire evaluation corpus using both the classical NaiveBayes approach (which proved to perform best among others we have tried: J48, SVM, RandomForest) and the method based on mining Class Association Rules. Classifiers have been built individually for each of the disambiguated words and in each case an attribute selection method has been employed to limit the size of feature vectors to less than 400 attributes. The accuracy of classification using the NaiveBayes method has been presented on Figure 5.

Figure 6 shows the results of classification using the CARs method. As may be seen from the overall accuracy results, shown in Table 3, the rule-based method is slightly less accurate, than the NaiveBayes approach. However, the classifier built using the CBA algorithm may be interpreted by a human expert and a potentially interesting knowledge can be extracted from it, which is not the case for the NaiveBayes method.

Table 3. Most Frequent Sense classification baseline, Inter-Annotator Agreement and classification accuracy for individual corpora

corpus	MFS (%)	ITA (%)	NaiveBayes (%)	CARs (%)
NCP subcorpus	77.65	91.97	87.67	84.14
market reports	94.31	96.82	98.86	97.26
overall	91.06	95.99	96.87	94.28

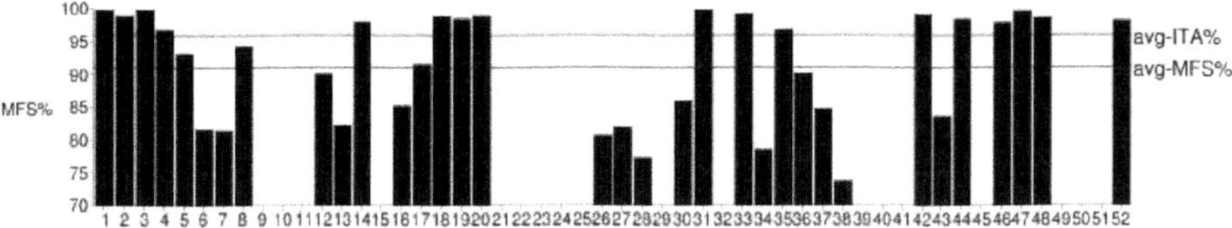

Fig. 4. Most Frequent Sense for each of the disambiguated words and Inter-Annotator Agreement for the entire corpus

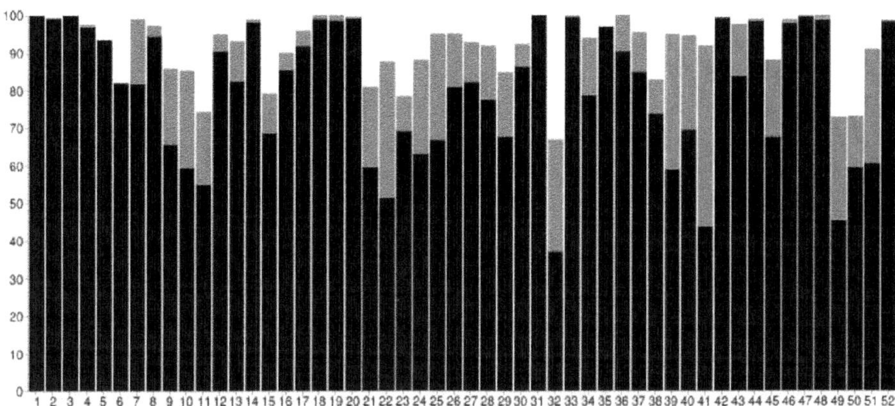

Fig. 5. Accuracy (%) of classification using the NaiveBayes method. Bottom bar (black): MFS baseline, top bar (gray): improvement over MFS.

As an example, below we present a rule generated by the CBA algorithm. Left-hand-side of the rule consists of attributes generated by particular feature generators. Here, the KFG generator provided an attribute pl_KFG (equal to 0), which indicates that the disambiguated word has a singular form. Similarly, noun-1_SFG2=1 noun+1_SFG2=0 attributes indicate that a noun should appear one place before the disambiguated word and no noun one place after the disambiguated word, for the rule to hold. If the rule holds, the selected sense is praca.2.

pl_KFG=0 pos+1_SFG2=0 noun-1_SFG2=1 noun+1_SFG2=0 →
→ SENSE=praca.2 [conf:0.93]

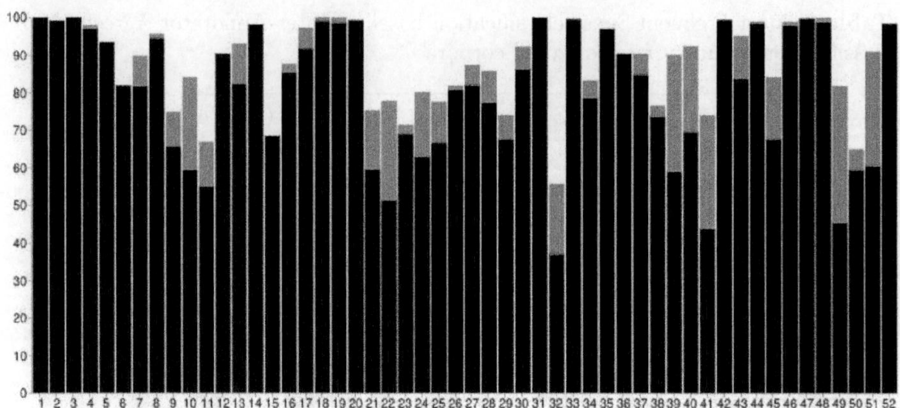

Fig. 6. Accuracy (%) of classification using the CARs method. Bottom bar (black): MFS baseline, top bar (gray): improvement over MFS.

7 Conclusions and Future Work

In this paper we have presented an application of Class Association Rules to the problem of Word Sense Disambiguation of Polish language texts from the domain of economy. We have created a hand-annotated corpus of economy-related textual resources, containing ambiguous lexemes, and used it to train a CARs-based classifier, using the CBA algorithm. Using the standard ten-fold cross-validation methodology we have evaluated the accuracy of the proposed approach and compared it with a well-known NaiveBayes algorithm. Achieved results, while showing the rule-based method to be less accurate than a purely statistical approach are encouraging, because for the cost of slightly lower accuracy we get a classifier that is understandable by human experts and may potentially be manually edited and enhanced.

It remains for future work to test the effectiveness and accuracy of other algorithms for building CARs-based classifiers and also increasing the number of features used to represent the disambiguated word in context.

References

1. Agirre, E., Edmonds, P. (eds.): Word Sense Disambiguation: Algorithms and Applications. Springer, Heidelberg (2006)
2. Agirre, E., Soroa, A.: Personalizing pagerank for word sense disambiguation. In: Proceedings of the 12th Conference of the European Chapter of the Association for Computational Linguistics, EACL 2009 (2009)
3. Agrawal, R., Imielinski, T., Swami, A.N.: Mining association rules between sets of items in large databases. In: Proceedings of the ACM SIGMOD International Conference on Management of Data, Washington, D.C., USA, pp. 207–216 (May 1993), `citeseer.csail.mit.edu/agrawal93mining.html`

4. Agrawal, R., Srikant, R.: Fast algorithms for mining association rules. In: Proceedings of 20th Interntaional Conference on Very Large Data Bases, Santiago, Chile, pp. 487–499 (September 1994), citeseer.csail.mit.edu/agrawal94fast.html
5. Antonie, M.L., Zaïane, O.R.: Text document categorization by term association. In: Proceedings of the 2002 IEEE International Conference on Data Mining, ICDM 2002, pp. 19–26. IEEE Computer Society, Washington, DC (2002), http://portal.acm.org/citation.cfm?id=844380.844745
6. Baś, D., Broda, B., Piasecki, M.: Towards word sense disambiguation of Polish. In: Proceedings of the International Multiconference on Computer Science and Information Technology, pp. 73–78 (2008)
7. Calzolari, N., Choukri, K., Maegaard, B., Mariani, J., Odijk, J., Piperidis, S., Rosner, M., Tapias, D. (eds.): Proceedings of the Seventh International Conference on Language Resources and Evaluation, LREC 2010. ELRA, European Language Resources Association (ELRA), Valletta, Malta (May 2010)
8. Ide, N., Véronis, J.: Word sense disambiguation: The state of the art. Computational Linguistics 24(1), 1–40 (1998)
9. Kobyliński, Ł., Walczak, K.: Class association rules with occurrence count in image classification. TASK Quarterly 11(1–2), 35–45 (2007)
10. Lesk, M.: Automated sense disambiguation using machine-readable dictionaries: How to tell a pine cone from an ice cream cone. In: Proceedings of the 1986 SIGDOC Conference, Toronto, Canada (June 1986)
11. Liu, B., Hsu, W., Ma, Y.: Integrating classification and association rule mining. In: Proceedings of the Fourth International Conference on Knowledge Discovery and Data Mining, New York, USA, August 27-31, pp. 80–86 (1998)
12. Mihalcea, R.: Co-training and self-training for word sense disambiguation. In: CoNLL 2004, Poznań, Poland (November 2004)
13. Młodzki, R., Przepiórkowski, A.: The WSD development environment. In: Vetulani, Z. (ed.) LTC 2009. LNCS, vol. 6562, pp. 224–233. Springer, Heidelberg (2011)
14. Ordonez, C., Omiecinski, E., Braal, L.d., Santana, C.A., Ezquerra, N., Taboada, J.A., Cooke, D., Krawczynska, E., Garcia, E.V.: Mining constrained association rules to predict heart disease. In: Proceedings of the 2001 IEEE International Conference on Data Mining, ICDM 2001, pp. 433–440. IEEE Computer Society, Washington, DC (2001), http://portal.acm.org/citation.cfm?id=645496.658043
15. Paliouras, G., Karkaletsis, V., Androutsopoulos, I., Spyropoulos, C.D.: Learning rules for large-vocabulary word sense disambiguation: a comparison of various classifiers. In: Christodoulakis, D.N. (ed.) NLP 2000. LNCS (LNAI), vol. 1835, pp. 383–394. Springer, Heidelberg (2000)
16. Passonneau, R.J., Salleb-Aoussi, A., Bhardwaj, V., Ide, N.: Word sense annotation of polysemous words by multiple annotators. In: Calzolari, N., et al. [7]
17. Piasecki, M.: Polish tagger TaKIPI: Rule based construction and optimisation. Task Quarterly 11(1–2), 151–167 (2007)
18. Pradhan, S., Loper, E., Dligach, D., Palmer, M.: Semeval-2007 task-17: English lexical sample srl and all words. In: Proceedings of SemEval 2007 (2007)
19. Przepiórkowski, A., Górski, R.L., Łaziński, M., Pęzik, P.: Recent developments in the National Corpus of Polish. In: Calzolari, N., et al. [7]

An Ontology-Based Method for an Efficient Acquisition of Relation Extraction Training and Testing Examples

Aleksander Pohl

Computational Linguistics Department,
Jagiellonian University, Cracow, Poland
aleksander.pohl@uj.edu.pl

Abstract. In this paper, we describe an ontology-based method of selection of test examples for relation extraction, as well as a method of their validation apt to be carried out by ordinary language-speakers. The results will be used to validate performance of various relation extraction algorithms. In performed tests we utilize the ResearchCyc ontology and demonstrate the method's performance in gathering examples from Polish texts.

Keywords: relation extraction, Polish, ontology, Cyc, corpus.

1 Introduction

The task of collecting test and training examples for relation extraction algorithms might be divided into two phases: the selection of the examples, then their annotation. In the first phase, the set of examples is built (usually) as a proper subset of some large corpus. In the second phase, that set is annotated with some meta-data.

There are several approaches to example selection problem: first of all, a proper subset of some larger, general-purpose corpus is selected without constraints; there might also exist an easily available special corpus, containing examples, the structure of which would indicate a number of semantic relations – such a database would be used directly as a source of the examples and finally, the corpus might be build specifically for a given relation.

The first approach usually takes place when the selection of the relation examples is integrated with other annotation tasks, such as named entity identification. E.g. in the National Corpus of Polish, it might be done parallel to the annotation of named entities (NEs) which are identified for its million-segment sub-corpus [16][1]. This style of work is also promoted in the GATE application [3], where the gold-standard examples are directly selected from the whole corpus (cf. http://gate.ac.uk/2mins.html).

[1] However, this is not done, at least it is not mention in the article.

P. Bouvry et al. (Eds.): SIIS 2011, LNCS 7053, pp. 318–331, 2012.

The second approach is popular in the context of semi-structured knowledge-sources like electronic dictionaries and encyclopedias, Wikipedia being the outstanding example. Characteristic structure of the entry or links between the entries are utilized and the examples are selected as results of pattern matching or more sophisticated methods (cf. [9], [18]).

The last approach seems to be particularly popular in the context of relation extraction. Seed patterns or seed examples are used to gather the examples for a particular relation and then these examples are verified by human judges or used directly as input for the statistic-based algorithms (cf. [2], [10], [7]). This allows for more focused examples acquisition and gives more certainty that the test examples would reflect the real world performance of the algorithm.

The second phase of the example collection namely the annotation (or verification) of the examples, depends on the method of their selection. The most traditional approach promoted in GATE assumes that the occurrences of relations are annotated as any other linguistic phenomenon. This is not very efficient, both in terms of the time required and the diversity of examples. Also, this method requires the annotator is trained well enough, to identify properly the occurring relation.

In the case of the second and the third approach, the training examples are automatically annotated as the patterns and seed examples are defined for particular relations and their arguments correspond directly to the arguments in the selected examples. However, the testing examples are usually verified by trained linguists, by asking if a given relation is present or not in a given example.

In this paper we describe alternative methods of both selecting the examples and annotating, i.e. verifying them. The primary idea is to use already available knowledge sources containing rich semantic knowledge, in order to select diversified relation examples. The second idea is to modify the verification task in such a way that even untrained language users would be able to accomplish it. We also present a tool, which is built according to the methodology and preliminary results of the method's performance. The direct results of the work will be used to assess various types of relation extraction algorithms and as a consequence this assumes maximization of the algorithm's coverage. The modified version of the algorithm will be used to gather training examples for hybrid relation extraction algorithms.

2 Related Work

There is a lot of research concentrating on the relation extraction both in the Natural Language Processing community and the Semantic Web community, still the compound potential of both these fields has not been fully utilized. We see our effort as a step in this direction.

Comparing it to the already available tools of which GATE [3] is definitely the most popular and robust, we have to state that its capabilities are in fact without competition in NLP. However, there are several issues connected with its application to the methodology described: the use of Poliqarp [14] server and the IPI PAN corpus [15], which would have to be integrated with the GATE infrastructure; the fact that GATE is designed according to the traditional information extraction pipeline[2], with a lot of attention put to the task of manual text annotation; the fact that the ontology we use – ResearchCyc – is so rich that it would be much impractical to use GATE user interface to select the ontology concepts to annotate the expressions and the fact that, although there is a web-based version of GATE, it is not yet available[3]. All these problems, the availability of our own NLP platform (developed for the Cyc translation task [13]) and our long-distant plans decided that we didn't use GATE.

Comparing our effort with other information extraction research we have to make the following observations. There is a lot of research concentrating on the acquisition of knowledge from Wikipedia. DBpedia [1] and YAGO [17] are efforts aiming at extracting structured knowledge from Wikipedia. DBpedia contains the knowledge extracted mostly from the Wikipedia infoboxes, while YAGO extends this approach, by building on the top of Princeton WordNet [4]. Both these efforts are restricted in the context of relation extraction by the type of relations found in the infoboxes and by their structure. PORE [18] seems to be an interesting alternative, since the relations are extracted from semi-structured Wikipedia contents (the articles' contents with their markup). Although PORE is limited to the contents of the encyclopaedia due to its size this allows for extracting various types of relations. PORE seems to be a very efficient method and we plan to investigate the combination of this algorithm with our idea.

There is also a lot of research related to relation extraction for Polish. First of all, semantic relations in the Polish WordNet [11] are determined semi-automatically. The authors developed an algorithm called *Estratto* which is a modification of *Espresso* [10] "developed mainly to cope with the significant differences between English and Polish" [11]. This algorithm was applied to extract instances of hypernymy in the semi-automatic extension of the Polish WordNet. We find our work complementary in the sense that our algorithm might be used to generate an initial set of seed examples which is then fed by the *Estratto* algorithm maintaining the semantic constraints defined in the ontology. We plan to test such a setting in the near future.

The second important project is the Polish National Corpus (PNC). As an important part of the research a 1-million segment corpus containing annotations of named entities is constructed [16]. Although the paper does not mention relation annotation and the tasks are different in nature, NE identification is related to the proposed method. Namely, the examples selected from the corpus might be identified via NEs and also the annotated corpus will be definitely used in information extraction experiments. But the important differences are: the scope of the annotation – limited to the 1-million sub-corpus in the case of PNC, while defined specifically for the relation in our case and the details level – covering syntactic structures and additional features in the case of PNC, while limited to identifications of the relations' arguments in our case.

---

[2] http://gate.ac.uk/2mins.html

[3] http://gate.ac.uk/teamware/

3 Methodology

3.1 Goals

The goal of this research is to provide a method and an application for an acquisition and verification of semantic relation examples for Polish. The samples collected with this tool will be primarily used for a verification and comparison of various relation-extraction algorithms. If the example set is large enough, they will be used as an input for statistics-based and hybrid relation-extraction algorithms for Polish.

3.2 Idea

The key feature of this method is to use the already available resources, containing rich semantic knowledge, such as ontologies. These serve as:

1. source of seed examples
2. source of hierarchical (hyponymy/hypernymy) relations
3. source of relation's arguments' constraints

The *seed examples* are used to select pairs of concepts maintaining a given relation. The *hierarchical relations* are used to extend the set of seed examples by substituting one of the concepts by its hyponyms. The *argument constraints*, with the disjointness relations found in some ontologies are used to further extend the set of relations by replacing some specified argument with the argument's constraint.

E.g. assume[4] that there is the `anatomicalParts` relation in the ontology, with the following arguments' constraints: `Organism-Whole` and `OrganismPart` and the following instance: `(anatomicalParts Fish Fin)`. The "Fish-Fin" words' pair is a seed example and is used to find examples of the relation in a corpus. The `Fish` concept might be further substituted with `Trout`, `Salmon`, `Hake` (via *hyponymy relation*), giving us "Trout-Fin", "Salmon-Fin", "Hake-Fin" and similar words' pairs. This concept might be also replaced with `Organism-Whole` concept and all of its hyponyms (such as `Dolphine`, `Person`, etc.) capturing words' pairs not present in the ontology (such as "Dolphine-Fin"), but yielding larger number of false positives. And it might be also replaced with any semantically related concept (e.g. a co-hyponyms) not disjoint with `Fish`, which is not its specialisation. In the case of biological taxa this will not bring fruitful combinations. But if we consider a different relation – e.g. `worksAtFacility` indicating that given type of person normally works at given type of facility, for the pair `Chef` and `RestaurantSpace` we could try different combinations, such as `Manager` and `RestaurantSpace`, since `Chef` is related to and is not disjoint with `Manager`. This might give better results than the previous option, if the arguments' constraints are too general.

The other important feature of the method is to provide the person which is responsible for judging if a given example is a valid example of a given relation,

[4] This example is taken from the ResearchCyc ontology.

with the most natural description of the problem. Instead of asking whether a given relation is present in the example, the user is presented with the example and with a rephrasing of the content, as if the relation was present in it. E.g. for the text "The *dog* wagged his *tail*" the description is shown as "The *tail* is an organism part of the *dog*". Although such a rephrasing seems to be trivial for English, it is not for an inflected language like Polish. Thus, the system has to correctly inflect the words in question, properly adjusting their numbers, cases and genders. For this task we use the Polish Inflectional Database [12].

3.3 Tools

The ontology we use in our application is ResearchCyc (a research version of the Cyc ontology [8]) – it contains hundreds of thousands of concepts and millions of assertions, covering hierarchical relations, disjointness relations and other semantic relations, such as the above mentioned `anatomicalParts` relation. This is the largest known ontology available for research.

It has to be stressed that the ResearchCyc ontology in its original version has only the English lexicon, that is the mapping between concepts and their natural-language counterparts. However, as a result of our earlier research we built a tool for mapping Cyc concepts to Polish expressions, which is integrated with the Polish Inflectional Database. The tool allows not only for selecting the Polish expression which best describes given concept, but also for selecting the semantic category or categories, extracted from the Polish Wikipedia, that corresponds to the concept. This allows for providing rich semantic characteristic for all the Wikipedia articles, which are instances of the category. Although only a fraction of the Cyc concepts was mapped to Polish expressions and Polish semantic categories, more than 200 thousands of Wikipedia articles is covered in the mapping. What is more – the tool allows for "pay-as-you-go" strategy, which means that it is easy to extend the mapping for a group of concepts which are important for the current research.

The last resource important for achieving the goal is a corpus of source texts. Regarding Polish, to this respect there are no many options:

1. The free IPI PAN corpus containing 250 millions of tagged segments
2. The Polish National Corpus
3. Internet + search engine

In this research we have chosen the first option, since it is the simplest and the cheapest one. The corpus is available free for research and is distributed with a corpus server, allowing for querying it not only by key-words, but also via lemmas and their tags. The Polish National Corpus [16] is a better option without doubt (it uses the same corpus server, by the way), but it is not yet finished and the access to it is restricted.

The last option is also tempting – there is a lot of research concentrating on the usage of search engines in NLP. There are also some problems connected with this approach. The first is the fact that this method is no longer free – e.g.

if you wish to use the Google API for searching, you have to pay for it[5]. Using the search engine directly violates the terms of use of the service. There is also the copyright problem – the examples found in the Internet would have to be stored in the original form locally and such a long-term storage is normally not allowed by the creators of the content.

The sites with free content, such as Wikipedia, are the special case of the last option. They seem to be a good alternative for manually built corpora (especially in terms of diversity of the content). Although we didn't use Wikipedia's text content as a corpus in this research, we plan to carry out such experiments in the near future.

3.4 Algorithm

Generally the algorithm is divided into several steps. These are: *relation selection*, *concepts mapping*, *data transformation*, *examples selection* and *examples verification*. The first three steps have to be performed in order to prepare the data for the work which is done in the last two steps. Even though they seem to be fairly simple, there are many practical problems, which have to be solved first.

Relation selection. The selection of relations is not as trivial as it seems, since there are about 20 thousands of predicates in Cyc. Many of them are used only to express relations between individuals, which are not as useful in our setting, since Cyc individuals (corresponding mostly to proper names) are not mapped to Polish expressions. On the other hand many of the predicates are used to express meta-knowledge and the corresponding relations are hard to extract from texts. However, there are two types of predicates in Cyc, which are well suited for this task:

1. *type* predicates – designed to relate concepts, e.g. `symmetricPhysicalPartTypes`, which allows for stating that `Crab` has symmetric `Arms`. This means that any (ordinary) instance of `Crab` has symmetric instances of `Arms`. Most of these predicates might be found in the `FirstOrderCollectionPredicate` collection or more general `SetOrCollectionPredicate`.
2. *instance* predicates – designed to relate instances of concepts, e.g. `properGeographicalSubRegions`, which allows for stating that `UnitedStatesOfAmerica` has `Alabama-State` as its proper geographical sub-region.

The first type of predicates might be used directly as a source of seed examples. On the other hand, due to the lack of mapping of individuals, the second type is harder to use. But many of these predicates have accompanying assertions in the form of `relationAllExists` and similar, which allow for stating the same facts as the predicates of the first type (e.g. that a country might be divide into first order administrative divisions, of which states are their specialisations).

[5] `http://code.google.com/intl/pl-PL/apis/customsearch/v1/overview.html`

These constraints substantially reduce the number of predicates to consider as a source of seed examples, but still there are many predicates occurring in typical relation extraction experiments, e.g. `agentTypePerformsWorkOfType` (meaning that instances of an agent type typically perform instances of an activity type as part of their jobs or commercial activity), `agentTypeUsesArtifactType` (meaning that instances of an agent type frequently or typically use instances of an artifact type), `physicalPartTypes` (meaning that every instance of some object type has at least one instance of the related type as a physical part), etc.

Concepts mapping. When the relation is selected, we have to check if all (or most) of the concepts appearing in its assertions are mapped to Polish expressions. Then we should provide the mappings for the missing concepts. It is also reasonable to look up and down through the hierarchy to map other related concepts in order to extend the concepts' coverage. This step is performed with the help of the application described in [13].

E.g. if there is an assertion in Cyc, that the country divides into first order administrative divisions, its specialisations (like US states) should be mapped to Polish expressions. It is also reasonable to create a new specialisation – voivodship – which has a corresponding semantic category in Polish Wikipedia that covers all the voivodships in Poland[6].

Data transformation. To limit the overhead in communication between the examples selection system, the ResearchCyc ontology and the database containing the Polish translations, the data is exported from these resources. A data model (depicted on figure 1 in UML notation) is defined in order to unify the models used in these resources.

There are two main classes: `Concept` and `Relation` in the model. The `Concept` captures both Cyc concepts and Wikipedia articles, forming a consistent concepts hierarchy, allowing for access to its direct `parents`, all its `ancestors` (generalisations), its direct `children` (specialisations or instances) and its `disjoints` (concepts it is disjoint with).

Every `Concept` is related to one or more `Spellings` – that is natural language expressions of the concept (e.g. "Stany Zjednoczone Ameryki Północnej" (*United States of America*) and "USA" for `UnitedStatesOfAmerica`). Each `Spelling` consists of one or more `Segments` (e.g. "Stany", "Zjednoczone", "Ameryki" and "Północnej" for the "Stany Zjednoczone Ameryki Północnej" spelling), each of which points to a corresponding `Lexeme` (e.g. "Ameryki" → AMERYKA) and have associated tags, indicating how the lexeme is inflected. Every `Lexeme` is linked with all its `Word_forms` and also have direct connections with all the `Concepts` it is a part of and `Relations` used to relate it to other lexemes. The `lemma` property indicates its lemma, while `frequency` indicates its frequency in the corpus.

[6] The Wikipedia article about *voivodship* mentions that the proper translation of the original term *województwo* is not *voivodship* but rather *province*. As a contrary, the article is linked to the Polish article *województwo*, while the English *province* is linked to Polish *prowincja*.

The `Relation` class captures both the Cyc relations and their instances (i.e. assertions). Each instance is connected with its relation via `meta relation` association, while each relation is connected with its instances via `instances` association. In the case of the former, the association with `Arguments` points to the concepts which are the arguments of the assertion and in the case of the latter, it points to the arguments' constraints. Every `Concept` is also directly connected with all the relations it is a part of.

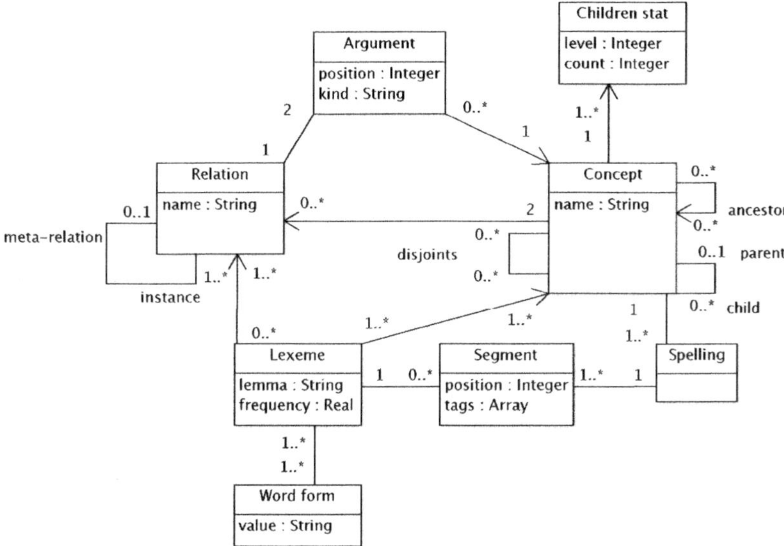

Fig. 1. Data model described in UML notation used in the algorithm

Examples selection. When the data is exported from the knowledge sources, it is used to select the text examples (algorithm 1). In general the algorithm iterates over the relation's instances (i.e. assertions) trying to generate as many as possible queries for each of the arguments (or concepts related to it) of the instance. The results of the query are then checked for the presence of the other argument (or concepts related to it) and are inserted into the return value accordingly.

SELECTCONCEPT function is used to allow for application of the different scenarios described in the section 3.2. Depending on the configuration it selects the argument itself, one of its direct children (specialisations) or the relation's argument's constraint. Then each of the spellings of the selected concept is used to query the corpus. If the spelling has one segment (i.e. is a single-word expression), the lemma of the lexeme linked with this segment is used as the query[7].

[7] The notation used to query the Poliqarp server is described in [14]. Here `[base=lemma]` means that the corpus will be searched for all the occurrences of lexemes with given `lemma`.

Algorithm 1. SELECTEXAMPLES(*relation*)

```
examples ← NEWARRAY()
corpus ← GETCORPUS()
for each instance in relation.instances do
  for each argument in instance.arguments do
    concept ← SELECTCONCEPT(argument)
    for each spelling in concept.spellings do
      if spelling has only one segment then
        segment ← spelling.segments[0]
        candidates ← QUERY(corpus,"[base="+segment.lexeme.lemma+"]")
      else
        candidates ← NEWARRAY()
        for each permutation in PERMUTATIONS(spelling.segments) do
          if INVALID(permutation) then
            next permutation
          else
            query ←"[base="+permutation[0].lexeme.lemma+"]"+
              "[]{0,SPACES}[base="+permutation[1].lexeme.lemma+"]"
            new_candidates ← QUERY(query)
            APPEND(candidates, new_candidates)
          end if
        end for
      end if
    end for
    for each candidate in candidates do
      if OTHERARGUMENTIN(argument, candidate) then
        INSERT(examples, candidate)
      end if
    end for
  end for
end for
return examples
```

If there are many segments in the spelling, each valid 2-element permutation of the segments is used to query the corpus. The validity of the permutation is checked by the INVALID function and might consider features such as the presence of the syntactic head of the spelling, open syntactic category membership of the segments and similar. Although such a method is naive, it is motivated by the free word order in Polish and the assumption of maximizing the coverage of the algorithm. E.g. for "Wojskowa Akademia Techniczna im. Jarosława Dąbrowskiego w Warszawie" (*Jarosław Dąbrowski Military University of Technology in Warsaw*) we are able to generate pairs such as "wojskowa – Warszawa" (*military – Warsaw*) allowing for selecting examples such as "On studiuje w Warszawie na wojskowej." (*He studies in Warsowa on a military [university].*), which will not be captured by any other, more sophisticated method. It is also partially enforced by the corpus server, which preserves the order of the segments in the results – generation of longer sequences would cause an unacceptable number of queries and unacceptable running time. SPACES is a parameter of the algorithm and indicates the number of other segments between the segments taken from the permutation.

When the candidates are selected, they are tested for the occurrence of the other argument via call to OTHERARGUMENTIN. Depending on the experiment configuration this might be one of:

1. direct occurrence of one of the spellings of the concept
2. occurrence of one of the spellings of children (specialisations or instances) of the concept
3. occurrence of one of the spellings of children of the other argument's constraint

The occurrence of a spelling in the example might be tested in various ways, especially if the spelling contains more than one segment. The researcher might define various constraints, such as the text distance between the selected argument and the other argument, the number or percentage of segments that have to occur, the presence of the syntactic head, etc.

The candidates which contain the other argument (or the concept related to it) are then recorded in the form of a corpus query and the result index since, according to the corpus license, the textual data should not be exported from it.

Verification. The last step of the algorithm is the manual verification of the gathered examples. As it was stated in the "Goals" section, the verification is done indirectly, i.e. the user is not asked if the text example and the highlighted segments are related via the relation in question, but there is a natural language rephrasing of the example, as if the relation was present. What is more, since the selected expressions might be ambiguous (e.g. "A *tree* has a *branch*...", where *tree* might be an organism or a mathematical construction), there are accompanying statements, indicating the semantic category or hypernym of concept in question. For instance, assuming that an excerpt "jako uderzenie *płetwy* *rekina* w morzu" (*as the blow of shark's fin in a sea*) was found in the corpus, the following description is produced:

1. Płetwa jest częścią ciała rekina. (*The fin is a body part of the shark.*)
2. Rekin jest drapieżnikiem. (*The shark is a predator.*)
3. Płetwa jest członkiem. (*The fin is an appendage.*)

The user is asked if the description corresponds to the excerpt. There are the following answers to the question:

1. **yes**
2. **no**
3. **don't know**
4. the description has a syntax error
5. the description doesn't make sense
6. the first argument doesn't fit
7. the second argument doesn't fit
8. both arguments don't fit
9. the usage of words in the example is metaphoric

By default only the first three answers are presented to the user and the others are displayed, when the user clicks the "other options" button. This is due to an assumption that most of the examples should follow the simple yes/no/don't know scheme and other answers indicate an error in the application (besides the last option) rather than a problematic example. In such cases the "don't know" option seems to be better.

4 Applications

Each step of the algorithm has an accompanying application, but we will describe only the application used for verifying the examples, since the others are out of scope of this paper.

The application allows for importing the data in JSON[8] format and organizes the examples into examples groups. These groups might be investigated and assigned to users. A regular user sees only the examples, which were assigned to him/her (fig. 2). The first field (*Tekst*) shows the original excerpt found in the corpus. The user might see the broader context by clicking the *szerszy kontekst* button. The second field (*Opis*) is the rephrasing of the relation identified in the text. The correspondence between the arguments in the text and in the description is established via font color. The third filed (*Czy opis odpowiada tekstowi?*) is the question: "Does the description correspond to the text?" and allows for selecting one of the answers described in section 3.4.

5 Results

Several preliminary tests were conducted in order to validate the general assumptions presented in this paper. As an example the `anatomicalParts` relation was

[8] JavaScript Object Notation is a lightweight data-interchange format. `http://www.json.org/`

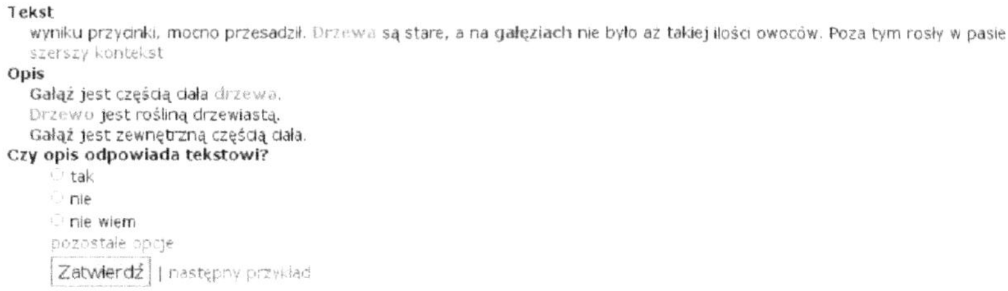

Tekst
wyniku przycinki, mocno przesadził. Drzewa są stare, a na gałęziach nie było aż takiej ilości owoców. Poza tym rosły w pasie
szerszy kontekst
Opis
Gałąź jest częścią ciała drzewa.
Drzewo jest rośliną drzewiastą.
Gałąź jest zewnętrzną częścią ciała.
Czy opis odpowiada tekstowi?
tak
nie
nie wiem
pozostałe opcje
Zatwierdź | następny przykład

Fig. 2. An individual example

selected, which is an *instance* relation (cf. 3.4), with 84 `relationAllExists` assertions. Most of the concepts appearing in the assertions were mapped to Polish expressions, as well as their specialisations. Many of these concepts were also mapped to semantic categories extracted from Polish Wikipedia. As a result, 16560 of Polish expressions were incorporated into the structure of the ResearchCyc concept hierarchy.

Then three different experiment configurations were tested with the Spaces parameter set to 3:

1. **root-root** where we queried the corpus for one of the arguments of the assertion, and the other has to appear in the example directly; this configuration gave 916 examples, of which **586** were unique
2. **root-any child** where we queried the corpus for one of the arguments of the assertion, while the other concept was recognized as the other argument or any of its children (i.e. any direct or indirect specialisation or instance); this configuration gave 3488 examples, of which **3102** were unique
3. **child-any child** where we queried the corpus for up to 10 direct, random children of one of the arguments of the assertion, while the other concept was recognized as the other argument or one of its children; this configuration gave 2274 examples, of which **2164** were unique

The same configurations were tested with the Spaces parameter set to 1 and 5. The results were the same for the first and the second configuration. In the third case the number of results was different (2259 and 2152 with Spaces = 1 and 1871, 1968 and 2300 with Spaces = 5), due to the fact that each time 10 random children of the concept were selected. For this limited setting it means that the parameter didn't have much impact on the number of examples.

821 examples[9] of the **root-any child** configuration were reviewed by an independent user with some linguistic training (not the author of this paper). The user recognized **323** of them as **valid** examples of the relation, **99** as **invalid** and **399** as **problematic**. Almost half (188) of the problematic examples were marked as having *invalid semantics*. It turned out that these examples had incomplete description, due to the fact that the lemma recognized in the IPI PAN corpus was ambiguous in the Polish Inflectional Database and some of the words

[9] The samle size was determined following the method described in [6] aiming for 95% confidence level and 3% error level.

in the description were missing. This means that we should put more attention to accommodate these resources. Another large group of examples (166) was marked as containing metaphoric usage. In fact, these examples could be treated as special kind of invalid examples. As a result more than a half (323 out of 588 valid+invalid) of the non-problematic examples were marked as valid.

It also turned out that, although the user interface encouraged the user to use the first three answers (yes/no/don't know), he preferred to give more detailed one, which caused several misunderstandings. First of all, the user marked several valid examples as metaphoric (as he understood the surname of a person not indicating the person itself), several invalid examples as having syntax error (an ambiguous concept was recognized erroneously by the system and it provided correctly inflected form for the wrong concept, but the user recognized it as incorrectly inflected form of the right concept) and the last but not the least – several descriptions like "Shoulder is an animal anatomical part" raised question if it is good for describing people's shoulders.

All in all, the verification of the 821 examples took 5 hours. Assuming that the problems with the examples with invalid descriptions were resolved and performance of one person might be used to estimate the performance of others, it should be possible to collect more than one thousand of threefold cross-validated positive examples for one relation within 40 hours. This seems to be both time-efficient and enough for a verification of a relation-extraction algorithm (cf. [5]).

6 Conclusions

The method presented in this paper augments the already known methods for the collection of relation extraction training and testing examples by utilizing ResearchCyc as a rich semantic knowledge source. The raw numbers obtained for a specific relation indicate that this method might multiply the number of examples several times compared to the simple method based on seed examples. It gives good results counted in thousands of positive examples, even for moderately sized, unbalanced corpora and a quite specific relation.

However, the novel method of examples verification has to be refined, since some of the results obtained were not foreseen by the author. The number of answers might be reduced, since some of them were not used by the user and some of them were wrongly understood. Also the message produced by the system should be rethought to provide the most natural description of the extracted information.

As a final remark we state that the general assumption, that the ontology is a good source of knowledge for selecting relation extraction examples (even for languages different than English) was proved.

References

1. Auer, S., Bizer, C., Kobilarov, G., Lehmann, J., Cyganiak, R., Ives, Z.G.: DBpedia: A nucleus for a web of open data. In: Aberer, K., Choi, K.-S., Noy, N., Allemang, D., Lee, K.-I., Nixon, L.J.B., Golbeck, J., Mika, P., Maynard, D., Mizoguchi, R., Schreiber, G., Cudré-Mauroux, P. (eds.) ASWC 2007 and ISWC 2007. LNCS, vol. 4825, pp. 722–735. Springer, Heidelberg (2007)

2. Brin, S.: Extracting patterns and relations from the world wide web. In: Atzeni, P., Mendelzon, A.O., Mecca, G. (eds.) WebDB 1998. LNCS, vol. 1590, pp. 172–183. Springer, Heidelberg (1999)
3. Cunningham, D., Maynard, D., Bontcheva, D., Tablan, M.: GATE: A framework and graphical development environment for robust NLP tools and applications. In: Proceedings of the 40th Anniversary Meeting of the Association for Computational Linguistics, ACL 2002 (2002)
4. Fellbaum, C.: WordNet: An Electronic Lexical Database. MIT Press (1998)
5. Hendrickx, I., Kim, S., Kozareva, Z., Nakov, P., Séaghdha, D., Padó, S., Pennacchiotti, M., Romano, L., Szpakowicz, S.: Semeval-2010 task 8: Multi-way classification of semantic relations between pairs of nominals. In: Proceedings of the 5th International Workshop on Semantic Evaluation, pp. 33–38. Association for Computational Linguistics (2010)
6. Israel, G.: Determining sample size. University of Florida Cooperative Extension Service, Institute of Food and Agriculture Sciences, EDIS (1992)
7. Jurafsky, D., Martin, J., Kehler, A.: Speech and language processing: An introduction to natural language processing, computational linguistics, and speech recognition, 2nd edn. Prentice Hall (2009)
8. Lenat, D.B.: CYC: A large-scale investment in knowledge infrastructure. Communications of the ACM 38(11), 33–38 (1995)
9. Markowitz, J., Ahlswede, T., Evens, M.: Semantically significant patterns in dictionary definitions. In: Proceedings of the 24th Annual Meeting on Association for Computational Linguistics, pp. 112–119. Association for Computational Linguistics (1986)
10. Pantel, P., Pennacchiotti, M.: Espresso: Leveraging generic patterns for automatically harvesting semantic relations. In: Proceedings of Conference on Computational Linguistics/ Association for Computational Linguistics, Sydney, Australia, pp. 113–120 (2006)
11. Piasecki, M., Szpakowicz, S., Broda, B.: A Wordnet from the Ground Up. Oficyna Wydawnicza Politechniki Wrocławskiej (2009)
12. Pisarek, P.: Słownik fleksyjny. In: Słowniki komputerowe i Automatyczna Ekstrakcja Informacji z Tekstu, pp. 37–68. Uczelniane Wydawnictwo Naukowo-Dydaktyczne AGH (2009)
13. Pohl, A.: The Semi-automatic Construction of the Polish Cyc Lexicon. Investigationes Linguisticae 21 (2010)
14. Przepiórkowski, A.: Korpus IPI PAN. Wersja wstępna. Instytut Podstaw Informatyki PAN (2004)
15. Przepiórkowski, A.: The potential of the IPI PAN corpus. Poznań Studies in Contemporary Linguistics 41, 31–48 (2006)
16. Savary, A., Waszczuk, J., Przepiórkowski, A.: Towards the Annotation of Named Entities in the National Corpus of Polish. In: Proceedings of the Seventh International Conference on Language Resources and Evaluation, LREC 2010 (2010)
17. Suchanek, F., Kasneci, G., Weikum, G.: Yago: a core of semantic knowledge. In: Proceedings of the 16th International Conference on World Wide Web, pp. 697–706. ACM (2007)
18. Wang, G., Yu, Y., Zhu, H.: PORE: Positive-only relation extraction from wikipedia text. In: Aberer, K., Choi, K.-S., Noy, N., Allemang, D., Lee, K.-I., Nixon, L.J.B., Golbeck, J., Mika, P., Maynard, D., Mizoguchi, R., Schreiber, G., Cudré-Mauroux, P. (eds.) ASWC 2007 and ISWC 2007. LNCS, vol. 4825, pp. 580–594. Springer, Heidelberg (2007)

Rich Set of Features for Proper Name Recognition in Polish Texts

Michał Marcińczuk, Michał Stanek, Maciej Piasecki, and Adam Musiał

Wrocław University of Technology, Wrocław, Poland

Abstract. In this paper we analyse the importance of data generalisation and usage of local context in the problem of the Proper Name recognition. We present an extended set of features that provide generalised description of the data and encode linguistic information. To utilize the rich set of features we applied Conditional Random Fields (CRF) — a modern approach for sequence labelling. We present results of the evaluation on a single domain following the cross-validation scheme and cross-domain evaluation based on training and testing on different corpora. We show that the extended set of features improves the final results for CRF and also this approach outperforms Hidden Markov Models (HMM). On the single domain CRF obtained 92.53% of F-measure for 5 categories of proper names, and 67.72% and 72.62% of F-measure for other two corpora in cross-domain evaluation.

Keywords: Named Entity Recognition, Proper Name Recognition Machine Learning, Hidden Markov Model, Conditional Random Fields, Classifier Ensamble, Polish.

1 Introduction

Proper name (PN) is a natural language expression that denotes one unique entity, its denotation does not depend on the linguistic and extra-linguistic context, at least to the extent of one possible' world [8], and, the most important, its denotation does not depend on its descriptive content (sense), if it has any. The basic difference between PN and a definite (referential) noun phrase is that the latter picks out one entity from the context on the basis of the identification information it conveys, but not the former. Thus, PNs are important links between language expressions and the interpretation contexts in which they are anchored by them.

Robust recognition of PNs in running text is essential in many tasks from the field of natural language processing, i.e. information extraction [14], text anonymization [5] or machine translation [6]. There are several linguistic markers that encode PNs, e.g. the use of big letters in text, however, the proper recognition of PNs is only a little bit easier due to them, and the problem is still unsolved. PNs are one of the main subclasses of *named entities* [10], thus in literature this task is also identified as Named Entity Recognition (NER).

The task of NER is well explored for many languages, especially for English. The top systems recognise names of people, locations and organizations with

P. Bouvry et al. (Eds.): SIIS 2011, LNCS 7053, pp. 332–344, 2012.

performance up to 94% of F-measure (MUC-7) and 97% of F-measure in MUC-6 [3] for cross-validation on a single domain on two corpora of news-wire articles. For Polish there is no common evaluation corpus, thus direct comparison of different approaches is not possible. In our previous work with machine learning methods [11] we obtained 89.67% of F-measure for 5 categories of names in a single-domain evaluation and up to 74.62% for cross-domain evaluation. With rule-based approaches tested on different corpora, [18] achieved ca. 87% and 57% for F-measure for persons and locations respectively. In turn, for the same categories, [1] obtained 72% and 65% of F-measure.

Statistical recognition of NEs in Polish is more difficult then in English mainly because of two factors: (1) *weakly constrained word order*, and (2) *rich inflection*. (1) causes that the same information can be encoded by many different sequences built from the same set of words. In turn (2) increases the number of unique symbols that can be observed in the text. Together these two factors cause that the number of proper word sequences corresponding to one multi-word NE is relatively high. A complex model is required to cope with this diversity. The level of diversity can be reduced by introducing a kind of generalisation over raw text, i.e. levels of lexical, grammatical or semantic information.

The analysis of the results obtained with HMM shows, cf [11], that in many cases HMM makes wrong decisions because the important premises appear in the close but right context — which is not available for HMM in the moment of making a decision. This problem also seems to be more serious for languages with less constrained word order than in English, and can be noted as the third one **(3)** to the above list. The sample errors are:

- "*siedziba w* ***Nowym Sadzie*** *w Republice Serbi*" ('office in Nowy Sad in Republic of Serbia') — HMM recognised *Republice Serbi* as a country name, but not *Nowym Sadzie* as city name. However a more sophisticated model could recognise that *Nowym Sadzie* is a city name from the left and right context taken together;
- "***Elektroproizvodnja****-ZPUE D.O.O.*" ('D.O.O.' is an abbreviation for *Limited liability company* in Serbian) — HMM recognised *Elektroproizvodnja* as a road name while *D.O.O.* in the right context indicate a company name;
- "*w* ***Republice Federalnej Niemiec*** *i Rzeczypospolitej Polskiej*" ('in Federal Republic of Germany and Republic of Poland') — HMM recognised *Rzeczypospolitej Polskiej* as country name, but not *Republice Federalnej Niemiec*.

CRF is a modern machine learning approach applied successfully to labelling sequence data in many Natural Language Processing tasks, e.g., in shallow parsing [22], NER [20], etc. The results obtained for NER with CRF models outperform generative models like HMM because CRF can utilise additional context features — encoding observations – in a non-linear manner. This can help to solve the problems (1) and (2). CRF is able to analyse a much broader context than HMM based methods, utilise features encoding both preceding and following observations — this can help to solve problem (3).

In this paper we investigate the best-practices for applying CRF models to PN recognition in Polish texts and our goal was to improve NER with respect to the three problems identified earlier. We aim at establishing a new set of features and their influence on NER recognition process. We ignore the problem of learning algorithms and normalization factors in CRF models assuming the application of the commonly used parameters for the English [16], and the state of the art stochastic gradiend descent learning method [23].

In the rest of the paper we will define a NER task limited to five categories of PNs which we consider here. Next, we will describe a rich set of features intended to be a basis for a generalised text description and for CRF application, as a CRF-based model that can make advantage of a rich set of features. Finally, we will describe the evaluation: a single-domain evaluation on the corpus of stock exchange reports and a cross-domain evaluation on another two corpora.

2 Task Definition

Our main objective of research is to develop a general method for NER in Polish texts. Due to the limited resources for Polish suitable for this task, that are still under intensive development (e.g. [11,21]), we have limited our scope to selected categories of PNs, i.e. *first names*, *surnames*, names of *countries*, *cities* and *roads*. The list of categories to be recognised will be extended in the future.

We aim at processing non-literary texts (newspaper articles, reports, brochures, etc.). Thus, the space of possible PNs is reduced and some orthographic constrains on PNs can be applied.

We consider the following PN types:

1. **first name** — (or given name) is a part of a personal name that differentiates members of the same family. We annotate separately forenames and middle names as *first name*. Nicknames, logins, pseudonyms (unless they have the form of a regular personal name) are not considered as *first name*.
2. **surname** — is a part of a personal name and is shared by members of the same family. We separately annotate family name and maiden name, if present. If family name and maiden name are joined with a hyphen, they are also separately annotated. Nicknames, logins, pseudonyms, names of non-humans are not considered as *surname*.
3. **country name** — official and short country names. Definite descriptions of countries (e.g. *kraj kwitnącej wiśni* 'Land of the Rising Sun') are not considered as *country name*,
4. **city name** — names of cities, villages, towns, etc.
5. **road name** — names of roads, streets, avenues, boulevards, highways, etc. Names are annotated without preceding key words like *ulica* ('street') or *ul.* ('st.') unless they are a part of the official name (e.g. *Al. Jerozolimskie*) — according to [7] the key words written from lower case letter are not a part of the road proper name.

3 Resources

3.1 Corpora

Three corpora were used during experiments: a corpus of stock exchange reports (CSER), a corpus of police reports (CPR) and a corpus of economic news (CEN). The corpora have been described in details in [11].

The corpus of CSER has been revised to correct errors found during the previous experiments. Numbers of annotation in the previous and contemporary versions of CSER are given in Table 1. The other two corpora (CEN and CPR) remain unchanged (also described in Table 1).

Table 1. Number of annotations in CSER, Revised CSER, CPR and CEN

	CSER	**Revised CSER**	**CPR**	**CEN**
first name	686	688	333	1097
surname	689	691	411	1517
city name	1827	1849	191	657
country name	414	484	27	1695
road name	395	395	42	31

3.2 Gazetteers of Proper Names

We have prepared 5 gazetteers for every PN category. The gazetteers comprise dictionaries collected by Piskorski [17] and PNs gathered from different Internet sources (detailed list of sources is presented in [11]). The gazetteers consists of: 22 435 person first names, 371 380 person surnames, 1 867 country names, 77 873 city names and 40 859 road names. 95% of all proper names are Polish PNs. 96% of all Polish PNs are in morphological base forms.

3.3 Gazetteers of Key Words

On the basis of the manual analysis of the NER rules proposed for Polish in [17] we have defined 5 sets of key words. The key words might indicate the presence of a proper name and its category in the given context. The sets of key words are:

- `country_prefix` — a list of common words that can occur in a country name, e.g. *republika* ('republic') in *Republika Czeska* ('Czech Republic'), *federacja* ('federation') in *Federacja Rosyjska* ('Russian Federation'). This list is be useful for country names that are not present in the dictionaries (especially their official names and inflected forms). The list consists of 17 entries.

- `person_prefix` — a list of positions and titles (full and short forms) that can precede person name. The list contains 1774 words collected manually and extracted from plWordNet.
- `person_suffix` — a list of words that might appear directly after person name. The list contains abbreviations of religious order, e.g. "*Francis Xavier SJ*". The list consists of 112 entries.
- `person_noun` — a list of expressions that can refer to people, e.g. profession names. The list consists of 6339 entries that were described as *nouns denoting people* in plWordNet.
- `road_prefix` — a list of words (full and short forms) that can precede road name, e.g. *ulica* ('street'), *ul.* ('st.'). The list contains 14 entries.

4 Conditional Random Fields

Conditional Random Fields (CRF) are undirected graphical models trained to maximize a conditional probability $Pr(y|x)$ [9]. CRF is commonly applied to problems of labelling sequence data such as NER [13], NP chunking [22], POS tagging [9].

In the case of NER the Markov Field in CRF is a chain, y is a linear sequence of labels from a fixed set, and x is a sequence of words and their corresponding features. The label set contains $2*n+1$ symbols which represents the entity types, where n is the number of entity categories (i.e. first name, surname, etc.). For every PN category A the set of labels contains: **B-**A — represents the beginning; **I-**A — intermediate; and one additional label **O** — out of entity labels.

CRF have to estimate a labelling Y from the observation sequence X. This is done through learning process in which parameters of CRF are tuned to maximize the likelihood of a (x, y) pairs given as training data.

Currently, in the sequence labelling tasks CRF outperforms other learning methods [4] such as classical probabilistic automata [15], Hidden Markov Models [2] and Maximum Entropy Markov Models [12]. CRF can achieve high performance in sequence labelling task because it can make use of many features by analysing them in non sequential manner that makes CRF one of the best method which can overcome label bias problem [9].

5 Features

5.1 List of Features and Their Motivation

We have defined a set of 34 features which are used to form a description of a word occurrence in the sequence. The features are:

1. Ortographic features:
   - **orth** — a word itself, in the form in which it is used in the text,
   - **base** — a morphological base form of a word,

- **n prefixes** — n first characters of the encountered word form, where $n \subset \{1, 2, 3, 4\}$. If the word is shorter than n, the missing characters are replaced with '_'.
- **n suffixes** — n last characters of the encountered word, where $n \subset \{1, 2, 3, 4\}$. If the word is shorter than n, the missing characters are replaced with '_'. We use prefixes to fill the gap of missing inflected forms of proper names in the gazetteers.
- **pattern** — encode pattern of characters in the word:
  - ALL_UPPER — all characters are upper case letters, for example "NASA",
  - ALL_LOWER — all characters are lower case letters, for example "rabbit"
  - DIGITS — all character are digits, for example "102",
  - SYMBOLS — all characters are non alphanumeric, for example "-_-"',
  - UPPER_INIT — the first character is upper case letter, rest are lower case letters, for example "Andrzej",
  - UPPER_CAMEL_CASE — the first character is upper case letter, word contains letters only and has at least one more upper case letter, for example "CamelCase",
  - LOWER_CAMEL_CASE — the first character is lower case letter, word contains letters only and has at least one upper case letter, for example "pascalCase",
  - MIXED — a sequence of letters, digits and/or symbols, for example "H1M1".

  In the future work, the list of patterns will be extended with new entries dedicated to other expressions (for example name of a web page, e-mail address, etc.).

2. Binary orthographic features — **8 binary features**, the feature is 1 if the condition is met, 0 otherwise. The conditions are: 1) *(word) starts with an upper case letter*, 2) *starts with a lower case letter*, 3) *starts with a symbol*, 4) *starts with a digit*, 5) *contains upper case letter*, 6) *contains a lower case letter*, 7) *contains a symbol* and 8) *contains digit*. The features are based on filtering rules described in [11], e.g., first names and surnames starts from upper case and does not contain symbols. To some extent these features duplicate the *pattern* feature. However, the *binary features* encode information on the level of single characters, while the aim of the *pattern* feature is to encode a repeatable sequence of characters.
3. Wordnet-base features — are used to generalise the text description and reduce the observation diversity. The are two types of these features:
   - **synonym** — word's synonym, first in the alphabetical order from all word synonyms in Polish Wordnet. The sense of the word is not disambiguated,
   - **hypernym n** — a hypernym of the word in the distance of n, where $n \subset \{1, 2, 3\}$

4. Morphological features — are based on NER grammars that utilize morphological information [17]. The features are:
   - **ctag** — complete tag with morphological information generated by TaKIPI,
   - **part of speech, case, gender, number** — enumeration types according to tagset described in [19].
5. Gazetteer-based features — one feature for every gazetteer. If a sequence of words is found in a gazetteer the first word in the sequence is set as *B* and the other as *I*. If word is not a part of any dictionary entry it is set to *O*. There are 5 features for every proper name category (see. Section 3.2) and other 5 for every list of key words (see Section 3.3).

A complete set of features for an example sentence is presented in Fig. 1 and 2.

5.2 Templates for CRF

We have prepared and tested CRF with the following set of feature templates:

- only *orth* features of the current, previous and next token — in order to compare with HMM and CRF based on a richer set of features,
- all features for the near context (previous, current and next token) — to check to what extent CRF can learn from the local information,
- all features for the wide context (3 preceding, current and 3 following tokens) — to check to what extent CRF can be improved with wider context.

6 Evaluation

6.1 Single-Domain Evaluation

In the single-domain evaluation we followed 10-fold cross-validation on the revised CSER. Due to changes introduced in CSER we had to repeat the baseline experiments and the results are presented in Table 2. We have used the best configurations reported in [11]. *10-fold HMM* is a cross-validation on all folds for HMM with re-scoring using heuristics and gazetteers and *HMM+post* is a cross-validation on folds 6–10 for HMM with re-scoring and rule-based post-processing. As can be observed in Table 2 the correction of errors improved slightly the evaluation results.

The single-domain evaluation of CRF was performed on the revised CSER. In the first configuration — *orth* feature only — CRF obtained 81.13% of F-measure what was worse by ca 8% than HMM using the same feature. However, the precision of CRF was significantly better than HMM by ca 6%. CRF learned discriminative observations very well but with the loss in the generality. With the extended set of features (see Section 5.1) CRF obtained better level of generalisation with only small loss in precision (ca 2%) and the final performance was better than HMM, i.e. 90.75% of F-measure. The best results were obtained for the wide context, i.e. 92.53% of F-measure with high precision 95.20% — this confirms the observation, that the discriminative information appears in a wide context (3).

n token	*translation*	*label*
1. Pan	Mr	O
2. Marek	Marek	B-PERSON_FIRST_NAM
3. Groszek	Groszek	B-PERSON_LAST_NAM
4. -	-	O
5. Prezes	chairman (of)	O
6. Zarządu	board (of)	O
7. BRE	BRE	O
8. Leasing	Leasing	O

(a) A sample sentence divided into tokens with assigned IOB labels

n token	**orth**	**base**	**pattern**	**p1**	**p2**	**p3**	**p4**	**s1**	**s2**	**s3**	**s4**
1. Pan	Pan	pan	UPPER_INIT	P	Pa	Pan	Pan_	n	an	Pan	_Pan
2. Marek	Marek	marek	UPPER_INIT	M	Mi	Mie	Miec	w	aw	ław	sław
3. Groszek	Groszek	groszek	UPPER_INIT	G	Gr	Gro	Gros	k	ek	zek	szek
4. -	-	-	SYMBOLS	-	-_	-__	-___	-	_-	__-	___-
5. Prezes	Prezes	prezes	UPPER_INIT	P	Pr	Pre	Prez	s	es	zes	ezes
6. Zarządu	Zarządu	zarząd	UPPER_INIT	Z	Za	Zar	Zarz	u	du	ądu	ządu
7. BRE	BRE	bre	ALL_UPPER	B	BR	BRE	BRE_	E	RE	BRE	_BRE
8. Leasing	Leasing	leasing	UPPER_INIT	L	Le	Lea	Leas	g	ng	ing	sing

(b) Ortographic features: orth, base, pattern, prefixes (p) and suffixes (s)

n token	**synonym**	**hypernym 1**	**hypernym 2**	**hypernym 3**
1. Pan	mężczyzna *male*	dorosły *adult*	człowiek_ze_względu_ _na_wiek *person in specified age*	człowiek *human*
2. Marek	marek	marek	marek	marek
3. Groszek	groszek *green peas*	kwiat *flower*	roślina_ozdobna *decoration plant*	roślina *plant*
4. -	-	-	-	-
5. Prezes	przewodniczący *chairman*	głowa *head*	człowiek_ze_względu_ _na_pełnioną_funkcję *person holding a position*	człowiek *human*
6. Zarządu	centrala *head office*	władza *authority*	grupa_ludzi *group of people*	zbiór *set*
7. BRE	bre	bre	bre	bre
8. Leasing	leasing	transakcja_handlowa *trade*	transakcja *deal*	transakcja *deal*

(c) Wordnet-based features: synonym and hypernyms

Fig. 1. Feature set for a sample sentence — part 1 (*columns in grey have been added for the sake of readability*)

n token	ctag	pos	case	number	gender
1. Pan	subst:sg:nom:m1	subst	nom	sg	m1
2. Marek	subst:sg:nom:m1	subst	nom	sg	m1
3. Groszek	subst:sg:nom:m3	subst	nom	sg	m3
4. -	interp	interp	null	null	null
5. Prezes	subst:sg:nom:m1	subst	nom	sg	m1
6. Zarządu	subst:sg:gen:m3	subst	gen	sg	m3
7. BRE	subst:sg:gen:n	subst	gen	sg	n
8. Leasing	subst:sg:nom:m3	subst	nom	sg	m3

(d) Morphological features: ctag, part of speech (pos), case, number and gender

n token	b1	b2	b3	b4	b5	b6	b7	b8	n1	n2	n3	n4	n5	k1	k2	k3	k4	k5
1. Pan	1	0	0	0	1	1	0	0	O	B	O	O	O	O	O	O	B	O
2. Marek	1	0	0	0	1	1	0	0	B	B	O	B	O	O	O	O	O	O
3. Groszek	1	0	0	0	1	1	0	0	O	B	O	O	O	O	O	O	O	O
4. -	0	0	1	0	0	0	1	0	O	O	O	O	O	O	O	O	O	O
5. Prezes	1	0	0	0	1	1	0	0	O	B	O	O	O	O	B	O	B	O
6. Zarządu	1	0	0	0	1	1	0	0	O	O	O	O	O	O	O	O	O	O
7. BRE	1	0	0	0	1	0	0	0	O	O	O	O	O	O	O	O	O	O
8. Leasing	1	0	0	0	1	1	0	0	O	O	O	O	O	O	O	O	O	O

(e) Binary orthographic features (b; in the same order as listed in Section 5.1), and gazetteer-based features: proper names (n; in the same order as listed in Section 3.2) and keywords (k; in the same order as listed in Section 3.3)

Fig. 2. Feature set for a sample sentence — part 2 (*columns in grey have been added for the sake of readability*)

Table 2. Base line evaluation on CSER

	CSER		Revised CSER	
	10-fold HMM	*HMM + post*	*10-fold HMM*	*HMM + post*
Precision	83.55%	85.28%	88.69%	89.84%
Recall	89.70%	88.56%	90.68%	89.66%
F_1	86.52%	86.88%	89.67%	89.75%

Table 3. Results of cross evaluation of CRF on CSER dataset

	road	*surname*	*first name*	*country*	*city*	*Total*
Orth feature for current, previous and next token + Filtering						
Precision	97.76%	97.22%	98.61%	92.59%	95.46%	96.06%
Recall	71.58%	57.85%	61.03%	64.94%	79.57%	70.21%
F_1	82.65%	72.54%	75.40%	76.34%	86.79%	81.13%
full set of features for current token+ Filtering Rule						
Precision	93.33%	95.78%	94.67%	81.22%	92.53%	92.07%
Recall	84.15%	87.60%	81.38%	86.15%	95.14%	89.47%
F_1	88.51%	91.51%	87.52%	83.61%	93.82%	90.75%
Wide contextual features + Filtering Rule						
Precision	96.67%	97.85%	96.89%	89.67%	94.74%	95.20%
Recall	95.08%	87.88%	80.23%	82.68%	95.35%	90.00%
F_1	95.87%	92.60%	87.77%	86.04%	95.04%	92.53%

6.2 Cross-Domain Evaluation

In order to analyse the ability of CRF models to generalise in the context of NER we evaluated them on cross-domain corpora. In the cross-domain evaluation we trained the CRF model using feature templates that produced the best results for the cross-validation on CSER. CRF model trained on CSER was next used to annotate CEN and CPR. Due to changes in the training corpus (CSER) we repeated the experiments from [11] using the best HMM configuration. The new baseline is presented in Table 4.

Table 4. Base line evaluation on CSER

	CPR	**CEN**
Precision	67.49%	54.83%
Recall	84.36%	76.95%
F_1	74.99%	64.03%

Results of the cross-domain evaluation for the first corpus (CPR) are presented in Table 5. CRF obtained 67.71% of F-measure what is less by 7.27% than HMM. However, CRF obtained significantly better precision than HMM, i.e. 92.88% but much lower recall. Application of the wider context resulted in precision improvement (by ca 2%) but also with recall reduction (by ca 4%) — the wider context tend to over-train the model.

Table 5. Cross-domain evaluation on CPR

	road	*surname*	*first name*	*country*	*city*	*Total*
All features for current, next and previous token						
Precision	100.00%	93.06%	93.89%	100.00%	89.05%	92.88%
Recall	50.00%	48.91%	50.75%	81.48%	63.87%	53.29%
F_1	66.67%	64.11%	65.89%	89.80%	74.39%	67.72%
All features for wide context						
Precision	100.00%	92.82%	94.08%	100.00%	95.69%	94.48%
Recall	54.76%	44.04%	47.75%	81.48%	58.12%	49.40%
F_1	70.77%	59.74%	63.35%	89.80%	72.31%	64.88%

In the second experiment we tested the model on the other corpora, namely CEN. The results are presented in Table 6. In this case overall F-measure was increased by 8.32%. On CEN dataset as well as on CPR dataset, CRF achieved very high overall precision. The worst results for CRF were achieved for the recognition of person names. The wider context improves precision for the cost of recall.

Table 6. Cross-domain evaluation on CEN

	road	*surname*	*first name*	*country*	*city*	*Total*
All features for current, next and previous token						
Precision	71.43%	93.06%	96.57%	91.19%	79.91%	91.15%
Recall	16.13%	51.29%	58.98%	70.86%	55.71%	59.98%
F_1	26.32%	66.13%	73.23%	79.75%	65.65%	72.35%
All features for wide context						
Precision	62.50%	94.42%	97.05%	90.31%	80.87%	91.41%
Recall	16.13%	49.11%	57.06%	68.73%	50.84%	57.53%
F_1	25.64%	64.61%	71.87%	78.06%	62.43%	70.62%

7 Summary

In the paper we presented some limitations of HMM in the task of Named Entity Recognition, i.e. a problem with encoding providing data generalised description of text data in terms of linguistic information and modelling contextual information from two-side context. To overcome these two limitations we applied CRF — a modern method for sequence labelling. We introduced a rich set of features: based on linguistic observation and applied to reduce the observation diversity.

In the single-domain cross-validation CRF outperformed HMM. CRF obtained 92.53% of F-measure, while HMM only 89.75%. On the cross-domain evaluation we have trained the model on CSER and evaluated on CPR and CEN. On both corpora we observed the same effect, the precision increased but also the recall decreased. In case of CEN the final results was improved from 64.09% to 72.35%, but for CPR was decreased by 7.27%. Cross-domain evaluation has shown that CRF models are capable to fit very good to the data in the training dataset. Unfortunately, CRF did not obtain high recall. The solution to this problem would be to extend currently used gazeetters, introduce another more generic features both for the tokens as well as for the context in which they are located. Another solution could be a combination of multiple classifiers trained on different domains.

References

1. Abramowicz, W., Filipowska, W., Piskorski, J., Węcel, K., Wieloch, K.: Linguistic Suite for Polish Cadastral System. In: Proceedings of the LREC 2006, Genoa, Italy, pp. 53–58 (2006) ISBN 2-9517408-2-4
2. Bikel, D.M., Miller, S., Schwartz, R., Weischedel, R.: Nymble: a High-Performance Learning Name-finder. In: Proceedings of Conference on Applied Natural Language Processing (1997)
3. Chinchor, N.A.: Overview of MUC-7/MET-2. In: Proceedings of the 7th Message Understanding Conference (1998)
4. Finkel, J.R., Grenager, T., Manning, C.: Incorporating non-local information into information extraction systems by gibbs sampling. In: ACL, pp. 363–370 (2005)
5. Graliński, F., Jassem, K., Marcińczuk, M.: An Environment for Named Entity Recognition and Translation. In: Márquez, L., Somers, H. (eds.) Proceedings of the 13th Annual Conference of the European Association for Machine Translation, Barcelona, Spain, pp. 88–95 (2009)
6. Graliński, F., Jassem, K., Marcińczuk, M., Wawrzyniak, P.: Named Entity Recognition in Machine Anonymization. In: Kłopotek, M.A., Przepiorkowski, A., Wierzchoń, A.T., Trojanowski, K. (eds.) Recent Advances in Intelligent Information Systems, pp. 247–260. Academic Publishing House Exit ((2009)
7. Karpowicz, T.: Kultura języka polskiego. Wymowa, ortografia, interpunkcja (2009)
8. Kripke, S.: Naming and Necessity (1972)
9. Lafferty, J.D., McCallum, A., Pereira, F.C.N.: Conditional Random Fields: Probabilistic Models for Segmenting and Labeling Sequence Data. In: Proceedings of the Eighteenth International Conference on Machine Learning, ICML 2001, pp. 282–289. Morgan Kaufmann Publishers Inc., San Francisco (2001) ISBN 1-55860-778-1
10. LDC: ACE (Automatic Content Extraction) English Annotation Guidelines for Entities (Version 6.6), Technical report, Linguistic Data Consortium (2008)
11. Marcińczuk, M., Piasecki, M.: Statistical Proper Name Recognition in Polish Economic Texts. Control and Cybernetics (to appear in, 2011)

12. McCallum, A., Freitag, D., Pereira, F.C.N.: Maximum Entropy Markov Models for Information Extraction and Segmentation. In: Proceedings of the Seventeenth International Conference on Machine Learning, ICML 2000, pp. 591–598. Morgan Kaufmann Publishers Inc., San Francisco (2000) ISBN 1-55860-707-2
13. McCallum, A., Li, W.: Early results for named entity recognition with conditional random fields, feature induction and web-enhanced lexicons. In: Proceedings of the Seventh Conference on Natural Language Learning at HLT-NAACL 2003, CONLL 2003, vol. 4, pp. 188–191. Association for Computational Linguistics, Stroudsburg (2003)
14. Mykowiecka, A., Kupść, A., Marciniak, M., Piskorski, J.: Resources for Information Extraction from Polish texts. In: Proceedings of the 3rd Language & Technology Conference: Human Language Technologies as a Challenge for Computer Science and Linguistics (LTC 2007), Poznań, Poland, October 5-7 (2007)
15. Paz, A.: Introduction to probabilistic automata (Computer science and applied mathematics). Academic Press, Inc., Orlando (1971) ISBN 0125476507
16. Peng, F., McCallum, A.: Accurate Information Extraction from Research Papers Using Conditional Random Fields. In: HLT-NAACL, pp. 329–336 (2004)
17. Piskorski, J.: Extraction of Polish named entities. In: Proceedings of the Fourth International Conference on Language Resources and Evaluation, LREC 2004 (ELR 2004), pp. 313–316. Association for Computational Linguistics, Prague (2004)
18. Piskorski, J.: Named-Entity Recognition for Polish with SProUT. In: Bolc, L., Michalewicz, Z., Nishida, T. (eds.) IMTCI 2004. LNCS (LNAI), vol. 3490, pp. 122–133. Springer, Heidelberg (2005) ISBN 3-540-29035-4
19. Przepiórkowski, A.: The IPI PAN Corpus: Preliminary version, Institute of Computer Science. Polish Academy of Sciences, Warsaw (2004)
20. Rosenfeld, B., Fresko, M., Feldman, R.: A systematic comparison of feature-rich probabilistic classifiers for NER tasks. In: Jorge, A.M., Torgo, L., Brazdil, P.B., Camacho, R., Gama, J. (eds.) PKDD 2005. LNCS (LNAI), vol. 3721, pp. 217–227. Springer, Heidelberg (2005) ISBN 978-3-540-29244-9
21. Savary, A., Waszczuk, J., Przepiórkowski, A.: Towards the Annotation of Named Entities in the National Corpus of Polish. In: LREC 2010 Proceedings (2010)
22. Sha, F., Pereira, F.: Shallow parsing with conditional random fields. In: Proceedings of the 2003 Conference of the North American Chapter of the Association for Computational Linguistics on Human Language Technology, NAACL 2003, vol. 1, pp. 134–141. Association for Computational Linguistics, Stroudsburg (2003)
23. Vishwanathan, S.V.N., Schraudolph, N.N., Schmidt, M.W., Murphy, K.P.: Accelerated training of conditional random fields with stochastic gradient methods. In: Proceedings of the 23rd International Conference on Machine Learning, ICML 2006, pp. 969–976. ACM, New York (2006) ISBN 1-59593-383-2

Similarity-Based Method of Detecting Diathesis Alternations in Semantic Valence Dictionary of Polish Verbs

Elżbieta Hajnicz

Institute of Computer Science, Polish Academy of Sciences

Abstract. In order to create semantic valence dictionary, in which semantically related syntactic verb schemata are connected, the information of diathesis alternations of verbs is needed. In this paper, first experiments concerning a method of automatic detection of alternation base on similarity between semantically interpreted (by means of selectional preferences) verb frames are presented.

1 Introduction

The primary task of our research is to create a semantic valence dictionary in an automatic way. To accomplish this goal, the syntactic valence dictionary of Polish verbs is supplemented with semantic information, provided by wordnet's semantic categories [4] or synsets [6] of nouns. In our present work we focus on arguments being nominal phrases NPs and prepositional-nominal phrases PrepNPs, whose semantic heads are nouns. We discuss the case of 25 predefined semantic categories of nouns.

In the current phase of work we have in our disposal an automatically created semantic valence dictionary (cf. section 3). It is a list of semantic verb frames, in which each argument is supplied with a semantic category. Each semantic frame can be viewed as an interpretation of the syntactic schema[1] it represents. However, no information is provided whether two schemata are used to express the same meaning, i.e., whether they are involved in a diathesis alternation.

In this paper a method to detect diathesis alternations is proposed. It is based on similarity between entries of semantic valence dictionary. In section 2 works on alternation detection are discussed, in section 3 valence dictionaries used for alternation detection are presented. Section 4 contains purely syntactic classification of alternations, section 5 describes the method used to detect alternation, whereas section 6 presents conducted experiments.

2 Related Works

There exist several works concerning automatic detection of diathesis alternation, mainly for English. Lapata [11] analyses verbs having double object

[1] We use the term syntactic *schema* instead of very popular syntactic *frame* in order to distinguish it from the term *semantic frame*.

P. Bouvry et al. (Eds.): SIIS 2011, LNCS 7053, pp. 345–358, 2012.

schemata and direct object plus prepositional phrase schemata. She identifies erroneous text realisations of three syntactic patterns extracted from a corpus using several linguistic heuristics. If a verb has both V NP1 NP2 and V NP1 *to* NP2 schemata afterwards, it is accepted as participating in dative alternation, whereas if a verb has both V NP1 NP2 and V NP1 *for* NP2 schemata, it is accepted as participating in dative alternation.

An alternation-based method of classifying verbs is proposed in [20, 17, 9, 10]. The authors take into account various features, like distribution of verbs between patterns, a level of consistency between arguments, animacy of arguments etc. The classification is performed using unsupervised hierarchical algorithm from SPlus 5.0 and supervised decision tree C5.0 and C4.5 algorithms for the whole set of features and its subsets.

Resnik [19] detects argument deletion alternation under the assumption that verbs participating in it have strong selectional preference for particular senses for deleted argument, and occurrences of corresponding (i.e., strongly preferred) anaphoric antecedents are rare in comparison with other verbs.

Gildea [3] clusters verbs under the assumption that occurrences of a noun on the particular syntactic slot of a verb are conditionally independent from unobserved variables representing a cluster and a semantic role. He trains the model using EM algorithm. The alternation takes place if the same role is attached to the similar set of nouns on different syntactic slots of the verb in the same cluster.

McCarthy [15, 16] presents a method of detecting alternations by means of optimal tree cuts in WordNet hypernymy hierarchy. A tree cut is a set of synsets not related by hypernymy. Tree cuts optimally representing selectional preferences between a verb, a schema and a syntactic slot were found using minimum description length principle (MDL) [1, 13, 14]. McCarthy applies MDL to detect alternations between corresponding syntactic slots of two schemata as well. She also compares probability distributions of synsets for the slots by means of Euclidean, rectilinear and cosines measures and α-skew divergence. For this sake she uses estimations of conditional probabilities $\hat{p}(c|v,r)$ obtained while finding optimal tree cuts, where c denotes a synset. Since the comparison has to be performed on the same set of synsets, a “union” tree cut was found, in which each hypernym from one cut substituted all its hyponyms from the other cut.

3 Valence Dictionary

A syntactic valence dictionary $\mathcal{D}$ is a set of entries representing schemata for every verb considered. Formally, $\mathcal{D}$ is a set of pairs $\langle v, g \rangle$, where $v \in V$ is a verb and $g = \langle r_1, \ldots, r_n \rangle \in G$ is a syntactic schema, with $r_i \in R$ being its arguments. The dictionary for 32 verbs chosen for experiment was prepared on the basis of Świdziński's [22] dictionary. Verbs were chosen manually in a way to maximise the variability of their syntactic frames (in particular, diathesis alternations) on one hand and the polysemy within a single frame on the other. Their frequency was the important criterion for this choice as well. Arguments are nomi-

Table 1. Predefined set of general semantic categories in Polish WordNet

name	acr	name	acr	name	acr	name	acr
act	ac	communication	cm	motive	mt	quantity	qn
animal	an	event	ev	person	pn	relation	rl
artifact	ar	feeling	fl	phenomenon	ph	shape	sh
attribute	at	food	fd	plant	pl	state	st
body	bd	group	gr	possession	ps	substance	sb
cognition	cg	location	lc	process	pr	time	tm

nal phrases (np:⟨case⟩), prepositional-nominal phrases (prepnp:⟨prep⟩:⟨case⟩), wh-clauses (sentp:wh) etc., and sie is a reflexive marker.

A semantic valence dictionary was obtained by supplementing the syntactic valence dictionary with selectional preferences. Here, we consider the simple case of the fix set of 25 semantic categories, which were assigned to nouns at the beginning of the preparation of the Polish WordNet [18], which was modelled on the Princeton WordNet and wordnets constructed in the EuroWordNet project. The list of categories can be found in Table 1 together with acronyms used in examples. The process of collecting a semantic valence dictionary for semantic categories was described in [5]. An exemplary subset of the set of frames connected with the schema `np:acc np:nom` of the verb *kończyć* (*to finish*) is shown on the left side of Figure 1.

Dictionaries existing for other languages, like VerbNet [2] for English or VerbaLex [8] for Czech, consider one most strongly preferred sense per argument. Such resources without frequency cannot be applied for our goal. In contrast, VALLEX [23] contains frequencies of schemata, but tectogrammatic functors are kinds of semantic roles, not semantic preferences.

Formally, a semantic dictionary $\mathfrak{D}$ is a set of tuples $\langle\langle v, g, f\rangle, m_f\rangle$, where $\langle v, g\rangle \in \mathcal{D}$ is a schema of a verb, $f \in F_g$ is one of its semantic frames and m_f is the frequency of $\langle v, g, f\rangle$. A frame $f = \langle a_1, \ldots, a_k\rangle$ is a list of arguments $a_i = \langle r_i, c_i\rangle$, among which NPs and PrepNPs are semantically interpreted, i.e., supplied with semantic categories c_i.[2]

4 Classification of Alternations

For Polish, there exists no comprehensive classification of diathesis alternations and verbs participating in them, as [12] serves for English. The analysis of accusative verbs was conducted in [21].

Our goal is to consider all potential alternations regardless of the fact whether they were already classified or not. Because of that we decided to start with very coarse purely syntactic classification of potential alternations, describing only how the alternation relate arguments in two schemata $g^A = \langle r_1^A, \ldots, r_{n^A}^A\rangle$, $g^B = \langle r_1^B, \ldots, r_{n^B}^B\rangle$ involved in it.

[2] For uniformity, we can say that semantic interpretation of other arguments is empty.

The alternations can be divided in two ways. The first concerns the occurrence of alternating arguments in both schemata:

- alternations preserving the number of arguments in both schemata,
- alternations in which one of alternating arguments is absent in one schema.

The second is characteristic for Slavic languages and concerns the voice of an utterance:

- alternations preserving the voice of an utterance,
- alternations changing the voice of an utterance from active to reflexive.[3]

According to this partition, we distinguish the following eight types of alternations.

A. Alternations preserving the number of arguments and voice
   1. *Simple* alternation occurs for schemata $g^A = \langle r_1, \ldots, r_k^A, \ldots, r_n \rangle$ and $g^B = \langle r_1, \ldots, r_k^B, \ldots, r_n \rangle$, where $r_k^A \neq r_k^B$. Alternating k-th arguments differ syntactically, but they are semantically consistent, as in dative alternation, see (1).
      (1) *Chłopak posłał książkę koledze.* (*A boy sent his friend a book.*)
      Chłopak posłał książkę do kolegi. (*A boy sent a book to his friend.*)
   2. *Cross* alternation occurs for schemata $g^A = \langle r_1, \ldots, r_k^A, \ldots, r_l, \ldots, r_n \rangle$ and $g^B = \langle r_1, \ldots, r_k^B, \ldots, r_l, \ldots, r_n \rangle$, where $r_k^A \neq r_k^B$. The schemata differ syntactically only in k-th argument as well, but $r_l \in g^A$ is semantically consistent with r_k^B, whereas $r_l \in g^B$ is semantically consistent with r_k^A, as in locative alternation, see (2).
      (2) *Rolnik załadował wóz sianem.* (*The farmer loaded the wagon with hay.*)
      Rolnik załadował siano na wóz. (*The farmer loaded hay onto the wagon.*)

B. Alternations changing the number of arguments and preserving voice
   3. *Argument deletion* alternation occurs for $g^A = \langle r_1, \ldots, r_k, \ldots, r_n \rangle$ and $g^B = \langle r_1, \ldots, r_{k-1}, r_{k+1}, \ldots, r_n \rangle$, which differ only in presence or absence of k-th argument, see (3).
      (3) *Matka pozmywała naczynia.* (*Mother washed dishes.*)
      Matka pozmywała. (*Mother washed.*)
   4. *Argument shift* alternation occurs for $g^A = \langle r_1, \ldots, r_k, \ldots, r_l, \ldots, r_n \rangle$ and $g^B = \langle r_1, \ldots, r_{k-1}, r_{k+1}, \ldots, r_l, \ldots, r_n \rangle$, which syntactically differ in presence of k-th argument, but r_k is semantically consistent with $r_l \in g^B$, so $r_l \in g^A$ is semantically absent in g^B, as in an unreflexive case of causative alternation, see (4).
      (4) *Jeździec pognał konia przez las.* (*The rider rode a horse across a forest.*)
      Koń pognał przez las. (*A horse rode across a forest.*)

C. Alternations preserving the number of arguments and changing voice

[3] We do not consider passive alternation because of the regularity of passivisation. Moreover, there are not separate passive schemata in $\mathcal{D}$.

5. *Reflexive simple* alternation occurs for $g^A = \langle r_1, \ldots, r_k^A, \ldots, r_n \rangle$ and $g^B = \langle r_1, \ldots, r_k^B, \ldots, r_n, \mathsf{sie} \rangle$, where $r_k^A \neq r_k^B$. Alternating k-th arguments differ syntactically, but they are semantically consistent. Additionally, reflexive marker *się* is present in schema g^B (and absent in g^A), see (5).
   (5) *Chłopak kocha dziewczynę / się w dziewczynie.* (*A boy loves a girl.*)
6. *Cross reflexive* alternation occurs for $g^A = \langle r_1, \ldots, r_k^A, \ldots, r_l, \ldots, r_n \rangle$ and $g^B = \langle r_1, \ldots, r_k^B, \ldots, r_l, \ldots, r_n, \mathsf{sie} \rangle$, where $r_k^A \neq r_k^B$, and constraints on r_k and r_l are similar to *cross* alternation. Additionally, reflexive marker *się* is present only in schema g^B, cf. (5).
   (6) *Córka niepokoi matkę.* (*A daughter worries (her) mother.*)
   Matka niepokoi się o córkę. (*A mother worries about (her) daughter.*)

D. Alternations changing the number of arguments and voice

7. *Reflexive deletion* alternation occurs for $g^A = \langle r_1, \ldots, r_k^A, \ldots, r_n \rangle$ and $g^B = \langle r_1, \ldots, r_{k-1}, r_{k+1}, \ldots, r_n, \mathsf{sie} \rangle$, in which k-th argument is replaced with sie, as in reflexive (7) and reciprocal (8) alternations.
   (7) *Żołnierz obronił towarzysza/się przed atakiem.*
   (*A soldier defend his comrade/himself from the attack.*)
   (8) *Chłopak spotkał dziewczynę / się z dziewczyną.* (*A boy met a girl.*)
   Chłopak z dziewczyną spotkali się.
   Chłopak i dziewczyna spotkali się. (*A boy and a girl met.*)
8. *Reflexive shift* alternation occurs for $g^A = \langle r_1, \ldots, r_k^A, \ldots, r_l, \ldots, r_n \rangle$ and $g^B = \langle r_1, \ldots, r_{k-1}, r_{k+1}, \ldots, r_l, \ldots, r_n, \mathsf{sie} \rangle$, and constraints on r_k and r_l are analogous to *argument shift* alternation, as in causative alternation, cf. (9).
   (9) *Kelner stłukł szklanki.* (*A waiter broke glasses.*)
   Szklanki stłukły się. (*Glasses broke.*)

The arguments not involved in an alternation have to be semantically consistent in both schemata.

Formally, the set of alternations $\mathfrak{A} = \{\langle \mathfrak{a}, g^A, g^B, r^A, r^B, r \rangle\}$, where $\mathfrak{a}$ is the alternation type, g^A, g^B is a pair of alternating schemata, whereas r^A, r^B, r are arguments involved in the alternation, $r^A, r \in g^A$, $r^B, r \in g^B$. According to alternation type, some arguments are empty.

5 The Method of Detecting Alternations

Potentially, all pairs of schemata satisfying one of constrains 1.–8. can participate in the corresponding alternation. The method of detecting which schemata actually participate in the particular alternation presented in this paper is an adaptation of solution proposed in [15, 16], concerning comparison of probability distributions imposed by tree cut models. In our case, we compare estimations of probability distributions formed by semantic frames, as in (1). The main difference is that McCarthy considers only arguments involved in an alternations, whereas we compare whole schemata. A minor difference is that we use a fixed set of semantic categories instead of tree cuts. Thus, for schemata g^A, g^B potentially involved in alternation $\mathfrak{a}$ we have corresponding distributions $\hat{p}^A_{v,g}, \hat{p}^B_{v,g}$ in our disposal, which are normalised frequencies of $\mathfrak{D}$, namely

$$\hat{p}_{v,g}(f) = \hat{p}(f|g,v) = \frac{m_f}{\sum\limits_{\langle v,g,f'\rangle \in \mathfrak{D}} m_{f'}}. \tag{10}$$

5.1 Preparing Frames to Comparison

The problem is that we are able to compare different distributions (frame sets) of the same schema, whereas alternating schemata differ from each other. However, an alternation itself brings information how to transform the frame set of schema g^A to uniform it with g^B. We implement this by means of two procedures: *Compact*, which deletes one argument and aggregates frames with consistent other arguments, and *Match*, which only changes the syntactic type of an argument.

(11) **procedure** *Compact* (g, r)
  let $g = \langle r_1, \ldots, r_k = r, \ldots, r_n \rangle$;
  let $g' = \langle r_1, \ldots, r_{k-1}, r_{k+1}, \ldots, r_n \rangle$;
  for each $f' = \langle a_1, \ldots, a_{k-1}, a_{k+1}, \ldots, a_k \rangle$ **do**
    $\hat{p}_{v,g'}(f') = \bigcup\limits_{f=\langle a_1,\ldots,a_k,\ldots,a_k \rangle} \hat{p}_{v,g}(f)$;
  od;
  return $(\langle g', \hat{p}_{v,g'} \rangle)$.

(12) **procedure** *Match* (g, r^A, r^B)
  let $g = \langle r_1, \ldots, r_k = r^A, \ldots, r_n \rangle$;
  let $g' = \langle r_1, \ldots, r_k = r^B, \ldots, r_n \rangle$;
  for each $f = \langle a_1, \ldots, a_k = \langle r^A, c \rangle, \ldots, a_k \rangle$ **do**
    $f' := \langle a_1, \ldots, a_k = \langle r^B, c \rangle, \ldots, a_k \rangle$;
    $\hat{p}_{v,g'}(f') = \hat{p}_{v,g}(f)$;
  od;
  return $(\langle g', \hat{p}_{v,g'} \rangle)$.

Using this two procedures, we can unify pairs of schemata involved in any alternation by modifying schema g^A. Procedure *Compact* is applied to the syntactically deleted argument r^A for argument deletion and r for shift alternations. The procedure *Match* changes the argument r^A to r^B for simple alternation and r^A to r for shift alternation. As for cross alternation, first argument r is changed to r^B and next r^A is changed to r by means of the procedure *Match*. The same procedures are applied to the reflexive counterparts of the above alternations.

We illustrate the procedure on example of reflexive shift (causative) alternation and schemata of verb *kończyć*. First, all pairs of schemata satisfying the

Frame	Prob.	Merged	Prob.		Result	Prob.
`acc: ac; nom: at`	0.002	`acc: ac`	0.386	$\Longrightarrow$	`nom: ac`	0.386
`acc: ac; nom: ac`	0.004					
`acc: ac; nom: gr`	0.049					
`acc: ac; nom: qn`	0.006					
`acc: ac; nom: pn`	0.303					
`acc: ac; nom: cm`	0.002					
`acc: ac; nom: ar`	0.004					
`acc: ac; nom: ev`	0.015					
`acc: cm; nom: gr`	0.002	`acc: cm`	0.087	$\Longrightarrow$	`nom: cm`	0.087
`acc: cm; nom: pn`	0.085					
`acc: ps; nom: pn`	0.002	`acc: ps`	0.004	$\Longrightarrow$	`nom: ps`	0.004
`acc: ps; nom: ev`	0.002					
`acc: ev; nom: gr`	0.011	`acc: ac`	0.179	$\Longrightarrow$	`nom: ac`	0.179
`acc: ev; nom: qn`	0.002					
`acc: ev; nom: pn`	0.143					
`acc: ev; nom: st`	0.002					
`acc: ev; nom: ar`	0.009					
`acc: ev; nom: ev`	0.013					

Fig. 1. The process of transformation of schema `np:acc np:nom` of verb *kończyć* for reflexive shift alternation

constraint 8. are chosen, which in particular concerns pairs ⟨`np:acc np:nom`, `np:nom sie`⟩ and ⟨`np:nom prepnp:z:inst`, `np:nom sie`⟩. In Figure 1 the process of transformation of frames of schema `np:acc np:nom` into schema `np:nom`[4] to match requirements of reflexive shift alternation. For simplicity, we write only a case for NPs (`acc`) and a preposition followed by a case for PPs (`na_acc`). This makes no confusion, as only these arguments are semantically interpreted. Nevertheless, schemata which differ in other arguments are not considered as candidates for alternations.

5.2 The Algorithm

From among the measures considered by McCarthy, we use in our experiments the Euclidean D_E, rectilinear L_1 and cosines cos measures. Applied to probability distributions $\hat{p}^A_{v,g}, \hat{p}^B_{v,g}$ of uniform schemata $g^{A\prime} = g^B = g$ of verb v:

(13) $$D_E(\hat{p}^A_{v,g}, \hat{p}^B_{v,g}) = \sqrt{\sum_f (\hat{p}^A_{v,g}(f) - \hat{p}^B_{v,g}(f))^2},$$

(14) $$L_1(\hat{p}^A_{v,g}, \hat{p}^B_{v,g}) = \sum_f |\hat{p}^A_{v,g}(f) - \hat{p}^B_{v,g}(f)|,$$

[4] At this level, schema `np:nom` cannot be distinguish from `np:nom sie`, as `sie` is not semantically interpreted.

$$\cos(\hat{p}^A_{v,g}, \hat{p}^B_{v,g}) = \frac{\sum_f \hat{p}^A_{v,g}(f) \cdot \hat{p}^B_{v,g}(f)}{\sqrt{\sum_f (\hat{p}^A_{v,g}(f))^2} \sqrt{\sum_f (\hat{p}^B_{v,g}(f))^2}}. \tag{15}$$

The first two measures are distance measures, whereas the third one is a similarity measure. Both $D_E(\hat{p}, \hat{p}) = 0$ and $L_1(\hat{p}, \hat{p}) = 0$ and they increase while the difference between the distributions increases. Moreover, $L_1(\hat{p}^A, \hat{p}^B) \in [0, 2]$, $D_E(\hat{p}^A, \hat{p}^B) \in [0, \sqrt{2}]$ On the other hand, $\cos(\hat{p}, \hat{p}) = 1$ and it decreases while the difference between the distributions increases, and $\cos(\hat{p}^A, \hat{p}^B) \in [0, 1]$. In order to normalise the measures, we transform the first two in the following way:

$$\tilde{D}_E(\hat{p}^A, \hat{p}^B) \equiv 1 - D_E(\hat{p}^A, \hat{p}^B)/\sqrt{2}, \tag{16}$$

$$\tilde{L}_1(\hat{p}^A, \hat{p}^B) \equiv 1 - L_1(\hat{p}^A, \hat{p}^B)/2. \tag{17}$$

After this modification, we deal with three similarity measures (denoted uniformly as μ) satisfying the conditions:

- $\mu(\hat{p}^A, \hat{p}^B) \in [0, 1]$;
- $\mu(\hat{p}^A, \hat{p}^B) = \mu(\hat{p}^B, \hat{p}^A)$,
- $\mu(\hat{p}^A, \hat{p}^B) = 1 \quad \text{iff} \quad \hat{p}^A = \hat{p}^B$.

This means that all the measures obtain minimal value 0 for maximally different distributions. For cos and $\tilde{L}_1$ this means that only one of them can obtain positive value for any frame f.[5] For $\tilde{D}_E$ this means that there exists f^A, f^B such that $\hat{p}^A_{v,g}(f^A) = 1$ and $\hat{p}^B_{v,g}(f^B) = 1$. Therefore, $\tilde{D}_E$ shows maximal difference much more rarely than two other measures.

All three measures increase while the similarity between the distributions increases, and obtain maximal value 1, when they are identical.

The main idea of the algorithm consists in computing the similarity measure μ between distributions representing a candidate pair of schemata. If μ exceeds a particular threshold η, then we assume that the particular alternation between them occurs.

6 Experiments

The experiments were performed using semantic valence dictionary $\mathfrak{D}$ containing 341 schemata of 32 verbs. However, since it was created completely automatically [4, 5], $\mathfrak{D}$ is quite noisy. In order to reduce this noise, we used a small dictionary $\mathfrak{D}^H$ containing 37 schemata of 5 verbs, which was prepared manually as a gold standard for evaluation of of $\mathfrak{D}$ [5, 7]. Since it does not contain frequencies, it was supplied with frequencies of corresponding frames from $\mathfrak{D}$. Frames absent

[5] Geometrically, this is orthogonality of vectors.

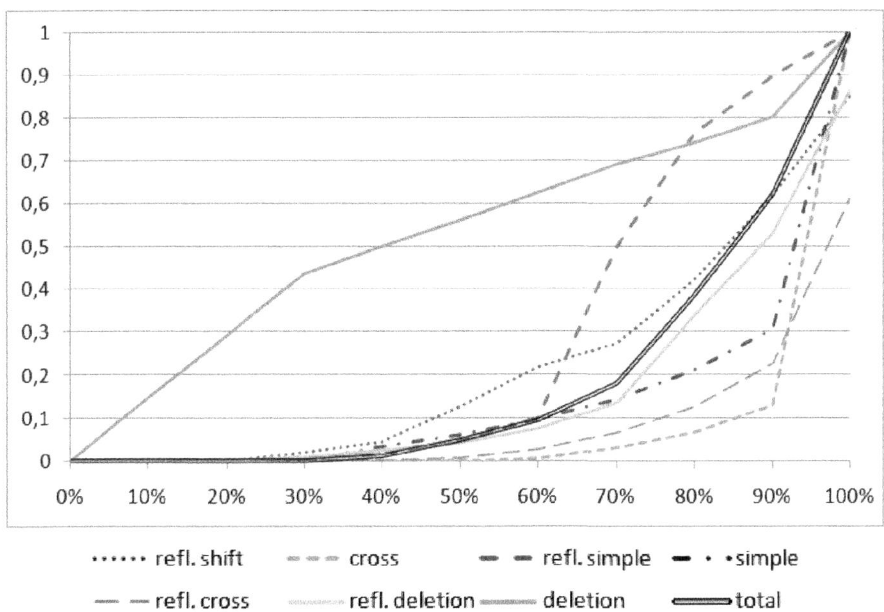

Fig. 2. Rectilinear measure L_1 computed for every 10th percentile for dictionary $\mathfrak{D}$

in $\mathfrak{D}$ were considered rare and hence they obtain an artificially small frequency 0.2. After this procedure both dictionaries were normalised to obtain estimations of probability distribution.

The method described in the previous section depends on the value of the threshold η. McCarthy [16] considered equal number of verbs participating in each alternation and not participating ones. Therefore, she considered the thresholds equal to the median or the mean of the values of similarity measure computed for all candidate verbs. However, this assumption is evidently artificial. McCarthy claims that she made it because she only wanted to test whether her method works.[6] In contrast, we decided to find the threshold experimentally. For this sake, we sort candidate pairs of schemata for each alternation accordingly to increasing μ, and we compute the value of μ for every 10th percentile. The value of μ for rectilinear measure L_1 computed for the dictionary $\mathfrak{D}$ is presented in Figure 2. The results are evaluated, and k-th percentile with the greatest F-measure[7] for a particular alternation is assumed the optimal percentile for this alternation. The F-measure for rectilinear measure L_1 and the dictionary $\mathfrak{D}$ is presented in Figure 3.

For a baseline, candidate pairs of schemata for each alternation were randomly ordered, and $k/10$ of them were selected accordingly to the obtained order. On the other hand, the random k was selected. Both these procedures were performed 3 times, and the results of their evaluation were averaged.

[6] Personal communication.

[7] F-measure was computed with neutral, default parameter value 0.5.

(a) the dictionary $\mathfrak{D}$

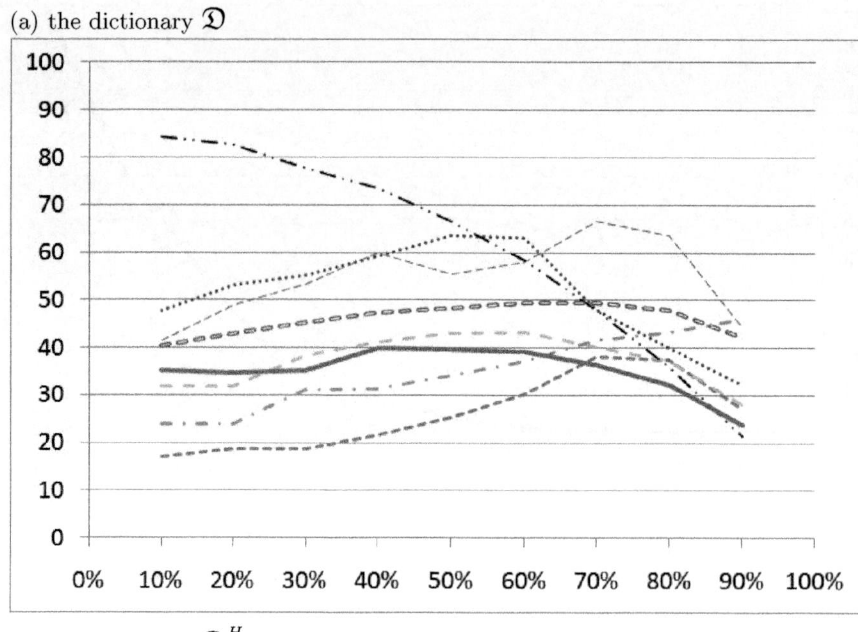

(b) the dictionary $\mathfrak{D}^H$

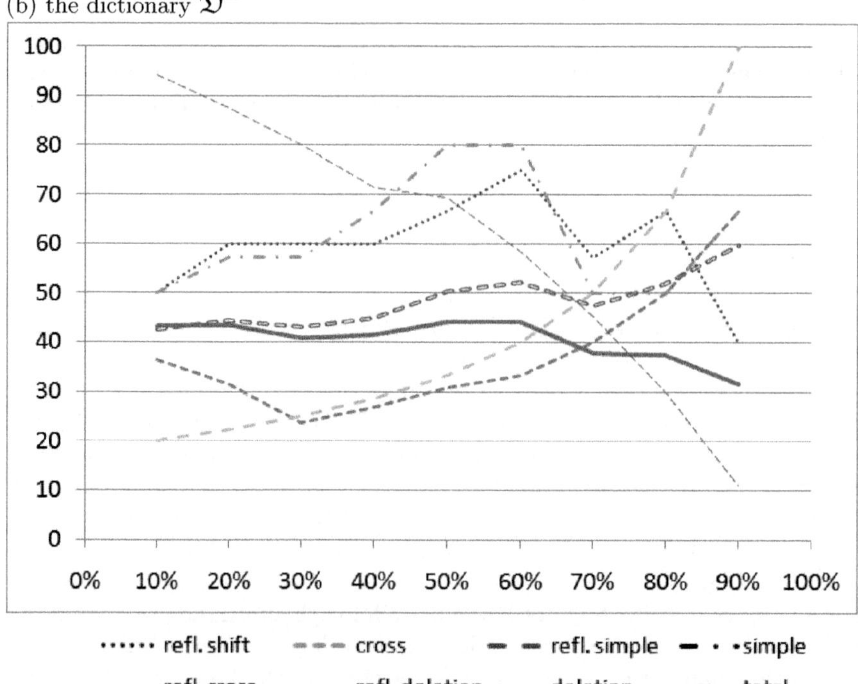

Fig. 3. F measure for all percentiles of rectilinear measure L_1

For the sake of evaluation, the repository of alternating verb schemata was manually prepared. Alternations, in which verb *rozpocząć* (*to begin*) participates, are presented in (18). Arguments participating in the alternation that are semantically consistent in both schemata are displayed as **np:nom**, and semantically dropped are displayed as np:nom.

(18) reflexive shift alternation

np:acc np:inst np:nom	np:inst **np:nom** sie
np:acc np:nom	**np:nom** sie
np:acc np:nom prepnp:od:gen	**np:nom** prepnp:od:gen sie

simple alternation

np:acc **np:inst** np:nom	np:acc np:nom **prepnp:od:gen**
np:inst np:nom sie	np:nom **prepnp:od:gen** sie

deletion alternation

np:acc np:inst np:nom	np:acc np:nom
np:acc np:nom prepnp:od:gen	np:acc np:nom
np:inst np:nom sie	np:nom sie
np:nom prepnp:dla:gen sie	np:nom sie
np:nom prepnp:od:gen sie	np:nom sie

reflexive cross alternation

np:nom **prepnp:dla:gen** sie	**np:acc** **np:nom**

The results of evaluation for the best percentiles for rectilinear, Euclidean and cosine measures, respectively, can be found in Table 2 and 3 for the automatically and manually created dictionaries. *Average* means average results for all alternations (including ones without true positives). *Cumulative* means treating the set of alternating pairs of schemata as a whole in spite of the type of an alternation. In parentheses, the evaluation for the baseline algorithm is presented.

The results obtained for the algorithm using similarity measures are substantially better than the baseline. The smallest differences concern deletion alternation, as it holds for most corresponding pairs of schemata (so it is unlikely to select a wrong pair).

The superiority of applying algorithm to hand dictionary $\mathfrak{D}^H$ in comparison with $\mathfrak{D}$ is striking, in spite of the small size of $\mathfrak{D}^H$. This shows the influence of data noise on the performance of the algorithm. $\mathfrak{D}$ is redeemed only by fairly good recall, which makes possible to use such noisy data in semi-automatic alternation detection.

7 Conclusions and Future Work

In this paper, a method of detecting diathesis alternations is presented. It is based on semantic similarity between two syntactic schemata of a verb. Thus, the participation of particular verb schemata in an alternation is actually considered. Alternations are classified much more coarsely than in other works (usually, the

Table 2. Evaluation of detecting alternation for automatically created dictionary $\mathfrak{D}$

alternation	percentile	precision	recall	F-measure
deletion	10/10/10	77.8/79.1/77.8	91.9/93.4/91.9	84.3/85.6/84.3
	(–)	(77.5)	(66.5)	(70.9)
simple	50/50/60	29.7/27.9/31.9	78.5/73.8/67.7	43.3/42.6/43.3
	(–)	(14.4)	(56.1)	(21.6)
refl. cross	90/50/90	54.5/20.0/45.5	53.3/73.3/33.3	46.2/31.4/38.5
	(–)	(13.3)	(47.4)	(18.6)
refl. deletion	70/40/60	64.3/33.3/61.1	69.2/69.2/84.6	66.7/45.0/71.0
	(–)	(26.9)	(45.5)	(29.6)
refl. shift	50/50/50	47.7/51.3/45.5	95.5/90.9/90.9	59.2/66.7/60.6
	(–)	(33.5)	(50.2)	(39.5)
refl. simple	70/80/70	25.0/31.8/25.0	80.0/70.0/80.0	38.1/43.8/38.1
	(–)	(8.3)	(45.6)	(13.8)
average	–/–/–	43.4/33.4/42.4	80.8/83.2/80.5	56.5/47.4/55.6
	(–)	(25.7)	(58.8)	(34.8)
cumulative	–/–/–	52.4/49.6/54.3	86.0/87.3/84.4	65.1/63.3/66.1
	(–)	(42.5)	(61.2)	(35.5)

Table 3. Evaluation of detecting alternation for manually created dictionary $\mathfrak{D}^H$

alternation	percentile	precision	recall	F-measure
deletion	10/10/10	88.9/83.3/88.9	100.0/93.8/100.0	94.1/88.2/94.1
	(–)	(82.8)	(67.4)	(73.5)
simple	90/90/70	100.0/100.0/33.3	50.0/50.0/50.0	66.7/66.7/40.0
	(–)	(23.1)	(66.7)	(32.0)
refl. cross.	90/90/90	100.0/100.0/100.0	100.0/100.0/100.0	100.0/100.0/100.0
	(–)	(0.0)	(0.0)	(0.0)
refl. deletion	50/90/50	66.7/100.0/66.7	100.0/50.0/100.0	80.0/66.7/80.0
	(–)	(60.0)	(77.8)	(52.9)
refl. shift	60/60/50	60.0/75.0/50.0	100.0/100.0/100.0	75.0/85.7/66.7
	(–)	(28.2)	(63.0)	(37.7)
average	–/–/–	59.4/65.5/62.7	92.9/84.8/92.9	72.4/73.9/74.9
	(–)	(27.7)	(67.8)	(39.1)
cumulative	–/–/–	75.0/78.6/68.6	92.3/84.6/92.3	82.8/81.5/78.7
	(–)	(30.9)	(65.0)	(41.8)

set of schemata and their arguments under considerations is fixed), which makes the task harder. However, the set of verbs for experiments is too small for more fine-grained differentiation of alternations.

Taking the above into account, the obtained results are promising, especially for manually filtered dictionary $\mathfrak{D}^H$. The main objection is that evaluation was performed on the same set of data as optimal percentiles were computed, which may lead to overestimation of the evaluation results. In order to obtain reliable results of evaluation, cross validation is needed. Unfortunately, corresponding experiments have given poor results, only slightly better from random. $\mathfrak{D}^H$ is evidently too small to be divided into parts (to be ordered and subdivided), whereas $\mathfrak{D}$ is probably too noisy.

The algorithm was performed for each type of alternation separately under the assumption that the similarity level between pairs of schemata for a particular type of alternation would be uniform. However, the similarity level depends on the number of NPs/PrepNPs in schemata as well (as this influences the number of frames per schema), and it is possible that this dependence is stronger than the dependence on the type of alternation. We plan to perform the algorithm for pairs of schemata classified w.r.t. their length (in the case of deletion and shift alternations, the length of a shorter schema is considered).

Experiments on a larger on one hand and less noisy on the other hand set of verbs are indispensable to obtain more cross-validation results.

Acknowledgements. This research is supported by the POIG.01.01.02-14-013/09 project which is co-financed by the European Union under the European Regional Development Fund.

References

[1] Abe, N., Li, H.: Learning word association norms using cut pair models. In: Proceedings of the 13th International Conference on Machine Learning (ICML 1996), Bari, Italy, pp. 3–11 (1996)

[2] Dang, H.T., Kipper, K., Palmer, M., Rosenzweig, J.: Investigating regular sense extensions based on intersective Levin classes. In: Proceedings of the 36th Annual Meeting of the Association for Computational Linguistics and 17th International Conference on Computational Linguistics COLING-ACL 1998, Montreal, Canada, pp. 293–299 (1998)

[3] Gildea, D.J.: Probabilistic model of verb-argument structure. In: Proceedings of the 6th Conference on Natural Language Learning (CoNNL 2002), Taipei, Taiwan, pp. 308–314 (2002)

[4] Hajnicz, E.: Semantic annotation of verb arguments in shallow parsed Polish sentences by means of EM selection algorithm. In: Marciniak, M., Mykowiecka, A. (eds.) Aspects of Natural Language Processing. LNCS, vol. 5070, pp. 211–240. Springer, Heidelberg (2009)

[5] Hajnicz, E.: Problems with pruning in automatic creation of semantic valence dictionary for Polish. In: Matoušek, V., Mautner, P. (eds.) TSD 2009. LNCS, vol. 5729, pp. 131–138. Springer, Heidelberg (2009)

[6] Hajnicz, E.: Generalizing the EM-based semantic category annotation of NP/PP heads to wordnet synsets. In: Vetulani, Z. (ed.) Proceedings of the 4th Language & Technology Conference, Poznań, Poland, pp. 432–436 (2009)

[7] Hajnicz, E.: Aggregating entries of semantic valence dictionary of Polish verbs. In: Bertinetto, P.M., Korhonen, A., Lenci, A., Melinger, A., Schulte im Walde, S., Villavicencio, A. (eds.) Proceedings of the Interdisciplinary Workshop on the Identification and Representation of Verb Features (Verb 2010), Pisa, Italy, Scuola Normale Superiore and Università di Pisa, pp. 49–54 (2010)

[8] Hlaváčková, D., Horák, A.: VerbaLex — new comprehensive lexicon of verb valences for Czech. In: Proceedings of the Third International Seminar on Computer Treatment of Slavic and East European Languages, Bratislava, Slovakia, pp. 107–115 (2006)
[9] Joanis, E., Stevenson, S.: A general feature space for automatic verb classification. In: Proceedings of the 10th Conference of the European Chapter of the Association for Computational Linguistics (EACL 2003), Budapest, Hungary, pp. 163–170 (2003)
[10] Joanis, E., Stevenson, S., James, D.: A general feature space for automatic verb classification. Natural Language Engineering 14(3), 337–367 (2008)
[11] Lapata, M.: Acquiring lexical generalizations from corpora: a case study for diathesis alternations. In: Proceedings of the 37th Annual Meeting of the Association for Computational Linguistics (ACL 1999), College Park, MA, pp. 397–404 (1999)
[12] Levin, B.: English verb classes and alternation: a preliminary investigation. University of Chicago Press, Chicago (1993)
[13] Li, H., Abe, N.: Generalizing case frames using a thesaurus and the MDL principle. In: Proceedings of the Recent Advances in Natural Language Processing (RANLP 1995), Borovets, Bulgaria, pp. 239–248 (1995)
[14] Li, H., Abe, N.: Generalizing case frames using a thesaurus and the MDL principle. Computational Linguistics 24(2), 217–244 (1998)
[15] McCarthy, D.: Using semantic preferences to identify verbal participation in role switching alternations. In: Proceedings of the 1st Meeting of the North American Chapter of the Association for Computational Linguistics (NAACL 2000), Seattle, WA, pp. 256–263 (2000)
[16] McCarthy, D.: Lexical Acquisition at the Syntax-Semantics Interface: Diathesis Alternations, Subcategorization Frames and Selectional Preferences. PhD thesis, University of Sussex (2001)
[17] Merlo, P., Stevenson, S.: Automatic verb classification based on statistical distributions of argument structure. Computational Linguistics 27(3), 373–408 (2001)
[18] Piasecki, M., Szpakowicz, S., Broda, B.: A Wordnet from the Ground Up. Oficyna Wydawnicza Politechniki Wrocławskiej, Wrocław (2009)
[19] Resnik, P.: Selection and Information: A Class-Based Approach to Lexical Relationships. PhD thesis, University of Pennsylvania, Philadelphia, PA (December 1993)
[20] Stevenson, S., Merlo, P.: Automatic verb classification using distributions of grammatical features. In: Proceedings of the 9th Conference of the European Chapter of the Association for Computational Linguistics (EACL 1999), Bergen, Norway, pp. 45–52 (1999)
[21] Szupryczyńska, M.: Syntaktyczna klasyfikacja czasowników przybiernikowych. Państwowe Wydawnictwo Naukowe, Poznań, Poland (1973)
[22] Świdziński, M.: Syntactic Dictionary of Polish Verbs. Uniwersytet Warszawski / Universiteit van Amsterdam (1994)
[23] Žabokrtský, Z., Lopatková, M.: Valency information in VALLEX 2.0: Logical structure of the lexicon. The Prague Bulletin of Mathematical Linguistics 87, 41–60 (2007)

Combining Polish Morphosyntactic Taggers

Tomasz Śniatowski and Maciej Piasecki

Institute of Informatics
Wrocław University of Technology
Wybrzeże Wyspiańskiego 27,
Wrocław, Poland
{157693@student,maciej.piasecki@}.pwr.wroc.pl

Abstract. This paper describes work on the construction of a morpho-syntactic tagger for Polish as an ensemble of the best performing Polish taggers: TaKIPI and Pantera. The tagger set was extended with RFTagger trained on the Polish corpus. Several methods of ensemble construction were tested with the best result, in terms of the tagging error reduction, achieved with simple, unweighted voting among the three taggers. Two evaluation metrics were used, namely: weak and strong accuracy. The ensemble-based tagger presented a significant increase in both evaluation metrics, achieving nearly 94% weak correctness. This represents a one percentage point increase over the best individual tagger tested, or an error rate reduction of over 15%.

1 Background

1.1 Morpho-syntactic Tagging

Morpho-syntactic tagging, or part-of-speech (POS) tagging, is one of the initial steps in automated text processing. It is concerned with assigning labels (*tags*) to words or, more generally, *tokens*. The notion of a 'token' is not always clear (Grefenstette and Tapanainen, 1994; Habert et al., 1998), The tags assigned to tokens correspond in a way to traditional linguistic parts of speech, but are not strictly equivalent, and might express additional morpho-syntactic information. In the latter case the tag might be referred to as a *morpho-syntactic description* (MSD) tag (although the name POS tag is sometimes used anyway). The set of all possible tags is called the *tagset*, its size ranges from several dozen to hundreds or even several thousand of different tags. The tagset depends primarily on the language processed, the formalism used to describe it, and the level of details.

Many important further steps of automated text analysis—such as word sense disambiguation, shallow or deep parsing, named entity recognition—all can benefit to a large extent from the tags assigned previously by a tagger. Errors during tagging can adversely affect the results of the later steps (Hajič et al., 2001). Usually the higher the complexity of the linguistic task at hand, the more high-quality tagging is required.

P. Bouvry et al. (Eds.): SIIS 2011, LNCS 7053, pp. 359–369, 2012.

1.2 Tagger Evaluation

Taggers are generally evaluated on *accuracy*, i.e. the percentage of tokens that are tagged correctly. There is a problem with imperfect or inherently ambiguous data, where there is more than one correct tag for a particular token (and a tagger might return more than one tag for a token). In this case the notion of accuracy requires adjustments, two simple measures can be used instead: *weak correctness* and *strong correctness* (Acedański and Przepiórkowski, 2010). Weak correctness (WC) considers a tagging correct if any of the tags returned by the tagger is appropriate in comparison with the manually annotated text. Strong correctness (SC), on the other hand, only counts a token as correctly tagged if the set of expected tags and the set of returned tags for it are equal. It follows that $SC \leq WC$. In the case in which there is only one valid tag for each token, and taggers always return one tag, WC and SC are equal and equivalent to accuracy.

Several other measures have been proposed, for example information retrieval based *precision* and *recall* by Van Halteren (1999), or complex, adjustable measures by Acedański and Przepiórkowski (2010) that allow evaluating taggers with a specific purpose in mind. That said, WC and SC seem better known and better suited for Polish tagger comparison, especially as recently the results of contemporary Polish taggers are presented in terms of these two measures.

1.3 Tagging Polish

POS tagging of Polish presents several challenges. The language is highly inflective with a free word order, which makes it difficult to use simple statistics-based methods operating on a narrow context (Sharoff, 2004). The English Penn Treebank tagset consists of 36 tags (Marcus et al., 1993), whereas the widespread Polish IPIC tagset spans 4179 theoretically possible tags (Przepiórkowski, 2005; Przepiórkowski and Woliński, 2003). The Polish tagset is *positional*, that is, apart from a general part of speech label, tags contain information about several grammatical attributes such as case, gender or number. The notion of *part of speech* is present in the first attribute of a tag, called the grammatical or flexemic class; each other attribute has a set of possible values, such as singular and plural for the number attribute (not all attributes are used in every part of speech). It should be noted, however, that a large number of attribute value combinations are impossible, and only 1054 different tags actually appear in the corpus we use for testing. This is on par with tagsets of other inflected languages such as Czech (Hajič et al., 2001).

The large number of possible tags is usually drastically reduced for known words by morphological analysis, which plays an important major role in tagging Polish. This processing step is well developed in the case of Polish and there are several available morphological analysers such as Morfeusz (Woliński, 2006) or the Morfologik (Miłkowski, 2010) dictionary. Unknown words pose a challenge, with morphology guessers such as Odgadywacz (Piasecki and Radziszewski, 2008) being useful.

1.4 Taggers of Polish

POS tagging is generally considered a nearly-solved problem for e.g. the English language, with accuracy exceeding 97% (Toutanova et al., 2003), and research focus has been shifted towards more advanced tasks such as sentence structure parsing or semantic analysis. For Polish, general-purpose taggers (often designed with English primarily in mind) present mild performance, not adequate for many applications. Usually at least some changes are needed in order to achieve reasonable results, but even though such adjustments are made, the accuracy of the contemporary Polish taggers is much below a typical result for English and even for Czech, e.g. Hajič et al. (2001).

Best published values (Acedański and Gołuchowski, 2009; Piasecki, 2007) for weak correctness lie in the range of about 93%, with strong correctness of about 90%. Moreover, looking at the evolution of the results published over the past several years one can come to a conclusion that progress has been somewhat slow. Scattered (unpublished) reports and our experience with TaKIPI tagger show that in real-world applications the perceived tagging accuracy is lower than what could be expected from the published results. One possible explanation is that there appears to be a sort of saturation in relation to the available training data, i.e. the manually disambiguated part of the The IPI PAN Corpus (henceforth MIPIC) and the limited accuracy of its manual disambiguation (Przepiórkowski, 2004).

A few Polish taggers of performance close to practical applications were proposed in literature, e.g. Dębowski (2004); Piasecki and Gaweł (2005), however, only two of them, and only recently, have been made publicly available. Fortunately, the contemporary trends in the language technology seem to favour openness in the area. TaKIPI (Piasecki, 2007) and Pantera (Acedański and Gołuchowski, 2009) are two state-of-the-art, readily and freely available taggers, designed specifically for Polish. Both these taggers can be used as provided, or trained by the user.

TaKIPI combines a limited number of hand-written tagging rules with a simple statistical classifier and a large number of decision tree based classifiers. The decision based classifiers utilise hand-written lexico-morphosyntactic constraints as a source of information, cf. Piasecki (2007). The TaKIPI architecture follows the general multi-classifier scheme: hand-written rules are applied first as a filter, followed by a statistical classifier that sets initial probability values for tags. The main work is then done by decision tree based classifiers organised in a sequence of three layers of disambiguation (each layer refers to different tag parts).

Pantera uses a variant of the Brill algorithm modified for the use with complex tagsets. For both these taggers weak correctness of 92% to 93% or slightly above 93% is reported and both are available under the terms of the GPL license.

In addition to the taggers dedicated to Polish, we have also selected a German tagger, based on Hidden Markov Models and adapted for positional tagsets, RFTagger (Schmid and Laws, 2008). RFTagger has been successfully trained and run on Polish linguistic data, with minor adjustments. Our initial tests showed that its weak correctness is about 89%, thus RFTagger is well behind the other two, but on a similar level to other Polish taggers, e.g. Piasecki and Gaweł (2005). As RFTagger has not been dedicated to Polish, the result can be considered promising.

2 Combining Taggers

Combining classifiers is a well known Artificial Intelligence method for improving the overall classification result that has been also successfully applied for various tasks in Natural Language Processing, e.g. (Henderson and Brill, 1999). As for the specific problem of POS tagging, several methods have been proposed, ranging from simple voting among different taggers (Van Halteren et al., 2001), to employing machine-learning methods such as boosting or bagging (Kuba et al., 2005).

A multi-classifier approach to tagging is far from a novel idea—indeed, TaKIPI itself is a multi-classifier tagger. However, a higher-level approach (where complete, different taggers are ensembled) has been researched for languages such as English (Brill and Wu, 1998), Swedish (Sjöbergh, 2003) or Italian (Søgaard, 2009), but, to the best of our knowledge, has not yet been successfully attempted for Polish on the basis of the contemporary taggers dedicated to Polish. A possible explanation could be the low number of Polish taggers that perform reasonably well and, even more importantly, are easily obtainable for experimentation. The recent development of the Pantera tagger, as well as the mildly successful test of RFTagger on Polish data open this new avenue for improving tagging accuracy for Polish.

A major prerequisite for successful tagger combination, and in fact any sort of classifier ensemble, is that the individual classifiers must be *different* in the sense of making different errors, preferably for different types of decisions. One way of attaining this feature is by choosing classifiers that operate on varied principles, with the hope that different algorithms will behave differently enough during classification. This is the case we are facing with the tested taggers of the Polish language: TaKIPI is decision-tree-based with some linguistic rules; Pantera is a strictly rule-based transformation tagger; RFTagger is an improved trigram HMM tagger.

2.1 Voting

Simple unweighted voting is often considered as an initial attempt to combine taggers. In this approach the taggers vote on each word, and the tag with the majority of votes is selected as the output of the combined tagger. A similarly plain tie resolution system is used, with a fall-back on one of the taggers, normally the one which performs best on its own.

Interestingly enough, simple voting can offer surprising and significant improvement over the best individual tagger, as long as the assumption about the varied types of errors of individual taggers holds. Even more interesting is the fact that more sophisticated combination methods can often offer little improvement over simple voting (Brill and Wu, 1998), especially when compared to the accuracy increase already achieved. In particular, weighted voting based on a tagger's confidence of the classification can reduce the overall accuracy, as discussed by Sjöbergh (2003).

2.2 Second-Level Classifier

Another approach is to choose a tagger on the basis of certain criteria – such as text type (Borin, 2000), some sort of word type, or contextual information about the word to be tagged. Alternatively, a second level classifier can be constructed for this purpose. Features such as the full tags returned by all the taggers in the ensemble for the word and N words surrounding it can be fed to this classifier in an attempt to train it for tagger selecting (or tag selecting) on top of the standalone taggers. The aim is to achieve results exceeding those of simple voting by selecting an outvoted tagger in some circumstances. Experiments by Brill and Wu (1998) suggest that choosing between taggers performs better than choosing between tags, even though such a method is in a way limited and will never tag correctly if all of the used taggers tag incorrectly.

3 Experiments

3.1 Training Data and Methodology

A version of MPIC (Przepiórkowski, 2004), which has been slightly corrected for the development of TaKIPI (Piasecki, 2007), was used. It consists of 884,273 tokens. Around 2.5% of tokens in the corpus have more than one correct tag assigned, making it impossible to use simple accuracy as a performance measure. Instead, the two already introduced measures of weak and strong correctness were applied. Both the training and testing data were fully tokenised and morphologically analysed beforehand; this was motivated by the intention to test taggers alone without having to account for e.g. different tokenisation behaviours.

Experiments were performed using repeated random sub-sampling cross-validation. The taggers were trained on 9/10 of the data and then evaluated on the remaining 1/10. Ten randomly split training-testing data sets were prepared, and each experiment was run on each of these training-testing data splits. The results reported are always the average of ten runs, and unless otherwise noted, were consistent across folds (the standard deviation was low).

3.2 Comparison of the Taggers Used

Three taggers were used: TaKIPI, Pantera and RFTagger. The manual disambiguation between the grammatical classes of nouns (`subst` tag in the IPIC tagset) and gerunds (`ger`) expresses a significant number of errors in MIPIC. That is why TaKIPI is not trained for this distinction in its default mode of use. However, in order to achieve a behaviour that is compatible with the other two taggers used, TaKIPI has been trained and used in a mode in which the internal merge of `subst` and `ger` was switched off.

It should also be noted that TaKIPI returns more than one output tag for around 0.3% of all tokens, while both RFTagger and Pantera always output one tag. All taggers were trained on the same modified version of MIPIC with the recommended parameter values as provided by the respective authors along with the taggers.

Several papers contain results for Pantera and TaKIPI, but since RFTagger has not been yet tested on Polish, and in order to provide a clear baseline for improvement, we have decided to first test all the taggers individually on our data. Table 1 presents the results, with TaKIPI and Pantera being very close, and significantly ahead of RFTagger. It should be noted that RFTagger was unable to use the morphological analysis information contained in the test corpora, which might account for some of the difference.

The difference between TaKIPI and Pantera is very slight. According to weak correctness there is no statistically significant difference (with a significance level of 0.05), and there is a statistically significant, but still small, advantage of Pantera in strong correctness. The result is different from that reported by e.g. Acedański and Przepiórkowski (2010), and might be caused by the corpus choice, tagset details, undisclosed assumptions or differences in test methodology, or plain bugs in the software—several implementation issues in both Pantera and TaKIPI were found in the course of performing the experiments described in this paper.

Table 1. Accuracy (Weak and Strong Correctness) of the tested taggers

Tagger	WC	SC
RFTagger	89.76%	87.43%
TaKIPI	92.93%	90.04%
Pantera	92.98%	90.33%

3.3 Tagger Complementarity

Brill and Wu (1998) proposed a measure of complementarity $comp(A, B)$ to evaluate how pairs of taggers relate in terms of errors made. Complementarity of tagger A and tagger B measures how often, when tagger A provides a wrong tag for a word, tagger B tags the word correctly. High values of tagger complementarity indicate that the two taggers err in different situations, thus indicating good candidates for combining. Conversely, low value of complementarity suggests that the two taggers are similar and there is likely little to be gained from combining them; $comp(A, A)$ is always zero.

Results of the complementarity analysis (on weak correctness) are presented in Table 2. The values are high across all tagger pairs, indicating that there is a good chance that a combined tagger will achieve results better than the best individual tagger.

Table 2. Tagger complementarity, $comp(A, B)$ indicates how often tagger B is correct in cases where A tags incorrectly (measured on weak correctness)

B \ A	RFTagger	TaKIPI	Pantera
RFTagger	0%	43.2%	42.2%
TaKIPI	62.7%	0%	40.9%
Pantera	62.5%	41.5%	0%

3.4 Oracle Accuracy

Another useful concept for measuring possible gain from tagger combination is the theoretical *oracle* which can, in all circumstances, choose the best tagger from a group of taggers. Essentially, the oracle tagger tags incorrectly only if no tagger produces a valid tag for a word. Accuracy of the oracle is the upper bound for accuracy of several tagger combination methods (all of those in which the algorithm chooses a tagger from the group).

In the case of the three taggers under test the calculated oracle accuracy is 97.10% weak correctness and 94.68% strong correctness, far higher than any of the individual taggers, again showing promise in a tagger combination.

3.5 Simple Voting

A simple voting tagger was constructed first. For each word it collects tags assigned by the three tested taggers, and outputs tags that were chosen by more than one tagger. In case of a tie (no shared tag chosen by the taggers), the voting system always falls back to the tagging decision of an initially specified tagger. The usual method (Brill and Wu, 1998) is to fall back on the best individual tagger, however we have decided to verify that assumption by testing all three possible choices of the voting tagger thrice, i.e. with each individual tagger as the fall-back one.

Table 3. Accuracy (weak and strong correctness) of all the tested voting tagger variants (parentheses indicate which tagger's output is used in case of a tie: P - Pantera, T - TaKIPI, R - RFTagger)

Tagger	**WC**	**SC**
Voting (P)	93.98%	91.28%
Voting (T)	93.93%	91.26%
Voting (R)	93.80%	91.12%

Table 3 presents the accuracy of the voting tagger variants, with the performance of the best voting tagger (all the other tested taggers and the oracle are shown once again for comparison in Table 5). There is a clear and statistically significant increase (with a significance level of 0.05; the P-value was below

0.001) in both weak and strong correctness when compared to the best individual tagger. In weak correctness the increase is close to one percentage point. When, instead of correctness, the number of errors is considered, there is a drop from around 7% to 6%—a decrease of roughly 14%.

The hypothesis that the fall-back tagger should be the best individual tagger seems confirmed in our experiments, however the differences are very slight (although statistically significant), especially when TaKIPI is considered instead of Pantera. It should be noted that a tie occurs only in 1.7% of decisions on average. It appears in general that there is not much to be gained from comparing different fall-back variants in voting, with the heuristic of choosing the best individual tagger performing best.

3.6 Ambiguity Class-Based Tagger Selection

Another approach we have investigated involved deciding which tagger to use based on the *ambiguity class* of the analysed word. Given how the tagset for Polish is positional, we define the ambiguity class as the set of possible tags a word can be assigned (based on the morphological analysis), but using only a subset of all the attributes. For example, using the number attribute and assuming the grammatical class is already known, we would end up with four classes of words: those that can be either plural or singular, those that are known to be plural, those that are known to be singular, and those that do not have a number attribute. We will be denoting ambiguity classes by listing the possible values within curly braces, for example `{sg,pl}` for the class of words that can be either singular or plural.

Hypothesising that such a split would uncover differences in behaviour between the taggers, we used the grammatical class (POS) attribute to identify ambiguity classes, so words were split into groups according to their possible POS. There are a bit over a hundred such classes in the corpus we used, with over a half of them rare (below 500 tokens). We analysed the accuracy of the three taggers on different classes, and considered a tagger that would choose the best result for each ambiguity class, expecting to see a result comparable with that of the voting tagger. A sample of the analysis data, including the performance of the voting tagger, is shown in Table 4 (the data in its entirety is far too spacious to be included here). Note that the values in the table do not measure just the ability to choose the correct POS for tokens within a class—should that be the case, we would expect near-100% correctness for tokens where the grammatical class is known unambiguously (such as the `{subst}` class) after morphological analysis (for taggers capable of using that information).

The initial hypothesis that taggers would not behave uniformly across POS ambiguity classes was confirmed. For example for words that are ambiguous between an adjective and a numeral (the `{adj,num}` class), the weakest tagger, RFTagger, offers a score increase of 5% over the otherwise best tagger, Pantera. This already allows an accuracy increase in a top-level tagger choosing an underlying tagger based on the ambiguity class. However, we were somewhat surprised to see that the voting tagger produces even better results for most of the ambiguity classes, and especially for the more common ones, such as the {subst} class (words known to be a noun). This class is the largest in our corpus, measuring roughly 190,000 instances, or 21% of the entire corpus. Within this class, the voting tagger achieves a weak correctness advantage of 1.2 percentage point over TaKIPI and Pantera.

We followed with an off-line analysis of the theoretical performance of a tagger that would choose between the three standalone taggers based on the ambiguity class of each tagged word. The total weak correctness of such a tagger was calculated as 93.26%, with strong correctness of 90.67%. While both these numbers are higher than those of the best individual tagger, the result is far lower than the one obtained by simple voting. This is further compounded by the fact that in order for the comparison to be fully valid, the ambiguity class analysis would have to be performed on the test corpora and then the choose-best tagger would have to be tested on a held-out portion. The proper result would have to be lower than the figures mentioned earlier, which should be treated as upper bounds for such a method.

Additionally, we investigated whether it is reasonable to resolve voting ties using ambiguity class information. We created a tie resolution mechanism that chose the best-performing tagger for the ambiguity class of the tied token. This approach failed to provide any statistically significant difference in the results obtained, despite again being favoured by using tagger performance information on the entire corpus including the test portion.

Table 4. Sample of tagger weak correctness (on full tags) split across ambiguity classes based on the morphologically possible grammatical class

Amb. class	Count	% of corpus	TaKIPI	Pantera	RFTagger	Voting
{subst}	190k	21.5%	92.3%	92.3%	88.9%	93.5%
{adj}	89k	10%	86.0%	85.2%	78.4%	87.5%
{prep,qub}	15k	1.7%	93.5%	95.1%	93.0%	95.6%
{fin,subst}	5k	0.6%	89.9%	86.7%	91.9%	92.2%
{adj,num}	0.3k	0.03%	68.5%	70.8%	74.3%	74.2%

Table 5. Accuracy of all the tested taggers, the voting tagger, the POS-ambiguity class based tagger and the oracle

Tagger	**WC**	**SC**
RFTagger	89.76%	87.43%
TaKIPI	92.93%	90.04%
Pantera	92.98%	90.33%
Voting	**93.98%**	**91.28%**
POS amb. class	93.26%	90.67%
Oracle	97.10%	94.68%

4 Conclusion

By combining two readily-available Polish taggers with a different tagger capable of working with Polish data, we have been able to achieve a significant increase in standard evaluation measures. The gain of roughly one percentage point of both weak and strong correctness corresponds to a 10–15% reduction in the number of errors made. The upper bound for a tagger-choosing algorithm lies even higher, indicating that a more complex method could yield even better results. The considered approach of selection based on the POS ambiguity class, however, failed to improve upon the simple voting tagger.

Further research should be directed at both employing more different taggers in the ensemble and investigating other approaches at combining the taggers. For instance, more ambiguity classes can be chosen and tested, possibly together with other word features fed to a classifier. It should also be investigated whether manual rules for choosing a tagger or amending the final output can have a significant impact on the evaluation metrics. We also plan to publish the source code for the voting tagger at `http://nlp.pwr.wroc.pl/votar`.

With regards to using different taggers, it would be useful to replace RFTagger, for two reasons. First, as shown in comparison with Pantera and Takipi, RFTagger performs below par for Polish; a better third tagger might yield even better overall results. More important from the practical point of view is the fact that RFTagger is not license-compatible with the other two taggers described, thus it is difficult to distribute and freely use a complete voting tagger program.

Acknowledgements. The work was co-funded by the European Union Innovative Economy Programme project NEKST, No POIG.01.01.02-14-013/09.

References

Acedański, S., Gołuchowski, K.: A Morphosyntactic Rule-Based Brill Tagger for Polish. In: Proceedings of Intelligent Information Systems, pp. 67–76 (2009)

Acedański, S., Przepiórkowski, A.: Towards the Adequate Evaluation of Morphosyntactic Taggers. In: Proceedings of COLING 2010 (2010)

Borin, L.: Something borrowed, something blue: Rule-based combination of POS taggers. In: Proceedings of the Second International Conference on Language Resources and Evaluation, pp. 21–26 (2000)

Brill, E., Wu, J.: Classifier combination for improved lexical disambiguation. In: Proceedings of COLING 1998, vol. 1, pp. 191–195. Association for Computational Linguistics (1998)

Dębowski, Ł.: Trigram morphosyntactic tagger for Polish. In: Proceedings of the International IIS: IIPWM 2004 Conference, pp. 409–413 (2004)

Grefenstette, G., Tapanainen, P.: What is a word, what is a sentence? Problems of tokenization. In: Proceedings of COMPLEX 1994, Budapest (1994)

Habert, B., Adda, G., Adda-Decker, M., de Mareuil, P.B., Ferrari, S., Ferret, O., Illouz, G., Paroubek, P.: Towards Tokenization Evaluation. In: Proceedings of 1st International Conference on Language Resources and Evaluation, vol. 1 (1998)

Hajič, J., Krbec, P., Květoň, P., Oliva, K., Petkevič, V.: Serial combination of rules and statistics: A case study in Czech tagging. In: Proceedings of the 39th Annual Meeting on Association for Computational Linguistics, pp. 268–275. Association for Computational Linguistics (2001)

Henderson, J., Brill, E.: Exploiting diversity in natural language processing: Combining parsers. In: Proceedings of the Fourth Conference on Empirical Methods in Natural Language Processing, pp. 187–194 (1999)

Kuba, A., Felföldi, L., Kocsor, A.: POS tagger combinations on Hungarian text. In: Dale, R., Wong, K.-F., Su, J., Kwong, O.Y. (eds.) IJCNLP 2005. LNCS (LNAI), vol. 3651, pp. 191–196. Springer, Heidelberg (2005)

Marcus, M., Marcinkiewicz, M., Santorini, B.: Building a large annotated corpus of English: The Penn Treebank. Computational linguistics 19(2), 313–330 (1993)

Miłkowski, M.: Developing an open-source, rule-based proofreading tool. Software: Practice and Experience 40, 543–566 (2010)

Piasecki, M.: Polish Tagger TaKIPI: Rule Based Construction and Optimisation. Task Quarterly 11(1–2), 151–167 (2007)

Piasecki, M., Gaweł, B.: A rule-based tagger for Polish based on Genetic Algorithm. In: Kłopotek, M.A., Wierzchoń, S.T., Trojanowski, K. (eds.) Proceedings of IIPWM 2005. Advances in Soft Computing. Springer, Heidelberg (2005)

Piasecki, M., Radziszewski, A.: Morphological Prediction for Polish by a Statistical A Tergo Index. Systems Science 34(4), 7–17 (2008)

Przepiórkowski, A.: The IPI PAN Corpus: Preliminary version. Institute of Computer Science, Polish Academy of Sciences, Warsaw (2004)

Przepiórkowski, A.: The IPI PAN corpus in numbers. In: Proceedings of the 2nd Language & Technology Conference, Poznan, Poland (2005)

Przepiórkowski, A., Woliński, M.: A flexemic tagset for Polish. In: Proceedings of Morphological Processing of Slavic Languages, EACL 2003 (2003)

Schmid, H., Laws, F.: Estimation of conditional probabilities with decision trees and an application to fine-grained POS tagging. In: Proceedings of COLING 2008, vol. 1, pp. 777–784. Association for Computational Linguistics (2008)

Sharoff, S.: What is at stake: a case study of Russian expressions starting with a preposition. In: Proceedings of the Workshop on Multiword Expressions: Integrating Processing, pp. 17–23. Association for Computational Linguistics (2004)

Sjöbergh, J.: Combining POS-taggers for improved accuracy on Swedish text. In: Proceedings of NoDaLiDa 2003 (2003)

Søgaard, A.: Ensemble-based POS tagging of Italian. In: IAAI-EVALITA, Reggio Emilia, Italy (2009)

Toutanova, K., Klein, D., Manning, C., Singer, Y.: Feature-rich part-of-speech tagging with a cyclic dependency network. In: Proceedings of the 2003 Conference of the North American Chapter of the Association for Computational Linguistics on Human Language Technology, vol. 1, pp. 173–180. Association for Computational Linguistics (2003)

Van Halteren, H.: Performance of taggers. Syntactic Wordclass Tagging 9, 81–94 (1999)

Van Halteren, H., Daelemans, W., Zavrel, J.: Improving accuracy in word class tagging through the combination of machine learning systems, vol. 27, pp. 199–229. MIT Press (2001)

Woliński, M.: Morfeusz — a practical tool for the morphological analysis of Polish. In: Kłopotek, M.A., Wierzchoń, S.T., Trojanowski, K. (eds.) Proceedings of IIPWM 2006, Ustroń, Poland, pp. 511–520. Springer, Berlin (2006)

Towards the Lemmatisation of Polish Nominal Syntactic Groups Using a Shallow Grammar*

Łukasz Degórski

Institute of Computer Science
Polish Academy of Sciences
ul. Ordona 21, 01-237 Warszawa, Poland

Abstract. While morphological analysers and taggers usually assign lemmata to wordforms, those tools focus on single words. For some tasks a tool that lemmatises (and thus normalises) whole phrases would be more appropriate. The paper presents, discusses and evaluates a set of tools to lemmatise nominal groups, based on a shallow grammar for Polish. The tools reach an overall success rate of over 58%, and almost 83% on the nominal groups that are correctly recognised by the grammar. The approach should be portable to other languages, especially those morphologically rich.

Keywords: lemmatisation, partial syntactic parsing, syntactic groups, nominal groups.

1 Motivation

The task of finding lemmata of word forms is particularly important for morphologically rich languages, such as Polish. This is mostly dealt with by morphological analysers and taggers, as lemmatisation is an inherent, while not trivial, subtask (or side effect) of tagging. Nonetheless, all those tools focus on single words, while for some tasks, such as indexing, computing statistical measures like TF-IDF, and machine learning, a tool that lemmatises whole phrases would be useful to generate intuitively correct normalised forms.

A lemmatising engine was also directly needed for the CMS designed to manage and publish multilingual content, currently in development in the Applied Technology for Language-Aided CMS project (ATLAS; `www.atlasproject.eu`).

Note that in a synthetic, free word order language a lemma of the whole phrase is rarely a simple concatenation of lemmata of the components. For Polish, that may happen for instance for simple groups matching the pattern `Adj+Noun` or `Noun+Adj` if the adjective is masculine (*krwiożerczego potwora 'bloodthirsty +*

* The work reported here was carried out within the Applied Technology for Language-Aided CMS project co-funded by the European Commission under the Information and Communications Technologies (ICT) Policy Support Programme (Grant Agreement No 250467).

P. Bouvry et al. (Eds.): SIIS 2011, LNCS 7053, pp. 370–378, 2012.

M+Gen monster + M+Gen'), for coordinations (*prezentacje i analizy 'presentations + Nom/Acc and analyses + Nom/Acc'* and also – by chance – for some forms unrecognised by the tagger. However, the simple concatenation will never work if the group contains, for instance, any non-masculine adjective/pronoun, or a nominal subgroup in genitive case:

`celem badania` *'aim+Inst+Sg research+Gen+Sg'*

should be lemmatised to

`cel badania` *'aim+Nom+Sg research+Gen+Sg'*

while the simple concatenation renders

`cel badanie` *'aim+Nom+Sg research+Nom+Sg'*.

The ongoing work in the National Corpus of Polish (NKJP[1]; `www.nkjp.pl`; see [7]) made it possible to deal with the task using a shallow grammar. An extensive grammar has been prepared for the Corpus, designed for the identification of various kinds of syntactic groups (among those – nominal) using the Spejd shallow processing tool (`nlp.ipipan.waw.pl/Spejd/`; [2]). The grammar has been handcrafted iteratively, using samples from a 1-million-word manually annotated subcorpus of the NKJP (see [3] for details).

Combining the lemmatisation task with shallow parsing has one great advantage - shallow parsing gives us structure, used as a base to write lemmatisation rules (or rather: schemata, as these are not rules in the sense of the grammar). The schemata are written separately for each rule of the grammar, and operate on the strings and structure matched by that rule.

2 Related Work

Previously a similar task was attempted for Czech (Pala et al., [5]) for the law domain. The paper does not get into details on the method used and achieved results. There were also some attempts for Mongolian [4], but it seems that Khaltar and Fujii focused more on lemmatising single words and on loanwords in the Mongolian language.

Other phrase lemmatisation-related research focuses mostly on named entities (for instance, Piskorski et al., [6]), which is a different task involving different methodology.

3 Implementation – The Processing Chain

In our approach, the lemmatisation process can be divided into four main steps: tagging, shallow parsing, generating additional needed wordforms and final post-processing.

Note that the input needs not to be a simple list of nominal groups – it can be any Polish text. Identifying the groups in a running text is a part of the task of the shallow grammar.

[1] In Polish: Narodowy Korpus Języka Polskiego.

3.1 Tagging

The input (text file) needs to be morphologically annotated before Spejd grammars can be applied. For this task we used a Brill-based tagger called Pantera. The tagger outputs information in TEI P5-conformant format used in NKJP. See `http://code.google.com/p/pantera/tagger` and [1] for more information.

3.2 Shallow Parsing

The main part of the lemmatisation process is applying the shallow grammar. The NKJP grammar mentioned before has been augmented with lemmatisation schemata for nominal groups, as well as for some adjectival groups, so that it is able not only to extract those groups, but also to assign them proper lemmata.

To do this in the Spejd formalism, we add a fourth parameter[2] to the `group()` operator in every relevant rule, as in the simple example below. The lemma of the whole group is constructed by smart concatenation of lemmata and orthographic forms of the constituents. The constituents, in turn, may also be syntactic groups – in which case their lemmata are results of similar operations performed at the earlier stages of parsing. Lemmata of single syntactic words (such as both nouns in the example below) are provided by the original NKJP grammar, based on the results of the tagging phase.

```
Rule     "NGk: Noun i Noun (koordynacja)"

Match:   [pos~"Noun"]
         [base~"i|oraz|ani|lub|albo|bądź|czy|a także"
          && pos~"Conj"]
         [pos~"Noun"];
Eval:    unify(case,1,3);

### Original NKJP grammar just marks the group
#      group(NGk,1,1);
### We added the 4th parameter for lemmatisation
       group(NGk,1,1,1.base " " 2.orth " " 3.base);
```

This particular rule recognises syntactic groups, consisting of two nouns with a conjunction in between. Both nouns must be unifiable for case. The lemma (called `base` in the Spejd formalism) of the conjunction must match one of the forms enumerated in the list, in addition to having a proper POS tag.

The lemma of this group is a concatenation of the lemma of the first noun, orthographic (unchanged) form of the conjunction and the lemma of the second noun.

Let's have a look at something more advanced:

[2] Only a new, prototype reimplementation of Spejd, still in development and not yet publicly available, supports syntactic groups lemmatisation and accepts this parameter.

```
Rule    "NGg: Noun + n-Noun w gen"

Match:  ([pos~"Noun" && case!~"gen"]
         | [type="NGa|NGk" && synh=[case!~gen]])
        ([pos~"Noun" && case~"gen"]
            | [type="NGa|NGk" && synh=[case~gen]]
            | [type="NGk" && semh=[case~gen]]
        )+;
### Original NKJP grammar
#Eval:   group(NGg,1,1);
### Added 4th parameter for lemmatisation
Eval:   group(NGg,1,1,1.base " " 2.orth);
```

This rule recognises syntactic groups that

- begin with a single non-genitive noun, or a syntactic group of type `NGa` or `NGk`, whose syntactic head's case is not genitive
- followed by one or more of the following: noun in genitive; nominal group of type `NGa` or `NGk` whose syntactic head is a genitive; nominal group of type `NGk` whose semantic head is a genitive

An example of a group matching this rule is *Instytut Podstaw Informatyki Polskiej Akademii Nauk – 'Institute (of) Computer Science (of the) Polish Academy (of) Sciences'*. The lemma of such a group is the concatenation of the lemma of the first (non-genitival) part with the orthographic form of the remaining genitival part.

More information about the NKJP syntactic grammar and examples can be found in [8].

3.3 Generating Forms

The tools we use (Pantera + Spejd) assign as lemma the nominative masculine singular positive form for adjectives and the nominative singular form for nouns. Perfectly simple in case of single words, it becomes more complicated in lemmatising multi-word expressions, such as nominal groups. For example,

`zielonej żabie` '*green+F+Dat+Sg frog+Dat+Sg*'

on a word-by-word basis would be lemmatised to

`zielony żaba` '*green+M+Nom+Sg frog+Nom+Sg*'[3],

while we expect `zielona żaba` '*green+F+Nom+Sg frog+Nom+Sg*' here.

For this reason we cannot always simply use the Spejd `.base` operator as in the example above. For adjectival groups, we protect the original gender information (extracted using the `.gender` operator) by returning a temporary string

[3] In fact, the gender system in the tagset is more complicated, with multiple flavours of the masculine tag; however, for the sake of clarity of the examples, it is simplified to M,F,N here.

like `ADJ(zielony,F)` instead of just `zielony`. In such cases, the appropriate line in the grammar may look like this:

```
group(NGa,2,2,"ADJ(" 1.base "," 1.gender ") " 2.base);
```

and render a "half-lemmatised" string like *ADJ(zielony,f) żaba.* These strings need to be converted later to proper forms. This is done using Morfeusz morphological analyser's (`http://sgjp.pl/morfeusz/`) wordform generation mode.

This implied deeper changes in the original NKJP grammar, as a lot of rules catch participles (imperfect and perfect) together with adjectives, whereas at the form generation level we need to treat them differently. Thus, some rules had to be multiplicated with various combinations of `ADJ`, `PPAS` and `PACT`.

3.4 Postprocessing

The final postprocessing deals with remaining simple problems that can be corrected on pure text level:

- all output is converted to lowercase for consistency, as some capital letters disappear during lemmatisation
- for some specific words two different forms (short and long, e.g. *me* and *moje*) are generated by Morfeusz; the short forms are removed using a regular expression

Technically this phase takes place together with form generation, in one Perl script. The script calls Morfeusz generator for each "half-lemmatised" string and processes its output.

4 Evaluation

For evaluation we used a subset of all nominal syntactic groups marked manually in the 1-million-word balanced subcorpus of the NKJP. From amongst almost 70000 we randomly chose a few hundred, and those have been manually lemmatised by a linguist. The linguist was instructed to skip groups that contain foreign names (Latin plant names, for instance) and names of people, unless they constituted only a small part of a longer phrase. After that we also removed a few groups for which the proper lemmatisation seemed very unclear, as we cannot expect the program to properly guess forms that even the linguists are not sure about.

In the end, 336 annotated phrases were left. They were divided into a development set of 112 and an evaluation set of 224. The development set was used to make final amendments to the shallow grammar, lemmatisation rules and postprocessing scripts. The program was then run with the final grammar and scripts on the unseen evaluation set.

The results were checked and divided into four categories:

1. program produced exactly the same result as the linguist (126)

2. grammar correctly recognised the group, but the produced lemma was different than the linguist's, and it was obviously incorrect (14)
3. grammar correctly recognised the group, but the produced lemma was different than the linguist's, however it was not obviously incorrect (18)
4. grammar incorrectly recognised the group, not giving a chance for proper lemmatisation of this group (66)

In case of any doubts, lemmata were classified to the third category. This category was later reviewed by another linguist, who marked 5 items as correct and 13 as indeed incorrect.

Thus, the evaluation results are as shown in Table 1.

Table 1. Results of the evaluation

Correct	131	58.5%
Group correctly recognised, bad lemma	27	12.0%
Group incorrectly recognised	66	29.5%
Total	224	

As a baseline we used a trivial algorithm that assigns the concatenation of lemmata of the constituents (single wordforms) as the lemma of the whole group. On the evaluation set it assigned 60 lemmata correctly (26.8%). It is worth noting that among those correctly lemmatised there were only 3 groups longer than 3 words.

The way of counting the success rate presented above may however be considered unfair to the algorithm, as it counts as an error not only wrong lemmatisation, but also wrong extraction of the nominal group (and that is, in fact, an error of the underlying grammar, not the lemmatisation patterns). It might be interesting to see how both the algorithm and the baseline performed on the subset of the evaluation set – those groups that have been correctly recognised by the grammar. In other words: to discard the 66 incorrectly recognised groups and look at the remaining 158 only. Table 2 shows these results.

Table 2. Comparison with baseline – with and without incorrectly recognised groups

	All groups in the eval set		Groups correctly recognised	
Number of groups	224		158	
Correctly lemmatised by our alg.	131	**58.5%**	131	**82.9%**
Correctly lemmatised by baseline	60	26.8%	43	27.2%

5 Errors and Potential Improvements

As can be seen in the previous section, there is plenty room for improvement, but most of it is at the level of the group recognising grammar itself, and not at the lemma generation level, as the success rate on correctly recognised groups reaches almost 83%.

5.1 Group Recognition

Among those 66 incorrectly recognised items, there are two basic types of error:

- catching only a part of the phrase as a nominal group
- catching a part of, or even the whole phrase, as two separate groups

It is worth noting that in many cases what has been marked as a group (a part or two separate parts of the input) is lemmatised correctly. In other words, the program correctly assigns lemmata to proper nominal groups being subsets of the provided input.

To solve this problem, we would have to use a completely different approach that takes into account the assumption that the whole input is a group and tries to match it top-down, while Spejd works bottom-up and makes no use here of the information that it is given a list of nominal syntactic groups (as opposed to free text).

In fact, using as input the manually extracted syntactic groups instead of whole sentences can make the results worse: the phrase *zielonej żabie* by itself is not lemmatised correctly, as it is not even recognised as a nominal group. However, it will be correctly marked and lemmatised in the sentence *Opowiedział historię zielonej żabie 'He told a story to a green frog'*.

Some errors, especially of the first type, can be corrected by adding specific rules to the grammar, such as a rule for dates, for ages (*40–letni '40-year-old'*, for groups with particular words (*zwłaszcza 'especially'*, *tylko 'only'*) etc. This is clearly a room for easy, however laborious, improvement.

5.2 Lemmatisation

Taking a more detailed look into the 27 correctly assigned groups for which the generated lemma is incorrect, we recognise the following sources of errors:

1. correct lemmatisation would require semantic information and/or knowledge that the shallow grammar does not have, as in *życia osobistego proroka 'personal life of the prophet'* that has been lemmatised as if it was *'life of a personal prophet'*, an intepretation that is formally correct, but very unlikely
2. plurale tantum nouns are treated as normal nouns (arguably a special case of the above): *prawa człowieka 'human rights'*, *uczucia religijne 'religious feelings'*, while retaining the plural form in the lemma is expected
3. participles caught by general (not participle-specific) rules are, according to the conventions used in Pantera, lemmatised to infinitives; in most cases this is wrong
4. part of the lemma is lost due to incorrect dealing with lower-level groups in the grammar (cascading)

The last one is a technical issue that can be corrected, albeit with a lot of work. The third can also be corrected in the grammar, but it involves deep changes in it. The first two are rather impossible to deal with in shallow grammar approach, unless we list every particular phrase like *prawa człowieka* separately. However, we should mention here the disagreements between the annotators, mostly regarding the way parts of the nominal group should (or not) be brought to singular form: should *polipy nosa i zatok 'nasal and sinus polyps'* be lemmatised to *'polip nosa i zatoki polyp (of the) nose and sinus)'* or rather *polip nosa i zatok 'polyp (of the) nose and sinuses'*?

6 Conclusions and Future Work

The first attempts to apply a shallow grammar to the task of lemmatising nominal syntactic groups give promising results, especially taking into account the fact that the task itself is not easy to define – even in the relatively small evaluation set we used, there is no undisputable "golden" lemma for many of the syntactic groups.

Although the grammar is obviously language-dependent, the whole approach is not. We know about a Spejd grammar being prepared now to extract syntactic groups from Modern Greek texts. That grammar can be augmented with lemmatisation patterns in the future.

An important conclusion, concerning at least Polish and the NKJP grammar, is that for the best results some parts of it should be rewritten with lemmatisation in mind (the grammar described in this paper was just quickly adapted to the task). Rewriting should be consulted with the authors of the original grammar.

Doing so, we may avoid some compromises, especially in dealing with adjectival phrases of various types (adjectives and participles) that form parts of the noun phrases.

More specific patterns (such as dates) should be added to deal with special cases.

Finally, the case of the lemmatised strings should be retained. This will be done by replicating the case pattern (regarding initial characters of words) to the lemmatised string.

References

1. Acedański, S.: A morphosyntactic brill tagger for inflectional languages. In: Loftsson, H., Rögnvaldsson, E., Helgadóttir, S. (eds.) IceTAL 2010. LNCS, vol. 6233, pp. 3–14. Springer, Heidelberg (2010)
2. Buczyński, A., Przepiórkowski, A.: Spejd: A Shallow Processing and Morphological Disambiguation Tool. In: Vetulani, Z., Uszkoreit, H. (eds.) LTC 2007. LNCS, vol. 5603, pp. 131–141. Springer, Heidelberg (2009)
3. Głowińska, K., Przepiórkowski, A.: The Design of Syntactic Annotation Levels in the National Corpus of Polish. In: Proceedings of the Seventh International Conference on Language Resources and Evaluation, LREC 2010 (2010)

4. Khaltar, B.-O., Fujii, A.: A lemmatization method for Mongolian and its application to indexing for information retrieval. Information Processing and Management: an International Journal 45(4), 438–451 (2009)
5. Pala, K., Rychlý, P., Šmerk, P.: Automatic Identification of Legal Terms in Czech Law Texts. In: Francesconi, E., Montemagni, S., Peters, W., Tiscornia, D. (eds.) Semantic Processing of Legal Texts. LNCS, vol. 6036, pp. 83–94. Springer, Heidelberg (2010)
6. Piskorski, J., Sydow, M., Kupść, A.: Lemmatization of Polish person names. In: ACL 2007 Proceedings of the Workshop on Balto-Slavonic Natural Language Processing: Information Extraction and Enabling Technologies. Association for Computational Linguistics Stroudsburg, PA (2007)
7. Przepiórkowski, A., Górski, R.L., Łaziński, M., Pęzik, P.: Recent Developments in the National Corpus of Polish. In: Calzolari, N., Choukri, K., Maegaard, B., Mariani, J., Odijk, J., Piperidis, S., Rosner, M., Tapias, D. (eds.) Proceedings of the Seventh Conference on International Language Resources and Evaluation (2010)
8. Waszczuk, J., Głowińska, K., Savary, A., Przepiórkowski, A.: Tools and Methodologies for Annotating Syntax and Named Entities in the National Corpus of Polish. In: Proceedings of Computational Linguistics - Applications (CLA 2010), Workshop at IMCSIT 2010, Wisła, Poland, October 18-20 (2010)

SyMGiza++: Symmetrized Word Alignment Models for Statistical Machine Translation

Marcin Junczys-Dowmunt and Arkadiusz Szał

Faculty of Mathematics and Computer Science
Adam Mickiewicz University
ul. Umultowska 87, 61-614 Poznań, Poland
{junczys,arekszal}@amu.edu.pl

Abstract. SyMGiza++ — a tool that computes symmetric word alignment models with the capability to take advantage of multi-processor systems — is presented. A series of fairly simple modifications to the original IBM/Giza++ word alignment models allows to update the symmetrized models between chosen iterations of the original training algorithms. We achieve a relative alignment quality improvement of more than 17% compared to Giza++ and MGiza++ on the standard Canadian Hansards task, while maintaining the speed improvements provided by the capability of parallel computations of MGiza++.

Furthermore, the alignment models are evaluated in the context of phrase-based statistical machine translation, where a consistent improvement measured in BLEU scores can be observed when SyMGiza++ is used instead of Giza++ or MGiza++.

1 Introduction

Word alignment is a key component of the training procedure for statistical machine translation systems. The classic tool used for this task is Giza++ [1] which is an implementation of the so-called IBM Models 1-5 [2], the HMM model by [3] and its extension by [1], and Model 6 [1].

All these models are asymmetric, i.e. for a chosen translation direction, they allow for many-to-one alignments, but not for one-to-many alignments. Training two models in opposite directions and symmetrizing the resulting word alignments is commonly employed to improve alignment quality and to allow for more natural alignments. The two alignment models are trained fully independently from each other. Symmetrization is then performed as a post-processing step. Previous work [4,5] has shown that the introduction of symmetry during training results in better alignment quality than post-training symmetrization.

The approaches from [4,5] as well as our method still require the computation of two directed models which use common information during the training. Employing a multi-processor system for the parallel computation of theses models is a natural choice. However, Giza++ was designed to be single-process and single-thread. MGiza++ [6] is an extension of Giza++ which allows to start multiple threads on a single computer.

P. Bouvry et al. (Eds.): SIIS 2011, LNCS 7053, pp. 379–390, 2012.

We therefore choose to extend MGiza++ with the capability to symmetrize word alignments models to tackle both problems in one stroke. The resulting tool SyMGiza++ is described in this work.[1] The paper will be organized as follows: Section 2 provides a short overview of Giza++ and MGiza++ and the above mentioned methods of symmetrized alignment model training. In Sec. 3 we give a formal description of our modifications introduced into the classical word alignment models implemented in Giza++ and MGiza++. The evaluation methodology and results are provided in Sec. 4. Section 4 is divided into two parts: in the first part we give results for alignment quality alone, the second part deals with the influence of the improved alignment method on machine translation results. Finally, conclusions are presented in Sec. 5.

2 Previous Work

2.1 Giza++ and MGiza++

Giza++ implements maximum likelihood estimators for several statistical alignment models, including Model 1 through 5 described by [2], a HMM alignment model by [3] and Model 6 from [1]. The EM [7] algorithm is employed for the estimation of the parameters of the models. During the EM algorithm two steps are applied in each iteration: in the first step, the E-step, the previously computed model or a model with initial values is applied to the data. The expected counts for specific parameters are collected using the probabilities of this model. In the second step, the M-step, these expected counts are taken as fact and used to estimate the probabilities of the next model. A correct implementation of the E-step requires to sum over all possible alignments for one sentence pair. This can be done efficiently for Model 1 and 2, and using the Baum-Welch algorithm also for the HMM alignment model [1].

For Models 3 through 6, a complete enumeration of alignments cannot be accomplished in a reasonable time. This can be approximated by using only a subset of highly scored alignments. In [2] it has been suggested to use only the alignment with the maximum probability, the so-called Viterbi alignment. Another approach resorts to the generation of a set of high probability alignments obtained by making small changes to the Viterbi alignment. [8] proposed to use the neighbour alignments of the Viterbi alignment.

MGiza++ [6] is a multi-threaded word alignment tool that utilizes multiple threads to speed up the time-consuming word alignment process. The implementation of the word alignment models is based on Giza++ and shares large portions of source code with Giza++. The main differences rely on multiple thread management and the synchronization of the counts collection process. Similarly, our tool in turn incorporates large portions of the MGiza++ source code extending MGiza++'s capabilities of using multiple processors with the ability to compute symmetrized word alignment models in a multiprocessor environment. Since the multiprocessing aspect is mainly a feature of the original

[1] SyMGiza++ is available at `http://psi.amu.edu.pl/en/index.php?title=Downloads`

MGiza++, we will not discuss it in this paper and refer the reader to the original paper on MGiza++ [6].

2.2 Symmetrized Word Alignment Models

The posterior symmetrization of word alignments has been introduced by [1]. This method does not compute symmetrized word alignment models during the training procedure, but uses heuristic combination methods after the training. We described it in more detail in Sec. 3.5. The best results of [1] for the Hansards task are 9.4% AER (using Model 4 in the last training iterations) and 8.7% AER (using the more sophisticated Model 6).

[4] improve the IBM alignment models, as well as the Hidden-Markov alignment model using a symmetric lexicon model. Similarly as in our approach, symmetrization takes both translation directions (from source to target and from target to source) into account. In addition to the symmetrization, a smoothed lexicon model is used. The performance of the models is evaluated for Canadian Hansards task, where they achieve an improvement of more than 30% relative to unidirectional training with Giza++ (7.5% AER).

In [9], the symmetrization is performed after training IBM and HMM alignment models in both directions. Using these models, local costs of aligning a source word and a target word in each sentence pair are estimated and graph algorithms are used to determine the symmetric alignment with minimal total costs. The automatic alignments created in this way are evaluated on the German–English Verbmobil task and the French–English Canadian Hansards task (6.6% AER).

Another unsupervised approach to symmetric word alignment is presented by [5] where "two simple asymmetric models are trained jointly to maximize a combination of data likelihood and agreement between the models". The authors restrict their experiments to IBM Models 1 and 2 and a new jointly trained HMM alignment model. They report an AER of 4.9% — a 29% reduction over symmetrized IBM model 4 predictions — for the Canadian Hansards task.

3 SyMGiza++ — Symmetrized MGiza++

In this section we will describe our modifications to the well known alignment models from [2] and [1].

We do not introduce changes to the main parameter estimation procedure. Instead, we modify the counting phase of each model to adopt information provided by both directed models simultaneously. The parameter combination step is executed in the main thread. In the following subsections, the formal aspects of the parameter combination will be outlined separately for each model. The notation has been adopted from [2] and we refer the reader to this work for details on the original models that will not be repeated in this paper.

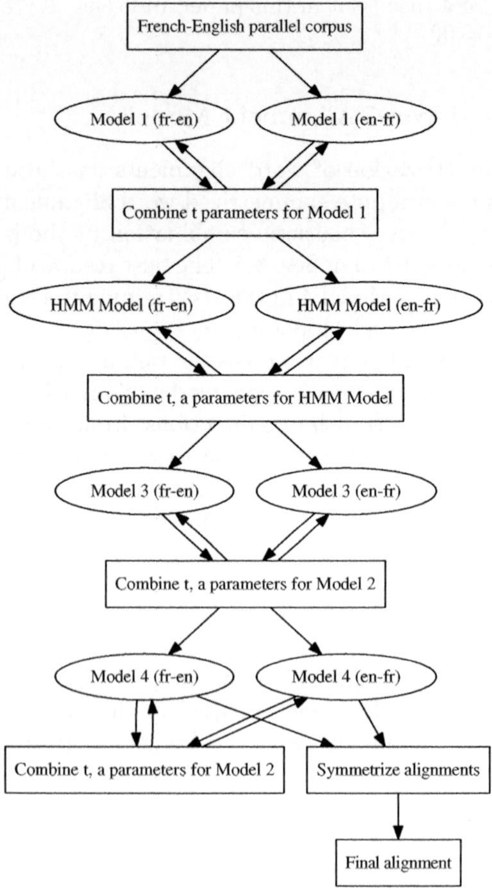

Fig. 1. General training scheme for SyMGiza++

3.1 Model 1

Model 1 is the first of the IBM models described extensively by [2] which have been implemented accurately in Giza++ and MGiza++.

In order to distinguish between the parameters of the two simultaneously computed alignment models we will use α and β as subscripts for the parameters of the first and second model respectively. For our English-French training corpus we compute the following two models:

$$Pr_\alpha(\mathbf{f}|\mathbf{e}) = \frac{\epsilon(m|l)}{(l+1)^m} \sum_{\mathbf{a}} \prod_{j=1}^{m} t_\alpha(f_j|e_{a_j}) \tag{1}$$

$$Pr_\beta(\mathbf{e}|\mathbf{f}) = \frac{\epsilon(l|m)}{(m+1)^l} \sum_{\mathbf{b}} \prod_{i=1}^{l} t_\beta(e_i|f_{b_i}) \tag{2}$$

where l and m are the lengths of the French sentence $\mathbf{f}$ and the English sentence $\mathbf{e}$ respectively, $\mathbf{a}$ and $\mathbf{b}$ are the directed alignments between the sentences and t_α and t_β the directed *translation probabilities* between the French and English words f and e. Due to the simplicity of this model, it is straightforward to introduce our changes in the counting method used during the E-step of the EM-algorithm. The only parameters of Model 1 are the translation probabilities t_α and t_β which are estimated by:

$$t_\alpha(f|e) = \frac{\sum_{s=1}^{S} c(f|e;\mathbf{f}^{(s)},\mathbf{e}^{(s)})}{\sum_{f'}\sum_{s=1}^{S} c(f'|e;\mathbf{f}^{(s)},\mathbf{e}^{(s)})}, \tag{3}$$

where S is the number of sentences in the parallel training corpus. $c(f|e;\mathbf{f},\mathbf{e})$ is the expected count of times the words f and e form translations in the given sentences $\mathbf{f}$ and $\mathbf{e}$, in the inverted model $c(e|f;\mathbf{e},\mathbf{f})$ is used.

In the original model, the expected counts $c(f|e;\mathbf{f},\mathbf{e})$ are calculated from the t values of the preceding iteration with the help of the following two formulas:

$$c(f|e;\mathbf{f},\mathbf{e}) = \sum_{\mathbf{a}} Pr_\alpha(\mathbf{a}|\mathbf{f},\mathbf{e}) \sum_{i,j} \delta(f,f_j)\delta(e,e_i), \tag{4}$$

and

$$Pr_\alpha(\mathbf{a}|\mathbf{f},\mathbf{e}) = \frac{\prod_{j=1}^{m} t_\alpha(f_j|e_{a_j})}{\sum_{\mathbf{a}}\prod_{j=1}^{m} t_\alpha(f_j|e_{a_j})}, \tag{5}$$

where δ is the Kronecker function[2]. Equations (3) and (4) are common for all models discussed in this section. Our modifications are restricted to (5) which is replaced by

$$\begin{aligned} Pr_\alpha(\mathbf{a}|\mathbf{f},\mathbf{e}) &= \frac{\prod_{j=1}^{m} \bar{t}(f_j,e_{a_j})}{\sum_{\mathbf{a}}\prod_{j=1}^{m} \bar{t}(f_j,e_{a_j})} \\ &= \frac{\prod_{j=1}^{m} \left(t_\alpha(f_j|e_{a_j}) + t_\beta(e_{a_j}|f_j)\right)}{\sum_{\mathbf{a}}\prod_{j=1}^{m} \left(t_\alpha(f_j|e_{a_j}) + t_\beta(e_{a_j}|f_j)\right)} \end{aligned} \tag{6}$$

Here we see the only difference between the standard Model 1 and our symmetrized version. By taking into account the translation probabilities from the previous iteration of both directed models we inform each model about the estimates of its counterparts. The following intuition applies: a French word is a good translation of an English word, if the English word is a good translation of the French word as well. This cannot be easily captured in the directed models without breaking up its sound probabilistic interpretation, as it happens here. However, since we modify only the way expected counts are obtained, the requirement imposed by [2] that

$$\sum_f t(f|e) = 1$$

[2] $\delta(i,j) = \begin{cases} 1 \text{ if } i = j \\ 0 \text{ otherwise} \end{cases}$.

still applies. Our modifications do not interfere with the EM procedure. The parameters for the inverted model are obtained analogously.

It should be noted that in most cases — despite the symmetry of the sum $t_\alpha(f|e)+t_\beta(e|f)$ occurring in both counts — $c(f|e;\mathbf{f},\mathbf{e})$ and $c(e|f;\mathbf{e},\mathbf{f})$ will have different values for the same words and sentences. This is due to the differences in the alignment direction. Therefore $t_\alpha(f|e) \neq t_\beta(e|f)$ in the general case.

3.2 Model 2

Although it is common practice to replace Model 2 during the training procedure with the HMM Model described in the next subsection, we need to modify its counting procedure as well. Model 2 is used to score a subset of alignments during the training procedure of the more sophisticated Models 3 and 4 which — in contrast to the lower models — cannot efficiently enumerate all possible alignments.

Model 2 introduces a second type of free parameters: the *alignment probabilities a*. These a parameters capture the probability that given the lengths of both sentences, a French word at position j is aligned with an English word at position a_j. The complete model is given by [2] as:

$$Pr_\alpha(\mathbf{f}|\mathbf{e}) = \epsilon(m|l) \sum_{\mathbf{a}} \prod_{j=1}^{m} \left(t_\alpha(f_j|e_{a_j}) a_\alpha(a_j|j,m,l) \right) \tag{7}$$

The general scheme described in (3) and (4) for the estimation of t values is the same for Model 2 as for Model 1. The alignment probabilities are estimated similarly:

$$a_\alpha(i|j,m,l) = \frac{\sum_{s=1}^{S} c(i|j,m,l;\mathbf{f}^{(s)},\mathbf{e}^{(s)})}{\sum_{i'} \sum_{s=1}^{S} c(i'|j,m,l;\mathbf{f}^{(s)},\mathbf{e}^{(s)})}, \tag{8}$$

$$c(i|j,m,l;\mathbf{f},\mathbf{e}) = \sum_{\mathbf{a}} Pr_\alpha(\mathbf{a}|\mathbf{f},\mathbf{e}) \delta(i,a_j). \tag{9}$$

Again, we only modify $Pr(\mathbf{a}|\mathbf{f},\mathbf{e})$ in (4) and (9) to obtain our symmetrized version of the alignment models:

$$Pr_\alpha(\mathbf{a}|\mathbf{f},\mathbf{e}) = \frac{\prod_{i=1}^{m} \left(\bar{t}(f_j,e_{a_j}) \bar{a}(a_j,j,m,l) \right)}{\sum_{\mathbf{a}} \prod_{j=1}^{m} \left(\bar{t}(f_j,e_{a_j}) \bar{a}(a_j,j,m,l) \right)} \tag{10}$$

where $\bar{t}(f,e)$ is defined as before for Model 1 and $\bar{a}(i,j,m,l) = a_\alpha(i|j,m,l) + a_\beta(j|i,l,m)$. The effect of information sharing between the two inverted models Pr_α and Pr_β is even increased for Model 2 since translation and alignment probabilities interact during the estimation of both types of parameters for the next iteration.

3.3 HMM Model

The HMM Alignment Model has been introduced by [3] and is used in the Giza++ family of alignment tools as a replacement for the less effective Model 2. The HMM alignment model is given by the following formula which at first looks very similar to (7):

$$P_\alpha(\mathbf{f}|\mathbf{e}) = \epsilon(m|l) \sum_{\mathbf{a}} \prod_{j=1}^{m} \left(t_\alpha(f_j|e_{a_j}) a_\alpha(a_j|a_{j-1}, l)\right) \tag{11}$$

The alignment probabilities from Model 2, however, are replaced by a different type of alignment probabilities. Here the probability of alignment a_j for position j has a dependence on the previous alignment a_{j-1} which turns the alignment model into a first order Markov model. The counts for the new a parameter are defined as follows:

$$a_\alpha(i|i', l) = \frac{\sum_{s=1}^{S} c(i|i', l; \mathbf{f}^{(s)}, \mathbf{e}^{(s)})}{\sum_{i''} \sum_{s=1}^{S} c(i''|i', l; \mathbf{f}^{(s)}, \mathbf{e}^{(s)})}, \tag{12}$$

$$c(i|i', l; \mathbf{f}, \mathbf{e}) = \sum_{\mathbf{a}} Pr_\alpha(\mathbf{a}|\mathbf{f}, \mathbf{e}) \sum_{j} \delta(i', a_{j-1}) \delta(i, a_j) \tag{13}$$

The definition of the t parameter and corresponding counts remains the same as for Model 1 and 2. Like before we only have to modify the definition of $Pr(\mathbf{a}|\mathbf{f}, \mathbf{e})$:

$$Pr_\alpha(\mathbf{a}|\mathbf{f}, \mathbf{e}) = \frac{\prod_{j=1}^{m} t_\alpha(f_j|e_{a_j}) a_\alpha(a_j|a_{j-1}, l)}{\sum_{\mathbf{a}} \prod_{j=1}^{m} t_\alpha(f_j|e_{a_j}) a_\alpha(a_j|a_{j-1}, l)} \tag{14}$$

is replaced by

$$Pr_\alpha(\mathbf{a}|\mathbf{f}, \mathbf{e}) = \frac{\prod_{i=1}^{m} \left(\bar{t}(f_j, e_{a_j}) a_\alpha(a_j|a_{j-1}, l)\right)}{\sum_{\mathbf{a}} \prod_{j=1}^{m} \left(\bar{t}(f_j, e_{a_j}) a_\alpha(a_j|a_{j-1}, l)\right)}. \tag{15}$$

$\bar{t}$ is defined as before for Model 1 and Model 2.

Here, the alignment probabilities a remain unchanged. For Model 2 we are able to find the symmetrically calculated a parameters just by swapping source and target values. Doing the same for the Markov model would change the interpretation of the alignment probabilities. We would require neighbouring source language words to be aligned only with neighbouring target language words which is too strong an assumption. Nevertheless, their values are still influenced by both models due to the appearance of $\bar{t}$ in the re-estimation.

3.4 Models 3 and 4

We already mentioned that the parameters specific for Models 3 and 4 are calculated from fractional counts collected over a subset of alignments that have been identified with the help of the Viterbi alignments calculated by Model 2. Therefore it is not necessary to revise the parameter estimation formulas for Models 3 and 4, instead we simply adopt the previous changes made for Model 2. This influences the parameters of Models 3 and 4 indirectly by choosing better informed Viterbi alignments during each iteration.

3.5 Final Symmetrization

Although the two directed models influence each other between each iteration, the two final alignments produced at the end of the training procedure differ due the restrictions imposed by the models. Alignments are directed and since alignments are functions, there are no one-to-many or many-to-many alignments for the respective directions. There are, however, many-to-one alignments. [1] have proposed a method for the symmetrization of word alignments, which they call *refined symmetrization* and which is reported to have a positive effect on alignment quality.

They first map each directed alignment into a set of alignment points and create a new alignment as the intersection of these two sets. Next, alignment points (i, j) from the union of the two sets are added to the newly created alignment if they occur in the first alignment or in the second alignment and if neither f_j nor e_i has an alignment in the new alignment, or if both of the following conditions hold:

- The alignment (i, j) has a horizontal neighbour$(i-1, j)$, $(i+1, j)$ or a vertical neighbour $(i, j-1)$, $(i, j+1)$ that is already in the new alignment.
- Adding (i, j) to the new alignment does not created alignments with both horizontal and vertical neighbours.

This method is applied as the final step of our computation and will also be applied to the directed alignments created by Giza++ and MGiza++, our baseline systems. Final symmetrization methods are included in SyMGiza++ and can be applied without the need for external programs. Apart from the mentioned refined method it is also possible to use multiple variants of *grow-diag* featured in the Moses training procedure.

4 Evaluation

4.1 Word Alignment Quality

Evaluating word alignment quality, we compare three systems on the same training and test data: Giza++, MGiza++, and SyMGiza++. For the Giza++ and MGiza++ we run both directed models separately and in parallel and recombine the resulting final alignments with the refined method described in 3.5. We experimented with different training schemes and found the following to work best for Giza++ and MGiza++: $5 \times$ Model 1, $5 \times$ HMM Model, $3 \times$ Model 3 and $3 \times$ Model 4. This is consistent with the findings of [1] for the same training data and test set.

Table 1. Results for the HLT/NAACL 2003 test set

Alignment Method	Prec [%]	Rec [%]	AER [%]
GIZA++ EN-FR	91.19	92.20	8.39
GIZA++ FR-EN	91.82	87.96	9.79
GIZA++ REFINED	93.24	92.59	7.02
MGIZA++ EN-FR	91.19	92.22	8.40
MGIZA++ FR-EN	91.84	87.96	9.78
MGIZA++ REFINED	93.25	92.60	7.01
SYMGIZA++	94.34	94.08	**5.76**

The training scheme for SyMGIZA++ has been determined as 5 × Model 1, 5 × HMM Model, 5 × Model 3 and 5 × Model 4. The models are symmetrized between model transitions. Using this training scheme for Giza++ or MGiza++ causes a small decline in alignment quality.

The standard metric *Alignment Error Rate* (AER) proposed by [1] is used to evaluate the quality of the introduced input word alignments. AER is calculated as follows:

$$\text{Precision} = \frac{|A \cap P|}{|A|} \qquad \text{Recall} = \frac{|A \cap S|}{|S|}$$
$$\text{AER} = 1 - \frac{|A \cap S| + |A \cap P|}{|A| + |S|} \tag{16}$$

where P is the set of possible alignment points in the reference alignment, S is the set of sure alignments in the reference alignment ($S \subset P$), and A is the evaluated word alignment.

In order to obtain results that can be easily compared with the work summarized in 2.2, we evaluated our system on the Canadian Hansards task made available during the HLT-NAACL 2003 workshop on "Building and Using Parallel Texts: Data Driven Machine Translation and Beyond" [10]. The training data comprises 1.1M sentences from the Canadian Hansards proceedings and a separate test set of 447 manually word-aligned sentences provided by [1].

Our results are summarized in Table 1. It is not surprising that there are no significant differences between Giza++ and MGiza++ when AER is considered. SyMGiza++ achieves the best AER results with a relative improvement of more than 17% compared to Giza++ and MGiza++.

In Sec. 2.2 we gave the results for a number of other symmetrization approaches. Although we use the same test set our results are not yet fully comparable to the results of other works. We tried but failed to reproduce the results from [5] where the authors reported an AER of 4.9% for the Hansards Tasks. We used the BerkeleyAligner which is based on the algorithms described by [5]. The results reported by [5] for their baseline alignments produced with Giza++, on the other hand, are more or less identical to our results. This requires further investigation.

Table 2. BLEU scores for WMT08 data and test sets

(a) Europarl (test2008)

	fr-en	en-fr	es-en	en-es	de-en	en-de	es-de	de-es
MGIZA++	0.3189	0.2944	0.3241	0.3184	0.2656	0.1982	0.1996	0.2706
SYMGIZA++	0.3193	**0.3000**	0.3231	0.3172	0.2657	0.1993	0.2014	**0.2741**

(b) News Commentary (nc-test2008)

	fr-en	en-fr	es-en	en-es	de-en
MGIZA++	0.2565	0.2339	0.3367	0.3220	0.2305
SYMGIZA++	**0.2630**	0.2359	**0.3380**	0.3234	**0.2381**

	en-de	es-de	de-es	cz-en	en-cz
MGIZA++	0.1531	0.1233	0.1775	0.2281	0.1285
SYMGIZA++	**0.1575**	0.1234	**0.1822**	**0.2369**	**0.1329**

(c) Hunglish (newstest2008)

	hu-en	en-hu
MGIZA++	0.0587	0.0449
SYMGIZA++	**0.0632**	0.0458

4.2 Machine Translation Results

We agree with [11] that the evaluation of alignment quality on its own may not be very meaningful. It should be considered good practice to include an evaluation of statistical machine translation models produced from the seemingly improved word alignment. In this section, such an evaluation is presented.

For our baseline systems, we configured Moses [12] as described by the ACL 2008 Third Workshop on Statistical Machine Translation (WMT-08) – Shared Translation Task guidelines. The data sets provided for the WMT-08 Shared Task[3] were used as training, tuning, and test data. Furthermore, training, tuning, and evaluation were performed in compliance with these guidelines. Several baseline systems were created to account for different language pairs, training corpora and translation directions. All baseline systems make use of MGiza++ to produce the word alignment models which serve as input to the bilingual phrase extraction phase of the Moses training process.

For our systems, we modified the training process only by replacing MGiza++ with SyMGiza++, no other parameters or steps were altered. Thus the *grow-diag* post-alignment symmetrization method is used and not the refined method introduced previously. We refer to the translation systems by the name of the alignment tool used. Thus the baselines are simply denoted by MGiza++, the systems created from the jointly trained alignment models by SyMGiza++.

The BLEU scores for all systems and language pairs have been compiled into Table 2. We split the results according to three different training corpora used. Bold figures mark results that are statistically significantly better than their counterpart. Significance has been calculated as proposed by [13].

[3] Available at `http://www.statmt.org/wmt08/`

In the case of statistically significant BLEU results (bold figures, 10 test cases out of 20), the translation quality of SyMGiza++ exceeds the results for the MGiza++ system. This effect seems to be more visible for small training corpora like the news commentary parallel corpus which comprises about 70,000 sentence pairs. The Europarl parallel corpus and the English-Hungarian corpus feature both more than one million sentence pairs. The very low BLEU scores for the English-Hungarian language pair result from the use of an out-of-domain test set provided with the WMT-08 data. The test set has been compiled from a news source while the training data consists of various legal texts and other data scraped from the internet.

5 Conclusions

We have presented SyMGiza++, a tool that computes symmetric word alignment models with the capability to take advantage of multi-processor systems. Our fairly simple modification to the well-known IBM Models implemented in Giza++ and MGiza++ achieves quite impressive improvements for AER on the standard Canadian Hansards task. Our symmetrized models outperform post-training symmetrization methods.

Improvements in translation quality — though less significant than in terms of pure AER — are also visible when SyMGiza++ is used as a drop-in replacement for Giza++ or MGiza++ in the training procedure of the phrase-based statistical machine translation system Moses. Translation quality improved on a statistically significant level for 10 out of 20 directions tested for three different training corpora and test sets provided for WMT-08. The results for the remaining test cases should be interpreted to be the same as the baseline, since they are not statistically significant.

It can be safely concluded that SyMGiza++ can be used anywhere instead of Giza++ or MGiza++ and in most cases will yield better results for word-alignment oriented tasks. For statistical machine translation, it seems to be a safe bet to use SyMGiza++ instead of Giza++ or MGiza++. There is a good chance that choosing SyMGiza++ will result in improved translation quality. In the worst case translation quality should not decrease.

References

1. Och, F.J., Ney, H.: A systematic comparison of various statistical alignment models. Computational Linguistics 29(1), 19–51 (2003)
2. Brown, P.F., Pietra, V.J.D., Pietra, S.A.D., Mercer, R.L.: The mathematics of statistical machine translation: Parameter estimation. Computational Linguistics 19(2), 263–311 (1993)
3. Vogel, S., Ney, H., Tillmann, C.: Hmm-based word alignment in statistical translation. In: Proceedings of ACL, pp. 836–841 (1996)
4. Zens, R., Matusov, E., Ney, H.: Improved word alignment using a symmetric lexicon model. In: Proceedings of ACL-COLING, p. 36 (2004)

5. Liang, P., Taskar, B., Klein, D.: Alignment by agreement. In: Proceedings of ACL-COLING, pp. 104–111 (2006)
6. Gao, Q., Vogel, S.: Parallel implementations of word alignment tool. In: Proceedings of SETQA-NLP, pp. 49–57 (2008)
7. Dempster, A.P., Laird, N.M., Rubin, D.B.: Maximum likelihood from incomplete data via the EM algorithm. Journal of the Royal Statistcial Society, Series B 39(1), 1–38 (1977)
8. Al-Onaizan, Y., Curin, J., Jahr, M., Knight, K., Lafferty, J., Melamed, I., Och, F., Purdy, D., Smith, N., Yarowsky, D.: Statistical machine translation. Technical report, JHU workshop (1999)
9. Matusov, E., Zens, R., Ney, H.: Symmetric word alignments for statistical machine translation. In: Proceedings of ACL-COLING, pp. 219–225 (2004)
10. Mihalcea, R., Pedersen, T.: An evaluation exercise for word alignment. In: Proceedings of HLT-NAACL, pp. 1–10 (2003)
11. Fraser, A., Marcu, D.: Measuring word alignment quality for statistical machine translation. Computational Linguistics 33, 239–303 (2007)
12. Koehn, P., Hoang, H., Birch, A., Callison-Burch, C., Federico, M., Bertoldi, N., Cowan, B., Shen, W., Moran, C., Zens, R., Dyer, C., Bojar, O., Constantin, A., Herbst, E.: Moses: Open source toolkit for statistical machine translation. In: ACL (2007)
13. Koehn, P.: Statistical significance tests for machine translation evaluation. In: EMNLP, pp. 388–395 (2004)

How Opinion Annotations and Ontologies Become Objective?

Aleksander Wawer[1] and Krzysztof Sakwerda[2]

[1] Institute of Computer Science, Polish Academy of Science
ul. Ordona 21, 01-237 Warszawa, Poland
axw@ipipan.waw.pl

[2] Institute of Computer Science, University of Wroclaw
ul. Joliot-Curie 15, 50-383 Wroclaw, Poland
ksakwerda@gmail.com

Abstract. We describe the methodology and the process of annotations of a corpus of reviews along with experiments on inter-annotator agreement. Our approach goes beyond "flat" sets of attributes and relies on more complex graph-alike ontologies to annotate the data. We propose and test an algorithm of automated induction of an ontology and compare the results with "manually" created ontologies and annotations. We conclude with a discussion of differences between the two approaches and annotator influence.

Keywords: opinion annotations, ontologies, ontology integration, inter annotator agreement.

1 Introduction and Existing Work

Many existing works, such as [3,5,4,6] deal with automated mining of product features (also referred to as attributes). This special type of opinion mining is concerned with various aspects of products under review rather than aggregated evaluations. Instead of asking: is the product review as a whole positive or negative, the approach here is more fine-grained, as it considers each feature or aspect separately. Popular methods of automated feature recognition typically involve part of speech patterns, frequency filtering and various sorts of supervised and semi-supervised classification.

Application of automated methods and computing their precision and recall demands resources: reliably annotated corpora of texts. At the moment no Polish resource meets these requirements[1].

Another motivation for our efforts is that none of existing works on recognizing attributes from text corpora that we are aware of has been preceded by an extensive inter-rater agreement study using attribute ontologies rather than simple sets of attributes. The intention of this work was to design and create such a reference resource for Polish.

[1] Customer review aggregators like for example `http://www.cokupic.pl` are of little use. Although the site provides placeholders for describing positive and negative attributes, there is no guarrantee that the features are ever mentioned in a review.

P. Bouvry et al. (Eds.): SIIS 2011, LNCS 7053, pp. 391–400, 2012.

Our use of the notion "ontology" only partially follows popular definitions like Sowa's [7]. We also apply it to describe organization of knowledge in a domain, modeled as a graph of linked concepts. However, in our case concepts are narrowed to product features only and associated with sets of fragments of texts where the attributes are mentioned.

2 Background

The general orientation of this work is inspired by the following two approaches to methodology and semantics. We discuss them briefly below, providing references to relevant parts of our work.

Grounded Theory [2,8]. In its essence, it can be described as developing a set of categories[2] from the data, rather than the other way around, analyzing the data through existing categories. In our case we read a corpus of reviews and "discover" or identify categories, product attributes in our case, as found in texts, and describe their interrelationships on a graph. The opposing approach is to create an ontology of attributes using expert knowledge and only then read and annotate texts.

The use of such a method seems to be justified by the nature of reviews that base solely on experiences with the object under review and rarely require any expert knowledge. Crafting a set of categories by experts and analyzing the reviews through these concepts may end up with omissions of numerous categories actually present in the data, perhaps even frequently mentioned.

Meaning as Use [10]. According to it, meaning is defined as patterns of usage. The main application of this idea was identification of similarly annotated categories despite their potentially different labels and descriptions. For example, annotator *A* may have referred to a category as *aesthetics*, annotator *B* as *outlook* and both may actually mean the same, which becomes apparent only after examination of both sets of annotations.

3 Annotation

3.1 Software

To annotatate the reviews we used Atlas.TI[3], a well-known tool for qualitative analysis of textual data. Main features that render Atlas.TI attractive are its ability to create and edit graph-alike ontologies, capability of annotating fragments of texts using any ontology node[4], and finally, handling overlapping and embedded annotations.

3.2 Types of Annotated Text Fragments

Fragments of text, at least one word long but in many cases longer, could be annotated as:

---

[2] Originally, also a theory or a set of explanations.

[3] `http://www.atlasti.com`

[4] By this statement we mean that a node – an attribute is assigned to a set of annotated fragments.

- **Attribute** - marked *a*.
- **Root Attribute** - marked with *!* - the most abstract attribute at the top of attribute hierarchy.
- **Attribute Value** - marked *wa*.
- **Implicit** - marked as *.im* when attribute name or value is not mentioned directly.
- **Polarity** - marked as +,-,*0* indicates positive, negative and neutral attribute values.

Naming convention was as follows: Attribute or Attribute Value mark, potentially Implicit, followed by a slash, name (a graph node label), in case of attribute values followed by another slash and polarity mark. In short:

[Attribute|Attribute Value] / name [/ Polarity]?.

For example: *wa/outlook/+* refers to positive value of attribute *outlook*. Let us illustrate it by providing examples from perfume domain, originally spelled. Fragments which denote attribute values are marked with square brackets and attributes with angle brackets.

Let us start with a somewhat simplistic piece with attribute values expressed by adjectives and attribute as a noun:

```
[dobry] [odswiezajacy] i [energizujacy] <zapach>
[good] [refreshing] and [energizing] <fragrance>
```

However, attributes can be also expressed simultaneously with attribute values (or in an evaluative way):

```
Gwarantuje, ze [<przyciagaja one kobieca uwage>]
I guarrantee, that it [<attracts female attention>]
```

In the above example, the same text fragment denotes an attribute (a/effect on others) and is given positive evaluation (wa/effect on others/+).

3.3 Relations

We defined four possible types of relations between attributes, represented as ontology nodes (relation symbols in parentheses):

- **is associated with** (==). The most general relation which does not specify exact semantics which links both nodes.
- **is part of** ([]). The well-known relation of meronymy. For example, attribute *bottle* may be linked using this type of relation with attribute *container*[5] .
- **is property of** (*}). This relation says that one attribute is a feature that describes a higher level attribute, for example *durability* may be a property of *fragrance*.
- **is type of** (##). This describes an attribute as a type of another, higher level attribute. For example, attribute *special occasion* is a type of *purpose*.

We encouraged annotators to suggest new types of relations that seem the most appropriate but it quickly became apparent that the list of four types mentioned above is sufficient.

[5] While bottle can be seen as a type of a container, this specific example is adapted from "perfume" domain, where perfume's container consists of a cartoon package and a bottle.

3.4 Annotation Cycle

In the first phase annotators read texts, create their own ontologies and then annotate – mark appropriate fragments and assign them to appropriate ontology nodes. We thus obtain four different ontologies and four different sets of annotated reviews. At the end of this phase annotators meet and create one, common, final ontology, a result of discussions and collective agreement over which attribute means what exactly, the most appropriate graph structure, attribute names (node labels) and relations. An example final ontology with English label translations is presented on Fig 1. As mentioned before attribute names follow the naming convention of *a/name*. The meaning of numbers in brackets, as in **{A-B}**, is as follows: **A** denotes how many annotated text fragments are assigned to a given attribute (a graph node), **B** represents degree of a node: number of attributes linked using any relation type.

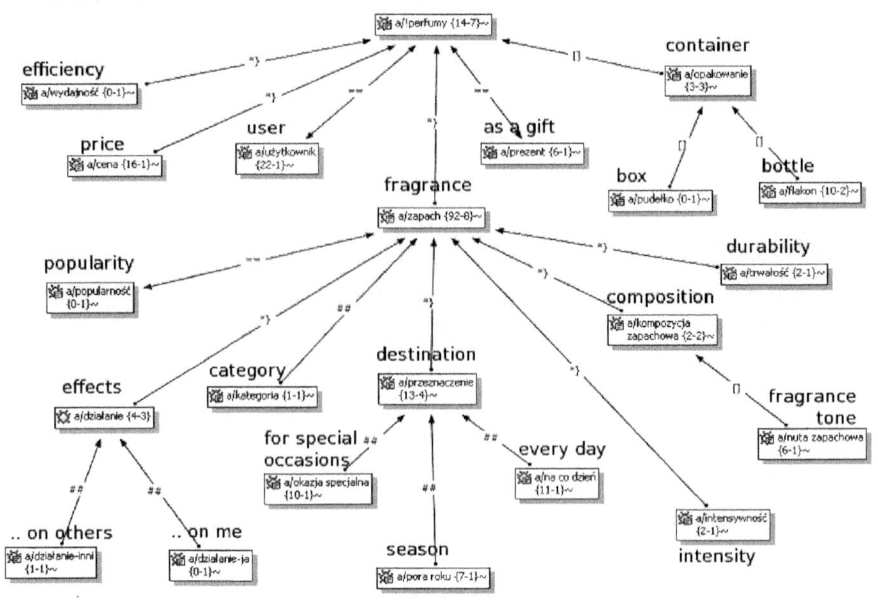

Fig. 1. Ontology graph in final form

Having created such an ontology texts are annotated again, but this time using the same set of attributes. This again results in four sets of annotated texts. Finally, annotators meet for the second time and produce one, final corpus of annotated reviews. For this purpose a special web application has been deployed, which visualizes annotation differences, allows to navigate, edit and select one of many possibly conflicting attributes for a fragment of text.

Decisions which attribute out of several possible ones is the most "correct" as well as selection of the correct span for each text fragment were collective. Annotators had an opportunity to convince one another and argue over the rationale of every selection.

The problem is similar to modeling common knowledge of multiple experts as described by [1], who proposed a method of solving conflicts between the expertise models of different experts. The models are represented as graphs of linked concepts using John Sowa's conceptual graph formalism [7]. The main difference that makes this method not applicable in our context is the definition of concepts and association with sets of annotations.

3.5 Annotator Instructions

The general principles governing annotation were as follows:

- As much context-free as possible: annotated fragment alone should be sufficient to understand its meaning.
- As little redundant as possible: no extra words should be added into annotated fragments.

In addition to this, annotators had two distinct sets of instructions on different levels.

The first set of general instructions covered understanding of what attributes and relations are, as in sections 3.2 and 3.3. Definitions provided initially have quickly proven not exhaustive enough to cover all possible cases so we expanded them with a new set of instructions added subsequently[6]. The second set of specific instructions contained explanations and definitions of attributes associated with a given ontology.

3.6 Dataset Description

Using this method we produced two sets of annotated reviews along with respective ontologies. Each set of reviews (for each domain or product type) has about 16 pages of A4 length. The second domain (woman's underwear) turned to be less wordy than the first (perfume) but ultimately the number of annotated fragments was not very different. In both cases, annotations turned out to be very dense, which is hardly surprising given the goal of product reviews. Table 1 presents numbers of annotated text fragments for both domains, for common final annotation referred to as ALL and each annotator separately.

4 Common Automated Ontology

Experiments on reviews of two product types confirmed not only existence of relationships between attributes, but also adequacy of hierarchical, graph based approach to attribute structure description. We believe that the resource created according to the described procedure provides the highest possible quality of annotations, attribute labels and ontology graphs.

[6] Perhaps the most notable example of such a rule is: *do not annotate attribute values for attributes involving product users*. This rule came out as an arbitrary settlement after a hot discussion of whether "fragrance for stylish people" tells something positive, neutral or maybe even negative about a perfume. An annotator can either try to guess writer's evaluation of "stylish people" or use her own experiences and judgements regarding the mentioned group.

Table 1. Numbers of words and annotated text fragments

	Domain 1	Domain 2
ALL	305	343
martas	277	273
magdab	204	283
tomaszz	310	292
annal	234	293
words	4232	2446

In the next part of this paper we focus on automated generation of a common ontology using annotated fragments of texts of four annotators as well as their ontologies. The intention is to compare automatically created ontologies to all human made annotations and ontologies, also the final ones (final in the sense of being a final product of each coding cycle). We hypothesize that the proposed method of building a geometrically central ontology graph and corresponding annotations is less prone to factors like personality influences or work organization and in this sense is more objective.

4.1 Ontology Comparisons

We begin by proposing a method of comparing two ontologies. Then we describe an algorithm of automated induction of a "central" ontology. By this we mean an ontology equivalent to the final product of annotation cycle as in section 3.4, but created automatically.

4.2 Ontology Similarity

Given any two ontologies from the same domain (referring to the same product type) we would like to tell how similar they are. One can ask when any two ontologies are similar and what does that mean? In the most intuitive formulation, two ontologies are similar if they have similar structure and corresponding attributes cover similar text fragments.

Comparing tokens. Most tokens carry associated base word forms and sets of morphosyntactic tags (such as *person*, *case*, *degree*, *gender* etc). To compare any two tokens we compare corresponding tags and count weighted mean number of equal ones. It is clear that lexical aspect should have precedence over morphosyntactics, therefore ortographic and base form identity have higher weights assigned.

Comparing text fragments. To compare two lists of tokens we used a greedy algorithm. Each token from the first text fragment is compared with each token in the second one. When the best match for a token is found, and of course each token can be only used once, we compute their weighted average similarity as described above. The method disregards word order and enables comparisons of slightly permuted token sequences.

Comparing attributes. To compare two sets of text fragments, related to two attributes, we apply the same greedy approach: for each text fragment of the first attribute we find its best match in the second one and use both to compute similarity. The measure may not be optimal but has two advantages: allows to compare sets of different length and is guarranteed to use all text fragments of a shorter set. We apply it only for pairs of attributes where the F similarity exceeds a provided threshold value.

We selected F-measure as the most appropriate following the discussion in [9]. The other popular measure of agreement, Cohen's Kappa seems more suitable for problems with the same set of objects, such as word sense tagging, for example. Comparing similarity of two sets of annotated text fragments requires evaluating the intersection between both sets. Precision and recall between sets A and B are in this case interchangeable which reduces F to mean value of recall(A $\|$B) and recall(B $\|$A).

Comparing ontologies. In the most naive approach, ontologies are comparable by comparisons of all attributes according to the procedure described above. This approach however disregards ontology graph structure. Our algorithm, proposed below, takes graph structure into account by limiting comparisons to sets neighbours.

Algorithm

- Input:
  1. two ontologies O_1 and O_2
  2. F–matrix of similarity between all attributes from both ontologies
- Procedure description
  1. convert ontologies to neigbour lists
  2. create a priority queue of vertices from two ontologies, with vertex outdegree as a priority
  3. while queue is not empty and there are unmarked attributes in each ontology:
     (a) take the first attribute a from queue and find S_n^a – set of (at most n) attributes most similar to a (none of them must be used) in the second ontology (using weighted mean of attributes comparison method discussed above and F measure).
     (b) for each $b \in S_n^a$ compare sets of neighbours of a and b and choose the best match b_a for a (using weighted average of attributes and neighbour similarity)
     (c) mark attributes a and b_a as used
  4. compute average of of best matches

5 Automatic Generation of Common Ontology

Given $\mathscr{O}$ – set of ontologies, we would like to generate one ontology being the closest to each $o_i \in \mathscr{O}$ and thus being the "geometric center" of $\mathscr{O}$. We can achieve this goal by looking at similar (in the sense of F–measure) sets of attributes and generate vertices for such groups. After generating verices we connect them with edges. Below we describe the procedure in detail.

Algorithm

- Input:
  1. set of ontologies $\mathcal{O}$
  2. F–matrix of similarity between all attributes from both ontologies
- Procedure description
  1. construct set family $\{A_i\}$. Each set A_i contains attributes, and each two members a^i_n and a^i_m of A_i are similar: $F(a^i_n, a^i_m) > k$, where k is a parameter treshold value[7].
  2. for each $A \in \{A_i\}$ choose its representative a as an attribute having highest average similarity value to other members of A and thus being geometric centre of the set (here we use only the measure of attributes similarity, described in 4.2)
  3. each representative selected in the previous step will become a vertex of the new, generated ontology[8]
  4. for each pair of veritces (a_i, a_j) an edge (relation) between them is set iff all of the following conditions hold:
     (a) there exists some attributes $v^o_i \in /A_i$ and $v^o_j \in /A_j$ such that v^o_i and v^o_j belongs to the set of vertices of the same ontology o.
     (b) there is an edge between v^o_i and v^o_j in o.
     (c) average number of attributes for which (a) and (b) hods in all ontologies is higher than a treshold value l

6 Results and Discussion

Distances between ontologies computed using the described algorithm, mapped into euclidean two-dimensional space, are presented on Fig. 2. **ALL** refers to common, final ontology and associated annotations created manually, **COMMON-AUTO** to automatically obtained ontology.

Compared to the first set of annotations and ontologies, distances between ontologies in the second, chronologically later sets of annotations and ontologies, are smaller about one third. In other words, annotations and ontologies were much more alike.

Initial examination of distances between points proves that all ontologies in Domain 2 were much more alike. This is explained by the fact that annotators went through a number of “difficult” cases and the number of rules mentioned in section 3.5 has been expanded. This is also apparent by F–measure matrixes which were not disclosed here.

Our assumptions that the designed algorithm should result in a geometrically central ontology have been found true. In fact, the automated ontology **COMMON-AUTO** is more central than than the manual ontology **ALL** in case of Domain 2. In Domain 1 however, **ALL** is very different not only from **COMMON-AUTO** (which is still the most central) but from all individual ontologies and annotations. This can be explained

[7] As similarity measure F is given as matrix construction of such set family is not difficult.

[8] The only exception is when an attribute appears already in some sets of $\{A_i\}$ and thus can not be selected as a representative. In such case the first most similar to the rest which has not yet been “demoted” is selected.

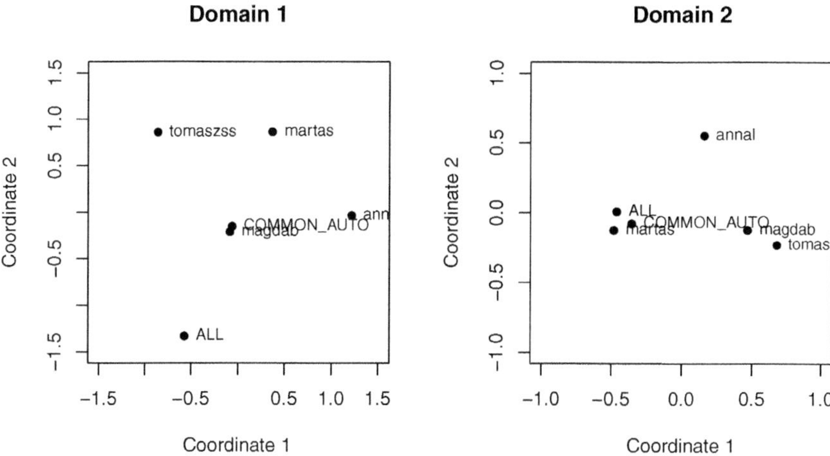

Fig. 2. Distances between ontologies and annotations

by several factors. When creating **ALL** for Domain 1, annotators confronted each other for the first time and the results resembled a work in its own rather than just "average" solution of all indivitual annotations.

The annotator that had the most influence on the manual ontology **ALL** for Domain 2 was the person that also held the responsibility to schedule meetings and organize annotator work, which probably also resulted in larger influence on the **ALL**. In the case of Domain 1, **ALL** is similarly distanced from any other ontology.

7 Future Work

The study described in this paper provides background for fully automated product attribute extraction: the corpus is necessary for subsequent developments and evaluations of algorithmic approaches. Further work will be continued in two directions. First, by efforts to identify fragments of texts referring to attributes. This problem, especially in case of certain abstract and difficult attributes, is far from trivial. Second, by supervised and semi-supervised experiments on assigning those fragments to appropriate attributes. Preliminary work on the latter using varius similarity measurements and multiple kernel learning method has already proven successful.

Acknowledgements. This research is supported by the POIG.01.01.02-14-013/09 project which is co-financed by the European Union under the European Regional Development Fund.

References

1. Dieng, R.: Comparison of conceptual graphs for modelling knowledge of multiple experts. In: Michalewicz, M., Raś, Z.W. (eds.) ISMIS 1996. LNCS, vol. 1079, pp. 78–87. Springer, Heidelberg (1996)

2. Glaser, B.G., Strauss, A.L.: The Discovery of Grounded Theory: Strategies for Qualitative Research. Aldine Publishing Company (1967)
3. Hu, M., Liu, B.: Mining opinion features in customer reviews. In: Proceedings of the 19th National Conference on Artifical Intelligence, AAAI 2004, pp. 755–760. AAAI Press (2004)
4. Hu, M., Liu, B.: Opinion feature extraction using class sequential rules. In: Proceedings of AAAI 2006 Spring Symposia on Computational Approaches to Analyzing Weblogs, AAAI-CAAW 2006 (2006)
5. Popescu, A.M., Etzioni, O.: Extracting product features and opinions from reviews. In: Proceedings of the Conference on Human Language Technology and Empirical Methods in Natural Language Processing, HLT 2005, pp. 339–346. Association for Computational Linguistics, Stroudsburg (2005)
6. Riloff, E., Patwardhan, S., Wiebe, J.: Feature subsumption for opinion analysis. In: Proceedings of the 2006 Conference on Empirical Methods in Natural Language Processing, pp. 440–448. Association for Computational Linguistics, Sydney (2006), `http://www.aclweb.org/anthology/W/W06/W06-1652`
7. Sowa, J.F.: Conceptual graphs for a database interface. IBM Journal of Research and Development 20(4), 336–357 (1976)
8. Strauss, A.L., Corbin, J.: Basics of Qualitative Research. Sage Publications (1990)
9. Wilson, T.A.: Fine-grained Subjectivity and Sentiment Analysis: Recognizing the Intensity, Polarity, and Attitudes of Private States. Ph.D. thesis, University of Pittsburgh (2008)
10. Wittgenstein, L.: Philosophical Investigations. Blackwell (1967)

Author Index

Author Index

GPSR Compliance

The European Union's (EU) General Product Safety Regulation (GPSR) is a set of rules that requires consumer products to be safe and our obligations to ensure this.

If you have any concerns about our products, you can contact us on ProductSafety@springernature.com

In case Publisher is established outside the EU, the EU authorized representative is:

Springer Nature Customer Service Center GmbH
Europaplatz 3
69115 Heidelberg, Germany

Batch number: 09490872

Printed by Printforce, the Netherlands